Beyond the Screen:
Institutions, Networks and Publics of Early Cinema

Cover image: Temple Theatre, January 1915, Canandaigua, NY. Exhibition of *The Girl of the Sunny South* (Dir. Travers Vale, 1913).
[Photograph courtesy of George Eastman House, Rochester, NY.]

Beyond the Screen: Institutions, Networks and Publics of Early Cinema

Edited by
Marta Braun, Charlie Keil, Rob King,
Paul Moore and Louis Pelletier

British Library Cataloguing in Publication Data

Beyond the Screen: Institutions, Networks and Publics of Early Cinema

A catalogue entry for this book is available from the British Library

ISBN: 9780 86196 703 2 (Paperback)

Published by
John Libbey Publishing Ltd, 3 Leicester Road, New Barnet, Herts EN5 5EW, United Kingdom
e-mail: john.libbey@orange.fr; web site: www.johnlibbey.com
Direct orders (UK and Europe): direct.orders@marston.co.uk

Distributed in Asia and North America by **Indiana University Press**, 601 North Morton St, Bloomington, IN 47404, USA. www.iupress.indiana.edu

© 2012 Copyright John Libbey Publishing Ltd. All rights reserved. Unauthorized duplication contravenes applicable laws.

Printed and bound in China by 1010 Printing International Ltd.

Contents

	Introduction *Marta Braun, Charlie Keil, Rob King, Paul Moore and Louis Pelletier*	1
PART I	**CHARITY AND RELIGION**	
Chapter 1	"Neutrality-Humanity": The Humanitarian Mission and the Films of the American Red Cross *Jennifer Horne*	11
Chapter 2	Early Missionary Filming and the Emergence of the Professional Cameraman *Stephen Bottomore*	19
Chapter 3	Mission on Screen: the Church Army and its Multi-Media Activities *Frank Gray*	27
Chapter 4	"Baits to Entrap the Pleasure-Seeker and the Worldling": Charity Bazaars Introduce Moving Pictures to Ireland *Denis Condon*	35
Chapter 5	Paroles éducatives et religieuses lors des projections de films en France avant 1915 *Martin Barnier*	43
Chapter 6	*Mütter, verzaget nicht!* (1911) [*Mothers, Despair Not!*]: Henny Porten's Promotion for Mothers' Welfare *Martin Loiperdinger and Holger Ziegler*	51
PART II	**GOVERNMENT AND CIVICS**	
Chapter 7	The Tsar and The Kinematograph: Film as History and The Chronicle of the Russian Monarchy *Oksana Chefranova*	63
Chapter 8	"Wheelbarrows" and "Real Soldiers": Advertising, Audiences and War Films of all Varieties *Liz Clarke*	71
Chapter 9	"What is a Picture?": Film as Defined in British Law Before 1910 *Ian Christie*	78
Chapter 10	Le cinéma et les élections au Québec: de l'attraction à la banalité *Germain Lacasse*	85
Chapter 11	A Moving Picture Farce: Public Opinion and the Beginnings of Film Censorship in Quebec *Louis Pelletier*	94

BEYOND THE SCREEN: Institutions, networks and publics of early cinema

PART III	EDUCATION AND ADVOCACY	
Chapter 12	Health Instruction on Screen: The Department of Health in New York City, 1909–1917 *Marina Dahlquist*	107
Chapter 13	John Collier, Thomas Edison and the Educational Promotion of Moving Pictures *Amanda R. Keeler*	117
Chapter 14	"And They Can See Half-Naked Dancers, Catching Young Men In Their Nets": Teachers and the Cinema in Norway, 1907–1913 *Gunnar Iversen*	126
Chapter 15	Documentaries, Family Film Nights and the First Film University: The Early Works and Big Ideas of Belgian Film Pioneer Hippolyte De Kempeneer (1876–1944) *Gerda Cammaer*	131
Chapter 16	The School of the Future or Ganot's *Physics*?: Edison's Foray into Educational Cinema *Oliver Gaycken*	143

PART IV	SCIENCE AND MAGIC	
Chapter 17	Multi-Purposing Early Cinema: A Psychological Experiment Involving *Van Bibber's Experiment* (Edison, 1911) *Marsha Orgeron*	153
Chapter 18	Dissecting the Medical Training Film *Scott Curtis*	161
Chapter 19	Corporal Permeability and Shadow Pictures: Reconsidering *Uncle Josh at the Moving Picture Show* (1902) *Amy E. Borden*	168
Chapter 20	Eroticism and Death: The Skeleton in the Trick Film *Murray Leeder*	176
Chapter 21	Magies en images, les prestidigitateurs et la machine *Frédéric Tabet*	184

PART V	ART AND AESTHETICS	
Chapter 22	Early Film Colour, Today and Yesterday *Charles O'Brien*	195
Chapter 23	Salvage Ethnography and the Exoticisation of Decay in Peter Delpeut's *Lyrical Nitrate* and Bill Morrison's *Decasia* *Nadia Bozak*	200
Chapter 24	Picture Craft, Visual Education and the Lantern: A Lecture Fantasy *Kaveh Askari*	207
Chapter 25	The Scope of Those Scopes: Production Diversity for the Mutoscope and Biograph During the Movies' Early Years *Paul C. Spehr*	214
Chapter 26	The High-Stakes History of the French Camera Operators' Union before the First World War *Priska Morrissey*	223

CONTENTS

PART VI   EXHIBITION AND SHOWMANSHIP

Chapter 27   Les séries culturelles de la conférence-avec-projection et de la projection-avec-boniment: continuités et ruptures
André Gaudreault and Philippe Gauthier   233

Chapter 28   Les "conférenciers de cinéma" en France (1896–1930): Historique à travers différents lieux de projection, genres filmiques et réseaux   *Thierry Lecointe*   239

Chapter 29   Les images en mouvement au théâtre de variétés: le cas de l'Apollo de Düsseldorf   *Frank Kessler et Sabine Lenk*   247

Chapter 30   Royals, Rembrandts and Luxors: Patterns and Clusters in the Nomenclature of Dutch Cinemas   *André van der Velden*   255

Chapter 31   Local Showmanship in the Early Feature Era: The Case of Stanley Mastbaum   *Joel Frykholm*   263

Chapter 32   A Transformative Moment: Samuel Rothafel and the Rise of Multi-Class Moviegoing in the Midwest, 1911–1913   *Ross Melnick*   271

PART VII   COMMUNITY AND THE PUBLIC SPHERE

Chapter 33   "This Splendid Temple": Watching Movies in the Wanamaker Department Store   *Caitlin McGrath*   281

Chapter 34   "Boost Your Town in the Movies": Municipal Film Companies in the United States, 1910–1917   *Martin L. Johnson*   288

Chapter 35   Early Cinema and the Public Sphere of the Neighbourhood Meeting Hall: The Longue Durée of Working-Class Sociability   *Judith Thissen*   297

Chapter 36   Trans-Inter-National Public Spheres   *Wolfgang Fuhrmann*   307

Chapter 37   Turning the Social Problem into Performance: Slumming and Screen Culture in Victorian Lantern Shows   *Ludwig Maria Vogl-Bienek*   315

Editors and contributors   325

Index of Films   329

Index of Names   332

Introduction

Marta Braun, Charlie Keil, Rob King, Paul Moore and Louis Pelletier

The roots of motion pictures exist as much in science and industry as in magic lantern shows and fairground exhibition. Indeed, the ultimate reputation of cinema as a medium devoted to entertainment was an eventual destination and not a foregone conclusion. In the novelty era – from its origins until around 1901 – cinema performed a range of functions: it provided its viewers with increased visual awareness of the natural world, access to remote corners of the globe, and immediate reports of pertinent events, both local and international. Even as it gained institutional status, cinema continued to be exploited for educational and civic purposes, and its reach extended beyond the four walls of the nickelodeon theatre to a wide variety of venues including churches, schools, department stores and charitable organisations. In such settings, from Dublin to Brussels, Quebec to Kyoto, cinema's impact exceeded the narrow conceptual confines dictated by its primary role as purveyor of entertainment for the masses. *Beyond the Screen: Institutions, Networks and Publics of Early Cinema* seeks to illuminate the range of early cinema and the ways in which it influenced and intersected with realms beyond the world of entertainment. Whether deployed for medical training, enlisted by missionaries, or debated by lawmakers, cinema insinuated itself into a range of institutions, the collective force of which we still scarcely comprehend. This volume is an important step toward our understanding of how early cinema defined itself through institutional interconnections, within a network of intermedial exchange and to a series of publics united by their interest in cinema: it shows just how the variety of motion pictures' aims and uses helped define the multi-faceted nature of the medium in its first decades.

Ironically, cinema's potential as a medium of social effectivity found itself constrained by an American legal decision. In 1915, near the end of the early cinema period, a U.S. Supreme Court decision declaring moviemaking a "business, pure and simple" entrenched the film industry's role as a producer of "harmless entertainment". Together with the concurrent establishment of the feature film, the growth of the star system and the consolidation of production companies, this decision ensured that movies would become the primary form of commercial entertainment in the new century. Just prior to this moment, however, the possibilities available to film – to educate, to influence public policy, to explore the natural world – were as open as they would ever be again in the medium's existence. The eleventh bi-annual Domitor conference held on the campuses of Ryerson University and the University of Toronto (13–16 June

2010), explored the various ways that a range of institutions, both commercial and non-commercial, shaped early cinema's cultural functions and social uses. As this volume attests, conference presenters confirmed the breadth and variety of interests that cinema served during the first few decades of its existence; in so doing, they extended the role of film far beyond that of the "entertainment" model eventually pursued by a maturing industry and championed by the Supreme Court in America.

To consider early cinema "beyond the screen" is to restore complexity to the historical account of film's social and cultural roles, its interactions with a variety of institutions and its ideological function and aesthetic impact. Examining the range of social networks in which cinematic practices operated provides insight into the many ways film was used within the domains of science, technology, education, and social uplift; it also reveals how those applications influenced the development of the medium while simultaneously shaping the public's idea of what cinema was capable of achieving. Moreover, the identification of those groups or institutions who saw the exploitation of cinema as a means to further their own aims – for Progressive-era social intervention or for capitalist expansion of industry, religious indoctrination or artistic education – gives us a clearer idea of how this new form of image production became integrated into the changing cultural landscape of the early twentieth century. One of the more striking insights afforded by this line of inquiry is the manner in which cinema's various features – its reliance on oversized images, its portability, its ability to be viewed by large numbers of people at a single screening – attracted the attention of groups just coming to terms with equally modern ideas of influencing the public on a large scale, thus aligning cinema with broad-based public policy and with the burgeoning mass media of journalism and advertising.

As much as cinema attracted the attention of groups and institutions outside the motion picture industry, those making and screening films within that industry reached out to the broader public realm in turn. Many early film producers and exhibitors explored how they could become more useful to a range of social agents, motivated either to improve cinema's public image or increase its earning potential. Projecting mainstream moving pictures in churches, convincing educators of the benefits of using film in the classroom, and collaborating with charitable organizations to produce movies meant to increase awareness of social ills – all of these gestures enlarged the role of cinema within the public sphere while also demonstrating its usefulness as a tool of instruction, advocacy and persuasion. If the Supreme Court decision of 1915 reinforced the film industry's tendency toward making frivolous films for a complacent audience, this volume's collective focus on cinema's early years of engagement with a wide range of social institutions documents a counterbalancing tendency that tested the boundaries of what was considered entertainment, and often opposed the expectations that the Hollywood studio era so forcefully created and fulfilled.

Institutions

All of the papers collected here contribute to what might be called a new "institutional turn" in the study of film cultures – an approach spearheaded in such work as Haidee Wasson's on the creation of MoMA's Film Library (*Museum Movies*, 2005), Peter Decherney's on *Hollywood and the Culture Elite* (2005), and Dana Polan's on the first university film courses (*Scenes of Instruction*, 2007), all of which examine how cinema has been put to use by institutions outside what is conventionally understood as the "film industry".[1] Before outlining the contents of the present volume, then, it is worth briefly considering this new emphasis in film history, and in particular its implications for the study of early cinema.

Introduction

If revisionist histories of pre-1915 cinema can be said to have had a founding gesture, it was surely the relabeling of what was once dismissively considered "primitive" cinema as, instead, "early" or "pre-classical". In great part an effort to rescue film history from a kind of Lamarckian schema – as though cinema's historical development was to be understood as a linear, unidirectional evolution from the first "primitive" scenes (Edison, Lumière) toward increasingly complex storytelling forms (Griffith) – this relabeling also placed the question of *context* firmly on the historians' agenda. Rather than a symptom of a primordial stage of development, the oft-noted difference of early film was now to be explained as deriving from the different contexts in which early cinema's uses and functions were first explored. Two lines of contextualizing inquiry here emerged. On the one hand, from the perspective of *social* history, there was an interest in relating the forms of nickelodeon-era cinema (1905–1912) to the needs and tastes of its largely immigrant, working-class audiences, as well as in examining cinema's emerging storytelling norms in terms of filmmakers' attempts to incorporate genteel cultural values into their films. On the other, from the perspective of *cultural* history, was the attempt to relate the attractions-based aesthetic of early film to the broader context of "modernity", which, like the films themselves, was characterized by the shock effects attendant on unprecedented technological and industrial change.

Both of these approaches, however, stumbled over a shared problematic; namely, the question of how social and cultural forms – genteel cultural values or the shocks of modernity – come to be implanted in film texts. We should not assume or expect to find social realities directly "reflected" in art, since historical context always passes through a process of mediation in which its content is changed in the very act of representation. But this observation, in turn, adds a further twist to the question of context, since it requires that the film historian direct attention to the various mediating processes through which social values and intentions have shaped the uses of cinema. And here, evidently, formal institutions have a profound role to play; it is, after all, through institutions (pedagogical, religious, commercial, etc.) that specific social meanings and practices are selected and transmitted. Indeed, specific interest groups seek to exert pressures on the conditions of social life precisely through institutions as the means of governance and enculturation. At no time, moreover, was the role of institutions within film culture more varied and open than during cinema's early period – before, that is, Hollywood and the other great national film industries had fully emerged to hegemonize the idea of film as "harmless entertainment". From this perspective, the institutional turn in film history represents a significant paradigm shift in the study of cinema's earliest years: it returns the study of early cinema's varied development and uses to the specific material contents and intentions of the social organisations, pedagogical disciplines, and cultural movements that sought to harness the new medium to new ends.

Yet the historiographic challenges that this line of inquiry raises are immense. Only the most unreconstructed Althusserian could imagine that a museum does the same kind of cultural and ideological work as a department store, or that charity administrators and commercial film exhibitors would have agreed on matters of cultural taste. To quote Raymond Williams: "[I]t can ... not be supposed that the sum of all ... institutions is an organic hegemony. On the contrary ... it is in practice full of contradictions and of unresolved conflicts".[2] There are, of course, variants in the intentions that different institutions bring to bear in their use of film, as well as differences in the volumes of economic and cultural capital incarnate in those institutions. To "uplift", to "legitimize", to "educate" – to name only some of the processes examined in this volume – these are not always synonyms, but speak to a diversity of

3

competing social interests and intentions of which any properly contextualized film history must take account.

Networks

The various institutions that appropriated the new technology of moving pictures at the turn of the twentieth century were typically associated with specific exhibition venues. The social context of viewing, as many of the authors assert, was instrumental in determining the uses and meanings of the films exhibited. Each of the various exhibition sites, however, gains its particularity in relation to the others as an alternative within a network of film practices. As with the work of institutions, the significance of particular audiences and their venues should neither be rigidly codified (e.g. a church leads to indoctrination) nor made synonymous through one conceptual dimension (the local). For example, animated views taken with the help of microscopes, X-rays or time-lapse photography could be framed as popular science when shown as part of a lecture or as sheer visual spectacle when screened in the commercial context of a nickelodeon. Conversely, narrative films produced to entertain a mass audience could be made to teach a moral or history lesson depending on the venue in which they were exhibited.

The research collected in this volume further demonstrates how deeply the practices of the first filmmakers were influenced by their own and others' pre-cinematic activities: most of the lanternists, lecturers, cartoonists, magicians and scientists who are found among the early adopters of moving pictures were typically more concerned with the enrichment and expansion of their traditional activities than with the creation of a new medium or art. As André Gaudreault and Philippe Marion have claimed, cinema was "born twice": during the first decade of its history, moving pictures were almost exclusively exhibited in venues primarily dedicated to other types of shows and performances, including lecture halls and legitimate or variety theatres. It took time for permanent exhibition sites to appear, gain autonomy from other theatrical networks, and develop standardised show formats. In most parts of the Western world, moving pictures' second decade – also covered by the essays collected here – saw the quick rise of a formidable network of venues dedicated primarily to cinema. Thriving on the new class of narrative films concurrently being developed, this vast theatrical network elevated cinema to the rank of leading attraction. It also, in the process, enlisted many of the established forms of entertainment in the service of cinema, maintaining the momentum of intermedial relations but reversing its direction. Magic lantern shows and vaudeville briefly became an essential part of the moving picture program through the standardised companion of the illustrated song. The advent of a theatrical network dedicated solely to film soon established the hegemony of cinema as a harmless form of entertainment, not least because the proliferation of the local picture theatre vastly outnumbered alternative venues and exhibition contexts – although it must be emphasised that it did not eliminate them. Nonetheless, it seems that from the moment venues dedicated to moving pictures appeared, non-fiction films such as newsreels, topicals and travelogues were routinely programmed by commercial exhibitors partly to assuage the industry's many critics by lending a degree of cultural capital and local content to commercial shows. This programming, in turn, facilitated the diffusion of the multireel fiction features cranked out of an increasingly limited number of production centres.

While the formation of a theatrical network established cinema as one of the most influential mass media of the young twentieth century, it also relegated many potentialities of film to the newly conjured non-theatrical ghetto. As part of Domitor's ongoing rediscovery and investigation of the continued use of moving pictures in a wide range of networks dedicated to education, science, reform or propaganda, *Beyond the Screen* is especially illuminating because of the emphasis it places on the intermedial environment in which cinema kept evolving – even after the institutionalisation of theatrical commercial cinema. Outside film palaces, moving pictures were still frequently made subservient to the speech of educators or lecturers, or made to play second fiddle to musical performances, variety acts, sporting matches, or even commercial displays of industrial wares. Beyond acting as a most useful – and humbling – reminder of the importance of context in film history, the increased attention given to "useful cinema" and non-theatrical networks demonstrates just how easily the lines between entertainment, education and uplift can be blurred when it comes to performances integrating film.

Publics

While describing film's emergence from within intermedial networks of other entertainments allows a sense of early cinema's circulation, and outlining the variety of institutions that strategically employed cinema as it established its own institutional autonomy provides a sense of the breadth of applications for the new medium, the specificity of any local cinematic practice still needs to be conceptualized as constituting a wider cinema culture. One framework in which the various cinema practices documented in this collection characterise a cultural capacity specific to moving pictures lies in the concept of "publics". As film historians, all of the authors in this volume give moving pictures a privileged place in modern culture, in part because it is simultaneously a commodity, technology and art form unlike others. But the unique character of the moving image perhaps can be best explored by interrogating how cinema existed as a mode of public address. To study the heterogeneous publics of early cinema is to see the moving image as not merely inscribed into other institutions, or circulating within other social networks, but rather as a novel social formation in itself – allowing a new way of being as well as a new way of seeing. The problem of defining cinema's publics, then, lies in generalising beyond local practices, or rather taking them as coordinated through the medium and its new way of addressing audiences. Just as cinema needs to be defined institutionally as more than a transparent reflection of social realities, its social significance needs to be understood beyond the particular local situations provided by individual case studies.

Defining a modern "public" has been subject to much consideration, perhaps most formally by Michael Warner, who articulates the concept as "a space of discourse" that comes to exist and is maintained in the very act of being addressed. A public is thus an imagined social formation, not an empirical one; a public is not necessarily addressed in a common space or time, or through a common identity. "Neither *'crowd'* nor *'audience'* nor *'people'* nor *'group'* will capture the same sense".[3] Modeled on his study of mass readerships, Warner's definition of publics depends upon an indeterminate formation: a reader's "partial nonidentity" with the subject being addressed, and therefore *an awareness* that masses of strangers are concurrently being addressed in the same fashion. The formulation is similar to Benedict Anderson's "imagined communities" but generalized beyond the vernacular address of nationalism.[4] For cinema in particular, the concept of a "public" unifies the many geographically and temporally dispersed audiences for particular films into a culture of film-going by recognizing the potential for different audiences to conceive of themselves as addressed in common by the film, or again more generally by the cultural practice of cinema going. The long shadow of Habermas' democratic public sphere and its rational debate over ideas looms large insofar as Warner's "publics" are reading publics. Miriam Hansen proposed – in her reading of Benjamin's "gamble with cinema" – that the key to a cinematic public sphere is "room-for-play", in part because of the very ambiguity and latitude for interpretive pleasure that viewing allows compared to reading.[5] The essays in the last two sections of this collection especially provide the groundwork to further such an understanding of how reading publics (such as those for newspapers) were transformed into viewing publics for cinema.

While revealing, and reveling in, the historical facts of local case studies, the papers in this volume collectively propose that early cinema culture was steeped in a sensibility of public service. Addressing a sense of public good, a moving picture show could draw an audience by appealing to its own best interests. Changing institutional or exhibition contexts could better match a specific public's sense of itself, its "imagined community". The limit of that generalization, ironically, lies at the point where film becomes art and develops its own institutions for aesthetic appreciation. Here is where the viewing public may be elided, in a sense, because parts of the film industry could turn inward to attend to professional standards and aestheticism with the institutionalization of the industry. Then again, taking the audience for granted could only occur as a result of the care, labour, invention, and attention that created cinema cultures beyond the screen in the first place.

From charity to the public sphere

The tri-partite emphasis on *Institutions*, *Networks* and *Publics* informs the organisation of these conference proceedings: section titles indicate the orientation of the papers included within each section and the sections themselves have been placed under one of the three rubrics contained in the volume's title. Under *Institutions*, the papers in the first three sections devoted to "Charity and Religion", "Government and Civics", and "Education and Advocacy" demonstrate the different ways in which cinema exerted influence on social agencies, government bodies and educational groups – and found itself affected by the forces of social improvement in its turn. Encompassing social uses that range from religious indoctrination to health instruction, these papers remind us that cinema's institutional interactions incited controversy and cultivated unlikely allies even as such connections expanded and challenged prevailing ideas about the medium's proper identity.

Under *Networks*, the papers in the sections "Science and Magic" and "Art and Aesthetics" investigate cinema's relationship to realms that found themselves increasingly defined by the presence of media. Whether it was the cinema's technologically-enhanced ability to document the unseen and the invisible or the manner in which cinema infiltrated art education as one of a range of technologies capable of image reproduction, the medium operated within a growing network of media practices and devices, whose collective force helped define how one might understand art and science. The technological basis of cinema – and its intermedial connections – continues to inform its aesthetic potential in the present, not least because of the archive's role in preserving and disseminating the extant fragments of the medium's past.

The role of *Publics* in shaping the culture of cinema during this period receives its fullest rehearsal in the collection's concluding sections, "Exhibition and Showmanship" and "Community and the Public Sphere". In these papers the emphasis shifts to the manner in which the exhibition venue and the practices employed in the screening of films aided in an expanded sense of cinema's effectivity and community presence. The varied ways in which spectators viewed and made use of films proved a vital element in perpetuating tendencies already evident at the levels of production and distribution. The public's willingness to embrace cinema's diverse social and cultural roles rein-

Introduction

forces how early cinema's potential for extending its purview beyond the realms of entertainment found its necessary corollary in an equally varied terrain of viewing and exhibition practices. Moreover, cinema's role in helping to create communities, whether films were projected in the neighbourhood theatre or a local meeting place, underscores the recurrent argument within this volume: that the medium's potential demonstrably extended "beyond the screen" to incorporate a series of institutional collaborators, tapping into a vast matrix of intermedial networks, and reaching an ever-changing set of publics. In our contemporary era of seemingly limitless connectivity, abetted by multiple delivery systems, social networking sites and virtual communities, the era of early cinema, with its counterbalancing examples of possibilities explored and opportunities lost, still has much to tell us.

Acknowledgements

The editors wish to acknowledge the assistance of the Social Science Humanities Research Council of Canada and the Office of the Dean in the Faculty of the Arts and Science at the University of Toronto. We are particularly grateful for the generosity and support of Ryerson University: its School of Image Arts, Faculty of Communication and Design, Office of Research and Innovation and Office of the Provost. We are deeply indebted to Alicia Fletcher for her expert and conscientious editorial assistance in the preparation of this volume. Finally, thanks to John Libbey for his ready support of this project.

Notes

1. Haidee Wasson, *Museum Movies: The Museum of Modern Art and the Birth of Art Cinema* (Berkeley: University of California Press, 2005); Peter Decherney, *Hollywood and the Culture Elite: How the Movies Became American* (New York: Columbia University Press, 2005); Dana Polan, *Scenes of Instruction: The Beginnings of the US Study of Film* (Berkeley: University of California Press, 2007).
2. Raymond Williams, *Marxism and Literature* (New York: Oxford University Press, 1977), 118.
3. Michael Warner, *Publics and Counterpublics* (New York: Zone Books, 2002), 67.
4. Benedict Anderson, *Imagined Communities: Reflections on the Origins of Nationalism* (New York: Verso, 1983).
5. Miriam Bratu Hansen, "Room-for-Play: Benjamin's Gamble with Cinema", *October* 109 (2004): 3–45.

PART I

Charity and Religion

"Neutrality-Humanity": The Humanitarian Mission and the Films of the American Red Cross

Jennifer Horne

In 1921 the American Red Cross in the east-central Ohio county of Muskingum took up motion picture exhibition, putting on an ambitious monthly film series to be shown at various community sites across the region. Announcements of the summer-long event promised viewers films of high quality made by the Red Cross, with each evening opened by guest lecturers on topics tied to the films and closed with rounds of community singing. The outreach film programming purported to offer discussion and illumination in areas of continuing education relevant to the immediate farming community: agriculture, health, schools, good roads, and child welfare. The Ohio Red Cross chapters mounted these screenings with portable projection equipment loaned to the organisation by a local enterprise hoping to draw sales interest from audience members – just the type of private-public partnership celebrated by pro-business advocates of visual education, who stood to gain from such tacit displays of public betterment.

While the touring films were touted as educational, individual film titles' relationship to each theme reveals a more relaxed curriculum. We might ask what the travelogue reel, *Venice* (1920), was doing in the "Schools" program? Or how *Father Knickerbocker's Children* (1920) supported the goal of "Good Roads"? Topical but residual in its conception of film reception, the entire summer program consisted of films released as many as three years earlier. These film programs confirm film historians' current conception of the nontheatrical distribution network as remedial and repertory-by-default, sustaining and sustained by an unfiltered and uneven flow of older and cheaper films.

Sponsored film exhibitions tied to charity fundraising and community education, simultaneously goodwill gestures and good publicity, offer us further evidence of the dynamic interplay between the varied publics of moviegoing. Mobile, makeshift, and enthusiastically civic-spirited screenings of motion pictures in public halls, schools, libraries, churches, lodges, and peripheral cinemas in urban locations were not only well-established by 1915, but they were a continuation of the screen practices of traveling showmen, lanternists, and lecturers before them. The circulation of Red Cross films and filmmaking by the Red Cross is a short-lived film example that would ordinarily be considered outside of the networks of entertainment but which is more properly understood as having taken place on the fringes of this sphere. What makes

Fig. 1. This publicity still shows American Red Cross Juniors in Father Knickerbocker's Children *(1920) arriving at Bellevue Hospital to distribute their handmade toys to infirm children. [Courtesy Library of Congress.]*

the example of the in-house production of films by the American Red Cross all the more notable as a nontheatrical endeavour is the agency's late entrance and sudden exit from film production, at the same time as production, distribution, and exhibition outlets for educational and instructional film in North America entered a period of relative stability and modest profitability. And the American Red Cross's filmmaking division addressed its audience with all of the authority of a semi-governmental agency, lending to any screening of its films an automatic public legitimacy.

Whether that summer screening in 1921 was a success or not – or whether it demonstrates a national but fragmentary cinema of civic happenstance – it is clear that this type of charity organisation film gathering has not yet been properly accounted for by film historians. That the American Red Cross produced short films during these years is a fact that still goes relatively unrecognised by scholars.[1] Regular but cursory mention is made by historians of the Red Cross photography units as willing purveyors of war propaganda, always in connection with its cooptation by the U.S. Office of War Information (OWI) and George Creel's Committee on Public Information (CPI).[2] Similarly, it is well-known that Pathé and other studios regularly purchased Red Cross footage of the European conflict for use in weekly newsreel and screen magazine programs. This kind of trafficking in footage might have been widespread during this period, but is not well documented (and so, not very often pursued as a meaningful topic for analysis). Several well-known documentary filmmakers (such as Ernest Schoedsack and Merl LaVoy) and photographers (Lewis Hine, for example) were given an officer's rank and uniform and sent to the field to make films for the unit or shoot stills for Red Cross publications and film publicity. Hamid Naficy has recognised the significance of the Red Cross to the career of Schoedsack and written about his fieldwork as cameraman for the Bureau.[3] Gerry Veeder, meanwhile, has published a detailed overview of the Red Cross's years in film production in the *Historical Journal*

1 "Neutrality-Humanity"

Fig. 2. Extension services offered by Berea College in Kentucky as depicted in Down in Lonesome Hollow *(1920). The Red Cross captioner noted that community organising was one of the skills offered to the "Kentuckey mountaineers" [sic] in the film. [Courtesy Library of Congress.]*

of Film, Radio, and Television. The most authoritative analysis of the Bureau's moving image work to date, her article raises a series of important questions about institutional filmmaking, educational film culture (broadly construed), and archival discovery that have yet to be fully responded to.[4] In what follows, I consider the ways that specific generic categories – beyond the familiar codes of objectivity and dispassionate enunciation usually applied to works of nonfiction – help us frame the agency's film work as specific to its humanitarian mission and quasi-governmental status. In the Red Cross's employment of motion pictures, *neutrality*, it appears, was both a filmic device and an ideological rationale.

The Red Cross Motion Picture Bureau was established in late 1916 primarily for the purpose of satisfying a publicity mission. Starting in 1917, the Bureau sent camera operators into war relief areas. Closing finally in 1922, it had produced motion pictures in the years after the war as part of its civilian public health campaigns. Due to its governmental status, the Red Cross's film unit was able to attract talented photographers and camera operators who had been called into military service. The unit produced over one hundred titles in all. Only seven titles are held in the collections of film archives today.[5]

The first Motion Picture Bureau chiefs envisioned Red Cross membership as the principal, if not exclusive, audience for its films. In 1917, the agency restricted exhibition of the films it produced to Red Cross chapters and special fundraising engagements.[6] But this exclusivity of address quickly evaporated as the agency's financial needs shifted and exhibitors exercised practical patriotism. *The Historic Fourth of July in Paris* (1918), featuring parades of Red Cross nurses, became the agency's inaugural public screening in August 1918. Its premier was held at the Rivoli Theatre in New York City and the film was subsequently booked into over two thousand vaudeville houses. To determine the full range of locations and spaces in which the

Red Cross films were shown would require research at the level of regional chapters. What is potentially most interesting about the Red Cross's film exhibition initiative is its close connection to community-based organisations that the burgeoning nontheatrical circuits sought to outfit with projection equipment and screens: Rotary halls, Kiwanis clubs, churches, schools, theatres, social clubs, and the like. The address to the audience must have been somewhat pluralising, seeking out among spectators the immediate Red Cross public and an aspirational sympathetic public as well.

Confusion about the intended audience for these films can be found both within the organisation's internal communication and in announcements for Red Cross films in trade papers of the day. One of the thornier issues of rhetoric circumscribing the visual campaigns of the Red Cross, however, was the professed ideal of political neutrality that bound the organisation to its humanitarian mission. Prior to 6 April 1917, the stated mission of the American Red Cross was to adhere to a notion of political neutrality in aid and humanitarian service; even its letterhead proclaimed "Neutrality-Humanity". When the organisation became an auxiliary to the armed forces, however, offering civilian relief and applying the "merciful hand" in neutral fashion was impossible. To further complicate matters, under the US Espionage and Sedition Acts of 1917 and 1918 it was unlawful to speak against the Red Cross or its war work. Other American relief and volunteer agencies – the YMCA, the Knights of Columbus, and the American Library Association, to name a few – provided educational and recreational services, including a steady stream of motion pictures, to soldiers in war camps. But the assistance given by the Red Cross was different in that it was specifically commissioned to perform patriotic duty.

The subject matter and stylistic range of the one- and two-reel agency films prove vexing for anyone seeking to dismiss the organisation's filmic output as shallow instruments of persuasion. Judging by the extant films, available stills, and catalogue descriptions, the films produced by the agency during its years of in-house operation had a remarkable consistency of voice and message. Generically and visually, the films balanced the foreign with the familiar. Film catalogues and printed brochures dispatched to regional chapters advertised the pictures using the most commonly used descriptors for topical film: "war picture", "action picture", "travel films", "scenic films", and "industrial films". Encouraging well-balanced film programs, the agency suggested themed programs such as "travel and science", or "the rehabilitation of veterans", or "health films", without regard for the specific needs of a region or chapter. Film titles were either poetic or emotionally-laden, in an attempt to draw attention away from graphic depictions of human suffering or destruction: *Of No Use to Germany* (1918) featured French and German civilian war refugees; *Your Boy* (1918) was composed of footage of wounded American soldiers under the care of Red Cross workers in France; *The Train at Havre* (1918; alternate title, *The Train of Horror*) contained graphic images of Russian war wounded returning from the front lines of the war;[7] and *New Faces for Old* (1918) showed the reconstruction of mutilated soldiers by French doctors. *Come Clean* (1918?), a dental hygiene film in two reels produced by the US Army but distributed by the Red Cross, found wider circulation, as did the home hygiene and public health nursing pictures, *Every Woman's Problem* (1921) and *Winning Her Way* (1921).

Lines between intellectual and popular audiences were blurred, as were the lines between information and spectacle. Reportage in the war pitched charity: information was combined with sentiment in order to soothe, comfort, and reassure the viewer that something good was coming of their benevolence and humanitarianism. In its final years of operation, the Bureau turned out nursing films and educational titles more germane to a sense of American neediness. Didactic films displaying domestic household hygiene addressed public health issues, advertised the teaching of first aid and water safety, and dramatized the history of Red Cross workers. Another series of shorts, produced for Junior Red Cross audiences, featured pen-pal narratives with war orphans abroad.

Closer examination of the Red Cross's catalogues in which these series were described and promoted can help us further refine our understanding of the morphology of educational genres in this period. If we take, for instance, those films presented to the public as travelogue pictures, we can usefully locate their imaginative power and manner of address as expressive modes that lay somewhere between the two key tendencies of early factual film: a cosmopolitan and globe-trotting cinema, dispatching camera operators to exoticised, far-flung regions with the intent to broaden spectatorial horizons, and a cinema that delighted in depicting the world just outside the theatre doors. The latter tendency would constitute what Tom Gunning refers to as "a cinema of locality", typified by an audience's amazement in seeing the recognisable and the familiar on screen.[8] In the hands of Red Cross photographers, that sense of familiarity might have been produced by the display of a procedure or a vocation as a humanising debut: the selling of wares in an outdoor market, for instance, in *The Fall of Kiev* (1919). Cinematic treatment of an everyday life during wartime found the familiar in the foreign by couching its documentary tourism in terms of a humanitarian mission. With conflict somewhere off-frame, but also operating in this mode of displaying everydayness, the organisation would be able to link its mission – as promoted to its supporters – to the magical immediacy of the cinema without trafficking in the spectacles of war photography. Indeed, the years of film production at the Red Cross coincide and track perfectly with the emergence of the paradoxical phenomenon of the "exotic mundane" in nonfiction films as described by William Urrichio. As the more spectacular novelties of early cinema gave way to serious subjects, the demand to capture and hold the audience's attention in a state of wonderment was tempered by more prosaic and familiar scenes. In the years leading up to the war, Urrichio explains, "[T]he motion picture's intimate visual access to remote cultures, famous persons, and historical events managed simultaneously to enhance its subjects' aura (putting them in the news, making them 'bigger than life') while transforming the exotic or exalted into a repeatable commodity – an ordinary, even trivial, encounter".[9] After the war, a more subdued approach dominated, one that Urrichio attributes to "a new cultural immune system".[10] It is no surprise, then, that at the stylistic core of the American Red Cross's filmmaking venture (a venture not isolated from the agency's other communications aims and divisions) we find a transitional enunciation, one that toggles between spectatorial distance and familiarity.

Looking at the catalogue descriptions, the lobby cards, and the publicity stills that remain from these films, one also sees evidence of the common generic strategy of asserting an Americanism that treats the rest of the world as its subordinate, its past, and its object of consumption. *The Red Cross Travel Series* (1920–21) most likely used highly conventional strategies to depict the geographically distant and culturally different. As Jennifer Peterson has observed, the early travel film's primary mode of address performs the "acting out of attraction and repulsion".[11] From this perspective, it makes sense that in the North African film, *Children of the Sahara* (1921), a title which is no longer extant, many of the scenes seem to have been composed to display rituals and beliefs that underscore stereotypes about the uncivilised and mystical ways of the Other. However, if the films in this series likely also conformed to standard expedition and scenic film conventions, using the most commercially successful and exploitative techniques to depict far-off places and peoples, it is also true that these were not simply

Fig. 3. The reverse side of this mounted photograph from the American Red Cross collection described the appearance of a "little Arabian girl", a non-actor in The Children of the Sahara (1920), in the more familiar terms of film stardom. [Courtesy Library of Congress.]

travel films but a hybridised version of the genre that would hardly encourage leisure travel, tourism, or unselfconsciously embody a tourist's subjectivity. In fact, it is more likely that titles such as *In Picturesque Romania* (1921), *Prague, City of a Hundred Towers* (1921), *Apple Blossom Time in Normandy* (1921), and *Beside the Zuider Zee* (1921) would have been presented to audiences as typical voyage-oriented views of the world when their humanitarian aid message unsettled the idea of venturing there; more likely, an excess of appeals pushed these films out of their conventional generic location entirely. If, as Peterson argues, a dynamic of fascination and ambivalence became the commercial travel genre's most characteristic quality, then in the Red Cross travel series especially, the underlying purpose of salvation and rescue would alter both the landscape and the gaze. After all, these films were meant to illustrate a charitable commitment to aid from afar for those living in the wake of conflict, with travel to these lands inadvisable and even dangerous.

Through its graphic association of action and participation through charity and aid, the Red Cross multiplied the burden of representation already contained in films from the front. As Gerry Veeder argues, spectators were promised that in these films they would see their kindness writ large: viewers were shown "the tangible results of their donations, medical supplies, bandages, kit bags, clothing, and food. Human drama, shown in the faces of the participants, was combined with the maternal image of the Red Cross, personified in posters as 'the Greatest Mother'".[12] Films that were not premised upon the actual circumstances of a refugee population, returning soldiers, or human catastrophe would employ sentimental devices of narration to associate patriotism with humanism.[13] Films that were, were more sensational; *The Land without Mirth* (1920), a depiction of war refugees in Belgium, adopted picturesque strategies of displacement in order to shift attention from referential documentary content to the hypertrophic heroic support network of the agency. The Red Cross film brochure promised viewers that *Land Without Mirth* would take them "into a land so dreary that the children have only cemeteries for playgrounds, into once comfortable homes now masses of ruins".[14]

Generic classification is but one of the interesting qualities salient to these films and their circulation through a civilian and civic mediascape that is less well understood than the more dominant commercial networks of entertainment. But it is an important starting place, as the question of how to classify such work is directly connected to its film-historical marginalisation. For this reason, I conclude with an ironic anecdote about historical oversight, one that demonstrates how personal the stakes of historical exclusion might be for a case like the Red Cross. Arthur Edwin Krows' "Motion Pictures – Not for Theatres", a panoramic history of nontheatrical film serialised in issues of *The Educational Screen* beginning in 1938, includes only a few glancing references to the American Red Cross's years of film production, and ignores the organisation's relationship with other nontheatrical interests such as Eastern Film or the Society for Visual Education. While I cannot explain Krows' ignorance of the Red Cross's Bureau of Motion Pictures, I was surprised to find a direct connection between the American Red Cross and this chronicler of nontheatrical media in the course of my research. Late in 1926, an announcement emanated from Red Cross Headquarters in Washington. Chapters were being encouraged to book, through the Society for Visual Education, a new Red Cross film titled *The Twister*, a dramatic short on the theme of disaster preparedness, to be shown to raise money for disaster relief in hurricane-stricken Florida. The synopsis tells a simple story of greed versus generosity, a tornado leveling a small town whose mayor had dismissed the usefulness of the Red Cross local chapter. The author of the film's story and scenario was Arthur Edwin

Krows, the man who would later leave the American Red Cross out of nontheatrical film history.

Notes

1. Recognition of the cultural importance of one Red Cross film was bestowed by the Library of Congress in 2009 when the title *Heroes, All* (1919) was added to the National Film Registry.
2. See Craig W. Campbell, *Reel America and WWI: A Comprehensive Filmography and History of Motion Pictures in the United States, 1914–1920* (Jefferson, NC: McFarland, 1985), 77–89, 130. The filmography also includes several American Red Cross titles.
3. Hamid Naficy, "Lured by the East: Ethnographic and Expedition Films about Nomadic Tribes – The Case of *Grass* (1925)", in Jeffrey Ruoff (ed.), *Virtual Voyages: Cinema and Travel* (Durham: Duke University Press, 2006), 117–138. As Naficy notes, and not merely in passing, Ernest Schoedsack shot several of the films in the Red Cross travel series, including *Children of the Sahara* (1921), *'Neath Poland's Skies* (1921), and *Shepherds of Tatra* (1921). *To the Aid of Poland* (1921) and *The Fall of Kiev* (1921) also contain Schoedsack's footage.
4. Gerry K. Veeder, "The Red Cross Bureau of Pictures, 1917–1921: World War I, the Russian Revolution and the Sultan of Turkey's Harem", *Historical Journal of Film, Radio, and Television* 10, no. 4 (1990): 47–70. Veeder's unprecedented access to the historical files at the Red Cross headquarters in the 1980s, prior to their relocation to the National Archives and Records Administration, enabled a meticulous and nuanced treatment of the Agency's internal records, from an optimal vantage point that no other historian is likely to have for some time to come.
5. These statistics are based upon a February 2010 search of the International Federation of Film Archives (FIAF) database. Duplicates of titles do exist in several locations, although, to my knowledge, the prints have not been compared.
6. Veeder, "Red Cross", 56.
7. The exhibitor's catalogue description for this film reads: "Think of a train which traveled a distance equal to that from New York to San Francisco and back to Chicago – more than five thousand miles – a train of crude box cars filled with ill and wounded Russian Soldiers! Scores of them as well as nurses and doctors, died before they could be reached by the hand of 'The Greatest Mother' [the Red Cross's self-personification]. This is an unusual picture, with the above title. It holds spectators from beginning to end". *A Descriptive Catalog of Fifty Motion Pictures Produced and Circulated by The Red Cross* (undated), Box 425, RG 200, Red Cross Collection, National Archives and Records Administration.
8. Tom Gunning, "Pictures of Crowd Splendor: The Mitchell and Kenyon Factory Gate Films", in Vanessa Toulmin, Patrick Russell, and Simon Popple (eds), *The Lost World of Mitchell and Kenyon* (London: BFI Publishing, 2004), 49–58.
9. William Urrichio, "Ways of Seeing: The New Vision of Early Nonfiction Film", in Daan Hertogs and Nico De Klerk (eds), *Uncharted Territory: Essays on Early Nonfiction* (Amsterdam: Stichting Nederlands Filmmuseum, 1997), 119–131.
10. Urrichio, "Ways of Seeing", 120.
11. Jennifer Peterson, "Truth is Stranger than Fiction", in Hertogs and De Klerk (eds), *Uncharted Territory*, 75–90.
12. Veeder, "The Red Cross", 55–56.
13. On this point in particular, see Kevin Rozario, "'Delicious Horrors': Mass Culture, the Red Cross, and the Appeal of Modern American Humanitarianism", *American Quarterly* 55, no. 3 (2003): 417–455. The focus of Rozario's analysis is the Red Cross Magazine, but his deft analysis of the sentimental modes at work in Red Cross multi-media publicity offers a useful analogy with the institution's film output.
14. *A Descriptive Catalog*, National Archives and Records Administration.

2

Early Missionary Filming and the Emergence of the Professional Cameraman

Stephen Bottomore

Introduction

In the early era, film found a variety of non-fiction uses, including for travelogues, for recording natural history and anthropology, and as political propaganda and advertising – and indeed for documenting missionary projects. In each case the aim of filming was to capture the essence of the activity in a visually understandable and interesting manner. To do this, the filmmaker needed to have both a general knowledge of the subject to be filmed, and a basic competence in using a film camera.

In this period, because there were so few trained cameramen, these two skills often came combined in one person who knew the subject and did the filming too. Hence one finds, for example, anthropologists like Alfred Haddon filming native customs, writers such as Frederic Villiers taking a film camera to a war in the 1890s, or travellers like C. Rider Noble filming the places he visited.[1]

I call these early operators "gentlemen amateurs", and almost by definition, they had limited camera abilities. But quite soon a new breed of specialist cameramen emerged, with more technical experience and skill, who often made an entire career in this role. I call these kind of cameramen "artisan professionals", and I'm thinking of such names as Oscar Depue, Joe Rosenthal, Leo Lefebvre, Joseph De Frenes, William Harbeck and John McKenzie. Sometimes such an "artisan professional" would be teamed up with a professional person ("gentleman") who knew the subject to be filmed, and the pair would work together, somewhat like a modern director and cameraman combination.[2]

I argue that this evolution of cameramen from amateur to professional, although not a steady progression, was fairly *general* in the film industry, and I suggest that some of the early missionary filmmakers offer persuasive examples of this developing trend.

Missionary societies

Overseas missionary societies were formed in Britain from the 1790s, and even earlier in some other western countries, and have continued until the present. Every denomination had its associated missionary organisation: whether Roman Catholic, Church of England, Salvation Army, Baptist or Methodist (as well as other Protestant groups).[3] At their peak in the late nineteenth century, these societies sent out hundreds of

19

missionaries each year to what we now call the developing world – but which was then called "the mission field".

Missionary organisations were avid users of the latest technologies for visual education and propaganda, including the magic lantern (from the 1830s) and photography. But while scholars have paid some attention to the missionary use of these earlier media, the use of film has received less attention.[4] Indeed, most of the missionary filmmakers I will discuss are scarcely mentioned in film history books (or indeed in books about mission history). Part of the reason for this neglect may be due to the complex nature of the missionary propaganda project, for missionaries had two targets: people in faraway countries whom they wished to convert to Christianity, and the flock back home *from* whom they wished to raise money.[5] In 1901, journalist William Stead defined this dual challenge of using film for missionary purposes:

> Mission work is another vast field which has hardly been attacked. The bioscope is useful at both ends. In the field at home, where funds are collected for missions, it would give a much more vivid, living interest to the details of missionary work than has hitherto been possible. The missionary meeting would be transformed, and become one of the most popular of all the week-night services if it were illustrated by living pictures introducing the audience to lifelike presentations of the far-off scenes and peoples amongst whom the proceeds of their collection boxes maintain the emissaries of the Cross. At the other end, a complete library of the films of the parables and living pictures of the Bible stories would be an endless and inexhaustible source of attraction to the simple children of Nature amidst whom missionaries labour. The picture itself would be little short of miraculous, and would probably do more to carry conviction as to the truth of the Christian religion to their untutored minds than the most eloquent discourses.[6]

Although I have found early examples of film being used in overseas evangelisation campaigns,[7] in this paper I will concentrate on the "reporting-back" aspect: films taken *of* overseas missions and their work, which were then screened back home to raise awareness and generate financial contributions.

J. Gregory Mantle, Methodist

The first person to use film to document mission work may have been the Rev J. Gregory Mantle, a dynamic minister in the British Methodist Church. An established author, magazine editor, and ebullient preacher, he was a master of publicity campaigns to attract congregations. It is not known how exactly he became interested in film, but possibly through personal contact, because, between 1896 and the turn-of-the-century, he lived and worked in the early cinema "hotspot" of Brighton/Hove.[8]

In 1902 Mantle was planning a lengthy trip to India to visit churches and missions, and he contacted Charles Urban and offered to film the Delhi Durbar ceremonials which were due to take place at the end of the year. All he asked (according to Urban's account) was the loan of a film camera and some training in how to use it. Urban had no qualified cameraman available to film the Durbar so he agreed to Mantle's plan.[9] The Rev Mantle did indeed take a film camera with him, and over the course of several months, managed to film various actuality scenes, not only of the Durbar but also of missionaries and mission hospitals and schools, projects to help orphans and widows, and general scenic views and activities of people at work and play in some eight locations in India and Burma.

Both Urban and Mantle benefited from the filming: Urban listed the films for sale in his catalogue, while Mantle showed them back in the UK (especially the missionary scenes) as publicity to support mission work in India. Three of the films survive, though sadly not the one which might have been most historically interesting, featuring a pioneer female Christian social-reformer, Pandita Ramabai, who was working for women's rights in India.[10]

At this time, 1903, Mantle was put in charge of a new Methodist Central Hall in south London near Deptford, and over the next five years or so he built up a formidable array of lantern and film projection equipment operated by a sizeable team of projectionists, who gave film/lantern shows in London and wider afield (including the films Mantle had shot in India).

Mantle undertook another trip to the east in 1907–08, this time to China, and again he did some filming, but there was much less to show for it than for his India trip: a mere handful of films emerged, showing the Wesleyan mission and foreign missionary in Fatshan, China. By this time film exhibition had become a regular event at Central Hall, especially at "concerts" on Saturday nights where the films included pure entertainment titles (such as *Rescued by Rover* and the *Dear Boys* series) largely to raise funds for foreign mission work.[11] However, quite suddenly in about 1908 the mission authorities halted film exhibition activities in Deptford, due to the growing competition from cinemas in south London, and believing that screen entertainment was inappropriate for a mission.[12]

As to those films Mantle shot in India, clearly these were, in a literal sense, the work of an amateur. After all, Mantle was a clergyman not a cameraman, and was travelling to India mainly to visit missions and liaise with other clergy, so camerawork would have been a relatively low priority. And although he shot quite a few films, and some sixty shots are listed in the Urban catalogue, Charles Urban himself recalled that, because Mantle had no previous experience as a cameraman, most of his films were "spoilt with the heat", for they should have been developed soon after being exposed. Mantle apparently didn't have the photographic skills to do this.

As I suggested above, this lack of skill was common in the early years of the cinema among these first proto-cameramen, the "gentlemen amateurs", and one wonders why they thought they could operate film cameras with so little training? In the case of missionaries, perhaps they felt that because they so often used stills cameras to record their mission activities, they would also be able to handle moving picture cameras, given the similarities between moving and stills photography.[13] However, in practice, film cameras are more complicated to handle than their stills equivalents, especially for a lone operator who must crank and simultaneously control the other functions of the camera, and then deal with (and possibly develop in the field) long lengths of delicate film.[14]

Grenfell & Forfeitt, Baptists

This apparent belief that a competence in *stills* photography might entail a similar competence in *film* shooting, also seems to have been current in the British Baptist Missionary Society. The Baptists had missions all over the world, and in 1906 the head office initiated a plan to film this work inexpensively by circulating a film camera to their projects. The bioscope was to be brought by a Mr. Oldrieve to Congo, and then would be sent to China and India. The idea was that when the camera arrived in the mission station in each country, the local missionary would use it to film his own projects, before shipping it on to the next missionary in the next country. The advantage of this peculiar "pass-the-parcel" system of filmmaking was that, with no accompanying cameraman, the society would save the man's salary and travel costs.

The bioscope camera duly arrived in the Upper Congo to be used by the Revs George Grenfell and William Forfeitt. These missionaries both had considerable experience in stills photography, having taken numerous photographs to document their African mission work, but had no experience with film.[15] After receiving the film camera, Grenfell expressed his doubts about the enterprise in a letter of 15 March 1906:

> I fear that really interesting pictures which could be shown at a missionary meeting at home are not very plentiful. I've taken a few at Bolobo, and hope they will turn out all right.[16]

That phrase, "hope they will turn out all right", scarcely suggests much confidence, and though some of these films were apparently shown at missionary meetings, there is no indication of quality; and at that time almost *any* images of the Congo would have been acceptable because the territory was then in the news, due to the ongoing scandal about atrocities.[17]

The CMS: Edward Cash

In contrast to the Rev Mantle and the Baptists, other missionary societies decided to employ *professional* cameramen to film their foreign mission activities. The Church Missionary Society (CMS) was originally formed by the Church of England, and had established a department dealing with magic lantern slides by the early 1880s, and became the most active missionary organisation in lantern use.[18] Perhaps it was this long experience with one screen medium which encouraged them to handle the new *cinema* medium in a more professional manner than Mantle or the Baptists. In 1904 the CMS sent a cameraman to India and then in 1906 another man to Africa, and in both cases these were professional operators from established film companies.

First to go was Edward Cash, working for the Autoscope Company, who set off for India in the Autumn of 1904. Cash was the brother-in-law of film pioneer Birt Acres, and was a competent technician who understood film cameras (and even knew how to fix his camera when it broke down). From a fairly humble background in Hackney, east London, he was, in my terminology, a classic "artisan professional".

This filming assignment took him from Bombay in the west, up to the Himalayas, to central India, then east to Calcutta and south to Ceylon, lasting some five months into early 1905. He wrote a diary of the trip, recording details of many of the places and events which he filmed. Edward Cash was assigned a travelling companion by the CMS, a medical missionary called Dr. Arthur Neve, who was a well-known authority on Kashmir. Their status seems to have been unequal: for example, a photograph taken during the trip shows the university-educated Neve sitting for breakfast while the technician Cash stands.[19] And we learn from the diary that there was indeed a strong differentiation of roles, with Neve acting as something like a "producer" and Cash as the cameraman-technician. It seems that Neve was advising on the choice of locations to be filmed and arranging details with missionary colleagues in the places they visited. He may also have been advising Cash about the kind of activity to be shot, though this general advice had already been communicated to Cash back in the UK.

According to initial press reports about the venture, Cash was expected to prioritise two kinds of scenes, and his diary entries indicate that he indeed filmed both.[20] Firstly, missionary activities (e.g. mission-run schools and hospitals), and secondly – and more interestingly – shots of non-Christian religion, or "heathenism". Cash filmed suitable shots including views of Muslims at prayer, and Hindus burning their dead and making stone idols. The idea was that these images of supposedly barbarous religious practices would be contrasted in screenings back in the UK with Cash's other shots of Christian mission hospitals and schools to indicate that the CMS was eliminating heathenism while bringing practical improvements.[21] In addition to religious practices, Cash also filmed many scenic or general shots of Indian life (e.g. elephants, a mountain railway, etc) – and his diary suggests that he was deeply impressed with Indian scenery and culture.

Edward Cash's films were apparently well received by the CMS, and were premiered in London in style. As the official history records: "The first exhibition of the first set was given in Exeter Hall on Jan. 24th, 1905, to an audience of 3000 people ...".[22] There were later screenings elsewhere in the UK.[23]

The CMS: Emile Lauste

The subsequent CMS filming expedition exemplifies, I think, a further step in a development towards professional camerawork. The cameraman was Emile Lauste, and, like Cash, he came from a famous early film "lineage", being the son of sound-film pioneer Eugene Lauste, and assistant for several years to W.K.L. Dickson. As with Cash, a diary of Lauste's CMS trip survives. He set off on a ship from Britain in September 1906, disembarking in Mombasa in east Africa, and then spent several weeks filming in parts of British East Africa and Uganda. He wasn't just working for the CMS but also had an assignment to make films for the Warwick Trading Company for their travelogue series about Africa, "Cape to Cairo". As far as we know, he travelled alone, without a guide/director (i.e. no equivalent of Neve), though to judge from a photograph in my collection it seems he employed a local African as assistant.

Emile Lauste was evidently a self-reliant and competent cameraman, who could be sent unaccompanied, with a "shopping list" of scenes to try and film, and then be left to his own devices. (This has some similarity to the way modern wildlife cameramen work). It suggests to me a new level of professionalism in the job of cameraman, and Lauste himself took his status as a professional very seriously. For example, he wrote to the trade press a few months before embarking on the Uganda trip about the problem of incompetent projectionists and cameramen, and then pronounced on "what I think is really an expert operator". In Lauste's view, such a professional would combine the skills of cameraman, projectionist and mechanic:

> ... a man who can photograph, develop, print, and project, with an exceptional experience of electricity and oxy-hydrogen work, and able to repair or make his own machines.[24]

In other words he saw the role of "operator" as being a real "hands-on" technician. Lauste indeed proved to be competent, and the CMS films he shot were of quite a high standard, as the organisation acknowledged in a letter of thanks.[25] In May 1907 the films were shown in London, and then again on other occasions during the next couple of years.[26] The CMS subsequently continued its film work with some success, as the organisation's official history, published in 1916, noted (in recalling the Edward Cash trip):

> Since then, of course, the whole kinematograph system has been much developed, and everything is quite familiar; yet even now the new pictures added year by year never fail to give thousands of people fresh and vivid glimpses of the actualities of missionary work. These exhibitions, it may be added, not only make an effective entry into Eye-gate [i.e. visual education], but yield a considerable financial profit. In eight tours they netted over £4000.[27]

With profits like these, the CMS might well have concluded that the trust they placed in companies like Warwick, with their professional cameramen Edward Cash and Emile Lauste, had been amply vindicated.

22. Stock noted of Cash's film of Dr. Lankester of Peshawar that "… the sudden sight of Dr. Arthur Lankester walking down the Khyber Pass among the camels will not soon be forgotten by those who were present that night". Eugene Stock, *The History of the Church Missionary Society … vol. 4* (London: CMS, 1916), 503.
23. A screening was reported at the Albert Hall, Sheffield: *Optical Lantern and Cinematograph Journal* [OLCJ] (March 1905): 102.
24. OLCJ (February 1906): 81. The term "operator" with its twin referents to camera and projection, has a direct parallel in the French terms "opérateur prise de vues" and "opérateur projection".
25. Letter from Ernest J. Staples, who ran the CMS lantern slide loan department, to Lauste, 21 May 1907 stating of Lauste's east Africa films, that they were "on the whole very good indeed", especially for photographic quality. Although he noted that "one or two are failures, and one or two not sharp", those were a low percentage. Lauste Collection, Screen Archive South East.
26. KLW (16 May 1907): 11; and KLW (5 September 1907): 263; KLW (12 December 1907): 75; KLW (5 March 1908): 311; KLW (25 November 1909): 145.
27. Stock, *Church Missionary Society, vol. 4*.

3

Mission on Screen: the Church Army and its Multi-Media Activities

Frank Gray

Poverty was the greatest social and economic problem in Britain at the end of the nineteenth century. The grave dilemma the country faced was that it was one of the wealthiest and most industrialised nations in the world with painfully high levels of poverty and social deprivation. The nation's first social researchers, men such as Charles Booth and Seebohm Rowntree, collected the evidence that described the nature of this crisis. Booth's "Life and Labour of the People in London" (1902), for instance, described in great detail the difficulties faced by the poor of this metropolis in terms of health, housing, unemployment and crime. Would this dilemma bring about the downfall of this civilised and advanced society? Would a century of 'progress' come to some terrible apocalyptic end as envisioned by H.G. Wells in his scientific fantasy, *The Time Machine* of 1895?

The immense scale of this social and economic crisis engendered a vigorous debate on the nature of its causes and the solutions. Opinion was divided between those who saw it as a result of the by-product of poor moral character and a lack of religious belief and others who conceptualised it as a failure of society and its organisation. The most well known religious organisation that dedicated itself to solving this crisis was the Salvation Army. Founded by William Booth (also known as 'General' Booth) in 1865, it was dedicated to the work to the "poor and lost" through a campaign "against the evils which lie at the root of all miseries of modern life".[1] Using Charles Booth's analyses, in 1890 he addressed his mission to that ten per cent of the nation that was made up of paupers, the homeless, the starving and the very poor. To quote General Booth, "A population sodden with drink, steeped in vice, eaten up by every social and physical malady, these are the denizens of Darkest England amidst whom my life has been spent, and to whose rescue I would now summon all that is best in the manhood and womanhood of our land".[2]

A parallel organisation was the Church Army. Inspired by the Salvation Army, it was founded in 1882 by the Reverend Wilson Carlile as the evangelistic arm of the Church of England. He created an army of laymen and laywomen who were devoted to "saving" the urban and rural poor. Carlile's philosophy, which still shapes the work of the Church Army to this day, was that Christian teaching combined with practical support in terms of food, clothing and shelter needed to be taken directly to the poor. His missionaries were therefore trained to work outside of the conventions of church buildings and formal services. An important difference between the Salvation Army and the Church Army was the latter's early commitment to integrate a range of screen practices into its daily practices.

The Church Army began its work in London and then it quickly spread first across Britain and then throughout the British Empire. Carlile's own beginnings as an evangelist had started in the early 1870s in London when he was stimulated and encouraged by the arrival of two Americans: the Christian evangelist Dwight Lyman Moody and the gospel singer Ira Sankey. Moody and Sankey performed to crowds of thousands in Britain in 1874 and 1875 and were in residence at the Agricultural Hall in London in 1875 for a number of months. Moody made use of the "Wordless Book". Invented by the London Baptist Minister Charles Spurgeon, it was designed as a visual device, usually a set of banners, to describe the journey to Heaven through colour and not words. It employed three colours: black (the state of sin), red (the blood of Jesus Christ) and white (the righteousness attained through belief in Christ). Moody added a fourth colour in 1875 – gold – to represent Heaven. Moody established an effective template for a very new kind of populist evangelism. It employed preaching, music, song and a visual aid (the 'Wordless Book') in an engaging and accessible manner that was tailored to a working class and illiterate audience. Carlile became part of their "shows" in 1875 by playing the harmonium and leading the singing. This experience led to his recognition that, "ornate surroundings and formal liturgies did not attract the people", positioning himself as "an apostle to the man in the street, rather than to the man in the pew".[3]

In the late 1870s, Carlile became attached to a number of churches in inner London and began to abandon the conventions of formal church services and to practice, first as a layman and then as an ordained Minister, in a manner that would connect with the poor. He designed open-air meetings in the evenings with song and encouraged participants to offer testimonials on the comfort they had received from the mission's work. He also began to integrate the projection of magic lantern slides into his informal weeknight services, recognising the value of combining both comic and religious slides into a presentation that would be attractive to the young working class. These formative experiences were vital to the establishment of the Church Army in 1882.

Carlile became Rector of St Mary-at-Hill in the City of London in 1892, a post he held until 1926. During this time, as Stephen Bottomore has detailed in his exemplary study of Wilson Carlile, he established this church as the flagship for the Church Army's particular understanding of how to deliver a new kind of religious service that made use of "new media" – the lantern and the cinematograph. The Church was located in the City of London, and like Wall Street, was busy during the daytime throughout the working week but deserted at night. Carlile's ambition was to fill the church on Sunday evenings by reaching "a class who went nowhere".[4] By 1894, his popular Sunday evening services began to attract audiences of over eight hundred (double the usual capacity) and became a much discussed and celebrated aspect of contemporary London life. Before each service and to attract the working class in the area to attend, a procession took place through the City with music from a brass band (often featuring Carlile on his trombone) and a women's concertina band. Once inside, an imaginative and innovative multimedia experience unfolded.

The lantern, presenting both sacred and secular imagery, was used throughout his services. Slides were made to represent all of the formal elements of the service including hymns, prayers and collects. No prayer or hymn book was required. The accompanying music included the bands involved in the procession as well as a string orchestra and the church's own pipe organ (a William Hill organ of 1848). Song was represented by soloists and a choir. Carlile directed all of these elements (the projec-

3 Mission on Screen: the Church Army and its Multi-Media Activities

Fig. 1. "The Evangelist points to the Gate", coloured lantern slide from the series, The Pilgrim's Progress, *c. 1890. [Screen Archive South East.]*

tions on screen and the music) and added a third: his own voice. His sermons were pointedly topical in nature, drawing upon subjects such as travelogue, nature, national sporting events and wars (such as the Anglo-Boer War and the Russo-Japanese War). The congregations were encouraged to actively participate through singing, hand-clapping and laughing: "The services are in fact one of the features of church-going London. They are designed chiefly to attract the working classes, and in this they succeed completely, probably beyond those of any other church in the metropolis".[5]

As Bottomore discovered, around 1900 Carlile began to integrate the cinematograph into his Sunday services. The films included Queen Victoria's funeral, the English football Cup Final, London Zoo and views of the world. Reflecting on his activities at St Mary-at-Hill, Carlisle said, "My experience, extending over many years, is that we must go out into the streets to bring the people in, and when we have them we must hold them. Therefore … I have never hesitated to make the most of music, to have a string orchestra, to have magic lanterns, to have the kinematograph, and to adopt other popular notions to attract the careless soul. I get men and women thoroughly interested … . The music and the pictures are but the beginning, and I feel fully justified in using such means to gain so desirable a result".[6]

Carlile was criticised by some fellow clergyman and some journalists for turning his church into what they saw as a fairground attraction. He was felt by his critics to have crossed the "boundaries of reverence" by encouraging "vulgarity" and promoting the "sensational", especially with the arrival of "the flickering 'cino', with its suggestion of the music-hall". His biographer came to his defense:

> With lantern, music, and topical sermons, Mr. Carlile manages to fill his church with one of the most remarkable congregations in the country. Some of the most gifted pens have attempted to describe these curiously informal and human services, and failed miserably, because you cannot set down in print the spirit that animates them. You read that Mr. Carlile clapped his hands to urge the people to sing the "Gloria" louder, and emphasised the "loud Amen" with his trombone, and it sounds very outrageous. And yet when you are in St. Mary-at-Hill Church … you feel that these things are perfectly natural and spontaneous, and make the act of worship seem more real.[7]

Carlile was an innovator in the use of both the lantern and the cinematograph by the Church. His other activities for the Church Army reveal not only his organisational skills but also his understanding of how to fight poverty on a very broad front. The Church Army's first training home for working class evangelists opened in London in 1886. It introduced the concept that those with the experience of poverty were deemed to most equipped to bring both empathy and conviction to, "the mighty army of suffering and outcast humanity".[8]

The trained "Officers" began to work across the country both distributing the Church Army's publications and being involved with its many missions. These included its missions to agricultural labourers (especially during harvesting), workhouses, racecourses, travellers including the Roma, fishermen, sailors, public houses, coffee houses, prisons, open-air slums, night rescue and public parks. In 1888, the Church Army Social System was created. As a complement to the missions that were developing across the nation, its primary expression was the building of Labour Homes that were designed to aid and benefit "the outcast – that vast multitude of tramps, criminals, inebriates, fallen men, women and youths". The Homes had four core principles, "cleanliness, hard work, total abstinence, personal religion", and their purpose was to prepare the "outcast" for a new life.[9]

Carlile, having established missions across the country and largely in poor urban areas, then began in 1892 to address the needs of the countryside by creating a fleet of travelling caravans. "He was much attracted by the system of preaching friars of the thirteenth century, and by the story of Wesley's journeyings, and it had for long been his desire to start a body of men who should travel through the country in twos and threes, preaching in the hamlets and villages".[10] Each horse-drawn van, painted in dark green with biblical quotations hand-painted in light green on every side, was led by an "Officer" (a trained evangelist) with one to two prospective evangelists who would serve on the vans as a form of probation before their entry into the Training Home. The vans toured for periods of up to nine months, with private prayer, bible study, bookselling and evening services for adults and children held outdoors and in churches and schools. Rowan noted the significance of the lantern to the peripatetic work. "A

3 Mission on Screen: the Church Army and its Multi-Media Activities

lantern and slides is a part of the equipment of each van, lantern services, and a lecture on Church Army work generally, being frequent features of the missions".[11] By 1912 there were seventy vans constantly travelling through rural areas and visiting urban slums. In the 1920s the horse-drawn vans were modernised by being replaced by motorised vans and mobile cinemas.

The Church Army also established a lantern and cinematographic department with studios and darkrooms for the making of new material and a salesroom for the hire and purchase of slides and apparatus to Church of England parishes. With its show-room, darkrooms and workrooms for hand-colouring slides, the lantern stock for hire was estimated in 1905 at 100,000 slides. Annual loans at the same time were estimated at one million, primarily to clergy around the world. All of the Church Army's vans and mission tents were equipped with lanterns and, where feasible, with film projectors. It is difficult to argue with Rowan's claim that Carlisle and his Officers by "refusing to abandon the lantern in days when it was almost universally condemned, they have helped to bring it into its present wide use. It is, therefore, fitting that the Church Army Lantern department should be in the front rank of the trade, both for the sale and hire of slides, and for supplying lanterns and all other accessories".[12]

Running in parallel was its publications department. The sheer volume of work, reflecting both the expansion of the Army's activities and its canny ability to take on commercial projects for other organisations, led to the establishment in 1905 of the Church Army Press at Cowley, Oxfordshire. Its modern, electrically-driven presses could address any requirement including lithography, die-stamping, block-engraving and colour printing. With a unionised staff of over one hundred, it produced books including Bibles and hymnals, parish magazines, stationery, pamphlets, brochures, catalogues and posters for the Church Army, the Church of England and commercial clients. Each week it printed the *Church Army Gazette* (it had a circulation in 1912 of 120,000 weekly copies). Collectively, the Church Army's Lantern, Cinema & Book Department represented the organisation's commitment to using text and screen to promote its mission. The Department's motto, captured this position very succinctly: "Through Eye to Heart/ By Picture and the Printed Page".[13] In this context, the Church Army's *Lantern and Slide Catalogue, 1913–14* is a valuable document as it gives a detailed description of this aspect of the Army's Lantern, Cinema & Book Department. Over almost 450 pages, much of it in eight point, it is densely packed with descriptions of sets of lantern slides. The catalogue begins with photographs of the Show Room within the army's headquarters on Edgware Road in London, testimonials from satisfied customers and a section on "Practical Hints on Lantern Work". It details how lanterns are operated with sections on screens, objectives, illuminants and the cinematograph. It is then followed by over fifty pages that illustrate and describe the range of apparatus and accessories available for purchase including lanterns (single-lensed lanterns, biunials and a triunial) cinematographs, objectives, oxygen generators, screens, arc lamps, screens and stands. It claims, "We are conducting the largest hire business in the country. You can trust us to execute your orders with promptitude and reliability". The section concludes with a notice that they can supply operators for lantern and cinematograph displays and that its slides are "artistically hand-painted by experienced artists".[14]

The remainder of the catalogue, approximately 375 pages, are descriptions of lantern sets, both for hire and purchase and available as plain and coloured. An estimated 45,000 are named with sets ranging from the sacred to the secular. They include *Old and New Testament Pictures*, *Views of Palestine*, *Allegorical Picture Stories* (including *Pilgrim's Progress*), *English Church History*, *The Church's Year* (illustrating the Collect, Epistle and Gospel for each week in the Church calendar), *Temperance Stories, Humorous Series, Illustrated Address Series* (for sermons), the illustrated Prayer Book and Hymn Book, *The Life of Christ* as illustrated by the artist James Tissot, *Travel and Lectures* (including *From London to Niagara*, *Westminster Abbey*, *With the Troops in South Africa*, *China and the Chinese*, *London Life including Slum Life* and *Wireless Telegraphy*). A very large section of plain text slides of the hymns, prayers, psalms, lessons and readings from the Bible are also described. They enabled a whole service to be delivered on screen without the need for either a prayer book or a hymn book.

Carlile had worked in his family's silk and fine clothing business for over a decade before he became a Minister and created the Church Army. His business background clearly played an important role in creating an organisation devoted to the training and administration of evangelists and the establishment and management of its own missions, homes, farms, travelling vans, a printing works and a Lantern & Cinema Department. It had the character of a vertically integrated business, engaged in all aspects of production from the acquisition of raw materials through to manufacturing to marketing and retailing. This was a very modern organisation which used charitable donations from the well-off to create a structure of inter-related activities that were devoted to "the rescue and uplifting of starving men from the streets".[15]

The scale of the organisation's activities in this period was remarkable. Their own annual figures for 1906, which reflected the Edwardian interest in measuring value through quantitative data, provided the scale of their work: meals supplied: 2.7 million; food and lodging: 330,000; day's work given: 537,000; visits paid by parochial evangelists and mission nurses: 1.4 million; mission services held by the travelling vans: 30,000; circulation of the *Church Army Gazette*: five million; publications sold: 360,000; meetings held: 120,000 and estimated audience at these meetings: 9.3 million. It was also noted that within the British Empire, the Army had expanded its activities to South Africa, India, Australia, Canada and the West Indies.[16]

William Thomas Stead provides a contemporary perspective on the Church Army and its uses of new media. Stead was a journalist, campaigner and publisher from the 1880s until the time of his death on the Titanic in 1912. He believed that positive social change in Britain would be brought about through the agency of modern communications. For him this meant newspapers, journals, pamphlets, the magic lantern and the cinematograph. His own publication, the *Review of Reviews*, founded in 1890, provided him with his national platform. Through it, he campaigned for education, social reform and Christianity and against all of contemporary society's problems including poverty, alcoholism and child prostitution. His organisation *Help*, with its army of national social service volunteers, served as one of his many attempts to change the nation's direction through the strength of its participants' altruism and charitable activities. Part of its work was expressed by what he called his "Magic Lantern Mission". Laid out in his article of 1890 with the same title, he advocated the significant role that 'pictures' had played and could play in education and evangelism. Here he championed the notion that the visualisation of the world through pictorial representation would transform society. "If we have to get ideas into the mind", he said, "they must enter by the gate of the eye".[17] For Stead, in 1890, this meant using the magic lantern and its role in educating the uneducated. He envisaged what he called a Magic Lantern Mission "with magic lantern missionaries in every town in the land", and proclaimed:

> When the Magic Lantern Mission is in full working order there will not be a single squalid slum in any great city which will not have its weekly visit from the peripatetic magic lantern missioner, who for an hour or two in the evening

would throw upon a sheet hung on some blank wall radiant shapes of grace and beauty.[18]

Stead's Magic Lantern Mission had little success but its concept did prove to be remarkably prescient as first the lantern and then the cinematograph began to change the nature of contemporary visual culture. In the 1890s, an ever-growing number of educational and religious organisations began to integrate the lantern into their daily practices. These included the Baptist Missionary Society, the Church Missionary Society, the Band of Hope Union, the Church of England Temperance Society, the Recreative Evening Schools Association and, as laid out here, the Church Army.

In 1912 and in a posthumously published article, Stead updated his understanding of the social role of screen practice by turning to the cinema. Using similar arguments to those expressed in 1890, he asked what part the nation's newly-built 4,000 cinemas, with their daily audiences of 4,000,000, could play in expanding the role and influence of the Church and the advancement of the nation. His answer was simple: the cinema, especially on Sundays, should exploit film's great power which was its representation of "Life". This was the new medium's inherent ability to capture the world in its diversity. He argued that if cinema could be steered away from "sensational spectacle" and be attached to the power of the lecture, its cultural power could be unleashed. "The approach to the mind is solely through Eye-gate; the approach by Ear-gate is entirely neglected. The Cinema challenges, but does not fix attention. It excites wonder, it does not allow time for reflection. Is it not possible", he asked, "… to make the Cinema useful for instructing, inspiring, and saving the people?".[19] "Can we, dare we, who are always bemoaning the dullness, the indifference, the lack of inspiration of the monotonous life of every day, refuse to avail ourselves of this greatest of all agencies devised by mortal man for rousing attention and stimulating imagination?".[20] Stead's hope was that cinemas on Sundays would become "Cinema palaces for ethical, educational and evangelical purposes".[21] This never came to be.

Carlile and the Church Army and campaigners like Stead expressed a serious commitment to addressing the problems associated with "Darkest England", recognising that new methodologies were required to engage with the poor and their plight. For them, this meant a particular form of Christian evangelism and direct action supported by new media. At this same moment there were also secular crusaders who had a radical agenda for improving contemporary society. Shaped by the forces of secularisation and democratisation, the rise of trade unions and the Labour Party and the analyses of a new generation of social scientists and social reformers, a new understanding emerged of the role that the State could play in the war against poverty. This *zeitgeist* had a profound impact on the drafting and passing of new legislation in the British Parliament. Enabled by the Liberal Government from 1906 to 1914, it was devoted to establishing a system of social security, old age pensions, health and employment insurance and the end of child labour. These laws reflected a profound shift in the dominant political discourse from one focussed on individual liberty and self-help to one in which the State was responsible for social progress and social justice by building new community-based structures devoted to caring for the needy and the vulnerable. This genuine revolution in the State's conception of social policy placed the efforts of the Church Army and its commitment to 'rescuing the fallen' through volunteerism, charity and emergency relief as a particular and limited solution to such a serious national issue.[22]

Notes

1. William Booth, *In Darkest England and the Way Out* (London: Salvation Army, London, 1890), Preface i.
2. Ibid., 14–15.
3. Edgar Rowan, *Wilson Carlile and the Church Army* (London: Hodder and Stoughton, 1905), 111.
4. Ibid., 447.
5. Leonard W. Lillingston, "The founder of the Church Army: a chat with the Rev. W. Carlile", *Sunday Magazine* 27 (December 1898): 813–814, cited in Stephen Bottomore, "Projecting for the Lord – the work of Wilson Carlile", *Film History* 14, no. 2 (2002): 198.
6. "The Kinematograph in Church", *Kinematograph and Lantern Weekly* (6 May 1909): 1539, cited in Bottomore, 204.
7. Rowan, *Wilson Carlile*, 450–451.
8. "Portraits of Celebrities at Different Ages - New Series: Wilson Carlile", *Strand Magazine* 32 (September 1906): 311.
9. "Wilson Carlile, My Life Work, The Story of the Church Army", *Quiver* 615 (January 1898): 350.
10. Rowan, *Wilson Carlile*, 353–354.
11. Ibid., 373.
12. Ibid., 432.
13. This motto is found on a Church Army bookmark c. 1913 now in the collection of Screen Archive South East at the University of Brighton.
14. Church Army Lantern Department, *Lantern and Slide Catalogue 1913–14* (London: Church Army, 1913), lxi–lxii. Church Army collection, Screen Archive South East.
15. "The Church Army", *The Times* (3 May 1912): 4.
16. "Portraits of Celebrities", 312.
17. W.T. Stead, "A Magic Lantern Mission", *The Review of Reviews* 2, no. 12 (December 1890): 561.
18. Ibid., 566.
19. W.T. Stead, "The Church's Picture Galleries", *The Review of Reviews* 46, no. 275 (November 1912): 534.
20. Ibid., 536.
21. Ibid., 534.
22. Two articles on the Church Army by scholars associated with the University of Trier complement this one: Karen Eifler, "Between Attraction and Instruction: Lantern Shows in British Poor Relief", *Early Popular Visual Culture* 8, no. 4 (November 2010): 363–384 and Torsten Gärtner, "The Church on Wheels: Travelling Magic Lantern Mission in late Victorian England", in Martin Loiperdinger (ed.), *Travelling Cinema In Europe, Sources and Perspectives* (Frankfurt am Main: Stroemfeld Verlag, 2008), 129–140.

    The current President of the Church Army is Archbishop Desmond Tutu and its website displays its continuing commitment to using new media in both its British and international work. The website features news, articles, blogs, a discussion forum, an interactive map, a gallery of photographs to view and download, video files to watch and download and a twitter feed.

4

"Baits to Entrap the Pleasure-Seeker and the Worldling": Charity Bazaars Introduce Moving Pictures to Ireland

Denis Condon

> From the first exhibition yesterday the animatograph drew large crowds of patrons. This is certainly, of the many things worth seeing at Cyclopia, one of the most entertaining. It is more so than the kinetoscope, for it shows the figures life size, and so imparts additional realism to the pictures. The Trilby scene is an excellent one, and so is the boxing match.[1]

So reported the *Irish Daily Independent* in May 1896 as part of its coverage of the third day of a large charity bazaar called Cyclopia then underway in Dublin, Ireland. Early cinema scholars will be familiar with practically all the elements of this brief review – the early moving-picture devices, the films, the type of venue – but contextual details illuminate the way in which the new entertainment form was adopted in Ireland. Originally known as the theatrograph, the animatograph was the stage name given by the manager of the Alhambra Theatre, Leicester Square, to the moving picture projector developed by British pioneer Robert Paul, when it debuted there in March 1896 for what would be an extended engagement.[2] For the *Daily Independent* writer, the animatograph represented an improvement over the peepshow kinetoscope on the basis of the increased verisimilitude of its life-sized projected images, but enhancements to the kinetoscope also garnered favourable comments because of *their* increased realism in reviews of Cyclopia. As well as this, because the writer was familiar with kinetoscopic moving pictures – and assumed his or her readers were also – they could be used as the basis of a comparison in an existing public discourse on moving pictures.[3] One of the films, too, can be identified with some certainty: the Trilby scene is one of the four films shot by Edison personnel in June 1895 that were available to exhibitors in Britain and Ireland through the London office of Maguire and Baucus.[4] These devices and films are elements of an already international trade at the very start of projected moving pictures' novelty year, a period often seen as lasting – in those countries where the projector made its first impact – at least through 1896, and to the end of the 1896–1897 theatrical season.

Accepting this chronology, charity bazaars become an important focus for early cinema research at precisely that moment. To the extent that charity bazaars have been discussed in the current literature, their image has been dominated by the disaster of the Paris Bazar de la Charité, which was held almost exactly a year after Cyclopia. On

35

Fig. 1. This advertisement for the animatograph at Cyclopia appeared in the Irish Daily Independent (21 May 1896): 4.

4 May 1897, at least 120 attendees of the Bazar de la Charité died in a calamatous fire caused by the carelessness of the operators of a cinématographe Joly when relighting the lamp illuminating the pictures.[5] Indeed, H. Mark Gosser has argued that the Bazar de la Charité fire is the third most significant event of cinema's early years, after the commercial debuts of the kinetoscope and Lumière cinématographe.[6] Unlike these debuts, however, the fire constitutes more an end than a beginning, a tragedy rather than a triumph, a moment of disastrously negative publicity for projected moving pictures. A brief account of the Bazar de la Charité fire will help to point up the similarities and differences with the Irish bazaars that will be the focus here. Founded in 1885, the Bazar de la Charité was an annual event at which the French elite congregated in great numbers to make a contribution to the relief of poverty. They came together in 1897 in a wooden building erected for the occasion whose hasty construction was disguised by stalls decorated with such readily flammable material as papier-mâché and fabrics designed to make the venue look like Old Paris. A long awning hid the roof, and under it, attractively costumed women – many belonging to the social elite – manned the stalls selling donated goods and raffle tickets and inviting attendees to participate in games of chance. One of the featured entertainments was a recent technical curiosity, a moving-picture projector, which was located in a side room. The building – which had only one main entrance – was particularly full on the bazaar's opening day. As the *Irish Times* commented the day after the fire: "It is [...] not unlikely that over 1,000 persons representing wealth, distinction, nobility, and diplomacy, were thronged within the building to contribute all that grace, beauty, and

money could do to succour the needy and distressed".[7] As this quote indicates, it was not just the scale of the tragedy but also and particularly the class origin and gender of most of the victims that made the fire such shocking news. This was a horrific event that disproportionately affected the *beau monde*, the leaders of fashion, the duchesses, countesses, baronesses and other elite women whose doings were reported in the society pages of the newspapers.

Notwithstanding the importance of these events for the early development of the French industry, they have nonetheless tended to occlude investigation of the role of charity bazaars elsewhere during this period, and it is here that a closer look at the previous year's Cyclopia proves useful. Although certain features of the Irish bazaars made them particularly important to the reception of moving pictures in Ireland, charity bazaars internationally should, I think, be considered among the multiplicity of venues where moving pictures found a more or less short-term home in the decade or so before they found their own dedicated exhibition spaces. Like those other venues – which in Ireland consisted principally of theatres of all kinds, trade shows, *conversaz-*

Fig. 2. *This illustration of Cyclopia appeared in the* Evening Telegraph *(16 May 1896): 8.*

ioni (meetings to discuss literary or scientific topics), waxwork exhibitions, and circuses – bazaars added contextual meanings and implied modes of behaviour that shaped how people received the entertainment novelty of 1896. The institutional meanings associated with bazaars would be of continuing importance in defining the cultural place of moving pictures in Ireland into the 1900s, rivalled only by the variety theatre in terms of number of attendees. Among the institutional connotations attached to bazaars were notions of consumerism and popular entertainment harnessed to social utility; the displaying of women's organisational abilities in the public sphere; and social consensus built on the acceptance of class divisions. Charity bazaars provided a context in which the carnivalesque world-turned-upside-down was domesticated to a display of *noblesse oblige* in which the leisured elite appeared to work for the common good. The charity bazaar was thus a site where the discussion of class and early cinema can identify the role not only of working- and middle-class audiences but also of the elite – particularly elite women – as both audience and impresarios.

Furthermore, although early film scholars may associate charity bazaars with France, it seems that they were particularly strong in Britain and Ireland, where in England alone more than a thousand bazaars were advertised in newspapers every year during the nineteenth century.[8] Most of these were relatively modest affairs, but the largest drew tens of thousands of attendees and raised tens of thousands of pounds for the charities concerned. These monster bazaars, as they were often called, were very lucrative sources of funding for charities, in large part because they placed a higher emphasis on spectacular entertainments than in the cases of the Bazar de la Charité or smaller bazaars, at which the selling of goods at stalls was the main activity. The mix of commerce, entertainment, and religion – because charities were always linked to one religious group or another – was not uncontroversial and was condemned by such churchmen as the Gloucestershire vicar J. Priestley Foster, whose 1888 book-length sermon *Fancy Fair Religion, or, the World Converting Itself* noted that "when a history was written of the latter half of the Nineteenth Century, it would not be complete unless it took notice of such institutions as Bazaars", but considered them not to be a creditable feature of the age because they were an obstacle to true Christian almsgiving.[9] Consumerism as such was not the focus of Foster's ire; far more pernicious was the fact that people attended a bazaar for the

> amusements offered, or because of the Patronage bestowed, or in order to join in the general fun, and be entertained by the concerts and theatricals, farces, nigger entertainments, or opportunities for gambling which the various programmes issued, hold out as baits to entrap the pleasure-seeker and the worldling.[10]

That bazaars required such a broadside from Reverend Foster indicates the established place they held in Victorian society in the late nineteenth century. And in true Victorian fashion, the bazaar would become highly codified, with such manuals as John Muir's 1896 *Bazaars and Fancy Fairs: Their Organisation and Management* instructing the new bazaar organiser on how to arrange all aspects of the event, from lighting the grounds at night, to booking sideshows, to seeking the endorsement of a titled patron.[11]

By 1896, Dublin had become a centre of expertise in bazaar organising. Looking back from 1909, the Irish women's journal *The Lady of the House* claimed that "Dublin is famous for its monster bazaars; in no city in the three kingdoms [England, Scotland and Ireland] are such gigantic fancy fairs held".[12] The benchmark for these very large events was a series of monster bazaars that had been held in the city between 1892 and 1896 at the exhibition grounds of the Royal Dublin Society (RDS) in a prestigious area south of the city called Ball's Bridge.[13] The RDS grounds consisted of a large exhibition

4 "Baits to Entrap the Pleasure-Seeker and the Worldling"

hall and extensive show grounds on which the most prestigious event of the city's social calendar, the Dublin Horse Show, took place during a week in August. It was the Horse Show that the bazaars' organisers sought to rival and outdo, and in this, they succeeded.[14] In a city of less than 400,000 according to the 1891 census, the attendances at these bazaars were in excess – sometimes well in excess – of eighty thousand, attracted by the things that Reverend Foster had complained about: entertainments and fashionable patronage.

"The larger the list of influential patrons and patronesses that can be secured", Muir advises neophyte bazaar organisers, "the more imposing does the bazaar become".[15] In an Ireland polarised along religious, political, and class lines that separated the majority population's Catholicism and nationalism from the largely Protestant peerage and gentry loyal to the British crown, the patronage of as prominent a titled person as possible served usefully contradictory ideological functions. On the one hand, a large social event organised and led by the elite classes, supported by those of the Catholic middle class with social aspirations, demonstrated the normality and loyalty of Ireland in relation to the British Empire. On the other hand, these elite classes displayed their utility and dedication to Ireland as a country with a distinct identity and social needs that had to be addressed. The chief patrons of Cyclopia were the Lord Lieutenant of Ireland, Earl Cadogan, who performed the opening ceremony, and his wife, Countess Cadogan. Alongside them, advertisements named seventy-seven titled women, listed in order of social rank, as patronesses of the bazaar, led by such royals as the Princess of Wales, Princess Christian of Schleswig-Holstein, and the Duchess of York. Under the rhetoric of social service, class hierarchy was maintained because these women lent their names to the event, sponsoring stalls at which women of lesser rank sold "pretty trifles of all lands from China to Peru, as well as the more substantial necessaries of life".[16] Of particular ideological importance was the fact that the Irish Industrial Stall, which sold Irish-made handcrafts, was under the patronage of Countess Cadogan, but was actually run by Lady Charlotte Stopford, Lady Bellingham, and Mrs Gore Cuthbert.[17] The unmarried daughters of such women did much of the selling, providing one of the attractions of the bazaar for male attendees, including the reporter who declared himself willing to be robbed in the cause of charity, if it meant that he would "be 'held up' by a blushing maiden armed with no more fatal weapon than a pair of witching eyes and an attractive book of ballot tickets".[18]

All but one of Dublin's monster bazaars were to aid the city's hospitals – a cause that could command widespread support – and all had an overarching theme on which the exhibition grounds were decorated and the "lady stallholders" were expected to be dressed – often in fanciful orientalist or peasant costumes. Cyclopia, the last of the monster bazaars of the 1890s, was organised to raise the estimated ten thousand pounds needed to fund the amalgamation of two Dublin hospitals, the National Eye and Ear Infirmary and St Mark's Ophthalmic Hospital. The name Cyclopia was a pun on this objective of producing "one eye" hospital for the city.[19] Therefore, this bazaar had a particular focus on visual and to a lesser extent auditory attractions, the visual attractions being epitomised by Sir Henry Grattan Bellew's Cyclopean Eye, a large mechanical eye whose pupil moved and lid blinked. Grattan Bellew might have expected that his locally invented device would be among the most prominent attractions, but by a historical coincidence that could not have been foreseen when the bazaar was original planned in the summer of 1895, two even more striking visual novelties became available for public display in the early months of 1896: moving pictures and X-rays.

The press had made Irish people aware of both of these startling discoveries, with X-rays particularly capturing the public imagination, at least as far as can be gauged from newspaper articles.[20] Public interest in X-rays had been raised and fuelled by reports of spectacular experiments by international and then Irish scientists, several of the latter of whom held public lectures and demonstrations. Moving pictures, by contrast, had received only modest press coverage in the early months of 1896, and there had been only one film show in Dublin, when the Star Theatre of Varieties had featured the Lumière cinématographe on the top of its bill in the week of 20 to 25 April. However, audiences had been disappointed by the indistinctness of the screened image, the result of the projectionist – who was not a genuine Lumière operator – using films printed on frosted kinetoscope stock. The manager of the Star, Dan Lowrey, noted in the theatre's engagement book that there had been "[n]ot enough light on the pictures".[21] As a result, these shows did not catch the public interest to the same extent as the X-rays had, receiving reviews that were more interested in the potential of moving pictures than in their current realisation.

Nevertheless, these first shows did contribute to what would be the successful launch of projected moving pictures just a month later. The Saturday matinee at the Star had in fact been a benefit in aid of Cyclopia, held under the patronage of the Countess of Mayo and attended by many of the bazaar organisers. The cause of charity brought members of the social elite to Dublin's best-known music hall, where they got their first view – however distorted – of a moving-picture show. At Cyclopia, projected film in Dublin would be sufficiently technically accomplished to achieve popular approval in a context in which it could be directly compared to other technological marvels. Although many bazaar-goers did return home with a souvenir X-ray of their own hands, interest in moving pictures would eclipse that in X-rays at Cyclopia and transform the public perception of cinematography.

In contrast to the poor reception of moving pictures at the Star, several accounts of Cyclopia emphasised the particular attractiveness of the animatograph shows, which garnered increasing attention as the bazaar progressed. This is especially revealing because here observers had the choice of patronising all the well-established and state-of-the-art novelties that the bazaar organisers had booked. As a report in the *Dublin Evening Mail* put it:

> [A]n effort has been made to bring together under the one roof everything to delight the eye, to please the ear, to soothe the appetite, to tickle the fancy, to excite curiosity and then allay it, and generally speaking, to put people into that glorious condition of being well satisfied with themselves, in which they are usually more disposed to part with money. Every reasonable penchant has been carefully considered, all tastes have been thought of, and an effort has been made to gratify them.[22]

Among the biggest attractions of Cyclopia, patrons could stroll around the mock-up Dutch village with its lady stallholders and fancy goods; ride the water chute, switchback railways, and merry-go-rounds; ascend in a hot-air balloon; and attend the café chantant, the Pembroke Concerts, the Olympia Variety Entertainment, and the ever-popular children's dances. Many of these were human-based entertainments, but technological ones, what one reporter called "the products of a highly developed state of civilization", were also enormously popular.[23] Among these, other moving-picture and projected visual novelties vied for attention with the animatograph. A kinetoscope synchronised to a phonograph – arguably the novelty that provided the best audio-visual spectacle – showed "a champion high-kicker perform[ing] a vigorous and graceful dance to the accompaniment of an orchestra".[24] After dark, a spectacular outdoor magic lantern show issued from the Lantern Tower in the grounds onto a thirty-foot screen, which raised some objections because "[m]ixed with the slides dealing with subjects of general interest were many others which partook of the nature of advertisements, and were calculated to make the spectator feel that he was being more or less imposed on".[25]

Even in this dazzling company, the animatograph stood out, receiving increasing attention in advertising and press accounts of the bazaar. A column-long advertisement that appeared in the daily newspapers on the bazaar's third day not only listed the animatograph first of the amusements as in previous days, but also ended with details of the films and from where they and the projector had been hired. Among the other attractions, only the café chantant, a bazaar staple, was afforded this special treatment. Of the nine named films – *Zaro, the Tumbling Clown, Interior of a Whiskey Saloon, Death of Svengali, The House on Fire, The Boxers, Scene from Comic Opera, Justice in the Far West, The Village Smithy,* and *The Dentist's Chair* – most are readily recognisable as Edison titles. The Trilby scene mentioned in the epigraph is here named as *Death of Svengali*, and of the others, *Zaro* is the only really puzzling title, but it may be Edison's *Grotesque Tumbling* of January 1895.[26] The exhibitor is listed as August Rosenberg from Newcastle in the north of England, who was part of a firm that launched a projector known as "Rosenberg's cinematograph" later in 1896.[27] Charles James, proprietor of Dublin's World's Fair Waxworks, had booked the animatograph from Rosenberg and would keep the projector in the city in the week after Cyclopia.

As well as the prominence given to the animatograph in advertisements, the press commentaries on each day of the bazaar also gave it sustained attention. An almost thousand-word article, titled "The Wonder of Cyclopia: The Animatograph", appeared in Dublin's most popular daily paper, the *Freeman's Journal,* and its *Evening Telegraph*, offering technical information on persistence of vision, projection speeds, and the operation of the shutter; notes on Edison and the Lumière brothers; and detailed descriptions of some individual films.[28] As the bazaar progressed, the newspapers reported that additional animatograph shows were required to cater to demand. The trajectory of this is clear when the *Irish Daily Independent*'s brief final notice of the bazaar revealed that during the Whit Monday holiday, "Cyclopia was still in full swing and had a fair attendance, the animatograph supplied by Mr C. A. James, of the World's Fair, being exceedingly well patronised, while the Children's Dances, and the Café Chantant did good business in the afternoon".[29] The animatograph had been the hit of Cyclopia, allowing James legitimately to advertise it as the "wonderful triumph of Scientific Research, [...] which has been patronised by the Nobility and Gentry of Ireland at Cyclopia", when he opened it at his World's Fair Waxworks in the week following the bazaar.[30] The change of venue could hardly have been more extreme; James charged two pence (2d.) admission to the waxworks and stage show at the World's Fair, a sixth of the one shilling (1s.) daily admission charged at Cyclopia. Those with just the minimum of disposable income could enjoy the entertainment that had been the spectacular success of the biggest social event of the year. Although over the coming years film projectors with other proprietary names would more often be exhibited at Irish venues associated with the lower-middle and working classes, they would also remain established features of both large and small charity bazaars. At these, moving pictures would continue to accrue the benefits of being associated with charity events organised by the most respectable members of society.

Notes

1. "Cyclopia: Third Day of the Fete", *Irish Daily Independent* (22 May 1896): 6.
2. John Barnes, *The Beginnings of Cinema in England* (Newton Abbot: David & Charles, 1976), 99. The spelling here – all the Irish references refer to the projector without a final "e" – may indicate that the projector used in Dublin was not manufactured by Paul. Advertisements nevertheless

claimed that this was the "[f]irst appearance of the original Animatograph in Ireland", specifying that it was currently "being exhibited nightly at the Alhambra Theatre, London".

3. Several kinetoscope parlours had opened in Dublin since the device's premiere on 4 April 1895; see Denis Condon, *Early Irish Cinema, 1895–1921* (Dublin: Irish Academic Press, 2008), 25–34.
4. Charles Musser, *Before the Nickelodeon: Edwin S. Porter and the Edison Manufacturing Company* (Berkeley: University of California Press, 1991), 52.
5. José Baldizzone, "L'Incendie du Bazar de la Charité", *Archives* 12 (March 1988); H. Mark Gosser, "The Bazar de la Charité Fire: The Reality, the Aftermath, the Telling", *Film History* 10.1 (1998): 70–89.
6. Gosser, "The Bazar de le Charité Fire", 70.
7. "Terrible Calamity in Paris: Fire at a Fashionable Bazaar", *Irish Times* (5 May 1897): 5.
8. F.K. Prochaska, "Charity Bazaars in Nineteenth-Century England", *Journal of British Studies* 16.2 (Spring 1977): 66.
9. J. Priestley Foster, *Fancy Fair Religion, or, the World Converting Itself* (London: Swan, Sonnenschein, and Co., 1888), 11.
10. Foster 1888, 18.
11. John Muir, *Bazaars and Fancy Fairs: Their Organisation and Management: A Secretary's Vade Mecum* (London: L. Upcott Gill, 1896).
12. "This Year's Great Bazaar at Ball's Bridge", *Lady of the House* (May 1909): 5.
13. For a more detailed account of the monster bazaars in relation to consumerism in Ireland, see Stephanie Rains, *Commodity Culture and Social Class in Dublin, 1850–1916* (Dublin: Irish Academic Press, 2010), 141–163.
14. No full attendance figures were published for Cyclopia, but the daily figures appear to indicate a falloff in comparison to previous years, a fact also noted by several commentators. Nevertheless, the admissions for the bazaar were considerably more than for the Horse Show, on the lines indicated by the attendance figures for the 1895 events: while fewer than 54,000 people attended the Horse Show that year, eighty thousand attended the Ierne bazaar. See "The Great National Horse Show: Opening Day", *Irish Times* (26 August 1896): 9; and *Lady of the House* (June 1895): 2.
15. Muir 1896, 11.
16. "Cyclopia", *Irish Times* (2 May 1896): 7.
17. Ibid.
18. "Cyclopia Bazaar: Opening Ceremony by the Viceroy", *Irish Daily Independent* (20 May 1896): 5.
19. Gearoid Crookes, *Dublin's Eye and Ear: The Making of a Monument* (Dublin: Town House, 1993), 45–46.
20. Denis Condon, "'Spleen of a Cabinet Minister at Work': Exhibiting X-Rays and the Cinematograph in Ireland, 1896", in John Hill and Kevin Rockett (eds), *Film History and National Cinema: Studies in Irish Film 2* (Dublin: Four Courts Press, 2005), 69–78.
21. Lowrey quoted in Eugene Watters and Matthew Murtagh, *Infinite Variety: Dan Lowrey's Music Hall, 1879–97* (Dublin: Gill and Macmillan, 1975), 166.
22. "Cyclopia Fete", *Dublin Evening Mail* (21 May 1896): 3.
23. "Cyclopia Fete", *Daily Express* (21 May 1896): 5.
24. "Cyclopia: A Big Attendance", *Irish Daily Independent* (21 May 1896): 6.
25. "Cyclopia Fete", *Dublin Evening Mail (21 May* 1896): 3.
26. Charles Musser, *Edison Motion Pictures, 1890–1900: An Annotated Filmography* (Washington, DC: Smithsonian Institution Press, 1997), 174.
27. Barnes 1976, 135–138.
28. "The Wonder of Cyclopia: The Animatograph", *Freeman's Journal* (20 May 1896): 5.
29. "Whit-Monday in Dublin", *Irish Daily Independent* (26 May 1896): 3.
30. Advertisement for World's Fair Waxworks, *Evening Telegraph* (26 May 1896): 1.

Paroles éducatives et religieuses lors des projections de films en France avant 1915

Martin Barnier

En France, avant la Première Guerre mondiale, dans un contexte de lutte entre l'Église et les tenants de la laïcité (lois de 1905), les projections de films permettent à la fois de diffuser des idées et d'attirer le public le plus jeune (patronages).[1] "Les conférences avec projections sont, sans contredit le moyen le plus simple et le plus efficace de parler au peuple" explique G.M. Coissac, dans un numéro de la revue *Le Fascinateur*, publié le 1 janvier 1903.[2] Si les projections dans les églises sont interdites par le pape à partir de 1912, les séances de films pendant les patronages sont vivement recommandées. Dans le camp laïc, les professeurs de lycée, ou d'université (particulièrement en médecine), se tournent vers ce nouveau moyen d'éducation par l'image. Les revues corporatives se font l'écho des initiatives qui introduisent les films dans les classes, et dans les patronages laïcs. Parfois la lutte se fait âpre entre les deux camps, par revues interposées. Mais le film éducatif est parfois aussi un élément de consensus. Les institutions aussi importantes que l'Église et l'Éducation nationale activent un processus de légitimation d'un certain type de "cinéma" (mot peu utilisé avant la fin de la période).

On pourra questionner cette façon de voir les films, de les projeter, et de les commenter. Les revues de l'époque, les journaux et autres bulletins paroissiaux nous donnent des exemples concrets de la façon dont les partisans du "cinéma éducatif" (comme on dira plus tard) ont propagé leurs idées. La parole "posée sur les films", par des prêtres ou des professeurs, reste un sujet à défricher pour comprendre comment ces images animées pouvaient être reçues par le public. Ce "son" laïc ou religieux, replacé dans le contexte de la Belle Époque, permet de saisir avec précision le travail de diffusion éducative et non commerciale des films avant 1915. Entre la voix professorale et la parole religieuse nous écouterons un exemple de voix magistrale de la période.

De l'école à l'université

Parallèlement aux conférences pour adultes, la voix des hommes de science accompagne les vues fixes et les films dans les écoles. Par exemple, dans quatre cantons de Lorraine, M. Denis présente, au cours de l'hiver 1913–1914, vingt-quatre conférences accompagnées de films. Dans le cadre de ces séances scolaires, ce conférencier avait alors parlé devant 4,000 élèves.[3] Les conférenciers opérant en dehors des circuits commerciaux, dans des salles dépourvues de cabines de projection, bénéficiaient de certaines faveurs. Ils pouvaient se passer de certaines mesures de sécurité, à condition d'utiliser des films ininflammables, ce qui pouvait difficilement être vérifié par les services municipaux de chaque commune. Par exemple, cet arrêté municipal pris à Villeurbanne en 1915, peut concerner des réunions dans des écoles ou des salles des fêtes. (Il est très proche d'arrêtés pris dans d'autres villes à la même époque):

> En dehors de projections fixes de clichés sur verre, l'emploi d'appareils cinématographiques ne comportant pas de cuve à eau pourra être exceptionnellement autorisé, au cours des conférences faites dans les salles dépourvues de la cabine réglementaire, mais sous la réserve expresse que les films utilisés seront ininflammables.
>
> Les organisateurs de ces conférences devront se prêter à toutes les mesures de contrôle nécessaires, notamment à des prises d'échantillons qui seront effectuées service d'incendie.
>
> Les appareils devront être de l'un des systèmes autorisés par la Commission. Ils devront comporter un dispositif renfermant complètement le film, et permettant de laisser ce dernier en projection fixe pendant un temps illimité sans courir de danger d'inflammation.[4]

Georges-Michel Coissac, directeur du *Fascinateur* et propagateur infatigable de l'utilisation des films pour l'enseignement religieux avant 1914, et Edmond Benoit-Lévy son homologue laïc, ont aidé au développement du cinéma des écoles aux universités.[5] Coissac nous dit:

> Dès 1906, se posait le principe de la mission scolaire du film; nous fûmes des artisans de la première heure avec M. Edmond Benoît-Lévy, sans oublier M. Léopold Bellon, ancien vice-président du conseil municipal de Paris.
>
> C'est en 1907 que fut donnée dans le préau de l'école de la rue de Vitruve (13e) la première séance de cinématographe. En 1911, M. Brucker, titulaire du cours d'histoire naturelle au lycée Hoche, à Versailles, illustrait ses leçons de projections animées.[6]

Cette citation est tirée d'un livre de Coissac, dont le titre bat des records de longueur: *Le cinématographe et l'enseignement: nouveau guide pratique, approuvé et adopté par le Ministère de l'Instruction publique, le Ministère de l'Agriculture, la Direction de l'Enseignement technique, la Cinémathèque de la Ville de Paris*. En incluant dans son titre qu'il était officiellement adopté par plusieurs ministères, il prouve la volonté de son auteur de représenter la ligne officielle de l'enseignement public (et laïc), dans les années 1920 (et non plus de l'éducation religieuse comme avant 1914). Il construit donc une "histoire officielle" de l'enseignement avec projections de films. Il oublie quelques projections isolées qui eurent lieu avant 1907, mais nous renseigne efficacement sur l'importance de la parole du maître accompagnant les images éducatives en mouvement. Dans les cours de M. Brucker, les projections auraient convaincu pour la première fois un inspecteur de l'Éducation nationale de la nécessité de développer l'enseignement "audio-visuel" (comme on ne disait pas encore) dans les écoles publiques. Coissac se promeut en tant que témoin et acteur de la propagation des films dans l'instruction:

> Nous-même utilisions des films en des conférences, après avoir longtemps pratiqué les projections fixes, et notre ami et collaborateur M. Émile Roux-Parassac, fut le premier à s'en servir pour la propagande touristique et l'enseignement de la géographie de la France en public. Ceci se place avant 1913, époque où quelques lycées parisiens, Condorcet, Louis-Le Grand, Voltaire, Fénelon, Jules-Ferry, imitèrent l'exemple de celui de Versailles.[7]

Les établissements parisiens d'enseignement secondaire ont donc adopté rapidement les cours avec des films. Mais nous ne savons pas la proportion de cours ainsi proposés. Les firmes privées se rendent compte du débouché possible dans l'Éducation Nationale. Le catalogue Gaumont des films documentaires signale que chaque film est accompagné de fiches pour permettre les "commentaires des professeurs".[8]

Un cours avec projections est décrit par *Cinéma-revue* en décembre 1913:

> M. Léopold Bellon, ancien président du conseil municipal de Paris, a fait, le jeudi 23 octobre [1913], à l'intention des jeunes élèves qui emplissaient la salle Villars, rue du Rocher, une intéressante démonstration du cinématographe appliqué à l'enseignement et à l'éducation. Le conférencier était M. Armand Gauley, professeur à l'École Normale primaire. Le thème, très original, était le trajet parcouru par une lettre qui, partie des lacs de l'Afrique centrale, parvenait enfin à Marseille en empruntant tous les moyens de locomotion particuliers aux pays traversés: caravane, pirogue, voie ferrée, paquebot, etc. Entre-temps, devant les yeux des jeunes auditeurs, passaient les vues, non seulement des grands lacs, mais aussi d'Assouan, de l'île de Philae, d'Alexandrie, etc.[9]

Notons la stratégie pédagogique remarquable de ce cours de géographie. On raconte une petite histoire pour accrocher les élèves et les faire voyager sans difficulté grâce au suspense: la lettre arrivera-t-elle à temps? L'utilisation de "panoramas" (selon le terme désignant alors les films documentaires) provenant du commerce s'intègre ici parfaitement à une séquence de cours. Il devient clair que la voix du maître, en donnant un sens nouveau à ces images exotiques est l'élément central de cette démonstration. Il est difficile d'évaluer le nombre de cours de ce type, à cette date. Il est certains que des professeurs d'école sont particulièrement motivés par cette nouvelle méthode: dans son ouvrage sur le cinéma et l'enseignement, Coissac précise que les instituteurs aussi utilisèrent le cinéma, avec un matériel "acquis le plus souvent de leurs propres deniers".

Par ailleurs, Coissac n'oublie pas que la première parole accompagnant doctement les films pour enseigner des connaissances et des pratiques fut celle du docteur Doyen: "En vérité, c'est au Dr Doyen qu'il faut accorder la priorité du cinématographe d'enseignement. En 1898, il tournait et projetait des films 'pour son enseignement personnel, déclarait-il, et pour celui de ses élèves'".[10] Dans son bref résumé Coissac cite également le professeur Garrigue-Lagrange qui utilisa les films pour ses cours de physique et de chimie. Il signale que le manque de films spécifiques pour l'instruction publique se fit sentir et que des films d'actualité et des documentaires produits pour des projections commerciales furent utilisés. Et surtout, Georges-Michel Coissac rappelle la règle d'or de l'utilisation des films en milieu scolaire: "La projection cinématographique ne se suffit pas à elle-même: elle fait partie d'une leçon et ne peut, en aucun cas, en tenir lieu. Elle doit être commentée par le maître et observée par les élèves".[11]

On pourrait noter la passivité des élèves dans cette imprécation. L'essentiel ici est la mise en avant de la parole doctorale. Sans doute pour ne pas effrayer les enseignants lecteurs de son ouvrage, mais également par conviction profonde, Coissac, qui avait commencé sa carrière par des projections de plaques fixes, assujettit les films aux mots du maître. Il cite un article de *La Revue critique de médecine et de chirurgie* qui montre l'enthousiasme de Doyen devant la possibilité de montrer ses films au public rassemblé dans d'immenses amphithéâtres: "Si vous photographiez au cinématographe une opération typique, vous ferez comprendre en moins d'une minute à un millier de personnes ce que toute une conférence ne pourra démontrer qu'à un petit nombre d'étudiants, placés à proximité du professeur".[12]

À part Doyen, et, à partir de 1906, d'autres professeurs obtiennent de montrer des films à leurs étudiants:

> Dans le courant de 1912, le médecin-major Henry Billet, professeur agrégé

de médecine opératoire et d'anatomie chirurgicale au Val-de-Grâce, résolut de pourvoir d'un cinématographe l'école d'application. Ses prédécesseurs s'étaient heurtés à des difficultés budgétaires qu'il parvint à aplanir, et en novembre 1913, il commençait ses cours.[13]

Ces précisions montrent que les universités ne purent pas s'équiper facilement en matériel de projection. Les divers exemples cités par Coissac prouvent néanmoins que des enseignements de toutes matières (mais surtout scientifiques) ont profité du cinématographe dans les années 1910.

Dans *Jérusalem*, film produit pour être diffusé dans des salles commerciales (et sans doute dans les établissements scolaires), nous avons un exemple de volonté pédagogique mêlant histoire et géographie.[14] Il s'agit d'un film parlant synchronisé avec le système Chronophone Gaumont. Ce cours magistral est aussi une voix d'imprécation presque religieuse, européo-centrée ("Cité sainte […] surtout pour les Chrétiens"). Il s'agit bien d'une vision catholique et française (anachronisme: "Royaume français de la Palestine"), comme un prêche, sans interrogation, qui ne propose que des affirmations: "tout cela nous intéresse mais ne nous émeut pas" dit le commentateur quand il s'agit de bâtiments juifs ou musulmans. L'ensemble de ce commentaire nous permet d'avoir une idée de ce que pouvait être la voix professorale posée sur un film dans la période précédant la Guerre de 1914–18. Cette voix nationaliste et catholique, dans le cas cité, n'est pas éloignée de celle du prêtre qui commente aussi des films.

Paroles religieuses

Quand le lieu de projection est une église, le recueillement est de rigueur lors des projections, sauf lorsque les fidèles laissent échapper des petits cris d'étonnement: "Les spectateurs gardaient un silence profond qui témoignait de l'émotion de leur âme; silence interrompu seulement par des exclamations de ce genre: Oh! Voyez donc le petit Jésus! Oh, qu'il est beau!".[15] Sous la nef de l'église, les paroles des paroissiens résonnaient. L'émotion partagée, dans un lieu religieux ou non, semble être une des caractéristiques les plus fortes des séances de projection de la période. Même dans une ambiance de recueillement, le public exprime ce qu'il ressent profondément.

Le Musée pédagogique et les sociétés d'instruction populaire, comme la très laïque Ligue de l'Enseignement, de même que des organismes catholiques comme la Bonne Presse, proposent de plus en plus de soirées de formation pour adultes. Les traditions anciennes du théâtre religieux placent souvent un commentateur à côté du tableau vivant représentant une scène de l'Évangile. Il est chargé de déclamer des dialogues complétant les scènes muettes.[16] Depuis les années 1870, les Catholiques ont utilisé les projections lumineuses pour "l'enseignement populaire de toutes les sciences et la propagation de la foi". Entre 1900 et 1908, pendant la période de séparation de l'Église et de l'État, les patronages paroissiaux se multiplient et proposent plus de 5,000 plaques pour projections variées. Vues fixes et animées sont encouragées par la revue catholique *Le Fascinateur* qui loue "les bons résultats [que] donne la projection pour l'enseignement du catéchisme aux enfants et pour jeter dans les âmes la 'vérité lumineuse'".[17]

Les projections de films s'insèrent dans ce dispositif et se font dans les églises, jusqu'en 1912. Le prêche précède la projection qui peut se faire dans le silence, comme à Pau, en 1904 quand *Vie et passion de Jeanne d'Arc* et *Apparitions de Lourdes* sont projetées dans une église. Le *Mémorial des Pyrénées* témoigne du silence recueilli de l'assemblée, mis à part quelques exclamations de surprise des paroissiens.[18] En juin 1905, dans l'église Saint-François d'Annecy, une conférence organisée par la paroisse propose de retracer la vie du Christ grâce à des photos et films pris en Palestine.[19] MM. Musant et Chevalier montrent 110 vues fixes et 600 mètres de vues cinématographiques sur le sujet "Au

5 Paroles éducatives et religieuses lors des projections de films en France avant 1915

Fig. 1. Image tirée du Fascinateur, *1er janvier 1904 [Collection Jean-Claude Seguin.]*

pays de l'enfance du Christ". Leur conférence est passée par Paris, Londres, Lyon, Amiens, Dijon, Besançon, Cannes, Monte-Carlo, Turin et Marseille d'après les journaux. Les séances sont chères, entre 1 et 3 francs la place. *L'Indicateur de la Savoie* note: "les explications sont aussi claires que sobres et érudites [...]. Il faut louer sans réserve l'initiative de ces prêtres distingués".[20] Les paroles accompagnant les films s'entendent donc dans les églises françaises jusqu'en 1912. À cette date, le Saint-Siège mit fin aux projections dans les lieux saints, mais il encouragea les films et les vues fixes dans les salles de patronage.[21] Dès 1898, les salles de patronage servent à projeter les *Passions*, avec explications par le prêtre local. Henry Fescourt se souvient d'avoir côtoyé un notable de Nancy, qui a vu, en 1898 ou 1899, une présentation de *La Passion de N. S. Jésus-Christ* dans un patronage.[22] La voix du curé de la paroisse accompagne les plaques et les films dans les salles paroissiales. Un historien du patronage catholique explique les réactions des spectateurs:

> Les appareils de projection n'eurent bientôt plus de secret pour maints directeurs de patronages. [...] Le vicaire, debout à gauche de l'écran, surveille le film et commente pour les spectateurs, l'orchestre du patronage assurant les intermèdes musicaux au grand dam du public: "que la musique nous laisse en paix. C'est mieux quand l'abbé raconte" [...]. Bien entendu, le commentateur ne se prive pas de critiquer au passage telle ou telle scène.[23]

La Société cinématographique de France s'est spécialisée dans les vues religieuses. En Lorraine, elle présente un programme édifiant, à Bar-le-duc, le 22 mai 1906, puis à Nancy, le 24 mai suivant, Grande salle de la passion, 146 rue Jeanne d'Arc. Les films et les vues fixes traitant de Lourdes s'enchaînent: *Lourdes en 1858*, *La genèse des apparitions*, *Enfance de Bernadette*, etc. Les projections sont suivies d'une conférence animée par l'écrivain Boyer.[24] Ces projections commentées peuvent être rapprochées de la tradition très ancienne de l'utilisation des vitraux et sculptures pour l'apprentissages des fidèles.[25] Le développement des projections cinématographiques dans les patronages paroissiaux se fait à partir de 1908. Il s'intensifie après que le Vatican ordonne de cesser les projections dans les églises en 1912.

Dès 1908, une véritable distribution de films pour les paroisses se met en place. "Le cinématographe de l'A.C.J.F., à Rennes, proposait ses services itinérants aux paroisses rurales".[26] La parole des curés continue d'accompagner plus des images fixes, aux sujets édifiants, que des vues cinématographiques. Le prêtre commente aussi les films burlesques (le plus souvent) et les quelques drames projetés, mais il ne s'agit pas de parole éducative. Le catéchisme reste majoritairement illustré par les plaques. Un exemple de séance de patronage, vers 1910 contient deux parties:

- Vues fixes: *La vie d'une famille chrétienne. Divine enfance de Jésus. Les guérisons de Lourdes. Vie intime de Pie X.*
- Cinématographe (petits films de 80 à 100 mètres): *Farces de frise poulet. Course des agents. Le chemineau. Course aux potirons. Passe-partout. Bonsoir fleur.*

D'après Michel Lagrée:

> peu de films proprement religieux apparaissent aux catalogues, y compris celui de la Bonne Presse. On peut donc considérer l'époque qui précède la Première Guerre mondiale comme celle du cinéma *concession*, pis-aller subordonné à l'image lumineuse fixe, plus facilement maîtrisable et plus proche de la culture iconographique traditionnelle du clergé (vitraux, images pieuses et catéchismes illustrés).[27]

Conclusion

Les églises, puis les patronages résonnent des voix des prêtres commentant des vues fixes et animées, mais les groupements laïcs semblent beaucoup plus nombreux à utiliser ces deux moyens de projections et à les disséminer dans les écoles publiques (pour les projections du jeudi par exemple). Dans les deux cas, la voix de l'adulte (ou du professeur face à ses étudiants) contrôle le défilement de l'image. Cette voix d'autorité empêche tout débordement, tout commentaire ... Dans nos recherches, nous avons constaté que les salles commerciales laissaient au contraire libre cours aux bavardages, à la même période. Certains projectionnistes devaient faire face à un brouhaha continu, des cris, des réactions vives du public.[28] Face à la voix du maître ou du prêtre, seuls le recueillement et l'écoute attentive sont autorisés. On remarque que les conseils officiels trouvés dans les plaquettes, articles et ouvrages trahissent une conception de l'éducation, religieuse ou laïque, ne laissant aucune part à une interaction maître/élève, ni même à un simple questionnement.

L'autorité impose une seule lecture possible des films. Mais quand, dans les patronages religieux ou laïcs, il s'agit non plus d'instruire, mais de distraire, les rires sont autorisés, puisque la sélection des films comporte principalement des burlesques. On constate donc, dans ces projections non commerciales, un balancement entre deux extrêmes: le cours magistral, avec un commentaire dictant la lecture des images et ne laissant place à aucune participation (ce qui serait considéré comme de l'indiscipline), ou le délassement avec des films comiques choisis pour le plaisir des enfants. Dans les deux cas, le film sert à canaliser l'attention des jeunes, à les encourager à revenir chaque jeudi au patronage, et à faciliter l'apprentissage (voir même l'endoctrinement).

L'accompagnement des films par la voix du maître allait continuer jusqu'à l'avènement de la télévision scolaire, et même dans ce cas, l'instituteur pouvait couper le son et commenter à sa guise. Dans les années 1930 et 1940, des films prévus pour l'enseignement, mais comportant une piste son, furent rendus muets pour ne pas gêner le pouvoir doctoral dans les classes. On peut encore voir aujourd'hui le trait noir qui "mate" la piste son, dans certaines archives.[29]

Notes

1. Merci à l'Équipe d'Accueil Passages XX-XXI qui m'a aidé à participer au colloque Domitor 2010 à Toronto.
2. George-Michel Coissac, *Le Fascinateur* no 1 (1er janvier 1903). Coissac cite à la fin de sa phrase Mgr Méronillod: "et le peuple est à qui lui parle".
3. *Lectures pour tous*, septembre 1917, cité par Blaise Aurora, *Histoire du cinéma en Lorraine: du cinématographe au cinéma forain, 1896–1914* (Metz/Nancy/Paris: La Serpenoise/Conservatoire régional de l'image/AFRHC, 1996), 25.
4. Arrêté municipal, du 1er juin 1915, concernant les dispositions de sécurité pour les salles de cinéma. Article 186. Archives municipales de Villeurbanne, Rhône. Merci à Mathias Chassagnieux.
5. Georges-Michel Coissac a dirigé *Le Fascinateur* de 1903 à 1914, luttant contre la propagande laïque de la Ligue de l'Enseignement, mais après la guerre il crée le *Cinéopse*. "Collaborant de près avec les éminents représentants du courant républicain, dont un certain nombre de francs-maçons, Coissac devient ainsi le promoteur de valeurs qui se situent totalement aux antipodes de ses premières activités rédactionnelles", explique le *Dictionnaire du cinéma français des années vingt*, sous la direction de François Albéra et Jean A. Gili, *1895* no 33 (juin 2001): 120.
6. Georges-Michel Coissac, *Le cinématographe et l'enseignement: nouveau guide pratique, approuvé et adopté par le Ministère de l'Instruction publique, le Ministère de l'Agriculture, la Direction de l'Enseignement technique, la Cinémathèque de la Ville de Paris* (Paris: Éditions du Cinéopse/Librairie Larousse, 1926), 3.
7. Ibid.
8. Frédéric Delmeulle, "Le rêve encyclopédiste: le cinéma documentaire chez Gaumont, 1908–1928", dans *Cinéma des premiers temps: nouvelles contributions françaises*, sous la direction de Michel Marie, Thierry Lefebvre et Laurent Mannoni, *Théorème* no 4 (Paris: Presses de la Sorbonne Nouvelle, 1996): 102.
9. *Cinéma-revue* 3e année, no 12 (décembre 1913).
10. Coissac, *Histoire du cinématographe des origines à nos jours* (Paris: Édition du Cinéopse/Librairie Gauthier-Villars, 1925), 527. Néanmoins, il semble que Boleslaw Matuszewski avait enregistré, avant le Dr Doyen, les travaux de chirurgiens français. Valérie Vignaux, "Contribution à une histoire de l'emploi du cinéma dans l'enseignement de la chirurgie", *1895* no 44 (décembre 2004): 73–74. Voir également: Thierry Lefebvre, *La chair et le celluloïd: le cinéma chirurgical du docteur Doyen* (Brionne: Jean Doyen Éditeur, 2004).
11. Ibid., 32.
12. Article du Dr Doyen dans la *Revue critique de médecine et de chirurgie* (15 août 1899), cité dans Georges-Michel Coissac, *Histoire du cinématographe*, 527.
13. Coissac, *Histoire du cinématographe*, 530.
14. Ce film est une phonoscène produite par Gaumont. Le disque et le film synchronisés font partie de la série "Enseignement" entre 1906 et 1914. Film visible dans le DVD accompagnant le livre *Le muet a la parole*, sous la direction de Giusy Pisano et Valérie Pozner (Paris: AFRHC, 2005).
15. *Le Mémorial des Basses-Pyrénées* (16–17 octobre 1904), cité dans Hélène Tierchant, *Aquitaine, 100 ans de cinéma* (Bordeaux: CRL d'Aquitaine, 1991), 39.
16. Deslandes et Richard donnent l'exemple du Théâtre religieux de Nouvalon, qui donnait des représentations dans les années précédant 1860. Les deux historiens citent le dialogue entre Caïphe et Jésus. Le bonisseur est chargé de faire les deux voix pendant que les acteurs sur scène forment des tableaux muets. Jacques Deslandes et Jacques Richard, *Histoire comparée du cinéma*, tome 2, *Du cinématographe au cinéma, 1896–1906* (Tournai: Casterman, 1968), 89.
17. *Le Fascinateur*, revue catholique des projections fixes et animées, citée dans *Phono-Ciné-Gazette* no 24 (15 mars 1906).
18. *Le Mémorial des Pyrénées* (16–17 octobre 1904), repris dans Tierchant, *100 ans de cinéma en Aquitaine*, 39.

19. Les deux conférenciers ont pris eux-mêmes les images et proposent dans les églises de France leur "reportage" commenté. Merci à Loris Thiel.
20. *L'Indicateur de la Savoie* (24 juin 1905), à propos de la séance du 14 juin. Cité dans Pignal, *Les premiers pas du cinéma en Haute-Savoie* (Annecy: Conseil Général de Haute-Savoie, 1997), 32–33.
21. Ces consignes semblent avoir été respectées en France, mais dans d'autres pays les projections eurent encore lieu dans les églises. Une enseignante portugaise m'a expliqué que son père se souvenait de séances dans les églises entre les années 1930 et 1950. Même si les films avaient du son, les prêtres portugais continuaient de commenter les images, traduisant et interprétant avec une très grande liberté les films français par exemple. Ils changeaient totalement le sens de l'histoire, pour accentuer une morale toute catholique. Témoignage de Graça Lobo, Cineclub de Faro, 4 décembre 2004.
22. Henry Fescourt, *La foi et les montagnes* (Paris: Paul Montel, 1959), 12–13.
23. Michel Lagrée, "Les trois âges du cinéma de patronage", dans *Le patronage ghetto ou vivier?*, sous la direction de Gérard Cholvy (Paris: Nouvelle cité, 1987), 220.
24. Aurora, *Histoire du cinéma en Lorraine*, 92.
25. Merci à Benjamin Labé. "Le curé de l'église Saint-Nicolas du Chardonnet, à Paris, déclare ne pas voir de différences entre les images de la Passion, qu'il projette à ses ouailles pour accompagner son prêche et les vitraux ou le chemin de croix qui ornent son église", cité par Christian-Marc Bosséno, "Le Répertoire du grand écran", dans, *La culture de masse en France*, sous la direction de Jean-Pierre Rioux et Jean-François Sirinelli (Paris: Fayard, 2002), 171.
26. Michel Lagrée, "Les trois âges du cinéma de patronage", 217.
27. Ibid., 218.
28. Martin Barnier, *Bruits, cris, musiques de film: les projections avant 1914* (Rennes: Presses Universitaires de Rennes, 2010). Une partie de cet article recoupe un chapitre de notre livre.
29. Films dans les Archives de la Cinémathèque de Saint-Étienne et dans celles de la Cinémathèque de la ville de Paris. Recherches inédites de Béatrice de Pastre, en 2007, montrant que les films parlants sont rendus muets par une bande opaque en laboratoire (la Cinémathèque de la ville de Paris avait payé pour cela, car les devis existent toujours!). Contrairement à ce que pensent Raymond Borde et Charles Perrin, dans *Les Offices du cinéma éducateur* (Lyon: PUL, 1992), ce ne sont pas pour des raisons économiques que les films muets sont préférés par les Offices.

6

Mütter, verzaget nicht! (1911) [Mothers, Despair Not!]: Henny Porten's Promotion for Mothers' Welfare

Martin Loiperdinger and Holger Ziegler

German film companies started to make silent features only after the end of the Tonbilder boom in 1910.[1] At that time, the leading film production countries – France, the USA, Italy, Great Britain and Denmark – had already been producing one-reel features for short film programmes for several years. Germany caught up quickly, however, by producing long features composed of three to five reels, by the exclusive system of film distribution – so-called *Monopolfilm*, and by introducing the star system.[2] From 1911, German companies had started to export long feature films and Asta Nielsen had become a well-known film star in many countries.

A sponsored long film to promote Berlin's Mother and Child Auxiliary Day

Henny Porten was Germany's second film star before the First World War. Whereas Asta Nielsen became famous in long, entertaining commercial films from the beginning, Henny Porten started as a leading character in five one-reelers. Her first long film was a sponsored film to promote mothers' welfare. *Mütter, verzaget nicht!*, a three-reeler with a projection time of forty-five minutes, was a milestone in Henny Porten's career, although her name was not credited by the producer, Messter's Projection. Henny Porten was not yet a film star when *Mütter, verzaget nicht!* was released in June 1911.

Sponsored films are made to improve public relations. Their purpose is information, education, advertisement or propaganda. The sponsor pays for the production of the film and for access to audiences. *Mütter, verzaget nicht!* was made on behalf of the Hauptstelle für Mütter und Säuglingsfürsorge in Groß-Berlin [The Central Office for Mother and Infant Welfare in Greater Berlin], on the occasion of the Hilfstag für Mutter und Kind in Groß-Berlin [Mother and Child Auxiliary Day in Greater Berlin]. This fundraising campaign took place on 24 and 25 June, 1911, with various public events, parades and concerts. Thousands of voluntary assistants with vendors' trays moved throughout town selling flowers. Although the proceeds were to benefit Berlin welfare associations and facilities, public donation requests of this kind were also subject to criticism. To forestall critics of this particular event, educational work was to be carried out by means of a "gigantic film", a "one-hour lecture"[3] demonstrating mother and child welfare achievements in Berlin.[4]

Fig. 1. Domestic violence: the evil of drink.

Fig. 2. Saved from suicide by the policeman.

6 *Mütter, verzaget nicht!* (1911) [*Mothers, Despair Not!*]

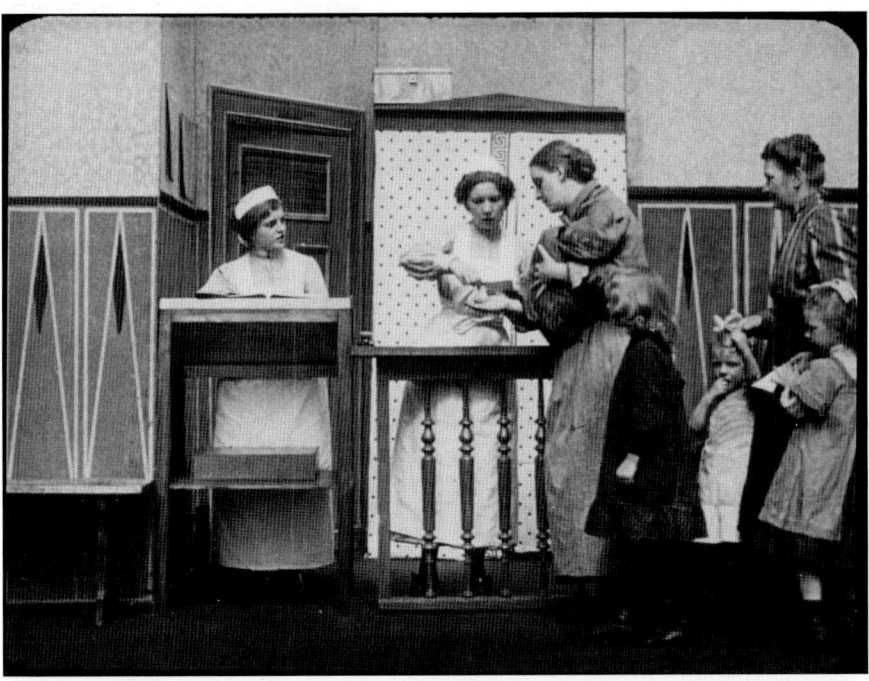

Fig. 3. Payment of the breast-feeding premium.

Fig. 4. The result of professional treatment.

Fig. 5. On location: in front of the Pestalozzi Fröbel House, Berlin.

Fig. 6. Gymnastic physical training: the Charité cure from drink.

6 *Mütter, verzaget nicht!* (1911) [*Mothers, Despair Not!*]

Fig. 7. In the new flat: the husband's return, accompanied by the temperance volunteer.

Fig. 8. Packshot: the family saved and unified at the cosy home.

55

Mütter, verzaget nicht! is a non-fiction film. Outdoor scenes were filmed on location while the interior scenes illustrating the procedures and achievements of Berlin welfare facilities were filmed in the studio of Messter's Projection. The first three minutes of the film are a condensed social drama – a formula well-known to contemporary audiences: A mother lives in a hovel with two hungry children. Her husband is a drunk who beats her up. The landlady shows up with the bailiff to impound the furniture. Exhausted from pain and sorrow, the mother is about to jump off the nearest bridge with her children when at the last minute a constable rushes over to save her and directs her to those who can help. Then, after only those three short minutes of the familiar touching scenes, a guided tour through the Berlin welfare facilities begins:

> Together with the unhappy woman we enter the helpdesk for mother and child welfare where all necessary information is given to her. We accompany her to the infant nursery and the rehabilitation clinic for alcoholics. We satisfy ourselves that the defenceless babies are well-treated and well-fed by professional hands. The five- or six-year-old daughter gets lodging in the Pestalozzi Fröbel House. The woman gets a job and is able to act for herself and the little ones, and her husband gets treatment in the rehabilitation clinic to restore his health. We follow him at every turn. [...] At last father, mother and children are happily united anew in cosy family life.[5]

In the last shot, a close-up, the laughing members of the family face the camera: Like the pack shot of a promotional film, this concluding shot displays the "happy family" – the product that the Berlin welfare facilities achieve through their services' efforts. At the premiere, according to a newspaper report, the film closed with the words, "All these welfare achievements require love, work and money. Hence, on June 24 and 25: Mother and Child Auxiliary Day!"[6]

Presentation of various welfare facilities

On her journey from attempted suicide to happy family life, the mother finds all doors open for the wife of a drunkard. The guided-tour portion of the film displays the smoothly operating wheelwork of the welfare bureaucracy: She is given papers permitting her to accept social services and guided into a neighbouring room where she submits them. Here, instead of money, she is issued authorisation notes that can be exchanged for welfare benefits. Only in one scene, in return for a slip of paper, does the mother receive money: four coins as a breast-feeding premium.[7]

Next, with a paper in her hand, the mother enters the infant nursery. In 1911, there were seven infant nurseries operating in Berlin. They were financed by the Berlin City Council to reduce the enormously high infant mortality rate, amounting in some quarters to more than twenty-five per cent. In the film, the infant nursery cares for an obviously malnourished infant whom we watch grow rather quickly into a healthy bouncing baby.

The five- to six-year-old daughter is accommodated in a day nursery at the Pestalozzi Fröbel House, which the Verein für Volkserziehung [Association for People's Education] had established with the help of a upper-class sponsor to carry out educational work in the spirit of Heinrich Pestalozzi and Friedrich Fröbel, the 'inventor' of the kindergarten. The alcoholic father is examined by the neurological polyclinic of the royal Charité (i.e. by a department of the hospital that was the leading medical research centre in the German Reich). Although the investigation methods and the cure brought forward in the film were familiar at that time to every country doctor, at least, the Charité takes action: A temperance volunteer visits the father in his local pub and persuades him to come along to the Charité. After measured moral pressure, the alcoholic agrees to become involved in treatment. "The cure" (intertitle) is as easy as it is effective: By doing gymnastics and carpentry work in the fresh air, the alcoholic turns into a healthy man capable of doing physical work. Before-and-after-treatment portraits demonstrate the successful cure made strikingly visible in the husband's stylish haircut and well-arranged clothes.

Presentation of living spaces

Dramaturgically the film works by consistently depicting scenes before and after the intervention of the welfare institutions, and not only of the protagonists but also of their environment. At the beginning, the living space of the mother is an old hovel. Her husband is shown primarily in the pub around the corner, a gloomy place, poky and sticky with bald, badly plastered, windowless walls. After the intervention of the welfare institutions, these living spaces are juxtaposed with the light-flooded work spaces of the couple: The mother works as a seamstress in a large, airy hall. Her husband finds work in a carpenter's workshop which is apparently clean and tidy – only fresh wood shavings cover the ground. Good working conditions are represented as the requirement for a healthy, carefree life and the influence of the surroundings on the condition of the people living in them is implicitly made clear. The respective rooms are used as dramaturgical devices: The old hovel of the couple is located at "Am Krögel 6" (intertitle). The Krögel lies in Old Berlin and to Berliners this ancient quarter was notorious for its narrow, unsanitary antiquated buildings. It was generally considered as the perfect example of oppressive housing conditions in the city.[8] The interior of the hovel looks miserable with its painted window and skewed entrance door, all of which suggests a depressing narrowness. When the landlady enters the room with the bailiff, she collides with the couple. The action before the camera is staged very flatly: within the hovel everybody crowds into the foreground. The spatial depth is hardly used at all for the action. As the main protagonist, the mother always remains in the foreground until she leaves the hovel with her children.

The mother's new apartment is located in "Turmstrasse 4". This street (today Brinkmannstrasse) is in Berlin-South End. In 1911, the South End with its villas and parks was considered an idyllic area outside the crowded town and had become a popular destination for weekend forays. Messter's studio set of the interior of the new apartment looks much more spacious and solid than the hovel. The window and door are no longer painted replicas on a flat backdrop. Near the window there stands a sewing machine: the mother may sew for her children, or try to earn some extra money by doing piecework at home. In contrast to the studio set of the old hovel, the whole space is now used for the action: When the husband enters the apartment he walks from rear left of the set to the right side of the foreground where his wife is sitting.

The front entrances of both houses suggest different living conditions as well. The front entrance of the house in Old Berlin has no door at all, but just leads into the interior of the house, reminiscent of a dark cave. When leaving the hovel, the mother rushes out of the darkness and upwards into the light to pause there again only to look back to the threatening darkness of the entrance. In the slightly raised front entrance of the new apartment house is a massive wooden door leading into the new cosy home. Happily chatting with her daughter, the mother approaches the entrance, then stops before the door to caress her daughter before she opens it and steps inside.

Various exhibition contexts

The ceremonial premiere of *Mütter, verzaget nicht!* was organised by the Kaiserin Friedrich Foundation, named after Empress Victoria (the wife of Emperor Friedrich who had died only a few months after his coronation in 1888). The premiere took place on 10 June, 1911, for invited guests in the lecture hall of the Kaiserin Friedrich House near the Charité. Established in 1906 with money donated by Berlin citizens, the neo-baroque building was and still is owned by the Kaiserin Friedrich Foundation which devotes itself to this day to medical training. High-ranking representatives from pertinent institutions and authorities such as the Reichsgesundheitsamt [Imperial Health Office], Reichsmarineamt [Imperial Naval Office], Kaiser-Wilhelms-Akademie [Emperor William Academy] and Königlicher Charité [Royal Charité Hospital] were present at the premiere.[9]

The sponsored film *Mütter, verzaget nicht!* was used first in Berlin to promote the Mother and Child Auxiliary Day. Physicians and medical professors arranged screenings for public relations purposes and for the instruction of the many volunteers. Whereas the middle-class Berlin newspapers still completely ignored commercial cinema programmes in 1911, their local correspondents covered *Mütter, verzaget nicht!* in a positive manner: "[In this film] we see the magic of the cinematograph which so often is damaged by trumpery and worse. Here we see it in the service of charity and education, a purpose that has raised it to the level of art".[10]

At that time, cinema reformers in Germany fiercely opposed cinema owners who offered entertaining stories of sex and crime that could be viewed by sensation seekers of any age. As seen from the cinema-reform perspective, *Mütter, verzaget nicht!* offered a welcome opportunity for exemplary presentations that were to be recommended to cinema owners for emulation: The first municipal cinema of the German Empire opened on 1 December 1912, in Eickel in the Ruhr area. As a local cinema, it committed itself to the service of Volkserziehung (people's education), and *Mütter, verzaget nicht!* was included in its opening programme.[11]

Besides screenings on behalf of charity, *Mütter, verzaget nicht!* was also exploited commercially. Cinema owners included the film in their programmes to mollify the critics of their entertainment business and to win over those sectors of the public that were put off by "sensation-based films". This sponsored film could be particularly recommended to women's circles, "in virtue of the absolutely discreetly presented story line".[12] The film rental company that offered *Mütter, verzaget nicht!* exclusively as a "Monopol Art Film", guaranteed entertainment together with inoffensive content: "Finally, there is a film that describes, nevertheless, an affecting drama, a sad big-city destiny, in brilliant rendition and with a pleasing solution without adultery, without a murder scene, without raw brutality".[13]

Different comments for differing audiences

In political terms, *Mütter, verzaget nicht!* is constructed as an umbrella that covers associations and facilities belonging to a wide range of the political spectrum. This sponsored film includes both private- and state-financed welfare institutions, from the conservative to the liberal middle class, as well as those with affiliations to the well-organized working class Social Democrats. At the beginning of the guided film tour through Berlin welfare facilities, the constable points the suicidal mother to the Deutsche Gesellschaft für Mutter- und Kindesrecht [German Society for Mothers' and Children's Rights], that provided "advice and support free of charge before and after the delivery", as a door plate says in the film. The feminist Adele Schreiber founded this organisation on 28 May 1910, after a conflict within the Bund für Mutterschutz [League for Mothers' Protection]. Affiliated with the Social Democratic Party, the Deutsche Gesellschaft für Mutter- und Kindesrecht acted primarily as a helpdesk for unwed mothers. At the time, one quarter of the children in Berlin were born to unwed women, and their babies were particularly endangered.

The presentation of politically heterogeneous welfare facilities under the umbrella of the film plot corresponded to the contemporary situation of film exhibition. For screenings of *Mütter, verzaget nicht!* there were changing demands on the lecturers who commented on the film. Each occasion, place, audience for, and purpose of the film's presentation required different welcoming addresses and different comments during projection. It made a great difference whether the sponsored film was shown to women supporters of the Social Democratic Party or to representatives from the ministries, imperial offices and medical professionals, as had been the case at the premiere. The poor were to be addressed differently than the well-to-do citizens who were asked for donations.

The narrative of *Mütter, verzaget nicht!* runs along one-dimensionally: Like a string of beads, the fateful chain of family problems is juxtaposed against the welfare agencies with their array of solutions. But depending on the specific context of exhibition, the audience's relations to *Mütter, verzaget nicht!* could be complex and ambiguous: The film evades the real problem of mother and infant care. The mother seeking help in the film is married. Without any blame on her part, she becomes a welfare case because of her husband's drunkenness. But it was the single mothers the Berlin child welfare agencies cared for and this care was contentious because segments of the conservative citizenry viewed it as promoting immorality and thus subverting the family as a state-supporting institution. *Mütter, verzaget nicht!* excludes single mothers – presumably out of concern for conservative circles and potential film censorship. What mattered was that the plot and its presentation in no way served to scandalize. Standard social dramas, in contrast to this film, often showed unwed mothers in need of welfare, and usually receiving none; instead they were sent away, repudiated and chased off; they were destroyed by illness, or alcohol or finished up by committing suicide. *Mütter, verzaget nicht!* clearly distances itself from such commercial entertainment attractions.

No film narrator, however creative he might have been, would have been able to reinterpret *Mütter, verzaget nicht!* as some exciting film entertainment. This sponsored film served to inform and educate viewers and if ever it was announced as a touching social drama in a commercial cinema programme its viewers would have certainly been disappointed.

Images: All the illustrations are frame enlargements taken by Gerhard Ullmann from the 35mm print of *Mütter, verzaget nicht!* which is kept in the vaults of the Bundesarchiv-Filmarchiv, Berlin.

Notes

1. See Martin Loiperdinger, "German Tonbilder of the 1900s: Advanced Technology and National Brand", in Klaus Kreimeier and Annemone Ligensa (eds), *Film 1900: Technology, Perception, Culture* (Herts. John Libbey Publishing, 2009), 187-199.
2. On Monopolfilm, see Corinna Müller *Frühe deutsche Kinematographie: Formale, wirtschaftliche und kulturelle Entwicklungen* (Stuttgart/Weimar: Metzler, 1994). On the beginnings of Asta Nielsen's career, see Martin Loiperdinger, "Der erste Filmstar im Monopolfilmverleih", in Heide Schlüpmann, Karola Gramann, Eric de Kuyper, Sabine Nessel and Michael Wedel (eds), *Asta Nielsen. Sprache der Liebe* (Vienna: Filmarchiv Austria, 2009), 177–186; and Martin Loiperdinger, "Afgrunden in Germany 1910/11 – 'Monopolfilm', Cinema-Going and the Emergence of Film Star Asta Nielsen", in Richard Maltby, Daniel Biltereyst and Philippe Meers (eds), *Explorations in New Cinema History: Approaches and Case Studies* (Forthcoming September 2011).
3. "Der Film im Dienste der Wohltätigkeit", *Berliner Morgenpost* 158 (11 June 1911); "Kinematographische Vorführung für den Hilfstag für Mutter und Kind", *Berliner Börsen-Courier* 269 (11 June 1911).

4. See K.J., "Fürsorge-Drama", *Vossische Zeitung* 281 (11 June 1911).
5. "Der Kinematograph als Helfer der sozialen Fürsorge", *Berliner Lokal-Anzeiger* 292 (11 June 1911).
6. K.J., "Fürsorge-Drama".
7. See ibid.
8. See Susanne Gänshirt-Heinemann, *Der Krögel: Eine Gasse im alten Berlin* (Berlin: Haude & Spener, 2000).
9. See "Der Kinematograph als Helfer der sozialen Fürsorge".
10. "Mütter, verzaget nicht!" *Berliner Tageblatt* 299 (11 June 1911).
11. http://www.lwl.org/westfaelische-geschichte/portal, accessed 19 July 2011.
12. Advertisement for the Trierisches Lichtspielhaus, *Trierischer Volksfreund* 52 (6 February 1912).
13. Advertisement for the Ostdeutscher Film-Vertrieb, *Lichtbild-Theater* 40 (5 October 1911).

PART II

Government and Civics

7

The Tsar and The Kinematograph: Film as History and The Chronicle of the Russian Monarchy

Oksana Chefranova

In Russia, cinema and the institution of the monarchy met as soon as new media entered the country's cultural landscape. In 1896, the Lumière cameramen filmed the coronation of the emperor Nicholas II in the Kremlin, marking the beginning of film documentation of political events, a significant part of which is known in Russia as the "Tsar Chronicle". The term refers to a body of actuality films about the monarchy, a multi-film record of official and private moments from the life of the Emperor systematically produced by various cameramen and film ateliers until 1917. At the turn of 1907–1908, the Tsar Chronicle had become widely used in the commercial cinema circuit to promote the monarchical idea.[1] The Tsar Chronicle offers an example of the alternative existence of early film within a particular territory of the imperial palace, remote from the environment of commercial mass entertainment. The palace, where film was more than just a pleasurable pastime, became the site of the first steps in the development and institutionalisation of cinema; one of the first film ateliers in Russia was located in Tsarskoe Selo and the first film collection was launched around the production of the Chronicle. The monarch occupied a unique position in relation to the new medium: a veritable staple of early Russian film and its irrefutable iconic figure, he is at once the subject and the object of film, a spectacle, whose screen images likely outnumbered those of anyone else in pre-revolutionary cinema, and a spectator, whose power beyond the screen could affect the production and circulation of images. In this paper, I am interested in exploring Nicholas II's taste for a particular type of cinematic representation and the implications that his attitude toward film may have had for its evolution. The monarchy was crucial in the development of actuality film, so my second concern is a sub-genre of actuality – the chronicle film – that originated around the monarch and became the first manifestation of domestic film production, by which the Russian monarchy inscribed itself both into history and into the history of film.

The monarch and the new medium: "historically true images" and an "agreeable method of studying the past"

Nicholas II established a strong and multifaceted relationship with film, which became a significant part of the publicity and mythology of the emperor. Biographers of the emperor referred to film and photography as a favourite leisure activity, as a pleasure that the entire imperial family shared and as an educational tool for the imperial children.[2] According to the diaries of Nicholas II, the kinematograph and photography became enjoyable and routine pastimes for him. Nicholas II appreciated different forms of spectatorship, with the Imperial Palaces functioning as principal sites for screenings. The most noted location was the spacious neo-classical Semi-Circular Hall in Alexander Palace in Tsarskoe Selo, the centre of the formal ensemble of parade rooms, which was regularly used to show movies and photographic slide shows. This location included screen images in close proximity to picturesque views of the garden revealed through the open doors and windows. This blending of the white, airy, ambient space of classical forms and the garden, later imitated by indoor plants, would be extensively replicated in the architecture of movie palaces in Russian cities during the 1910s. Another locale was a mobile screening room in the dining salon on the modern yacht *Standart* used for summer travels of the imperial family. On *Standart*, actual mobility afforded by the boat's movement past landscapes and picturesque sights was juxtaposed with the cinematic experience of virtual movement and travel by means of film images. The yacht also served as a favourite shooting location for the imperial family, bringing together filming and screening spaces. Occasionally, the emperor watched films on his private train. Moreover, the monarch never missed chances to attend local movie theatres, especially during the war years.

The emperor was a photographer himself and all members of the family, including his children, had their own cameras and practiced photography, especially while traveling. The Tsarevich Alexey even filmed his own amateur movies. The patronage of the imperial family was crucial for initiating and establishing Russian film production: acknowledging the fact that private shows in the palace could ensure future success, major film producers such as Aleksandr Drankov and Aleksandr Khanzhonkov screened their films there and even had a chance to discuss issues of film production with the emperor. The monarch was one of the first film censors who controlled exhibition of the Chronicle since his permission was essential for releasing the films for any public screenings.[3] He also assembled film programs by selecting pictures for film séances inside, and sometimes outside, the palace. Another example of such professional universality, pertaining to the formative years of cinema, is Aleksandr Jagelskiy – the court cameraman, the court projectionist, a distributor, and the first Russian film archivist.[4] For the monarch, multi-faceted participation in film was fundamentally a continuation of his supervision of all domains of the empire.

Nicholas II never left an expanded account of his position regarding film in general, nor did he directly formulate his response to the Chronicle. Nonetheless, occasional and brief statements, dispersed throughout different sources, reveal the complexity of his view that oscillated from hostility toward the potentially dangerous medium to the possibility of its deployment as a political tool for larger nationalistic projects. "I consider the kinematograph as an empty, unnecessary and even harmful entertainment. Only an odd person can put this farcical trade on the same level as art. It is nonsense, and one should not attach any significance to those trifles …".[5] Expressions that Nicholas II used in his diary, however, show his fascination with film: "remarkably interesting moving photographs on the screen", "amusing", "entertaining", "cheerful", "historically true images". In a conversation between the emperor and the Russian film producer Aleksandr Drankov after the demonstration of the film *The Tercentenary of the Rule of the House of Romanov 1613–1913* (production Drankov & Taldykin, 1913) in 1913, the monarch praised the producer for "the accurate representation of the historical chronicle of the events", and contrasted the film with another picture – a historical reenactment *The Defense of Sebastopol* (production of Aleksandr Khanzhonov, 1911), in which "in the background of the shot, representing a historical marine battle, one can see contemporary battleships and weapons". The emperor approved the next project of Drankov – a historical chronicle of the Russian army – but asked him "not to inhabit images with props".[6]

For the emperor, the modern battleships, seen on the screen, betrayed the historical truth and the truth of images, transforming film into a carefully crafted artefact removed from reality "out there". Nicholas II's vision of film was shaped by his contact with Bolesław Matuszewski, among other factors, who worked as a photographer and cameraman at the court of the Russian emperor from July 1897 to November 1898.[7] Although Matuszewski was never an official court cameraman, his work at the Russian Imperial Court provided a kind of workshop for the development of his theoretical ideas. Matuszewski aimed to donate a collection of historically significant films to establish a film library, which would then be a part of the private library of Nicholas II.[8] Most likely, the emperor was also familiar with Matuszewski's texts on cinema, *Une nouvelle source de l'histoire: création d'un dépôt de cinématographie historique* and *La photographie animée, ce qu'elle est, ce qu'elle doit être*, published in France in 1898, since the cameraman attached them to one of his letters to the Ministry of the Imperial Court to prove the seriousness of his intention to organise the film depository.[9] In both texts, Matuszewski explains how a film's representation of a military or naval manoeuvre allows the viewer to discover and recreate meticulous and tiny details of the event. In a similar manner, the emperor refers to the shot containing the re-enactment of the marine battle, noticing small particularities of the image. Nicholas II's preoccupation with elucidating visibility and rendering images transparent, and his rhetoric of documentation and the truth value of the image resonate with Matuszewski's insistence on animated photography having "authenticity, exactitude and precision which belong to it alone. It is the epitome of the truthful and infallible eye-witness".[10] The emperor's preference and support for actuality and for pictures of the historical genre stem from his recognition of the historical value contained in the film image, whose degree of certainty and clarity can promise the "incontestable and absolute truth".

This idea of film as a historical document and reliable evidence, the notion of cinema shared by Nicholas II and Matuszewski, was a paradigm based on absolute trust in the indexical cinematographic image, and differed from other contemporaneous responses to the image as a lifeless and opaque shadow of reality. Both Matuszewski and Nicholas II looked at cinema through the lens of the Enlightenment ideal of didactic and purposeful entertainment. As "a singularly effective teaching method" and "an agreeable method of studying the past" that permits seeing the past directly, film was called upon to play a part in the imperial nationalistic project for the historical education of the nation. Russian production between 1908 and 1912 experienced a proliferation of non-fiction filmmaking and pictures of the historical genre. At this early stage, film contributed to the reconfiguration of the institution of history, and the imperial palace became a territory where the ideas of recording history and the film depository were formulated and made possible. Monarchies played a role in developing this particular philosophy of film – film as history. At the court of the Russian monarch, it was realised as the Tsar Chronicle, a fulfilment of Matuszewski's project and his method of writing modern history with the camera.

The Chronicle genre

By establishing the position of the court cameraman in 1900 and encouraging regular and systematic film recording of the life inside and outside the palace, the emperor facilitated the production of the Tsar Chronicle. The word "chronicle" has been applied to this group of films from the beginning. Although in the Russian language, "chronicle" is normally synonymous with "documentary", and one may hesitate to describe these early films as documentaries. Theorising about early non-fiction film-making, some scholars point to basic distinctions between the phenomenology of actuality, associated with early cinema's descriptive mode, and documentary, pertaining more to the period after the First World War and based on montage interpretations of material.[11] This difference became apparent when the Chronicle was reshaped into a propagandistic artefact by Esfir Shub in her 1927 documentary *The Fall of the Romanov Dynasty*, for which the director manipulated and re-arranged the films using montages and speed distortions. Another connotation of "chronicle" refers to a particular literary genre: medieval chronicles and other manifestations of non-fiction literary narratives (as memoirs and family chronicles) that occupy a significant place in Russian literature. I propose that the body of films known as the Imperial Chronicle constitutes a specific sub-genre of actuality film.

Russian literature adapted the chronicle from the Byzantine Empire, where it recorded episodes arranged around the figure of the monarch. More generally, "chronicle" refers to a method of writing history that provides an extended chronological account of events without the interference of an authorial interpretation, different in kind than the analytical scholarly tradition of writing history, which goes back to antique authors like Herodotus. The formal aspects of the Tsar Chronicle films – the camera's descriptive mode of recording and the employment of editing for clarity and logic through the relaying of information as successive events – resonate not only with the properties of the literary chronicle, but also with Nicholas II's vision of cinema. That vision was reinforced by the style of his diary, which consisted of non-interpretive, unvarnished enumerations of repetitive everyday events. The emperor's diary and the Chronicle films envisioned history as a non-hierarchical panoramic stream with no beginning and no end, as fragments arbitrarily pulled out of the stream of life. Another notable aspect of the chronicle is its reliance on a vernacular form of writing that employs a widely understood language. The claim of being accessible and reaching those who could not read was a central aim of the films, testimony to the universal language of cinema. As a vernacular form, the chronicle synthesises a historical record with spectacular and sensational elements; the Byzantine and Russian literary chronicles were based on the accumulation of facts of such "very diverse nature as the body and souls of famous people, wondrous and catastrophic events".[12] This generic hybridity is reflected in the dual functions of the film Chronicle as both didactic entertainment, representing ceremonial events of historical significance, and a spectacle with sensational potentiality appealing to vernacular taste. This dual function finds its echo in the varied reception that the Chronicle films invited from different audiences: while the emperor envisioned the Chronicles in terms of the ideal of educational purposefulness, believing in the ideological, cultural and uplifting role of film, the mass audience expressed a new visual curiosity and a longing for image-based displays of the emperor. An advertisement of one of the Chronicles by Drankov's company states that "the monarch is clearly and distinctly visible on the screen".[13] "Clearly and distinctly visible" figures the emperor as a spectacle, locating his power in visibility and indicating the look as one of the main sites of the construction of the modern empire.[14]

As an approach to non-fiction filmmaking and a form of presenting history as an endless panoramic expanse, the Chronicle aimed to provide an exhaustive anthology of views. Jagelskiy, who positioned himself as the imperial chronicler, articulated the idea of the perpetual and systematic character of the recording as "pursuing a special goal to represent photographically ALL outstanding and eminent moments and events during the reign of the last emperor".[15] This intention echoes Matuszewski's call for assembling the "exterior manifestations of history so later they can be unfolded before the eyes of those who did not witness them".[16] The term itself has a temporal connotation and refers to the chronological accumulation of filmic recordings, so the Chronicle is constituted not by a single film but by a continuous accumulation of separate and autonomous pictures linked together by the figure of the emperor. This quality appears to be the major element of the genre's temporality and narrative nature. Brought together into a collection, different film pieces develop discursive connections through the juxtaposition of different views of various events or through the collation of several views of the same event (especially after 1908, when several domestic and international companies, such as Drankov, Khanzhonkov, Pathé and Gaumont, were allowed to join Jagelskiy in filming the Imperial family). The rhetorical meaning of the films - the myth of the emperor and the narrative of the Russian monarchy – emerges only out of the totality of many pictures. The view of the chronicle as a collection and of film as a document implies the idea of an archive as a phenomenological feature of the genre. It is no accident that Jagelskiy, who shot, preserved and catalogued the films, also initiated a prototype of the Russian film archive. The logic of the chronicle is the logic of a depository of images, from which it later would be possible to select some films for exhibition. As a form of exhibitor-based control, this act of selection dictated what would be seen, yet it also rendered some images invisible. In producing the Chronicle, attention was placed on the shooting process, on producing as many films as possible without necessarily making them all available through exhibition and circulation. The invisibility is a constituent of the chronicle genre that separates it from the newsreels, which were filmed to be seen, and, crucially, seen at the time of their filming.

Defined by unstable genre boundaries, the Chronicle presents a heterogeneous phenomenon that exists at the intersection between reportage on the life of the empire and a hagiographic portrait of Nicholas II. The polyphonic nature of the Chronicle is reflected in the existence of several sub-genres developed throughout the body of the films. The first distinction can be made between the official chronicle of the Russian empire (the ceremonial views) and the chronicle of private life of the imperial family (the family views). As a literary genre, the chronicle resurfaced in Russian literature in the eighteenth and nineteenth centuries as the family chronicle novel and memoir, the purpose of which was to preserve memory and to set an example for future generations. The films from the private life of the Imperial Family were made in this mode. A significant amount of the footage, shot for internal circulation and never intended for public screening outside of the palace, was devoted to the life of the family in the mode of a family album, recording such private pleasures as summer voyages, and time spent with the children and playing tennis.[17] The ceremonial and family views generally had the same objects for the camera – the imperial family. They differ slightly in the camera distance and framing, as the family views offer more medium-close shots of the emperor. However, the differences in contact with and response to the camera on the part of the people being filmed are more profound; this is especially visible in the films with the children, who incorporated the film apparatus into their games. The differentiation between the ceremonial and family views involves consideration of the issue of spectatorship: answering the question of *for whom* a film is made – for the general public or for private family viewing – becomes more meaningful in defining the sub-genre than does the question of *what* is actually being filmed. In *Animated Photography*, Matuszewski refers to his filming of Nicholas II during a stroll in Petergof as "constituting rather property of history than episodes of private family life".[18] Besides being recordings of private memories, the family views belong to history, a history that includes not only privileged moments of staged ceremonial spectacles but unexpected events that usually elude the camera. The cinematic private history of the Russian Imperial Family was in line with Matuszewski's vision of history as "far from being composed uniquely of planned ceremonies, organised in advance and ready to pose for the cameras".[19] The family views help to represent and evoke history as an unfolding process.

The ceremonial views can be divided into several sub-genres: official ceremonies and events; military parades and visits to the army; political and diplomatic contacts; visits to European countries and different regions of Russia; inaugurations of monuments; religious holidays, pilgrimages, and cathedrals; chronicles of the war; agriculture; sport; festivities. These sub-genres are equally defined by their objects (the particular events being filmed) and by the ideological implications of the official imperial mythology. Besides being a historical document, the Chronicle played a role in the formulation of the myth of the emperor and expression of the monarchical ideology. The practicality of the Chronicle for making an ideological statement is linked to the transparency and truth value of its images that force the audience to perceive the imperial mythology as authentic and trustworthy. These structural series consolidate political, sacral, commercial, cosmopolitan and popular aspects of the empire and directly correspond to sections of the celebratory biography of Nicholas II that was released for the tercentenary Jubilee of the Romanov's dynasty.[20] Drawing on the myth of the emperor, both the biography and the films present different facets of the monarch: the emperor as the sovereign, "the crowned toiler", an orthodox Christian, the father of his nation, the head of the army and a family man. (The promotion of the institution of the family in the Tsar Chronicle emerged as a counterpoint to contemporaneous film melodrama's narrative of the dissolution of the family in modernity.) The military films about Nicholas II's visits to different regiments, and the accompanying army parades and celebrations, constitute an extensive part of the Tsar Chronicle and reflect the emperor's great interest in the history of the Russian army. In his *Animated Photography*, Matuszewski devotes a section specifically to the cinematic history of army regiments. For him, those films are crucial not only from the documentary perspective but also from the pedagogical standpoint – film as a means to elevate soldiers' morality and reinforce their patriotism. A more direct link can be made between Matuszewski's screenings of his films in Russian and French barracks and Nicholas II's compilation of film programs for the army. In January 1907, Nicholas II ordered a set of twelve positive copies of the Tsar Chronicle and the War Chronicle for screening in a Sebastopol garrison.[21]

The representational aspects, advertisement strategies and responses of viewers to the Chronicle films reveal the hybrid aspirations of the genre manifested, for instance, in the potential of one film (especially after 1908) to speak simultaneously to different audiences. In filming the Chronicle, one goal was to balance recording an event happening in a particular place with providing the sense of locale by including architectural backdrops of historical monuments and landmarks. First and foremost, *The Opening of the Monument to Alexander III in Moscow on May 30, 1912* offers a ceremonial view. It displays the monument that represents sacralisation of the imperial power through the symbolic sculptural body, and also fulfils the program of historical education of the nation by projecting the history of Russia through figures of its monarchs. A reverse shot, showing the parade from another position, also opens up a panoramic backdrop to the event – a view towards the Kremlin, familiar to readers of contemporaneous tour books. The film simultaneously functions as a city film, a travelogue presenting a landmark place, and a kind of touristic advertisement using the imperial ceremony taking place there to attract visitors. Moscow received an unprecedented visibility in the Tsar Chronicle that displayed an ideologically charged and somewhat pre-modern image of the city, focusing more on historical monuments, cathedrals and monasteries, the timeless archaeology of which conveyed the imperial identity, and avoided modern urban development. A film's relation with location can be figured as a travelogue: films of the 1913 Jubilee Volga river tour of the imperial family include views of picturesque scenery and panoramas from a moving boat. These point to another specialty of A.K. Gan-Jagelskiy's film company: the series of topical and travelogue films collectively labelled *The Picturesque Russia*. In some films, topicality and locality intersect, so a ceremonial event of a broader historical significance can be simultaneously infused with a local interest, featuring a particular place with its inhabitants who then can see themselves or familiar places on the screen. In *The Visit to Evpatorija* (1916), several pans over citizens of the town, waiting for the emperor's arrival, reveal that for them being filmed is no less important than seeing the monarch. After two weeks, the film was exhibited in a local film theatre, called "Science and Life", with the audience filled with the local spectators.

The Tsar Chronicle exposed an ambiguity between transparency of indexical cinematic images and opacity of symbolic aspects of the imperial representation, between public and private, sacred and profane. Using film for the purpose of imperial representation and for mediation between the monarch and his subjects revealed a paradox between the Chronicle's documentary nature in its relation to history as an unfolding dynamic process and the exclusive status of the monarch. In 1913, these paradoxical relations appeared visible in Drankov's *The Tercentenary of the Rule of the House of the Romanov*. The film itself is structured as a chronicle narrating the lineage of Russian tsars and emperors and their achievements in a series of separate and artificial tableaux. The common rule for such historical recreations was that the more distant monarchs could be portrayed as semi-legendary personages, and more recent emperors had to be presented with dignity. The latter could not be portrayed by actors, only by symbolic substitutes. In the film, a series of such substitutes includes sculptural busts for Alexander I and Nicholas I and painted and photographic portraits for Alexander II and Alexander III. Nicholas II, on the contrary, is represented as himself through several inserts from the Chronicle: the coronation, the dedication of the monument to Alexander II in 1909, and the Borodino celebration. These filmic fragments display the emperor through emblematic acts and relics of monarchical authority – through the spectacle of Nicholas II receiving power during the coronation at the Kremlin or presented as the head of the army on the Borodino field parade. Within the film, this coexistence of the hieratic artefacts with the living presence of the emperor rendered through cinematic images, making everything and everyone look similar on the screen, shows that the myth of the emperor began to lose its monological dimension. The acquiring of mass publicity through film has accelerated the erosion of the monarchical sovereignty as being immutable and constant throughout centuries, a price paid for an attempt at gradual integration of the monarchy into the flow of historical time.

Notes

1. The Tsar Chronicle constitutes one third of all Russian non-fiction films made prior to 1917 that are preserved at The Russian State Documentary Film and Photo Archive in Moscow. Vladimir Magidov refers to thirty-nine thousand metres and about 363 films in V.M. Magidov, "Dorevolujtsionnaja kinockronika Archivnogog Fonda Rossijskj Federatsii i ejo istoricheskoe znachenie", *Deloproizvodstvo* 2 (2009).

2. Aleksandr Elchaninov, *Tsarstvovanie Gosudaraj Imperatora Nikolaja Aleksandrovicha* (Moscow, 1913), 52–53; "Kinematograf na stranitsakh dnevnika Nikolaja II", *Kinovedcheskie zapiski* 28 (1995): 233–255.

3. The section of film censorship in the Ministry of the Imperial Court was established in 1899 in response to the showing of films of the Tsar's visit to Paris in 1897. Rachid Ianguirov, "The 'Tzar's Pastime': The Russian Royal Family and Cinema. The Early Years (1896–1908)", in C.

Dupré la Tour, A. Gaudreault, R. Pearson (eds), *Le cinéma au tournant du siècle* (Lausanne-Québec: Editions Payot-Editions Nota Bene, 1999), 381.

4. On Jagelskiy's efforts to establish a special archive under the Ministry of the Imperial Court see Ianguirov, "The 'Tzar's Pastime'", 379.
5. From Nicholas II's resolution on a report of the police department. Cited in S. Ginzburg, *Kinematografija dorevolujtsionnoi Rossii* (Moscow, 1963), 34.
6. V.I. Fomin and A.S. Derajbin (eds), *Letopis' Rossiiskogo Kino, 1863–1929* (Moscow, 2004), 126.
7. Vladimir Magidov refers to nineteen film and photo sessions in Vladimir Magidov, "Itogi kinematograficheskoi i nauchnoi dejatelnosti B.Matushevskogo v Rossii", *Kinovedcheskie zapiski* 43 (1999): 280.
8. Ibid., 274.
9. Ibid., 275.
10. Bolesław Matuszewski, "A New Source of History: The Creation of a Depository For Historical Cinematography", *Cultures* 2, no. 1 (1974): 219–222.
11. Tom Gunning, "Before Documentary: Early Nonfiction Films and the '"View Aesthetic"', in Daan Hertogs and Nico de Klerk (eds), *Uncharted Territory: Essays on Early Nonfiction Film* (Amsterdam: Stichting Nederlands Filmmusem, 1997), 9–24.
12. F.A. Brokgauz and I.A Efron, *Entsiklopedicheskii slovar* (St. Petersburg, 1890–1904).
13. *Cine-Fono* no. 19 (1908).
14. Recognising the power of images, including filmic, and facing the Jubilee year of 1913, Nicholas II lifted the prohibition against representing the Tsar on stage, in mass-produced objects, and in souvenirs. Richard Wortman, *Scenarios of Power: From Alexander I To the Abdication of Nicholas II* (Princeton: Princeton University Press, 2000), 484.
15. Fomin and Derajbin (eds), *Letopis' Rossiiskogo Kino*, 43.
16. Matuszewski, "A New Source of History", 219–222.
17. Jagelskiy compiled a catalogue of films of 1900–1903, in which six pictures out of seventy-six were prohibited as public screenings. The catalogue is published by V.K. Belajkov, *Kinovedcheskie zapiski* 18 (1993): 98.
18. Bolesław Matuszewski, "Animated Photography", *Kinovedcheskie zapiski* 83 (2007): 145.
19. Matuszewski, "A New Source of History", 219–222.
20. Elchaninov, *Tsarstvovanie*.
21. Fomin and Derajbin (eds), *Letopis' Rossiiskogo Kino*, 52.

8

"Wheelbarrows" and "Real Soldiers": Advertising, Audiences and War Films of all Varieties

Liz Clarke

In the classified section of the *New York Clipper* on 9 April 1898 – less than two months after the explosion of the USS Battleship *Maine* in Havana harbour sparked the Spanish-American War – Siegmund Lubin, Manufacturing Optician, advertised a business opportunity. For just one hundred dollars, a would-be entrepreneur could purchase a projecting machine, films, and slides, and begin at once a career as exhibitor and showman. Yet, reference to the projector is found only in the fine print; if font size is any indication, the real interest to potential showmen rested in the films Lubin had to offer: "Films of the Battleship *Maine*". And while the films were likely not even of the actual *Maine*, because it could have been any warship, the message is clear that the war was the star attraction of the show.

Analysed together, the advertisements in the *New York Clipper* and the film catalogues distributed by a number of companies at the time reveal the intended reaction to these films, which not only assumes a homogeneous, white, male audience but also overwhelming support of American expansionist efforts. More specifically, these sources indicate for contemporary scholars how audiences were *supposed* to understand and react to the films in their historical context – not necessarily how they were always interpreted. During the Spanish-American War the notion of American identity was in flux and the acceptance of military expansion overseas was a highly debated topic; yet, promotion of these films illuminates ways in which support for the war was naturalised through various methods. First, advertisers emphasised a participatory and active audience reaction even for films that focused on routine and discipline, and second, travelogues were repackaged and used freely as war films.

Representing American expansionism: war films and films for wartime
In the introduction to the "War and Militarism" issue of *Film History*, Stephen Bottomore discusses the context from which film emerged, arguing that cinema's early years must be re-evaluated based on the masculinist and militaristic ideologies that dominated the socio-political landscape. Film was invented and predominantly produced by those individuals and companies that shared expansionist sentiments, Bottomore suggests, and thus we must understand the development of early film as intrinsically tied to those ideologies.[1] An example to demonstrate this point would be the war with Spain and the incidents in Cuba and the Philippines from 1898 to 1899.

The topic of war was not just one of many subjects of interest to viewers but, rather, the Spanish-American War became central for film distributors during those years. In fact, for a brief period during 1898, the film projector was advertised under the title of "wargraph".[2] From 1898 through to 1900, cinema can be described as a visual newspaper, presenting audiences with views (whether actual or staged) of current events not only designed to inform but also to engage and foster particular ideological viewpoints. In short, the films intended to encourage support for American expansionist efforts extended beyond those directly presenting views of battle to include a variety of subjects. War films of this period should not to be confused with the contemporary war genre that most frequently contains battles and other generic staples. These are films *for* wartime: brief, yet exciting, visual references to well-known topical events, which required the audience to know popular news items but also reflected the norms of filmmaking, distribution and exhibition of the time.

Tom Gunning proposes a concept of early film as global and encyclopaedic rather than national and finite.[3] In other words, film catalogues of this era were similar to encyclopaedias in their ever-expanding nature, and included examples of all subject matter, like the information contained in an encyclopaedia. While Gunning views early cinema as a form of global media, the encyclopaedic analogy is not irreconcilable with an examination of the predominance of military subjects in early film catalogues and trade journals as contributing to the development of national narratives. American imperial efforts, of which the Spanish–American War was a central example at the end of the nineteenth century, were contestable issues. American film entered into the entertainment market at a time when its ability to oscillate between the fragmentary and the unified benefited its ability to play numerous roles – as the idea of the American nation itself continued to shift. Gunning argues that an examination of film catalogues demonstrates that films of national interest were balanced with a myriad of other subjects; however, one must consider the predominance of expansionist and militaristic films and the symbiotic relationship existing amongst the subjects, the ideologies and the constant redefinitions of early cinematic viewing practices. From the encyclopaedic nature of the catalogues, specific films were chosen and advertised as war films, which in turn contributed to the cultural formation of national and patriotic identities at the turn of the century.

These war films functioned as supplements to already-known news items; they were visual spectacles complementary to the narratives of war and imperialism familiar to contemporaneous audiences.[4] The Spanish-American War was not just a topical news item of the period, but also tapped into larger expansionist ideologies of the period. The well-known American myth of the frontier, including the idea of Manifest Destiny, was in a process of adaptation to include international imperial efforts. While the Western frontier had recently been declared closed in 1890, the war with Spain, fought in Cuba and the Philippines, facilitated the continuance of expansionist beliefs by securing for the United States a number of new colonies, such as the Philippines and Puerto Rico. But to suggest that this shift from the Western frontier of America to overseas empire-building was a seamless endeavour is to ignore the extreme efforts exerted both on the political and cultural field to make that transition. In *Anarchy of Empire in the Making of U.S. Culture*, Amy Kaplan emphasises the complexity of synthesising the notion of American empire-building with the democracy on which it had previously constructed its identity.[5] Kaplan argues that the nation was envisioned and represented, through a number of rhetorical and cultural texts, as a male body. After the closing of the frontier this body faced a crisis that was alleviated through the alignment of nation and empire. According to Kaplan, nation and empire are linked because of a rhetoric that defines the home through its foreign exploits. Thus, the representation of the Spanish-American War for American audiences was an integral part of the discourse surrounding nation and empire in the late 1890s.

Furthermore, film plays an important role as one of many cultural forms defining an idea of American identity by presenting itself as a representation of "truth", both in the texts themselves and also through the promotional materials. Rather than discussing "truth" in relation to whether audiences knew or cared if these films were actualities or recreations, what is more traceable is the rhetoric and phrasing used in the advertisements to naturalise the popular sentiment in relation to an imagined, unified audience. The analysis of trade journal advertisements and catalogue descriptions during the late 1890s demonstrates a distinctly pro-expansionist vision of American identity through a variety of types of film used to represent war; however, Kaplan demonstrates at length in her study of American culture and politics of this time period that this ideology was not so strictly entrenched. The extra-filmic material examined in this paper reveals a concerted effort on the part of producers and distributors to elicit a particular response to the films – one that may or may not have been experienced by exhibitors or audiences of the time.

From military routine to the rowdy crowd

One type of film used predominantly during 1898 in representing the Spanish-American War was the military routine film. These specific films demonstrate and construct a very particular image of the military as organised, structured, disciplined and triumphant. This type of film could involve drills, loading or unloading gear, men working on battleships, or a representation of any number of everyday activities related to the military. One can attribute the interest in these films that appear to show relatively mundane tasks to the contemporaneous audience's pre-existing knowledge of the war in Cuba and the participating American soldiers. Kristen Whissel argues that in early war films the pleasure derives from "images of an ideal machine-made military masculinity already immune to the pathologies of modern life" and from the viewer's power over the scene and desire to see routine.[6] Whissel links the fear of a weakened, inactive male body to the increase of technology in the workplace that confines the male body to desks and offices.[7] The anxiety that results from this relocation in the workplace is, for Whissel, countered through the representation of everyday military activities that display the male body in a constant state of movement and discipline. First, the subject matter presents order and discipline; and, second, the spectator feels empowered through the surveillance of these hard-working men. However, the advertisements do not simply encourage the spectator to regard this scene with a sense of power but, rather, to become physically involved in the patriotic fervour connected with these scenes through the social experience of the crowd setting.

Early films – whether shown in a vaudeville theatre, a church or a public hall – engaged with direct address not just of the individual spectator but also of the *social group* of the crowd. Analysis of promotional materials reveals that viewings were meant to be a chance for audiences to gather together and participate in the cheers of approval for the American military and the jeers at Spanish soldiers. Rather than just representing patriotism and heroism *on the screen*, the advertisements present the possibility and desirability of the communal experience of this patriotic fervour *within the crowd*, created by fostering a social experience in which audience members could connect over shared beliefs and feelings of national pride. Not only are the men on screen "immune to the pathologies of modern life", but also the spectators, once they had entered the crowded vaudeville houses or the lecture hall or church social room, could engage in their own form of patriotic support through cheers elicited by the sudden presence of moving images depicting military routine.

The Spanish-American War film *10th U.S. Infantry Disembarking From Cars* (Edison 1898) is an example of a military routine film. In this short film, a group of soldiers march forward from behind a train and to the right out of the frame, all the while being watched by a group of bystanders. The film highlights the order and precision of the military unit, the authenticity of their uniforms and gear as well as the contrast between the men and the bystanders. Add to this the catalogue description and we can imagine how this film might have been introduced to the viewers in a vaudeville house, a church auditorium or any other community event at which films were presented to the crowds:

> A stirring scene; full of martial energy. No ordinary dress parade this, but a picture of soldiers – men with a high purpose. They march up the platform in fours, and left wheel just in front of the camera, passing out of sight in a cloud of dust. The customary small boy is in evidence in great numbers. While the rear guard passes, the train pulls out of the station. Literally "out of sight".[8]

The catalogue entry stresses that this is *not* the kind of scene you could encounter at a military parade in your hometown. These are *not* men in decorative uniforms on display for their fellow countrymen and women, but rather these are soldiers *as they are* during battle. The descriptions suggest that these men are not just marching past as they would during a parade – merely marching for the sake of the display – but are in fact marching somewhere, "with a high purpose". The appeal of this film is that these men are on their way to "battle", despite the falsity of this assumption. The film is staged as any parade, yet the presentation and description suggest otherwise. And if the audience of this film were used to seeing local regiments in annual parades, dressed in ornamental uniform, this film allowed the recreation of that experience – to be within a crowd watching a military spectacle – with the added bonus that these men were in the midst of a war when the film was taken. The routine is nothing new, nor is the popular opinion it draws from, but it reflects a desire to see a visual representation of the soldiers that audiences were reading about in contemporaneous newspapers.

The promotional material for early films continually emphasised the social experience of film viewing as central to the films' impact. For example, the description for *10th U.S. Infantry Disembarking From Cars* – "A stirring scene; full of martial energy" – indicates how this film may have been introduced to audiences. The film itself depicts a column of men marching through the frame, yet with the addition of a lecturer's energy and introduction of these men, the film becomes a scene of celebration. It is important to note, though, that the celebration derives as much from the experience in the theatre as from what is depicted on screen. A second film, *10th U.S. Infantry, 2nd Battalion, Leaving Cars* (Edison, 1898) aims to convey even more patriotic fervour based on its catalogue description:

> Hurrah – here they come! Hot, dusty, grim and determined! Real soldiers, every inch of them! No gold lace and chalk belts and shoulder straps, but fully equipped in full marching order: blankets, guns, knapsacks and canteens. Train in the background.[9]

These descriptions allude to the energetic response from audiences that are confirmed in vaudeville reviews of the day, but also indicate that film producers were assuming their audience to be predominantly white and male. A presenter, exhibitor or lecturer of some kind is necessary to elicit these responses from audiences, drawing from the surrounding discourse of patriotism available in newspapers of the time. The patriotic response is encouraged and spelled out in these catalogue descriptions through the way these soldiers are described in conjunction with audience response. The "hurrah" stands in not for the cheers of the soldiers, but the cheers of the audience members as they see the men arrive. Tom Gunning has described the temporality of the cinema of attractions as being the alternation between presence and absence.[10] In this description such temporality is made explicit: rather than the act of marching having narrative importance, the audience is cued to respond to the sudden presence of 'real' soldiers on view. The patriotic energy is roused through the direct connection between the viewer and the scene that is accomplished by the attraction-style scene. The spectators are not meant to identify with the soldiers but rather to find camaraderie and community in the group that cheers them on; hence, whether soldiers are physically present is not a concern precisely because of the presence of the moving images and the participation of the crowd. These promotional descriptions suggest that producers were not only attempting to create a homogeneous audience but rather an active crowd in support of American empire-building.

Imperialism and China as the exotic locale

Moreover, while the Spanish-American War was an extremely popular news item and, as a result, has often been addressed as a popular subject in cinema's development, comparing films of the American military with films about wars involving little American presence – *the Boxer Rebellion* – yet made by American companies, provides a new angle from which to examine how early filmed representations of war were tied to expansionist impulses.[11] The varying subject matter used to represent each war – for example, travelogues of China used in lieu of battle films for the Boxer Rebellion – sheds light on ways in which imperial and expansionist ideologies were presented in ways other than simply showing American militaristic endeavours.

The Boxer Rebellion was yet another international conflict that captured the attention of American citizens through journalism and film. The rebellion included a group of Chinese peasants fighting against the colonisation and Westernisation of their country. On 30 June and 18 August 1900, references to the Boxer Rebellion appeared in Edison advertisements in the *New York Clipper*. Many of the films advertised – although, in total there were only seven films advertised in June and three in August – were, in fact, just travelogues about China. The combination of discourse about the "Boxer massacres" and the visual depictions of tourism resulted in the representation of China as an exotic locale, meant for the enjoyment of Western culture, and the Chinese as cruel and savage, inflicting unwarranted slaughter on the innocent and well-meaning colonisers.

The films of the Boxer Rebellion are by no means extensive, nor were they overly detailed in the first months following the events. What is of interest, though, is the means by which these films were advertised in the *New York Clipper*. Rather than a discussion of the troops, as was evident in the Spanish-American War films, the Boxer Rebellion is discussed as an event of interest to the world by rendering China an exotic locale in need of and destined for colonisation. For example, the *Clipper* advertisement from 30 June 1900 states:

> The Boxer Massacres in Pekin [sic]
>
> Have turned the eyes of the civilized world toward China. Public interest is now thoroughly aroused, and people will appreciate any pictures that relate to the localities in which the present war in China is being prosecuted.[12]

This last statement – "people will appreciate any pictures that relate to the localities" – is further emphasised in the Edison catalogue from July 1901. Three films are listed relating to the rebellion specifically, with an additional statement: "A Complete List of

Chinese Picture Films is found on Page 37 under the heading Occidental and Oriental Series".[13] Thus, interest in the war could be sustained through the interest of picturing an exotic locale.

In an advertisement from 18 August 1900, the Edison Company lists three films under the large headline, "Chinese Pictures Just Received": *Bombardment of the Taku Forts by the Allied Fleets*; *Street Scene in Peking*; and *Scene in Legation Street, Shanghai*.[14] Furthermore, the description for *Scene in Legation Street, Shanghai*, wherein "a number of Europeans and Americans being driven down the thoroughfare, in native rickshaws and wheelbarrows" are shown, seems strikingly similar to the description for *Shanghai Street Scene, no. 2* from 1898, which also stresses the use of wheelbarrows:

> Here is another view on the Bund, with the Garden on the left, with its high arched conservatory. As in the former scene, the peculiar wheelbarrows prove to be the central attraction. Evidently some tourists are enjoying the novel vehicle, as shown by the hilarity of the party that passes in front of our artists. A barrow is often loaded with three or four passengers, although but one man propels it.[15]

This, in fact, is not a film of battle at all, but yet another example of the expansionist mentality that is provided by showing Europeans and Americans making themselves at home in another country. This film shows colonisers exploiting native modes of transportation for their own pleasure, and yet it is presented, in this advertisement, as a positive picture demonstrating for American audiences their countrymen and women enjoying the exotic locale. However, what is more interesting than the use of a film about tourists to represent the current rebellion is the fact that this film seems to have been repackaged and advertised in light of the public's knowledge of the events. Again, the advertisements demonstrate the naturalisation of expansionist ideologies through the assumed audience acceptance of travelogues as exemplary of the conflict in foreign locations.

I would like to use this example of the Shanghai street film to conclude by stating that while the catalogues may have indeed been "global" and "encyclopedic", as Tom Gunning argues, we can see through the chronology of the advertisements and the phrasing used that distributors and exhibitors of early cinema had the ability to use films to further particular nationalist discourses of civilisation and empire-building. This example demonstrates that a film's significance could change significantly based on audience associations and the way in which exhibitors and showmen introduced films to audiences. While I do not mean to suggest that any subject could be repackaged for audiences in light of current events, these advertisements and catalogue descriptions reveal how surrounding news items about current events and the ways in which the subjects were presented to audiences could alter particular texts' meanings. Further work on alternative reactions to early American films involving the military will expand our understanding of how audiences reacted to, engaged with, or resisted these texts. In what ways did the encyclopedic and non-narrative characteristics of these early films allow for differences in the construction of military-themed programs? How did these films function when shown within non-military-themed programs? Finally, if the notions of American identity and masculinity were such hotly contested issues, as Kaplan suggests, how – if ever – were these films used by exhibitors to run counter to the producers' and distributors' intended meanings? Current trends in reception and regional studies will likely provide fruitful analyses of reactions that stand as alternatives to those encouraged by early film promotions.

Notes

1. Stephen Bottomore, "War and Militarism: Dead White Males", *Film History* 14, nos. 3/4 (2002): 240.
2. *New York Clipper*, (9 April 1898): 92. "The patriotic feelings of the audience invariably get plenty of fresh and sterling material for frequent outbursts in the splendid biograph views of Cuban occurrences, this motion picture machine still continuing a most heartily appreciated feature of the programme"; *New York Clipper*, (23 April 1898): 126. "The National Wargraph, improving with use, is still a potent factor in attracting the public, its pictures of U.S. warships and scenes in Cuba continually rousing patriotic sentiment"; *New York Clipper* (30 April 1898): 144. "The Edison war-graph still retains its hold on the public, the pictures it throws upon the screen eliciting signs of hearty approval or disapproval as they depict American or Spanish subjects".
3. Tom Gunning, "Early cinema as global cinema: the encyclopedic ambition", in Richard Abel, Giorgio Bertellini and Rob King (eds), *Early Cinema and the "National"* (New Barnet, Herts: John Libbey Publishing, 2008), 11.
4. Charles Musser, *Before the Nickelodeon: Edwin S. Porter and the Edison Manufacturing Company* (Berkeley: University of California Press, 1991), 7.
5. Amy Kaplan, *The Anarchy of Empire in the Making of U.S. Culture* (Cambridge, MA: Harvard UP, 2002), 97.
6. Kristen Whissel, "Gender and the Empire: American Modernity, Masculinity, and Edison's War Actualities", in Jennifer M. Bean and Diane Negra (eds), *A Feminist Reader in Early Cinema* (Durham: Duke UP, 2002), 150.
7. Ibid., 144.
8. *Edison War Extra* (20 May 1898): 3.
9. *Edison War Extra* (20 May 1898): 3–4.
10. Tom Gunning, "'Now You See It, Now You Don't': The Temporality of the Cinema of Attractions", in Richard Abel (ed.), *Silent Film* (New Brunswick, NJ: Rutgers UP, 1996). 75–76.
11. Charles Musser discusses the Spanish-American War in relation to ongoing competition between film companies in *Emergence of Cinema* (New York: Maxwell Macmillan International, 1990); Robert Allen discusses the popularity of the war in *Vaudeville and Film 1895–1915: A Study in Media Interaction* (Diss. U of Iowa, 1977. New York: Arno Press, 1980); Kristen Whissel discusses the representation of American militarism in the context of new experiences of modernity in "Gender and the Empire", 141–165.
12. *New York Clipper* (30 June 1900): 408.
13. *Edison Films* (July 1901): 16.
14. *New York Clipper* (18 August 1900): 564.
15. Charles Musser, *The Phonoscope* (August 1898): 15, reprinted in *Edison Motion Pictures, 1890–1900: An Annotated Bibliography* (Washington, D.C.: Smithsonian Institution Press, 1997), 474.

9

"What is a Picture?": Film as Defined in British Law Before 1910

Ian Christie

> The film was neither a print nor a book, nor – in fact, everybody could say what it was not, but nobody could say what it was. The scheme was not exactly pigeonholed. The real trouble was that nobody could say to which particular pigeonhole it belonged.[1]

This wry comment appeared in the British showmen's newspaper *The Era*, in October 1896, referring to a widely reported proposal by Robert Paul to deposit samples of his Animatograph films at the British Museum as a record of contemporary history. The affair was reported in an article by Stephen Bottomore as long ago as 1995, incorporating research by Richard Brown.[2] Whatever Paul's motives for making this proposal, and also for publicising the Museum's delay and confusion over its response, it is clear that he was *not* trying to register the film's copyright. To do this in Britain in 1896 would have required a deposit and or registration of the films at Stationers Hall. And indeed a number of early British filmmakers did deposit copies of single frames from their films at Stationers Hall, apparently believing this to be the best – or only – way to register copyright in the new medium.[3] We know that other manufacturers were doing likewise in other countries, according to the requirements of their national copyright legislation: Edison had started sending films to the Library of Congress as early as 1893, while the Lumières in France were also depositing copies in order to establish *droit d'auteur* on their films as publications.[4]

But *was* a film a publication? To what "pigeonhole" did these anomalous new objects belong? One of the legal cases from this early period that offers some insight is the 1901 prosecution of Walter Gibbons by Charles Urban for duplicating or "pirating" films owned by Urban's Warwick Trading Company. Urban's memoirs recount how he came to suspect Gibbons of making unauthorised copies; Gibbons' print order from Warwick had gone down even as he was increasing the scale of his exhibition business around the London music halls. But Urban needed evidence, which he eventually managed to get in a suitably melodramatic way – by forcing one of Gibbons' employees to take him to the scene of the crime, where, by candlelight, he found "three short duplicated films, even bearing the Warwick trade mark at each beginning".[5]

Finding the trade mark was important, since Urban intended to accuse Gibbons of "forging the company's trade mark by photography" in this 1901 case.[6] Trademark protection was certainly a clearer legal issue than the status of films around 1900.[7] In the course of recounting the Gibbons affair, Urban stated: "The copyright of a picture according to English law belongs to the man who operated the camera" – followed by: "Our camera men however understood that all films they took while in our employ were the copyright of the company".[8] Here is indeed one of the first problems in arriving at a legal definition of film – a problem that went back to the difficulty originally raised by photography. The legal status of photographs was first defined in English law by the Fine Arts Copyright Act of 1862, which stated that the author of a photograph has "sole and exclusive right of copying, reproducing and multiplying" the photograph; but also that this right may be assigned to another person, and that neither copyright nor assignment is valid unless registered at the Hall of the Stationers' Company.

Robert Paul seems to have been the first British filmmaker to register copyright in this manner in March 1897, as shown by a registration form for the most popular item in his series *A Trip through Spain and Portugal* (and here I must pay tribute to Richard Brown for his pioneering work on copyright and for providing me with copies of Paul's copyright claim forms).[9] In the case of the *Sea Cave near Lisbon*, Paul records the "date of assignment" from his cameraman Henry Short to himself as January 1897 (Figures 1 and 4). Six years later, in July 1902, Paul is again registering copyright on a film of the Prince and Princess of Wales and their children, filmed by "G. Francis"; but there has been a dispute, as Paul's accompanying note reveals: "I am quite unable to give his full name, legal proceedings being pending between us [however] the assignment to us has been signed and such assignment has been legally approved of".

We might wonder how much of a problem protecting the copyright of early films was. Back in 1985, André Gaudreault described film piracy as "extremely common" between 1900 and 1906 amongst all the major production companies in England, France, and the United States. "All producers at the time [1900–06] enthusiastically pirated (by duping a print) the films of competitors who had not taken the precaution of copyrighting them at the Library of Congress".[10] Richard Brown has subsequently challenged Gaudreault's "sweeping statement", noting that he offered no evidence, and suggesting instead that "whilst film 'duping' probably existed in England before 1912, it was certainly not the high-profile activity it was in the United States".[11]

This is probably correct, due in part to the British film trade being relatively collegial and highly concentrated in London's West End, with similarly concentrated regional distribution centres. Certainly there had been extensive unauthorised copying of films in the earliest period: Edison copied Acres and Paul's first films, notably their *Rough Sea at Dover*, which was the hit of his 1896 Broadway debut screenings;[12] and Paul may have copied Edison's films, or at least the purchasers of his replica Kinetoscopes could have done so. But by the early 1900s, systematic piracy would almost certainly have been detected – as it was by Charles Urban's threatened prosecution of Gibbons and a 1903 case in the United States brought by Edison against Lubin. Early producers were increasingly concerned to protect their investment. Further evidence of this concern comes in a four-part series of articles that appeared in the United Kingdom's *Kinematograph and Lantern Weekly* in November 1907. This most substantial attempt to clarify the copyright position of film outside an actual case at trial does not seem to have had the attention it deserves.

The articles were based on a paper by barrister William Jago, read to the newly formed Kinematograph Manufacturers Association (Figure 3). It seems likely that Jago had been commissioned by the association's first president, Robert Paul, as part of efforts to develop the infrastructure of the new industry. These efforts included, for example, a certificate course for projectionists in partnership with the Northampton Polytechnic Institute. The journal was itself new, having been launched in May 1907, as successor to the *Optical Lantern and Cinematograph Journal*, which had collapsed in bankruptcy.

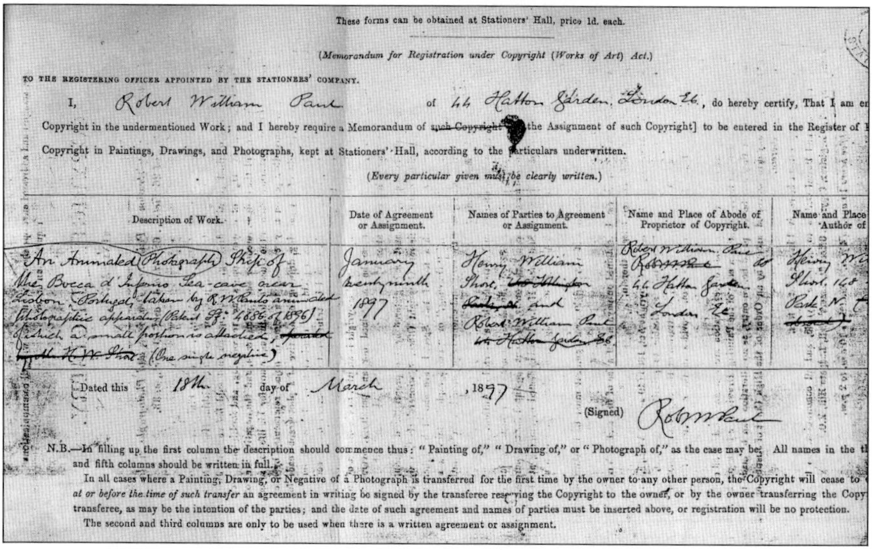

Fig. 1. Robert Paul's registration of A Sea Cave near Lisbon *under the Fine Arts Copyright Act.*

The extended survey of "The Law of Copyright in Kinematograph Pictures" was thus something of a platform statement, both for the new association and its would-be trade journal.

Jago starts by distinguishing two senses of copyright. The first is "the right which a man has to control, and if he wishes, to prevent the publication of his literary publications". The second sense is "the exclusive right of multiplying the copies of such production after publication". Once published, a work was protected by the Copyright Act of 1842, although as Jago admits "there is nothing legally literary about a kinematograph picture". There would, however, be redress under common law if someone was shown to be "passing off" their work as that of another. But what protection might there be for the subject or performance embodied in a film?

Jago cites an important historical case, that of Turner vs. Robinson, dating from 1860, and heard at the Rolls Court in Dublin, Ireland (then part of Great Britain).[13] Robert Turner was a print seller in Newcastle, who had bought the engraving rights to Henry Wallis's hugely popular painting *The Death of Chatterton* (1856). James Robinson, of the Polytechnic Museum and Photographic Galleries in Dublin, was one of the first generation of stereographic publishers to cash in on the new fashion for stereoscopic views. He had published a stereograph of "The Death of Chatterton" in 1859, which Turner claimed was a "piratical imitation" of the Wallis painting.[14] We learn from a contemporary account of the case that this had come about when Turner shipped the painting to Dublin in order to attract subscriptions for his engraving, whereupon Robinson had announced that he would soon offer "the beautiful stereoscopic figure of the last moments of Chatterton".[15]

When Turner applied for an injunction, Robinson's defence was that "his stereograph was not copied from Mr Wallis's picture, but was an independent study from the biography of Chatterton" and that he had "from recollection built up the subject in his studio and made a stereoscopic photograph of it". At a second hearing, he further argued that "it is impossible to take pictures for stereoscopic slides from a plain surface such as a picture".[16] Despite this, Turner succeeded in getting an injunction against

9 "What is a Picture?": Film as Defined in British Law Before 1910

Fig. 2. Robert Paul pictured with his camera in 1897.

Robinson on the grounds that, although "the stereographic slides are not photographs taken directly from the picture, in the ordinary sense of copying; but they are photographic pictures of a model, itself copied from and accurately imitating in its design and outline the petitioner's painting".[17]

Jago pursues at length the two – let us say "ontological" – issues that continued to perplex those seeking to apply statutes introduced before moving pictures appeared: whether sequences of photographs could be regarded as "a picture"; and whether the

> **Nov. 7, 1907.** THE KINEMATOGRAPH AND LANTERN WEEKLY. 441
>
> ## The Law of Copyright in Kinematograph Pictures.
>
> *Paper read before the Members of the K.M.A. by*
> WILLIAM JAGO, F.I.C., F.C.S., of Lincoln's Inn, Barrister-at-Law.
>
> It was with very great pleasure that I accepted the invitation of your Association to read a paper at one of your meetings on the Law of Copyright in its relation to Kinematograph pictures.
> The Kinematograph is a new invention and was unknown and probably unthought of at the time of even the most ... the present effective statute is the Copyright Act of 1842, on which the existence of literary copyright in this second sense depends.
> The application of this Act to literary productions only concerns us in so far as the principles laid down in its administration have some application to our present subject.
> There is nothing which is legally literary about a kinemato-

Fig. 3. *The first installment of Jago's article.* Kinematograph and Lantern Weekly *(7 November 1907).*

representation of a performance can be treated *as* a performance. On the first, he argues that although the negative of a film consists of a series of pictures, "their sole use is for the purpose of producing when exhibited one picture only". And on the latter, he suggests that "no one who has heard the roars of laughter caused by a comic moving picture can doubt that a Kinematograph exhibition may certainly cause the same emotions as those produced by a representation by actors of the same scene or event".

Jago does not mention, but may well have been aware of, the landmark US Federal Court ruling in Edison v. Lubin in 1903. This has often been characterised as one pirate taking another to court, although in truth American copyright law at this time was radically unclear about the status of film. Lubin's defence against the Edison charge of piracy was that Edison should have registered each frame of his films individually to secure protection under the 1870 US Copyright Act. This was upheld in the lower court, before being reversed in the Federal appeal court, which held that "while the advance in the art of photography has resulted in a different type of photograph, yet it is none the less a photograph".[18]

Citing judgements in which "scenic entertainments" and "producing emotions" had been regarded as criteria for something being considered a "dramatic representation", Jago concludes that "a kinematograph representation can claim the protection afforded by the Dramatic Copyright Act of 1833, while the Fine Arts Act protects the film itself from all trafficking, whether by copying, multiplying or exhibiting". But whatever satisfaction the Kinematograph Manufacturers might have felt after this learned analysis of their situation was about to be rudely disturbed in April 1908 the following year.

Fig. 4. *Frames from* A Sea Cave *near Lisbon.*

9 "What is a Picture?": Film as Defined in British Law Before 1910

The landmark case of *Karno vs. Pathé Frères* has been shrewdly analysed by Richard Brown.[19] This turned on the impresario Fred Karno's claim that the Pathé film *At the Music Hall* infringed his copyright on the music hall sketch "The Mumming Bird", which he had registered in 1906. After the court visited the Oxford music hall to see the sketch performed, and viewed the film, the judge found that the film was indeed "a representation of the plaintiff's sketch", but that this sketch did not qualify as a "dramatic or musical performance"!

Although the judgement disappointed Karno and left open the question of who might be liable if such a case *were* proved (the producer or the exhibitor of the film?), it established that no "legitimate" dramatic work could be filmed without the author's permission. A parallel case in the United States, Harper Brothers vs. Kalem Company and Kleine Optical (1908), which arose from Kalem's unauthorised filming of Lew Wallace's Ben-Hur, already a popular stage and arena entertainment, turned on whether Kalem's dialogue-free adaptation of a literary work could be considered a "dramatization". In an eventual Supreme Court ruling delivered by Justice Holmes, Kalem's screen version was judged to infringe Harpers' copyright, thus establishing the rights of the owners of the source-work of a film.[20]

Later the same year, an international copyright conference in Berlin revised the original Berne Convention of 1886 and its 1896 Paris revision, including for the first time only now in 1908 an article that referred to film. In Britain, a new Copyright Act followed in 1911, which incorporated the Berlin provisions, thus giving film formal copyright status for the first time.[21] America, meanwhile, continued to reject the principles underlying the Berne Convention until nearly the end of the twentieth century.[22]

So much was changing within both the business and the art of film in 1908 and 1909 – from the launch of the *film d'art* in France, which would eventually transform production everywhere, to Edison's formation of the Motion Picture Patents Company – that it is hardly surprising that clarifying copyright should have become an urgent priority at this moment. Films were getting longer, more expensive to produce and distribute, and increasingly worth protecting – or pirating.[23] Stabilising and harmonising copyright would indeed prove crucial to building the new industry for producers prepared to stay in the business and for the authors who would start to reap major rewards from this increasingly dramatic medium. Robert Paul, however, was one of the pioneers who read the signs and decided to bow out.

Notes

1. *The Era* (17 October 1896).
2. Stephen Bottomore, "'The Collection of Rubbish', Animatographs, Archives and Arguments: London 1896–97", *Film History* 7 (1995): 291–297.
3. This collection, transferred from Stationers Hall to the Public Record Office, and thence to the National Archives in Kew, was reported in 1993 by Richard Brown.
4. Under French law, the Lumière films are still "protected" by a variety of rights – patrimonial rights (until 2039), rights of artistic property, and moral rights, which are vested in the "Lumière succession" of descendants.
5. Charles Urban, *A Yank in Britain: The Lost Memoirs of Charles Urban, Film Pioneer*, Luke McKernan (ed.) (East Sussex, UK: Projection Box, 1999), 57–59.
6. Ibid.
7. Richard Brown mentions an earlier case of "unauthorised use of a registered trademark" in *Koopman v. The Manchester Palace Theatre of Varieties* (K. 365 of June 1897), in "The British Film Copyright Archive", in Colin Harding and Simon Popple (eds), *In the Kingdom of Shadows: A Companion to Early Cinema* (London: Cygnus Arts, 1996), 241.

8. Urban, *A Yank in Britain*, 58.
9. Brown, "The British Film Copyright Archive", 240–245.
10. André Gaudreault, "The Infringement of Copyright Laws and its Effects (1900–1906)", *Framework* 29 (1985): 4.
11. Brown, "The British Film Copyright Archive", note 6, 244.
12. On Edison's unscrupulous use of European films in his Vitascope screenings, see Charles Musser, *The Emergence of Cinema: The American Screen to 1907* (Berkeley and Los Angeles: University of California Press, 1990), 118.
13. Turner v. Robinson, 10 Ir. Ch. 121, 510.
14. Additional information on this celebrated early case in photographic history from Heinz K. Henisch and Bridget Ann Henisch, *The Photographic Experience, 1839–1914: Images and Attitudes* (State College: Pennsylvania State University Press, 1994), 306.
15. "The Death of Chatterton", *Athenaeum* 1652 (25 June 1859): 841–842.
16. Ibid.
17. Judgement in *Turner* v. *Robinson*, 10 Ir. Ch. 121, 510.
18. *Edison v. Lubin*, 122 Fed. Rep. 240.
19. Brown, "The British Film Copyright Archive", 242–243.
20. See Charles Musser, *Before the Nickelodeon: Edwin S. Porter and the Edison Manufacturing Company* (Berkeley: University of California Press, 1991), 421 and 552. See also a discussion of this case in L. Trotter Hardy, "Copyright and 'New-Use' Technologies", *Faculty Publications* 187 (1999), available online through the College of William and Mary Law School. I am also grateful to Jon Solomon for shedding further light on the significance of this case.
21. Copyright Act, 1911, Part III, Section 35: "'Dramatic work' includes any piece for recitation, choreographic work or entertainment in dumb show, the scenic arrangement or acting form of which is fixed in writing or otherwise, *and any cinematograph production where the arrangement or acting form or the combination of incidents represented give the work an original character*" [my italics].
22. The United States remained outside the Berne Convention until 1952, when a special Universal Copyright Convention was created to meet its requirements. This was then overtaken by America's Implementation Act in 1988, which brought the U.S. fully into the Berne process, and led eventually to the foundation of the World Intellectual Property Organisation in 1996.
23. As long films became central to exhibition, and were sold at auction to distributors for unprecedented sums, so efforts to "pass off" inferior or pirated copies occurred. For an account of this practice in the Netherlands in 1913–14, see Ivo Blom, *Jean Desmet and the Early Dutch Film Trade* (Amsterdam: Amsterdam University Press, 2000), 228–232.

10

Le cinéma et les élections au Québec: de l'attraction à la banalité

Germain Lacasse

Introduction

À Montréal et au Québec, au cours de la première moitié du 20ème siècle, les grands journaux organisaient de grands rassemblements publics pour diffuser les résultats des diverses élections nationales ou régionales. Le cinéma faisait partie des nombreux dispositifs utilisés pour attirer et captiver les spectateurs. Ce texte fera d'abord l'historique de ces projections singulières, surtout à partir de l'exemple de celles organisées par le quotidien montréalais *La Presse*. On commentera ensuite cet exemple afin d'analyser quelle y fut la place du cinéma en tant que "nouveauté" et comment cette pratique peut éclairer la position du cinéma dans ce que Thomas Elsaesser appelle une "archéologie des médias".[1] Nous essaierons de montrer que nous ne pouvons pas toujours récuser la téléologie dans une histoire du cinéma et des médias, mais que si nous pouvons parler de déterminisme nous devons suggérer qu'il est aléatoire. Seront aussi étudiées les réflexions de Frank Kessler sur le "dispositif du spectaculaire" qui correspondent assez bien au rôle que le cinéma joua dans ces rassemblements publics, où il n'était la plupart du temps qu'une distraction narrative dans un dispositif multimédia d'information participative.[2]

Aspects historiques

Les rassemblements organisés par les journaux quotidiens pour annoncer les résultats des élections (nationales ou autres) sont probablement issus des grandes assemblées que les partis politiques organisent pendant les campagnes électorales. Celles-ci mobilisant beaucoup l'opinion et l'attention, leur conclusion est un événement très attendu par les citoyens anxieux de connaître les résultats. L'intervention des journaux d'opinion et de la presse de masse dans ces événements est donc tout sauf fortuite. La causalité en est complexe mais liée à la modernité politique et culturelle: avènement de gouvernements élus par la masse, liberté d'opinion, diffusion d'information par des entreprises privées, etc.

À Montréal les grands journaux quotidiens apparaissent vers 1880 et connaissent rapidement un succès considérable. Vers 1910 le journal *La Presse*, celui qui a le plus servi pour cette étude, tirait environ 125,000 copies par jour, dans une ville comptant 500,000 habitants. La poste lente de cette époque rendait les quotidiens inadéquats dès que le lecteur était éloigné, mais dans la ville le journal était extrêmement populaire et publiait trois éditions par jour, auxquelles s'ajoutaient même parfois des éditions spéciales.

À ses débuts vers 1890 la "soirée des élections" ne comportait que la communication des résultats, mais graduellement la pratique s'est raffinée et diversifiée en ajoutant différentes attractions et innovations: projection de photographies des candidats; projection de dessins et caricatures;[3] projection de vues panoramiques;[4] intégration d'une partie récréative montrant des vues animées; films montrant certains candidats. Il y eut souvent aussi la présence de fanfares qui jouaient des airs patriotiques ("Vive la Canadienne", "God Save the King", etc.).[5] La confirmation des résultats finaux était par ailleurs couramment suivie des discours des candidats gagnants, qui s'installaient à la fenêtre d'un édifice ou sur une tribune installée sur place.[6]

Cette pratique ressemblait beaucoup aux émissions de télévision actuelles qui suivent aujourd'hui en temps réel le dépouillement des résultats d'élections. L'organisation et le déroulement le montrent très bien. Le journal recevait par téléphone ou télégraphe les résultats des bureaux de vote; les résultats étaient inscrits sur des plaques de verre déjà préparées comportant des tableaux avec les noms des candidats, où il ne restait qu'à ajouter les chiffres des résultats, qui étaient projetés par la lanterne magique sur un très grand écran tendu sur la façade des bureaux du journal ou sur un bâtiment voisin.[7] La présentation des résultats locaux était entrecoupée périodiquement par une mise à jour de l'ensemble des résultats et de la position des partis.[8]

Pour l'élection fédérale canadienne du 7 novembre 1900, *La Presse* fit installer sur le toit de son édifice un très grand tableau lumineux (probablement fait de rangées d'ampoules électriques): "D'après ce système, on pourra lire de toutes les parties élevées de la ville les rapports des élections à mesure que nous les recevrons à nos bureaux. Ce nouveau système est un ensemble de lettres formées par des lampes électriques que l'on fait jouer à volonté selon la phrase que l'on veut écrire."[9] Mais les résultats et les photos des candidats étaient également projetés à l'aide de lanternes magiques sur un écran tendu sur la façade. *La Presse* organisa aussi des soirées de ce genre devant ses bureaux de Québec, sur la rue St-Joseph.[10] Selon *La Presse* et les autres journaux qui les organisaient, des milliers de personnes se déplaçaient pour assister à ces projections. Au moment de leur plus grande popularité, il fallait détourner la circulation urbaine parce que la foule y occupait toute la place. Les lieux ne suffisant pas à contenir tout le monde, d'autres sites furent ajoutés ailleurs dans la ville, où on projetait également les résultats.[11] *La Presse* a aussi présenté parfois les résultats des élections états-uniennes.[12] Un million de Québécois ont émigré vers l'est des États-Unis à la fin du 19ème siècle mais maintenaient des liens avec leurs familles et leur pays natal, et les journaux québécois commentaient régulièrement l'actualité politique états-unienne.

Les vues, d'abord fixes et ensuite animées, étaient perçues comme un divertissement:

> Dans le champ lumineux passeront les portraits des différents candidats, des nouveaux députés, des principaux personnages politiques et religieux de la province de Québec, ainsi que des vues de la vieille cité de Champlain, édifices du Parlement, Citadelle, Terrasse Dufferin, Hôtel de ville, etc. À l'occasion de la Sainte-Catherine il y aura des caricatures amusantes et des vues typiques, représentant des scènes dont plusieurs ont déjà été témoins déjà dans cette "fête de la tire canadienne".[13]

Mais en 1908 le cinéma prend une place importante, qu'il n'eut jamais avant et semble n'avoir jamais eu après dans ces événements. Cela est lié à la très grande popularité qu'il connaît alors: depuis 1906 ont ouvert à Montréal une vingtaine de "scopes" dont le premier et plus populaire, le Ouimetoscope, montre à ses clients les films documentaires tournés à Montréal par son propriétaire, Léo-Ernest Ouimet, devenu une célébrité locale très souvent mentionnée par les journaux. Le journal *La Patrie*, principal concurrent de *La Presse,* lui demande de fournir des vues animées pour la soirée des élections provinciales en juin 1908.[14] L'attraction semble avoir été très appréciée et *La Patrie* la répète en octobre lors des élections fédérales canadiennes.[15]

Pour la même occasion *La Presse* s'associe elle aussi à Ouimet pour présenter des vues animées: "En effet, pour que la foule ne ralentisse pas ses acclamations, pour que les quelques minutes d'attente qu'il pourrait y avoir entre les divers rapports paraissent plus brèves, la 'PRESSE' [sic] s'est assurée le concours de M. L.-E. Ouimet. [...] Pas n'est besoin [sic] non plus d'ajouter que les vues animées seront de l'inédit".[16] On ne dit pas quels films furent présentés, mais cette semaine là au Ouimetoscope on annonçait "*Le cœur de la bohémienne et pris avec les marchandises* [sic]. *Le talisman de Pierrette*, superbe vue en couleur. *Pour un royaume*, grand drame à sensation. *Une héroïne de l'auto et le chevalier mystérieux*, autre superbe vue en couleur".[17] Le Ouimetoscope projetait aussi cette semaine là "*Mes espérances en 1908*" film de Ouimet montrant ses enfants. Mais pendant la soirée des résultats, le cinéaste-producteur ne montra pas seulement des films divertissants, il ajouta un choix judicieux, un film tourné peu avant montrant le premier ministre Wilfrid Laurier s'adressant à une foule de partisans.[18] Le Ouimetoscope présentait également les résultats des élections "à l'extérieur et à l'intérieur de la salle", et fut imité par d'autres théâtres: His Majesty's, Académie de Musique, National Français, Bennett, Princess, Français, et Royal.[19] Les résultats étaient présentés par des projections à la lanterne magique, à mesure qu'ils étaient reçus par télégraphe.[20]

Pour la soirée des résultats de 1911 *La Presse* fit construire sur le toit de son édifice une plate forme où s'installa la fanfare du journal, dirigée par Albert Goedike.[21] Le programme de la soirée comportait aussi des feux de Bengale et le lancement de ballons aux couleurs des partis. Les projections fixes annoncent les résultats, mais les projections animées sont encore de la partie: "Nous verrons défiler sur l'écran les vues, illustrations et portraits des hommes et les choses de la politique canadienne y compris les vues animées du plus grand intérêt, agrémentées de quelques scènes comiques. Sur l'écran passeront des vues de la capitale du Canada (Ottawa), des édifices du Parlement, et autres".[22]

Pour l'élection fédérale de 1921 *La Presse* annonçait encore la projection de vues animées, ainsi que de caricatures de son dessinateur Albéric Bourgeois.[23] (Le journal reproduit d'ailleurs plusieurs de ces caricatures des candidats dans l'édition du mercredi 7 décembre.) En 1923 la projection a encore lieu, et *La Presse* annonce que des vues animées seront projetées comme divertissement.[24] Mais les résultats de l'élection étaient aussi transmis par CKAC, la station de radio de *La Presse* entrée en ondes l'année précédente.[25] Les résultats semblent rarement avoir été annoncés verbalement avant l'arrivée de la radio; le seul exemple trouvé est lors de l'élection fédérale de 1917: le *Montreal Daily Star* installa une plateforme devant l'Hôtel Windsor et y posta un annonceur à la voix très puissante ("whose voice enabled him to discard the megaphone") qui communiquait les résultats dès réception.[26]

En 1925 les résultats de l'élection fédérale du 29 octobre furent l'occasion pour *La Presse* de vanter sa station de radio.[27] Mais le journal installe aussi des haut-parleurs qui servent à faire entendre les résultats par les spectateurs trop éloignés des écrans; pour qu'eux aussi aient droit à des distractions dans les temps morts, le journal offre un programme musical attrayant: l'orchestre "Chesterfield" du Cinéma Capitol, dirigé par Bud Fischer, ainsi que la troupe du folkloriste Conrad Gauthier et des chanteurs dont Charles Marchand et Ernest Patience. Le même programme était offert aux auditeurs de CKAC qui écoutaient les résultats sur leur récepteur radio.[28] Sur les écrans un programme de divertissements visuels amusait les gens entre l'annonce des résultats: des films comiques, des caricatures de candidats, et même une série de caricatures simulant un combat de boxe entre les deux chefs des principaux partis, Mackenzie King et Meighen!

En 1931 *La Presse* présentait une soirée où accourut encore une très grosse foule. Les résultats sont toujours projetés sur un écran, et des candidats gagnants viennent faire des discours.[29] Taschereau, premier ministre élu, vint faire une brève déclaration devant la foule, puis se rendit aux bureaux de CHRC et de CKAC afin de lire son discours pour les auditeurs qui ont suivi les élections. Les résultats étaient présentés à toutes les quinze minutes, entrecoupés d'attractions musicales. Pour la foule réunie à l'extérieur autour des bureaux du journal, les temps morts étaient occupés par des projections de caricatures et de films comiques.[30]

L'élection de 1935 fut encore l'occasion d'une telle soirée, même si la radio était maintenant devenue très répandue et permettait aux citadins qui le voulaient de recevoir à domicile les résultats. Pour cette occasion le dispositif semble avoir été encore plus sophistiqué: d'après *La Presse* un écran était consacré aux élections et projetait à intervalles de 30 secondes des "rapports, résumés, photos et caricatures" pendant que sur un autre écran "passèrent une quinzaine de films de voyage, de sport, d'amusants dessins animés qui, pendant toute la soirée, amusèrent ou instruisirent la foule qui marqua d'applaudissements sa satisfaction".[31] Des haut-parleurs avaient aussi été installés et diffusaient des commentaires pour les gens qui ne pouvaient pas bien voir les écrans.

L'élection provinciale du 25 octobre 1939 donna lieu à une autre soirée du même genre. Le dispositif est semblable à celui des années précédentes : projections de photographies, de dessins et de films, et annonce des résultats à la radio qui est retransmise à l'extérieur par des haut-parleurs. Les résultats du vote étaient projetés sur un écran avec les photos ou dessins des candidats, alors que sur l'autre écran étaient projetés "des fantaisies, comédies, dessins animés qui firent oublier la fatigue et les minutes. Plus de 16 000 pieds de film furent ainsi déroulés devant les spectateurs amusés. Ces bobines avaient été fournies par United Amusement et M. Roméo Vandette et leur présentation avait été organisée par M. Vandette".[32] Ailleurs dans le journal il était écrit qu'une vingtaine de "courts films fantaisistes" furent projetés.

Pour l'élection de 1940 le public eut encore droit à la projection de films: "*La Presse* n'avait pas oublié de présenter une bonne douzaine de films comiques en couleurs. Le temps passa ainsi plus rapidement à suivre les aventures fantaisistes de 'Popeye the Sailor', du canard 'Donald', du 'Captain and the Kids'".[33] Mais à cette occasion le journal mentionne une technique singulière pour la projection des résultats électoraux: "Les renseignements obtenus par fils télégraphiques et téléphoniques spéciaux étaient dès leur arrivée tapés à la machine sur les pellicules mêmes qui devaient passer sur l'écran une minute plus tard".[34] La même technique semble avoir été décrite précédemment une autre fois: "À droite M. Eugène Picard, chef du service de l'illustration de la '*Presse*' croqué sur le vif au moment où il remet une dépêche filmée à l'opérateur de cinéma".[35] L'expression opérateur de cinéma désigne probablement ici le projectionniste chargé à la fois des vues fixes et des vues animées. Il semble qu'on dactylographiait le texte sur de la pellicule pour le projeter, tandis qu'auparavant les résultats étaient écrits à la main sur des plaques de verre. Le commentateur de radio agissait en guise de "bonimenteur" donnant au micro des explications sur les résultats projetés: "Au centre: M. Jacques Demers, commentateur de CKAC, expliquant à la multitude les bulletins-éclairs qui étaient projetés sur l'écran et simultanément communiqués par haut-parleurs".[36]

Le 9 juin 1945 paraît à la une de *La Presse* un petit encadré qui fut sans doute l'acte de décès de ces soirées d'annonces électorales, du moins sous cette forme. "Coin St-Jacques et Saint Laurent, en face des bureaux de la 'Presse', aucun résultat ne sera affiché et il ne sera pas davantage donné de renseignements par téléphone, tant à CKAC qu'au journal. Sous les auspices de la *'Presse'*, la publication des résultats complets du vote du 11 juin ne sera donc faite que par radio, soit par le poste CKAC".[37] Dans la page que le journal consacre à la programmation radiophonique, un article encadré souligne que le programme du lundi à CKAC sera modifié pour être consacré aux résultats des élections.[38] Les longs textes que le journal consacrait jadis à la soirée de projection des résultats sont remplacés par un article et des photos montrant au travail les journalistes de *La Presse* et les commentateurs de *CKAC* à l'œuvre pendant la soirée.[39] Il est possible que cette fin abrupte des soirées électorales ait été demandée ou même ordonnée par les autorités. Au cours des mois précédents les préparatifs de l'annonce de la victoire des Alliés en Europe avaient été encadrés soigneusement afin de minimiser les débordements.

Aspects théoriques

(1) Archéologie et hiérarchie des médias

Dans un article intitulé "New Film History as Media Archaeology" Thomas Elseasser écrit que la nouvelle histoire du cinéma a revitalisé l'étude des origines, mais n'a pas obtenu autant de succès dans l'analyse de la conjoncture multimédiatique du tournant du 20e siècle.[40] Pour répondre à cette lacune il appelle à faire une archéologie des médias. D'inspiration foucaldienne, cette archéologie consisterait en une étude non des filiations mais plutôt des parentés et des familles. Pour ce il propose de s'inspirer du présent pour examiner le passé, plutôt que l'inverse. Plus précisément il veut comparer la conjoncture nouvelle suscitée par l'arrivée du numérique, et celle du cinéma des premiers temps: "Practically, this means considering the history of image and sound technologies as made up less of a family tree and more of 'family relations' – belonging together, but neither causally or teleologically related to each other".[41] Selon lui les technologies électroniques et numériques sont des phénomènes hybrides, développés pour des besoins militaires avant de devenir des objets culturels. Il faudrait donc examiner l'arborescence de leurs possibilités autant comme le résultat d'une détermination plurielle qu'en tant que virtualités permanentes. Une archéologie des médias devrait donc tenter d'identifier les conditions de possibilité du cinéma en parallèle avec son ontologie : "I suggest adding an archaeological 'turn' in order to describe the emergence and development of cinema, not in its own terms or when competing with television, but within the technical and electronic media of the 20th century generally".[42]

Si nous appliquons cette proposition à la pratique que nous avons décrite, nous pouvons constater qu'une vision téléologique du cinéma y perd encore la plupart de ses prétentions. Cette pratique est placée sous l'hégémonie du journal quotidien, technologie plus ancienne. Celui-ci s'adjoint des médias récents et pré-cinématographiques (la téléphonie et la télégraphie) pour obtenir de l'information, et des technologies contemporaines du cinéma pour diffuser cette information (amplification sonore, radio, etc.). Au moment où le cinéma connaît sa fulgurante poussée d'émergence, les journaux montréalais lui accordent plus d'importance dans l'arsenal déployé au cours de ces soirées et publicisent largement sa participation et ses agents. Ainsi lors de l'élection de 1908 Ernest Ouimet est-il l'objet de nombreuses mentions dans les journaux qui soulignent la projection de son film sur le premier ministre Wilfrid Laurier, mais aussi celle du film montrant ses propres enfants.

C'est cependant la seule occasion où le cinéma obtient autant de place et de visibilité; d'autres films sont projetés mais on n'en connaît ni le titre ni l'origine, ils ne sont là qu'à titre de divertissement visant à amuser ou occuper les spectateurs dans l'attente des résultats des élections. On pourrait dire qu'au moment où il devient dans une autre institution et d'autres pratiques l'art narratif majeur du 20ᵉ siècle, le cinéma n'est ici qu'un amusement trivial, comparable à l'orchestre de *La Presse* ou aux caricatures du journal. Son statut le ramène à ce que William Uricchio appelle média d'enregistrement par opposition à média de transmission:[43] le film peut servir à montrer des choses survenues auparavant, mais il ne correspond pas au besoin de simultanéité qui est recherché par les technologies utilisées pour une pratique du type étudié. Il correspond à la nouveauté qui est associée à la modernité, mais ici au lieu d'être au sommet d'une hiérarchie des médias il n'en est qu'un des éléments inférieurs, les places plus élevées étant dévolues aux médias de transmission: télégraphie, imprimerie et radio, qui seront plus tard supplantés dans cet événement par la télévision, laquelle intégrera toutes ces technologies antérieures et suscitera la fin, ou le déplacement, de ces rassemblements publics, qui se font aujourd'hui surtout dans les locaux des partis politiques, comme avant que les journaux ne les prennent en charge.

(2) La banalité du cinéma
Dans ces projections multimédia le cinéma semble n'avoir qu'une valeur de divertissement. Les titres des films ne sont jamais mentionnés (les seules exceptions: le court film sur Wilfrid Laurier en 1908, et les dessins animés en 1939) les articles de journaux se bornant à annoncer des "vues animées instructives ou divertissantes". Le cinéma qui est l'attraction majeure dans le monde du spectacle semble ici n'être qu'un secondaire complément; l'élément central est l'annonce des résultats de l'élection le plus rapidement possible, et la possibilité de réagir collectivement à ces annonces, le summum étant atteint quand le candidat préféré est élu et se présente sur place pour s'adresser à la foule. L'élément principal est peut-être la rencontre avec la collectivité, et les médias sont le moyen de rendre cette rencontre plus attrayante en apprenant les résultats rapidement. Le cinéma ne joue presque aucun rôle dans cette communication, ce sont d'autres médias qui sont employés: le téléphone, le télégraphe, la lanterne magique et la photographie pour montrer les images des candidats; plus tard arrivera la radio, et plus tard encore la télévision.

On est donc ici dans une pratique intermédiatique où le cinéma ne peut presque imposer ou susciter aucune règle ou norme. Il doit au contraire se plier à celles de cette pratique elle-même, où il ne se voit accorder qu'une petite place. La seule fois où le cinéma se retrouve plus en évidence est lors de l'élection de 1908: les journaux embauchent Ouimet pour gérer les projections, mettent ensuite en évidence cette coopération comme qualité supplémentaire de leur organisation, et signalent le seul film documentaire explicitement mentionné dans toute l'histoire de cette pratique, le film d'actualité sur Laurier. Le cinéma est alors en expansion fulgurante à Montréal et Ouimet est devenu une célébrité locale. Mais jamais dans les élections suivantes les vues animées n'auront cette visibilité, elles retombent rapidement au rang des attractions destinées à divertir les électeurs qui attendent les résultats.

Les films projetés semblent avoir été souvent destinés à illustrer des aspects de cette épopée nationale en direct que constitue la soirée des élections: on y montre des vues, fixes ou animées, des capitales et des édifices parlementaires, des politiciens en lice, mais aucune de ces vues n'est le point focal de l'attention. Cette dernière est centrée sur le résultat du scrutin, et sur la coprésence des électeurs venus attendre les résultats. Il est cependant un peu étonnant de découvrir que cette présence n'a jamais été aussi intense qu'à ce moment où les médias sont intensément utilisés. L'utilisation conjointe de plusieurs technologies rend possible l'annonce rapide des résultats, et c'est cette possibilité qui semble attirer autant de gens ensemble au même moment et au même endroit. Comme pour bien souligner ce fait les journaux publient le lendemain de nombreux dessins, et plus tard de nombreuses photos, montrant la foule sur les lieux. Les journaux publient aussi de longs articles où ils racontent la soirée, décrivant non les résultats (qui sont résumés dans d'autres articles) mais la façon dont ils sont communiqués à la foule, et les réactions de celle-ci. L'épopée devient celle du journal, qui s'accorde autant d'importance que les candidats élus, comme si le média lui-même avait rendu possible l'élection, plutôt que sa simple narration.

L'analyse de la place du cinéma dans la pratique que nous venons d'étudier montre qu'au sein d'un dispositif intermédiatique à but informationnel, le cinéma occupe une place bien restreinte comparée à celle qu'il occupe dans le champ de la fiction. Dans une soirée d'élection, sa nouveauté et son attrait n'étaient que bien relatifs... Pour revenir à ce que proposait Elseasser en disant qu'une histoire du cinéma doit comporter une archéologie intermédiatique, cette pratique montre que dans un contexte intensément centré sur l'information le cinéma, même documentaire, prend une place assez minime. C'est un peu comme si on montrait aujourd'hui des courts métrages comiques pendant une soirée de résultats électoraux offerte par une chaîne télévisée d'information continue. Peu importe leur qualité ou leur pertinence, ces films seraient de l'ordre de la banalité.

(3) Déterminisme aléatoire

Considérer l'histoire de cette pratique en la comparant avec les soirées d'élections télévisées permettrait certes de dire qu'elle les anticipait : le journal s'associait toutes les techniques qui feront plus tard partie du dispositif de la télévision. Mais par contre la radio et la télévision sont venues supprimer un des aspects fondamentaux de cette pratique: la présence physique des citoyens venus assister à cette présentation. La réception est encore simultanée, mais la rétroaction est maintenant différée: chacun peut réagir et commenter, mais il est séparé de la masse et ne peut manifester physiquement, sauf pour ses proches dans son domicile. Cette pratique avait donc des traits de communication orale qui sont disparus: télévision et radio transmettent images et sons, mais les citoyens sont dispersés. Ces rassemblements passés seraient-ils une des "possibilités" non déterminées résultant d'une utilisation aléatoire des médias? Il faudrait alors parler de déterminisme aléatoire, puisque les rassemblements ont persisté longtemps après la possibilité d'informer à distance en simultanéité, et montrent que la tradition des rassemblements ne s'efface que longtemps après la réalisation de cette possibilité. Cette pratique n'existe plus, sinon pour des auditoires restreints: pendant les soirées d'élections, les partisans des différents partis se rassemblent dans des locaux où ils attendent les résultats, qu'ils peuvent saluer et discuter entre eux; mais ce n'est plus le média qui organise la rencontre, c'est le parti politique.

Cette pratique disparue, dans laquelle le cinéma devenait une attraction mineure, semble un bon exemple de "déterminisme aléatoire". On pourrait penser que l'impressionnante popularité de ces grands rassemblements aurait mené à leur pérennité et qu'ils auraient duré pendant des décennies. Pourtant elles n'existent plus; on pourrait penser que la télévision a suscité leur déclin, mais cela ne peut être la seule raison, puisque la télévision ne suffit certes pas à remplacer la présence physique, et que ces rassemblements ont persisté bien après que les citoyens pouvaient obtenir les résultats chez eux par la radio. Sans oublier, bien entendu, que ces rassemblements disparaissent avant l'arrivée de la télévision. Pour reprendre les termes de Elsaesser, nous dirions que ces rassemblements sont davantage le fruit de "possibilités" plutôt que de "virtualités permanentes". Les citoyens sont attirés par la possibilité d'apprendre rapidement une chose qui les intéresse au plus haut point; les journaux rassemblent toutes les technologies disponibles pour informer le public, y compris le cinéma qui permet d'ajouter des images animées. Les technologies nouvelles ont permis l'organisation de tels événements, qui semblent donc causalement déterminés par la logique du progrès des moyens d'information; mais cette virtualité "réalisée" se dissipe ensuite dans ce qu'on peut appeler l'aléatoire du déterminisme: d'autres configurations de technologies viennent supplanter les précédentes. On peut penser, par exemple, que la télévision est devenue le média dominant, qu'elle a supplanté les journaux autant que le cinéma, et que cette position hégémonique a poussé les citoyens à se regrouper ailleurs, hors des lieux d'hégémonie médiatique, pour apprendre les résultats des élections. Les partisans des principaux partis politiques se réunissent dans des locaux réservés pour eux, et regardent à la télévision les reportages des journalistes qui sont sur place; on les verra faire des discours, on montrera des "vues" de leurs actions antérieures, mais jamais d'extraits de fiction comme *Primary Colours* (Mike Nichols, 1998) et encore bien moins *Farenheit 9/11* (Michael Moore, 2004).

La fonction du cinéma dans ces rassemblements correspond beaucoup, comme nous le disions dans l'introduction, à ce que Frank Kessler appelle "dispositif du spectaculaire".[44] Il entend surtout réviser la notion de dispositif pour en atténuer l'aspect essentialiste; il dit vouloir l'historiciser mais aussi la déplacer du champ de la métapsychologie (Baudry et Metz) vers celui d'une pragmatique historique. Il propose de voir alors la cinématographie comme dispositif du spectaculaire: "Il s'agit avant tout de 'donner à voir' beaucoup plus que de raconter, de démontrer ou de faire savoir [...] La technologie n'est plus elle-même l'attraction principale [...] elle sert avant tout à montrer du spectaculaire, participant de la sorte à d'autres séries culturelles, tout en utilisant les possibilités techniques du média".[45]

Cette approche convient assez bien à l'exemple que nous avons documenté et étudié. Les films y sont utilisés comme une attraction nouvelle, attrayante, divertissante, contribuant à rassembler les gens pour une activité dont la finalité est toute autre. La presse à grand tirage semble avoir récupéré à son profit une activité d'abord dominée par les partis politiques; pour mousser ces activités et le rôle qu'elle y joue, elle mise au maximum sur la nouveauté et le perfectionnement technique (associés à la présence médiatisée) et le cinéma y est pendant quelques années un appareil attrayant qui est au sommet de sa capacité spectaculaire. Le cinéma demeure ensuite présent dans ce dispositif, mais il est vite associé à d'autres nouveautés plus récentes: la radio, l'amplification électrique du son, le téléscripteur, qui seront bientôt tous supplantés par la télévision, dont pourtant l'hégémonie est maintenant disputée par l'ordinateur et les médias numériques.

Notes

1. Thomas Elsaesser, "The New Film History as Media Archeology", *Cinémas* 14, nos 2–3 (printemps 2004): 75–117.
2. Frank Kessler, "La cinématographie comme dispositif (du) spectaculaire", *Cinémas* 14, no 1 (automne 2003): 21–34.
3. "Les élections", *La Presse* (22 juin 1896): 1.
4. Ibid.
5. "Les nouvelles à Montréal", *La Presse* (12 mai 1897): 2. (L'article parle aussi de *La Patrie*.)
6. Ibid.
7. "How Montreal Citizens Received the Results of the Elections; Working of *Star*'s Bulletin Service", *Montreal Daily Star* (4 novembre 1904): 6.
8. "Les élections", *La Presse* (23 juin 1896): 1.
9. "Les élections", *La Presse* (7 novembre 1900): 1.
10. "Le résultat des élections", *La Presse* (6 novembre 1900): 1.

11. "Les élections", *La Presse* (10 mai 1897): 1.
12. Ibid.
13. "Les élections", *La Presse* (25 novembre 1904): 1.
14. "Nos projections: les bulletins affichés sur l'écran lumineux de '*La Patrie*'", *La Patrie* (9 juin 1908): 1.
15. "La journée d'hier aux bureaux de *La Patrie*", *La Patrie* (27 octobre 1908): 1.
16. "Les rapports des élections", *La Presse* (24 octobre 1908): 1.
17. "Musique, comédie, drame: le Ouimetoscope", *La Presse* (24 octobre 1908): 8.
18. "Le parti libéral remporte la victoire", *La Presse* (27 octobre 1908): 1.
19. "Les élections et les théâtres", *La Patrie* (26 octobre 1908): 5.
20. "Musique, comédie, drame: le Nationoscope", *La Presse* (24 octobre 1908): 8.
21. "L'élection de jeudi", *La Presse* (19 septembre 1911): 16.
22. "Rendez-vous en foule à *La Presse* pour le résultat du scrutin ce soir", *La Presse* (21 septembre 1911): 1.
23. "En foule à *La Presse* demain soir", *La Presse* (5 décembre 1921): 1.
24. "En foule ce soir à *La Presse*…", *La Presse* (5 février 1923): 1.
25. "Les élections par le radio", *La Presse* (5 février 1923): 12.
26. "Throngs Cheered Election Returns at Windsor Hotel", *Montreal Daily Star* (18 décembre 1917): 1.
27. "Les résultats de l'élection d'hier transmis par le poste CKAC sont entendus par toute l'Amérique", *La Presse* (30 octobre 1925): 1.
28. "Le radio de *La Presse*", *La Presse* (28 octobre 1925): 2.
29. "La foule réunie près de *La Presse* acclame les discours des vainqueurs", *La Presse* (25 août 1931): 1.
30. "Plusieurs milliers de personnes devant *La Presse*", *La Presse* (25 août 1931): 1.
31. "Une foule énorme acclame le résultat des élections de *La Presse*", *La Presse* (15 octobre 1935): 1.
32. "Les péripéties de l'Austerlitz libéral: une foule immense réunie à *La Presse*", *La Presse* (26 octobre 1939): 1.
33. "Les résultats à *La Presse*", *La Presse* (27 mars 1940): 1.
34. Ibid.
35. "Le service d'information de la '*Presse*' hier soir", *La Presse* (26 octobre 1939): 2.
36. Ibid.
37. "CKAC donnera le résultat complet du vote lundi soir", *La Presse* (9 juin 1945): 1.
38. "Émission de rapports électoraux par CKAC", *La Presse* (9 juin 1945): 2.
39. "Succès de la 'soirée d'élections' à CKAC", *La Presse* (11 juin 1945): 1.
40. Elsaesser, *New Film History*.
41. Ibid., 93.
42. Ibid., 104.
43. William Uricchio, "*Phantasia* and *Technè* at the *Fin-de-siècle*", *Intermédialités* no 6 (automne 2005): 32.
44. Kessler, *La cinématographie*.
45. Kessler, *La cinématographie*, 30.

II

A Moving Picture Farce: Public Opinion and the Beginnings of Film Censorship in Quebec

Louis Pelletier

Attending the world premiere of his latest film, *I Confess*, on 13 February 1953, Alfred Hitchcock vowed he would never set foot in Quebec again. Back in Quebec City, where the film had partly been shot the previous summer, the famed director had just found out that no less than nine cuts had been made by the Quebec Provincial Board of Cinema Censors. The cuts came in spite of taking pains during production to soothe Quebec's Roman Catholic Archdiocese – known to be very close to the Censors – by submitting the script for their approval.[1] Hitchcock's anger was probably less about the stringency of the Quebec Censors, as he no doubt had been aware of their reputation as being among the world's toughest, but rather the sheer unpredictability of their decisions. The master of suspense had tried to follow the rules, only to discover that there were no clear rules.

Hitchcock's difficulties with the Quebec Board of Censors were neither unique nor new. Indeed, a survey of the Board's first year of operation back in 1913 reveals that within months of its creation, the Censors' rulings had sparked at least two major controversies bringing out charges of inconsistency and lack of transparency. Using the extensive contemporary press coverage of the creation and first year of operation of the Quebec Board of Censors, this paper will argue that the events surrounding the advent of film censorship suggest that the province's public opinion and nascent film industry were both less concerned with protecting free speech and the artistic potential of cinema than calling for transparent standards in the regulatory activities conducted by the government institution. In other words, moving picture censorship – contrary to vigorous opposition to censorship of drama or literature[2] – was widely perceived as being necessary, and even possibly beneficial to the film industry. What ended up being so strenuously denounced almost as soon as the Censors began to examine films was the alleged corruption of the political machine to which the Provincial Board of Censors was subordinate. The controversy was less the fact of film censorship than the resulting lack of consistency and public accountability characterising the activities and decisions of the Board.

This relative lack of concern for cinema's expressive potential might have been fed by the fact that nearly all films exhibited in Quebec were foreign productions and that, as a result, cinema had come to be associated more with passive consumption than with creation. In fact, one of the arguments invoked in favour of the creation of a provincial board of censors was to prevent some of the more objectionable foreign productions from entering the Quebec market. Censorship, it was thought, would create a void that would be filled by a national film industry. Others hoped more realistically that the creation of the Board would help the industry by simplifying things. Centralised provincial censorship was anticipated as a means of overriding the demands of countless groups aiming to exert control on films and moving picture shows, and give some degree of protection to the distributors and exhibitors under the guise of an official stamp of approval by the Board.[3] Many individuals and organisations had indeed argued for increased control on moving picture shows since the appearance of the first *scopes* and nickel shows back in 1906, including the Montreal chief of police, the Montreal Aldermen, the Parks and Playgrounds Association, and many religious organisations.[4] Most of the criticism directed at picture shows by these organisations derived from concerns over the safety of the establishments dedicated to film exhibition, from the moral panic surrounding children and the movies, and from concerns over the perceived Americanisation of Quebec's population (Figure 1).

While these concerns were by no means specific to Quebec, they were exacerbated by the fact that the province (and more particularly the city of Montreal, then Canada's metropolis) was in fact a bicultural territory where Francophones and Anglophones, Catholics and Protestants strove to control institutions, including the municipal, provincial and federal administrations. Fresh in the memory of the Province's exhibitors at the time of the creation of the Board of Censors was the fight over Sunday shows, drawn out over no less than six years, from 1907 to 1912. Initiated by religious groups and opposed by a coalition of workers' unions, progressive groups and film industry representatives, this campaign had been complicated by a jurisdictional fight between the three levels of government. This protracted battle over Sunday shows had severely strained the resources of exhibitors, and nearly bankrupted Quebec film pioneer Léo-Ernest Ouimet, whose legal team had eventually secured the exhibitors' right to do business on Sundays.[5]

No doubt sensing that centralised provincial censorship could prevent showmen from getting mired in endless litigation, Quebec's film distributors and exhibitors did not oppose the creation of the Board of Censors. Support for censorship extended to Montreal's leading daily newspapers, which all argued in favour of film censorship in the months leading to the creation of Board, instituted by a provincial law passed on 4 December 1912.[6] Most of the city's newspapers agreed that movies could well stand the scrutiny of censorship, and that this form of control could even help make this new form of mass entertainment more legitimate by weeding out the few truly objectionable films. Even the *Montreal Daily Star*, which would soon become one of the Censors' fiercest critics, at first expressed the belief that censorship "could do no harm and might do some good".[7] Quebec's largest two French dailies, *La Patrie* and *La Presse* also initially came out as firmly pro-film censorship, and even argued for the Board's jurisdiction to be extended to the songs and live acts presented in picture houses.

The circumstances leading to the creation of the Quebec Board of Censors thus generally reflected those documented by historians all over North America. Daniel Czitrom for instance quotes Frank L. Dyer, president of the Patents Company, as declaring in May 1909 that: "the proposition of a single National Censorship Board strikes me as being the only solution of the problem, admitting there must be censorship, which I think everyone having the best interests of the business at heart must admit".[8] Jan Olsson similarly notes that in Los Angeles "a censorship ordinance came into effect in August 1911 in an amicable atmosphere".[9] In the neighbouring province of Ontario, Paul S. Moore's research has documented the support of pioneer exhibitor Peter Griffin, who believed the creation of an Ontario Board of Censors would improve upon municipal police censorship, which he claimed was "demoralizing the business".[10] Created in 1911, the Ontario Board would eventually serve as the main model and point of comparison for the Quebec Board.[11] It should further be reminded that one of the main aims of the Motion Picture Producers and Distributors of America (MPPDA) – created some time later in 1922 – would also be the centralisation of censorship, this time through the creation of an internal production code and certification system.

The crisis triggered by the first controversial decisions of the Quebec censors had more to do with issues of governance than with freedom of speech. The original members of the Quebec Board of Censors were all political nominations: President Louis-Joseph Lemieux, a Sheriff, had represented the Liberal party then in power at the provincial *Assemblée nationale* between 1904 and 1910; Vice-President Michael James Walsh, an insurance salesman by trade, was a recently defeated liberal candidate; and G. Maxwell Sinn was a journalist.[12] None of them had had any kind of experience with film, theatre or literature, leaving room for their decisions to be attacked as ill-informed. Since the film industry had yet to organise collectively as a political lobby in Quebec, opposition to the Censors' first controversial decisions was largely led by the daily press. Most newspapers at the time had only recently transformed from political organs to commercial enterprises relying on advertising – and thus mass readership – for revenues. Coincident with this modern transition was a shift in allegiance from political organisations perpetuating a lack of transparency and accountability in public affairs to the vast reading public that also patronised moving picture shows, and further to film exhibitors and distributors as clients – just beginning to buy advertising on a regular basis in 1913. In short, newspapers had ceased to align themselves with for parties and interest groups, and started to define themselves more as an extension of public opinion.[13]

The newly appointed members of Quebec Board of Censors first met early in April 1913 at their Montreal office to establish a list of prohibited images and themes. As was to be expected, violent and immoral scenes made the list, as also did divorces, suicides, "scenes injurious to patriotism", and "scenes where religion and its ministers were mocked".[14] The Board finally began to review films on April 15, two weeks before the day – 1 May – where its tag would become mandatory on all films exhibited in Quebec. The Censors announced that their activities would be held in private, but nevertheless invited journalists, politicians and religious leaders to attend a few initial screenings.[15] Archbishop Bruchési paid them a visit, as also did Quebec Premier Lomer Gouin, and public works minister Louis-Alexandre Taschereau.[16] For a few weeks, the press remained entirely sympathetic to the Board and its mission. Articles on the ordeal of having to sit through so many moving pictures regularly appeared in newspapers. *La Patrie* for instance reported that the huge backlog of films waiting to be approved had forced the censors to organise marathon screenings lasting from 9am to 11pm from days on end, and that, as a result, two of them had been forced to seek treatment from an oculist.[17] The press kept cheering when the first films were ordered cut or banned. Newspapers did report a first minor controversy provoked by the Censors' decision to ban Ambrosio's *Satan*, a film that had been deemed to contain "a lesson at once wholesome and subtle" by the Ontario Board of Censors, but newspaper editors at first chose not to inflame the situation.[18]

The honeymoon between the Censors and the Quebec press, however, was brief. The Board of Censors was barely entering its second month of activity when its May 15 decision to reject two of the five reels of *Cleopatra*, a prestigious production featuring

11 A Moving Picture Farce

Fig. 1. *Arthur Racey,* Montreal Daily Star *(7 May 1913): 3.*

Helen Gardner, sparked public debate. Initially, *La Patrie* simply explained that "unfortunately, some incidents taken from Cleopatra's love life could prove somewhat troubling for some chaste viewers", and that, after much discussion (and no less than four screenings), the Censors had decided to ban the most offensive reels.[19] But then the film's distributor, the Canadian Film Company, decided to go public with its displeasure with the Board's decision. According to the Censors' records, the distributor had first tried to get the decision reversed by offering a bribe, and it is only after this method had failed that it had changed its tactics and threatened legal action.[20] The ensuing events were closely followed by the local film industry, as it became obvious that *Cleopatra* would become a test case of the authority and jurisdiction of the Board of Censors. The Montreal exchanges knew that an Ontario judge had just reversed a decision of the provincial Board, and were most anxious to see if a similar precedent could be established in Quebec.[21]

The campaign mounted by the Canadian Film Company in the following weeks cleverly shifted the burden of the proof back to the Censors. As framed by the distributor, the *Cleopatra* case was not so much about the moral value of the film as it was about transparency of the activities of the Board of Censors. Realising that its main ally was public opinion rather than the institutions represented by Gouin and Bruchési, Canadian Film chose to make the press a major player in its campaign. Its first move consequently was to gather a select group of journalists and public officials to a private screening of *Cleopatra* held at the Théâtre Français, one of Montreal's most prestigious theatres. The fact that this screening was tolerated by Board of Censors despite being announced in advance clearly reveals some of the more undemocratic biases of the Censors, as this selective broad-mindedness posited two classes of citizens: the educated elite, whose members were capable of rational debate, and the masses, whose emotional reactions were to be feared and tightly controlled.[22]

In order to demonstrate the Board's lack of transparency and troubling inconsistencies, the screening organised by Canadian Film at the Français paired *Cleopatra* with the Biograph comedy *Just Kids*, which had just been approved by the Board in spite of being full – according to subsequent reports by the *Star* and *La Patrie* – of debased clergymen, elderly voyeurs, and "emancipated American girls" in bathing suits.[23] The publicity stunt generated predictable results: journalists denounced *Just Kids* and praised *Cleopatra* for its artistic value, striking sets and remarkable mise-en-scène. *La Patrie*'s reporter further observed that nothing he had seen in *Cleopatra* could be described as scandalous, while the *Star* journalist reported that "the consensus of opinion [at the screening] was that the [picture] receiving the approval of the Board was the more immoral".[24]

Commentary on the *Cleopatra* case soon gave rise to criticism of the Censors' methods and decisions. The *Star* led the way with what would soon blossom into a months-long campaign of ridicule against the Censors. Sheriff Lemieux's first reaction to this increased scrutiny of the Board's activities was to meet with various members of the press in order to defend the Censors' decisions. To a *Star* representative, he explained that "the morality or immorality of a reel [depended] upon whether it [depicted] comedy or tragedy".[25] The Censors nevertheless implicitly acknowledged their error by recalling the two prints of *Just Kids* being exhibited in Quebec and requesting that several cuts be made.[26] This failed to make much of an impression on the *Star*, whose humour-column sarcastically commented: "Sheriff Lemieux and his companions license a film: that is tragedy. Then they withdraw their license: that is comedy. Afterwards they give reasons for their action: that is farce".[27] In yet another editorial dealing with censorship, the *Star* simultaneously expressed its disapproval for both the "repulsive" fun of *Just Kids* and the Censors' "metaphysical distinction" between comedy and drama.[28] Perhaps unsurprisingly, the controversy actually ended up boosting *Just Kids*' commercial career: two days after making the headlines, this "much talked of" comedy was the featured attraction at Montreal's most prestigious show place, His Majesty's Theatre – a rare feat for a short split-reel film.[29]

The *Cleopatra* case eventually ended up in court on June 13, 1913.[30] Attorneys for the two parties mostly argued about the nature of the censors' activities during the court hearing. Canadian Film's lawyer claimed that the Censors acted as judges, whereas the King Counsel representing the Board went for a somewhat unfortunate comparison: he argued that "the Censors passed the films just as the inspectors at the abattoirs pass the meat, and that their judgment in the matter was [consequently] final".[31] In a decision rendered two weeks later, the Court upheld the Board's decision and explained that the Censors' work constituted "an act of administration" which could only be appealed to the Lieutenant Governor of the Province.[32] The Canadian Film Company finally decided to leave the King's representative out of the decision, and to simply release the three reels out of five that had been approved by the Board back in May.[33]

Although overt controversy appeared to wane for the next few weeks, press and public opinion kept scrutinising the Censors' decisions. Early in September, complaints from Jewish citizens forced the Board to recall the Keystone comedy *The Firebugs*, which it had approved for exhibition.[34] The Board's decision to "reject without comment" *The Wages of Sin*, a film deemed to be "a masterpiece of kinetic art" with a "strong moral" by the *Star*, also gave rise to some criticism, but no major controversy ensued.[35] For a short while, it even seemed like the Board had won the battle for public opinion. In an

HIS MAJESTY'S THEATRE

To-day at 3   To-night at 8.30

9—BIG FEATURES—9

Including
THE MUCH-TALKED-OF

JUST KIDS

Entire Dress Circle 10 Cents. Lower Floor (all reserved) 15c, 25c and 50c.

NEXT WEEK—DEBORAH
Seat Sale Friday.

138

Fig. 2. Montreal Daily Star *(12 June 1913): 2.*

article reviewing the Board's first four months of operation, *La Patrie* reported that several religious and social organisations, as well as many public officials had nothing but words of praise for the Board. Sheriff Lemieux himself was quoted as saying that the Board of Censors now ran like a clockwork, and that, for the time being, everything was *"pour le mieux dans le meilleur des mondes"*.[36]

This relative serenity was a brief respite for the Quebec Censors. By the end of the summer, Lemieux, Walsh and Sinn would find themselves in the middle of the worst controversy of their short career as moving picture Censors. The new crisis was brought about by the capture in the Quebec town of Coaticook of notorious American escaped convict Harry K. Thaw, who had just fled from the New York state asylum where he had been confined after his second trial for the murder of the famed architect Stanford White. As soon as news of Thaw's arrest had gotten out, hordes of journalists, photographers and newsreel cameramen had descended upon the city of Sherbrooke, where Thaw was being held captive while the legal fight over the extradition procedures was going on. The many films dealing with Thaw's sensational life and escape released over the next few weeks were however soon banned in several states and cities across the U.S., as many local Censors were of the opinion that anything associated with the Thaw affair was not fit to be seen by the public.[37]

In the Province of Quebec, the first images of Harry Thaw's captivity submitted to the Board of Censors were deemed innocuous by their examiner, Maxwell Sinn, who approved them for exhibition. In an interview to the *Star*, Sheriff Lemieux initially defended his subordinate's decision, in spite of not having seen the films himself.[38] The Board's President nevertheless decided to request a screening after learning from the *Star*'s reporter that the views had been banned in New York and Boston. What Lemieux ended up seeing unexpectedly upset him, but for reasons entirely different from those of the various U.S. Censors who had condemned the Thaw films. The lead Quebec Censor was not offended by the scabrous overtones of the Thaw case, but rather by the actuality footage showing the good citizens of Sherbrooke cheering Thaw, who had by then become something of a folk hero. Lemieux was compelled to withdraw his public support of Maxwell Sinn's decision. He tried to justify this change of mind by telling the *Star* that Canadians were "playing the fool" in the Thaw films, and that he did not intend to let "our people [become] a laughing stock for Americans".[39] Somehow, Lemieux seemed to have been oblivious to the fact that the decisions of the Quebec Board of Censors had no impact over whether the film was shown South of the border.

Still, the Board's troubles over the Thaw pictures were not caused by Lemieux's rather dubious logic, but by Maxwell Sinn's refusal to toe the party line and consent to the ban of the films. Worse still, Maxwell Sinn did not hesitate to publicly express his disapproval, going as far as calling Lemieux's position "bosh" in an interview with the *Star*.[40] The first consequence of this most embarrassing and most public quarrel was a Board decree on September 12 that its members were henceforth prohibited from making public statements. The Censors were subsequently required to swear under oath that they would not divulge the Board's proceedings.[41] But newspapers still kept publishing all through the month of September unflattering reports on the deadlock situation generated by the Board's hazy procedures in case of disagreement. At some point, it looked like the Lieutenant-Governor would have to be called in to decide if the Thaw picture could be exhibited in Quebec or not.[42]

While the Censors were fighting over the Thaw films, exchanges had to watch their most valuable commodity sit idly on their shelves. When a final decision banning all Thaw films was finally reached on 1 October, more than twenty-nine days after the first film dealing with the affair had been submitted to the Board, and some three weeks after Thaw had been deported to the United States, most of the interest for the case had dissipated.[43] Had the films been approved, it is likely that they would have attracted but a fraction of the audiences they would have drawn a few weeks prior. The situation prompted the *Star* to ask: "When is a picture not a moving picture?" The answer was, of course: "When it is waiting for Sheriff Lemieux's approval".[44] The *Star*'s mocking of the moving picture censors did not relent over the last few months of 1913. Indeed, irritation and distrust would arguably remain the two most commonly held attitudes toward the Quebec Board of Censors over the following decades. In just a few months' time, the three Censors had managed to lay waste to the vast support for their mission initially demonstrated by the province's public opinion and film industry.

Ironically, the last notable controversy of the first year of operation of the Quebec Board of Censors was triggered by a film explicitly showing the effects of bad municipal governance in Montreal with consequences far more tragic than Censors' cuts. The film in question was a U.S. Pathé newsreel containing images of the water famine that had disrupted the life of Montrealers between 25 December 1913 and 2 January 1914 and brought fear of major calamities such as fires and epidemics. Everybody knew that the direct cause of the event was the sudden collapse of the city's sole water intake conduit, but many believed that the real cause of Montreal's woes was the negligence and incompetence of a municipal administration plagued with corruption, patronage, and rivalries between francophone and anglophone cliques. Anger directed towards the alleged shortcomings of the administration had even bred rumours of an imminent rebellion and of the formation of a *"comité de salut public"* in the midst of the water famine.[45]

The Pathé newsreel dealing with the event was passed without discussion by the Quebec Board of Censors on 5 January 1914, and first screened at Montreal's Imperial theatre two days later.[46] The film however drew strong criticism from "a number of businessmen of the city" and "some of the 'city fathers'", who were of the opinion that the spectacle defiled Montreal's reputation and ought to be banned. Sheriff Lemieux soon countered that he had no intention of recalling the film, as it was not "immoral".[47] For once, the Censors' decision was supported by newspapers like *La Patrie*, who published an editorial defending right of exhibitors to show the film and echoed Lemieux's declaration by imploring the Board to limit itself to issues of morality.[48] Good sense may have prevailed in the end, but while influential citizens were using cinema as a scapegoat and trying to sweep the inconvenient views under the carpet, no real efforts were made to reform the administration and political system that had created the conditions where such a potentially catastrophic situation could occur.

While cinema was routinely labeled a bad influence during this transitional period of its history, my research demonstrates how its legitimacy could suffer as much from being regulated by corrupt institutions as from depicting corruption on screen. In the light of the multiple controversies documented in contemporary sources and exposed here, there is no doubt that the Quebec Board of Censors' repeated inconsistencies over its first year of activity were detrimental to the affairs of the numerous exchanges and exhibitors active in Quebec. However, the most significant damage inflicted on the Quebec film industry by the Board of Censors' erratic decisions was possibly on the films never made rather those banned and not exhibited. In the years and months leading up to the creation of the Board, many commentators had expressed the belief that the censoring of the violent, vulgar and exceedingly patriotic pictures imported from the U.S. would create a vacuum that would soon be filled by "Canadian scenes".[49] In reality, it could very well be that the first victims of the Quebec Censors' inconsistencies were not the U.S. producers, who could stomach the occasional arbitrary banning of one their pictures in a minor foreign market, but the Québécois and Canadian producers for whom a ban on their home market would have simply meant bankruptcy. The Censors' obsession with making moving pictures safe thus managed to make a risky business even riskier for Canadian entrepreneurs.

Acknowledgment

I would like to thank Yves Lever for answering all of my questions dealing with the complex history of the Quebec Board of Censors. This project was funded by research grants from the Social Sciences and Humanities Research Council of Canada and Bibliothèque et Archives nationales du Québec.

Notes

1. Andrée Hudon, "Mon histoire: hommage à un maître", *Le Beaver*, Quebec 400th Anniversary Special Issue (2008): 92–93; Yves Lever, *Anastasie ou la censure du cinéma au Québec* (Montreal: Septentrion, 2008), 164; Bibliothèque et Archives nationales du Québec, Régie du cinéma collection (E188), *I Confess* file, 4 February 1953. Régie du cinéma collection will hereafter be abbreviated BAnQ.
2. *Montreal Daily Star* (30 September 1913): 9.
3. Even Quebec film pioneer Léo-Ernest Ouimet, notorious for his multiple fights with the authorities, had pleaded for the creation of a Board of Censors. See: "Un propriétaire de scope conteste la légalité de la taxe qu'impose la cité", *Montréal La Presse* (27 May 1913): 11.
4. "Want Censors to Pass on All Films and Plays", *Daily Star* (29 May 1912): 7; "Les vues animées et la censure", *Montréal La Patrie* (18 October 1912): 7; "Ontario Censors Say Certificates Are Wrongly Used", *Daily Star* (28 October 1912): 11.
5. Germain Lacasse, *Histoires de scopes: le cinéma muet au Québec* (Montreal: Cinémathèque québécoise, 1988), 21–33.
6. "Censorship of Picture Films", *Daily Star* (12 November 1912): 13; "La censure surveillera étroitement les scopes", *La Presse* (4 December 1912): 16.
7. "Censoring Moving Pictures", *Daily Star* (28 October 1912): 10.
8. Daniel Czitrom, "The Politics of Performance: Theater Licensing and the Origins of Movie Censorship in New York", in Francis G. Couvares (ed.), *Movie Censorship and American Culture* (Amherst / Boston: University of Massachusetts Press), 34–35.
9. This local board of censors was destined to be short-lived, as the industry came to be of the opinion that its work was merely duplicating that of the National Board of Censorship of Motion Pictures. Jan Olsson, *Los Angeles Before Hollywood: Journalism and American Film Culture, 1905 to 1915* (Stockholm: National Library of Sweden, 2008), 219–221.
10. Paul S. Moore, *Now Playing: Early Moviegoing and the Regulation of Fun* (Albany: State University of New York Press, 2008), 144.
11. "La censure des vues animées", *La Patrie* (18 February 1913): 12.
12. "Le Gouvernement nomme trois censeurs pour les salles de vues animées", *La Presse* (31 January 1913): 1; Lever, *Anastasie*, 32–33.
13. For an overview of the modernisation of newspapers and the history of journalistic objectivity, see Michael Schudson, *Discovering the News: A Social History of American Newspapers* (New York: Basic Books, 1978); Minko Sotiron, *From Politics to Profit: The Commercialization of Canadian Daily Newspapers, 1890–1920* (M ontreal & Kingston: McGill-Queen's University Press, 1997).
14. "Movie Censors Condemn Their First Picture", *Daily Star* (18 April 1913): 22; Lever, *Anastasie*, 34–35, quoting BAnQ, minutes of the meetings of the Board of Censors.
15. "Le travail des censeurs", *La Patrie* (14 April 1913): 12; "Dame censure commence à tailler dans les rouleaux de films cinématographiques", *La Patrie* (18 April 1913): 1.
16. "La censure a de bons ciseaux", *La Patrie* (19 April 1913): 32; "La censure des films", *La Patrie* (15 May 1913): 8; "Le travail énorme des censeurs", *La Patrie* (17 May 1913): 32.

17. "Movie Censors Condemn Their First Picture", *Daily Star* (18 April 1913): 22; "Le travail énorme des censeurs", *La Patrie* (17 May 1913): 32; "Le travail des censeurs", *La Patrie* (24 May 1913): 9.
18. BAnQ, examination file, 18 April 1913; "La censure a de bons ciseaux", *La Patrie* (19 April 1913): 32; "Claims Moral in Satan Film", *Daily Star* (25 April 1913): 22.
19. *La Patrie* (22 May 1913): 1.
20. BAnQ, minutes of the meetings of the Board of Censors, 30 May 1913; "To Appeal Decision of Censors", *Daily Star* (9 June 1913): 3.
21. "Des procédures contre le Bureau de censure", *La Patrie* (10 June 1913): 8.
22. "To Appeal Decision of Censors", *Daily Star* (9 June 1913): 3.
23. "Morality Depends Upon Whether It Is Comedy of Not", *Daily Star* (10 June 1913): 3; "Another Crack at Censors", *Daily Star* (13 June 1913): 3; "Chronique des cinémas", *La Patrie* (14 June 1913): 24.
24. "À propos de 'Cléopâtre'", *La Patrie* (10 June 1913): 2; "Morality Depends Upon Whether It Is Comedy or Not", *Daily Star* (10 June 1913): 3.
25. "Morality Depends Upon Whether It Is Comedy or Not", *Daily Star* (10 June 1913): 3.
26. BAnQ, examination file, [2?] June 1913; "Another Crack at Censors", *Daily Star* (13 June 1913): 3.
27. "Another Crack at Censors", *Daily Star* (13 June 1913): 10.
28. "The Basis of Censorship", *Daily Star* (11 June 1913): 12.
29. *Daily Star* (12 June 1913): 2.
30. "Cléopâtre en cour de justice", *La Patrie* (13 June 1913): 12.
31. "Another Crack at Censors", *Daily Star* (13 June 1913): 3.
32. "Cette décision des censeurs de vues est maintenue en cour", *La Presse* (30 June 1913): 11; "Can Make Appeal from Decision of the Censors", *Daily Star* (1 July 1913): 3.
33. "Cleopatra Comes Minus the Bad Parts", *Daily Star* (4 August 1913): 2.
34. "Have Recalled Film Said to Be Offensive", *Daily Star* (5 September 1913): 11.
35. "Ban on a Film Censors Passed in London Town", *Daily Star* (16 August 1913): 3; BAnQ, examination file, 14 August 1913.
36. "L'oeuvre du Bureau de censure", *La Patrie* (7 August 1913): 1.
37. "Thaw Pictures Fit to Be Seen Here Says Censor", *Daily Star* (13 September 1913): 38.
38. Ibid.
39. "Thaw Pictures Cause Fall Out Among Censors", *Daily Star* (13 September 1913): 3.
40. Ibid.
41. BAnQ, minutes of the meetings of the Board of Censors, 12 September 1913; "Thaw Pictures Wait for Censor", *Daily Star* (15 September 1913): 2.
42. "Thaw et le cinéma", *La Patrie* (17 September 1913): 1.
43. BAnQ, examination file, 2 September 1913; *La Patrie* (10 September 1913): 1; "Les vues animées de l'affaire Thaw", *La Patrie* (1 October 1913): 5.
44. "The Passing Hour", *Daily Star* (16 October 1913): 10.
45. "Des arrestations imminentes", *La Patrie* (31 December 1913): 14.
46. BAnQ, examination file, 5 January 1914; *Daily Star* (7 January 1914): 2.
47. "Unless Immoral, Water Famine Films May Go on", *Daily Star* (9 January 1914): 5; *Moving Picture World* (14 February 1914): 828.
48. "La censure", *La Patrie* (10 January 1914): 4.
49. "Dame censure commence à tailler dans les rouleaux de films cinématographiques", *La Patrie* (18 April 1913): 1.

PART III

Education and Advocacy

12

Health Instruction on Screen: The Department of Health in New York City, 1909–1917

Marina Dahlquist

As cinema became a medium for social activism, public health discourses adopted films as a means to achieve the wider aim of Americanisation. In Progressive era New York City, didactic initiatives on the part of the Department of Health between 1909 and 1917 brought together a cross-section of civic movements and organisations at a time before government leadership in health and quality of life was assumed either at the federal or municipal level. In New York City, moving pictures were used to raise awareness about the link between sanitary and civic conduct in efforts to reshape both types of behaviours. Cultural integration and Americanisation are thus inextricable from images of citizens proactively keeping their bodies clean and healthy, and the body politic as well.

Manhattan's hundreds of moving picture theatres, combined with its polyglot mix of ethnic immigrant communities, have long been a touchstone for research in early cinema. Discussions have primarily focused on the composition of audiences in terms of class, gender, ethnicity and age. Ben Singer's essay on Manhattan nickelodeons in *Cinema Journal* in 1995 reignited an extensive debate about questions of class and ethnicity, following the earlier round of late 1970s research by Robert C. Allen, Charles Musser and Robert Sklar among others.[1] Further research considered working women's leisure, as well as attending specifically to Jewish and Italian picture show audiences.[2] This study is indebted to those efforts to map film culture in New York City, as I attempt to further explore conditions concerning the film market with an eye on pedagogical programming by reformers, drawing upon cinema's usefulness for civic education. These didactic initiatives, particularly prominent in the United States during the Progressive Era of 1910 to 1930, would have decisive socio-political importance and were widely emulated.

The Health Department in New York City emerged as a key progressive hub, embracing a multi-media sweep for attention in theatrical venues as well as using film at their own non-theatrical activities. As Kevin Brownlow and Eileen Bowser have shown, this discourse ran in tandem with concerns about the screen offering detrimental instruction, as it were, by representing immoral and undesirable scenes.[3] Utopian and dystopian perspectives blend in the debate as regulation and policing cinema through censorship became contrasted against the possibilities of the medium.[4] Film's ability to reach a wide audience did, however, lead to its use in an array of informational and educational projects, managed primarily by private organisations. Moving pictures' pedagogical might infused high hopes for its potential in civic education to raise awareness about the social evils and physiological ills of modern society. As Robert T. Eberwein and Martin Pernick have demonstrated, film was integrated into the wider discourse of health issues, and social problems more generally.[5] In these educational pieces, for example, someone careless with his cigarettes causes a devastating forest fire, or draining marshlands fights mosquitoes and malaria. Such productions contributed to a more nuanced view of the social importance of cinema. Kevin Brownlow stresses the political importance of depictions of social problems in mainstream films. For example, the settlement worker Sophie Irene Loeb succeeded in her campaign for a New York State Widows' Pension Law partly due to her involvement in Vitagraph's 1914 film *The Silent Plea for a Widowed Mother's Allowance*, produced in cooperation with the East Side Protective Association. The same topic was taken up by Pathé's 1915 film *The Pardon*.[6]

Progressive-era projects sought to improve and modernise metropolitan everyday life. These uplift campaigns profiled sanitation measures, working conditions, childcare, education, and healthy recreation. In Progressive America, the ideology of improvement was laden with middle class aspirations, aimed primarily at workers and immigrants – in a form of disciplinary pruning. Professional activists and bodies acted as self-appointed vanguards.[7] Many forms of communication and media were enlisted in the process, but cinema was often central.

Modern health education dates to the mid-1800s. In order to assist physicians' work and fight quackery in all its guises, scientifically sound hygiene and health information was published and distributed widely for the welfare of the general public. Morris Fishbein's *History of the American Medical Association 1847 to 1947* follows its national efforts in health education. The National Medical Convention, precursor to the American Medical Association, worked to get state governments to adopt a compulsory registration of births, marriages and deaths, vital for any statistics concerning death and sickness rates.[8] In the first report presented by the Committee on Public Hygiene in 1849, the most important findings concerning public hygiene were "deficient drainage, street cleaning, water supply, ventilation, housing, and nuisances such as slaughter houses, factories, butcher shops, cotton mills, and other factories".[9] Many of these problems were still unresolved at the turn of the twentieth century.

New York City was singled out in such public health surveys for being especially unsanitary because of the overwhelming congestion of its ethnic tenement districts. Sanitary work was carried out first and foremost to reduce the death rate amongst children. The Department of Health in New York City was established in 1870.[10] Around 1910 the most pressing issues for the Department were sanitation, food and milk inspection, controlling contagious diseases such as rabies, cholera, trachoma, smallpox, and communicable diseases such as typhoid fever and tuberculosis. The Department gradually mapped the city for such sanitary dangers as dirty water, impure milk, contagions, in addition to suggesting measures to battle these health hazards. Recommendations and alerts from the Department of Health were posted publicly on its office and on billboards. In 1915, the district office for Manhattan's Lower East Side (Figure 1) initiated an experiment of administering public health issues at the neighbourhood level. The experiment was soon extended to other areas of New York, enabling Health Officers to provide neighbourhood services combining children's care with instruction for fighting communicable diseases. A set of bullet points list the major concerns of the work conducted by the Department of Health at the time: Infant Milk Stations, vaccinations, Clean Up and Starve the Fly campaigns.[11]

In exhibitions and campaign work, visual material was often used in order to gain public attention. Fliers and circulars in different languages together with posters and billboards came with dashing slogans such as "Don't Spit" or health leaflets about "How to Make a Home-Made Milk Refrigerator" or "How to Make a Home-Made Fly Trap".[12] As early as 1894, Dr Herman M. Biggs initiated a Department program to help control tuberculosis through newspaper publicity, leaflets and public illustrated lectures.[13] From 1906 and onwards, the Department of Health in New York organised annual lantern slide exhibitions on a large scale in public parks to teach the masses about the prevention of tuberculosis. In July 1911, exhibitions in public parks and on recreational piers across Manhattan, the Bronx and Brooklyn consisted of 125 coloured lantern slides, describing the essential facts about the disease – its causes, symptoms, methods of infection and treatment, as well as the work of the Department to stamp out the disease. The Committee on the Prevention of Tuberculosis of the Charity Organisation Society collaborated with the Health Department to provide lecturers accompanying the pictures and to answer questions from the audience.[14]

The Health Department began to incorporate moving pictures even as it took on the responsibility of inspecting moving picture theatres' ventilation and water closet facilities.[15] Lantern exhibitions as well as popularised scientific films or "health films" were shown in schools, scientific societies, free of charge in public venues such as parks and recreation piers – apart from in movie theatres – all to instruct and educate New Yorkers about public health. Around 1910, moving pictures were taken up as a pedagogical tool for campaign work in different contexts across the U.S. on a more regular basis. Using films to illustrate scientific theories and inform the public concerning matters of sanitation as well as other aspects of modern society signalled that the medium finally had found its supposed true mission. Preventative knowledge and scientific observations, which had been restricted to health professionals, could potentially now reach the entire public directly. Film became the medium *par excellence* for depicting, demonstrating and disseminating knowledge and insights and thus became a powerful tool as an instrument of social integration and civic betterment. Conceptions of proper class, race, and gender norms, of course, shaped much of the Department's work.

The New York Health Department's exemplary efforts in fact sanitised film culture during the transitional era. In 1907, Progressive reformers intensely criticised moving pictures as an immoral influence on children, both picture shows as social spaces and film content for portraying crime and sensationalism. Measures were taken by film producers against such apprehension; one of the reasons for creating the Motion Picture Patent Company was to regulate the film business, or as Eileen Bowser phrased it, to "improve the motion-picture industry and its customer at the same time".[16]

Obviously, the Edison Company became prominent in this respect by producing social-interest films in collaboration with a multitude of welfare organisations and institutions such as American Red Cross, Russell Sage Foundation and the National Association for the Study and Prevention of Tuberculosis. *The Man Who Learned*, for example, was produced in cooperation with The New York Milk Committee for their campaigns to regulate the purity of milk through pasteurisation; *Children who Labor* was produced in cooperation with National Child Labor Committee; *The Street Beautiful* in cooperation with the General Federation of Women's Clubs; *Dangers of the Street* in cooperation with the Public Service Corporation of New Jersey. Edison also produced films about the work of the Department of Health draining marshes to control mosquitoes. These Edison films attracted attention in the daily press and were used in health campaigns and welfare exhibits all over the country. In the beginning of the

1910s, Edison also produced a number of educational subjects about the infrastructure of New York City such as the Fire Department, The Police Department, Street Cleaning, and Water Supply.

Debates at the time over food purity and hygiene in food preparation came to centre on milk for its importance to the welfare of babies and ability to specifically lower infant mortality. Unclean, unpasteurised milk had devastating effects on infants by spreading diseases like dysentery, typhoid fever, cholera, tuberculosis; intestinal disorders caused a large number of babies' deaths every summer, with 7,000 children annually estimated to die from such diarrhea-causing diseases in New York City alone.[17] One strategy to improve upon the situation was information campaigns; another was to organise milk stations placed around the city of New York. The improvement of the quality of milk delivered to retailers was of singular importance. To achieve this, the New York Milk Committee was established in 1907, and soon went to the source of problems by showing instructional films to farmers. Stations were set up to sell safe milk at the lowest market prices, attracting mothers who could be educated and prompted to bring in their young children to be examined for diseases on site. The successful experiment of fifteen milk stations in 1911 was expanded to fifty-five locations the next year.[18] They were later renamed Baby Health Stations to clarify that the overall objective of the stations were to educate parents in baby care.[19] As Jacob Sobel at the Department of Health explained in 1916:

> The milk station clientele, with few and far between exceptions, are of the poorer financial element, as would be expected from the fact that these stations have been established in sections where the infant mortality has been highest and the congestion greatest.[20]

To be able to obtain the confidence of their "clientele" and to better understand their needs, nurses were encouraged to learn to speak in whatever language was dominant near their stations.[21] One of the major concerns of the Department of Health was child hygiene and the education of so-called ignorant mothers.[22] And many campaigns were especially singling out young mothers and older girls. Little Mothers' Leagues consisted of girls over twelve years of age on the subject of the care of babies, as many girls in fact acted as the main caretakers of their younger siblings. The Leagues were organised in a multitude of schools were the need seemed urgent.

According to the Department of Health in 1908, "ignorant" mothers in New York were found almost exclusively in tenement houses, and infants were to be monitored over several visits. Children living in "private houses, high-class apartment houses, under the care of trained nurses", or whose parents "the nurse endorses as fully capable of following out the instructions given" did not need more than one visit.[23]

The film *Summer Babies*, produced by Essanay Film Manufacturing Company in 1911, showed the Chicago Health Department's work safeguarding babies during the hot summer months. In these educational films, cinematic qualities seem at times subordinate to factual accuracy. According to *Moving Picture World*, "no continued narrative is attempted; it merely pictures what the corps of visiting nurses is doing to give the young children of the very ignorant a chance to grow up into healthy men and women. It is a very commendable educational film".[24] As was common practice, the film was released as a split reel along with a comedy, in this case Essanay's *Gossiping Yapville*. According to Ernest A. Dench, the author of *Motion Picture Education*, the Chicago Health Department also initiated a motion-picture campaign for comprehensive birth registration with the film *Somebody's Birth Certificate* after a scenario by Dr C. St. Clair Drake.[25]

Despite these efforts filmed in Chicago, New York took a prominent position in

12 Health Instruction on Screen

Fig. 1. The Department of Health in New York City. Office of District no. 1 in the Lower East Side.

municipal health campaigns.[26] Under the reform administration of Mayor John Purroy Mitchel, the New York Department of Health inaugurated a large-scale clean-up effort in 1914. A first step was a clean-up campaign begun by the Department in May 1914 under the commission ship of Dr Samuel S. Goldwater. The campaign was promoted through lantern slides shown in over eight hundred moving picture theatres, with text in English, Italian and Yiddish stating: "Dirt Breeds Flies", "Flies Carry Disease", "Disease Means Doctors' Bills", "Avoid Disease and Doctors' Bills by Cleaning Up". New slides soon addressed other aspects of health instruction such as typhoid fever and infant healthcare.[27] In 1912, the Department of Health also began its own free outdoor exhibitions of health-themed moving pictures.[28] In June 1913, *Moving Picture*

News devoted editorial space to this "new" method of using cinema for public education fighting tuberculosis almost nightly at 8pm in a mix of parks and piers in Manhattan and the Bronx.[29] These screenings were arranged by the Department of Health with the Committee on the Prevention of Tuberculosis.[30] In 1912, attendance was estimated at one hundred thousand with many more expected in 1913, according to *Moving Picture News*[31]. According to Frank H. Mann, the secretary of the Committee:

> Recognizing the popularity and general educational value of the moving-picture show, we have determined to use this as a means of reaching the great number of people who assemble in the parks every night.[32]

Almost 20, 000 people attended the open-air moving picture shows during their first week in 1914. For the third season, titles included *The Story of a Consumptive*, *The Production and Handling of Milk*, *The City Beautiful* and *The Little Cripple*, with many instructive lantern slides shown between films.[33] The health film programs were expanded to include a more middle-class audience through meetings in Brooklyn.[34] Although considered a success with the public at large, the audience consisted especially of immigrants and children who could not afford to pay to attend movie theatres. Dench, for one, reflected back on the campaign's success and surmised that moving pictures could communicate with New York's many immigrants who neither spoke nor understood English.[35]

Outdoor screenings featuring health films continued in New York City throughout the 1910s, except for 1916 due to a polio epidemic. Even in that situation, the Department of Health tapped into commercial theatres to actually increase its total number of screenings from 270 in 1915 to 431 in 1916. The following three films, for example, were shown in approximately 250 Brooklyn theatres: *Long Haul vs. Short Haul* on the advantages of breast feeding; *The Life History of a Fly* about the fly menace; and Edison's *The Price of Human Lives* on tuberculosis after a script by Epes Wintrop Sargent. Health pictures were also extensively added to movie theatre programs during Anti-Mosquito Week.[36]

In the summer of 1914 New York organised its first Baby Week, an intensive campaign to fight infant mortality featuring lectures by visiting nurses on baby care in every public school and at Milk Stations. Schools and two major life insurance companies distributed one million leaflets in three languages.[37] In addition, a Better Baby Competition and a Baby Parade were organised with prize-winning babies. Public interest was immense. Department stores distributed literature; milk companies sent Baby Week tags with their deliveries of milk, and many public and private organisations contributed. Practically all services and materials were donated. All forms of media were used: moving pictures, ads in newspapers, billboards, and posters on streetcars in shop windows. The adopted slogan: Better Babies – Better Mothers – Better City.[38] Turning Baby Week into a national concern, the New York Milk Committee distributed post cards to Health officers all over the country with the provocative headline "Are You Satisfied With the Infant Death Rate in Your City?"[39] The Health Department's own work was presented as a model in widely-distributed films marketing their efforts in making antitoxins, vaccines, mosquito extermination and food inspection.[40] Such efforts were not, of course, limited to urban areas. As Kevin Brownlow points out, the Board of Health in Vermont used a horse-drawn wagon carrying a projector to reach more remote areas. In Maryland and Wisconsin, anti-tuberculosis associations used motorcars.[41] But mobile and itinerant exhibitions were also done in New York as an effective and popular way of communicating health information.[42]

In 1914, the Bureau of Public Health Education was established as a specialised branch within the Department of Health. Among the stipulation of their responsibilities:

"prepare and exhibit moving picture films dealing with public health work".[43] The Bureau received a fully equipped moving picture machine as a gift. The machine was temporarily brought to the Annual Convention of the American Public Health Association in December 1914 in Jacksonville, Florida, where films were shown in co-operation with the New York Milk Committee and the Fly-Fighting Committee of the American Civic Association. Arrangements were also made for films of the Health Department activities to be shown as part of the New York City exhibit at the Panama Pacific Exhibition in San Francisco.[44] The Department's activities were widely advertised and publicity was regularly supplied to New York newspapers and journals such as *Moving Picture World, The Survey*, and *Scientific American*.[45] Weekly radio programs on health issues began in 1922, when New York City opened its own radio station, WNYC.

In connection with Clean-Up Week and Baby Week in 1914 the Bureau had prepared a large number of lantern-slide announcements, which according to the Department were screened in "all" moving picture theatres in the city.[46] In 1915, health reels were shown in moving picture theatres in connection to Staten Island Baby Week, and loaned to schools and settlement houses.[47] In 1916, ten films about infant health were shown in large moving picture theatres throughout the city, and four hundred lantern slides with references to the different phases of infant diet, hygiene and care were distributed to moving picture theatres in areas of the city with high infant mortality.[48] New York was considered especially prone to disease outbreaks and poor health conditions because of congestion in tenement districts. However, a Special Health Commission report in 1913, noted that the city's mortality rate had begun to decline from 1.771 per 1000 population in 1902 to only 1.455 in 1912. Aside from recent provisions to isolate contagious patients at hospitals, the decline was thought to be a result of reformed regulations and inspection, the centralised responsibility of the Health Department, and the expertise of professional sanitation and health professionals.[49] According to the Health Department's annual report for 1914, the death rate for infants had gone down to an all-time low of 94.6 per 1000 births, and claimed to be lowest of any of the large cities in the world.[50] By 1917, it had declined further to only 89 infant deaths per 1000 births. Although the Department took such figures as an indication of the success of its own educational work, immigration had begun to wane and improved health statistics were also the effect of economic and cultural integration of immigrant families, many of whom had now lived in the United States for two decades or more.[51]

In the January 1913 issue of *Photoplay Magazine,* Williard Howe emphasised the enormous importance of moving pictures for getting out information to the public about hygiene and thus aiding in the prevention of contagious diseases.[52] Howe claimed that even though this knowledge had been around and practiced for some time by health professionals, it had become a concern for the public only with the use of motion pictures. Sanitation and hygiene thereby became part of the household economy:

> The sterilisation of water has been preached for years, but not until the reel of "Boil Your Water" [produced by Pathé in 1911] made its appearance did the people realise its full significance. The normal housewife never dreamed of the *animated* life that was being consumed, until this was viewed on the screen. The hosts of people who went directly home and boiled the water after this demonstration it would be impossible to calculate.[53]

The "milk films" had also made the public take notice of the importance of pasteurisation. Howe claimed that these films had a tremendous effect on the quality of the milk sold in markets: "With the people having this knowledge of sanitary dairies, diseased cows and pure milk, health departments were greatly assisted in their labours. The dairyman soon discovered that he could not so easily fool his customers, though he might evade the law".[54] Thus, motion pictures were the best way health departments could inform the public, and get people to change their behaviour.

The Department of Health of the City of New York held its own open-air moving picture shows; films were exhibited in regular theatres; films and lantern slides were provided free to schools and associations; films were occasionally scripted and produced. Most of these educational moving pictures were shown outside moving picture theatres, but close collaboration with the industry was vital. The majority of these films were produced by major production companies, often in collaboration with public welfare organisations and institutions. New York's Health Department collaborated with production companies such as Edison, Universal and Pathé, and the Motion Picture Exhibitors' Association of Greater New York. In particular, moving picture theatres were perhaps the most important venue for showing lantern slides announcing campaigns and publicising slogans. Picture houses were also used as venues for educational mass meetings. The motion picture was the most efficient way to inform the public of the vicissitudes of modern life, the latest inventions and improvements in science, as well as the most up-to-date measures in dealing with metropolitan everyday life. In short, film was positioned as a civic primer for how to navigate and negotiate a modern urban context.

Notes

1. Robert C. Allen, "Motion Picture Exhibition in Manhattan 1906–1912: Beyond the Nickelodeon", *Cinema Journal* 18, no. 2 (Spring 1979): 2–15; Ben Singer, "Manhattan Nickelodeons. New Data on Audiences and Exhibitors", *Cinema Journal* 34, no. 3, (Spring 1995): 5–35. For a first round of debate concerning related issues see: Robert Sklar and Charles Musser (eds), *Resisting Images: Essays on Cinema and History* (Philadelphia: Temple University Press, 1990).

2. See for example Melvyn Stokes and Richard Maltby (eds), *American Movie Audiences: From the Turn of the Century to the Early Sound Era* (London: BFI Publishing, 1999); see also Kathy Peiss, *Cheap Amusements: Working Women and Leisure in Turn-of-the-Century New York* (Philadelphia: Temple University Press, 1986); Judith Thissen, "The Emergence of Cinema in Jewish New York; How the Movies Came to Rivington Street" in Corinna Müller and Harro Segerberg (eds), *Kinoöffentlichkeit (1895–1920): Cinema's Pubic Sphere 1895–1920* (Marburg: Schüren Verlag, 2008), 196–209, and Giorgio Bertellini, "Shipwrecked Spectators: Italy's Immigrants at the Movies in New York, 1906–1916", *The Velvet Light Trap no.* 44, (Fall 1999) 309–353.

3. For a discussion on motion pictures during the progressive era see: Kevin Brownlow, *Behind the Mask of Innocence: Sex, Violence, Prejudice, Crime: Films of Social Conscience in the Silent Era* (New York: Knopf, 1990) and Eileen Bowser, *The Transformation of Cinema, 1907–1915* (Berkeley: University of California Press, 1994).

4. Lee Grieveson, *Policing Cinema, Policing Cinema: Movies and Censorship in Early-Twentieth-Century America* (Berkeley: University of California Press, 2004); Charles Musser, *The Emergence of Cinema: The American Screen to 1907* (Berkeley & Los Angeles: University of California Press, 1994)

5. Robert T. Eberwein, *Sex Ed: Film, Video, and the Framework of Desire* (New Brunswick, N.J.: Rutgers University Press, 1999); Martin Pernick, *The Black Stork: Eugenics and the Death of "Defective" Babies in American Medicine and Motion Pictures Since 1915* (New York: Oxford University Press, 1996), and Pernick, "More than Illustrations: Early Twentieth-Century Health Films as Contributors to the Histories of Medicine and of Motion Pictures"; Leslie Reagan, Nancy Tomes and Paula Treichler (eds), *Medicine's Moving Pictures: Medicine, Health, and Bodies in American Film and Television*, (Rochester, NY: University of Rochester Press, 2007), 19–35.

6. Brownlow, *Behind the Mask of Innocence*, 266.

7. For a discussion on the progressive era in the United States, see Maureen A. Flanagan, *America Reformed: Progressives and Progressivisms, 1890s–1920s* (New York: Oxford University Press, 2007) and Lewis L. Gould, *America in the Progressive Era, 1890–1914* (New York: Longman, 2001).

8. W.W. Bauer, Sylvia B. Martin, and Audrey McKeever, "The Bureau of Health Education", in

Morris Fishbein (ed.), *A History of the American Medical Association 1847 to 1947* (Philadelphia & London: W.B. Saunders Company, 1947), 996–1009.
9. Bauer et al., "Bureau of Health Education", 997.
10. For a chronology of the department see, Arthur Bushel, *Chronology of New York City Department of Health and its predecessor agencies, 1655–1966* (New York: The Department of Health, 1966).
11. About the national fly campaigns see Marina Dahlquist "'Swat the Fly.' Educational Films and Health Campaigns 1909–1914", in Corinna Müller and Harro Segerberg (eds), *Kinoöffentlichkeit (1895–1920): Cinema's Pubic Sphere (1895–1920)* (Marburg: Schüren Verlag, 2008), 211–225.
12. "Publications", *Annual Report of the Department of Health of the City of New York 1915* (New York: The Department of Health, 1916), 109.
13. Arthur Bushel, *Chronology of New York City Department of Health*, 9.
14. "Public Exhibitions on Prevention of Tuberculosis", *Monthly Bulletin of the Department of Health of the City of New York* 1, no. 7 (July 1911), 168–169.
15. "Work During the Year 1914", *Annual Report of the Department of Health of the City of New York 1914* (New York: The Department of Health, 1915), 35.
16. Bowser, *Transformation of Cinema*, 38.
17. Daniel D. Jackson", The Transmission of Disease by Flies", *The House-Fly at the Bar* (New York: Commerce and Industry Association of New York, 1909), 31.
18. "Infants' Milk Stations", *Monthly Bulletin of the Department of Health of the City of New York* 3, no. 12 (December 1913), 248.
19. *Annual Report of the Department of Health of the City of New York 1916* (New York: The Department of Health, 1917), 49.
20. Jacob Sobel, "Social Service Work in Connection with the Infants' Milk Stations", *Monthly Bulletin of the Department of Health of the City of New York* 4, no. 1 (January 1916), 9.
21. Sobel, "Social Service Work", 10.
22. There were complaints about the department's "parental attitude" and their interference with the legitimate practice of medicine that possibly could lead to loss of practice for the private physician. Jacob Sobel, "The Relation of the Baby Health Stations of the Department of Health to the Private Physician", *Monthly Bulletin of the Department of Health of the City of New York* 8, no. 4 (April 1918), 74.
23. "Child Hygiene", *Annual Report of the Department of Health of the City of New York 1908* (New York: The Department of Health, 1909), 329.
24. *Moving Picture World* 9, no. 8 (2 September 1911), 629.
25. Ernest A. Dench, *Motion Picture Education* (Cincinnati: The Standard Publishing Company, 1917), 181.
26. For example, see *Monthly Bulletin of the Department of Health of the City of New York* 2, no. 3 (March 1912), 68–73.
27. "Movies Teach Health Work", *Weekly Bulletin of the Department of Health. City of New York* 3, no. 19 (16 May, 1914), 153: Florence Margolies, "Promoting Public Health", *Moving Picture World* 22, no. 10 (5 December 1914), 1359.
28. Dench, *Motion Picture Education*, 192–193: "Health in Moving Pictures", *New York Times* (21 June 1912): 10.
29. "Films Will Show How to Fight Tuberculosis", *Moving Picture News* 7, no. 26, (28 June 1913), 31.
30. "For Free Moving Pictures", *New York Evening Post* (23 June 1914), 4.
31. "Films Will Show How to Fight Tuberculosis", 10.
32. "Moving Picture for Health", *New York Evening Post* (20 June 1912), 4. For a schedule of the screenings in July, see "Picture Campaign for Health", *New York Evening Post* (28 June 1912), 16.
33. Dench, *Motion Picture Education*, 193: Margolies, "Promoting Public Health", 1359; *Annual Report of the Department of Health of the City of New York 1916*, 58; "Free Movies have begun", *Weekly Bulletin of the Department of Health, City of New York* 3, no. 26 (4 July 1914), 213–214.

34. "Moving Picture Activities", *Annual Report of the Department of Health of the City of New York 1914*, 96.
35. Dench, *Motion Picture Education*, 196. For a description of how a Clean-Up campaign was organized in the city of New Britain, Connecticut, where eighty per cent of the population were foreign born see, Herbert A. Jump, "A Municipal Spring House-Cleaning", *Independent* (27 April 1911), 884–888.
36. "Bureau of Public Health Education", *Annual Report of the Department of Health of the City of New York 1916*, 83–84.
37. "Baby Week", *Weekly Bulletin of the Department of Health, City of New York* 3, no. 24 (20 June 1914), 193. Moving pictures became one of the most important ways of reaching a large number of people. However, repeatedly searching for new ways to promote public health one can read a very enthusiastic announcement in the Health Department's Weekly Bulletin in the spring of 1914 about an upcoming cooperation with life insurance companies. Accordingly the agents of the Metropolitan Life Insurance Company and the Prudential Life Insurance Company could reach the homes of 750,000 families weekly with public health literature which would by far be more effective than press bulletins, lectures, exhibitions and even moving pictures. "Educating 750,000 Families in Public Health", *Weekly Bulletin of the Department of Health, City of New York* 3, no.16 (25 April 1914), 121.
38. "Baby Week", *Annual Report of the Department of Health of the City of New York 1914*, 82–83; "Stimulating Others to Emulate", *Weekly Bulletin of the Department of Health, City of New York* 3, no. 28 (18 July 1914), 229–230.
39. "Stimulating Others", 229.
40. "Bureau of Public Health Education", *Annual Report of the Department of Health of the City of New York 1916*, 58 and 84.
41. Brownlow, *Behind the Mask of Innocence*, 271. For the use of healthmobiles showing moving pictures see for example: S.R. Winters, "The Picture of Health", *The Independent* (5 February 1917), 5; "Healthmobile Begins Work for Mother and Children", *Atlanta Constitution* (16 July 1922), C4; "Statewide Tours by Healthmobile", *New York Times* (19 September 1920), E13.
42. "Exhibits", *Annual Report of the Department of Health of the City of New York for the Calender Year 1919* (New York: The Department of Health, 1920), 236.
43. "A New Bureau of Public Health Education", *Weekly Bulletin of the Department of Health, City of New York* 3, no. 22 (6 June 1914), 179.
44. "Moving Picture Activities", *Weekly Bulletin of the Department of Health, City of New York* 4, no. 6 (6 February 1915), 50. Margolies, "Promoting Public Health", 1359.
45. "Publications", *Weekly Bulletin of the Department of Health, City of New York* 4, no. 6 (6 February 1915), 49.
46. "Baby Week", *Weekly Bulletin of the Department of Health, City of New York* 3, no. 24 (20 June 1914), 193; "To Head Health Teachers", *New York Times* (29 May 1914), 11.
47. "Moving Picture Activities", *Annual Report of the Department of Health of the City of New York 1915*, 110.
48. "Bureau of Child Hygiene", *Annual Report of the Department of Health of the City of New York 1916*, 49.
49. Public Health Commission of New York State, *Report of Special Public Health Commission to Governor William Sulzer Transmitted to the Legislature February 19, 1913* (Albany: J.B. Lyon Co. 1913), 14–16.
50. "Reduction of Infant Mortality", in *Annual Report of the Department of Health of the City of New York 1914*, 80.
51. This was especially noticed when it came to registered cases of tuberculosis. See "Division of Tuberculosis", in *Annual Report of the Department of Health of the City of New York 1917* (New York: The Department of Health, 1918), 29.
52. Williard Howe, "Sanitation and the Motion Picture", *Photoplay Magazine* (January 1913): 91–92.
53. Ibid., 91.
54. Ibid.

John Collier, Thomas Edison and the Educational Promotion of Moving Pictures

Amanda R. Keeler

By the early 1910s, the debates over using moving pictures for education coalesced into a seemingly influential discursive presence in the United States.[1] Film was still a relatively new technology in the early twentieth century and accordingly, experimentation with the medium continued to explore uses beyond theatrical screenings. The promotion of moving pictures for educational purposes grew out of several concerns, including the popularity and influence of moving pictures, the subject matter they covered and the spaces in which they were shown.[2] By 1910, several individuals and businesses attempted to expand film screenings to nontheatrical spaces and produce moving pictures for use in classrooms.

The rhetoric touting the use of films in education found its way into general interest magazines, newspapers, books and moving picture trade journals. Four men were at the centre of this first wave of the promotion of film for education: Charles Urban, George Kleine, Thomas Edison and John Collier. In this short essay I will focus briefly on two of these men, Thomas Edison and John Collier. Urban and Kleine's careers, though integral to the larger discussion around this historical exploration, have been examined in detail in other places. Edison has been written about extensively as well, though from the perspective of the inventions that emerged from his laboratory. To understand Edison's promotion of film for educational purposes, I will discuss several articles published in general interest magazines and film trade journals that featured his philosophy around moving pictures and education. Next, I will examine John Collier, whose work promoting the educational power of moving pictures was detailed in a number of articles he wrote beginning in 1908. Though both Edison and Collier encouraged the educational use of moving pictures, each had his own contrasting ideas about whom these films should educate, and where they should be utilised. Moreover, they also represent two disparate perspectives: Edison, working within the industry, privileged business interests; Collier from outside the industry, operated with a reform agenda in mind.

One should not be surprised that Thomas Edison, the master of self-promotion, was featured so heavily in general interest magazine articles touting the educational future of the moving picture. Up to this time, Edison had been widely celebrated for his pioneering work on electricity, phonographs and moving picture cameras and projectors. His notoriety from these previous endeavours may have propelled the discussion of educational film further into the national consciousness. In the 1910s Edison unveiled his Home Kinetoscope with an accompanying catalogue of moving pictures designed for "Education and Entertainment at home, in schools, Sunday-schools, clubs, lodges, etc".[3] To promote the projector and catalogue, Edison agreed to be interviewed in a number of magazines, as well as appearing frequently in the film industry trade journal discourse. Magazines like *The Survey* and *Harper's Weekly* detailed Edison's ideas about the endless possibilities for moving pictures in schools. Featuring Edison allowed these articles to equate the abstract concept of moving pictures for education with a highly respected name in the film industry.

Edison's basic principle behind his promotion of moving pictures for educational use was simple: he felt that they would make school more attractive for students. For example, in a 1911 interview with Edison, William Inglis wrote that Edison's latest development was "going to make school so attractive that a big army with swords and guns couldn't keep boys and girls out of it".[4] Edison told Inglis that his plan to keep children interested in schools was "education by moving picture. Teach the children everything from mathematics to morality, by little dramas acted out before the camera, and reproduced in the schoolroom at very low cost. Sort o' swing the education in on them so attractively that they'll *want* to go to school".[5] To convince readers and educators that making school more fun would in turn help students learn better, Edison emphasised that if teachers used moving pictures in the classroom it might help prevent young people from skipping school.

Making school more attractive to students was just one step in Edison's plan to revolutionise learning in the classroom. Edison also claimed that moving pictures would bring subjects to life and help keep children focused on classroom subjects. In the July 1911 issue of *Moving Picture World*, Edison stated that "above all else, the fact must not be lost sight of that for educational purposes the moving picture possesses the tremendous advantage of not only giving the more correct and vivid idea of a subject than can possibly be obtained in books, but it places the knowledge before the child in an attractive and entertaining way ... I shall not be surprised to see the school children of the future clustered on the steps waiting for the door to open".[6] This assessment of films pointed to the way that moving images unleashed the potential vividness of school lessons. The benefit of using moving pictures to bring subjects to life for learning purposes would, according to Edison, additionally keep students focused on the subject matter, which would facilitate the learning process. Winthrop Lane agreed with Edison's proclamations about the powers of moving pictures for education. Lane attested that moving pictures "will teach the elementary branches throughout the eight years of the public school; staging the laws of physics and giving line and form to the processes of chemistry; teaching arithmetic by pictures and letting grammar in through the eye".[7] By "letting" subjects in "through the eye", Lane and Edison suggested that the visual learning achieved through moving pictures had a more direct link to knowledge acquisition than other methods.

Another advantage Edison saw in moving pictures in schools was illustrated in the article "Edison's Substitute for Schoolbooks". In it Edison invoked a nameless son, a twelve-year old boy who hated school.[8] Edison proclaimed that "while schoolbooks are made for children, children were never made for schoolbooks. If this were not true, schools would be the universal delight that they really should be".[9] He used this point repeatedly to help persuade readers that moving pictures accomplished something that textbooks never could: they brought images to life before the eyes of curious school children. Edison told Mary Master Needham for the *Saturday Evening Post* that "I intend to do away with books in the school, that is, I mean to try to do away with schoolbooks

... How? By Moving pictures ... Well, this will certainly change education – will it not?" Needham replied, "Change education? It will revolutionize education!"[10] Edison also opined that watching moving pictures was "always a thousand times as powerful as the effect of a thing described".[11] This notion was a radical retooling of school through the elimination of textbooks, which Edison felt were no longer an ideal teaching tool. Though he clamoured for the elimination of textbooks, his rhetoric here may have been polemical, attempting to convince the reader to rethink his ideas about classroom technology rather than proposing a complete overhaul of existing procedures.

In September 1913 *The Survey* published a piece titled "Edison vs. Euclid, Has He Invented a Moving Stairway to Learning?" The fourteen-page collection consisted of several smaller articles by notable people and institutions, such as Leonard Ayres from the Russell Sage Foundation and John Dewey from the Department of Philosophy at Columbia University. This article again spends several pages touting Edison's feelings on the vast educational potential of moving pictures. It also featured discussions by men and women that Edison invited to his laboratory to check out his latest invention. However, alongside the usual hyperbolic insistence on the educational power of moving pictures from the articles discussed above, the article featured the opinions of several of his guests, who did not necessarily agree that "pictorial education" was "revolutionary" and did not reach consensus as to the usefulness and viability of moving pictures in the classroom.[12] In line with Edison, Henry W. Thurston, of the New York School of Philanthropy, wrote that he was "greatly impressed by the educational possibilities of the motion picture".[13] R. R. Reeder, Superintendent of the New York Orphan Asylum, saw the potential in using moving pictures to "reduce truancy...and hold in school those hundreds of thousands who every year drop out on account of lack of interest in study and a desire to go to work".[14] Leonard P. Ayres claimed that "the new motion pictures are an educational tool of great potential value".[15] Marietta L. Johnson, of the School of Organic Education, observed that "Mr. Edison has found a way ... in which children may acquire education without the stress and strain that endangers the nervous system".[16]

Other visitors, however, were less hopeful about Edison's educational experiment. Henry H. Goddard, of the Vineland Training School, feared that "lazy teachers" might utilise moving pictures in the classroom to avoid having to labour over lesson plans, and that manufacturers might produce "unwise" films not well suited for pedagogy.[17] John Dewey expressed worry about the passivity of students watching activities rather than participating in them. He suspected that the "widespread adoption of motion pictures in schools might have a tendency to retard the introduction of occupations in which children themselves actually do things".[18] Since Dewey's educational philosophies privileged experiential and interactive learning processes, the passive viewing of moving pictures was not necessarily in accord with the way he wanted classroom education to occur.

Overall, the men and women who participated in the visit to Edison's laboratory to view his moving picture experiment were impressed by what they saw and agreed with its potential for the classroom. While some had concerns and reservations, most found the possibilities of films in the classroom to be a welcome addition to existing teaching methods, rather than operating as a replacement of the teacher or some other radical pedagogical intervention. Nonetheless, the inclusion of counterpoints in this article ran counter to the earlier interviews with Edison, which had highlighted only the positive attributes of moving picture education; opposition to his plans suggested that his name alone was not enough to convince all the visitors.

Overall, Edison's vision of using film for educational purposes was targeted towards young boys, to keep them interested in attending school. In terms of subject areas to cover, he suggested that there was potential in the classroom for moving pictures to demonstrate scientific experiments and principles, for teaching mathematics, geography and history. He employed hyperbole to show the vaunted superiority of moving pictures as a teaching tool. Edison frequently noted the dull, rote nature of book-based learning and contrasted it to the living, moving example of moving pictures. In the articles discussed here Edison attempted to convince the public that moving pictures brought life, the world, excitement and entertainment to the classroom, experiential qualities that a mere teacher could not provide. But the question of what exactly students were supposed to learn from moving pictures remained: Historical facts? Scientific principles? The lessons for students may have been more exciting via moving pictures, but nonetheless Edison's promised drastic improvement over textbooks remained unclear.

The promotion of film for education retained prominence in these articles, and it was sometimes easy to forget that they were written in support of Edison's new, low cost, portable projector. Many of the writers found ways to mention the projector, claiming that it was not just that Edison was now promoting the educational use of moving pictures, but that he had successfully created the projector and the associated films to bring pictorial education to classrooms everywhere. William Inglis wrote that Edison put the Home Kinetoscope "within the reach of every school in the country" and that Edison's company had many films available for rent "for eight dollars a week".[19] E.B. Lockwood proclaimed that "the Edison Company has recently perfected a small moving picture machine and film which will do a great deal in making moving pictures one of the great mediums of education".[20] Allen Benson remarked that "Edison has made the machines safe by inventing a non-inflammable film".[21] Henry Lanier wrote that Edison made "films that his great company can market successfully".[22]

Edison's claims about the superiority of visual learning raise suspicions because of their connection to the marketing of his new Kinetoscope projector. At face value, Edison's rhetoric seems insistent on the possibilities for real educational reform and progress if moving pictures were to be employed in the classroom. At the same time, this promotion of moving pictures for schools hints at the vast, untapped market of nontheatrical sites that Edison and others like him might exploit if they were able to convince the thousands of schools in the United States that films and projectors were a worthwhile investment. Though his business interests seem at the forefront of his educational promotion of moving pictures, similar discourse was occurring in many other magazines, from a number of other writers and supporters who saw the benefit of moving pictures in classrooms. Edison created a vibrant dialogue through his interviews, which may have helped to propel the discussion further.

Edison's discourse on the educational uses of film was in line with that of many other people from the time, like John Collier, who saw the moving pictures as possessing great power to influence and educate the populace, though film needed to be properly harnessed so that this education was helpful rather than hurtful towards society. Collier was not a businessman like Edison, and therefore approached moving pictures and education from a different angle. He was, however, just as excited and hopeful that film could be used to help educate people. Collier formed his ideas on the educational uses of moving pictures beginning in 1907, when he joined the People's Institute, a progressive neighbourhood organisation. There he served first as Civic Secretary and Editor of the People's Institute weekly newspaper, *The Civic Journal*, and later as the Secretary of the Recreation Department. With the People's Institute, Collier also served

13 John Collier, Thomas Edison and the Educational Promotion of Moving Pictures

on the National Board of Censorship through 1914. At the People's Institute he pursued a diverse reform agenda that focused primarily on moving pictures, theatre reform and regulation, appropriate family leisure, and education.[23] His career promoting the positive aspects of moving pictures paralleled much of the discourse that Edison had advanced, though the two men saw the educational benefit of moving pictures quite differently.

John Collier's tenure at the People's Institute was notable for the programs and studies in which he participated, beginning with an investigation into New York City's "cheap amusements", looking at nickelodeons, arcades and other popular amusement venues. Collier's investigation led to the 31 January, 1908 report, "Cheap Amusements Shows in Manhattan: Preliminary Report of Investigation". Collier wrote that "each day, and night after night, I visited, again and again, the more than 250 film houses in the city, studying their shows".[24] While Collier specifically took umbrage with the conditions of the moving picture theatres, he was able to separate his problems with them from his opinion of the films themselves, which he felt had tremendous educational potential. He opined that the moving pictures possessed a "constructive influence, meeting a genuine need in the people".[25] Collier wrote that the films might prove to be an "important opportunity for schools, settlements, churches, and educators generally", if and when they might be utilised outside of existing theatres, or when theatres were properly cleaned and ventilated.[26]

The "cheap amusements" investigation led to multiple articles and public appearances where Collier reported his findings. For example, he detailed his report in an article in *Charities and the Commons*, where he proclaimed that the "cheap amusement problem" of low-class activities like "cheap vaudeville" and "burlesque" could be remedied with more wholesome leisure activities.[27] For one, he observed that "the nickelodeon's the thing", meaning it was an acceptable place for leisure that offered "history, travel, [and] the reproduction of industries".[28] Collier was aware that movies allowed working-class New Yorkers to spend leisure time with their families at a very low cost. He reasoned that "all the settlements and churches combined do not reach daily the tithe of the simple and impressionable folk that the nickelodeons reach and vitally impress every day".[29] Collier described the moving picture theatre as "a true theatre of the people ... an instrument whose power can only be realised when social workers begin to use it".[30] Collier counted himself among these qualified social workers, and would spend the next several years promoting his educational vision.

Collier served for several years on the National Board of Censorship, a self-regulatory group that was described as being "made up of representatives from several civic bodies and certain individuals, none of whom were financially interested in motion pictures".[31] Collier wrote in 1909 for *Moving Picture World* that "the National Board of Censorship has been organised for the improvement of motion pictures and for their further extension in this country as social and educational forces. Its work consists of censoring moving pictures and dealing constructively with the social, civic and educational problems connected therewith ... The Board also sees in the moving picture an agent which can educate ... capable of use in direct pedagogical ways".[32] Cinema historian Lee Grieveson writes that "censorship was never the sole aim of the National Board of Censorship, though, for it sought also to promote an educative cultural function for cinema".[33] To this end, Collier wrote that "the prevailing view at the People's Institute, among its Board of Censorship, and at that time among the exhibitors and producers at large, was that the cinema was 'the people's theater,' and held great potential for education and for life".[34] Notable in these statements Collier made is the reference to education, for, in his opinion, the Board had a dual responsibility, not only to persuade manufacturers to continue working towards a "better program", but also to convince the public of the educational potential of moving pictures, a goal Collier pursued vigorously.[35] As Graham Taylor wrote in 1909, "Mr. Collier predicted that in the very near future motion pictures will be used in schools and playgrounds for both their educational and recreational value".[36]

In order to entice schools to show moving pictures, both during the day and evening, Collier reported that "the People's Institute plans to establish one or more 'model' moving picture theatres, which will be run on a cooperative basis. They will give emphasis to the educational side of moving pictures, and will dramatize subjects like tuberculosis, the Consumer's League plea, [and] the distribution of immigration".[37] The experiment he described was affiliated with a local school in New York, where the Institute investigated the use of commercial amusements, among them motion pictures, "within the educational atmosphere of the school".[38] The hope was that this initiative would help transform the school into a "family gathering place", where appropriate leisure could be emphasised, like "motion pictures ... folk dance ... civic clubs ... [and] public meetings".[39] Collier noted that "motion pictures are an adjunct of teaching along a great many lines, including biology, history, geography, literature, social science…the motion picture appeals to the whole family".[40] He concluded that "the social and political possibilities of this idea are too evident to require statement".[41] This experiment eventually brought New York educators, People's Institute founder Charles Sprague Smith and the Board of Education to the school to observe a "model moving picture show" showcased by the Board.[42] The group watched a number of films deemed to be educational, including *The Life of Washington*, *A Lesson in Chemistry*, and *East Indian Temples*.[43] *Moving Picture World* reported that the "notable gentlemen", Dr Maxwell, "recently witnessed an exhibition of moving pictures by Mr. Charles Sprague Smith and was very favourably impressed with the idea of using them to help educate the children".[44]

In May 1912, under the leadership of the People's Institute's new managing director, Frederick C. Howe, Collier wrote a summary of the Institute's good works to date for *The Independent*. He reiterated the work that the People's Institute has done "to transform the motion picture theater into an educational agenda".[45] Collier suggested that the work done by the National Board of Censorship had contributed greatly to the increased quality of moving pictures in the previous several years. He claimed that "motion pictures have been transformed into perhaps the cleanest and most educational form of public amusement at this time available in America, and a remarkable impetus has been given to the production of strictly educational films".[46]

Collier's vision of educational film aligned to a degree with that expressed by Thomas Edison. He predicted that "moving pictures will be used generally in the school room" in the near future.[47] There were, however, several ways in which Edison's and Collier's views of the educational function of moving pictures differed. Collier, like Edison, readily pointed out that he was interested in the educational uses of moving pictures, though unlike Edison, he was working outside the film industry, and did not have the same agenda to sell projectors and films. Collier and Edison agreed on the range of subjects that the moving picture might treat to aid the educational system. Unlike Edison, however, Collier felt that in addition to their classroom use for young boys, moving pictures "will be used also to afford evening entertainment for the parents and thus interest them in schoolwork".[48] According to Collier, whole families in New York City were looking for education and activities suitable for all ages. Collier writes that moving picture shows were an inexpensive and effective way "for filling the leisure time of the people with wholesome and educational activities".[49] This notion was radically different from Edison's vision of using moving pictures to placate and entertain restless little boys in school classrooms. Rather, Collier envisioned using moving pictures in multiple spaces to provide education, entertainment and leisure for children and their parents, bringing families together for their educational benefit.

Conclusion

After Collier resigned from the Board of Censorship in 1914, he continued to write about moving pictures and drama for *The Survey*. In 1915 he wrote ten articles as part of the series "The Lantern Bearers", which was billed as "a series of essays exploring some thoroughfares of the people's leisure".[50] *The Survey* remarked that Collier's articles would "offer the experience and state the philosophic positions of a writer who is at once a student of the drama, a practical censor and a seer of visions".[51] The series of articles, which formed the bulk of Collier's later statements on moving pictures and education, together contextualised his continued interest in the subject while also conceding that his vision for it had not yet been realised. Over the course of the series, Collier explained how he continued to see the educational merit in moving pictures. However, circumstances surrounding the moving picture industry were hindering the educational potential of moving pictures, particularly the growing implementation of state-sanctioned censorship, and the failure of film manufacturers to make adequately educational moving pictures for school use.

Likewise, Thomas Edison's experiments with the educational use of moving pictures failed to achieve the success of his earlier filmic endeavours. According to historian Ben Singer, Edison Home Kinetoscope was "an unqualified commercial disaster" because both the projector and its films were cost-prohibitive, and the projector had many design and performance flaws.[52] Edison was not someone who was accustomed to failure, though an event occurred soon after that meant that he did not have to address this business defeat. On 9 December 1914 there was a fire at his laboratory and factory that eventually shuttered his film equipment manufacturing business. Edison made no attempts to rebuild this aspect of his business. The closure of this arena of his business suggests that his educational initiatives had proved unprofitable and unsustainable.

This paper touches on the complexity of these two men's philosophies on the educational use of moving pictures, and how each defined their specific vision. Using Edison and Collier as case studies illustrates some of the parallel and contrasting ideas that permeated the discourse during the 1910s. Interestingly, while both Edison and Collier avidly promoted the educational aspects of moving pictures for a number of years, by the end of the decade both had essentially abandoned this pursuit.[53] Regardless, their discourse represents contrasting voices on the nontheatrical uses of moving pictures. It also helps to elucidate that this first wave of interest in using moving pictures for education was not monolithic, but offered disparate visions regarding how to promote and utilise nontheatrical moving pictures.

Notes

1. I use the phrase "moving pictures for educational purposes" because the period literature conflates many different types of films when speaking of film as educational, including what we now call science films, industrial films and instructional films. In this context "educational film" refers not just to the films themselves, but the spaces in which people hoped to use them, such as schools, churches, community spaces and moving picture theatres. "Educational moving pictures" were often theatrical films repurposed for nontheatrical use, and therefore not specifically produced for purely educational use.

2. Eileen Bowser, *The Transformation of Cinema: 1907–1915* (Berkeley: University of California Press, 1990), 37–52.
3. Thomas A. Edison, "Catalogue for Motion Picture Films for use on Edison Home Kinetoscope", 1913: front cover.
4. William Inglis, "Edison and the New Education", *Harper's Weekly* (4 November 1911): 8.
5. Inglis, "Edison and the New Education", 8.
6. Frank Parker Hulette, "An Interview with Thomas A. Edison", *Moving Picture World* (22 July 1911): 104–105.
7. Winthrop D. Lane, "Edison vs. Euclid: Has He Invented a Moving Stairway to Learning?", *The Survey* (6 September 1913): 681.
8. Edison had a son that would have been around this age, but I am unaware if he is speaking truthfully about his actual son.
9. Allen L. Benson, "Edison's Substitute for Schoolbooks", *World To-Day* (March 1912): 1925.
10. Mary Master Needham, "Going to School at the 'Movies': An Interview with Thomas A. Edison", *Saturday Evening Post* (30 November 1912): 16.
11. "Education by Films", *Motography* (August 1911): 57.
12. Lane, *"Edison vs. Euclid"*, 682.
13. Henry W. Thurston, "Dangers of Short Circuits", in Lane, *"Edison vs. Euclid"*, 692.
14. R.R. Reeder, "Words, Words, the Besetting Sin", in Lane, *"Edison vs. Euclid"*, 686.
15. Leonard P. Ayres, "Ladling Learning into Children", in Lane, *"Edison vs. Euclid"*, 687.
16. Marietta L. Johnson, "Insincere Work the Root of Evil", in Lane, *"Edison vs. Euclid"*, 689.
17. Henry H. Goddard, "Pedagogy Plus Science Needed", in Lane, *"Edison vs. Euclid"*, 688.
18. John Dewey, "Cut-and-Try School Methods", in Lane, *"Edison vs. Euclid"*, 691.
19. Inglis, "Edison and the New Education", 8.
20. E.B. Lockwood, "Motography as a Medium of Education", *Motography* (May 1912): 225.
21. Benson, "Edison's Substitute for Schoolbooks", 1927.
22. Henry W. Lanier, "The Educational Future of the Moving Picture", *The American Review of Reviews* (December 1914): 729.
23. Thomas M. Todd, "Love, Science and Social Justice: Voices and Conversations from the Urban Community Movement Before the Great War", diss., University of Minnesota, 1981, 287; Robert B. Fisher, "The People's Institute of New York City 1897–1934: Culture, Progressive Democracy and the People", diss., New York University, 1974, 290.
24. John Collier, *From Every Zenith: A Memoir and Some Essays on Life and Thought* (Denver: Sage Books, 1963); John Collier, "Cheap Amusement Shows in Manhattan", Subject Papers, Papers Relating to the Formation and Subsequent History of the National Board of Review of Motion Pictures, Box 170, New York Public Library, 31 January 1908.
25. Collier, "Cheap Amusement Shows in Manhattan", 3.
26. Ibid.
27. John Collier, "Cheap Amusements", *Charities and the Commons* (11 April 1908): 74.
28. Collier, "Cheap Amusements", 74.
29. Ibid., 75.
30. Ibid.
31. "National Censorship of Motion Pictures", *The Survey* (1 July 1911): 469.
32. "John Collier", *Moving Picture World* (16 October 1909): 524.
33. Lee Grieveson, *Policing Cinema: Movies and Censorship in Early-Twentieth Century America* (Berkeley: University of California Press, 2004), 101.
34. Collier, *From Every Zenith*, 71–72.
35. "Censorship for Moving Pictures", *The Survey* (3 April 1909): 9; Vachel Lindsay, *The Art of the Moving Picture* (New York: Liveright Publishing, 1970), 233.

36. Graham Romeyn Taylor, "City Neighbors at Play", *The Survey* (2 July 1910): 564.
37. John Collier, "The People's Institute", *The Independent* (30 May 1912): 1147.
38. Ibid.
39. Ibid.
40. John Collier, "Moving Pictures: Their Function and Proper Regulation", *Playground* (October 1910): 239.
41. Collier, "The People's Institute", 1147.
42. Fredrick Dunbar, "Scientific and Educational Films", *Nickelodeon* (15 April 1910): 200.
43. Ibid.
44. "Superintendent of New York Schools Favors the Picture", *Moving Picture World* (12 March 1910): 375–376.
45. Collier, "The People's Institute", 1146.
46. Ibid.
47. "Collier Advocates Moving Picture Instruction", *Nickelodeon* (11 March 1911): 282.
48. Ibid.
49. "Wants City to Run Movies and Dance Halls for Poor", *New York Times* (27 April 1913): SM7.
50. John Collier, "Back of Our Footlights: The Half-Forgotten Social Functions of the Drama", *The Survey* (5 June 1915): 213.
51. "Editorials", *The Survey* (5 June 1915): 229.
52. Ben Singer, "Early Home Cinema and the Edison Home Projecting Kinetoscope", *Film History* (1988): 56. See also Singer 56–63.
53. See Amanda R. Keeler, "Sugar Coat the Educational Pill: The Educational Aspirations of Film, Radio, and Television", diss., Indiana University, 2011. Chapters One and Two discuss the promotion of the educational uses of film during the 1910s.

"And They Can See Half-Naked Dancers, Catching Young Men In Their Nets": Teachers and the Cinema in Norway, 1907–1913

Gunnar Iversen

In April 1907, shortly after the opening of several permanent cinema theatres in the Norwegian city of Trondheim, the city's two newspapers both printed the same angry letter from Sven Svensen, vice principal of one of the city's schools. In the letter, Svensen attacked the newly established cinemas, the Kinografen theatre in particular, accusing them of showing "disgusting images".[1]

What triggered Svensen's attack was the release of a new film, *Den første nat efter brylluppet* (The First Night After the Wedding, 1907). Not only had the local police superintendent declared the film fit for all audiences, but he had also, according to Svensen, allowed the Kinografen's owner, Martin Carstens, to print the word "pikant" (piquant or spicy) in newspaper ads – a word signaling sexually explicit material, and obviously intended more as a lure than as a warning. Svensen was furious. He wrote: "What school and home laboriously have built, is systematically being broken down by speculators without conscience".[2] Svensen ended by calling for a protest by all thinking people, especially parents, against the city's theatres.[3] This short letter not only resulted in the banning of the film the very next day, but also marked the start of what would become a nationwide "crusade" against cinema.

During these years, elementary and high school teachers represented the single most influential group shaping public perceptions of cinema in Norway. In 1907, teachers' organisations began to debate the harmful effects of moviegoing on young people, as well as how movie theatres were changing the nation's cities. Letters from teachers were sent to newspapers, public meetings were arranged, committees formed, all complaining about cinema's harmful effect on learning and upbringing, and damning it for corrupting the younger generation. Local initiatives by school authorities and individual teachers, like Sven Svensen in Trondheim, were followed by attacks on a nationwide scale, resulting in the passage of the Film Theatres' Act by Parliament in 1913, establishing municipal control over movie theatres and a Central Board of Film Censors in Norway. Yet, although many teachers were hostile to the new medium, other more favorable voices were also raised. In the journals of teachers and educators, moving pictures were often celebrated as a perfect tool for education, and especially for providing mediated object lessons that would change teaching in the future and should be adopted as soon as possible.

This short essay will discuss the different attitudes voiced by teachers about cinema as a medium, as well as the relationship between teachers and motion picture exhibitors, with special emphasis on the small city of Trondheim in the middle of Norway.

The teachers' crusade against cinema

As Nils Klevjer Aas has shown, letters complaining about cinema's harmful effects on learning and upbringing began appearing in educational journals like the *Norsk Skoletidende* (Norwegian Educational Times) and *Norsk Skoleblad* (Norwegian Educational Journal) from 1905 onward[4]. During this period, most educators' criticisms centered on media *content*; and, indeed, it was this hostility to content that triggered the initial "crusade" against the cinemas. This crusade started in 1907, and the city of Trondheim was important.

In the city of Trondheim, the activities of vice principal Sven Svensen were crucial. By 1907, Svensen had completed several books on Norwegian grammar and, that year, published a small, well-reviewed book about Trondheim's history. So he was more than just a "pillar of society" and vice principal; he was also a well-known and familiar name outside of educational circles. Svensen was very active during the first year of his crusade, discussing the detrimental effects of cinema on children in newspapers and public meetings. During a meeting of the Folkeskolens Pædagogiske Forening (Primary School Society), for instance, Svensen talked about cinema's harmful effects and how it often drove children to steal.[5] He continued his attack in another meeting a couple of weeks later, this time arranged by the Kvindesagsforeningen (Women's Society), and then in April, in the aforementioned newspaper letter.[6] Finally, Svensen sent another letter in June, once again accusing cinema of driving young children to theft as well as attacking the industry's businessmen and entrepreneurs.[7]

These activities helped launch the wave of teachers' protests against cinema in Norway, although it was not until 1910 and 1911 that these local attacks escalated to the national level. This expansion of the debate followed resolutions from the Foreningen til Sædelighetens Fremme (The Society for the Promotion of Morality) and Norske Kvinders Nasjonalraad (The National Council of Norwegian Women), spurring nationwide discussions around censorship as well as the control and ownership of cinemas.[8]

During these later years public meetings were arranged in several Norwegian cities, where concerned citizens and, again, especially teachers complained about motion pictures.[9] In Stavanger, Bergen, and Trondheim these meetings resulted in initiatives from the cities' Lærerlag (Teachers' Societies), while, in Trondheim, vice principal Svensen continued to advocate censorship and municipal control over motion picture theatres. A letter from a concerned citizen in one of the city's newspapers in February 1911 led to a public meeting at one of the schools, where Svensen harped once again on his favorite themes – the immoral content of most films, how moviegoing led to theft, and the need for a local censor board.[10] His speech was later printed in the journal *Norsk Skoletidende* (Norwegian Educational Times) and reached many teachers in Norway, not just those who attended the meeting.[11]

The Trondheim meeting in fact led to a heated discussion in the newspaper *Dagsposten*. In a series of letters, cinema owner P. Skytte countered Svensen's attack, pointing out that Svensen had never visited his cinema, and could not know much about what was shown and the number of children attending. In the first of these, Skytte wrote that the number of children was lower in 1911 than it had been in 1907. He also countered the claim that moving pictures caused delinquency, writing that films easily could have the effect of *preventing* crime, by showing its consequences. Finally, he referred to the recent aesthetic and technological progress of film art: back in 1907, it had been the French and Danish sensational melodramas that Svensen had singled out for attack; but Skytte pointed to the new American films, and especially those from Vitagraph and Biograph, as constituting a more "natural", "true", and "realistic" film art.[12] Skytte also reacted negatively to Svensen's proposal for a local censor board. After another long letter from Svensen, repeating his attack, Skytte again countered by pointing to the moral values articulated *within* films, through established narrative conventions and especially "moral" endings: "Evil will always be punished, good prevails", he wrote.[13]

These discussions, along with Svensen's broader criticisms of motion picture theatres and the films they showed, did not result in a functioning local censor board. In Trondheim, by 1911, the police superintendent already regulated all aspects of the cinema: moving pictures could be cut or banned by the local police, after consultations with police superintendents in other cities; cinema buildings were controlled for safety; and the number and locations of the cinemas were also regulated (indeed, no cinemas were allowed in the eastern part of the city, because of their potential proximity to working-class residential areas).[14] However, the crusade did result in a special Film Act in Norway in 1913, establishing a Central Board of Film Censors in the capital Christiania (Oslo) and municipal control over cinemas. After 1918, all cinemas in Trondheim were run by the municipality, with no private cinemas allowed to operate.

The cinema as educational tool

Despite most teachers' hostility toward cinema, exhibitors and itinerant showmen had from quite early on arranged special shows for children, often highlighting the educational value of actualities from Norway. In Trondheim, for instance, Paul Kräusslich organised a special children's show as early as December 1904 – a year before the first permanent cinema was established – and in the newspaper described the actualities, displaying scenes from the northernmost part of Norway, as "a whole small course in the geography of northern Norway".[15] By 1907, Kräusslich was Trondheim's leading exhibitor in organising screenings of educational films, and continued to promote their particular value for children.

Nor was it only exhibitors who discussed cinema as an educational tool. Before 1910, the educational journal *Vor Ungdom* (Our Youth) had shared in the general attitude of indignation at motion pictures, making frequent reference to German and American analytical studies about moviegoing's harmful effects.[16] Subsequently, however, the journal began publishing more positive notes about cinema as an educational tool, pointing to the fact that the medium could offer didactic object lessons of great value. An article in 1910 referred to an American study from a teacher's college in Cleveland by one Dr. Wallin, illustrating the harmful effects of cinema on young women.[17] But, in spite of the study, the Norwegian author ended the article by praising cinema's possibilities: "The nineteenth century gave the school the laboratory, the twentieth century has offered the school living pictures. The importance of these for engaging lessons can hardly be overestimated, but the school has not yet managed to incorporate living pictures into its lessons".[18] The writer continued by mapping out the ways in which schools could use motion pictures, especially for classes in geography, history and the natural sciences. Two approaches seemed possible. First, specific cinema theatres for school children could be founded, or special shows arranged at commercial cinemas once or twice a week. Second, central school authorities could establish a system of itinerant projectionists, who would travel from school to school showing educational films. These suggestions were later followed by the launching of several school cinema projects along the lines of the second alternative, especially in the capital Christiania in the late 1910s and early 1920s.[19]

Similar discussions about cinema as education formed an important part of the mass meetings and newspaper discussions of 1911. Even vice principal Svensen, in a meeting in March of that year, allowed for possibilities in cinema shows accompanied by lectures; and, in the discussion after Svensen's address, one school director – identified in press reports simply as Mr. Aas – said that cinema would most certainly "offer valuable things" in the future. Aas concluded by suggesting a special cinema for children.[20]

These ideas about the functions and effects of the new medium – the ways theatres could be used as educational sites as well as how films shown in schools could offer advantages in learning – persisted through the 1910s. In a 1918 article in the educational journal *Norsk Pædagogisk Tidskrift* (Norwegian Pedagogical Journal), a writer characterised the motion picture theatre as "a school where one learns spiritual laziness and indifference", but, like other teachers, ultimately ended by praising the possibilities of educational film shows accompanied by lectures.[21]

Teachers and film in Norway between 1907 and 1913

These interactions between the discourses of teachers, cinema owners, and regulatory authorities had lasting effects on the way the Norwegian cinema was perceived and organised. Anxieties about individual films, where one could see, as one school teacher wrote, "half-naked dancers, catching young men in their nets", as well as a more general concern about the moral dangers of cinema, were coupled with discourses about the potential of cinema as an institution to strengthen the pedagogy of Norwegian schools.

Many Norwegian teachers early on saw the educative potential of cinema, and attempts to regulate the medium most often came with an impulse to reposition it as something other than mere entertainment. Concerns about the child audience, as well as with imitative responses from "suggestive" audiences, triggered intense anxieties about socialisation and citizenship. The elite response of teachers to modernity, and to the cinema in particular as a problematic site of new ideologies about sexuality and morality, is familiar, for example, from the United States in the same period; and, like their Norwegian counterparts, American teachers also were interested in the unique potential of film as an educational tool.[22] Amongst Norwegian educators, however, these discourses around the need to manage the new mass entertainment form were further linked to the question of private enterprise versus municipal ownership of cinemas. It was not only the question of cinema's educational possibilities that was debated, but also of who would be permitted to own and manage movie theatres.

And in their battle against the new medium, the teachers were to some extent victorious. The municipalities took over the control of the cinemas, a central board of film censors was established, and film was frequently used in schools as an educational tool.[23]

Notes

1. Sven Svensen, "Hvor længe skal det taales?" *Adresseavisa* (5 April 1907), and *Dagsposten* (5 April 1907).
2. Ibid.
3. About local police censorship in Norway before 1913, see Gunnar Iversen, "Cutting Bordello Scenes and Dances: Local Regulation and Film Censorship in Norway before 1913", *Film History* 17, no. 1 (2005): 106–112.

4. Nils Klevjer Aas, "Municipal Cinemas, 1910–1925: Building a Unique Exhibition", *Levende Bilder* 1 (1994): 56–57.
5. "Fristelser for børnene", *Adresseavisen* (1 March 1907).
6. "Skoleinspektør Svensen", *Adresseavisen* (18 March 1907).
7. Sven Svensen, "Forretningsfolk og Børn", *Adresseavisen* (3 June 1907).
8. Aas, "Municipal Cinemas", 56–57.
9. Jan Anders Diesen, *Eit hugtakande læremiddel? Undervisningsfilmen i norsk skole* (Trondheim: Institutt for Drama, Film og Teater, 1995), 39–50; Bjørn S. Utne, *Kunst og kasse: Stavanger Kinematografer 75 år* (Stavanger: Stavanger Kinematografer, 1995), 25–34; Sigurd Evensmo, *Det store tivoli*, (Oslo: Gyldendal, 1967), 53–71; and Aas, "Municipal Cinemas", 56–57.
10. "Kinematograferne. Til overveielse", *Dagsposten* (19 February 1911); "Kinematograferne. Massemødet igaar", *Dagsposten* (25 February 1911).
11. Diesen 1995, 49.
12. P. Skytte, "Kinematograferne", *Dagsposten* (28 February 1911).
13. P. Skytte, "Hr. Skoleinspektør Sven Svensen", *Dagsposten* (8 March 1911). This was the answer to Sven Svensen's "Barn og kinematografer", *Dagsposten* (4 March 1911).
14. Iversen, "Cutting Bordello Scenes and Dances", 106–112
15. "Det vil bli et helt lidet Kursus i det nordlige Norges Geografi", *Dagsposten* (9 December 1904).
16. Diesen 1995, 34–35.
17. This was likely the psychologist J. E. Wallace Wallin, and the study referred to probably "The Moving Picture in Relation to Education, Health, Delinquency and Crime", *Pedagogical Seminary* 17, no. 2 (June 1910). See Lee Grieveson, *Policing Cinema: Movies and Censorship in Early-Twentieth-Century Cinema* (Berkeley: University of California Press, 2004), 12 and 223.
18. Georg Bruun, "Biografteatrene", *Vor Ungdom* (1910), 312.
19. Diesen 1995; Per Kviberg et al., *Innførelse av filmundervisning ved skolene i Oslo* (Oslo: Innstilling fra Oslo skolestyres filmkomité, 1927).
20. "Kinematograferne. Massemødet igaar", *Dagsposten* (25 February 1911).
21. Søren Nordeide, "Kinematografane og upplysningsarbeidet", *Norsk Pædagogisk Tidskrift*, vol. 2, 83–89.
22. See Grieveson 2004.
23. Gunnar Iversen, "The Norwegian Municipal Cinema System and the Development of a National Cinema", in Richard Abel, Giorgio Bertellini, and Rob King (eds), *Early Cinema and the "National"* (London: John Libbey Publishing, 2008), 195–198.

15

Documentaries, Family Film Nights and the First Film University: The Early Works and Big Ideas of Belgian Film Pioneer Hippolyte De Kempeneer (1876–1944)

Gerda Cammaer

Introduction

At the time of the birth of cinema in the 1890s, Belgium, the small bi-lingual country squeezed between The Netherlands, Germany and France, was already a sixty-five-year old industrial state and a nascent colonial power.[1] In its social, economic and technological aspects, the country was well prepared for its film industry to expand rapidly and its citizens were renowned for their entrepreneurial spirit, efficiency and inventiveness.[2] Yet despite these favourable conditions and presence of talent, there was almost no Belgian film production until the 1920s. This can be attributed to the country's subservient position toward the French with regards to cultural matters – a consequence of the ruling class being francophone, even in Flanders – as well as to the dire economical situation of the country during World War One.[3] The absence of a vibrant national cinema prior to 1920, explains why only two filmmakers are listed as the pioneers of Belgian cinema: Hippolyte De Kempeneer and Alfred Machin. Machin (1877–1929), was a Frenchman recruited by the Charles Pathé Company to run its Belgian production office and to develop a local market for Pathé films.[4] Hippolyte De Kempeneer, on the other hand, was a Flemish entrepreneur who was interested in all the new inventions of the day including radio, airplanes and film. In contrast to his contemporary Machin, he was interested in cinema's educational and cultural function over its value as a medium for entertainment. With the outbreak of World War One, Machin was forced to leave Belgium for France, effectively making De Kempeneer a key figure in Belgian cinema for years to come.[5] During the war, De Kempeneer produced newsreels and some of his best documentary work clandestinely under German rule. Despite the harsh times, he also came up with several ambitious film-related educational projects, such as founding a national film library for educational films he even developed plans for the first European film university.

Early beginnings: newsgathering, a weekly show and other ambitious film projects

Hippolyte De Kempeneer was born in 1876 in Anderlecht, a village near Brussels. He began his career as a wine and beer salesman, but he was an astute businessman who quickly realised that typical Belgian news items had as much, if not more, commercial potential than alcoholic beverages. He learned this lesson with the popular success of his first short film shot in 1897, less than two years after the première of the Lumière films in Belgium.[6] De Kempeneer's film was his own unedited reportage of King Leopold II's visit to the "Tervuren Exhibition".[7] A few years later, in 1908, De Kempeneer attended an air show in Zellik, a village north of Brussels. An aviation aficionado, he aspired to have his own moving images of the show. He hired a cameraman to film the event and asked an editor to edit the images with intertitles, like a true "actuality film". This air-show film was a hit, and De Kempeneer was converted for good.[8] He gave up his wine and beer business entirely and turned his attention full time to film production.

Hippolyte De Kempeneer clearly understood that the most lucrative opportunity for his nascent film business, and one in tune with his personal interest in news reportage, was to present short actuality films for cinema theatres. He therefore started to produce and distribute *La semaine animée*, a weekly newsreel that ran in different theatres from 1912 to 1914. With the help of three other cameramen, he shot and produced numerous short actuality films in and around Brussels, Liège and surrounding provinces about typical Belgian topics. These included *The Abbey of La Cambre*, *The Castle of Gaasbeek*, *The Funeral of City Mayor Demot* (all 1909), a flower show staged by a worker named "Jenny" on the Place the la Monnaie in Brussels, *The Arrival and Stay of the Danish King and Queen in Brussels*, a horse competition, a cattle exhibition, a national agricultural show in Brussels and the transformation of the city of Brussels by the new line connecting the North and South train stations. He made these films in 1914 and he showed them in a small theatre he opened that year, the *Cinéma des Familles*.[9] Unfortunately, most of these short documentaries and newsreels are lost. De Kempeneer is recorded as having sold some of his films to the city of Brussels in 1918; thus, perhaps, at least part of his *œuvre* is preserved in the city archives.[10]

With the making of his various actuality films, De Kempeneer was doing very similar work to what news-gathering cameramen such as Alfred Machin did for Pathé. But for De Kempeneer, there was more to cinema than just offering news. A devout Catholic, De Kempeneer started other film-related projects early in his career that he considered just as crucial for a Belgian national cinema as the recording of daily events. For example, in 1913 he founded *La ligue du cinéma moral* (League for a Moral Cinema) with which he tried to pressure city mayors to give film exhibition permits exclusively to those film theatres that were league members.[11] He thus attempted to prevent "immoral" films from exhibition (mostly films with "sexual" content).[12] However, this particular initiative of De Kempeneer's was met with a lot of protest and, consequently, never implemented.[13]

The trials and tribulations of World War One

World War One broke out on 4 August 1914. The troops of the German empire invaded Belgium and soon the country experienced a "total" war: soldiers as well as civilians were completely drawn into the war experience. Except for a small part on the left bank of the Yser river in the far north of Flanders – the famous Flanders Fields – the entire country was occupied by the German army. The occupation regime was harsh, characterised by a constant and severe repression of the local population and a very

15 Documentaries, Family Film Nights and the First Film University

Fig. 1. Fragment of the pan showing all the workers of the Brussels Restaurants, focussing on some of the cooks.

strict regulation of public life; goods were confiscated and men who were not conscripted were simply deported to German labour camps.[14]

Remarkably in this context of an all-encompassing war, De Kempeneer continued to film "actualities". To be able to do this, he clandestinely installed a laboratory for film processing and printing in the basement of his *Cinéma des Familles*. The lab enabled De Kempeneer to keep production going, when most other film activities in Belgium had ceased – fiction film production in Belgium had come to a complete halt by 1914.[15] Most of the films shown in theatres were images made by the occupied forces or imported films, except for some coverage of the activities of the Belgian forces made by the film service of the Belgian army – this service was founded in 1915 and operated from behind the Yser frontline.[16] In this restrictive environment, it is notable that De Kempeneer maintained his role as a film exhibitor at his *Cinéma des Familles*, where he screened matinées of newsreels and "documentaries for schoolchildren".[17] Unfortunately, no programmes or posters of these screenings remain, which makes it difficult to know what is meant by "documentaries" and how these might have differed from regular news reportages or actualities. This absence of programme information means there is also no way to prove how often Kempeneer's *actualités* were shown, but I assume that screenings occurred on a regular basis.

Throughout the war period, De Kempeneer also remained concerned with the moral and intellectual well-being of film audiences, especially youth. In 1917 he founded the *Compagnie Belge des films instructifs* specifically targeting young audiences. He wanted film theatres to show educational films instead of fiction films, which he believed were corrupting Belgian youth. He also had plans to start a *National School Library of Didactic Films*, a loan service that would make educational films available to schools all over the country. However, this idea did not come to fruition until much later. The war

133

Fig. 2. Farm activities of the Brussels Restaurants: loading flour at the miller's house.

prevented De Kempeneer from realising his noble intentions as a film educator. Nevertheless, given the circumstances, his activities as film producer and exhibitor during the war years are all the more remarkable.

It is unclear how much of De Kempeneer's work from this era is lost, but in most filmographies there is a gap between the films he made in 1914 on such mundane topics as a horse race or the funeral of a celebrity, and his films on the hardships and the relief efforts during the war. Almost all the latter films are dated 1918, most probably because they surfaced – or were given an "official release date" – only after the war had ended. However, they must have been filmed during the war since they deal directly with various war experiences in and around Brussels.[18] Translated, these titles include *Fresh Supplies for the City: Distribution of Butter and Mussels in the Central Halles*, *The National Committee Warehouses in the Vergote Bassin: the Arrival of the Ships and the Unloading of Fats and Lard*, *A Bake for Schools in the People's House*, *An Open-Air Cure for Infants in Bosvoorde*, *Day Camp for Weakened Girls in Zellik*, *The Distribution of Flour*, *French Refugees in Brussels*, *A Flower Sale for the Orphans*, *Distribution of Unemployment Benefits*, *Check-point for Infants and Canteen for Mothers* and *Brussels during the Occupation*.[19] De Kempeneer was careful to ensure these actuality films conformed to the rules imposed by the war censor and they were devoid of any subversive material. Nevertheless, according to René Michelens, the films had the virtue of capturing the war experience in an authentic way.[20] This claim is confirmed on viewing the documentary titled *Brussels Restaurants* (1919), a longer film De Kempeneer also shot during the war. It is a remarkable work that deserves recognition as a key film in the history of Belgian cinema.

Les Restaurants Bruxellois / De Brusselse Spijshuizen / Brussels Restaurants

De Kempeneer's *Brussels Restaurants*, a 752 metre (ca. 29 minutes) 35mm film, survives in excellent condition. The work is considerably longer than the typical De Kempeneer

15 Documentaries, Family Film Nights and the First Film University

Fig. 3. Inter-title explaining the organization of the Brussels Restaurants.

actuality films. The film shows the distribution of free meals to those in need in Brussels during the war by the community restaurants (a type of soup kitchen), which were organised by a humanitarian cooperative called *La société intercommunale*. The film shows people working for the organisation in 1915 and has intertitles referring to the organisation's activities in 1917, confirming that despite the 1919 release date for this film, De Kempeneer obviously worked on it for several years during the war. As we learn from the intertitles at the beginning of the film, each meal offered to the needy by the "société intercommunale" was composed of a bowl of soup, one hundred grams of meat, five hundred grams of potatoes, one hundred grams of vegetables, sixty grams of bread, a glass of beer and a coffee. These meals were in high demand, and the need for them grew as the war continued. According to the film, by 1917 this organisation was providing no less than sixty-five thousand meals per day, and in total over the four years of war, the "société intercommunale" delivered forty-one million meals.

The tone of the film and the exhaustive detail with which De Kempeneer catalogues the activities of these Brussels Restaurants confirms an impression of him as a devoted and patriotic documentary filmmaker concerned with getting the facts right: the film at times feels like it is the work of a bookkeeper. De Kempeneer devotedly reports the growing poverty and hunger in the streets of Brussels, and he shows how these Brussels restaurants worked hard every day to get hundreds of cheap meals ready and distributed to those in need. The film opens with title cards explaining the workings of the organisation and giving us the figures mentioned above, followed by aerial views of Brussels. De Kempeneer used similar images in his later patriotic melodramas, and as he obtained those aerial views from the army's film service, I assume the ones in *Brussels Restaurants* came from the same source.[21] After this opening, images follow of people receiving tickets for meals and a presentation of all the people who work for the different restaurants of the cooperative: the cashiers, the cooks and kitchen chefs, the

Fig. 4. One of the clients leaving Restaurant O^2.

servers etc. These images are all large group portraits, and the sequence ends with a slow pan over the entire staff – 860 people in total. Except for this last pan, it is unclear whether the portraits are filmed still images or moving images of people standing very still, locked in a pose for De Kempeneer's camera.

The film continues with an action-packed overview of all the activities involved in running soup kitchen operations: we see people at work on farms, follow a veterinary inspection of all the animals (horses, cows and dogs), we visit the cow stables ("les vacheries"), the pig sties ("les pocheries") and then witness how the pigs recycle the kitchen garbage. De Kempeneer even takes the viewer to a pig show and sale. Following these shots, a visit to the fields and the vegetable gardens conclude the first part of the film. Part two starts with the hay harvest. We then follow the arrival of potatoes at one of the storage locations in Brussels and distribution from storage to the seventy restaurants. From that moment, the film leaves behind the countryside to detail activities of the organisation in the city. Trucks leave the storage yards to deliver imported goods from "the commission for relief in Belgium" (also known as just "Belgium Relief"), a United States organisation that supplied food to occupied Belgium. An inter-title announces that by 1917, forty animals were consumed every day, which is swiftly illustrated with the slaughter of a cow and a tour of the coop's own meat plant. The film also shows how furniture is collected and distributed and how the meals are transported and delivered both with trucks, horse-drawn carriages and dogcarts.

At this point the film takes an interesting turn. The film crew passes by the fire brigade racing off to respond to an emergency call: the coop's food caravan has to stop and we see how the cooks help the fire brigade get through traffic. An inter-title announces this "interruption" in the story with an apologetic "duty called". After this, the film quickly wraps up with the presentation of the actual restaurants, all prefaced by the number "0" (e.g. 0^{24}) and listed with their respective addresses, and a rare glimpse of some of the indigent. A very brief shot of the board of directors of the organisation, one that is actually too short to see the individuals clearly, ends the film. It is worth noting that the last shot is short because the camera ran out of film (the film flares out), while it looks like the shots of the "bénéficiaires" are kept short and distant on purpose, as to protect the poor and not expose them in their misery. It is difficult to prove this hypothesis, but it fits the overall portrait of Hippolyte De Kempeneer as filmmaker and as concerned citizen.

Brussels Restaurants is a valuable historical document that gives contemporary scholars an interesting glimpse of real life during World War One outside of army footage or propaganda. Moreover, it is obvious that the maker thought about a logical structure for the film (from provisions to final product and delivery to the clients) with attention to detail and story flow. The scene in which the delivery of the food is interrupted by the fire brigade testifies to a concern for continuity, narrative structure and a heightened sense of drama. Because of the care with which De Kempeneer filmed and assembled *Brussels Restaurants*, the label "pre-documentary" that Jacques Polet ascribes to the film seems limiting.^{22} In Polet's view, De Kempeneer's documentary work is relegated to a "pamphlet film" that shows little aesthetic concern or knowledge of filmic structure. However, De Kempeneer's *Brussels Restaurant* is a lovely early instance of direct cinema and documentary, pleasing to watch for the craftsmanship with which it is made and edited.

Conclusion: after the war

After the war, De Kempeneer helped to re-launch the Belgian fiction-film industry with the production of patriotic war films and adaptations of famous Flemish literary works. In 1919 he released *La Belgique martyre* directed by Charles Tutelier, a film he is believed to have started during the war.^{23} The success of this fiction film overshadowed his previous work, accounting for the lack of information about his documentary *The Brussels Restaurants* in the trade press. Despite the success of *La Belgique martyre*, De Kempeneer began to scale down his activities as a film producer. A fire in his studio in 1923 and in-fighting amongst his colleagues drew a near-complete halt to his work in fiction film. The arrival of sound forced an end to his work as a documentarian. The advent of sound in cinema made film production in bilingual Belgium terribly expensive: one always had to make two versions of a sound film, while filmmakers who made silent films needed only to re-edit their films with alternate language intertitles.

Although De Kempeneer moved away from film production, he continued his support for educational films and film education. In 1925 he founded the first Belgian Film University, an organisation with the aim of making documentaries, industrial and educational films available to its members and to distribute them internationally. By 1928 this Film University had no fewer than 40,000 members who rented films on a regular basis. In 1932, for reasons that are unclear, De Kempeneer closed the university. He did, however, continue with his film lab which became his main business. When he died in 1944, his wife and five of his thirteen children continued the company. The "De Kempeneer Family Film Lab" was a cornerstone of the Belgian film industry until the 1960s.

While the technical contributions and the patriotic war films of Hippolyte De Kempeneer are most frequently cited, I consider his actualities and documentary films made before and during the war, his most important contribution to Belgian film history.^{24} De Kempeneer offers us a fascinating glimpse of a part of history and of film history that is fading away all too quickly, and of which very few film records remain. Despite the fact that there are limited sources available, studying De Kempeneer's documentary work proves to us that there is still a lot to discover from this era of Belgian cinema.

Notes

1. For an excellent brief overview of the political history of Belgium with all its linguistic and cultural complexities, see Philip Mosley, *Split Screen: Belgian Cinema and Cultural Identity* (New York: State University of New York Press, 2001), 14–25.
2. For example, Joseph Plateau (1801–1883), a physicist who contributed to the invention of cinema with his phenakistoscope and other experiments.
3. "[J]usqu'à la veille de la Première guerre mondiale, la Belgique était considérée par l'industrie cinématographique française comme un prolongement normal du marché français". Guido Convents, "Le Cinéma français en Belgique à la veille de la Première guerre mondiale", in *1895*, hors série, *L'année 1913 en France* (October 1993), 1959. In the entire country, both in Flanders and Wallonia, French was the language of the bourgeoisie and the language for education, publications, politics, commerce etc.
4. For a brief illustrated overview of Alfred Machin (in French), see Jacqueline Aubenas (ed.) *DicDoc: le dictionaire du documentaire* (Brussels: Service général de l'audiovisuel et des multimédias de la communauté française de Belgique, 1999), 287–288.
5. Cinéma Belge, *Grand Angle* 59 (November 1983): 82. Machin had just released his war film *Maudite soit la guerre* (produced in 1913, released in 1914 under the title *Mourir pour la patrie*), a Griffith style pacifist and visionary melodrama about a woman who waits for her loved one to come back from the front.
6. On 10 November 1895, the Lumière brothers had an avant-première in Belgium of their film *La sortie des usines* at the École supérieure de l'industrie in Brussels for a small group of people including many important personnages. More than a month later, on 28 December 1895, they had their big première in Paris, which is now generally recognised as the event that marked the beginning of film history. The introduction of the Lumière films to a bigger audience in Belgium took place in the Royal Gallery of Brussels on 1 March 1896. Marianne Thys, "The First Decades: The First Screenings", in *Belgian Cinema/Le Cinéma Belge/De Belgische Film* (Brussels: Royal Film Archive, 1999), 31–32.
7. Known as the "Royal Museum for Central Africa" founded by the same King.
8. Paul Geens, "De Kempeneer: het einde van het artisanale tijdperk van de pellicule", *Film en TV* 418 (1992): 38.
9. René Michelens, "The First decades: Hippolyte De Kempeneer", *Belgian Cinema/Le Cinéma Belge/De Belgische Film* (Brussels: Royal Film Archive, 1999), 62–63.
10. According to René Michelens, "The First World War: Hippolyte De Kempeneer", *Belgian Cinema*, 89. The claim needs to be verified on site at the city archives of Brussels.
11. This League for a Moral Cinema was actually the forerunner of the highly contested Belgian Control Commission which De Kempeneer also helped organise. The Belgian Control Commission was a national film censorship board notable for its conservatism. Geens, "De Kempeneer", 38.
12. In a 1992 interview about their family business, Hippolyte's son Maurice De Kempeneer explained that his father was a profoundly religious man who was in favour of censorship.
13. Ibid.
14. Leen Engelen, "History on Film? What Belgian Fiction Films (1918–1924) tell us about the Great War and its Aftermath", in Hannu Salmi (ed.), *History in Words and Images: Proceedings of the Conference on Historical Representation Held at the University of Turku, Finland, 26–28 September, 2002* (Turku: University of Turku, Department of History, 2005), 211. It is relevant to a history of filmmaking of this era that the chemicals used to produce raw film stock were confiscated for the manufacturing of gunpowder. See Mosley, *Split Screen*, 34.
15. By 1916 the Germans had installed their "Flamenpolitik", a set of rules to exploit the longstanding linguistic problems in Belgium, particularly the systematic discrimination towards the Dutch language (Flemish) that existed before World War One. As part of this political program,

15 Documentaries, Family Film Nights and the First Film University

distributors were forced to subtitle and intertitle all films exhibited in Flanders in Flemish. See Fréderic Sojcher, *La kermesse héroique du Cinéma Belge: de documentaries et des farces 1896–1965* (Paris: L'Harmattan,1999), 94. As Mosely states, "World War One devastated a number of growing film industries in Europe, while at the same time allowing the United States to gain a domination that it has never since relinquished". Mosely, *Split Screen*, 34. See also Paul Geens, "L'Armée et le Cinéma en Belgique", *Forum* 2 (1983): 83.

16. Known as S.C.A.B.: Service Cinématographique de l'armée Belge. This agency is still active today, and it is also one of the bigger film archives in Belgium. See Guido Convents, "Service Cinématographique de l'armée Belge (SCAB)", in *Belgian Cinema/Le Cinéma Belge/De Belgische Film*, Marianne Thys (ed.) (Brussels: Royal Film Archive, 1999), 92. According to Mosely, this agency was founded in 1915 by the Belgian Government in exile in France. Mosely, *Split Screen*, 34.
17. Mosley, Ibid., 38; Michelens, "The First World War", 89.
18. Francis Bolen confirms this in *Histoire authentique, anecdotique, folklorique et critique du cinéma belge depuis ses plus lointaines origines* (Brussels: Memo & Codec, 1978), 54.
19. Michelens, "The First World War", 90–91. Note that the original titles for these films were in either Flemish or in French with no consistency.
20. Michelens, Ibid., 89.
21. See Leen Engelen, *Verbeelding van de Eerste Wereldoorlog in de Belgische Speelfilm (1913–1939)* (Leuven, KUL. Nieuwe reeks van doctoraten in de Sociale Wetenschappen vol 84, 2005), 74. Engelen notes that the S.C.A.B. started to sell their images of the war freely for one Belgian franc per metre, which explains why so many post-war films contain these documentary images that impart a sense of credibility. See also Bolen, *Histoire authentique*, 54.
22. Jacques Polet, "Le Predocumentaire", in *DicDoc*, 17–20. Note that this encyclopedia of Belgian documentary dedicates an entire chapter to Alfred Machin but, except for a brief note in the introduction titled Pre-documentaire nothing describes De Kempeneer's work. The book treats only Francophone filmmakers and while most of his films were (also) released in French, Hippolyte De Kempeneer himself was Flemish, and thus he falls outside the book's scope. Overall, apart from language issues, there is a decided lack of studies and references about De Kempeneer's (documentary) work, compared to, for example, his contemporary Alfred Machin, even in specialised cinema journals. Yet the unique and difficult historical context in which De Kempeneer produced his work warrants further attention in historical accounts.
23. According to Frédéric Sojcher (but not confirmed by other sources) De Kempeneer made this film clandestinely during the war. Also in 1919, De Kempeneer produced Charles Tutelier's *Le Belgique Martyre*. Sojcher, *La kermesse héroique*, 96.
24. See, for example, Mosley, *Split Screen*.

PART IV

Science and Magic

16

The School of the Future or Ganot's Physics?: Edison's Foray into Educational Cinema

Oliver Gaycken

Thomas Edison's attempt to create a form of cinema for use in schools constituted one of the more significant efforts to realise the vision of cinema as a modern educator, an idea in wide circulation during the period of early cinema.[1] Although the incorporation of cinema into educational systems would not become a widespread reality until the 1920s with the rise of the visual education movement and the introduction of 16mm, there were myriad attempts to integrate film into the classroom in the first two decades of the medium's existence. These first steps constitute a crucial phase that in many ways set the agendas of cinema's use as an educational device. Edison's desire for this kind of cinema partook equally of Progressive conviction in the potential for betterment through education and of an entrepreneurial zeal that sought to monetise a potentially massive new market.

Along with his prodigious achievements as an inventor, Edison was a modern celebrity and master of publicity.[2] His repeated proclamations in the early 1910s that he would revolutionise education through motion pictures demonstrate this gift for self-promotion. In a series of press pronouncements, Edison claimed that his new series of educational motion pictures would replace textbooks – teachers, even, in his more radical formulations – and that this innovation would change the relationship of students to schooling. The titles of some of these articles gave the sense that Edison's plans involved a fundamental change in educational practice: *Harper's* wrote about "Edison and the New Education;" *The World Today*'s headline read "Edison's Substitute for School Books;" and *The Literary Digest* entitled its excerpt "Edison's Revolutionary Education".[3] Edison's foray into educational cinema reprised ideas that had been in circulation for the better part of a decade, and it did not represent, as he claimed, a revolutionary departure. Nonetheless, it did constitute an example, or what Edison might have termed an "object lesson", in the dynamics of adapting the new medium to the tasks of instruction.

Edison envisioned film providing an educational paradise characterised by enthusiastic voluntarism: "Sort o' swing the education in on them so attractively that they'll *want* to go to school. You'll have to lick 'em to keep 'em away", one article quoted him as saying.[4] This ethos was carried over into a publicity image, where the project is pitched as not just child-friendly but in fact partially child-generated (Figure 1). Here the stern associations of censorship are submitted to a playful inversion, with high moral

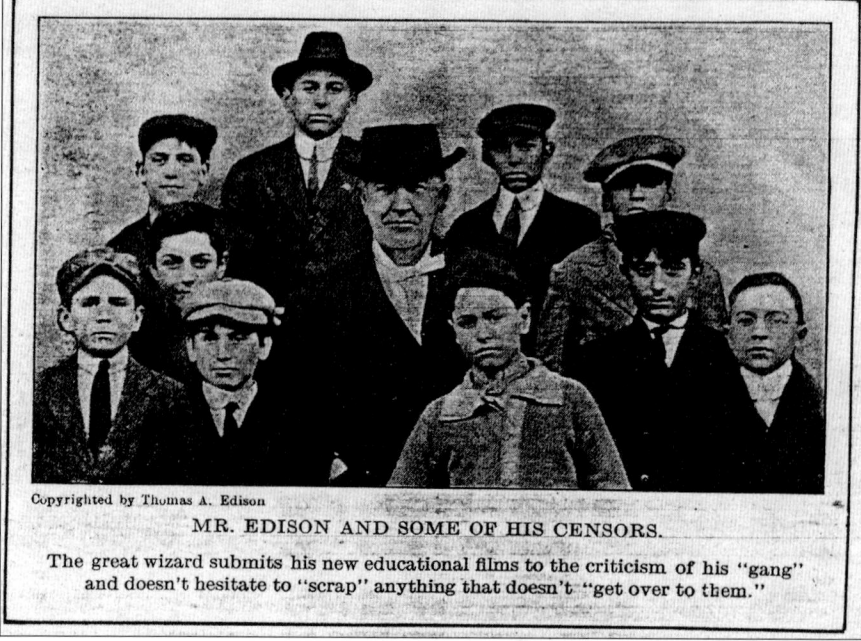

Fig. 1. Publicity image of Edison's "gang"; from The Literary Digest (4 October 1912): 576.

standards replaced by the "gang's" sense of whether a film "gets over to them". Another illustration envisioned the scene of the new education by depicting three young boys watching an animated film about spelling, which is described in the accompanying article: "The alphabet, which you had such a hard time learning when you were a youngster, will be presented so attractively to your children in picture form that they will know it almost 'before they know it'. Instead of the dull, uninteresting letters your teacher wrote for you on the blackboard, Johnny and Mary will sit spellbound watching a little picture play that the youngest child can understand" (Figure 2).[5] This depiction is also a good example of the omnipresence of Edison's own image in the publicity campaign; here his portrait forms a background to the screen, and in a way suggests that the film is an emanation of his thoughts – Edison's technological dreams as the future of learning.

The rhetoric of better living through technology had, of course, served Edison well elsewhere, and his image had long been synonymous with technological progress. It is all the more surprising, perhaps, that Edison's actual achievements in creating a scholastic cinema fell far short of his stated goals – the grand plans of a vast library of cinematic records ultimately resulted on the production of only a handful of films. One reason for the brevity of the project was that Edison's insistence on the superiority of cinema for educational uses flew in the face of much of American educational culture. Many educators were uneasy about claims that they were outmoded and could be replaced by a machine. Ultimately, this public-relations miscalculation may even have contributed to the slowing of momentum in the nascent field of educational cinema, which would not hit its stride until the early 1920s.

The multiple failures of Edison's enterprise are undoubtedly a reason it has received so little attention in film history. Nonetheless, both the existing films and the considerable archival materials related to their production contain a fascinating story about

16 The School of the Future or Ganot's *Physics*?

Fig. 2. Illustration accompanying 1911 Chicago Tribune *article "How Thos. A. Edison Plans to Cure 'Hookey".*

an early episode in the history of what we now would refer to as nontheatrical cinema. In this essay, I will focus on one aspect of this enterprise, namely, the rhetorical opposition between motion pictures and textbooks. Edison returned to this notion repeatedly; for example, in 1913, the *New York Dramatic Mirror* quoted him as saying, "Books will soon be obsolete in the public schools. Scholars will be instructed through the eye. It is possible to teach every branch of human knowledge with the motion picture. Our school system will be completely changed in ten years".[6] However, where Edison posited a radical rupture with previous modes of pedagogy, there was in fact a profound continuity between a certain strand of educational culture and Edison's vision for a new educational appliance. Was Edison's school of the future little more than a filmic version of existing textbook materials? Was Edison serving old wine in new bottles? A look at the history of late-nineteenth century scientific display culture and Progressive educational theory illuminates this seeming contradiction.

Production on Edison's educational films began in early 1912 and continued until August of 1913, and the films were part of a concerted effort to create the necessary materials for Edison's vision of a transformed American educational system. Along with producing new films, the effort also involved going through the extant Edison catalogue with an eye toward repurposing films that could serve educational purposes; and it had a significant interface with the introduction of the Home Kinetoscope.[7] Finally, in a manner typical of early nonfiction, the films the Thomas Edison Company created in the early 1910s would continue to circulate in a variety of guises and configurations for decades to come (as part of the Conquest series, via George Kleine's involvement in the visual education movement, and beyond).

The men tasked by Edison to realise the announced breakthrough in educational technology came from backgrounds in astronomy, chemistry, and biology. W.W. Dinwiddie, a key figure in the Education Film department, came to Edison from the Alvan Clark & Sons Corporation, where he was a member of the "Mechanical Department". Clark & Sons was one of the foremost makers of large telescopes in the United States, grinding lenses for the largest refracting telescopes in the world, including the 1000mm lens for the Yerkes Observatory, which remains the world's largest. Dinwiddie was, in other words, a skilled technician working for one of the leading companies in a scientifically and technologically advanced field.

Given these backgrounds, it comes as no surprise that these men drew on their own experiences with learning about science, which involved existing educational methods. Many of the images in the films can be traced to pre-existing visual teaching tools, including textbook illustrations and demonstration experiments. So, for example, in one of Dinwiddie's weekly reports to Edison (probably December 1912), he wrote, "All of the experiments on effect of electric current mentioned in Ganot's Physics except the electric furnace and Galvani's experiment with frog legs, have been photographed".[8] Tracking down and elaborating on this reference will illuminate some core features of the Edison educational motion picture project.

Adolphe Ganot wrote two physics textbooks in the 1850s, the *Traité élémentaire de physique expérimentale et appliquée* (1851) and the *Cours de physique expérimentale à l'usage des personnes étrangères aux connaissances mathématiques* (1859). The textbooks emerged out of Ganot's teaching practice, which relied heavily on his extensive instrument collection. Glass cases around the lecture hall of his school displayed the collection and served as a continual reminder to students of the lessons they had learned.[9] Placing special value on the quality and verisimilitude of its illustrations, the textbooks were conceived of as what Josep Simon terms a "replication of the classroom experience.... Illustrations were thus supposed to act as substitutes for real instruments and experimental demonstrations whenever those were not available".[10] This goal of providing an equivalent experience to actual classroom demonstrations was achieved in large part through collaboration with printers who employed the most advanced methods available at the time – Jules Claye, Ganot's Parisian printer, was renowned for his high-quality, low-cost wood engravings (he exhibited his work for Ganot's *Traité* at the first Paris World's Exhibition).[11]

In addition to the importance of the illustrations, Ganot's textbooks were characterised by a limited amount of mathematical formulas, a policy that emphasised accessibility. This tendency was more pronounced in the second book, the *Cours Élementaire*, which was advertised as, "A course of physics divested of mathematical formulae, expressed in the language of daily life".[12] The importance of verisimilar illustrations and accessible language allowed the textbooks to target "self-taught readers and those bringing science into social conversation".[13] These attitudes that prized simplicity, accessibility, and autodidacticism make Ganot's textbooks a precursor to Edison's educational ethos. Edison shared the aim of making certain classroom experiences more widely accessible (travel, views through the microscope, physics demonstrations, etc.), and he also argued, as did Ganot, that modern technology could provide a superior educational experience. Edison saw his films as helping to bring about a more modern and efficient educational system, a rationalised, technologically sophisticated approach that emphasised visual over verbal processes. Indeed, efficiency engineering in educational reform is an important intertext for Edison's work; in 1922 he talked about how the motion picture will allow for "100-per-cent efficiency" in education.[14] So the rhetoric of the romantic overthrow of the tyranny of learning by rote is only one aspect of Edison's interest in motion pictures in the schools. He was also interested in what we might now call the social engineering of the educational institution. A contemporary journalist married these insights elegantly:

> There is a touch of the romantic in the sight of this veteran inventor devoting the later years of his life to the more intelligent education of youth. Perhaps the memory of his own childhood, spent largely on the railroad where he sold newspapers as a train boy, comes back to him as he works. Having contributed so much through his work on the incandescent electric light to illumination for the physical eye, he is now hoping to turn a finer ray on the mind itself. Much has been done in the way of scientific management in the field of bodily toil. Perhaps Mr Edison thinks of himself as the efficiency engineer reaching into the mental processes – for, of course, time-saving and greater efficiency in education are of the very essence of his dreams.[15]

We can recall here a detail from Edison's biography. The book that supposedly started him on his path to scientific achievement was R.G. Parker's *School of Natural Philosophy* (1848), which preceded Ganot and contained a number of core similarities. Illustrations were incorporated into both texts as opposed to being reproduced in plates at the end of sections; both had an overall emphasis on do-it-yourself science.[16] Of course, Ganot's books were only one example of a larger tendency in nineteenth-century educational practice. Another equally important source for the Edison educational films was Milliken and Gale's *Practical Physics*, a textbook first published in 1906 and the most widely adopted textbook in use in the U.S. at the time. Dinwiddie's report from 1912 mentioned this book as a guide for the physics films, and he hoped, by following its structure and sequencing, that the films would fit more easily into existing curricula.

In addition to these similarities on the level of pedagogical philosophy, Edison's science filmmakers had recourse to specific visual strategies of late-nineteenth century textbook culture, of which the films on the topic of magnetism are a good example.[17] Magnetism was a subject that received extensive treatment in Edison's educational film effort; four reels were produced on this topic, and this footage was configured in a variety of ways. One of the later versions, *The Wonders of Magnetism*, was a film for general audiences released in 1913.[18] Fully half of this film's eight scenes have precedents in prior scientific demonstration culture.[19] The sixth shot, a demonstration of the "lines of force" generated by magnetic fields, is a staple of textbook illustrations and consistently recommended for teaching demonstrations (Figure 3). As the visual similarities of the "lines of force" demonstrations illustrate, Edison's educational films overlapped significantly with existing methods of visual demonstration in science education. Dinwiddie acknowledged this reliance on existing demonstration culture in one of his reports to Edison: "I believe this educational series will be a tremendous success, but it should be so well done that there will be no room for a word of criticism. The demonstration apparatus should not be recognised as a copy of Queen & Co. or Max Kohl, etc.: It can improve on all of them a little and its newness will add greatly to its popularity".[20] The films should not be recognised as copies of Queen & Co. or Max Kohl (both leading manufacturers of demonstration equipment for science teaching), but the difference is one of degree, not of kind. Indeed, a look at a Kohl's catalogue illustrates the proximity of the film's demonstrations with the established material culture of demonstration experiments for magnetism (Figure 4).[21]

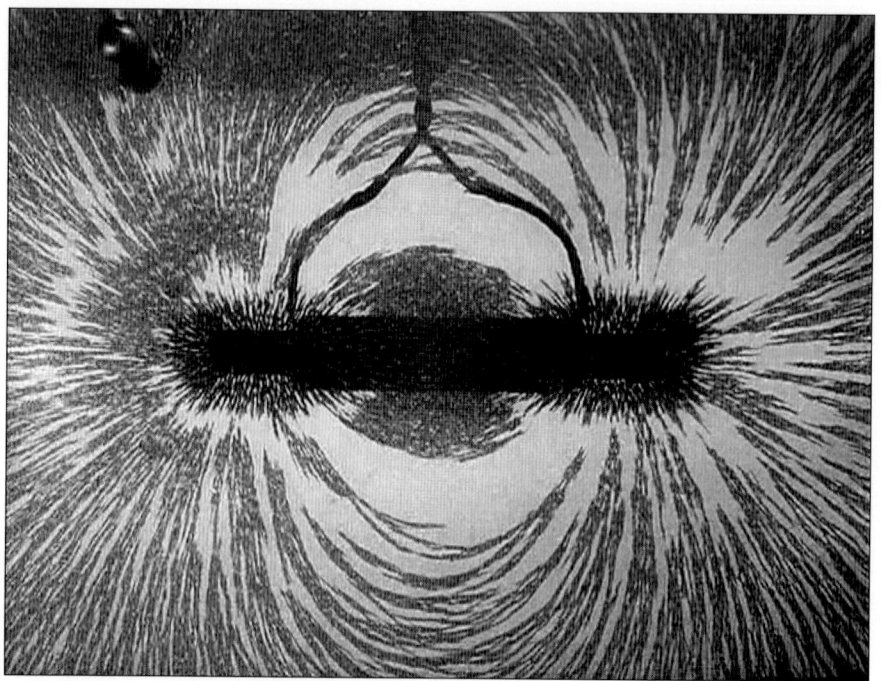

706. **Magnetic curves.**—If a stout sheet of paper stretched on a frame be held over a horseshoe magnet, and then some very fine iron filings be strewn on the paper, on tapping the frame the filings will be found to arrange themselves in thread-like curved lines, stretching from pole to pole (fig. 663). These lines form what are called *magnetic curves*. The direction of the curve at any point represents the direction of the lines of magnetic force at this point.

To render these curves permanent, the paper on which they are formed should be waxed; if then a hot iron plate be held over them, this melts the wax, which rises by capillary attraction (131) between the particles of filings, and on subsequent cooling connects them together. They may also be fixed by carefully placing on them a sheet of paper coated with paste, which is then

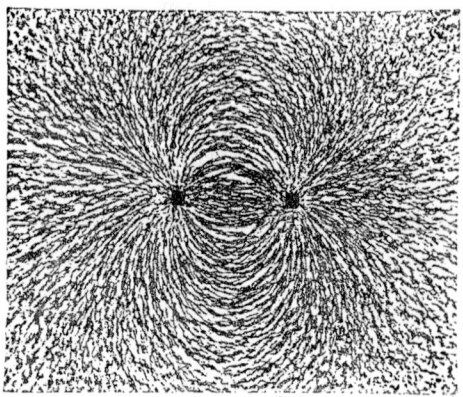

Fig. 663.

Fig. 3. Demonstrations of the principle of magnetic "lines of force"; from The Wonders of Magnetism *(Edison 1913);* Milliken and Gale, Practical Physics *(1922).*

16 The School of the Future or Ganot's *Physics*?

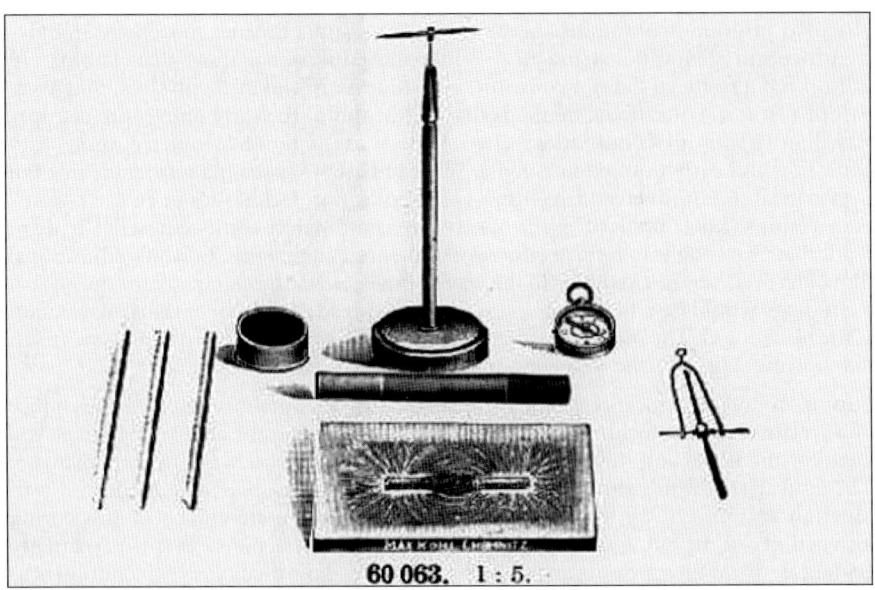

Fig. 4. An "apparatus for explaining the fundamental laws of magnetism – magnetic needle on stand, compass, simple dipping needle, bar magnet, steel bars for breaking, iron filings in box, with sieve and slab for sprinkling the same" (Max Kohl catalogue).

The familiarity of Edison's approach was not lost on other companies engaged in providing visual products to schools. Late in 1911, B.L. Singley, the President of the Keystone View Company, wrote to ask Edison whether he might like to partner in an educational motion picture venture.[22] Keystone had begun production of its 'Six Hundred' set in 1906, and the company would become one of the most prominent providers of visual instruction materials in the first half of the twentieth century; by 1935, their archive of produced and purchased stereoscopic and lantern slide views would total over 2 million images. Tellingly, Singley saw Edison's plans as in line with his own undertaking.

Similarly, J.H. Hanson, president of the Hanson-Bellows Company, contacted Edison late in 1912 to ask whether he had made plans yet for the marketing of the educational cinema products. Hanson-Bellows had published *The New Practical Reference Library* in February of 1907, and this illustrated reference work, which would later become the *World Book Encyclopedia*, distinguished itself from competitors such as *Encyclopedia Britannica* by its more accessible language and profuse illustrations. In his letter to Edison, Hanson wrote, "The Hanson-Bellows Company ... has worked in the school field ever since its organisation and has met with remarkable success, largely due, we believe, to the fact that its publications have presented, as nearly as it is possible to do so in book form, the ideas which you expect to bring graphically before teachers and pupils by means of the moving pictures. ... It will make school a delight, study as interesting as play".[23] Here, too, an established company saw Edison's "radical" plans as perfectly in line with its own goals. Additionally, Hanson's invocation of making school a delight not only repeats a component of Edison's pitch (his claim that schools equipped with motion-picture machines would have to beat children with sticks to keep them away) but it also recalls the venerable tradition of "instructive amusement".[24]

The rhetoric of futurity with which Edison surrounded his educational film enterprise obscured profound continuities between the films and a broader movement in nineteenth-century educational practice. While the educational films that Thomas A. Edison Inc. produced did not constitute a revolution in and of themselves, they were part of a shift in educational methods that had begun in the early nineteenth century, revealing significant continuities between the visual culture of nineteenth-century education and early nonfiction cinema. What initially may seem a retrograde or even hypocritical use of nineteenth-century visual education techniques in an early-twentieth-century "most modern" piece of software is ultimately consistent with a body of work that also sought to reform educational theory and practice. Edison's educational film enterprise was not a success in the way he envisioned; the cinema as an educational technology would have to wait to become as widespread a medium of visual instruction as the blackboard. The methods of conveying information established by Edison's team did, however, presage the strategies of subsequent educational cinema.

Edison's foray into educational cinema relied on a mixture of the revolutionary promise of a (relatively) new technology with time-tested strategies of educational display, a blend of the novel and the familiar characterises much of early nonfiction cinema.[25] The educational film's simultaneously radical and conservative aspects allowed it to function at times as an agent of stultification, as in the stereotype of the boring instructional film, but also as a source of inspiration, a response that is particularly evident in the avant-garde attraction to these images. This duality, which continues to operate in contemporary educational media, allows the early educational film to be characterised by repeated failures as well as by the promise of a continually novel future.

Notes

1. For an account of the rhetoric of educational cinema before 1910, see my "The Cinema of the Future: Visions of the Medium as Modern Educator", in Dan Streible, Marsha Orgeron, and Devin Orgeron (eds), *Learning with the Lights Off: Educational Film in the United States* (New York: Oxford University Press, 2011), 67–89. Recent attention to early nonfictional cinema has begun to reveal the considerable territory at the intersection of cinema and education. For an overview, see: Luke McKernan, "Education", in *The Encyclopedia of Early Cinema*, Richard Abel (ed.) (New York: Routledge, 2005), 214–15; *The Educated Eye: Visual Pedagogy in the Life Sciences*, Nancy Anderson and Michael R. Dietrich (eds) (Lebanon, NH: University Press of New England, 2012); and Jennifer Peterson, *Education in the School of Dreams: Travelogues and Early Nonfiction Film* (Durham, NC: Duke University Press, forthcoming). I cover other aspects of the current chapter in Gaycken, "'The Swarming of Life': Moving Pictures, Education, and Views through the Microscope", *Science in Context* 24, no. 3 (September 2011): 361–380.

2. See Charles Bazerman, *The Languages of Edison's Light* (Cambridge, Mass.: MIT University Press, 1999), which details how Edison's introduction of electric light included an intricate and well-orchestrated publicity campaign; and Charles Musser, "Before the Rapid Firing Kinetograph: Edison Film Production, Representation and Exploitation in the 1890s", in *Edison Motion Pictures, 1880–1900, An Annotated Filmography* (Washington, DC: Smithsonian Institution Press, 1997), 19–50, esp. 31–33, which discusses the mixture of commercialism and research in Edison's introduction of the kinetoscope.

3. William Inglis, "Edison and the New Education", *Harper's Weekly* (4 November 1911): 8; Allen L. Benson, "Edison's Substitute for School Books", *The World Today* (March 1912); "Edison's Revolutionary Education", *The Literary Digest* (4 October 1913).

4. Inglis, "Edison and the New Education", 8.

5. "How Thos. A. Edison Plans to Cure 'Hookey'", *Chicago Daily Tribune* (10 December 1911): G4; my thanks to Paul Moore for drawing this article to my attention.

6. Edison quoted in Frederick James Smith, "The Evolution of the Motion Picture", *New York Dramatic Mirror* (9 July 1913): 24; quoted in Anthony Slide, *Before Video: A History of the Non-Theatrical Film* (New York: Greenwood Press, 1992), 2.

7. See Ben Singer, "Early Home Cinema and the Edison Home Projecting Kinetoscope", *Film History* 2, no. 1 (1988): 37–69.
8. W.W. Dinwiddie, "Educational Series Motion Pictures Report" [December 1912?], in *Thomas A. Edison Papers: A Selective Microfilm Edition, Part V (1911–1919)*, reel 252, image 951.
9. See Josep Simon, "The Franco-British Communication and Appropriation of Ganot's *Physique* (1851–1881)", in *Beyond Borders: Fresh Perspectives in the History of Science* (Newcastle: Cambridge Scholars Press, 2008), 148.
10. Ibid., 148 and 151.
11. Ibid., 148. Furthermore, Ganot stayed abreast of current research by attending the numerous Parisian World Exhibitions, by being involved in journal culture, as well as through his friendship with the well-known scientific populariser the Abbé Moingo. And Ganot's illustrations circulated widely – Moingo's *Cosmos* reproduced images from an updated version of the *Traité,* and Moingo's collaboration with Molteni led to the creation of a physics set of 138 lantern slides, which were all based on the illustrations from Ganot's *Cours*; see Simon, "Communication and Appropriation", 151. Important for these pedagogues were "demonstration, experimental manipulation and observation, and illustrati[on]", as quoted in Simon, "Communication and Appropriation", 149.
12. Advertisement for *Ganot's Natural Philosophy for General Readers and Young Persons*, E. Atkinson (ed.); in *Nature* 47 (6 April 1893): cixxxiv.
13. Simon, "Communication and Appropriation", 159.
14. Edison quoted in Larry Cuban, *Teachers and Machines: The Classroom Use of Technology Since 1920* (New York: Teachers College Press, 1986), 9; for more on the concept of efficiency in the discourse of cinema and education, see Jennifer Peterson, "Concrete Civilization: Industrial Films and Progressive-Era Political Economy", paper presented at the 11th DOMITOR conference, Toronto, 16 June 2010; and Scott Curtis in this volume.
15. Winthrop D. Lane, "Edison vs. Euclid: Has He Invented a Moving Stairway to Learning?" *The Survey* 30, no. 23 (6 September 1913): 681–695.
16. For the anecdote about Edison being inspired by reading Parker, see Matthew Jopheson, *Edison: A Biography* (New York: McGraw Hill, 1959), 20.
17. Dinwiddie first mentions working on films of magnetism in "Educational Series Motion Pictures, Report", 24 August 1912, *Thomas A. Edison Papers, A Selective Microfilm Edition*, reel 252, image 918.
18. *The Wonders of Magnetism* was released on 20 January 1913, and it is accessible on the fourth DVD of *Edison and the Invention of the Movies,* distributed by Kino Video. Other versions of this material include an earlier, longer version held at the Library of Congress, *Magnetism* (Edison, 1912) 382ft., 10m12s; and a later version, *Magnetism and Electromagnets,* which is in the George Kleine collection at the Library of Congress. This version, which dates from 1923, consists of two reels and has a runtime of twenty-one minutes. The opening titles provide the following information, which suggests that the Edison material had undergone revision: "George Kleine / Educational / Film Productions / Magnetism and electro-magnets / Film and text arranged and edited by William H. Dudley, professor of Visual Education and Fred H. Batcheler, Assistant Professor of Electrical Engineering University Extension Division The University of Wisconsin, Madison".
19. Shots: 1: where the length of magnet is shown to relate to how strong it is (Ganot); 2: which shows the tank with magnetised needles and how they respond to polarity (Milliken); and 3: showing the floating needle experiment (Ganot). These scenes correspond, but not precisely with textbook illustrations, which raises a question about their usefulness.
    The other scenes – 4: an electromagnet demonstration; 5: a demonstration of how an electromagnet is stronger than steel magnet; 7: a demonstration of the power of a large electromagnet; and the final shot, which demonstrates the Edison magnetic ore separator – attest to the importance of Edison's investment in all things electrical.
20. W.W. Dinwiddie, "Educational Series Motion Pictures, Report", 5 March 1912, *Thomas A. Edison Papers: A Selective Microfilm Edition,* reel 252, image 898.
21. Max Kohl, A.G., *Physical Apparatus / Vol. II. Apparatus for General Use. Introduction to Physics. Mechanics. Wave Theory. Acoustics. Optics. Heat. Meterology. Cosmology* (Chemnitz: 191-), 787. This catalogue, and many others, have been placed online by the Smithsonian at http://www.sil.si.edu/digital-collections/trade-literature/scientific-instruments/intro.htm

22. Singley to Edison, 12 December 1911, *Thomas A. Edison Papers: A Selective Microfilm Edition*, reel 250, image 315.
23. Hanson to Edison, 2 December 1912, *Thomas A. Edison Papers: A Selective Microfilm Edition*, reel 252, images 932–933.
24. The frontispiece of the aforementioned Parker's *Natural Philosophy* cites the Horatian motto: *Delectando pariter que monendo* ("To please while instructing").
25. See Bazerman, *The Language of Edison's Light* for a similar story; Bazerman argues that the discourse Edison employed to introduce electric light succeeded in part because it was able to clothe a transformative technology in familiar and comforting terms.

17

Multi-Purposing Early Cinema: A Psychological Experiment Involving Van Bibber's Experiment (Edison, 1911)

Marsha Orgeron

Thomas Edison's *Van Bibber's Experiment* (1911) is one of many Edison Manufacturing Co. films considered lost. Traces that remain of the film include a short synopsis in Edison's *Kinetogram*, a review in *Moving Picture World*, a photograph in the 1914 *Cyclopedia of Motion Picture Work*, and four seven-frame paper print photographs, which were used to register copyright.[1] Beyond these small clues, this film came and went with relatively little notice or record of its existence.

This might have been the final word on *Van Bibber's Experiment* were it not for a pioneering instance of cinema's use beyond entertainment. Film's educational and instructive purposes were being proposed, implemented, tested, and hotly debated in the early years of the twentieth century, which witnessed the widespread utilisation of moving pictures outside of entertainment venues in classrooms, churches, businesses, and – in the case of *Van Bibber's Experiment* – laboratories. In the March 1916 issue of the *Journal of the American Institute of Criminal Law and Criminology*, American psychologist and, in later years, historian of psychology Edwin G. Boring published a study entitled, "Capacity to Report upon Moving Pictures as Conditioned by Sex and Age. A Contribution to the Psychology of Testimony". His experiment – actually conducted in 1912 while Boring was completing his doctoral studies at Cornell under the supervision of Guy Montrose Whipple – employed a one-minute scene excerpted from Edison's *Van Bibber's Experiment*, which Boring described in detail in his report.[2] The scene depicted a burglary foiled by an upper-class club member, and was screened to assess the ability of viewers to accurately report what they witnessed. However, Boring's experiment – conducted four years before the publication of Hugo Münsterberg's *The Photoplay: A Psychological Study* (1916) and seven years prior to what has generally been considered "the first psychological research project involving movies", conducted by John B. Watson and Karl Lashley in 1919 – is a study not just of how these subjects responded to witnessing a criminal act, but also, as the title of the published report indicates, of the very act of viewing motion pictures.[3]

Boring's experiment was almost certainly the first time that a commercial film was used in a psychological experiment. Significantly, it transformed *Van Bibber's Experiment* from an entertainment film into a useful scientific, pedagogical tool. Unlike other films that were being made for specifically educational or scientific reasons (for example, films documenting psychiatric problems, which appeared as early as 1905), *Van Bibber's*

Experiment was repurposed by Boring to study the very nature of spectatorship and memory.[4] This reorientation of an entertainment film exposes intriguing aspects of the era's scientific experimentation, including its intersection with the development of film form and narrative structure. How else, one can imagine Boring and Whipple pondering, could subjects in a psychological study "witness" a crime other than by way of moving images?[5]

The motion picture, it seems, offered a realist mode with which to tackle any number of social science challenges, though its employment by the scientific community in the pre-1915 era remains relatively untouched by film historians as well as by those working in the history of psychology.[6] When discussing his studies at Cornell in *A History of Psychology in Autobiography* (published in 1952), Boring mentions the experiment only in passing, despite the fact that his use of film appears to be a – if not *the* – truly pioneering aspect of this study.[7] Whipple's introduction to his *Manual of Mental and Physical Tests*, first published in 1914, just on the heels of the *Van Bibber's Experiment* study, comments on Boring's conclusions but not, except in passing, on his methodology.[8] This essay, then, considers Boring's extra-theatrical use of Edison's film in part to restore the importance of Boring's pioneering work to the history of psychology as well as to film history, especially with regard to film's early twentieth-century multipurpose functionality.

The film

Van Bibber's Experiment is an adaptation of Richard Harding Davis's short story, "Van Bibber's Burglar", first published in December 1890 in the New York *Evening Sun* and subsequently in Davis's collection, *Gallegher and Other Stories* in 1891.[9] The film depicts a "burglar" (played by Marc McDermott) being released from the State Penitentiary (Figure 1). He returns home to his wife (Mary Fuller) and promises "to begin a new life" by leaving his criminal ways behind him, but struggles to find work. In the meantime, the film introduces us to Van Bibber (Robert Conness, in his third turn at the role in an Edison Co. production) – an upper-class character about whom Davis wrote numerous stories, many of which were adapted into films in the 1910s. At a club, Van Bibber encounters a detective wielding photographs of jewel thief suspects, paving the way for his experiment. Walking home, he spies a suspicious character in the act of burgling. Van Bibber pounces on the man, removes his gun, and recognises his face from the detective's photographs. After forcing him to return the stolen goods, Van Bibber feels sympathy for the unfortunate soul and so embarks upon his experiment: he takes the burglar home with him, clothes him properly, and shows him "his new self in the mirror", which causes "his confidence and his belief in his own manhood" to return. After testing the burglar's resolve, Van Bibber gives him enough money to take his wife out west to start anew. *Moving Picture World* described the "very effective climax" as follows: "The reformed burglar sends Van Bibber a fine picture of himself and wife and child, happy in the free and breezy West and a check, paying back the money Van Bibber had given him".[10]

The experiment

Edward Garrigues Boring was an engineering major at Cornell when he used elective hours to take his first psychology course with E.B. Titchener in 1905. Following a stint as an engineer with Bethlehem Steel in 1908, Boring taught science and mathematics and then returned to Cornell to earn his Ph.D. in Psychology in 1914 under Titchener's direction. During his course of study, he had four minor subjects and published in each of these areas, including educational psychology with G.M. Whipple, at whose

17 Multi-Purposing Early Cinema

Fig. 1. The burglar is released from prison in Van Bibber's Experiment. *Frame from the paper print in the copyright file for* Van Bibber's Experiment.
[Courtesy U.S. Dept. of the Interior, National Park Service, Thomas Edison National Historical Park.]

suggestion he "completed a study of the fidelity of report on moving-picture incidents" (the *Van Bibber's Experiment* experiment).[11] Whipple had already moved from the psychology to the education department to pursue psychological testing methods by the time of Boring's doctoral work, partly in response to Titchener's advocacy for a purely scientific psychology.[12] Tantalisingly enough, Boring's experiment was conducted in 1912, the same year that Louis Leon (L.L.) Thurstone – another future preeminent psychologist and recent Cornell graduate in Engineering – began to work as Thomas Edison's assistant prior to attending the University of Chicago to pursue a Ph.D. in Psychology.[13]

Though the "how" of Boring's acquisition of *Van Bibber's Experiment* is unclear, the "why" is less so. As his published study suggests, Boring was not only testing the memory of his human subjects but also – quite deliberately – film's efficacy as a scientific tool. He begins his published report by questioning the value of still pictures or live events to gauge the "reliability of report" (the ability of witnesses to accurately report facts in a deposition situation). Boring proposes that moving pictures are a solution to the "disadvantage of both" of these other forms, offering a greater capacity to represent "human action" than photographs and more "accurate control" than a standard "event-test".[14] Boring's subjects for the study were forty-four in number, including Ithaca public school children, Cornell undergraduates, five psychology graduate students, and, interestingly enough, two psychology professors, all of whose identities are unknown.[15]

The scene screened from *Van Bibber's Experiment* lasted around one minute, beginning with Van Bibber's sighting of the burglar – who "is crouching before the gate with a sack of plunder beside him" (Figure 2). The published report's summary of the scene explains that Van Bibber is "well-dressed, wearing a silk hat and a light overcoat" and that the burglar is "very uncouth with ragged clothes, unkempt hair partly covered by

Fig. 2. Van Bibber (standing) catches the burglar red handed. This image was originally published with the caption, "Scene from Photoplay 'Van Bibber's Experiment'. Courtesy of Thomas A. Edison, Inc. Orange, N.J.", in David Hulfish, Cyclopedia of Motion Picture Work (Chicago: American Technical Society, 1914).

a cap, and a face lined and rough". The excerpt included Van Bibber's discovery and disarming of the burglar, a conversation between the two men, the burglar returning the "bag of plunder", and finally Van Bibber's escorting of the burglar, at gunpoint, out of the scene. Boring notes that this scene was "colored blue, in order to produce a moonlight effect, a condition which renders the detail slightly less distinct than it would otherwise be", although he never reflects upon the possibility of the tinting impeding or otherwise influencing his subjects' comprehension or retention of the scene's details.[16]

Boring borrowed a hand cranked "kinematograph" from Cornell's Department of Physics and projected the film from just behind the subjects, who were instructed as follows: "Sit in this chair and watch the wall over there. I am going to show you a picture upon the wall. I want you to watch it with your best attention. Be sure to watch it carefully all the time".[17] Following the screening, each subject gave an oral report of everything they remembered, swore to their degree of confidence in the veracity of their statements, and answered a twenty-six question questionnaire. The questions, with correct answers in parentheses, were published in the report, ranging from "Where did the man get the revolver with which he controlled the burglar? (From the ground; indirectly he got it from the burglar)" to "What sort of a neck-tie did the man wear? (White)" and "How long did it take to show the picture? (About one minute)".[18]

The questionnaire is a fascinating document. While Boring did not publish the subjects' answers, the questions provide a compendium of details from the lost scene as well as insight into the methodology of a psychological experiment of the period. Most of the questions are open; but some are implicative, offering a misleading possibility as in

"Did the burglar resist when the man grabbed him by the throat? (The man did not take the burglar by the throat)". Since the spectators were unaware that they would be tested on the details of the screening (note that they were not alerted to anything beyond the fact that they should pay close attention to the images), they were in essence being drilled on both memory and, perhaps even more so, on their individual attention to detail. Much of this detail was fairly microscopic in nature and would certainly not have been the type of information retained by an ordinary spectator of a motion picture, who would presumably have been focused on the characters and story. Perhaps this is the reason that the scene Boring selected was also not filled with much in the way of dramatic action – in essence it depicts an encounter, a conversation, albeit one involving a criminal (note also that the "questionary" uses the terms "man" and "burglar", linguistically assigning roles to the characters). Furthermore, the very act of excerpting robbed the test subjects of what, to the viewer of the whole, would have been essential narrative context: of potential identification with Van Bibber, sympathy for the downtrodden burglar, and satisfaction with the film's happy ending when the burglar attains a new life for himself and his family.

Although the results of Boring's study are not my focus here, especially given the experiment's many variables and acknowledged flaws (for example, "The men included more graduate and fewer under-graduate students than did the women"), it is worth noting that Boring concludes that "there is considerable presumption of a difference in excellence of report between men and women in favour of the former; that no such sex-difference is apparent in childhood; and that the reports of adults are more adequate and accurate than those of children".[19] Given the many permutations of data that Boring assesses to arrive at this conclusion, there is one especially noteworthy omission in the published report: despite the ambitions articulated at the beginning of the publication with regard to the superiority of moving pictures as experimental stimuli, Boring makes no comment about this methodology – or of its potential influence on the experiment's outcome – in his conclusion or summary beyond the rather pat, if prominent, "summary statement #1", which reads: "The moving picture presents a satisfactory and an easily and accurately controlled form of event-test".[20] This matter-of-factness is curious, especially given the titling of Boring's report and his framing of the experiment in terms of the method's novelty. Boring's ultimate downplaying of the role of the motion picture as stimulus may be symptomatic of any number of things. Despite his reticence, Boring's use of film clearly deserves comment, especially given its implied assumptions about film spectatorship as well as scientific methodology. Taken out of its context, the scene is not meant to invoke a larger narrative for the spectator-subjects, but rather to be replete with reportable temporal, spatial, and even sartorial details. The assumption here, then, is that film viewing habits reflect observational habits of daily life, and vice versa. This purports to be a study of witnesses' abilities to report in a deposition-like scenario, but is more accurately a study of spectators' ability to remember details from a moving picture scene.

Boring clearly perceived this film fragment as a convenient container of information, and the experiment thus amounts to a kind of viewing retention examination. Because film was used as a vehicle for this information there lurks an underlying assumption that it is closer to the experience of real-life witnessing than other available options. However unintentionally, the experiment anticipates several decades of theories about cinematic realism and the spectator's relationship to moving images. In its presumed faith in the correspondence between real life and cinematic witnessing, Boring's test suggests an early subscription to a line of thinking that André Bazin and Siegfried Kracauer would surely have appreciated: that film is an especially fit vehicle for preserving reality. Furthermore, the test relies upon – presumes, in fact – the notion of a wholly immersed viewing subject, even as it fails to acknowledge that such immersion is, even at this relatively early moment in film history, facilitated by a narrative context that is here dismantled. "Correct" responses, Boring suggests, are a product of "watching with (one's) best attention". Boring, however, seems unbothered by the possibility that there might be another mode of viewing that might bypass details like preferred neckwear, especially when belonging to the character who is *not* the criminal. Had his subjects viewed the film *as a film*, surely other factors – emotional, identificatory, and so on – would have played a role in their responses, a variable curtailed by the very act of excerpting.

Still, Boring's choice of films – perhaps even of this particular scene from this film – is curious: he does not select a scene depicting a crime in progress, but rather what happens after a crime has been committed. The fact that this scene was chosen – rather than one depicting, say, a family quarrel or people shopping – seems a deliberate selection in which is implicit the belief that the images reflect something worth deposing a witness about. Additionally, surely the more methodologically sound approach would have been to show the entire film and then to ask about details selected from the larger narrative whole. Instead, participants were primed to focus attentively on the one scene they were tested upon, an experience that deviates both from real-world observation as well as from moviegoing behaviour.

Some conclusions

Film's use in the laboratory offers us just one instance of its dynamic existence beyond conventional exhibition sites and entertainment purposes. The fragmenting of *Van Bibber's Experiment* into an especially useful one-minute scene and its reduction, in the experiment, to a series of potentially memorable details (actions, attire, duration, props) forces us to rethink film's purposefulness and functionality in an era replete with such non-theatrical uses. Where *Moving Picture World*'s review applauded *Van Bibber's Experiment* – despite disparaging Davis's skills as an author – for its "real Americanism, the noble sentiment, which in this newer and fresher world of ours, freer from the taint of caste and social prejudice, holds out a larger hope to erring or oppressed humanity", Boring's experiment stripped the film of its redemptive message and narrative integrity, borrowing only actions surrounding the criminal act that, the same review observed, was "not supposed to occur in moving pictures, however largely … [burglars] may figure in the daily press". Noting that audiences easily understood the plot and literally applauded the burglar's new lease of life at the film's end, the review held up *Van Bibber's Experiment* as the kind of film that "moving picture audiences everywhere are hungry for".[21]

In one context then, *Van Bibber's Experiment* can be considered a noteworthy example of uplifting narrative cinema, a well-made, socially redemptive story that was deemed particularly satisfying for American audiences. It was also part of a wave of literary adaptations by well-known contemporary authors (Edison's *Kinetogram* touted this in the film's publicity), in this case constructed around a recurring character in almost serial form. But *Van Bibber's Experiment* was also successful in part, as *Moving Picture World* pointed out, because the film "follows a very clever conception of the film maker, which he did not find in the story and which is entirely his own".[22] In fact, comparison between the short story and the film suggests many transformations and inventions which, the review claimed, facilitated the film's success.

In another context, the film functioned as a differently malleable text, valued for the ease with which it could be taken apart and removed from its originally intended context, presented not as entertainment but as stimulus. Boring's disregard for the film as a finite product, his use of it as a means of conveying reportable information to a group of subjects, offers an opportunity to rethink film's multi-purpose functionality in the 1910s. Given its originality, perhaps what is most intriguing about Boring's experiment is that it did not appear to set any methodological trends and has so completely disappeared from the history of psychological experimentation. The lack of contemporary and even retrospective commentary on the moving picture aspect of this experiment suggests that this was only a novel – and not a particularly effective – methodology.

But let us not forget that *Van Bibber's Experiment* also depicts a social experiment, and a successful one at that. The New York club man – now making his third appearance in an Edison production – enacts his experiment because he recognises the burglar from a *photograph*, not a motion picture, that he has been shown earlier in the evening. This, then, is a story about detection, which is what Boring's experiment was in some ways testing, and it revolves around a character with whom audience members – though perhaps not test subjects – were clearly meant to identify. Of course, Boring's subjects would not, presumably, have known about these aspects of the film they were watching (although one wonders if any of them might have seen a previous or even this Van Bibber film, all of which starred Conness in the leading role, and what that recognition might have done to the nature of their responses). Edison's film thus provides a simplified model within itself for a successful version of Boring's experiment – one with implications involving class and gender that would, in fact, end up figuring prominently in psychological research on the subject of witnessing to the present day.

Acknowledgements: Leonard De Graaf of the Edison Historic Site provided me with essential information and images, without which I could not have written this essay. For their generous assistance – especially regarding the history of psychology and the use of film in psychological experiments – I would also like to thank Scott Curtis (Northwestern University), Jonathan Auerbach (University of Maryland), Lynne Baker-Ward and Jeffery Braden (North Carolina State University), Susan Carey (Harvard University), Arlie Belliveau (York University), Bob Rieber (Fordham University), and Ludy Benjamin (Texas A&M).

Notes

1. "Van Bibber's Experiment", *Kinetogram* 4 (15 June 1911): 3–5; "Van Bibber's Experiment", *Moving Picture World* (1 July 1911): 1492; David Hulfish, *Cyclopedia of Motion Picture Work* (Chicago: American Technical Society, 1914), 68. The paper print photos survive in the Edison legal files at the Edison National Historic Site.

2. Whipple both "suggested and supervised" Boring's research plan. Edwin G. Boring, "Capacity to Report Upon Moving Pictures as Conditioned by Sex and Age: A Contribution to the Psychology of Testimony", *Journal of the American Institute of Criminal Law and Criminology* 6 (March 1916): 820.

3. Leslie Y. Rabkin, *The Celluloid Couch* (Lanham, MD: Scarecrow Press, 1998), 4–5. See also Benjamin Harris, "The Role of Film in John B. Watson's Developmental Research Program", *Contributions to a History of Developmental Psychology* (New York: Mouton Publishers, 1985), 359–366. For more on Münsterberg, the films he worked on for the Paramount Pictographs series (which are not extant), and experimental psychology see Scott Curtis's "'Like a Hailstorm on the Nerves of Modern Man': Cinema, Legibility, and the Body in Germany, 1895–1914" (Ph. D. dissertation, University of Iowa, 1996).

4. On earlier examples of film's use in documenting psychiatric conditions, see Rabkin, *The Celluloid Couch*, 3.

5. As recently as 2006, a study was published that used a film (produced explicitly for the experiment) to study the relationship between stress and memory: "Films come very close to mimicking verbal and visual stimuli as they naturally occur during an experience and for this reason have been used extensively in eyewitness memory and false memory research". Victoria Beckner, David Tucker,

Yvon Delville, and David Mohr, "Stress Facilitates Consolidation of Verbal Memory for a Film But Does Not Affect Retrieval", *Behavioral Neuroscience* 120.3 (2006): 519.

6. Films do, in fact, have a long history as tools in psychological experiments, especially those involving memory. I have, however, found only two psychological studies that engage with Boring's early film use, which did not set an immediate methodological trend. One claims that "The use of cinematic material to probe memory can be traced to the early days of cinema (Boring 1916), but did not catch on, a few exceptions notwithstanding". Orit Furman, Nimrod Dorfman, Uri Hasson, et al., "They Saw a Movie: Long-Term Memory for an Extended Audiovisual Narrative", *Learning & Memory* 14 (2007): 457. The other reference is reported in a series of articles by Herbert S. Conrad and Harold E. Jones, "Psychological Studies of Motion Pictures", published in *Parent Teacher*, *University of California Publications in Psychology*, and *The Journal of Social Psychology* between 1928 and 1931.

7. "Edwin Garrigues Boring", in Edwin G. Boring et al. (eds), *A History of Psychology in Autobiography*, vol. 4. (Worcester, MA: Clark University Press, 1952), 33.

8. G.M. Whipple, *Manual of Mental and Physical Tests* (Baltimore, MD: Warwick & York, 1921 [1914]), 32–34.

9. Henry Cole Quinby (ed.), *Richard Harding Davis: A Bibliography* (New York: E.B. Dutton & Co., 1924), 216.

10. This and all other quotes in this paragraph are from "Van Bibber's Experiment", *Moving Picture World* (1 July 1911): 1492.

11. "Edwin Garrigues Boring", 31–33.

12. Whipple is also the author of the two-volume *Manual of Mental and Physical Tests* (Baltimore, MD: Warwick and York, 1910). See Frank S. Freeman, "A Note on E.B. Titchener and G.M. Whipple", *Journal of the History of the Behavioral Science* 20 (April 1984): 178.

13. "L.L. Thurstone", in Boring, et al. (eds), *A History of Psychology in Autobiography*, vol. 4, 297–300. Thurstone would go on to write about educational uses of motion pictures and was involved in the 1930s Payne Fund studies of motion picture influence on high school students. For more on Boring's relationship to and influence on the field of psychology – especially on positivist psychology – see John J. Cerullo, "E.G. Boring: Reflections on a Discipline Builder", *American Journal of Psychology* 101 (Winter 1988): 561–575. Unfortunately, Harvard University's collection of Boring's papers dates back only to 1919; materials documenting his early years are uncollected.

14. Boring, "Capacity to Report", 820.

15. Ibid., 821.

16. Ibid.

17. Ibid., 822.

18. Ibid., 823.

19. Ibid., 833.

20. Ibid.

21. "Van Bibber's Experiment", *Moving Picture World* (1 July, 1911): 1492.

22. Ibid.

18

Dissecting the Medical Training Film

Scott Curtis

As we know, educators of all stripes immediately recognised the pedagogical value of motion pictures. Projected film, like slides, could reach a much larger number of students than could any individual demonstration. And unlike slides, films could present a moving record of the event or object under study; they could thus function effectively as a convenient substitute for the object. Furthermore, many advocates favourably compared film to books because film's moving record, they claimed, had an impact that was not only more powerful than the written word, but also more immediate. In other words, many of the claims for educational film are variations on one theme: efficiency. Reaching more people in less time, communicating with greater impact and more convenience, the motion picture was hailed as the ultimate appliance for learning, a device that could cut educational work and waste in half. In both Europe and the United States, the rhetoric of efficiency influenced just about every statement on the advantages of film as a pedagogical tool, which is not surprising considering that "efficiency" was a mantra chanted by nearly every reformer, ideologue, or would-be manager from around 1900 to 1920. Social engineers of all types hoped to increase productivity and reduce waste through techniques designed to get the most out of the energy put in.

Medicine also shared this agenda, especially but not exclusively in the United States. Efficiency was a key concept in transforming the turn-of-the-century hospital from "a well of sorrow and charity" into a "work place for the production of health".[1] In the United States from around 1900 to 1920, health officials were increasingly dissatisfied with the duplication of services, the lack of coordination of units, and the generally low level of effectiveness in patient care among clinics, dispensaries, and hospitals nationwide. "Efficiency" became an institutional logic to promote standardisation of facilities, services, and administration. In fact, in the United States at least, efficiency was the rubric through which the modern hospital adopted business practices in order to establish itself as a more acceptable place for treatment and to attract paying patients.[2] For example, *Modern Hospital*, the organ of the American Hospital Association, devoted itself to promoting economy and efficiency in hospital management, while the American College of Surgeons was established initially to focus on the standardisation of tools and techniques within surgical practice.

During this period, the medical training film stood at the intersection of medicine, efficiency, and cinema. Given its admittedly esoteric status, it is fair to wonder why we should be interested in this genre. First, as the international medical community adopted motion pictures as an educational device, health professionals made especially clear statements about the value of film for pedagogy. These statements expressed, explicitly or implicitly, a nascent theory of film, one that can also be inferred from examples in other educational arenas. So if we were to excavate a history and theory of educational film, its appropriation by the medical community would need to be included. Second, the discussions of film as a training medium are especially intriguing, because they shared a common assumption about the efficacy and effect of the moving image on the viewer; I will call this the "presumption of mimesis". Descriptions of the uses and advantages of training films implied that the spectator was to "follow" the film by way of inner mimesis or kinesthetic empathy. That is, the descriptions noted especially clearly the visceral effect of moving images. We *move* with the film; the discussions implied that a training film triggered some aspect of muscle memory and that spectators "learned" the appropriate gestures from the image, almost directly. Some statements about the educational value of motion pictures were quite explicit in this regard. In other words, if we were interested in early discussions about embodied spectatorship, the discourse about training films would be a good place to start.

So medicine, efficiency, and film intersected in two ways: film was used to train surgeons to use more efficient techniques, and film was applauded as an especially efficient training tool. According to its advocates, the training film could efficiently tutor viewers to be efficient. This essay will outline the connections between the rhetoric of efficiency and assumptions about the pedagogical value of the medical motion picture, focusing on pioneers in Germany, France, and the United States. There were other uses of film in medicine, of course, such as research films or health education films aimed at lay audiences, but this essay will focus on educational uses within the medical community. By "training film" I mean films that instructed for specific skills, as well as more general educational films designed for medical students or professionals; specifically, I am interested in two early (and familiar) proponents of the medical training film, Parisian surgeon Eugène Louis Doyen and American efficiency experts Frank and Lillian Gilbreth. Through these filmmakers we can see the extent to which the cinematic image was held as a model of efficiency.

Frank and Lillian Gilbreth were well-known efficiency experts in the United States, especially prominent between 1910 and 1920.[3] They adopted Frederick Taylor's principles of scientific management, but they differentiated their methods from his by rejecting Taylor's use of a stopwatch as the primary means of measuring worker efficiency. Instead they employed what they considered more "objective" devices, including the motion picture camera, to record, analyse, and improve worker movement; they argued that the stopwatch depended too much on the operator for results (the time for a task, for example, depended on when the operator started and stopped the watch, which many claimed was inconsistent from case to case), while they viewed their approach as more independent of operator error because they could record the entire task and deduce the time from calculations based on the recording. Other tools included their ubiquitous chronometer, in order to gauge distance to time; and a white, grid-pattern wallpaper, against which the subjects were filmed and which served simultaneously as a reflective surface and as a rough guide for measurement of hand motions (although not always useful, depending on the camera angle). They also used what they called a "cyclegraph": they attached light bulbs to the subject's hands and then photographed the movements through an open shutter. The resulting exposure would serve as the basis for a wire model that gave a visual, tactile rendering of the most efficient movement. With these devices, the Gilbreths deconstructed movement into different elements and rendered them graphically, which ultimately helped them determine the most efficient use of worker energy and time. They employed this method to a number of tasks, from bricklaying to typing to golf.

It is not well-known, however, that between 1912 and 1917 the Gilbreths focused their attention and technologies primarily on surgeons.[4] This move was, in part, a clever publicity strategy; the Gilbreths felt that if they could persuade surgeons of their methods, they could persuade anybody.[5] In fact, they did have some influence; a number of surgeons considered themselves disciples of Gilbreth efficiency and peppered journals with articles extolling the benefits of motion study and proper workplace organisation.[6] In their own writings, the Gilbreths focused on standardisation of surgical tools and techniques, on the one hand, and operating room efficiency, on the other.[7] The Gilbreths made their pitch to a number of hospitals on the east coast, and were successful in bringing surgeons to their home in Providence for "standardisation conferences". There is some question, however, about the role of film in their approach. The films that I have seen – which are by no means the only ones – are inconclusive.[8] In certain films, the camera is placed in such a way that the viewer cannot see anything but the backs of the surgeons hunched over the operating table, so it is unclear what help the filmed record could be. Other films focus on operating room organisation; the surgeons and nurses are numbered and coded, for example. In fact, the Gilbreths urged the establishment of the now-standard system whereby nurses hand surgical instruments to the physician during the operation. The Gilbreths were hired as consultants and they used film as part of a larger system for recommending changes in workplace design. In this sense, their use of film as a training device was atypical. Much more typical was the use of films as an educational tool in medical school curricula and in professional settings, such as conferences.

Indeed, film's potential for pedagogy was its most intriguing feature for the medical community, and most medical filmmakers at this time cited their desire to improve teaching. In Paris in 1897, Eugène Louis Doyen, a maverick surgeon known for his innovative techniques and disdain for the academy, employed two cameramen to film his surgeries. These films were meant to illustrate and publicise Doyen's tools and techniques, but they were also to serve as training films for surgeons and as a means to improve Doyen's own performance.[9] In 1899, Doyen wrote: "It has been with the object of completing our means of teaching the art of surgery that I have been led to study and employ the cinematograph".[10] In Germany, too, medical filmmakers had been working since the turn of the century, but the watershed moment came at a February 1910 demonstration of "Film in the Service of Medicine", which focused on educational uses. Representatives from the Berlin medical establishment, including the Imperial Board of Health, were so tightly packed into the lecture hall that the organisers had to turn people away.[11] While it was not the first time that such films had been shown in Germany, the event received much attention from the national and international medical community and helped to focus awareness on the educational potential of medical film.[12] The organiser of the event, prominent physician Robert Kutner, praised the power of cinematography:

> And how convenient, how effortless! ... [Cinema] has a persuasive evidentiary power beyond that of any other document, beyond even the most vivid description. ... The motion picture projector demonstrates its most spectacular educational applications in auditorium demonstrations of microscopic or macroscopic images of movement. In a normal lecture-room demonstration of movement, especially that of small objects (think, for example, of a frog's beating heart), only a small part of the audience really sees anything, while in a film demonstration everyone present can observe the presentation equally well. Without the assistance of the motion picture projector, almost all X-ray motion pictures and certainly all motion pictures taken from a microscope could be shown to only a small circle or to only one person at a time.[13]

Kutner describes the pedagogical advantages of motion pictures in a language common to advocates of educational film at the time. But Kutner also emphasises the efficiency of the moving image for the pedagogical task; in fact, he implies that there are a variety of efficiencies. First and most obviously, Kutner here refers to economies of scale: the simple claim that more people could see a large projected image than could see a small demonstration. As medical school enrollments in Europe and the United States grew steadily toward the turn of the century, this claim gained traction – lecturers used projected images more and more from the 1870s onward.[14] A number of famous physicians from the turn of the century, such as Vienna's Theodor Billroth, collected medical photography and film for precisely this purpose.[15]

But Kutner also hints at another kind of efficiency. When he says "how convenient, how effortless!" he is probably not referring to the motion picture apparatus, which was definitely not convenient and effortless. Instead, he is referring to the efficiency of the image itself. It has a "persuasive evidentiary power beyond that of any other document, beyond even the most vivid description". For Kutner and others, that power came naturally to the image, especially to the photographic image; they assumed that motion pictures worked quickly and effortlessly on the spectator. When Doyen insisted that "with the cinematograph we can make hundreds of people follow in one minute what a whole lecture could not make clear to a limited number of students", he was making a similar claim.[16] The issue here was not simply about numbers of students – it was about the immediacy of the image versus the indirectness of the spoken word. If the image was considered direct, instantaneous, vivid, and penetrating, then the written or spoken description was perceived as aloof, dull, circuitous. In a way, Kutner and Doyen's preferences echoed a bias common in modern medical education. The nineteenth century continued a long transformation in medical education (and education in general) that emphasised direct perception of the objects of study over their presentation in books. The discussion of film as an educational tool made this bias even more explicit. Educators viewed the direct perception of objects as a much more effective and efficient mode of learning. The image was efficient because it was presumed to affect the viewer immediately, like a drug, or a blow to the head, whereas reading or speaking and then cognitively processing words supposedly took (too much) time. The image was considered physical and immediate, while the word was seen as intellectual.

What was the presumed ontological basis for this immediacy? What characteristic of the image gave it this apparently direct, instantaneous persuasive power? For many writing about the educational or scientific benefits of film during this time, it was summed up in the concept of "vividness". Kutner writes, "Cinema has a persuasive evidentiary power beyond that of any other document, beyond even the most vivid description", implying that film was even more vivid than words, or more pointedly, book-learning. What exactly was this "vividness"? As we know, the clarity, texture, and abundant detail of the photographic image combine with projected movement to give the image a *presence* unlike any previous representational form. Its level of detail allows the photographic image to reproduce patterns of texture and variation, hence to represent the structure and randomness of the natural world, while the movement of the image presents this world in real time in a particularly striking way. The object "lives" onscreen. This is perhaps obvious, but it is all to say that "vividness" referred to the sense of presence that the moving image evokes. For early advocates of educational film, it was as if the thing itself were there in the room, available to direct perception.[17] Film thus functioned as an object lesson, an acceptable substitute for the thing itself, which was especially helpful in medical demonstrations, where the use of live patients was always logistically and ethically troublesome.

Cinema's vividness permitted Doyen to extol the virtues of the motion picture over not only books but even cadavers. Complaining about the inadequacy of the long-standing practice of rehearsing surgical techniques on cadavers, Doyen asks, "Do our books fill the gap thus left? Certainly not. The most detailed descriptions, the best diagrams or photographs of the various steps of an operation are inadequate. ... It is not sufficient to follow the operation, as it were, secondhand; rather, the author of the technique, the master himself, must be seen at work. The surgeon is judged by his work, and no text-books, however well-illustrated, can sufficiently express his personality".[18] In motion pictures, on the other hand, Doyen found a perfect medium to express vividly the personality of the "master himself". Movies were not "secondhand"; they allowed Doyen to be "present" to the students. This, then, is another cinematic efficiency: to be at more than one place at a time. Even more noteworthy is Doyen's concept of "personality". Doyen was not publicity shy, by any means, but he was not concerned to convey via a medical film his charisma and good looks, or not only those things. Primarily, his films were meant to promote his custom-designed surgical instruments and to present his technique – how Doyen held himself and how he moved in order to accomplish his task. Film provided, better than any previous medium, a demonstration of the actual movements required in surgery. Doyen's personality was his "posture" or "attitude" – his *embodied* technique. And to convey that personality was to presume that the student would copy it, that while the student watched the film, there would be a kind of kinesthetic empathy whereby the movements seen were somehow felt or incorporated into the student's own body. This is the mimetic presumption of most training films, it seems; most training films expect us to copy the movements they depict, and that the student will take on the "personality" or "attitude" of the master.

Doyen also extended this presumption to himself. He had in mind another form of efficiency: the power of film to improve his *own* technique. Doyen explains, "When I saw for the first time one of my operations reproduced on the screen, I recognised how far I fell short of my ideal. Many of the details of technique that had seemed satisfactory I now saw to be defective, and the cinematograph has thus enabled me considerably to correct and simplify, and to perfect my operative technique".[19] Fifteen years before the Gilbreths, Doyen claimed to have used film to study and correct the performance of work in the name of production efficiency. Whether he actually used film in this way or not is unclear, but the rhetoric is intriguing. "You will notice that each operation is done methodically. ... The surgeon is calm; his movements are precise and calculated. When he makes a muscular effort, you can see his biceps harden, his face contract, his whole body place itself in the most favourable position. The cinematograph registers the whole scene as it takes place, faithfully, rapidly, and in detail. Each step can thus be studied, analysed, critiqued. The surgeon can assist at and calmly study his own operations".[20] The drama of life and death shapes the practiced movements of the surgeon, giving them an urgency we might not encounter in other training film genres. It is noteworthy that, for Doyen, the cinematograph recorded details of the surgeon's "personality": the posture, the muscular effort, the position, as if the student could be somehow imprinted with this attitude or orientation. Anticipating Jean Epstein's thoughts on the close-up, Doyen similarly evoked the power of film to literally move us. And recalling Gilbreth and other scientific uses of film, he noted the power film gives the analytic eye to examine movement at leisure. Here and elsewhere, the educational film provided fertile ground for early discussions of scientific disinterestedness *and* embodied spectatorship.

So the medical training film presents an opportunity to discuss the relationship between film, education, and efficiency. In this essay, I have outlined three main varieties of filmic efficiency. First, film was often touted as an instrument that could provide a faithful record of the thing or event, and thus function as a convenient substitute. I do not mean to say that the *apparatus* was itself convenient, only that compared to, say, live medical demonstration, film was held up as a potentially suitable alternative, even if rarely acted upon during the early years. Second, advocates appreciated that film could reach more students or viewers with less effort. This took two forms: in the lecture hall, bounded by a particular time and space, and in distribution, where the reproduction and circulation of film could address audiences potentially anywhere and anytime. And finally, film was perceived to be "direct". Gilbreth said that efficient motion does not go from A to B to C when it could find the best way to go directly from A to C.[21] For many advocates of educational cinema, film worked in the same way: it bypassed the cognitive faculties and imprinted itself directly and immediately on the mind *and* body, prompting a voluntary or involuntary mimesis. We have heard variations of this theme: cinema and hypnosis, cinema and suggestion, cinema as Mabusian puppetmaster.[22] The paradox of the rhetoric of the educational film is that even though the moving image exemplified the very image of efficiency, that efficiency seemed to cut both ways, for good and for ill.

Notes

1. Paul Starr, *The Social Transformation of American Medicine* (New York: Basic Books, 1982), 146.
2. See George Rosen, "The Efficiency Criterion in Medical Care, 1900–1920", *Bulletin of the History of Medicine* 50, no. 1 (Spring 1976): 28–44; Margarete Arndt and Barbara Bigelow, "Toward the Creation of an Institutional Logic for the Management of Hospitals: Efficiency in the Early Nineteen Hundreds", *Medical Care Research and Review* 63, no. 3 (June 2006): 369–394.
3. On Gilbreth, see Brian Charles Price, "One Best Way: Frank and Lillian Gilbreth's Transformation of Scientific Management, 1885–1940" (Ph. D. dissertation, Purdue University, 1987); Richard Lindstrom, "'They All Believe They Are Undiscovered Mary Pickfords': Workers, Photography, and Scientific Management", *Technology and Culture* 41, no. 4 (2000): 725–751; Sharon Corwin, "Picturing Efficiency: Precisionism, Scientific Management, and the Effacement of Labor", *Representations* 84 (2003): 139–165; Elspeth H. Brown, *The Corporate Eye: Photography and the Rationalization of American Commercial Culture, 1884–1929* (Baltimore: Johns Hopkins University Press, 2005); and Scott Curtis, "Images of Efficiency: The Films of Frank B. Gilbreth", in Vinzenz Hediger and Patrick Vonderau (eds), *Films that Work: Industrial Film and the Productivity of Media*, (Amsterdam: Amsterdam University Press, 2009), 85–99.
4. I thank Caitlin Gainty, University of Chicago, for pointing me in this direction.
5. Albert Jay Nock, "Efficiency and the Highbrow: Frank Gilbreth's Great Plan to Introduce Time-Study into Surgery", *American Magazine* 75, no. 5 (March 1913): 48–51.
6. See Robert L. Dickinson, "Standardization of Surgery: An Attack on the Problem", *Journal of the American Medical Association* 63, no. 9 (29 August 1914): 763–765; Robert L. Dickinson, "'Efficiency Engineering' in Pelvic Surgery: One and Two-Suture Operations", *Surgery, Gynecology and Obstetrics* 18 (1914): 559–571.
7. Frank B. Gilbreth, "Scientific Management in the Hospital", *The Modern Hospital* 3 (1914): 321–324; Frank B. Gilbreth, "Motion Study in Surgery", *Canadian Journal of Medicine and Surgery* 40 (July 1916): 22–31. For an overview, see A. Baumgart and D. Neuhauser, "Frank and Lillian Gilbreth: Scientific Management in the Operating Room", *Quality and Safety in Health Care* 18 (2009): 413–415.
8. The Gilbreth films are collected at the Purdue University Libraries Archives and Special Collections, West Lafayette, Indiana, USA. Brief snippets from the surgical films are included on Purdue's DVD collections *The Original Films of Frank B. Gilbreth, Odds and Ends #2* (2006) and *Odds and Ends #3* (2006).
9. Eugène Doyen, "Le Cinematograph et l'Enseignement de la Chirurgie", *Revue critique de médecine et de chirurgie* 1, no. 1 (15 August 1899): 1–6, translated as "The Cinematograph and the Teaching of Surgery", *The British Gynæcological Journal* 15 (1899): 579–586. On Doyen, see Robert Didier,

Le Docteur Doyen: Chirurgien de la Belle Époque (Paris: Librairie Maloine, 1962); and especially the work of Thierry Lefebvre, including "Le cas étrange du Dr Doyen, 1859–1916", *Archives* 29 (February 1990): 1–12; "Le Dr Doyen, un précurseur", in Alexis Martinet (ed.), *Le cinéma et la science* (Paris: CNRS Éditions, 1994), 70–77; and *La Chair et le celluloïd: Le cinéma chirurgical du Docteur Doyen* (Brionne: Jean Doyen éditeur, 2004). On the films themselves, see Lefebvre, "La collection des films du Dr Doyen", *1895* 17 (December 1994): 100–114; and Tiago Baptista, "'Il faut voir le maître': A Recent Restoration of Surgical Films by E.-L.Doyen (1859–1916)", *Journal of Film Preservation* 70 (November 2005): 42–50.

10. Doyen, "The Cinematograph and the Teaching of Surgery", 581.
11. See the report in *Zentralblatt für Röntgenstrahlen, Radium und verwandte Gebiete* 1, no. 2 (1910): 78–80.
12. See "Special Correspondence: Berlin", *The British Medical Journal* (5 March 1910): 598, for another report of the evening. In England, Dr William Stirling was the primary early advocate of the use of film for medical education. See reports of Stirling's film presentations on medicine and biology in "Medical News", *The Lancet* 177 (27 May 1911): 1470, and *The Lancet* 182 (11 October 1913): 1083–1084.
13. Robert Kutner, "Die Bedeutung der Kinematographie für medizinische Forschung und Unterricht sowie für die volkshygienische Belehrung", *Zeitschrift für Ärztliche Fortbildung* 8, no. 8 (15 April 1911): 250.
14. For discussion of the projection of images in medical education, see Sigmund Theodor Stein, *Das Licht im Dienste wissenschaftlicher Forschung: Handbuch der Anwendung des Lichtes und der Photographie in der Natur- und Heilkunde* (Leipzig: Spamer, 1877); and Sigmund Theodor Stein, *Die optische Projektionskunst im Dienste der exakten Wissenschaften: ein Lehr- und Hilfsbuch zur Unterstützung des naturwissenschaftlichen Unterrichts* (Halle: W. Knapp, 1887). See also Henning Schmidgen, "Pictures, Preparations, and Living Processes: The Production of Immediate Visual Perception (Anschauung) in Late-19th-Century Physiology", *Journal of the History of Biology* 37, no. 3 (October 2004): 477–513.
15. On Billroth's enthusiasm for new media technologies, see Ernst Kern, *Theodor Billroth, 1829–1894: Biographie anhand von Selbstzeugnissen* (München: Urban & Schwarzenberg, 1994), 73–75.
16. Doyen, "The Cinematograph and the Teaching of Surgery", 581.
17. Alongside this discourse of "seeing as" – film as an extension of direct perception and the moving image as a substitute for the thing itself – there was another discourse of "seeing differently" – film as a technology for representing things in ways that the naked eye could not perceive. Educators regarded both features of cinema to be pedagogically useful, while film theorists such as Jean Epstein and Béla Balázs prioritised the latter. Thanks to Rob King for reminding me of the difference.
18. Doyen, "The Cinematograph and the Teaching of Surgery", 580–581, translation modified.
19. Ibid., 582.
20. Ibid.
21. Frank B. Gilbreth and Lillian Moller Gilbreth, "The Waste of Getting Tired", *The Independent* 91 (15 September 1917): 427.
22. See Stefan Andriopoulos, *Possessed: Hypnotic Crimes, Corporate Fiction, and the Invention of Cinema* (Chicago: University of Chicago Press, 2008); and Rae Beth Gordon, *Why the French Love Jerry Lewis: From Cabaret to Early Cinema* (Stanford: Stanford University Press, 2001).

19

Corporal Permeability and Shadow Pictures: Reconsidering Uncle Josh at the Moving Picture Show (1902)

Amy E. Borden

During research into how motion pictures were written about in late-nineteenth and early-twentieth century periodicals marketed to the American middle class, I found that photochemical motion pictures and X-ray images were discursively linked by writers via the repeated use of descriptive phrases such as "photographic shadow", "shadow-image", and, often, just plain "shadow".[1] The similarities in the way each technology was written about shows how projected motion pictures and X-ray images were discursively linked for American readers who were potential motion picture spectators. Viewing Edwin S. Porter's 1902 film *Uncle Josh at the Moving Picture Show* in a cultural context where "shadow pictures" simultaneously named the photochemical and the screen images both technologies produced, allows us to re-experience Porter's film, which a colleague affectionately refers to as "that old chestnut of film studies", as an exhibition of the process by which shadow bodies are created in their interaction with image-producing machines.

Tracing how the term "shadow" described images produced by each technology from 1895 – the year of both Wilhelm Röntgen's discovery of X-rays and the public debut of projected motion pictures – to 1929, the final year the *Los Angeles Times* published a regular feature advertising current films, entitled "Shadow Speakers", allows me to reconsider how the interaction between the human body and projected images highlighted in the pre-cinematic practice of shadowgraphy is carried over in coverage of early film and X-ray images. As a prehistory of photochemical moving pictures, shadowgraphy presents a visible relationship between the human body and its projected image that reveals the body to be made transient in its relationship with projection technologies. This relationship between body and machine is preserved in the essays and articles I located that write about X-ray and motion picture technology.

As we know from Lisa Cartwright's work, X-ray images were exhibited in urban centres.[2] The attraction of viewing a "shadow cast upon the fluorescent screen" is written about widely in the popular press.[3] In the news articles, essays, advertisements, and reviews that I examined I was struck by the centrality of the human body in the discourse produced by the American popular press about new image-producing technologies; these technologies included motion pictures and X-ray images produced by fluoroscopes – where part of a body is made visibly permeable on a luminous screen to reveal the body's interior movement for a viewer. Often writers understood the body as an exchange point between X-ray and motion picture technologies and the subsequently produced images, be they imprinted on photographic paper or presented on a screen.

This centrality is predictable for X-rays when we bear in mind how their discovery allowed for the penetration of corporal boundaries made visible on a screen or in photochemical images. Röntgen explains how the phenomenon he discovered creates "regular shadow pictures produced by the interposition of a more or less permeable body between the source and a photographic plate or fluorescent screen….a kind of relationship between the new rays and light rays appears to exist; at least in the formation of shadows [and] fluorescence".[4] The relationship Röntgen points to is due to the fact that dense materials, for example metal or the calcium in bones, absorb the high-energy X-rays, creating a fluorescent quality on exposed photographic paper. A photographic image is formed when the paper reacts to the rays emitted from the dense matter.

The human body as a site of exchange between screen and projection apparatus is less obvious when we think about motion pictures. Jonathan Auerbach argues that the bodies photographed in actualities or pre-narrative staged films such as the Corbett-Fitzsimmons fight "invite and compel us to pay attention to the more meagre shapes and traces, puzzling shadows and outlines struggling to realise some sort of coherence … apart from traditional categories of subject matter or personal identity (but not outside of history)".[5] Like Auerbach I find that there is difficulty in articulating how early cinema was experienced as a "medium of incarnation … populated by bodies placed in motion by the new technology because that view seems maddeningly obvious".[6] What may be less obvious is that once we consider these bodies as they were written about at the time – as shadows – a corporal instability is reintroduced into the way they are seen. Filmed bodies are visible incarnations of transience once we consider their shared discursive history with shadowgraphy and X-rays.

Describing the images produced by these two different image-producing technologies as shadows is held over from explanations of photographic methods earlier in the nineteenth century and from the pre-cinematic screen practice of shadowgraphy. Shadow pictures carry two immediate cultural associations. An example of the first may be taken from an 1839 report issued by the Commission of the Chamber of Deputies concerning pension awards for Louis Daguerre and the son of Joseph Niépce that reminds contemporary scholars of a photographic pre-history where the impression left by objects was understood to arise from a "contrast between light and shade" created by an exposure that revealed "the shadows of the objects".[7] This is a fundamental misunderstanding of the photographic process where the ability to fix an image relies on an emanation of light from an object's surface and not on the obstruction of a light source creating a shadow, yet this understanding of the photographic process is echoed in many of the American articles concerning photochemical images that I have examined.

The placement of a body or object between light source and exposure to create "shadows", be it on photographic paper or a screen, can be traced to shadowgraphy, the second cultural association that is vital to understanding the context in which *Uncle Josh at the Moving Picture Show* was released. One aspect of this theatrical tradition is defined by the manipulation of the human body between a light source and screen. In addition to the use of silhouettes, shadowgraphy displays the dexterous transformation of a performer's hands into an infinite number of figures. This practice offers narratives in motion and the ability to witness the transformation of a performer's hands into objects and characters within scenarios in motion.

Images of the transformation from recognisable human hands to such projected images as animals, a fisherman in a boat, or a fight between a janitress and a tenant were published in the periodical *Scientific American* and compiled in an 1897 anthology selected from the magazine's articles. Included in the anthology are chapters about the practices that produce the shadow images I discuss in this paper: descriptions of how X-rays were used in theatrical conjuring tricks, descriptions of the technology of projected moving pictures, and descriptions of shadowgraphy that describe the practice as producing a "collection of figures capable of being made with the shadow of the hands" that can be given "motion and life".[8]

Illustrations of shadowgraphic staging included in the anthology emphasise the projected light, the screen on which the figures will appear, and the shadowgraphist positioned amidst the audience, manipulating his hands within a beam of light. By obstructing a portion of the light source, the shadowgraphist creates figures on the screen. By being visible to the audience, the transformation of the corporal form of the shadowgraphist's hands occurs onscreen. The relationship between the bodily form that was – hands – and what that form has become – the onscreen image – is preserved by the visibility of the relationship between light source, performer's body, and onscreen image in the viewing environment.

Turning now to *Uncle Josh at the Moving Picture Show* (January, 1902), we can see a similar visibility in Josh's attempts to interact with projected motion picture images that he mistakes for the vaudeville actors that had previously occupied the stage.[9] His attempts to interact with the onscreen images depict how a performer's body is made shadow-like in its interaction with motion picture technology in an exhibition space. In the previous two *Josh* films Porter directed for the Edison company – *Uncle Josh's Nightmare* (March, 1900) and *Uncle Josh at a Spooky Hotel* (March, 1900) – he establishes a pattern: Uncle Josh physically confronts apparitions whose physical forms are present and not present. They are able to affect Josh but are visible only in certain spatial and temporal states: dream-life or the midnight witching hour.

The third *Uncle Josh* film continues this pattern of unstable bodies with its inclusion of filmed and spectator bodies that appear permeable. When read alongside published descriptions of onscreen bodies as shadow-like, this pattern asks how we might consider registers of corporal display, such as permeability, that present bodies made unstable in their interaction with image-producing technologies – even when that interaction occurs offscreen during filming. Coupled with these published accounts, the final *Uncle Josh* film explicitly suggests that filmed bodies were distinct due to this interaction. This points to the possibility that early trick films were a site for the display of these distinct and unstable bodies; accordingly, we can understand such films as more than simply a cinematic translation of stage illusions adapted to the new technology via framing and the deliberate presentation of a single view that Tom Gunning writes about.[10]

In the film Uncle Josh weaves into the space of the staged superimposed projection. He is reacting to an onscreen train's approach in what I first assumed was an attempt to look behind the screen to see if the train was actually about to steam into the theatre, a mocking poke at the realism of the image. However, repeated viewings have convinced me that Josh is not investigating the verisimilitude of the scene; rather, he is getting a closer look at the image of the train as it steams by. Acting on a similar desire to interact with an onscreen Parisian dancer projected at the beginning of the film, Josh gets a closer look at the train when he crosses into the screen. His body dematerialises within the screen's frame as he breaks its horizontal plane. Half of Josh's body appears as before: solidly rooted to the stage, but with his torso becoming a shadow-like image

19 Corporal Permeability and Shadow Pictures

Fig. 1.

Uncle Josh visibly becomes a shadow image. Uncle Josh at the Moving Picture Show. *Edwin S. Porter.*

as it crosses into the projected image of the Black Diamond Express. A portion of his onstage body disappears from the stage setting, but it simultaneously reappears in the projected image. This creates a double presence: Josh is both onstage and onscreen; he is both a solid body and a pale shadow-like image of the body we have just seen. Much like the 1895 description Röntgen provides of X-rays interacting with a body, Josh's presence creates the appearance of permeability between his body and the images on the screen.

Most likely this double-presence is an accident of an exuberant Charles Manley entering the space where the onstage screen will be superimposed; however, this effect is repeated with the next set of images in an instance that is clearly diegetically motivated. Josh emerges from his theatrical box after getting a closer look at the locomotive to take his place at stage left to continue watching the projection of *The Country Couple* – a film-within-Porter's film. As he views the film, Josh believes he recognises his daughter onscreen.[11] Seeing her with an unknown man, he throws down his coat, pushes back his sleeves, and prepares to confront the onscreen suitor. Once Josh removes his coat his appearance matches that of the onscreen male figure.[12] His body dematerialises as he jumps at the screen. This dematerialisation is again marked as a faded shadow-like corporal form that appears to have penetrated the projected image, entering the narrative. Once he enters the space of the superimposed Edison kinetoscope images, his body is itself projected into the screen world, like the shadow of a body caught in the projector's beam, but his grayed shadow-image is simultaneously shadow and solid body because he occupies both the onstage diegesis and the onscreen diegesis (Figure 1).

When Josh penetrates the projected image Porter abruptly ends the superimposition effect to allow for the completion of the film: Josh pulls down the screen, revealing Edison's operator behind it. This staging calls to mind the rear-projection of a silhouette show and animates the space occupied by the superimposed screen within the actual space of the diegetic stage set. It also recalls an 1896 description of the Vitascope published in *North American Review*, in which George Parsons Lathrop uses the term shadow to describe filmed bodies; at the same time he also argues that these shadows are illuminated moving bodies "that have all the naturalness ... of reality".[13]

Lathrop's ability to move between shadows and illumination as if they exhibited the same characteristics hints at the way shadows were used to name both the illuminated bodies seen on fluoroscopes and movie screens and reminds his readers of the physical bodies that cast those now-illuminated images.

I refer to Lathrop's article in relation to this *Uncle Josh* film because in his explanation of how the Vitascope projects illuminated shadows he suggests that these images could be used for onstage productions as long as the machine was placed behind a muslin screen, as in a silhouette show, "so that there would be no possibility of its radiance causing shadows from the figures of the living actors in front of the screen".[14] Porter enacts this exact staging, and Josh's onscreen entrance places his body in the space that published accounts identified when writing of the ability of a film performer's body to cast a shadow onscreen. Josh creates the same effect as a would-be shadowgraph performer who obstructs a light source to create onscreen shadow images. As in the articles that refer to the bodies of cinematic performers as shadows, Josh's onstage body and onscreen shadow image reinforce the fact that onstage bodies are now generated and projected by machines.

One way to consider why the figure of the shadow described both X-ray and motion picture images is via the visibility of this relationship made familiar by shadowgraphy and echoed in the way X-ray technology positioned the body in the production of images. In the months following Röntgen's discovery, the American press repeatedly featured stories describing possible uses for the new rays that draw from shadowgraphy as a means to explain these new uses with images and ideas that would be familiar to readers. In an April 1896 article in *McClure's* that publicised Edison's intention to use X-rays "to photograph the human brain", the produced images are exclusively referred to as "shadow pictures" and are described as similar to those produced by a shadowgraphist: "It is with these pictures as with a shadow of the hand thrown on the wall – the nearer the hand to the wall, the more distinct becomes the shadow".[15] The following month *Century Magazine* published a twelve-page symposium on the uses of X-rays led by Thomas Edison that repeatedly uses the term shadow pictures to describe photochemical images produced by X-ray exposure. The article also refers to the use of a "luminous screen" on which the "transient shadows" of moving bodies may be seen.[16]

At the end of the nineteenth and beginning of the twentieth century, X-rays allow the exhibition of a living body such that the body itself is present alongside the "shadow of [its] moving parts ... clearly visible upon the screen".[17] The presence of a screen, a ray-emitting machine, and a body is highlighted in Röntgen's own description of a fluoroscope. In article after article the description of how X-rays may display the internal movement of bodies in motion shares space with the production of photochemical still images. Each form provides evidence of the X-ray's ability to penetrate corporal boundaries and presents the imaged body as shadow-like in two ways: (1) sharp, clear photochemical images referred to as shadow pictures and (2) "transient shadow" images seen against a luminous background.[18]

By 1896 both viewing forms are sufficiently pervasive that one writer argues that "[the] screen is so luminous that the shadows are clearer than in the X-ray photographs", and suggests that fluoroscope viewing conditions are only satisfactory "if the room is quite dark, the screen in the closed tube appears immediately, upon putting the eye to the hole in the tube, to be perfectly luminous. It will be more luminous under these precautions ...".[19] Retrospectively this description feels deeply filmic. In fact, periodicals repeatedly theorised the new technology and experience of photochemical motion pictures as an interaction between image-producing machines and the human body that created shadow images that were also described as "illuminations".[20] The use of shadows to describe the appearance of an X-rayed body is particularly pertinent when considering how *Uncle Josh at the Moving Picture Show* displays Josh as a moving, transient shadow when he attempts to interact with the projected kinetoscope image.

Describing moving pictures as shadows is part of cinema's early history, so much so that writers could depend on a reader's familiarity with the use of shadows to describe projected motion pictures in articles that were not primarily concerned with the new amusement.[21] In one such use, a reviewer of Kipling's 1901 novel *Kim* refers to Kim's reflection on his perceptions as similar to "a shadowy jostling throng of images … [that] calls to mind the mechanic marvels of the vitascope, when the *photographic shadow* of moving scenes is thrown on the canvas before us".[22] Beginning in 1896 and accelerating in the pre-sound era of the 1920s, there are a number of references to motion pictures in fiction and nonfiction that suggest that the filming experience has cast its shadow onscreen.[23] For instance, a 1924 review of DeMille's *The Ten Commandments* refers to the film as one of the "most powerfully effective spectacles that has yet cast its shadow on the screen".[24] The description of DeMille's epic production is unusual in its focus on spectacle. Most examples I found fuse the image of the shadow with the figure of the body interacting with projection and filming technology. The descriptions may be characterised in two ways: (1) illuminated onscreen figures and (2) literal shadows cast by stage performers. These are often combined in later descriptions that use shadows to literally and figuratively describe motion pictures. Often, as in the examples that follow, this combination highlights an interaction between motion picture machines and the body of the performer much like that seen in *Uncle Josh at the Moving Picture Show*.

From 1909 to 1919 the *Los Angeles Times* published a regular column about the movie business entitled "The Shadow Realm" and from 1925–1928 the monthly magazine *The Independent* published a regular column about motion pictures titled "Shadow Stage". The title of *The Independent*'s column draws on the fact that early films were screened during vaudeville performances and on the pre-cinematic history of shadow plays. This directs reader's attention to the stage as a site of display for motion pictures and suggests that the stage itself is a shadow. Both columns remind readers and potential viewers – as they were, after all, columns about the motion picture industry – of the onstage objects and bodies of performers made into shadows via motion picture technology.

A 1920 announcement of the Abbey Theatre Company's recent film work similarly remarks on the placement of its actors' bodies in the creation of motion picture shadow images: "Dublin will not have the opportunity of comparing the Abbey players on the boards of their theatre with their shadows on the cinematograph screen [for those films are solely meant for American distribution]".[25] As in the "Shadow Stage" column, this use of *shadows* to describe motion picture images draws attention to the actors whose bodies cast their shadow on the screen once they are photographed by the cinematograph. A comparable conception of onscreen shadows cast by an actor's body can be found in the *Los Angeles Times'* announcements publicising a film's opening and screening around the city. Beginning in September 1926 and continuing until May 1929, the newspaper regularly published pictures of Hollywood stars grouped under two alternating headings: "Shadow Screen" and, beginning in May 1929, "Shadow Speakers".[26] Like the notice about the Gate Theatre, the suggestion of the *Times'* headings is that the bodies of Hollywood actors – stars – intervene to produce shadows on the screen; their onscreen presence is the shadow of their corporal form.

Revisiting this era to ask why the figure of the shadow was used to identify different types of images suggests that the human body acted as a common site of exchange for multiple image-producing technologies and points to a similarity that allows us to see how these technologies overlapped in popular discourse. Viewed within the then-contemporary cultural discourse of bodies represented as shadows as the result of interacting with x-rays and light, *Uncle Josh at the Moving Picture Show* acknowledges that the corporal boundaries of bodies are transient and motion pictures help create that state. Like the permeable bodies that produce "shadow pictures" or "transient shadows" when bombarded with X-rays, when Uncle Josh enters the onscreen world he makes his body permeable via an interaction with projected rays and a screen.[27] Considering the staging of Josh's movements within a discourse about bodies become shadows published prior to and concurrent with the film's release expands our understanding of how this film may have been seen as something more than a comedy about a "rube" going to the movies.

Notes

1. "The Rise of Photography and Its Service to Mankind", *The Arena* 28, no.1 (January 1902): 29.
2. Lisa Cartwright, *Screening the Body: Tracing Medicine's Visual Culture* (Minneapolis, University of Minnesota Press, 1995), 130–132.
3. E. Fleischman-Asceim, "Practical Radiography", *Frank Leslie's Popular Monthly* 54, no. 6 (October 1902): 550, 551.
4. Wilhelm Roentgen, "On A New Kind of Rays", *Science* 3, no. 59 (14 February 1896): 227–231. In contemporary discourse Röntgen's name is spelled as it is here. I retain the earlier spelling when used in citations to ease bibliographic searches.
5. Jonathan Auerbach, *Body Shots: Early Cinema's Incarnations* (Berkeley, CA: University of California Press, 2007), 2.
6. Ibid.
7. Dominique François Arago, "Report", in Alan Trachtenberg (ed.), *Classic Essays on Photography* (New Haven, CT: Leet's Island Books, 1980), 16–17.
8. Albert E. Hopkins, (ed.) *Magic: Stage Illusions and Scientific Diversions, Including Trick Photography* (New York: Munn and Co, 1897), 173, 175.
9. *Uncle Josh at the Moving Show*, Edison Film Catalogue, no. 135 (September 1902), "American Memory - Edison Motion Picture and Sound Recordings", Library of Congress, Washington, D.C., accessed 3 February 2009, http://memory.loc.gov/ammem/edhtml/ujmps.html.
10. Tom Gunning, "'Primitive Cinema' – A Frame Up? Or, The Trick's on Us?" *Cinema Journal* 28, no. 2 (Winter 1989): 9.
11. *Uncle Josh at the Moving Picture Show*, Edison Film Catalogue.
12. I am indebted to Marc Robinson for pointing this similarity out to me.
13. George Parsons Lathrop, "Stage Scenery and the Vitascope", *North American Review* 163, no. 478 (September 1896): 377.
14. Ibid.
15. Cleveland Moffett, "The Röntgen Rays in America", *McClure's Magazine* 6, no. 5 (April 1896): 415.
16. "Photographing the Unseen, A Symposium on the Roentgen Rays", *Century Illustrated Magazine* 52, no. 1 (May 1896): 125.
17. Edward P. Thompson, "Application of X-rays for Exhibiting Invisible Objects in Motion", *Medical News* (7 March 1896): 268.
18. Ibid.
19. Thompson 268.
20. Lathrop, 377.
21. *The Original Movie*, released in April 1922 as part of *Tony Sarg's Almanac* – a 1921–1923 animated

short film series, cuts between back-lit silhouettes depicting Muybridge's famous experiments to sequentially photograph a horse's gait with an intertitle that explains, "This is how people think the movies began". Sarg depicts two founding stories: Muybridge's motion experiments and moving narrative created via silhouettes. Tony Sarg, *The Original Movie*, 1922 (Treasures From American Film Archives: National Film Preservation Foundation, 2005), DVD. Also see: Maxim Gorky, "The Lumière Cinematograph", 4 July 1896, in Richard Taylor and Ian Christie (eds), *The Film Factory: Russian and Soviet Cinema in Documents 1896–1939* (New York: Routledge, 2002), 25; Charles Musser, *The Emergence of Cinema: The American Screen to 1907* (Berkeley, CA: University of California Press, 1990), 15–54; Stephen Herbert, *A History of Pre-Cinema*, Volume 2 (New York: Routledge, 2000).

22. My italics. "Literature", Review of *Kim*, *The Independent* 53, no. 2758 (10 October 1901): 2415. In a longer version of this essay I consider how the use of motion pictures to describe a process of self-reflective thought suggests that in the era of their public debut motion pictures were understood as a kinetic model of thinking.

23. I think that there are two possibilities for this acceleration: the waning of shadowgraph performances alongside the establishment of nickelodeons and, later, increasing film exhibition and the relative shift of discourse about X-ray technology from mass public texts to specialised scientific and medical journals. Once the dangers of X-rays are established, their presence as a new and intriguing image-producing phenomenon becomes specialised in medical discourse, leaving motion pictures the single, popular image-producing technology to be written about in the popular press.

24. "*The Ten Commandments* ", *Outlook* (30 January 1924): 169.

25. "Life, Letters, and the Arts", *The Living Age* (4 September 1920): 590.

26. "Motion Pictures", *Los Angeles Times* (30 September 1928): C17; "Motion Pictures", *Los Angeles Times* (26 May 1929): C14.

27. "Photographing the Unseen", 125; *Roentgen*, 230.

Eroticism and Death: The Skeleton in the Trick Film

Murray Leeder

Even the most casual survey of early cinema would find a fascination with skeletons on the part of trick film makers like Georges Méliès, Walter R. Booth, George Albert Smith, Émile Cohl and Segundo de Chomón. Skeletons in trick films are generally nimble, sprightly creatures that dance, tip off their skulls, and often fall to bones and then magically reform for further merriment. Frequently enough, there is a transformation scene in which a skeleton is turned into living flesh or vice versa, often switching back and forth several times.[1] This essay will not survey the appearances of skeletons in early cinema, but rather contextualize the first and most famous of them, from Méliès's *Escamotage d'une dame chez théâtre Robert Houdin* or *The Vanishing Lady* (1896). Méliès's film stands at the juncture of cinema as an emergent phenomenon, stage magic and the broader cultural fascination with skeletons in the 1890s, and in this essay it will serve as a conceptual nexus for exploring related historical trends. Following Elizabeth Ezra's remarks that *The Vanishing Lady*'s "hide and seek anatomy lesson perfectly emblematized the popular combination of masculine scrutiny (masquerading as 'X-ray vision') and sensationalized eroticism",[2] I argue that the sexual and misogynistic implications present in the "vanishing woman" magic act are amplified through Méliès's inclusion of the female skeleton, an image infused with surprising erotic implications in the 1890s.

Cinema was one participant in what we might call a "skeleton vogue" in the 1890s, a time when, as Roberta McGrath says, "[f]ormerly out of sight in the living world, [skeletons] were now ever present".[3] Skeleton-themed entertainment proliferated. One dramatic example is the gloomy Cabaret du Néant, which had chapters in Montmartre and New York. It allowed patrons to be served by waiters dressed as monks on tables shaped like coffins, drinking wine from skulls, in a room lined with paintings cleverly designed to reveal skeletons behind them when seen from the correct angle. For the floor show, patrons were invited on a stage to stand inside an upright coffin, where they would appear to transform into skeletons for the amusement of their friends. After describing this entertaining effect, an article by *Scientific American* on the New York Cabaret closes by saying that "the Röntgen rays are utilised in the advertising matter also, although John Henry Pepper, of the old London Polytechnic, may lay some claim to discovering the full utilisation of the rays actually used in the Cabaret du Néant" (153).[4] This statement provides a neat articulation of the skeleton vogue's double lineage. On one hand, it was in large part consistent with the use of skeleton imagery in theatrical devices like Pepper's Ghost, the "ghosts" of which were typically ambulatory skeletons in shrouds who would materialise and vanish like vapour.[5] This imagery descended from *danse macabre* imagery stretching back at least to the Middle Ages,[6] which had been kept alive through the nineteenth century via practices in the magic lantern,[7] the stereoscope[8] and stage magic,[9] among other means. Similar phantom skeletons occasionally appear in the literature on spiritualism and psychical research as well: a letter from a Miss Emma Foy of Manor Park, Essex, to the Literary Committee of the Society for Psychical Research, recounts that a skeleton dragging its own coffin appeared in her bedroom at 10:30pm every night for a two-year period in the 1870s.[10]

On the other hand, the discovery of the Röntgen or X-ray late in 1895, perhaps the single most sensational scientific discovery prior to the splitting of the atom, is a significant context for the skeleton vogue. A commentator in 1896 remarked in *The Quarterly Review* that "Never has a scientific discovery so completely and irresistibly taken the world by storm. Its results were of a kind sure to acquire prompt notoriety. The performances of 'Röntgen's rays' are obvious to the 'man in the street'; they are repeated in every lecture-room; they are caricatured in comic prints; hits are manufactured out of them at the theatres".[11] Such was the cultural excitement generated by X-rays that cinema was overshadowed in its nearly-contemporaneous debut. The two sensational new forms of photography quickly merged, not only through the literal X-ray films pioneered by Scottish scientist James MacIntyre in 1897,[12] but also through the use of X-rays to frame trick effects that were in reality accomplished by other means (rather like those at Cabaret du Néant).

Reactions to the X-ray varied considerably. Some hailed it as a new scientific wonder that might eventually spell the end of all disease.[13] For occultists and spiritualists, the X-ray seemed to confirm one of their commonplace assertions: normal human vision proved inadequate to assess the invisible world surrounding us.[14] In others, the rays inspired a sort of moral panic, a reaction to the X-ray's implicit threat to privacy and the erotic implications of its ability to profoundly undress its subjects. The erotics of bone can be subtle (the implications of Miss Foy's nocturnal skeleton bedroom visitor) or brazenly obvious (the skeletal showgirl featured in advertising for the Paris Cabaret du Néant). And let us consider what one commentator wrote in the *Pall Mall Gazette* in May 1896: "We are sick of the Röntgen Rays ... you can see other people's bones with the naked eye, and also see through eight inches of solid wood. On the revolting indecency of this there is no need to dwell".[15] The author then goes on to argue that X-rays should be banned, their discoverers executed, and all the material necessary to create them ever again should be dumped into the deepest part of the ocean. The threat of the X-ray, which promises to pierce through all of those layers of Victorian clothing in an instant, is palpable. Others welcomed the X-ray for that same reason: in the less famous of the two reviews he wrote of the Lumière programme in 1896, Maxim Gorky remarked "Possible tomorrow X rays will also appear on the screen ... used in some way or other for 'belly dances'",[16] endorsing a sort of skeleton pornography.

The X-ray represented a major shift in thinking about skeletons, as it was now possible to conceive of and examine a "living skeleton". Previously the skeleton was thought of as a relic and for this reason skeletons took on ghostly dimensions; in various artistic traditions, they were insubstantial figures that vanished like mist, and even in anatomy manuals they were conventionally drawn floating in midair like a ghost. In the *danse macabre* imagery they also tend not to be clearly gendered, perhaps because they are generally not skeletons of anyone in particular, but come closer to being allegorical figures of death itself. Where once female skeletons were a subject of so little interest that few reliable diagrams existed, suddenly, in the age of the X-ray, skeletons became

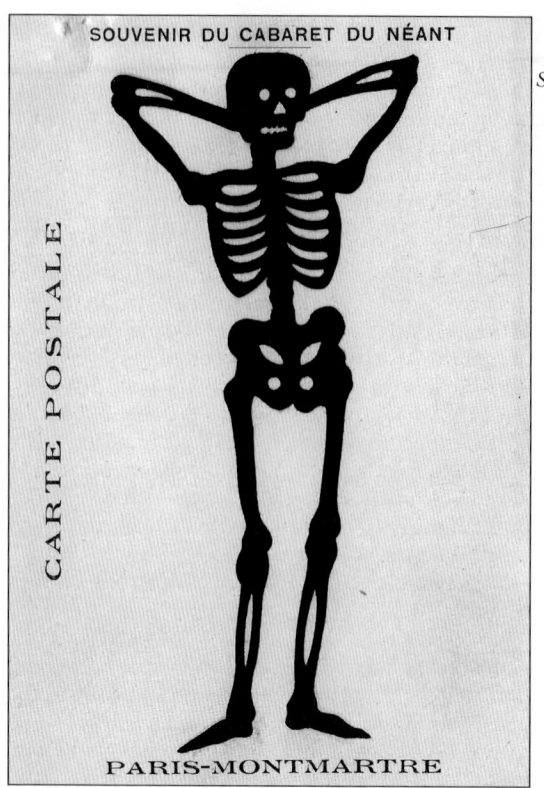

Fig. 1.

Souvenir postcard from the Paris Cabaret de Néant, 1890s, displaying a skeletal showgirl. (Author's private collection)

predominantly female.[17] Hack poets of the late 1890s mocked the eroticisation of "indecent" X-ray images, one writing:

> I'm full of daze,
> Shock and amaze;
> For nowadays
> I hear they'll gaze
> Thro' cloak and gown – and even stays,
> These naughty, naughty Roentgen Rays.[18]

Even more striking is the travesty of a love poem that appeared in *Life* magazine on 12 March, 1896, which facetiously describes a woman's skeleton with faux-erotic details:

> She is so tall, so slender, and her bones –
> Those frail phosphates, those carbonates of lime –
> Are well produced by cathode rays sublime,
> By oscillations, amperes and by ohms.
> Her dorsal vertebrae are not concealed
> By epidermis, but are well revealed.
>
> Around her ribs, those beauteous twenty-four,
> Her flesh a halo makes, misty in line,
> Her noseless, eyeless face looks into mine,
> And I but whisper "Sweetheart, Je t'adore."
> Her white and gleaming teeth at me do laugh.
> Ah! Lovely, cruel, sweet cathodograph![19]

20 Eroticism and Death: The Skeleton in the Trick Film

Fig. 2. Souvenir postcard from the Paris Cabaret de Néant, 1890s. The person in the coffin would appear to be transformed into a skeleton and back.

This facetious (or perhaps not so facetious) eroticisation of X-ray images of woman can be understood within the context of the fin-de-siècle fascination with dead and dying women, which Bram Dijkstra describes in *Idols of Perversity: Fantasies of Feminine Evil in Fin-de-Siècle Culture* as an alarmist reaction to incipient feminist movements. There is a distinct fascination in the last decades of the nineteenth century with monstrous female figures and tragic, dying ones like Tennyson's Lady of Shallot; Dijkstra draws on, for instance, clearly sexualized paintings of female corpses produced by German artist Albert von Kellar to talk about "how literal an equation late nineteenth-century males made between virtuous passivity, sacrificial ecstasy, and the erotic death as indicative of 'feminine fulfillment'".[20]

As Kelly Hurley writes, fin-de-siècle thinkers were perfectly capable of "identifying women as dangerously defined by their bodies on the one hand and ethereal, essentially disembodied creatures on the other",[21] so it is perhaps no surprise that women were allied with the ambulatory skeleton, similarly caught between life and death. Early filmmakers were well aware of cinema's paradoxical power in this regard: film had the potential to endow its subjects with life by animating them, and even bestowing on them a sort of immortality, but at the same time this filmic existence became a brand of living death. This paradox often manifests in decidedly gendered terms. Lynda Nead says:

> In the many transformation films of this period, the sexualized female body provides the matter through which the power of film magic is displayed. Women's bodies are fragmented and annihilated and their flesh turned to bone. In the American Mutoscope and Biograph Company's *The Artist's Dream* (1899), a beautiful, fleshy life model in a leotard is transformed into a skeleton, while an artist dozes at his easel.[22]

The Vanishing Lady, which also concerns the erotically-tinged "skeletonisation" of a woman, the first of Méliès's many trick films, more than a few of which contain skeletons in some capacity.[23] Only one is known to directly invoke X-rays, 1898's lost

Les Rayons Röntgen or *A Novice at X-Rays*,[24] but a poster survives from a theatrical act also named *Les Rayons Röntgen*, staged at the Théâtre Robert-Houdin under Méliès's management. The poster is crowded with familiar tropes: the male magician/scientist allied with the magical technologies of the X-ray while a shining female figure adorned with multiple X's stands as an embodiment of the X-ray itself. The skeletal hand on a placard reflects the fact that human hands were the first widely distributed X-ray images, starting with that of Röntgen's wife Berthe; a trend resulted of society women getting their hands X-rayed, the denser-than-bone wedding ring prominently visible.[25] It is easy to surmise that Méliès seized onto the potential of the spectacular X-ray aesthetics in his brands of magical and cinematic showmanship, and that this fact is not irrelevant to the appearance of his use of skeletons in films like *The Vanishing Lady*.

Only about a minute long, *The Vanishing Lady* is the first cinematic rendition of inarguably the most prominent magic trick of the late nineteenth century, in which a magician makes a woman disappear and reappear. *The Vanishing Lady* figures centrally in analyses of gender in the trick film, starting with Lucy Fischer's influential arguments about masculine magic and its reduction of the woman to a decorative, passive object, which she describes as a function of "womb envy" and the need to contain women's own magic.[26] I have not, however, encountered much scholarship foregrounding the importance of the skeleton. It is with the sudden appearance of the skeleton that the cinematic vanishing woman trick distinguishes itself from the conventions of its theatrical predecessor. Méliès's iteration begins like a faithful rendition of the vanishing woman trick: the magician, Méliès himself, places his assistant under a drape, makes her disappear, and tries to prompt her return. But the assistant comes back in the wrong form, as an inert skeleton. Gaby Wood writes, "If you play the film again and slow it down at the moment when the skeleton appears, you notice that Méliès ... is shocked by its arrival. He looks surprised, shakes his head, and tries to shoo the skeleton away, as if that wasn't supposed to happen. Clearly, even he thinks he has unintentionally killed the woman, instead of simply making her vanish" (194).[27] As James Frazer explains, "The first part of the trick substituted a film device for a stage device.[28] However, when the skeleton appears out of nowhere, a different order of thinking is involved. There is no longer a stage drape to cover the action. The magical appearance is entirely dependent on the ability of the camera to interrupt and reconstruct time".[29] Méliès enacts the theatrical vanishing woman trick cinematically but punctures its conventions too, and the point of that disruption is the skeleton. One might venture to say that the specifically cinematic dimension of the trickery is embodied in the skeleton, reflecting the close cultural proximity of cinema and the X-ray that existed at the time.

The sudden transformation of flesh into bone is a common scenario during the skeleton vogue, and it is common to find the "skeletonisation" of a woman framed in distinctly sexual terms.[30] When one considers that Méliès's vanishing lady, Jehanne D'Alcy, was also his usual assistant on stage, not to mention his mistress, the sexual implications become amplified.[31] Adelaide Herrmann, Gay Blackstone, Nani Darnell and Bess Houdini were notable examples from the early history of magic of the combined assistant-lover. The memoirs of Carl Hertz, magician and early cinema exhibitor, describe the beginnings of his relationship with his assistant: "The [oath of secrecy] was duly administered, and the contract signed, and thus Emelie D'Alton became the original Vanishing Lady, and, a little later, to make my secrets more secure, she became Mrs. Carl Hertz".[32] Hertz here articulates several dimensions of the magician's relationship to his assistant. No matter how many illusions she participates in, her identity *is* the "vanishing lady". Hertz describes, however facetiously, marrying Mademoiselle D'Alton in order to secure the secrets of his tricks, attesting to the essential danger women pose in their ability expose the magician and the need to contain that danger through strictures like marriage. Just as nature is often gendered female in western culture and represented by a woman in the process of being unveiled or dissected,[33] so is the magician's assistant often figured as the passive subject upon which male (scientific) magic is performed. From this perspective, one of Méliès's functions in *The Vanishing Lady* is to act as a surgeon, penetrating his assistant/mistress's body and displaying its secrets to prurient audiences. Twenty-five years later, British magicians Horace Goldin and P.T. Selbit would take up a saw and become perverse surgeons in a more undisguised way, cutting women in two on stage. The fact that Selbit invited feminist leader Christabel Pankhurst to take part in his sawing illusion shows just how undisguised the spectre of misogynistic violence truly was.[34]

Transforming a woman into an inert skeleton, as Méliès does in *The Vanishing Lady*, may be a milder expression of the eroticised violence common in magic acts, but it is an appropriate one for the skeleton vogue, when the X-ray made the skeleton into a figure that could titillate and shock. This would not last, and later trick films would replace the inert skeleton of *The Vanishing Lady* with sprightly and whimsical (and less obviously gendered) creatures perhaps more reflective of earlier lantern traditions than the X-ray's deathly stillness. However, as tempting as it might be describe the erotic and provocative potential of the female skeleton as a curiosity of the bygone skeleton vogue, the fact that it continues today was testified to by a minor online sensation in the summer of 2010. Imaging company EIZO released a calendar of apparent X-ray images of a woman, wearing only high heels, in classic stripper poses; lying with her back arched, or legs splayed with her hands at her crotch. Occasionally she is posed so that the fleshy outline of her breast juts into the frame, or her buttocks appear as a shapely halo framing her pelvic bones. Debate about these images no doubt generated substantial free press for EIZO, and the calendar shots appeared on sites like MSNBC.com that would not normally reproduce images of a nude woman. Blogger Phil Plait wrote:

> [W]ould someone consider these to be racy pictures? ... In many of the pictures, you can see a hint of flesh, and in many cases, those particular body parts are considered to be, um, secondary sexual characteristics ... In a lot of the pictures the model is posed provocatively. In most of them she's wearing some killer stilettos, which is more of a pinup thing than medical imaging thing.
>
> On the other hand, these are freaking X-rays.[35]

Certainty, a naked man's skeleton would not have the same impact. Though the skeleton vogue is long past, the constellation of nudity, voyeurism and "scientific" dismemberment recognizable in *The Vanishing Lady* applies just as strongly to EIZO's skeleton stripper.

Notes

1. These scenes are a subset of the transformation scenes that persist throughout the trick film. For an excellent treatment, see Matthew Solomon, "'Twenty-Five Heads under One Hat: Quick-Change in the 1890s", in Vivian Sobchack (ed.), *Meta Morphing: Visual Transformation and the Culture of Quick-Change* (Minneapolis: University of Minnesota Press, 2000), 3–20.

2. Elizabeth Ezra. "Becoming Woman: Cinema, Gender and Technology", in Diana Holmes and Carrie Tarr (eds), *A "Belle Epoque"?: Women in French Society and Culture, 1890–1914* (New York: Berghahn Books, 2006).

3. Roberta McGrath. *Seeing Her Sex: Medical Archives and the Female Body* (New York: Manchester University Press, 2002), 191.

4. "The Cabaret du Néant", *Scientific American* (7 March, 1896): 152–153. For the Paris cabaret, consult W.C. Morrow, *Bohemian Paris of Today* (London: Chatto, 1898), esp. 264–276.

5. See Jeremy Brooker, "The Polytechnic Ghost: Pepper's Ghost, Metempsychosis and the Magic Lantern at the Royal Polytechnic Institution", *Early Popular Visual Culture* 5, no. 2 (2007): 189–206; Helen Groth, "Reading Victorian Illusions: Dickens' *Haunted Man* and Dr. Pepper's 'Ghost'", *Victorian Studies* 5, no. 10 (Autumn 2007): 43–65; Dassia N. Posner, "Spectres on the New York Stage: The (Pepper's) Ghost Craze of 1863", in Lucy Elizabeth Frank (ed.), *Representations of Death in Nineteenth-Century U.S. Writing and Culture* (Aldershot, Hants: Ashgate, 2007): 189–204.

6. Leonard P. Kurtz, *The Dance of Death and the Macabre Spirit in European Literature* (Geneva: Slatkine, 1975).

7. Stephen Herbert, *A History of Pre-Cinema* Vol. 2 (London: Routledge, 2004), 173–174; Mervyn Heard, *Phantasmagoria: The Secret Life of the Magic Lantern* (Hastings: The Projection Box, 2006), esp. 211–246; Laurent Mannoni, *The Great Art of Light and Shadow: The Archaeology of Cinema* (Exeter: University of Exeter Press, 2000), 38. The dancing skeleton of the lantern tradition is echoed in the Lumière Brothers' stop-motion experiment *Le squelette joyeux* (1897).

8. See Jac Remise, *Diableries: La vie quotidienne chez Satan à la fin du 19e siècle* ([Place not listed]: Balland, 1977). Thanks to Frank Kessler and Sabine Lenk for pointing me to this resource.

9. See Albert A. Hopkins, *Magic: Stage Illusions, Special Effects, and Trick Photography* (New York: Dover, 1976), esp. 64–68, 96–99.

10. "Cases Received by the Literary Committee", *Journal of the Society for Psychical Research* 7, no. 66 (1891): 10.

11. Quoted in Allen W. Grove, "Röntgen's Ghosts: Photography, X-Rays and the Victorian Imagination", *Literature and Medicine* 16, no. 2 (Fall 1997), 143.

12. Lisa Cartwright, *Screening the Body: Tracing Medicine's Visual Culture* (Minneapolis: University of Minnesota Press, 1995), 131–141. For other sources on the relationship of cinema and X-rays, see Richard Crangle, "Saturday Night at the X-Rays – The Moving Picture and 'The New Photography' in Britain, 1896", in John Fullerton (ed.), *Celebrating 1895: The Centenary of Cinema* (Sydney: John Libbey & Company Pty Ltd, 1998): 138–144; Solvig Jülich, "Media as Modern Magic: Early X-Ray Imaging and Cinematography in Sweden", *Early Popular Visual Culture* 6, no. 1 (April 2008): 18–33; Akira Mizuta Lippit, *Atomic Light (Shadow Optics)* (Minneapolis: University of Minnesota Press, 2005); Yuri Tsivian, "Media Fantasies and Penetrating Vision: Some Links Between X-Rays, the Microscope, and Film", in John E. Bowlt and Olga Matich (eds), *Laboratory of Dreams: The Russian Avant-Garde and Cultural Experiment* (Stanford: Stanford University Press, 1996), 81–99; Simone Natale, "Le specttacolari origini di cinema e radiografia", *Mondo Niovo* 2 (2006): 55–62.

13. Nancy Knight, "'The New Light': X-Rays and Medical Futurism", in Joseph J. Corn (ed.), *Imagining Tomorrow: History, Technology, and the American Future* (Cambridge, MA: The MIT Press, 1986), 10–30.

14. See "Rontgen's Vindication of Reichenbach", *Borderland* 4, no. 1 (January 1897): 35–36, which argues that the X-rays were in fact the discredited Odic or Odylic postulated by Baron von Reichenbach some forty years earlier. For a useful treatment of the blurring of atomic science and the supernatural in the last decades of the nineteenth century, see Mark S. Morrisson, *Modern Alchemy: Occultism and the Emergence of Atomic Theory* (Oxford: Oxford University Press, 2007).

15. Quoted in Philip C. Goodman, "The New Light: Discovery and Introduction of the X-Ray", *American Journal of Roentgenology* 165 (1995): 1043.

16. Maxim Gorky, "Gorky on the Films, 1896", in Herbert Kline (ed.), *New Theatre and Film 1934 to 1937* (San Diego: Harcourt Brace Jovanovich, 1985), 231.

17. McGrath, *Seeing Her Sex*, 95.

18. Otto Glasser, *Wilhelm Conrad Rontgen and the Early History of the Roentgen Rays* (San Francisco: Norman, 1934), 44.

19. Lawrence K. Russell, "Lines on an X-Ray Portrait of a Lady", *Life* 27 (12 March, 1896): 191.

20. Bram Dijkstra, *Idols of Perversity: Fantasies of Feminine Evil in Fin-de-Siècle Culture* (New York: Oxford University Press, 1988), 56. For more on the gloomy character of Victorian eroticism,

see Deborah Lutz, *Pleasure Bound: Victorian Sex Rebels and the New Eroticism* (New York: Norton, 2011).

21. Kelly Hurley, *The Gothic Body: Sexuality, Materialism, and Degeneration at the Fin de Siècle* (Cambridge: Cambridge University Press, 1996), 10.

22. Lynda Nead, *The Haunted Gallery: Painting, Photography, Film c. 1900* (New Haven: Yale University Press, 2007), 90. For more on the theme of animation in early cinema, see Tom Gunning, "The Ghost in the Machine: Animated Pictures at the Haunted Hotel of Early Cinema", *Living Pictures* 1, no. 1 (2001): 3–17.

23. Tsivian identifies nine human/skeleton transformation tricks before 1904 ("Media Fantasies", 293 n.41); subsequent discoveries such as *The Prolific Magical Egg* (1902) extend this list.

24. A man is transformed into a skeleton in this lost film, which is less common but not unheard of; *The Prolific Magical Egg* even ends with Méliès himself turning into a skeleton.

25. Reproduced in Tsivian, "Media Fantasies", 90.

26. Lucy Fischer, "The Lady Vanishes: Women, Magic, and the Movies", *Film Quarterly* 33 (Fall 1979), 30–40. See also Linda Williams, "Film Body: An Implantation of Perversions", *Cinétracts* 12 (Winter 1981), 19–35; Karen Beckman, *Vanishing Women: Magic, Film and Feminism* (Durham: Duke University Press, 2003), esp. 62–69; and Stephen Waldow, "Women Objectified, Manipulated, and Exploited: The Central Attractions in Méliès's 'Cinema of Attractions'", *Film Matters* 1, no. 3 (July 2010): 20–25.

27. Gaby Wood, *Edison's Eve: A Magical History of the Quest for Mechanical Life* (New York: Alfred A. Knopf, 2002), 194. The film thus stages a "trick gone wrong", which complicates Lucy Fischer's claim that the magician in the trick film transparently represents masculine authorial power. For the traditions of staged failure in magic, see Peter Lamont and Richard Wiseman, *Magic in Theory: An Introduction to the Theoretical and Psychological Elements of Conjuring* (Hatfield: University of Hertfordshire Press, 1999), 119–120.

28. The newspaper that Méliès places on the floor at the beginning of the trick is a theatrical convention meant to defray suspicions of a trap door, but which actually conceals one. In the film, it exists as a vestigial trace of the stage act.

29. John Frazer, *Artificially Arranged Scenes: The Films of Georges Méliès* (Boston: G.K. Hall, 1979), 60.

30. Another key cinematic example is in G.A. Smith's *The X-Ray Fiend* (1897), where the eponymous voyeur, a new brand of camera fiend (played by Smith himself!) armed with a device resembling a motion picture camera, turns a courting couple on a bench into a pair of skeletons.

31. The next year, D'Alcy would be "stripped" again in Méliès's stag film *After the Ball* (1897).

32. Carl Hertz, *A Modern Mystery Merchant: The Trials, Tricks and Travels of Carl Hertz, the Famous American Illusionist* (London: Hutchinson, 1924), 29. For more on the magician's female assistant, see Francesca Coppa, "The Body Immaterial: Magicians' Assistants and the Performance of Labour", in Francesca Coppa, Lawrence Hass, James Peck (eds), *Performing Magic on the Western Stage: From the Eighteenth-Century to the Present* (New York: Palgrave Macmillan, 2008), 85–106.

33. Ludmilla Jordanova, *Sexual Visions: Images of Gender in Science and Medicine between the Eighteenth and Twentieth Centuries* (Madison, WI: University of Wisconsin Press, 1989).

34. Jim Steinmeyer, *Hiding the Elephant: How Magicians Invented the Impossible and Learned to Disappear* (New York: Carrol & Graff, 2003), 292.

35. Phil Plaitt. "X-rayted pinup", *Discover Magazine* (21 June, 2010) http://blogs.discovermagazine.com/badastronomy/2010/06/21/x-rayted-pinup; 24 July 2011.

21

Magies en images, les prestidigitateurs et la machine

Frédéric Tabet

Prestidigitation, illusionnisme, physique amusante: l'art magique est un spectacle paradoxal qui questionne les limites de la représentation et joue en dissonance entre la perception d'une situation et la connaissance du spectateur. Dès la naissance du cinématographe, cette machine constitue pour les artistes magiciens un nouvel outil d'écriture et de dissonance. Leur utilisation des images animées est basée sur ce même principe, exploitant l'écart entre la perception du spectateur et sa connaissance / reconnaissance de l'illusion cinématographique.

Le cinématographe intègre des pratiques préexistantes dont ses usages sociaux et culturels dépendent: il est utilisé dans la continuité de ce que les artistes présentent, selon les mêmes "règles" de présentation ou de construction. Ainsi pour André Gaudreault:

> le cinématographe fut à la fois numéro de vaudeville, spectacle de lanterne magique, numéro de magie, spectacle de féerie, ou numéro de café concert.[1]

Partie intégrante du spectacle, le cinématographe est loin d'être une attraction autonome, ses vues concourent à construire plus largement l'ensemble d'un discours et à prolonger les effets magiques présentés. Si les vues animées des artistes magiciens semblent autonomes aujourd'hui, elles ne sauraient être étudiées en dehors de leur contexte d'élaboration. Bien que souvent considérées comme des attractions supplémentaires, les vues animées servent un effet général et entrent dans un rapport dialectique avec la scène. L'utilisation des images animées *insinue* la pratique spectaculaire.

Autour de 1900,[2] l'art magique entre dans une période de mutation et de crise. Cette crise n'annonce ni un déclin, ni la mort d'une pratique venant à la suite d' "un âge d'or" irrémédiablement perdu.[3] Du *Prestidigitateur* à l'*Illusionniste* puis au *Manipulateur*, ces glissements dans les dénominations sont associés à des pratiques présentées comme novatrices. Or, l'étude des techniques utilisées par les magiciens montre que ces ruptures ne sont qu'*apparentes*, et que les termes cherchent à renouveler le regard du spectateur.

Dans le cadre de cet article, nous tenterons de montrer une diversité d'approche de la part des artistes magiciens à travers l'étude de la constitution des syndicats corporatifs de l'art magique. Les questionnements de ces groupements permettent de percevoir de nouvelles fonctions culturelles associées au cinématographe. Nous prendrons deux exemples ponctuels dans la carrière d'artistes magiciens emblématiques des films à trucs français: Georges Méliès et Gaston Velle. Une étude de leurs pratiques de la scène et les contextes d'élaboration de leurs vues animées montre qu'ils répondent chacun à des recherches et des positionnements très différents. Les analyses présentées montrent que chaque artiste conçoit différemment le spectateur auquel il destine ses vues animées.

A la fin du XIXème siècle, les spectacles magiques font partie des représentations les plus populaires. Le succès et les bénéfices qui s'en dégagent attirent de nouveaux venus et permettent aux artistes établis d'augmenter leurs investissements. De 1891 à 1904 naissent des syndicats professionnels qui visent à réguler et contrôler les usages et les pratiques associés à l'art magique. Ces groupements tentent, en rassemblant les magiciens, de faire front contre des usages de leur art qu'ils jugent non conformes à leur éthique.

Un premier groupement, *l'Académie de Prestidigitation*, est fondé en 1891.[4] Présidé par Georges Méliès, ce groupement est formé essentiellement par les magiciens engagés au Théâtre Robert-Houdin. En janvier 1902, la première revue corporative française afférente au monde de la prestidigitation, *l'Illusionniste* voit le jour sous l'impulsion de Jean Caroly,[5] marchand de matériel pour magiciens. Certaines chroniques de ce journal mensuel permettent alors de suivre les préoccupations de cette profession, mais *l'Académie de Prestidigitation* est sans activité.[6] En novembre 1902 un magicien indigné par une concurrence déloyale de "vandales" qui dévoilent le fonctionnement d'illusions, lance un appel au sein de la revue afin de "reconstituer sur des bases nouvelles l'Académie disparue".[7]

Mais c'est un an plus tard que *l'Association syndicale des artistes prestidigitateurs* verra le jour en décembre 1903. Les amateurs n'y sont pas acceptés et la revue n'explique pas de trucs. Agosta Meynier,[8] un ancien membre de *l'Académie de prestidigitation* est président, et Charles De Vere,[9] un marchand de matériel pour magiciens, en est le président d'honneur.

Cinq mois plus tard, le titre et les statuts de *l'Académie de prestidigitation* sont changés: la *Chambre syndicale de la prestidigitation* acquiert une existence légale par sa mise en conformité avec la loi des associations de 1901.[10] *L'Illusionniste* devient son organe officiel et une chronique régulière rend compte des réunions syndicales. La Chambre accepte les amateurs et la revue explique des nouveaux "trucs".

Par la suite ces syndicats perdent leur but premier et se transforment en groupes sociaux. Leurs activités sont essentiellement liées à l'organisation de rencontres amicales, de conférences données par des membres étrangers, de spectacles de charité, et de banquets annuels. Ils votent des blâmes et des décorations qui n'ont pas de portée effective. Cette tentative d'institutionnalisation et de normalisation du spectacle magique n'aboutit pas. Les pouvoirs des associations syndicales sont limités en raison de leur manque d'union, selon Raynaly.[11] Les groupements sont en rivalité, étant formés d'hommes opposés par des intérêts commerciaux, mais surtout des pratiques et des réseaux différents dans lesquels Georges Méliès tient une position bien particulière.

Lorsque Méliès devient en 1888 propriétaire du Théâtre Robert-Houdin, cette salle est un théâtre de répertoire où l'on conserve et présente les illusions et les automates de son créateur. Robert-Houdin, en épurant sa représentation, a déplacé l'art magique pour en faire un divertissement de salon destiné à un public bourgeois. Ses écrits ont contribué à asseoir sa renommée, le théâtre est alors une curiosité incontournable de Paris et un lieu tout aussi important pour les magiciens. Georges Méliès, directeur de ce théâtre, est au centre de l'attention de la profession, étant alors perçu comme un "historien qualifié".[12] Sa première collaboration à la revue *l'Illusionniste* est justement une biographie de Robert-Houdin. Puis il disparaît presque totalement des colonnes de la revue, dans laquelle il n'est mentionné qu'une seule fois comme impresario.[13]

Or un an plus tard, un article monographique dans cette même revue lui est consacré. On admire tant son inventivité que "les notes personnelles dans tout ce qu'il touche".[14] Georges Méliès est peu présent en tant qu'artiste-opérateur sur la scène de son théâtre, mais très actif lors des réunions syndicales, où il prononce discours d'introduction et poèmes, présente des automates et des illusions de Robert-Houdin. Dans l'ensemble des explications techniques qu'il donnera, il prête une attention toute particulière au regard de ses confrères. Certaines des vues animées de Méliès semblent, elles aussi, adressées à un public de spécialistes. En plus des magiciens itinérants qui proposent des projections, les forains présentent des illusions dans leurs baraques: fantasmagories, spectres, décapités …[15] Les forains sont des spécialistes de l'illusion mais aussi des clients à convaincre. Méliès développe ses truquages et ses mises en scène en fonction des yeux avertis de ce premier auditoire, qu'il cherche à brouiller et à confondre. Les mises en scène de ses vues animées se développent afin de mettre en valeur les effets magiques,[16] mais aussi – et surtout – afin de se démarquer des truquages utilisés sur scène pour ces mêmes illusions, trompant ainsi le connaisseur.

Sa vue animée *L'escamotage d'une dame chez Robert-Houdin* est largement reconnue comme étant une adaptation de l'illusion la *Femme enlevée*. Or, depuis 1886, date de la première représentation à Paris de l'illusion, Buatier de Kolta, son inventeur, a développé de nouvelles disparitions, sans chaise, puis sans voile. Quand Méliès reprend la présentation de la *Femme enlevée* dans son film, l'illusion a dix ans d'existence et a été maintes fois révélée dans la presse généraliste:[17] dès juin 1886, Frimousse annonçait dans *Le Gaulois*: "Je ne vous raconterai pas une fois de plus ce truc déjà fort expliqué. Vous connaissez l'histoire du journal, de la chaise, du foulard et de l'escamotage qui s'ensuit".[18]

La force de la vue animée de Méliès s'appuie en partie sur la connaissance des principes de l'illusion de scène par ses spectateurs, elle prend le spectateur à contrepied dans ses suppositions. Le film présente un réel mystère, y compris pour les spécialistes de l'illusion, acheteurs potentiels. Cette reprise et réécriture du truquage relève alors d'une stratégie commerciale.

Cependant, on ne citera pas le nom de Méliès dans la revue de la prestidigitation avant 1928, date à laquelle les deux associations tentent un rapprochement,[19] le journal usant de périphrases et de surnoms codés à peine voilés pour désigner l'association concurrente et Méliès (difficilement escamotables du paysage magique parisien).

Les groupes sont opposés en particulier par les pratiques. La magie développée par Méliès au sein de son théâtre, reconnu et établi, est à l'opposé de celle que proposent les magiciens itinérants qui doivent s'adapter continuellement à des espaces de représentation très variés. C'est le cas de Gaston Velle qui réalisera des vues animées pour les frères Lumière, pour la firme Pathé puis, après son départ en Italie, pour la firme Cinès à Rome. La recherche n'a mis à jour que très peu de données sur la carrière magique de Gaston Velle. À la suite de la mort subite de son père, le Professeur Joseph Velle, Gaston reprend en 1889 le titre, le répertoire et l'itinéraire de ses tournées. Il présentera en particulier deux numéros éprouvés: *La disparition d'un cheval vivant et de son cavalier* et *La chanteuse coupée en deux*. Les débuts de Velle ont vraisemblablement lieu en Italie. On le retrouve pendant l'été 1891 en tournée en Afrique du Nord à la tête d'une "troupe excentrique".[20] Velle est alors âgé de vingt et un ans. Il reprend ensuite l'itinéraire des tournées européennes de son père, misant sur la notoriété de son titre, "Professeur Velle." De 1896 à 1903 il passe la saison des fêtes hivernales à Lyon, salle Bellecour à l'hôtel du Progrès, et part au printemps dans les Alpes[21] et en Provence.[22] Il part ensuite en Suisse, passe vraisemblablement l'été en l'Italie, avant de retourner à Lyon pour les fêtes de Noël. Ses spectacles présentent différentes formes de magie: de la magie théâtralisée, appelée dès 1874 "magie bouffe" par son père,[23] des "grands trucs" exploitant entre autres les brevets de Buatier De Kolta,[24] des démystifications d'expériences spirites, puis de la "magie moderne" dans des séances de "haute prestidigitation".[25] Il présente aussi des projections d'ombres animées et de la transmission de pensée, épaulé par d'autres artistes: marionnettistes, comiques excentriques, puis par Fregoli II, un plagiaire du transformiste italien Leopoldo Fregoli. La récurrence de son public l'amène à devoir changer chaque année son spectacle ainsi que ses illusions. Cette nouveauté est entretenue par un changement de titres: Velle passe de manière indéterminée de prestidigitateur à illusionniste, et de magicien à enchanteur.

Les premiers films attestés de Gaston Velle inaugurent une nouvelle série au sein de la filmographie des frères Lumière: les vues fantasmagoriques.[26] Plus longues et plus élaborées, elles présentent des transformations réalisées grâce à des arrêts de caméra. Chez les frères Lumière, il succède au magicien Félicien Trewey peut-être puisque depuis 1896 Gaston jouit d'une réputation locale: "Jamais spectacle de ce genre n'obtint pareil succès à Lyon".[27] Ces vues sont tournées vraisemblablement fin 1902 et sont annoncées à la vente début 1903.[28] Mais après ces premières réalisations, l'artiste a déjà repris ses spectacles au moment où ses films sont mis en vente.[29] Le 22 février 1903, il quitte la ville et reprend son itinéraire habituel: Annecy en mai, Genève en septembre, Montreux en octobre. Et moins de deux mois plus tard, on trouve pour la première fois son nom dans le journal comptable de la firme Pathé en novembre 1903.

Était-il déjà engagé pour la tournée de 1903? Considérait-il alors les images animées comme une opportunité accessoire et temporaire avant de s'engager chez Pathé? Ou faut-il suivre son indication, lorsque dans une note manuscrite il décrit les vues tournées chez Lumière comme des "premiers films d'étude",[30] avant de réaliser des "créations cinématographiques" chez Pathé? Quoiqu'il en soit, ses carrières magique et cinématographique sont imbriquées et se chevauchent.[31]

Une analyse des circonstances de cette tournée de 1903 permettrait de mieux comprendre l'implication de Gaston Velle dans la firme Pathé. Les différentes illusions que Gaston Velle présente au cours de la tournée de 1903 permettent ainsi de considérer sous un nouveau jour certains de ses premiers films Lumière. D'abord au niveau des influences possibles de Méliès car certains films reprennent les titres de vues de la Star Film: *La tentation de Saint Antoine*,[32] et le *Château hanté*.[33] Gaston Velle avait déjà puisé au Théâtre Robert-Houdin des sources d'inspiration: en mai 1896 il présente à Lyon *La caverne des gnomes*[34] qui reprend le titre et les effets de la "scène fantastique" présentée au théâtre de Méliès de 1893 à 1895.[35] Ensuite, d'autres vues animées de cette série reprennent les titres des illusions de son répertoire. Le spectacle de la "scène musico-fantastique" *Les sorcelleries de Pierrot*[36] que Velle présente en scène dès 1899, est à mettre en relation avec la vue lumière *Pierrot et la flûte enchantée*[37] qu'il nomme *Les mésaventures de Pierrot*[38] dans sa liste manuscrite. Il en va de même pour *Un repas diabolique* présenté sur scène en 1899,[39] et la vue lumière *Le repas fantastique*.[40] Gaston Velle pourrait donc voir dans le cinématographe une manière "d'archiver" ses propres créations tout en en rénovant la forme: les effets magiques y sont réalisés par des trucages cinématographiques.

Le Prestidigitateur au café, film 2004 du catalogue Lumière, présente une approche singulière au vu des groupements syndicaux qui se forment. Un prestidigitateur couvert de médailles nommé IXOF s'installe sur la terrasse d'un restaurant dont le nom est "Riche," et entreprend d'y exhiber son programme avant de se faire mettre à la porte par un garçon. Très mécontent, le prestidigitateur transforme ses habits pour ne pas être reconnu et s'installe à nouveau. Il fait disparaître successivement les deux cafés que lui apporte le garçon, puis la cafetière et le sucre. Le garçon pris de fureur tente de frapper le prestidigitateur à l'aide d'une chaise puis de la table, qui disparaissent tour à tour dans ses mains. Il se décide finalement à chercher un agent de police, mais quand celui-ci arrive tout est en place et c'est le garçon de café qui est emmené par le policier.

Ce film ne fait pas référence à un tour de répertoire ni à une pièce de magie théâtrale. Le film présente une séance au café telle qu'il s'en déroule dans la ville de Lyon.[41] Le magicien médaillé à outrance (y compris dans le dos) est une référence à Marius Cazeneuve, en représentation à Paris pendant l'été 1900,[42] tandis que le nom IXOF semble être une inversion des initiales de Imro Fox, I. Fox, manipulateur américain, présent en mai 1902 au Casino de Paris.[43] Décorations fictives, utilisation de pseudonyme obscur ou étranger: ce personnage de magicien est loin de la sobriété prônée par Jean Eugène Robert-Houdin,[44] se rapprochant plutôt des magiciens itinérants en quête de légitimité.[45]

Velle, opérateur Lumière, saisit ici par le biais du cinématographe l'opportunité de prendre une revanche fantasmée et de dénoncer les difficiles conditions de travail des artistes itinérants[46] dont il a souffert lors de ses premières représentations.[47] Au-delà du divertissement ce film dénonce l'impuissance des artistes face aux autorités. Il devance ici la prise à partie des autorités par les associations syndicales. Au-delà du simple divertissement ce film est une critique et une dénonciation politique.

> Ma carrière cinématographique est tellement intimement liée à celle du Théâtre Robert-Houdin, qu'on ne peut guère les séparer ... .[48]

C'est précisément *l'intimité* qu'il est important de saisir dans les films réalisés par les magiciens. La connaissance intérieure du parcours des artistes permet de mettre à jour des utilisations qui dépassent le simple divertissement. Les films s'inscrivent dans le prolongement d'une pratique générique bien implantée. L'art magique est une"série culturelle"[49] au sein d'un paradigme plus vaste, celui de spectacle du scène de la fin du dix-neuvième siècle. L'étude de cet art montre que dans le détail il se divise en de multiples sous-séries (*illusionnisme, prestidigitation, pièces magiques*), subdivisées encore au point que chaque artiste poursuit d'abord sa propre pratique. Il n'y a pas une magie mais de multiples formes à explorer, il n'y a donc pas non plus une seule mise en images: bien que les magiciens soient groupés en corporations, chaque magicien utilise les vues animées à ses propres fins.

Pour faire émerger un nouveau regard sur les vues animées des artistes magiciens il est donc nécessaire de remonter très en amont, d'étudier le détail des sous-séries et leur légitimité face aux spectacles proposés. De même, il est nécessaire de refuser une approche simpliste des films à trucs et de leur reconnaître un statut autre que celui de récréation scientifique: c'est seulement ainsi que le chercheur pourra questionner à nouveau les rapprochements qui ont déjà été réalisés et interroger l'évidence trop visible du lien entre l'art magique et le cinématographe.

Il convient de ne pas adopter le regard profane du spectateur de l'art magique, celui qui ne voit qu'un *truc*, qu'un détail dans l'ensemble plus vaste du spectacle. À la conception de *fenêtre ouverte sur le monde* d'Alberti, on pourrait opposer l'idée que l'écran du film à trucs est une *trappe* qui, bien qu'ouverte sur les coulisses, arrête le regard critique et ne permet pas de voir, à travers elle, les rouages plus complexes de la scène.

Communication réalisée dans la cadre de mon doctorat "Circulations techniques entre l'art magique et le cinématographe", dirigé par Giusy Pisano, à l'Université Paris Est-Marne la Vallée au sein du LISAA EA4120, rendu possible grâce à une subvention de L'École Doctorale Culture et Sociétés.

Notes

1. André Gaudreault, *Cinéma et attraction: Pour une nouvelle histoire du cinématographe, suivi de Les vues cinématographiques* (Paris: CNRS Editions, 2008), 113.
2. Voir Matthew Solomon, "Up-to-Date Magic: Theatrical Conjuring and the Trick Film", *Theatre Journal* 58, no. 4 (décembre 2006): 595–615.
3. Erik Barnouw, *The Magicians and the Cinema* (New York: Oxford University Press, 1981), 9.
4. Un premier groupement, une "société filomagique", a vu le jour en 1820. Voir: Guy Lamelot, *AFAP, 100 ans d'histoire, 100 ans de magie* (Paris: Association française des artistes prestidigitateurs, 2004), 10.
5. Jean Auguste Faugeras, dit Caroly, avant d'installer sa boutique, a effectué des projections lumineuses à l'aide d'un cinématographe. Voir l'affichette reproduite dans Jacques Deslandes, *Le boulevard du cinéma à l'époque de Georges Méliès* (Paris: Éditions du cerf, 1963), 63; et Laurent Mannoni, "Méliès magie et cinéma", dans *Méliès magie et cinéma*, sous la direction de Laurent Mannoni et Jacques Malthête (Paris: Paris musées, 2002), 63–65.
6. Un critique (vraisemblablement Jean Caroly) suppose l'Académie dissoute en 1902. "Les prestidigitateurs célèbres, Jules Legris", *L'Illusionniste* (septembre 1902): 2. Cependant, ce n'est qu'en 2007 que cette dissolution a eu lieu, à la suite du décès du magicien Jean Ludow, dernier membre vivant du Bureau.
7. Berry, "Les vandales", *L'Illusionniste* (novembre 1902): 5–6.
8. Agosta Meynier présente des séances de prestidigitation en alternance avec les séances de cinématographe dans les grands magasins Dufayel. Voir l'affichette reproduite dans Jacques Deslandes et Jacques Richard, *Histoire comparée du cinéma*, tome 2 (Tournai: Casterman, 1968), 17.
9. Charles De Vere Herbert Shakespeare Gardiner Williams vend des vues animées dans sa boutique d'appareils de prestidigitation. Voir l'annonce publiée le 16 septembre 1899 dans la revue *The Era*, citée dans: John Barnes, *The Beginning of Cinema in England*, vol. 4 *1899* (Exeter: University of Exeter Press, 1996), 69.
10. Georges Méliès, "Le quart de siècle de la chambre syndicale de la prestidigitation", *Passez Muscade* Numéro spécial no 56bis (1929): 5–7.
11. Edouard Raynaly, "Causerie", *L'Illusionniste* (mars 1906): 130–131.
12. Georges Méliès, "Les prestidigitateurs célèbres: Robert-Houdin", *L'Illusionniste* (mars 1902): 1–3. Le numéro précédent le qualifie de "plume autorisée".
13. "Prestidigitateurs célèbres: E. Raynaly", *L'Illusionniste* (avril 1902): 2. Jusqu'en 1908 Georges Méliès est mentionné dans les revues corporatives étrangères comme spécialiste de Robert-Houdin, sans allusion à ses vues animées. En 1908, dans le cadre de sa campagne de dénigrement de Robert-Houdin, Houdini mentionne Méliès et son activité ("maker of motion picture films") auprès de son lectorat américain, tout en déplorant l'absence de spectacle magique dans le théâtre. Harry Houdini Erich Weiss, *The Unmasking of Robert-Houdin* (New York: The Publishers Printing Co., 1908), 48.
14. "G. Méliès", *L'Illusionniste* (septembre 1903): 169–170.
15. Pour une étude exhaustive de ces illusions voir: Christian Fechner, *Les entresorts* (Paris: Editions Georges Proust, 2010), pour une étude des échos entre les films de Méliès et les illusions présentées par les forains, voir: Solomon Matthew, "Fairground Illusions and the Magic of Méliès", dans *Travelling Cinema in Europe*, sous la direction de Martin Loiperdinger, *KINtop Schriften* no 10 (2008): 34–45.
16. André Gaudreault introduit le néologisme de "trucalité", alternative entre la narrativité et la théâtralité. Voir André Gaudreault, "Théâtralité et narrativité dans l'œuvre de Georges Méliès", dans *Méliès et la naissance du spectacle cinématographique, colloque international de Cerisy, août 1981*, sous la direction de Madeleine Malthête-Méliès (Paris: Kincksieck, 1984), 211.
17. Sur une décennie nous pouvons citer une dizaine de dévoilements, dont le premier semble être Brignogan, *La sorcellerie amusante* (Paris: Librairie Louis Chaux, 1890), 121.
18. Frimousse, "La soirée parisienne", *Le Gaulois* (1er juin 1886): [3].
19. "… suite à la rénovation du bureau et à la disparition des éléments de discorde qui avaient pesé

jusqu'ici sur notre Association". Jules Dhotel, "L'Union fait la force", *Journal de la prestidigitation, organe officiel de l'Association syndicale des artistes prestidigitateurs* (septembre 1928): 1.

20. Alger, Constantine, Oran, Mascara, Mostaganem, et finalement Bel Abbès (pour les trois dernières villes voir respectivement), "Arrivée de M. Gaston Velle", *L'Indépendant de Mascara* (21 juin 1891): [2]; "Théâtre. – Troupe G. Velle", *L'Indépendant de Mostaganem* (1er juillet 1891): [2]; "Velle", *Le Bel-Abbèsien* (19 juillet 1891): [2]).

21. À Lyon, Saint-Étienne, Villefranche sur Saône, Saint-Chambond, villes auxquelles nous pouvons ajouter Annecy. Voir Michelle Aubert et Jean-Claude Seguin, *La production cinématographique des frères Lumière* (Paris : Bibliothèque du Film, 1996), 146. Un programme de Gaston Velle datant de 1901 est reproduit dans Danielle Teil et Roger Heyraud, *Saint-Étienne et le théâtre* (Saint-Étienne: Éditions X. Lejeune, 1990), 81.

22. Pour Toulon et Aix, voir Guy Olivo, "Vers la sédentarisation: du cinématographe au cinéma. Les premières tentatives ambulantes et urbaines du cinématographe à Toulon (1897–1905)", *Cahiers de la Méditerranée* nos 16–19 (Nice: Université de Nice, Centre de la Méditerranée moderne et contemporaine, 1978): 13.

23. "Alcazar d'été", *L'Orchestre* (17 décembre 1876): [4].

24. Joseph Buatier, *Mémoire descriptif à l'appui d'une demande de brevet d'invention de 15 ans pour mode d'apparition et disparition de spectres ou autres sujets réels par Monsieur Joseph Buatier*, brevet français no 179906, 26 novembre 1886.

25. "Salle Bellecour", *Le Passe temps et le parterre réunis* (31 janvier 1897): 7.

26. Michelle Aubert et Jean-Claude Seguin, *La production cinématographique des frères Lumière* (Paris: Bibliothèque du film, 1996), 128.

27. "Le professeur G. Velle", *Le Passe temps et le parterre réunis* (6 février 1898): 7.

28. "Nouvelles vues fantasmagoriques", *L'Industriel forain* (18 janvier 1903), cité dans Gaudreault, André et Lamotte, Jean-Marc, "Fragmentation et segmentation dans les 'vues animées': le corpus Lumière", dans *Arrêt sur image, fragmentation du temps: aux sources de la culture visuelle moderne / Stop Motion, Fragmentation of Time: Exploring the Roots of Modern Visual Culture*, sous la direction de François Albera, Marta Braun et André Gaudreault (Lausanne: Payot, 2002), 239, note 9.

29. Il est en représentation salle Bellecour du 4 janvier au 22 février 1903. "Le Professeur G. Velle", *Le Passe temps et le parterre réunis* (4 janvier 1903): 7.

30. Gaston Velle, liste manuscrite reproduite dans: Henri Bousquet, *Catalogue Pathé des années 1896 à 1914*, vol. 1, *1896 à 1906* (Bures-sur-Yvette: Éditions Henri Bousquet, 1996), iii–iv.

31. Gaston Velle reprend son métier de magicien lors d'une tournée en Suisse en 1914. La fin de la carrière de Gaston Velle n'est pas documentée. Ce n'est que très récemment que sa date de décès, le 12 janvier 1953 à Pantin, à été découverte. Sa date de naissance n'a toujours pas pu être établie précisément.

32. Film 2011bis, et Star Film 169, 1898.

33. Film 2001, Star Film 96, 1897.

34. "Le professeur G. Velle", *Le Passe temps et le parterre réunis* (6 décembre 1896): 7.

35. Pour une description de l'argument de cette scène, voir "Robert-Houdin", *L'Orchestre* (21 décembre 1893): [4].

36. "L'enchanteur Velle", *Le Passe temps et le parterre réunis* (12 février 1899): 7.

37. Film no 2005.

38. Gaston Velle, liste manuscrite.

39. "Le professeur G. Velle", *Le Passe temps et le parterre réunis* (6 décembre 1896): 7.

40. Film no 2007.

41. Voir les vues nos 119 et 762 du catalogue Lumière: *Prestidigitateur I, Prestidigitateur II*.

42. "Théâtre des Capucins", *Le Figaro* (30 juin 1900): 4. Il restera programmé jusqu'au 3 juillet 1900.

43. "Chronique théâtrale de la prestidigitation", *L'Illusionniste* (mai 1902): 7.

44. Jean-Eugène Robert-Houdin, *Les secrets de la prestidigitation et de la magie: comment on devient sorcier* (Paris: Michel Lévy frères, 1868), 47.

45. Ces lourdeurs ont été décrites par Édouard Raynaly, *Propos d'un escamoteur: étude critique et humoristique* (Paris: C. Noblet, 1894), 48–51.
46. Les démarches que devaient effectuer les artistes magiciens itinérants sont détaillées dans Norbert Thiels, "Bavardages d'un vieux prestidigitateur", *Journal de la prestidigitation*, no 1 (1er avril 1905): 2–4; et no 2, (1er juillet 1905): 2–5.
47. Certains comptes-rendus de spectacles sont sans équivoque quant à la réception de ses spectateurs. Le critique de *la Tafna* conclut son article "Adieu donc, cher monsieur, mais pas au revoir. Nous ne voulons plus de Gaston ni Velle". Voir: "Était-il malade?", *La Tafna: journal de l'arrondissement de Tlemcen* (1er juillet 1891): [2].
48. Lettre de Méliès à Robelly, datée du 4 mai 1937, reproduite dans Robelly Robert Rouet, "Georges Méliès", *L'Escamoteur: revue confidentielle d'informations et de documentation magique* (février 1948): 118.
49. L'expression "série culturelle", a été introduite initialement par André Gaudreault dans le domaine des études cinématographiques: André Gaudreault, "Les vues cinématographiques selon Georges Méliès, ou: comment Mitry et Sadoul avaient peut-être raison d'avoir tort (même si c'est surtout Deslandes qu'il faut lire et relire)", *Georges Méliès, l'illusionniste fin de siècle*, sous la direction de Jacques Malthête et Michel Marie (Paris: Presses de la Sorbonne Nouvelle, 1997), 111–131.

PART V

Art and Aesthetics

22

Early Film Colour, Today and Yesterday

Charles O'Brien

The understanding of colour in early cinema has undergone a basic revision in recent years. Since the 1930s and continuing for the next seventy years, early cinema, by and large, was encountered strictly in black-and-white. This circumstance has changed over the past decade, when digital technologies have facilitated both the restoration of early colour films as well as their rapid distribution globally, with the consequence that today early cinema is likely to be encountered as a colour medium first and foremost. It's an exciting time. Great colour films are being restored and made available, and our sense of film history, in certain respects, is being transformed. At the same time, the rapid changes raise new questions and challenges regarding the role of restorations in conditioning current understanding of the aesthetics of early cinema. I will approach the question of the impact of digital technologies on early cinema history via what my research suggests was a major change in stencil colour practice evident in the summer of 1909, when Pathé released its first films made with the new mechanised system. My presentation has two parts. First, I define the aesthetic change in stencil practice wrought by mechanisation at Pathé. Second, I raise the possibility that the change might either be displayed or concealed by digital restorations of early films. This paper thus combines research into early film colour with reflection on how that research is mediated by current restoration practices.

Pathécolor
The aesthetics of applied colour underwent a major shift in 1909 with the mechanisation of stencil colour at Pathé. The change, some six years in the making, was linked to Pathé's emergence in the first decade of the twentieth century as the world's largest film producer and exporter. The pre-eminence rested on the creation of "Pathé" as the foremost brand name in the motion picture field. Essential in establishing the brand was Pathé's investment in colour technique, beginning with the red logo and intertitles that became standard for Pathé films circa 1903 and continuing through the mechanised stencil colour system of the late-aughts, the only polychrome motion picture system to be successfully industrialised prior to the 1920s. Other companies had experimented with stencil colour, notably Méliès and Gaumont; but they did so on a small, cottage-industry scale compared to Pathé, whose mechanised stencilling was used when at least 200 colour copies of a film were to be made.[1] For certain titles, as many as 400 colour prints were struck.[2] The high production volume was needed to recover the massive costs invested in the new electric technologies, increased plant size and expanded labour force – all unique to stencil colour as undertaken at Pathé.

Mechanisation of the stencil process reached its limit in 1909 when Pathé adopted Jean Méry's electric stencil cutter and colour application machine. Méry's cutter enlarged

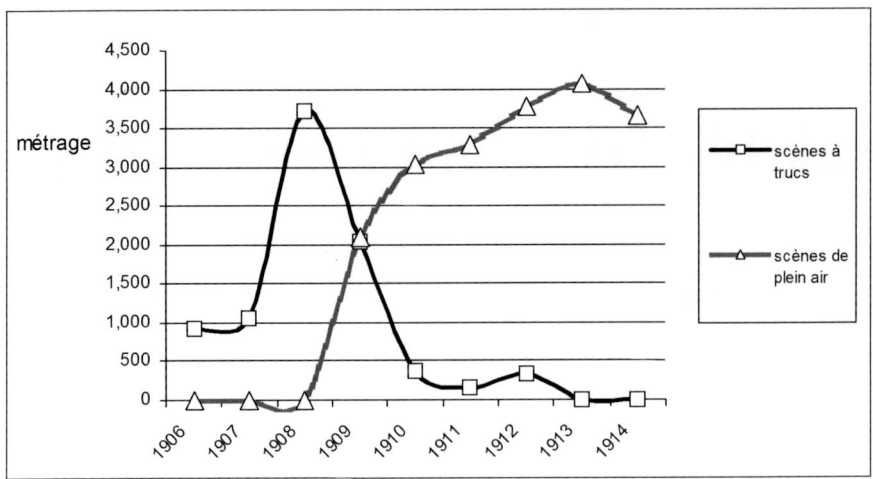

Chart 1. The colour métrage for Pathé's two main colour genres, arranged by year of release.

the film image on a screen where a worker traced it using a pantograph, a series of bars on pivots that reproduced an analogous shape on the 35mm print. The tracing was then punched out of the 35mm film strip by a stylus driven by an electric sewing-machine-like apparatus, thereby creating the stencil. The first films made with the electric cutter were released in June 1909 in Paris and soon after in London and New York where they drew much interest in the film community.[3] Operation of the Méry system was in full swing by 1910, when 400 workers were employed at Vincennes entirely for colouring films.[4] In creating a stencil whose outline matched the shapes of the film's representation more reliably than any preceding system, Méry's pantograph gave the applied colour images a more even finish. Adding to the uniformity was the other main component of the Méry system: the automatic colour-application device, whose felt-covered rollers further reduced the hand-coloured look of earlier stencil films. In their relatively uniform, machine-made look, the new stencil films approached the look of photographic colour.

Bregtje Lameris, in an important article on Pathé's stencil films, draws upon the Pathé catalogues compiled by Henri Bousquet to track the rise and fall in popularity of specific colour genres and hence changes in Pathé's stencil-colour aesthetic.[5] The catalogues were compiled by Bousquet in the 1990s from various primary sources, including Pathé company bulletins, company inventories, theatre programs, film scenarios and trade press reports, as well as secondary sources such as lists of films compiled by other scholars.[6] The catalogues list for each title whether it includes colour images, and if so, how many metres of colour film relative to monochrome. Lameris points out that the catalogues reveal that prior to 1909 Pathé used stencil colour mainly for films designated in its promotional literature as *"scènes à trucs"* and *"scènes de féeries et contes"*. Films belonging to these categories, Lameris claims, were typically filmed indoors with a static camera and with the principal action centred in the frame, which made them easy to stencil. Descendants of the trick and magic films produced a decade earlier by Méliès, these films display colour as a wondrous special attraction.

Retracing Lameris' steps, my research involved going through the catalogues and compiling numerical data pertaining to Pathé's output of colour films. A sample of this research is presented in Chart 1, which displays the colour métrage for what appear to have been Pathé's main colour genres over the period 1906–1914: the *"scènes à trucs"* and the "*scènes de plein air*". These genres represent a tiny fraction of the dozens of genres listed in the Bousquet catalogues; but they contain the greatest number of films issued in colour editions.

The "*scènes à trucs*", for instance, had dominated Pathé's stencil film production until 1908 but became increasingly less common thereafter, to the point of disappearing in 1913 and 1914, when no colour "*scènes à trucs*" were released. The same holds for the "*scènes de féeries et contes*" (not pictured in Chart 1), the output of which peaked in 1908 and then fell steadily afterward. Conversely, non-fiction genres rarely coloured before 1909 became the dominant colour genres afterward – at least in the number of titles. 1909 again stands out as the turning point. Before the summer of 1909 only one colour version of the location-filmed "*scènes de plein air*" is listed in the Bousquet catalogues; for the second half of 1909, however, twenty-two such films are listed. In subsequent years the number of colour "*scènes de plein air*" grew continuously to the point of more than doubling by 1913, when forty-three films in that category were released. With respect to Pathé's colour investment, the "scènes de plein air" that proliferated after 1909 functioned as replacements of sorts for the "scènes à trucs" prevalent until then, so that the previous emphasis on colour as a spectacular attraction can be said to have given way to a new stress on the simulation of phenomenal reality.

Supporting such an interpretation are trade-press reports on the realism and naturalism of the new stencil films. A critic in London, for instance, commented on excitement in New York over "the new Pathé colour films" by noting that "[t]he colours are not slobbed on, but are imparted to the pictures with reticence and restraint. The result is a beautiful naturalness of effect that converts the Pathé film into an unobtrusive work of art which does not 'hit you right between the eyes'."[7] The change has been evident also to recent observers such as Paolo Cherchi Usai, who singles out "a refinement of colour and precision of outline unequalled in the period" in the "Pathé series 'Film d'Art' and the adaptations from drama and literature produced by the company's 'Film d'Arte Italiana' between 1909 and 1912".[8] Film d'Art and Filme d'Arte Italiana were independent producers that had contracted for Pathé to serve as the "*editeur*" whose duties included colouring the release prints. The aesthetic characteristics associated with these prints – the precise matching of colour and image shape and the restrained, muted hues – allowed Pathé to stress in its advertising the "realism" of its stencilled films and thus compete with Kinemacolor and potentially other photochemical colour systems.[9]

Digital restoration

Essential to the restoration issues raised by stencil films is the role of digital tools. Prior to 1997, the range of restoration options was highly limited. Restoring a film, Paul Read and Jean-Paul Meyer observe, involved "using whatever modern film stock the film stock manufacturer currently supplied for modern production purposes, in order to copy an old image".[10] Damage to the emulsion in the form of ripped celluloid and embedded dirt, scratches and patches, was impossible to remove, Giovanna Fossati explains, with the consequence that "[u]p to 1997, all restorations of silent films were done photochemically and, therefore, they all contained a great deal of visible damage".[11] Over the past decade, however, digital tools and methods have enabled restoration projects unthinkable before. Digital tools, for instance, make it possible to "remove absolutely every scratch", including those that had been printed into the original film. They also allow restorers to control the amount of flicker at will.

This new potential for radically modifying the original film has raised contentious issues in archive ethics. Because scratches can be removed, should they? As Read and

Meyer note, "Scratches are sometimes regarded as part of the 'patina' produced by time, much as it is seen on a fine piece of furniture".[12] The issue came to a head with David Shepard's restoration of *Nanook of the North* (1922) for the 1998 Criterion DVD release. Shepard digitally removed the flicker that had resulted from mechanical defects in Flaherty's camera and he erased animal hairs and other foreign matter that had been printed into the negative.[13] At the First International Trier Conference on Film and New Media in 2002, Shepard's account of his restoration sparked a discussion over the ethics of restoration comparable to what occurs in cases involving famous paintings. Martin Koerber agreed with Shepard that restorers ought to remain true to the original but he challenged Shepard's decisions by invoking a different notion of what counts as the original film.[14] Whereas Shepard regards the original *Nanook of the North* as what director Robert Flaherty had intended (Flaherty presumably did not want animal hair in his negative), Koerber sees it as the film that audiences actually saw, flicker, stray hairs, and all.

Likewise for stencil colour: what the filmmakers presumably were aiming for – the exact alignment of colour with represented shape – can be distinguished from what they actually achieved. The women in Mme. Thuillier's workshop who hand-painted the Méliès films were not trying to mismatch the colour with the representation; they did so inadvertently given the technical constraints. As a consequence of the virtual impossibility of a precise match, applied colour, whether hand or stencil, often looked like a separate layer on top of the photographic image. Brush strokes dance on the surface, flicking and roiling, and thus accentuating the flatness of the screen surface. The appeal of colour lay in realism, it was often said. Colour supposedly rounded out the motion picture experience in ways that brought the sensory display of the moving image closer to ordinary perceptual experience. Stencil-colour images, however, like their hand-coloured antecedents, often inclined toward two-dimensionality and abstraction, whatever the intentions of those who did the colouring.

In this paper I have argued that the aesthetics of applied-colour changed to some extent in the late aughts with the mechanisation of stencil work at Pathé, claiming that viewers in 1909 saw the new stencil films from Pathé as an aesthetic improvement over previous applied colour films. The question I will pose now is whether the aesthetic change wrought by the mechanisation of stencil technique will be evident today to viewers of digital restorations of early colour films. Would I have noticed it myself if I had not been cued by the extra-filmic documentation I relied upon in my research such as trade-press reports, transcripts of the meetings of Pathé's Conseil d'Administration and the Bousquet catalogues? A great virtue of digital colour technology is its capacity for altering a single element in the image while leaving the rest untouched. This extraordinary potential for selectivity has made digital devices essential for the restoration not only of stencil colour but polychrome film colour of virtually any sort. How do those involved in restoring stencil films made prior to 1909 deal with the tendency for colour in these films to exceed the represented shapes? Do they preserve the mismatch or do they "correct" it digitally? The answer will no doubt vary depending on who does the restoration. Exemplary have been the efforts of the Nederlands Filmmuseum and its partner laboratory Haghefilm, whose personnel are highly sensitive to the dangers of restoring early films in ways that end up revising their aesthetic character. Commercial DVD producers, however, are likely far more willing to compromise. Thus the task of researching early film colour requires that digitally restored applied-colour films be compared to the 35mm prints to which they refer – preferably original nitrate prints like the frames in the Turconi and Joye collections examined by Joshua Yumibe.[15] At this point 35mm prints of one sort or another will continue to exist given their superiority as storage media.[16] Whether researchers have access to the prints is another question, which leaves us with the proposal that studying early film colour means examining not only the cinema's past but how our relation to that past is mediated by archival practices currently very much in a state of transition.

Notes

1. In "Colour Cinematography: Recent Advances", *The Times* 8, no. 37 (3 April 1912): 23.
2. In Paul Read and M.P. Meyer, *Restoration of Motion Picture Film* (Oxford, England: Butterworth Heinemann, 2000), 181.
3. See G. Fagot, "La cinématographie en couleurs", *Ciné-Journal* 3, no. 97 (2 July 1910): 17.
4. See Henri Destynn, "How Pathé Films Are Colored", *Nickelodeon* 3, no. 5 (1 March 1910): 121–122.
5. In B. Lameris, "Pathécolor: 'Perfect in their Rendition of the Colors of Nature'", *Living Pictures* 2, no. 2 (2003): 46–58.
6. See Henri Bouquet, *Catalogue Pathé des années 1896 à 1914: 1896–1906* (Bures sur Yvette, France: H. Bousquet, 1996).
7. In Thomas Bedding, "News from America", *The Bioscope*, no. 157 (16 September 1909): 35.
8. In Paolo Cherchi Usai, *Silent Cinema: An Introduction* (London: British Film Institute, 2000), 22.
9. See Lameris, "Pathécolor", 51–54.
10. In Read and Meyer, *Restoration of Motion Picture Film*, 224.
11. In Giovanna Fossati, *From Grain to Pixel: The Archival Life of Film in Transition* (Amsterdam: University of Amsterdam Press, 2009), 216.
12. In Read and Meyer, *Restoration of Motion Picture Film*, 224.
13. See J. Shepard, "Silent Film in the Digital Age", in Martin Loiperdinger (ed.), *Celluloid Goes Digital: Historical-Critical Editions of Films on DVD and the Internet* (Proceedings of the First International Trier Conference on Film and New Media, October 2002; Trier: Wissenschaftlicher Verlag, 2003), 23.
14. In M. Koerber, "Inside and Outside the Bubble: Archival Standards and the DVD Market", in *Celluloid Goes Digital*, 34–35.
15. See, for instance, J. Yumibe, "From Switzerland to Italy and All Around the World: The Joseph Joye and Davide Turconi Collections", in Richard Abel, Giorgio Bertellini and Rob King (ed.), *Early Cinema and the "National"* (New Barnet, Hertfordshire, U.K.: John Libbey, 2008): 321–331.
16. See John Belton, "Digital Cinema: A False Revolution", *October* 100 (October 2002): 114.

23

Salvage Ethnography and the Exoticisation of Decay in Peter Delpeut's *Lyrical Nitrate* and Bill Morrison's *Decasia*

Nadia Bozak

The nature of decay

Cinema, as Paolo Cherchi Usai has described it, has always been an ephemeral art form; indeed, in commercial, technological and material terms moving images are characterised by high rates of obsolescence and, consequently, disposal.[1] Our quickness to discard images – whether a damaged DVD or a bulky download from a hard drive – is an historical constant; Cherchi Usai reminds us, for example, that in cinema's first decade audience demand for new movies grew so high that by 1905 films that had exhausted commercial interest were thrown out.[2] But nowhere is the moving image's inherent transience more evident than in the composition of *film* itself – the stuff stored in canisters, spooled on reels. For the surface used to support the image will, ironically, perhaps tragically, eventually come to destroy it. Nearly every film from the era of early cinema was made on nitro-cellulose film stock, a practice that continued until the 1950s. Though not immediately detectable, as soon as it is produced, nitrate begins to break down. This inherently organic quality limits nitrate's average shelf life outside of a climate-controlled environment to approximately one hundred years.[3] This time span perhaps seems generous when compared to the short shelf life of magnetic video tape, say, or the rapidity of format migration that renders digital files vulnerable to illegibility. Stock that survives from cinema's first two decades will now have begun to shrink and curl, the perforations to fuse, making projection and copying problematic if not impossible. As Cherchi Usai describes it, and with poetic appeal, the decomposition of nitrate turns the base brown, the emulsion sticky; it produces a pungent smell. Eventually an eruption of "soft dark matter" will spread across the film and turn to a brown crust before reducing the material into "a white mass or even a powder".[4] That the moving image, and in whatever format – nitrate cellulose, video, digital – even has a shelf life is a vital if often overlooked component of cinematic history in general and of the relationship we have to early cinema in particular. Film's ephemeral quality produces a set of ideological questions about the ways in which we regard the past – not necessarily through what is visible in its images but through the very technology that makes them possible, or impossible, to access. That cinema is so materially transient lends it a vitality in and of itself; the slippery impermanence of this "flawed" or "half-way" technology produces a discursive longevity all its own, for the very disappearance and ontological flux of film is responsible for producing cinema as history in the first place.[5]

Of course in addition to and in contrast with film's inherent transience, the relatively contemporary urge to preserve fading cinema – or at least certain portions of it – is as vital a cinematic characteristic as the habit of tossing it out. The challenge to the archivist embodies some of this dialectic tension, for while there is an over-abundance of deteriorating films, the resources necessary to preserve them are limited, a fact that comes at the expense of those films that are partial or unidentifiable and thus unwanted.[6] Those films deemed unworthy of saving are culled – thus enlarging the sizeable population of so-called "lost" films. Statistics differ somewhat, but in general it is agreed that eighty per cent of films from cinema's first three decades and 20–50 per cent of all films produced have vanished.[7] But just as discarded early films were once mined for their metal and mineral components, discarded images find a way out of the trash bin, mined, this time, for memories, their striking visual quality and the discursive power they leverage. So in the end their very state of deterioration is preserved, exploited even, and so damaged nitrate is lent a fresh commercial and aesthetic value, only because of the fact that it has been deemed valueless in the first place.

Peter Delpeut's *Lyrical Nitrate* (1990) and Bill Morrison's *Decasia: The State of Decay* (2002) are found-footage films that document, narrativise, aestheticise and exoticise nitrate's deterioration process. Delpeut's film assembles fiction and non-fiction fragments culled from the archives of Jean Desmets, an early Dutch film distributor, while American Bill Morrison's *Decasia* can be situated as a response to Delpeut's influential work. While the earlier film meditates upon time and memory, and allows the decay process to slowly unfold, the American follow-up is a veritable extravaganza of decaying nitrocellulose. Set to an original and appropriately haunting score, this self-described "fantasy of decay" employs materials sourced from several ambiguously credited archives, including private collections and large public ones, and many of the images – though the viewer is not told specifically which ones – are, like Delpeut's, the fragile survivors from film history's first decades. While much differentiates these films, what ultimately binds them together is their lament for a lost cinema and the inadequacy of technology to retain our cultural memories. Taken together, the pair speaks to how contemporary cinematic culture continues to exploit early cinema's vanishing film texts as a way to critique our present and envision a bleak cinematic future. Implicitly, the films also foreground how analog technology itself – rather than the subjects of images – is perhaps early cinema's more viable and valuable form of cultural patrimony.

Enduring primitives

As Bart Testa has written, beginning in the late 1960s a succession of avant-garde filmmakers such as Ernie Gehr and Ken Jacobs began casting glances back, towards their medium's origins, the so-called primitive cinema. With wonder and exhilaration such practitioners plumb images from these formative decades, highlighting early cinema as one of pure possibility – and our own as one shot through with the strictures and limitations of narrative and aesthetic convention. Such experiment is also a means of historic exploration; as Testa writes, the exercise transforms raw stock into subject matter[8] and the filmmaker into what Hollis Frampton terms a "meta-historian" in that the filmmaker is inventing a tradition of historical discourse while likewise critiquing it.[9] In much the same spirit, Delpeut and then Morrison present themselves as anthropologists of a lost visual culture; and they are likewise archaeologists, if not grave diggers, for their stock is not raw, it is rotten, and magnificently so. Indeed, that these images have physically run their course, are cast out of the movie theatre, the archive, and potentially history, is precisely what compels us to watch them; for as the process of decay unfolds, it draws these images right back into the theatre, the archive and history, reinstating their lost status.

The marriage between the avant-garde and the primitive cinema that Testa pointed to in 1985 persists. Michelle Pierson describes a recent current in "avant-primitivism" that makes marked use of the live performance. Drawing examples from the films of Guy Maddin and Gustav Deutsch, as well as Bill Morrison, Pierson argues that the live film events these practitioners favour are re-enactments of the viewing circumstances of the early period. The evocation of an experience of in-the-moment "liveness", she argues, evokes in spectators a visceral sense of the past while implicitly critiquing contemporary viewing conditions, typically characterised by the fragmentation and repetition that accompany an on-demand, highly mobile multimedia landscape.[10] Such limited-run screenings, complete with live musical accompaniment and even spoken narration, are not just immersive, as Pierson calls them, but also instructive. As digital technology renders images endlessly and exactly reproducible, the experience of cinema as a live event reinstates its ebbing aura, and underwrites it with an economics of scarcity. The depleted celluloid image, therefore, is inflated with a newfound historical, cultural and commercial worth.

But before such reinscription occurs, discarded celluloid must be rescued, repurposed within a fresh context and a new set of politics. Such is the job of the museum, the art house and the avant-garde more generally. Importantly, the early footage that is Delpeut and Morrison's raw material has not been "found" so much as actively rescued from cultural and historical oblivion. What, this paper asks, might be a more productive way of describing the grand acts of resuscitation that inform *Decasia* and *Lyrical Nitrate*? In the spirit of the "avant-primitives" in particular and experimentation in general, this paper attempts to uncover some options, primary of which casts the meta-historian filmmaker as meta-ethnographer as well.

Ethnographers of decay

The primitive cinema, as Noël Burch theorises, is the cinema before it was co-opted by commercial interests and its expressive possibilities suppressed by the drive to satisfy audiences with standardised forms of storytelling.[11] Burch's evocative term "primitive" suggests the modernist, turn-of-the-century propensity to romanticise the exotic Other as an alternative to an increasingly industrialised reality. A similar tendency is evidenced in Delpeut's and Morrison's contrast between cinema's present and an ideal "primitive" past and what might be called its bleak future. As both filmmakers transform the archive's detritus into narratives of loss, they instill a longing for a cultural patrimony that at least *seems* to be, as Delpeut puts it, "disappearing before our very eyes". The analogy between human mortality and nitrate's inevitable passing is obvious, and might be seen to connect our contemporary film reality and the world from which cinema sprang. But the sense of loss for cinema's inevitable decay that drives these works does not simply fuse contemporary viewers to our cinematic point of origin; it also creates an important distance from that quintessentially modern invention. In other words, this rescued footage works according to an ethnographic logic, creating as it does an encounter between two distinct visual cultures – a contemporary "us" and a historical "them".

Salvage ethnography describes the colonial program of rescuing the "primitive" Other from the corrupting forces of industrial civilisation via its technological and institutional mechanisms: the movie camera, the phonograph, the natural history museum. When juxtaposed against the aesthetic of decay that characterises these two films, the term salvage ethnography comes to reveal something about contemporary avant-gardism, avant-primitivism and the attempt to reclaim the pre-digital authenticity that textures early cinema's aging legacies – battling against while also championing celluloid's inherent transience. But here, the so-called "primitive" subject being rescued is nitrate stock itself rather than the human subjects it supports – or supported at one time, until time and oxygen got in the way. The grand extent to which this pair of films aestheticises decay, turning it into raw matter, narrative structure and ontological discourse, frames early film culture as an exotic one, if only because it is fading so fast. What these films have in common with their damaged images is the paradoxical spirit of using modern means to salvage the receding past, a spirit that underwrites early cinema's ethnographic portraits and travelogues and, implicitly, the ideology of the salvage.

As Alison Griffiths has noted, the turn-of-the-century colonial imagination that fuelled an intense curiosity in the primitive Other is indivisible from cinema's beginnings.[12] Indeed, until about 1909 when narrative-driven films gained ascendancy, travelogues, and/or what we now call ethnographic films, were among the moving image's most popular brands of non-fiction. Those exotic images that glimpsed a pre-modern world were of course not neutral but, as Jennifer Peterson points out, heavily imbued with a sense of inevitable loss and pathos.[13] So, given their popularity, it is not surprising then that such views of exotic tribesman or disappearing wilderness are woven into *Decasia* and *Lyrical Nitrate*'s salvaged fabric; occurrences add a layer of self-reflexive meta-ethnography, wherein our encounter with "vanishing" images mirrors how their contemporary viewers regarded the "vanishing" cultures that the movie camera seemed to freeze in time.

Delpeut and Morrison represent their fragments of time past with an air of tragedy similar to what Peterson ascribes to early ethnographies and travelogues. But while Delpeut's and Morrison's salvaged shards bear some resemblance to our reality and we are encouraged to see in their disintegration a distinct, natural beauty, at the same time the depth of the nitrate's contagion – in Morrison's film in particular – keeps us at a distance. As Catherine Russell notes, the "salvage paradigm" that persists throughout ethnographic cinema bears conflictive tendencies: on the one hand the filmmaker takes a hierarchical approach to the exotic Other, representing her as unsophisticated and therefore relegating her to an undesirable historical distance; while on the other hand, the filmmaker romanticises that same primitivism, rendering the exotic's pure authenticity as a desirable alternative to the industrial, urban condition.[14] In a similar fashion, Delpeut and Morrison's rescued images fascinate the viewer while similarly alienating her. These films exoticise the process of decay, by allowing its infection to blossom, bloom and spread. Decay must remain monstrous; after all, if the audience looks away from the horror or is lulled by the beauty, the urgency of the message quickly disappears.

Contagion in the archive

Rendered of the moving image fragments that have washed up on the shores of our post-modern (apocalyptic) imagination, Delpeut and Morrison's films together illustrate the inherent fallibility of the archive as the saviour of our cinematic heritage and, attendant to that, arbiter of its future. Haidee Wasson has masterfully described how the turn towards film archiving in the 1930s transformed our culture's relationship with moving images. By collecting and screening films within the space of the art museum, the MoMA Film Library, for example, lent cinema a cultural pedigree and curbed its disposability factor. MoMA's initiative turned movies into *films*, in other words, a harmless entertainment into an elevated form of artistic production, forgotten features into invaluable cultural records.[15] When, in the early 1940s, nitrate's decay became apparent, a film strip's claim to being a precious artefact was further buttressed. It is within this climate of film as culture rather than mere commodity that early cinema could become a "primitive" cinema, a lost world, a cinema increasingly authentic and – as it disappears – ever more painfully pure.

But housing cinema within the protected space of the gallery, museum, archive or university was not a universal practice; Morrison's film testifies to precisely that, as it takes its raw stock from the Library of Congress's own discarded archives. Like Delpeut's film, Morrison's can be read as an ethnographic narrative featuring a filmmaker as social scientist who chances upon a lost cluster of primitive images and determines to capture their fading ways before they succumb to extinction. But of course neither filmmaker is attempting to restore the image to an original "pre-contact" or authentic state. Rather, the decay itself is exploited for all its narrative, aesthetic and emotional appeal. Music selections, for example, are consistently persuasive: Delpeut's lamentable song cycles and bouts of silence, *Decasia*'s unremitting atmosphere of apocalypse (Michael Gordon's accompanying symphony is played on mistuned instruments and salvaged car parts). Editing decisions such as consistent use of slow motion and freeze frames also contribute emotional charge, as does the provocative organisation of fragments into life cycles – from creation to disintegration to rebirth – that characterises both films.

Unlike Morrison's, Delpeut's project maintains fidelity to the historical context of his sources. A concise explanation of the archive's discovery introduces the film, and each fragment is credited with a title and production date at the end. Morrison, by contrast, does no such thing. Rather, *Decasia* overrides periodisation and contextualisation, mixing fragments of early cinema with shards from as late as the 1950s. What is being salvaged is less the image – or its original subject – than the decay itself, the homogenising force which makes no distinction between historical qualifiers that separates out films made in 1895 from those made in 1915, or in 1945 for that matter. Both filmmakers group clips thematically, according to the cycle of life and death and rebirth, and so the history they forge is about continuity, patterns, repetition. *Decasia*'s extravagance does a particularly good job foregrounding film as organic, a substance whose history and culture are indivisible from the nature of its support surface. By overlooking the historical context of his fragments, Morrison celebrates how decay cuts across our neat delineations of historical periods and likewise nullifies our perceptions of cultural difference. Indeed, decay infects us all; it is a universalising force. Morrison's radical response to Delpeut's comparably measured meditation suggests that decay's contagion has spread in the decade since *Lyrical Nitrate* was made. Time and atmospheric exposure have extended their tentacles from beyond the Desmets archive and film's first decades and continue to indiscriminately engorge all that is not adequately sheltered. So, what is for Delpeut a narrative of death, loss and longing for a primitive past is for Morrison a full-on cultural apocalypse and, perhaps, an end of cinematic and human history.[16]

Survival of the apparatus

Drawing on the work of Pierre Nora and Roland Barthes, André Habib describes cinema as an externalisation of memory, and the moving image archive as industrial culture's rejection of the permanent monument, if not history itself: that which retained the records and memories of pre-industrial European societies. While Barthes considered photography at once the "mortal" witness of our past and also its renunciation, the same can be said of cinema; like the photograph, the moving image is characterised by the paradoxical fact that it both captures and then cancels out industrial culture's historical record and so inherently jeopardises the patrimony we might leave for the future.[17] This, however, is only a partial consideration of cinema, for it speaks only of the moving image, but not of the larger support systems that make them possible. What enables those frustratingly delicate images to live, if only for a time (cameras, projectors, theatre complexes, clunky VHS players), will not readily fade away. There is, therefore, another force at work here implicitly bubbling under the surface, and that is technological innovation, format transition and – now in particular – the unstoppable march of digitisation. Primitive cinema is an analog cinema and analog technology is perhaps the more viable and immediate legacy of cinema's formative years. As Leo Enticknap pointed out relatively recently, if chemical decomposition is removed as a factor, "a moving image manufactured in the 1890s could be viewed and copied using equipment in widespread use in 2005, with only minor modifications".[18] But the infrastructure of early cinema is left out of Delpeut and Morrison's films. Perhaps we should extend the discourse to include analog mechanics as well, for this too is being subsumed, not by the ravages of time, but by digitisation and what might be called the homogenisation of viewing platforms. While analog machinery was characterised by staying power, the same cannot be said for the DVD players, laptops and television monitors that enable the majority of our direct encounters with cinema's early history, for this equipment quickly becomes outmoded and extinct, and is thus unable to support earlier formats of image capture and storage. Nitrate stock, therefore, is just one part of a primitive and/or analog cinema that is being subsumed by the forces of time, atmospheric conditions as well as the dominance of digital technology.

So while problems of technological obsolescence and rapid format migration make digital an unreliable archival medium, it is its inferior and/ or less authentic image quality that is more commonly highlighted as the threat posed to the viability of the archive. So far the commercial dimensions of technological innovation guarantee that digital technology is no more resilient than nitrate. And our images are no more precious than nitrate either, for we rip and burn and download – and delete – with as much zeal as early cinema mongers tossed reels in the trash once they'd been deemed tiresome. This disposability factor obviously represents a distinct continuity with the early cinema audiences rather than a rupture. So while digital replication and high rates of image turnover might add to the distance between our moment and the authentically analog primitive cinema, it also closes the gap in the first place. But, conversely, early cinema culture did not throw away cameras or projectors as readily as images, for these did not wear down or become unfashionable according to the season: herein, perhaps, lies the difference between this moment and the analog past. Perhaps it is the analog apparatus itself that is early cinema's unique patrimony, the longstanding legacy of the moving image's so-called primitive origins.

Notes

1. Paolo Cherchi Usai, *Silent Cinema: An Introduction* (London: British Film Institute, 2000), 161.
2. Ibid.
3. Ibid., 12.
4. Ibid., 13.
5. Paolo Cherchi Usai, *Death of Cinema: History, Cultural Memory and the Digital Dark Age* (London: British Film Institute, 2001), 89.

6. Cherchi Usai, *Silent Cinema*, 166.
7. André Habib, "Ruin, Archive, and the Time of Cinema: Peter Delpeut's *Lyrical Nitrate*", *Substance* 35, no.2 (2006): 125.
8. Bart Testa (with Charlie Keil), *The Avant-Garde and Primitive Cinema* (Toronto: The Funnel Film Centre, 1985), 6.
9. Quoted in Ibid., 3.
10. See Michelle Pierson, "Avant-Garde Re-Enactment: *World Mirror Cinema*, *Decasia*, and *The Heart of the World*", *Cinema Journal* 49, no. 1 (2009).
11. See Noël Burch, *Life to those Shadows*, trans. and ed. Ben Brewster (Berkeley: University of California Press, 1991).
12. See Alison Griffiths, *Wondrous Difference: Cinema, Anthropology, and Turn of the Century Visual Culture* (New York, Columbia University Press, 2002).
13. Jennifer Lynne Peterson, "Travelogues and Early Nonfiction Film: Education in the School of Dreams", in Charlie Keil and Shelley Stamp (eds), *American Cinema's Transitional Era: Audiences, Institutions, Practices* (Berkeley: University of California, 2004), 207.
14. Catherine Russell, *Experimental Ethnography: The Work of Film in the Age of Video* (Durham: Duke University Press, 1999), 56.
15. Haidee Wasson, *Museum Movies: The Museum of Modern Art and the Birth of Art Cinema* (Berkeley: University of California Press, 2005), 2.
16. Michelle Pierson astutely points out how in an age of ecological crisis, the apocalyptic tenor imparted in *Decasia*'s parallel between historical and organic decline is particularly resonant. See her "Avant-Garde Re-Enactment", 17.
17. Habib, "Ruin, Archive, and the Time of Cinema", 126.
18. Leo Enticknap, *Moving Image Technology: From Zoetrope to Digital* (London: Wallflower, 2005), 5.

24

Picture Craft, Visual Education and the Lantern: A Lecture Fantasy

Kaveh Askari

Max Weber's 1916 *Slide Lecture at the Metropolitan Museum* will probably never be mistaken for a major work. By most standards, this curious pastel on paper does not stand up to the more ambitious paintings created in New York in the wake of the 1913 Armory Show, including Weber's own prolific output during this period. But while it might not constitute a significant milestone in the history of modern American painting, in the history of modern visual education it offers a representation of instruction in the 1910s as illuminating as it is curious. Somewhere in the relationship between its style and the scene it depicts, Weber's pastel revisits the experience of the slide lecture in a compelling way. Its eccentric energy challenges assumptions about the lantern's role as a tool for teaching viewers how to contemplate pictures.

Art historians who discuss the picture in any detail usually group it with the better-known oil works from Weber's cycle of 1910s modernist paintings.[1] He completed this cycle after returning to New York from Paris, and this apprenticeship is evident in many of these cubist and futurist-influenced depictions of life in Manhattan. Scholars of Weber's work have used this group of paintings to position him among those who related moving picture devices to the dynamism and distraction of the city.[2] And with good cause. Projected images, motion pictures, and screening spaces figure prominently in his paintings and drawings. The windows on his skyscrapers in *New York 1913* run in single file up the buildings, resembling sprocket holes in celluloid. Cones of light fill works like *Russian Ballet* (1916), and projection surfaces dominate the frame with reflections of abstract shapes in works like *The Screen* (1913).

Weber was certainly fascinated with devices of projection. But while a technical fascination energises these works, it is not the only story that the slide lecture picture tells. When one addresses the event represented by the work, it begins to raise more questions than Weber's other modernist urban fantasies can answer. Its explosive suggestion of sensory immersion is clear, but just as clear is the pedagogical context. It is a picture about teaching with pictures, reflecting Weber's work with educational institutions, their lecture halls, devices and archives. With an approach to abstraction that seems more descriptive than truly cubist, it diagrams the components of an art lecture: from lantern slide, to projector beam, to screen, and then to the seating wrapped around the screen in concentric circles. These were pressing subjects of interest for Weber, who was in fact spending much of his time in the 1910s teaching art appreciation. His slide lecture picture suggests a compatibility between his painting and his pedagogy, and this compatibility seems to run counter to common assumptions about each. Much of his 1910s work depicts projection technologies as a kind of twentieth-century phantasmagoria. But in this particular composition he indicates a more specific interest in these technologies. He celebrates a scene of instruction, an art lecture. Weber's *Slide Lecture* picture may remain an anomaly in the history of New York modernist art, but its ambivalent depiction of the modernity of art education brings to light the stakes of a much broader movement.

One of the main pedagogical traditions that energised Weber's teaching efforts was known as "picture study". Historians of art education like Mary Ann Stankiewicz have provided detailed maps of this tradition and its influences in North America by the turn of the century.[3] They have shown how picture-study lectures in the US had, since the 1880s, appropriated John Ruskin's and William Morris's principles of craft labour and contemplation.[4] But while art educators depended on craft principles, the way their lectures transformed these traditions speaks directly to interests central to early cinema studies. Picture-study educators did not necessarily hold up craft as a means of resistance to the changes that were taking place in the world of art and design. Through a subtle sleight of hand, picture study actually revitalised craft ideals by transforming them into a modernised program of art appreciation. While art educators' craft rhetoric often resembled that of traditionalist reformers, ultimately they reversed the anti-modern goals of earlier proponents of American craft by redefining how and why students should contemplate the basic pictorial components of line and shape.

Such a pervasive tradition in art education deserves to have its intersections with the lantern and moving pictures more thoroughly explored, especially now. As cinema and media historians focus more attention on orphaned educational moving pictures, early cinema studies would do well to get acquainted with the picture-study tradition. Weber's pastel provides one opportunity to explore this acquaintance. It unites an awkward mix of forces. Weber's work may be a quasi-cubist study about the velocity of modern urban experience. But it is one that also reflects on the traditions of contemplation and craft that might appear at first glance to contradict the picture's more obvious themes. It is precisely in this act of reflection that Weber's pastel can offer a vantage point for understanding how slide series and moving pictures complemented, and in some cases accelerated, art education's changing relationship to craft.

Craft and the lantern

Before considering how theorists of art education drew from and transformed concepts of craft, one should note a few of the ways that this tradition of craft education influenced the collection and distribution of art slides. Many of these educational slide collections have not been preservation priorities, but there remains an excellent collection of slides and letters about the Brooklyn Museum lantern-slide department, a major lender of educational slides in New York. These documents show how hands-on the curators could be in creating these teaching collections. The Brooklyn Museum's first fine-arts curator, rubber tire heir William Henry Goodyear, carefully managed minute details of the collection. He made decisions about everything from the shape of the collection to how the slides should be coloured for educational purposes, making analogies between his slide collection and his hall of cast sculpture.[5]

A craft aesthetic was written all over Goodyear's slide collecting practices, and was even written on the slides themselves. Many of the slides bear handwritten notes about the faults or greatness in the craftsmanship of a particular cabinet or carving.[6] Beyond the decorative arts, Goodyear's interest in the lantern as an instrument of craft education was just as strong. If he had one overarching research project throughout his career, it

24 Picture Craft, Visual Education and the Lantern: A Lecture Fantasy

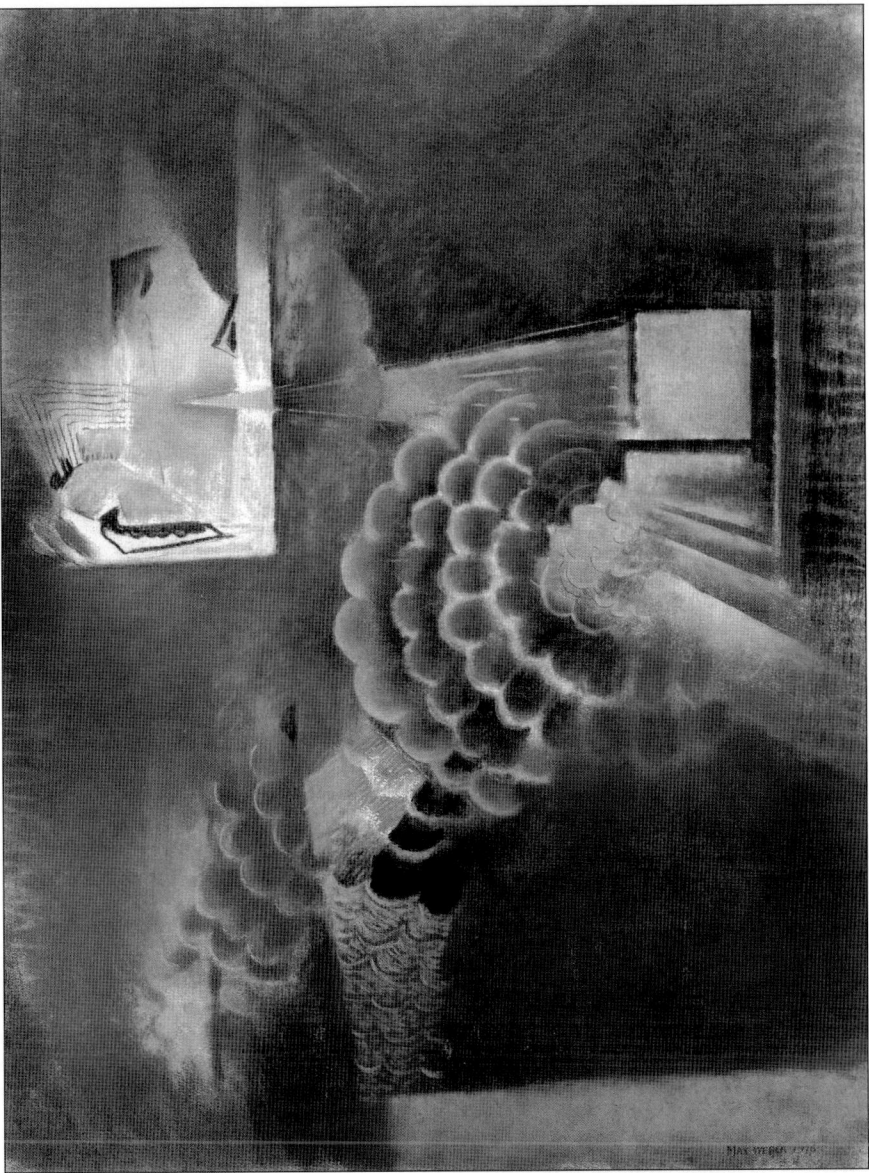

Fig. 1. Slide Lecture at the Metropolitan Museum *(Max Weber, 1916).*
[Courtesy of the Metropolitan Museum of Art.]

was to use the lantern to develop John Ruskin's idea that asymmetries in ancient and medieval architecture marked intentional moments of refined craft.[7] What had changed in Goodyear's project was not Ruskin's basic argument so much as the modernisation of Ruskin's methods. Goodyear systematically ran plumb lines through cathedrals and pen lines across his slides to measure and demonstrate these craft refinements. This idea of using the slide to illustrate the work of the craftsman reappears in Goodyear's published work as well as in his memos to slide suppliers.

Returning to Weber's slide lecture picture with a sense of this broader field of craft education, one can begin to make sense of its traces of a craft-focused aesthetic. In Weber's own description of the picture, he first made sure to note that this was a lecture on Giotto. Museum records indicate that this lecture was most likely given by Osvald Siren, a Swedish art historian who was completing a monograph on Giotto at Harvard.[8] The text of the lecture bears the influence of its home institution, where the famous Ruskinians Charles Elliot Norton and Denman Ross had brought the appreciation of craft design in thirteenth century Italian art and architecture to its height in the U.S.[9] Ruskin's influence on art educators in Boston and New York made Giotto slides a favourite in lectures like these. Art educators helped to circulate these images widely as examples of craft-guild production in contrast to the lurid visual effects of later Renaissance art (and, by analogy, factory-produced images that more conservative critics would denounce as part of the chromo-civilisation). These lectures on craft refinements did much to move craft education out of the workshop and into the lecture hall. Increasingly they worked to link craft with the contemplation of pictorial form projected on screen.

From craft to composition

Like many painters in his circle in New York, Weber's art pedagogy was at least as influential as his painting. He had focused on pedagogy during his early work at the Pratt Institute and had trained there under its most influential theorist of art education, Arthur Wesley Dow.[10] Dow's picture-study pedagogy emphasised composition above the more compartmentalised approaches to teaching art. Drawing from his colleagues in art education like Ernest Fenollosa and Denman Ross in Boston, Dow defined composition as a content-free and non-medium-specific paradigm that reconciled divergences among artistic practices. He taught that the same basic principles of line, shading and colour could apply to work from any nation and in any pictorial medium.

When picture-study educators like Dow and his protégés like Weber introduced their foundational theories of composition, they streamlined art education for the coming decades. They sought to address tired divisions and imbalances between the representational arts and the decorative arts, as well as between the appreciation and production components of art education. They could now freely adapt their basic methods of analysis to discuss media and works as far-reaching as Persian rugs, Arts and Crafts furniture, and even modernist paintings, so long as they taught aesthetics as a basic arrangement of line, shading and colour. The records of these art lectures clearly show how picture-study educators created a methodology for using lantern slides that diverged from older models. It was not about teaching rote copying of the masters, or really even about a sense of their traditions. Picture study focused instead on foregrounding abstracted principles of composition inherent in any object or scene. The adaptability of this composition-focused approach was, indeed, its greatest strength. It gained momentum between Dow's 1899 first edition of his *Composition* textbook and the 1910s. Influence in the U.S. ranged from higher and secondary education training programs like the Columbia Teacher's College, to public extension-course lectures, to educational publishing programs by companies such as Prang in Boston.[11] Composition offered a model by which educational institutions could effectively cooperate, and by which slide collections could be put to work predictably.

Weber had his first significant opportunity to implement this approach at Clarence White's school of photography, founded in 1914 after White's seven years of teaching with Dow at Columbia.[12] Weber described how each day he visited the Metropolitan Slide Library in the morning and assembled the slides that he would present in his afternoon lectures at the Clarence White School.[13] Existing copies of the lectures and their course materials indicate that, despite his flair for spiritual rhetoric, Weber followed Dow's model almost to the letter. Like Dow, Weber brought to his lectures Turkish string instruments and household items of formal interest. He placed these next to his lantern slides of famous paintings to demonstrate the translatability of composition.[14] He created exercises in art appreciation for his photography students that diverge from pictorialist photography, but do not quite fit with the modernist photographs that would go on to circulate in gallery settings. These compositions stay closer to an educational deployment of photography than to White's fine arts compositions. Like Weber's slide lecture picture, they sit between the lecture hall and the gallery and do not seem completely at home in either. But by the same token, they bring the intellectual history of aesthetic education, art practice and institutional circulation together into one, oddly fascinating, constellation. In their dissonance they evoke Weber's slide lecture picture: a cubist pastel, of a Ruskinian slide lecture, by a painter, teaching modern composition, to pictorialist photographers. Constellations like these, and the histories of the intellectual traditions that produced them, provide a vital complement to the work currently being done to reconstruct the institutions surrounding these courses. As the venues and materials for these lectures gain significance in the field, so does the content of the lectures themselves. And the picture study tradition provided methodologies and standards to systematise much of this content in an effective fashion.

Picture study and visual education

The traditions that Weber draws together in *Slide Lecture* have continuing and varied influences on the following generation of film criticism and filmmaking, from the pictorial art films of the 1910s and 20s so adored by the art educators who wrote about cinema to the work of art directors trained by many of these same educators in New York. But instead of gesturing beyond the scope of this paper and this volume, I will conclude with two points about picture study's connections to a movement engaged by several of the case studies in this volume: visual education. One point seems to follow directly from basic picture-study principles and the other takes account of the consequences of a modernised notion of contemplation.

First, we must be careful not to lump together the teaching of aesthetics and aesthetically (visually) motivated teaching. The Department of Visual Instruction of the Board of Education in Albany (which supplied the Met and the Brooklyn Museum with many of their art slides) had a strong interest in the effects of images, but these effects fell within the broader domain of visual rhetoric. Visual instruction departments were not primarily interested in aesthetics, but rather in how the aesthetics of projected images made them more attractive vessels for other subjects.[15] Meanwhile, art educators who taught courses in aesthetic contemplation did not necessarily support its use in subjects like chemistry and geography. But granting this distinction (and occasional mutual suspicion) does not mean that the type of art instruction systematised by Dow and his circle could not generate support for visual education. Dow's diagram method, by disentangling aesthetic instruction from a hierarchy of genre, supported an increasingly useful notion of beauty. It could free contemplation from a reverence for great works, as well as from a merely ornamental understanding of aesthetics. Even the urban shop window could be requisitioned by art educators as an opportunity to teach the values of proper citizenship that result, in part, from a feel for composition. As early as 1864 art critic and educator James Jackson Jarvies held that attractive shop windows are often "the first suggestions that the recipient has of a positive aesthetic faculty .... Everywhere these shop-schools are potent auxiliaries of the great art-galleries, and which, in

America they must supply the place of, until we can found them".[16] Carrying this sentiment into the twentieth century, picture study could bring aesthetic education closer to the familiar democratic ideals espoused by visual instruction departments. When aesthetic education focuses on the cultivation of aesthetic desire, it overlaps with visual rhetoric. They each emphasize, albeit through different means, the way that composition begets motivation. Design fosters interest. A content-free aesthetic of composition linked to viewer interest could indeed work well as theoretical support for visual educators whose democratic goals ultimately converged with those of aesthetic educators.

My last point about picture study and visual education has to do with the relationship between aesthetics and work noted in the above discussion of craft. It appears that, in some cases, the didactic composition redirected some of those earlier craft-based notions of work so prevalent in the preceding decades.[17] Dow and Weber were not really trying to discard older types of craft labour for a new art pedagogy. They simply wanted to revise those teaching methods that they thought had fallen out of synch with the expanding field of art education. Rather than abandon thoughtful, individual work, they sought to migrate the craft ideal to the domain of contemplation. There is a real irony to this move, because they indirectly helped to diminish craft labour in the design industries that their courses inevitably supported. In other words, as craft labour continues to recede in artistic production, it seems to re-emerge as an abstracted ideal in the theory of composition. A contributor to a 1910 issue of the *School Arts Book*, an influential Arts and Crafts periodical first published in 1901 as the *Applied Arts Book* (the American arm of the movement relied heavily on mail-order dissemination) illustrates how this transformation of craft labour could work in an everyday classroom.

> Appreciation
> A dextrous line, the work is done.
> That work a million eyes hath won!
> But few see the weary years
> Of struggle 'mid a mist of tears.
> That lay enshrouded in that line.
> And fewer trace
> Through realms of space,
> The yearning of the spirit fine
> That grasped the potencies of line.[18]

In this piece of amateur verse that would be easy to imagine written on a classroom wall, an artwork, a composition, is broken down to one of its fundamental components. Romantic sentiments notwithstanding, this component, a line, is described as an expression of work. But the real work moves to the domain of appreciation and the cultivation of aesthetic desire that Dow professionalised at places like the Teacher's College at Columbia.

Picture study, from its initial theorisation to its broad circulation in school arts magazines, retooled art education by casting appreciation as a kind of modernised craft labour. The educational lantern and motion pictures complemented this effort. Looking at these projected pictures was work, but not necessarily work as a form of self-denial promoted by the antimodern critics who saw the lyceum lecture as another component of the chromo-civilisation. It was a compelling craft experiment. Understanding contemplation in this way helped visual educators to calibrate an aesthetic experience, a measured feel for composition able both to serve classroom and lecture hall practice and to provoke Weber's ecstatic slide lecture fantasy.

Notes

1. See R. Scott Harnsberger, *Four Artists of the Stieglitz Circle: A Sourcebook on Arthur Dove, Marsden Hartley, John Marin, and Max Weber*, Art Reference Collection (Westport, Conn.: Greenwood Press, 2002); Percy North, *Max Weber: The Cubist Decade, 1910–1920* (Atlanta: High Museum of Art, 1992).
2. See Joan Ramon Resina and Dieter Ingenschay, *After-Images of the City* (Ithaca: Cornell University Press, 2003).
3. Mary Ann Stankiewicz, "A Picture Age: Reproductions in Picture Study", *Studies in Art Education* 26, no. 2 (1985).
4. ———, "From the Aesthetic Movement to the Arts and Crafts Movement", *Studies in Art Education* 33, no. 3 (1992).
5. Correspondence File, William Henry Goodyear Collection, Brooklyn Museum Archives.
6. Lantern Slide Collection, Brooklyn Museum Archives. Thanks to Angie Park for her guidance through this collection.
7. See John Ruskin, *The Seven Lamps of Architecture* (New York,: J. Wiley, 1849); ———, *The Stones of Venice*, 3 vols. (New York: J. Wiley, 1860); W. H. Goodyear, *Architectural Refinements* (London, 1907). For a discussion of Ruskin's influence in art education in the U.S. see Stankiewicz, "From the Aesthetic Movement to the Arts and Crafts Movement".
8. Siren gave two lectures on Giotto in 1916, one on 29 February and the other on 3 March. Metropolitan Museum of Art Archives.
9. See Denman Ross, *A Theory of Pure Design: Harmony, Balance, Rhythm* (Boston: Houghton and Mifflin, 1907); Linda Dowling, *Charles Elliot Norton: The Art of Reform in Nineteenth-Century America* (Lebanon: University of New Hampshire Press, 2007).
10. The most detailed description of Weber's work with Dow can be found in a transcribed series of audio interviews with Weber conducted by Columbia University in the 1950s. Max Weber and Carol Gruber, "Reminiscences of Max Weber", in *Oral History* (New York: Columbia University, 1958).
11. See Mabel Emery and Stella Skinner, *How to Enjoy Pictures, with a Special Chapter on Pictures in the Schoolroom* (Boston: Prang Educational Company, 1898).
12. Marianne Fulton et al., *Pictorialism into Modernism: The Clarence H. White School of Photography* (New York: Rizzoli, 1996).
13. Weber and Gruber, "Reminiscences of Max Weber". Met records indicate that the teachers at the Clarence White School frequently borrowed their teaching materials from the museum's slide library.
15. In addition to the Weber oral history recordings, Weber's published essays help to give a sense of the content of the lectures. Most of these essays from the 1910s were revised versions of his lectures from the Clarence White School. See Max Weber, *Essays on Art* (New York: Printed by W.E. Rudge, 1916).
16. Metropolitan Museum Archive. Thanks to Mellissa Bowling for her knowledge and help with collections here.
17. James Jackson Jarvies, *The Art Idea* (Boston: Houghton, Mifflin, & Co., 1864).
18. For a discussion of the modernisation of craft labour in the university outside the domain of art education see Christopher Newfield, *Ivy and Industry: Business and the Making of the American University, 1880–1980* (Durham: Duke University Press, 2003).
19. Minnie Hays, "Appreciation", *School Arts* 9 (1910).

The Scope of Those Scopes: Production Diversity for the Mutoscope and Biograph During the Movies' Early Years

Paul C. Spehr

In this paper I would like to take us back to the beginnings of film in America, specifically to examine film production at the American Mutoscope Company, the company that evolved into the Biograph Company, though I will confine my examination primarily to the early years, 1896 to 1904. My intention is to demonstrate that both in concept and practice, the company had a much broader approach to the potential of moving pictures than would be evidenced by treating the cinema primarily as a theatrical, i.e. entertainment medium. Entertainment was an important element, but the company had several other objectives, among them, advertising, news and information. For much of the period that I am covering, news and information were significant factors in the company's business plan and I hope to show that those activities – and the films made for them – involved more creativity and skill than is evident from judging the company's output by the comedies and occasional melodramas produced as entertainment.

Biograph's origins

The company was founded on 30 December, 1895 as the American Mutoscope Co. The founders were four friends (Elias B. Koopman, Harry N. Marvin, Herman Casler and William Kennedy Laurie Dickson) in a syndicate named KMCD after the initials of their last names. They attracted the funds to establish the company by licensing patents they owned, primarily for the Mutoscope, a flip-card "peepshow" device and a camera called the Mutograph (later called the Biograph). After the company was established, they added a projector that they called the Biograph. The original intent was to market the flip card viewer, hence the name American Mutoscope Co., but the interest in projection flowered as the company was organising, which led to the rather hasty development of the projector. The Mutoscope was a simple, versatile and durable device but the camera and projector were devilishly large and complicated. The company's system, designed to evade Edison's patents, used roll film intended for Eastman's Kodak still camera. The film was not advanced by sprockets and the image was large, two inches high and almost three inches wide.

When the projector using this large format was introduced in New York in the fall of 1896, it created a sensation and was immediately regarded as superior to that of any competitor.[1] In December 1896 Benjamin Keith contracted with the company to provide projections at his variety theatres in New York, Boston, Providence and Philadelphia. Early in 1897 the Biograph opened at the Palace in London and by October was featured at leading variety houses in Paris and Berlin.[2] In the summer of 1897 the company established an affiliated branch in London, which set up related companies in Paris, Berlin, Vienna, Amsterdam, and Milan. Dickson moved to Europe to establish film production in England and studios were subsequently opened in Paris and Berlin. By 1898 the company was international in scope and regarded as the gold standard in film exhibition. But Biograph's reputation was based as much on the quality of its productions as on the quality of the image on the screen.

To serve its customers the company provided a complete entertainment package: a projector, projectionist and an ever-changing program of films. In contrast to most of its competitors, the company did not sell films, projectors or cameras. A similar program existed for the peep show Mutoscope. This restrictive marketing pattern continued until 1902, when, as the market was changing and after receiving a favourable ruling in its legal battle with Edison, the company began producing, distributing and selling films in the 35mm format.[3]

While entertaining the public was the company's dominant concern during these years, its approach to film production was broadly based. Variety theatres expected variety in the program of films and that is what the company supplied. Comic turns were part of a program that also included scenics, information, news and advertising. This comprehensive approach suited the character of the company's founders. The KMCD group had been drawn together by a mutual interest in exploring diverse and novel projects and its interests were not confined to moving images.[4]

Advertising was, in fact, one of the initial purposes of the company. The first investors – railroad owners, bankers and other businessmen – found advertising a more attractive investment than show business. They were shown moving images of a pump, a threshing machine and a man sawing to demonstrate that movies could illustrate actions that were hard to describe. Entertainment films could also be advertisements, a practice borrowed from Edison's Kinetoscope films. The company's first film programs featured Niagara Falls and the New York Central Railroad's Empire State Express running towards the audience at sixty miles per hour carrying passengers to visit the Falls. Phantom rides were a specialty and audiences enjoyed seeing – and riding on – the Pennsylvania, Canadian Pacific, Union Pacific, Main Central, Illinois Central, Grand Trunk, Boston & Maine and other routes. The Mutoscope Company also promoted the theatres that booked its films as when the audience at the Wonderland Theatre in New Haven was entertained by a comic arrest of Joe Poli, the brother of the theatre's owner, S. Z. Poli. It was staged with the theatre prominently visible in the background.[5]

Films were also made for a variety of commercial concerns, some very obscure. General Electric, Westinghouse, H. J. Heinz and National Cash Register are well-known, but the Gold Dust Twins and Mellin's Baby Food have vanished from grocery shelves. The most spectacular advertising images were made for National Cash Register and Westinghouse, both of whom exhibited them at the Louisiana Purchase Exposition in St. Louis in 1904. Each set was about an hour of film, shot in segments that could be exhibited on Mutoscopes but also projected in groups.[6]

The public wanted news

> "...[We assumed] that what the public would desire would be a series of finished and artistic pictures representing a scene or event of historic interest

or artistic value – but the public wanted news". (Harry Marvin, testifying in July 1901 in Equity 6928 Edison v. American Mutoscope Co.)

Advertising was a complementary activity to other productions. The studio in New York kept busy supplying comic diversions to theatres and Mutoscopes, but it was reporting news that became the company's most important and rewarding function. One might suppose that filmed news was, at best, an incidental, supplementary record and, at worst, marginal and insignificant. In reality, movies were much closer to mainstream news reporting than has been generally assumed. Those early views of public events and prominent citizens may seem a mere curiosity today, but they played a significant role in what was, at the time, a revolution in news and information provision – the introduction of photojournalism.

While photographers had been recording events since the 1850s, the ability to easily and quickly print photographs in newspapers and journals was a recent development. Offset printing and reproduction of photos by the halftone process were developed in the 1880s and were still novelties. In fact, in the late 1890s many papers chose not to use illustrations at all, and most of those that were illustrated used drawings, sometimes adapted from photographs. Although they did not enjoy universal acceptance, illustrated journals were gaining in popularity.

Interestingly, during these early years, instead of regarding the movies as a novelty or an inferior rival, publishers welcomed the movies, and the American Mutoscope Company cultivated a close relationship with the press. Camera crews took still photos and the company supplied them to a variety of newspapers and magazines. The British Mutoscope company had three prominent publishers on its board of directors and the American company worked with both Joseph Pulitzer (*New York World*) and William Randolph Hearst (*New York Journal*), the controversial publishers who were actively experimenting with illustrations as a means of entertaining and informing.

Authentic photographs of current events were a novelty and newspaper readers were more accustomed to cartoons and etchings than naturalistic photographs. Some were artistic, such as drawings that Frederick Remington made for the Hearst papers, but Hearst and others also published outrageously jingoistic images. To a public accustomed to interpretive images, those presented by the Biograph were welcomed as realistic and exceptional.

The Spanish-American War

The company's coverage of the Spanish-American War is a case in point. The stereotypical impression of Spanish-American War movies is of ship models firing puffs of smoke at each other in a tub of water, or a motley collection of uniformed men with an American flag held aloft charging across a field in New Jersey to overwhelm a group posing as Spaniards. There were a number of such films, of course, but it is not necessarily true that the public, accustomed to interpretive images, was fooled into thinking it was seeing the real thing. Rather than engage in deceptions, the American Mutoscope Company was conscientious about producing realistic images of the war and did not "fake" battles in New Jersey fields.

When the company received news of the explosion of the *Maine* on 15 February, 1898, it dispatched its most experienced cameraman, Billy Bitzer, to Cuba. Bitzer arrived in Havana three days later, on the 18th, and stayed five days. His films of the wreckage of the *Maine* were in New York on the 24th and would have been on screen in other East Coast locales a day or two later. The trade magazine *Phonoscope* commented: "The series of pictures thus obtained strikingly indicates the value of the biograph [sic] in presenting to the public scenes of current interest in a manner more graphic than is possible by any other means".[7] As war preparations progressed, audiences saw Captain Charles D. Sigsbee, the commander of the *Maine*, and the Secretary of the Navy, Theodore Roosevelt, as well as warships preparing to move to the Caribbean and soldierly activities including simulated battle exercises.[8]

War was declared on 25 April, 1898, and Bitzer was sent back to Cuba. He made a sincere effort to record the action but was severely hindered by the huge, cumbersome Biograph camera and restrictions imposed by the military. He was manoeuvring a ton of equipment and the size of the camera made it conspicuous and an unwelcome potential target. He was able to make two films of troops landing and one of wounded being put in rowboats. He had better luck at sea where he filmed several American warships, the wreckage of the Spanish warship *Vizcaya*, and the *Lorenzo*, which the Americans had captured. He was forced to leave because he was coming down with yellow fever, the disease that caused more American casualties than combat. Bitzer claimed that he was taken to Baltimore aboard Hearst's yacht, *Sylvia*.[9]

The duration of the war was mercifully brief. The Spanish sued for peace on 26 July and a peace protocol was signed 12 August. Public enthusiasm was intense so the company continued filming military activities as well as the orgy of celebratory parades that took place in subsequent weeks.[10] The end of the war had a dark side; combat casualties were light, but the fever that felled Billy Bitzer afflicted much of the military and returning units were filmed at camps where they were being kept in isolation for fear that the fevers were contagious. The company's descriptions of these films stressed the woeful condition of the units they filmed.[11] When a bloody rebellion broke out in the Philippines, Raymond Ackerman was sent to the Philippines to record activities.

All told, the Mutoscope Company produced more than one hundred and sixty films in 1898 and 1899, recording activities related to the war with Spain. They were short, less than one minute long, and though they did not record actual combat, they still covered a remarkably diverse panorama of activities.

But what impact did these films have? Who saw them and how did they react?

By 1898 the Mutoscope Company had projection units in pre-eminent cities of the East and in many other major cities and it exercised some control over the selection and sequencing of the films that could be shown at theatres that subscribed to its service. In the spring of 1898 the company issued a publicity broadside describing the successful programs of films that it was exhibiting as the war was heating up. The broadside reported that audiences cheered, rose to their feet and waved hats as they viewed films of the *Maine* and Consul General Fitzhugh Lee in Havana.[12] On 20 February, five days after the *Maine* exploded, the audience at the Hopkins Theatre in Chicago cheered a film of the warship made the previous fall and audiences at the Orpheum in San Francisco joined the cheering a few days later. The program in Chicago was augmented two weeks later with pictures of the Spanish warship *Vizcaya* and the American flag. Spain sent the *Vizcaya* to New York to counter the visit of the *Maine* to Havana and withdrew the ship after the explosion of the *Maine*. The *Vizcaya* was hissed when it appeared on screen, then cheered when it seemed to sail away from the American coast. The broadside reported that there were equally passionate reactions when images of the wreckage of the *Maine* were added to this program. While we have less specific information about subsequent showings of war films, this seems to have been an established pattern.

The company had an efficient timetable for production. New films were sent to New York by express; they were developed and printed at a lab in Hoboken, New Jersey; then prints would be shown in New York as soon as lab work was done. Copies were rushed to Boston, Providence and Philadelphia. Chicago and other cities in the

Midwest would have them a day or two later and they would be on the West Coast about a week after that. In July 1898, at the height of the war, *Leslie's Weekly* called the Biograph a "modern wonder" and praised the company for going "... hand in hand with the daily press in presenting to nightly audiences events which they have seen during the day or read of in the evening papers. .... The quickness of the delivery of this news (for such scenes can properly be termed news) is exceeded only by the telegraph".[13]

In addition to the projections at variety theatres, some of the films were exhibited on Mutoscopes. The extent of these showings is difficult to determine. In May 1898 the trade magazine *Phonoscope* reported that the company opened a large Mutoscope parlour at 1193 Broadway in New York City "... having [previously only] exhibited in saloons and places of amusement".[14] One regional Mutoscope company had been created, but before 1898 the distribution of Mutoscope machines seems to have been restricted largely to "places of amusement" showing the company's extensive library of risqué subjects. An effort to upgrade the image of its peepshow programming appears to have been launched during this war-time period.

Interest films

The public's fascination with news, events and persons of note had an offshoot: films that, for want of another term, I will call "interest" films. These are films of people, places and things that were not news, but were interesting to watch and that fell outside of the more common interest categories: fire departments, railroads, military and marine activities, parades, and children. They were a forerunner of films made for education, instruction, public relations and general information. A few, such as demonstrations of fire ladders and breeches buoys, were derivations of the popular fire and maritime genres, but what to make of three films of eggs hatching, made in 1899, or three other films titled *Treating Spinal Curvature with Exercise* made in 1901?[15] Theatre audiences might have been entertained by eggs hatching, but even though there was a boom of interest in physical culture, treating curvature of the spine would not have attracted many nickels. The Mutoscope Company had another constituency in mind, and while scientific research and audiovisual education were only concepts, the company understood that there was real potential in using films to inform and instruct.

The company found a natural outlet for such films in the international expositions in Paris (1900), Buffalo (1901) and St. Louis (1904). The public was excited about the expositions, so the fairs provided an opportunity to demonstrate the versatility of moving images. The company's cameramen filmed opening ceremonies, visits of prominent personalities, panoramas of the grandiose buildings and amusement areas and exotic visitors from lands familiar and unfamiliar. It was a new opportunity to exhibit films, Biograph's own and ones made for clients such as the sets of films created for National Cash Register and Westinghouse, which were shown in St. Louis. In addition to its commercial clients, the company did an active business supplying visuals for the U.S. Government and local governments in Missouri. Since it is not generally known, I will elaborate on this early involvement of the government in film.

We usually think of government involvement in film as happening much later, but government agencies showed interest in films almost from the beginning. It started with the military and then spread to other branches. It might have begun in late 1896 or early in 1897 when W.K.L. Dickson made eleven films of the 13th Infantry Regiment and two films of a ten-inch coastal artillery cannon firing a shell. There is no record that these were made at the request of the military, but the consent and co-operation of the military was necessary. The variety of manoeuvres is more detailed and more didactic than standard theatre fare, which usually consisted of visually exciting scenes of a parade, cavalry charging or cannons firing.[16] The intent is not clear, but the two films of the cannon were made to show the projectile being fired and then striking a target. In slow motion or frame-by-frame they could be used for analysis or training – or both. Audiences liked military films so they remained a staple in peace and war. The co-operation of the military was necessary to produce them and both parties benefited from maintaining a cooperative alliance.

In 1901 the U.S. Fish and Fisheries Commission asked the Mutoscope Company to provide films of commercial fishing for possible display at the Pan American Exposition. Films were shot in Kittery, Maine; Gloucester, Massachusetts; Edenton, North Carolina; Road Bridge, Virginia; and the Fulton Fish Market in New York City.[17] Before the fair opened in Buffalo, Arthur Marvin was in Washington, D.C. to document activities in the public schools of the District of Columbia. At the Indian School at Carlisle Barracks in Pennsylvania, Marvin filmed the students in physical education activities.[18] These were filmed in the large format and were probably exhibited on Mutoscopes at the fair.

In 1903 the Post Office Department commissioned a series of films showing how mail was received, transported, sorted and delivered. Twenty-eight films were shot in Washington, D.C. and Philadelphia, as well as Westminster and St. Georges in Maryland, and Marceline in Missouri. They were filmed in 35mm rather than the large format and the coverage was carefully planned and comprehensive. Planning is evidenced by scenes showing mail being picked-up and received by a running train which fit with a film of a Santa Fe Railroad mail train running at full speed. The latter was made in Missouri, the only one made there. The series was probably intended for exhibition at the St. Louis Fair, but the coverage was so comprehensive that it appears that the Post Office had other uses in mind. This is confirmed by its ordering additional films after the fair closed.

St. Louis's Louisiana Purchase Exposition was a fertile stimulant for production for the Mutoscope and Biograph. The U.S. Fisheries Commission asked for more films and some were made on the West Coast.[19] Forty-five films were made in New Mexico, Arizona, California, Montana and Wyoming for the U.S. Department of the Interior (which administered the national parks) and the Office of Indian Affairs (which administered the lands reserved for Native Americans). The parks were an important element of President Theodore Roosevelt's program to conserve – and use – America's natural resources, while the status of Native Americans continued to be a source of interest and controversy.[20] A film series made for the Navy Department is noteworthy because of the scenes showing how seamen were recruited, processed and trained. The films seem to have been intended for recruiting rather than training or public information.

The nature of production had been changing for a number of years and after 1904 the number of these "interest" films declined. By 1905 audiences wanted longer productions and they were seeing them projected in venues that only showed films. Imported films, particularly those from France, had a significant impact on the American market. To meet the increased competition, the company's theatrical productions became longer and more complex. Somewhat hesitantly, the American Mutoscope & Biograph Company was evolving and would soon drop both Mutoscope and American from its name.

The name was changed in 1909, after D.W. Griffith joined the company. Prior to that, during a period of transition, the company made occasional advertising, news and "interest" productions, but these had become increasingly more sporadic. In keeping with the trend towards longer productions, most of these films were several minutes in duration and most were made in 35mm rather than the larger format. News coverage dwindled and became more local. The company filmed the delegates at the Russo-Japanese Peace Conference at Portsmouth, New Hampshire (1905), but did not send a cameraman to film the war in Asia. After films of the aftermath of the San Francisco earthquake (1906), coverage of the tri-centennial celebration of the Jamestown, Virginia colony (1907) was the final national news event that the company filmed.[21] Advertising films were made for Mellin's Food, General Electric and New York Life Insurance Co., and additional films were made for the Post Office and Navy. There was still some large-format production for the Mutoscope. While it was always low-key, the company produced a stream of titillating subjects for its peepshow. The production records indicate that the large-format Biograph camera was still in use in the 14th Street studio when Griffith began directing. On 21 May 1908, almost six months after Griffith began acting in Biograph productions, Arthur Marvin filmed *Girls Boxing Match*, *Too Many in Bed* and *Fluffy's New Corset*, and on 1 June he filmed the intriguingly titled *Soul Kiss*, the final film made in the large format.

Griffith's arrival was symptomatic of major changes at the Biograph Company. The management was evolving and with the settlement of the protracted Edison lawsuit the company committed to a new system of film marketing. After the settlement, story films dominated production – but that is another story, not part of this one.[22]

My point in examining the "other side of the scopes" is to demonstrate that despite the interest in narrative film, there are other aspects of film that have value and are worth thoughtful examination. This was true from the beginning of film as we know it. In fact, narrative entertainment was only a part of the early film experience. I have concentrated on the American Mutoscope and Biograph Company, but it was not unique in providing early audiences with diverse fare. The Edison Company covered the wars in Cuba and China, filmed Native Americans, promoted America's railroads, and produced scenics and other subjects of general interest. This rich heritage has suffered neglect through the emphasis on the movies' theatrical tradition. The crude, often unimaginative comedies of the early years seem uninspired predecessors of the more sophisticated cinema that came a generation later. But there was more to early cinema than people's dignity being squelched by torrents of water, flour or soot. For the people who launched the industry – and the audiences they attracted – cinema represented more than a medium designed to provide entertainment. It was a new way of seeing the world. and the pioneers of the industry sought to explore and draw on the variety of ways that movies could be used to record life and the variety of experiences that life afforded; the aim of these pioneers was to influence, inform and enlighten the people attracted to watch their films. They understood that the camera was a versatile instrument that could – and would – change the world.

Notes

1. During September 1896 the Biograph toured for three weeks to Pittsburgh, Philadelphia and Brooklyn with Eugene Sandow's show *Olympia*. Sandow's show closed after a week at the Grand Opera House in Manhattan. The following week, on 12 October 1896, the Biograph had an "official" opening at Oscar Hammerstein's Olympia Theatre in Longacre Square, better known today as Times Square.

2. Gordon Hendricks Collection, National Museum of American History, Smithsonian Institution. The Biograph opened at the Casino de Paris on 16 September, 1897 and moved to Folies-Bergère in the fall of 1898 after a brief summer interlude at Théâtre Marigny. The Biograph opened at the Wintergarten, Berlin on 15 August 1897.

3. Thomas Edison Papers, Edison Historic Site, West Orange, N.J., in Equity 5/167, Thomas Edison v. American Mutoscope Co. & B.F. Keith. A decision in this case by the judge in the U.S. Circuit

Court of Southern District, New York reversed a previous decision favourable to Edison and invalidated several provisions of Edison's patent for a motion picture camera. Although Edison revised his patent and prolonged the lawsuit through 1907, the American Mutoscope & Biograph Co. felt it could now market films in the 35mm format used by Edison and a large number of competitors. However, the 35mm camera they used did not use sprockets to guide the film.

4. The members of KMCD had patents for products as diverse as belt buckles, miniature cameras, mining lamps and safety devices for gas lighting fixtures. Harry Marvin had opened a factory to make his mining drill and Elias B. Koopman was selling two miniature cameras designed by Herman Casler and W.K.L. Dickson. In later life, Casler patented various machine tools, Dickson dabbled in rides for amusement parks, automobile parts and lighting fixtures, and Marvin designed a push-button tuner for radios.

5. Gordon Hendricks Collection, National Museum of American History, Smithsonian Institution, Washington, D.C. Hereafter Hendricks, NMAH. *An Arrest* was filmed by W.K.L. Dickson in New Haven, Connecticut on 16 November, 1896 with G.W. "Billy" Bitzer operating the camera. Reported by the *New Haven Evening Register*, 18 November 1896, which also mentioned that Dickson filmed workers leaving the Winchester Repeating Arms Factory the same day.

6. Only still frames from the Cash Register series survive, but much of the Westinghouse film exists and can be viewed on the web page of the Library of Congress.

7. *Phonoscope*, April 1898, p. 10.

8. All the production information comes from the files of the American Mutoscope & Biograph Co. at the Museum of Modern Art, supplemented by entries in Elias Sevada (ed.), *American Film Institute Catalog, Film Beginnings, 1893–1910* (Metuchen, N.J. & London: The Scarecrow Press, 1995). Bitzer made ten films in Cuba, and while filming *Reconcentrades* at Los Fosas Relief Station in Havana, Bitzer was threatened by a mob until the police aided him. Roosevelt and Sigsbee were filmed separately, but at the same location and probably on the same day, though the camera set-up is different. The navy was filmed in Hampton Roads, Virginia and Key West, Florida. Military training was filmed at camps in Florida.

9. G.W. Bitzer, *Billy Bitzer, His Story* (New York: Farrar, Straus and Giroux, 1973), 33–40.

10. The Caribbean fleet paraded in New York Harbour on 20 August and there were welcoming parades in several cities where the Biograph was playing.

11. Films of Theodore Roosevelt and his Rough Riders and visits by Secretary of War Russell A. Alger and President McKinley were made at Camp Wikoff, near Montauk, Long Island. Similar films were made at Camp Meade near Harrisburg, Pennsylvania.

12. Karl Malkames Collection. Karl's father, Don Malkames, probably received the broadside from his friend and fellow cameraman, G. W. Billy Bitzer. It mentions articles from papers in New York, Chicago, San Francisco and Dayton, Ohio.

13. *Frank Leslie's Weekly*, 6 July, 1898. *Biograph Bulletins, 1896–1908*, comp. Kemp R. Niver (Los Angeles: Locare Research Group, 1971), 46. The article, reprinted in the *Springfield [Mass.] Republican*, 5 July, 1898, is in a scrapbook in the Van Guysling Collection, Los Angeles County Museum of Natural History. *Leslie's*, a leading illustrated journal, frequently used photos supplied by the Mutoscope Company.

14. *Phonoscope*, May 1898.

15. *Jumping Net Practice* (1898); *Shooting the Life Line* and *The Breeches Buoy* (1899); *Eggs Hatching, Two Hours After Hatching* and *Chickens Coming Out of the Shell* (1899).

16. The 13th Regiment was filmed at Governor's Island, N.Y. and the disappearing cannon was at Sandy Hook, N.J.

17. Eleven films were made for the United States Commission of Fish and Fisheries, which was an independent government agency created in 1871 to investigate and report on the decline of commercial fishing and marine life. In 1902 it became the Bureau of Fisheries, a branch of the newly created U.S. Department of Commerce and Labor (Wikipedia).

18. The films were made for the Department of the Interior. Marvin shot fifteen films in Washington, and among the subjects were kindergarten students, laboratory activities, physical education and a deaf student signing "The Star-Spangled Banner". He made seven films in Carlisle.

19. The Miles Brothers of San Francisco were commissioned to film salmon fishing in Washington State and Billy Bitzer filmed shad fishing near Annapolis.
20. Francis Armitage was sent west to film the Grand Canyon, Yosemite and Yellowstone Parks. He filmed Indian schools in Phoenix and Albuquerque as well as activities at several tribal locations in New Mexico, at Keams Canyon, Arizona and the Crow Agency in Montana.
21. Records of parades and events of interest in cities showing the company's films were also produced. Some, such as the opening ceremonies for New York's subway, had national interest and a spectacular trip on the subway, *Interior N.Y. Subway, 14th St. To 42nd St.*, filmed with artificial light, captured national attention.
22. *Moving Picture World*. After settlement of the Edison-Biograph lawsuit, the Motion Picture Patents Company was organised on 26 December 1908. Member companies were Edison Manufacturing Co., American Mutoscope and Biograph Co., Pathé Frères, George Méliès Co., Selig Polyscope Co., Vitagraph Co. of America, Kalem Co., Essanay Co., George Kleine, and Lubin Mfg. Co. In addition to the Edison and AMB Co. patents, the MPPC also claimed Jenkins patents, Pross patents, Vitagraph patents and the Campbell patent. A new licensing agreement took effect 1 January 1909.

26

The High-Stakes History of the French Camera Operators' Union before the First World War

Priska Morrissey

Focusing attention only on what is projected onto the screen risks neglecting several vital aspects of the historical transition from the cinema of attractions to cinema as an institutionalised art form. One element in this change beyond the screen was the shift away from grouping all types of projector and camera work as the job of "operators" to a clear distinction between projectionists working in exhibition spaces and camera operators working in production spaces. In its first years, the *Union des opérateurs cinématographistes de France* was a labour association defending the interests of projectionists without explicitly addressing those who actually photographed motion pictures. At the end of 1913, however, camera operators took a giant step toward establishing the legitimacy of their professional field of shooting moving pictures – their *métier* of the *prise de vues* – by organising their own, exclusive subsection of the *Union*, a step toward distinguishing their work from that of projectionists. Creating their own subsection testifies to the increasing awareness that their professional world was undergoing specialisation requiring a greater degree of expertise about lighting and composition, distinct from the optical and electrical knowledge and workplace fire hazards that concerned projectionists.

Five years earlier in 1908, the first labour union of camera operators in France was established. By the outbreak of the First World War in 1914, camera operators had been included and were able to assert the importance of their role in the film industry. As I review in the remainder of the chapter, this transition is inseparable from two factors: the camera attaining a privileged, central status in studio shoots with the invention of the art of studio lighting, and perhaps more importantly the creation of a professional portfolio in the filmography. Among the bylaws of the camera operators' subsection of the *Union* was the requirement that each member keep a personal filmography, a significant and step toward recognising filmmaking as a genuine art form. The separation of projectionists from camera operators, then, has less to do with the distinction of a projector from a camera on technological terms than with the professional esteem that studio filming gained as creative work compared to the labour done in projection booths. As I will show, the irony is that the first collective associations for camera operators in France originated within projectionists' labour unions.

The emerging recognition of film as an art form in France has been the focus of several researchers. Richard Abel has studied the transition to a narrative construction and the question of copyright, Alain Carou has considered the concept of the *auteur*, and Christophe Gauthier has done likewise for French film historiography.[1] Other historians have focused on aspects of the professionalization of cinema's *metiers,* such as Timothy Barnard's consideration of projectionists, Janet Staiger's delineation of Hollywood's mode of production, Charles Musser's work on Porter and the collaborative system, Paul C. Spehr on Dickson, or Laurent Le Forestier on the industrial organisation of Pathé.[2] Jean-Jacques Meusy's research on film exhibition in France is particularly valuable for shedding light on the history of the first projectionists' unions.[3] I propose that one of the important characteristics of cinematic *métiers* is their early interdependence, and I retrace the stages of distinction as "camera operators" become "cinematographers" and establish a legitimate profession.[4] The history of labour organisation offers an excellent vantage point to see how the sometime public persona of the cinematographer began to stand apart from the indistinct labour of projectionists hidden in booths. The establishment of the filmography as a public record of unique works is thus key in the recognition of cinema as the Seventh Art.

1908: Le Syndicat des opérateurs cinématographistes de France

In April of 1908, Paris's projectionists first established their own trade union, *Syndicat des Opérateurs Cinématographistes de France*. The need for collective organisation came from the anchoring of the cinema business in permanent exhibition sites, which led to both a proliferation of work and a clearer labour hierarchy between cinema owners as employers and projectionists as employees. Projectionists were subject to problematic hiring and firing practices and unsafe work conditions, and wasted no time organising collectively, instituting policies to control admission to their ranks and guaranteeing members' basic professional competence (no small matter, given the persistent concern about fire safety due to film's flammability). The same process occurs in the three other countries that also dominated the film industry at the time; projectionists in many parts of the United States, England and Italy established their own trade unions, guilds or protective associations in 1907.

In the course of 1908, the French projectionists' union first raised the issue that preoccupied members' debates until the start of the First World War: whether and how to issue a license certifying members' professional capacities and thus guarantee the cinema manager, and thereby the public as well, a minimum standard of mechanical and electrical knowledge. Many felt a license was necessary as a guarantee of safety, but it also could control the number admitted to a field of work still suffering from the instability and insecurity of rapid growth and competition. The same debate happened in the other countries at the time, but licensing was legislated only regionally or at the municipal level. If permanent theatres and exhibition sites prompted the first unions of projectionists in many places, one can add some specifically French context by noting the outburst of trade-union activism reaching its height around 1906, known in France as the moment of "revolutionary trade unionism".

This "revolutionary" form of trade unionism was characterised by several features. First was a spectacular increase at the start of the new century in the number of trade unions and strikes, part of what has been called the Second Industrial Revolution. In just eighteen months between June 1905 and January 1907, the number of trade unions rose from 4,625 to 5,322.[5] Industrial production soared at the same time, especially the modern industries of automobile and aviation, aluminium production and electric power generation. The second feature of this boom in trade-union activity and other social movements was their unprecedented reach into every corner of the nation assisted by new forms of communication. The 1884 law legalising trade unions, including those that had long existed outside the law, also authorised the coordination of related trade unions under an umbrella organisation, allowing nationwide collective action. The third feature was aggressive tactics aiming to sabotage and paralyse the national economy. Many strikes followed the uniting in 1902 of the *Confédération générale du travail* and the *Fédération nationale des bourses du travail*, two powerful labour federations.

Among the best-known strike actions was that of Paris's electricians in 1907. Formed in 1904, and almost immediately boasting a thousand members, the electricians created a network of solidarity with other workers that proved to be most effective. Major players in general strikes in 1905 and 1906, the electricians launched the "Pataud strike" on 7 March 1907, employing the surprise tactic of plunging the "City of Lights" into darkness by simply cutting the current citywide. Theatres were forced to shut down, newspapers to stop presses. Just twenty-four hours later, the striking electricians declared victory. Between 1907 and 1909, several similar tactical strikes left a deep impression on both trade-union activity and its regulation. Cinema projectionists, operating the projectors' arc lights, no doubt felt a greater affinity with the Opéra's electricians than with its "artistes dramatiques, lyriques et musiciens", who had been unsuccessful at organising a union since their first effort in 1890.[6] The term *opérateur-électricien* became widely used to refer to film projectionists, and electricians' and projectionists' unions benefited from such affinities. Projectionists in Lyon, in fact, created a union for themselves as a division within the city's electricians' union in 1913.[7]

1912: Projectionists in the Union des opérateurs

The trade-union movement in France suffered several serious setbacks following its "revolutionary" period in the first decade of the new century. The common term for labour groups became "association" (*union*) instead of the more assertive "labour union" (*syndicat*).[8] The semantic shift was significant: in order to maximise the number of members, political neutrality became the norm, negotiating with employers became routine. The projectionists' union of 1908 was short-lived, part of a steep drop in the number of unions, and in the activity of those remaining. In 1911 and 1912 several associations and umbrella groups vied to bring projectionists into their fold, but their own association was created in 1912 – this time overtly addressing camera operators as well as projectionists as part of its purview. The *Union professionnelle des opérateurs cinématographistes de France (prise de vues et projection réunies)* welcomed all *opérateurs*, of projectors and of cameras alike, indeed claimed to reunited them, at first without regard to age or nationality (although a minimum age of eighteen was soon set). The association's declared purpose was to "come to the aid of projectionists and camera operators [identified by one and the same term, *opérateurs*] who are unemployed or sick; all trade-union and political issues will be strictly excluded from the Union's program".

Did the *Union* actually succeed in drawing together Paris's projectionists and camera operators? Reliable figures are few and far between, let alone the means to check them. Georges Mariani, president for its first two years, spoke of forty-five members just weeks after the *Union* began in May 1912.[9] Membership had more than tripled to 142 at a meeting a year later, according to *Le Cinéma et l'Echo du cinéma réuni*.[10] Although six thousand camera operators were reported to have received a copy of the *Union* magazine in July 1913, the magazine's official circulation does not grow beyond the small circle of official members.[11] While the figure of six thousand was probably exaggerated, it still seems safe to say the magazine helped increase *Union* membership. A few months later, the October 1913 issue of *Film-Revue* announced that eight more *opérateurs* had joined.[12] Moreover, at the end of 1913 came the new, special section of the *Union* titled "Prise de vues", which clearly enjoyed considerable success; forty camera operators from the most important production companies attended the *Union*'s general meeting in December. Such specialisation no doubt increased membership.

Such efforts to explicitly include camera operators stand apart from the generic terms used back in 1908. Thanks largely to the dynamic rhetoric of Mariani, insisting on the need for a license to guarantee professional qualifications, the *Union* made it clear that it was an organisation aiming to elevate the status of all *opérateurs*, projectionists and camera operators alike. Mariani told his members that it was their duty to "enhance the prestige of one of the foremost branches of cinematography, shooting and projection, and rid the profession of a multitude of *tourneurs de manettes* [crank-turners]". He continued, "bid good riddance to this horde of invaders who are steadily tarnishing the reputation of those who have mastered the craft of cinematography, and the related ones of electricity and mechanics as well".[13] In fact, the Union went even further to help coordinate the various groups and associations of *opérateurs* at the national level by appealing to regional branches. National scope was intended from the very start of the *Union*'s existence, and it was open to working on an international level, too; in August 1913 Mariani was invited to Belgium to help establish the *Fédération internationale des opérateurs du cinématographe*. The integration of camera operators into the ranks of operators should be taken as part of a general effort to include all potential members. Whereas there is no indication that the term *opérateurs* included *prise de vues* in 1908, this had clearly changed by 1912 with the new *Union professionnelle des opérateurs cinématographistes de France (prise de vues et projection réunies)*.

Recall from my introduction that the camera operators created their own separate subsection of the *Union* at the end of 1913. The recognition of the special field of *prise de vues* was perhaps inevitable, encouraged by the *Union*'s efforts in fair representation: camera operators were firmly ensconced in the statutes from its very inception, as well as the name (albeit within brackets). Although the uniting of the two *métiers* was signalled with the one word *opérateur*, there was no concealing how the association was a merger of two distinct professional fields, a distinction that only widened further with time. But what was the position of camera operators within this Union in 1912 leading up to their creating a separate division? In the minutes of general membership and other meetings reported in the press (endless debates over licensing), there is a clear discrepancy between the presence of projectionists and the absence (or at least the invisibility) of camera operators. Certainly, projectionists outnumbered camera operators by a wide margin.

Accepting Meusy's estimate of 180 cinemas in Paris in 1913, there were perhaps two hundred to three hundred projectionists; the number of camera operators was significantly lower, perhaps between fifty and one hundred based on the number of production companies started between 1906 and 1909.[14] With somewhere between a quarter and a third of the association made up of camera operators, their position in leadership was nonetheless assured. Positions on the executive board, including some of the most important ones, were filled according to parity between the two types of *opérateurs* on each successive board. In 1912, the president is a projectionist (Mariani); the vice president is a cameraman (Ducot); the secretary is a projectionist (Leroy); and the treasurer is Georges Asselin, a camera operator who started out at Eclipse the year before. Everything changes on 7 December 1913; at a special general assembly a special section devoted to *prise de vues* was approved by a unanimous vote. This section grows in strength over the following year as camera operators' membership soars. Major production companies become well represented, and about sixty camera operators are members in 1914, a number that, if not a majority, at least provided for strong representation of the emerging *métier*.

The appearance of specialised professional associations just before the First World War is not restricted to France. In the United States, too, 1913 is decisive since camera operators created their first two clubs or associations, separately on the East and West Coasts.[15] To understand the appearance of cameramen's organisations, sometimes unaffiliated with projectionists' trade unions at this point, requires some reflection on other transformations in camerawork. An industrial mode of production coalesced around 1906 with the proliferation of permanent exhibition sites, including new strategies for the rational organisation of filming itself. One effect, in practice as well as in theory, was the creation of a new, autonomous area of professional competence in the *prise de vues*. Any analysis of changes in the discourse of the *métier* of the camera operator needs also to consider technical developments in the science of sensitometry imposed at this time on camera manufacturers and photography studios, as well as the moving picture industry. Studio lighting also shifted to artificial, electric lamps and away from glass-roofs and sunlight. Further, cinema's becoming a legitimate art form – the shift toward longer features, the star system – led to a public desire to know behind-the-scenes details.

Still printing and editing as well as shooting scenes, at least in France, the camera operator literally became the film's photographer, responsible for both its technical and aesthetic qualities. Working at Gaumont or Pathé, a camera operator would have attended weekly production meetings. A single mistake could have meant the end of his career. One of his duties was making preliminary still photographs, and he would have needed to master the darkroom, too, illuminated only by its little red light. Recruitment into the field of camera operators intensifies between 1905 and 1910. Before this, operators were hired on the basis of physical strength, family connections, or local business links, but with the development of the industrial film industry came a preference to hire camera operators with a background in photography or other visual arts. A perfect example of this new trend is Alphonse Gibory, winner of several medals in photography competitions before turning to the moving picture camera. A few years later Léonce-Henry Burel was a graduate of Nantes' Ecole Nationale des Beaux-Arts before his career in the film industry.

Camera operators' early trade association activities and filmographies

What were the activities of the first camera operators' subsection of the *Union* in its first year? In the course of 1914, its members were apparently silent on the subjects of wages, working conditions, and professional training or licensing. Those topics preoccupied projectionists, but there are no reports of cameramen being concerned about such labour conditions. Instead, their reported discussions are entirely focused on elevating their professional status. In February 1914, Eclair's camera operators introduced a plan, signed by every one of them, to distinguish internal standards for the *Union*'s *prise de vues* subsection. Following a long discussion, most of the proposed articles were accepted. Of particular note is a clear departure from the labour concerns regulated by the *projection* section: "Each camera operator must maintain, in the *Union* archives, an individual file of all the shoots that he has completed, including a list of the main screenplays". The adoption of this article signals the precise moment cinematographers' filmographies came into existence. The creation of the filmography signals the awareness that camera operators were not the same as other workers and labourers; the terms "career", perhaps even "oeuvre", could be applied to this *métier*. In fact, the demand for filmographies came primarily from their employers, the film studios, who wanted catalogues of past work to act as a guarantee of any operator's competence. This marks the start of cinematography as a legitimate profession of individual artists with higher status and a distinct character from the other type of *opérateur,* projectionists. The camera operators' trade union emerged largely due to a gradual divergence from the prestige and concerns of projection operators. Despite remaining a subsection of an umbrella association, it is difficult to overstate the importance of this first operators' union in delivering awareness – within the membership and in the public at large – that photographing moving pictures was the distinct art form of cinematography.

Recall *Union* president Georges Mariani's scornful description of earlier *opérateurs* as mere *tourneurs de manettes;* similar rhetoric appeared in 1916–17, now aimed at the early generation of cameramen. From 1917, the modern cinematographer is presented as a genuine artist and juxtaposed against a mythical "common crank-turner" of old times. Between 1914 and 1918, camera operators had their professional identities transformed into elite members of a new major industry. Their esteem is confirmed, on the one hand, by members of the *Service cinématographique de l'armée,* who brought back films of fighting from the front, and on the other hand, the development of technologies and techniques of film exposure and lighting for motion pictures. A milestone came in 1918 when the credits of a French film first named the person responsible for *prise de vues*: Léonce-Henry Burel, cinematographer of Abel Gance's *La Dixième Symphonie.* At war's end, projectionists resume trade-union activities, but it is now inconceivable that camera operators will remain satisfied to remain a mere subsection under the collective umbrella of *opérateurs.* They create their own trade union in 1919, *Le syndicat des opérateurs de prise de vues cinématographiques.*[16]

Translated from French by Julie Smith.

Notes

1. Richard Abel, *The Ciné Goes to Town: French Cinema, 1894–1914* (Berkeley and Los Angeles: University of California Press, 1994); Alain Carou, "Le procès des auteurs, 1906–1909. Questions au cinématographe", *1895* 29 (1999): 39–60; Carou, *Le Cinéma français et les écrivains: histoire d'une rencontre, 1906–1914* (Paris: Ecole nationale des chartes/AFRHC, 2002); Christophe Gauthier, *Une composition française: la mémoire du cinéma en France des origines à la Seconde Guerre mondiale,* Ph.D. Dissertation (Université Paris 1, 2007).

2. Timothy Barnard, "The 'Machine Operator': Deus ex Machina of the Storefront Cinema", *Framework* 43 (2002): 40–75; Janet Staiger, "The Hollywood Mode of Production to 1930", in David Bordwell, Janet Staiger and Kristen Thompson, *The Classical Hollywood Cinema: Film Style and Mode of Production to 1960* (New York: Columbia University Press, 1985), 85–153; Charles Musser, *Before the Nickelodeon: Edwin S. Porter and the Edison Manufacturing Company* (Berkeley and Los Angeles: University of California Press, 1991); Paul C. Spehr, *The Man Who Made Movies: W.K.L. Dickson* (Eastleigh, UK: John Libbey, 2008); Laurent Le Forestier, *Aux sources de l'industrie du cinéma: le modèle Pathé, 1905–1908* (Paris: L'Harmattan/AFRHC, 2006).

3. Jean-Jacques Meusy's research on early exhibition in France includes consideration of projectionists' unions. See Meusy, "Losque le Cinématographe est devenu une industrie culturelle: le grand boom des années 1905 à 1908 en France", in Jacques Marseille and Patrick Eveno (eds), *Histoire des industries culturelles en France, XIXe–XXe siècles* (Paris: ADHE, 2002), 343–366; Meusy, "Palaces et bouis-bouis, état de l'exploitation parisienne à la veille de la Premiere Guerre mondiale", 1895 (1993 hors-série): 66–99; and Meusy, Paris-Palaces ou le temps des cinémas, 1894–1918 (2nd edn) (Paris: AFRHC/CNRS, 2002).

4. My terminology and understanding of professionalization is from Andrew Abbott, *The System of Professions: An Essay on the Division of Expert Labor* (Chicago: University of Chicago Press, 1988).

5. Institut national de la statistique et des études économiques, *Annuaire statistique de la France* (Paris: Imprimerie nationale, 1906 and 1907).

6. On account of the inherent instability of their professions, dramatic and lyric artists and musicians were among the first to organise. In August 1890 the café-concert Raymond Broca establishes in Paris the *Chambre syndicale des artistes dramatiques, lyriques et musiciens*. Its fortnightly mouthpiece, *La France théâtrale*, began on 15 December 1890, lasting four years. In August 1894, the *Syndicat fédératif du spectacle* is created, but it remains inactive. In 1899, Edouard Guillaumet created the *Association générale des artistes dramatiques et lyriques de France*; its president is the tragedian Sylvain. It soon proved to be another failure. Finally, in 1903, the *Syndicat des artistes dramatiques* is formed and is granted the "prud'homale" jurisdiction over stage artists in 1907, but does not survive the First World War. In 1917, the *Union des artistes dramatiques et lyrique des théâtres français* is founded by the actor Félix Huguenet (1858–1926); in 1936 it is affiliated with the *Fédération nationale du spectacle*. See the two sets of introductory remarks of the archivist Naïla Kebbati, titled "Syndicat français des artistes interprètes (CGT) 1917–1997" (157J) and "Gala de l'Union des artistes, 1923–1981" (183J), available at the departmental archives of Seine-Saint-Denis in Bobigny.
7. *Cinéma-Revue* 5 (May 1913).
8. The French term for such an association, or umbrella group, is *union*, whereas the French term for a union, in the specific sense of a labour or trade union, is *syndicat*. To minimise the risk of confusion, this paper does not translate the French word *union* as "union" but either keeps it untranslated (if part of a proper name) or uses instead "association", "umbrella group", or the like.
9. Georges Mariani, "Tribune libre", *Le Cinéma* 14 (31 May 1912): 3.
10. Mariani, "Union mutuelle des opérateurs cinématographistes de France (prise de vues et projection réunies)", *Le Cinéma et l'Echo du cinéma réunis* 59 (11 April 1913): 6.
11. "Union professionnelle des opérateurs cinématographistes de France", *Le Cinéma et l'Echo du cinéma réunis* 72 (11 July 1913): 6.
12. "Union professionnelle des opérateurs cinématographistes de France (prise de vues et projection réunies)", *Film-Revue* 47 (31 October 1913): 7.
13. Mariani, "A propos de l'Union mutuelle des opérateurs cinématographistes", *Ciné-Journal* 204 (20 July 1912): 27.
14. See Meusy, *Paris-Palaces*, 276; and Youen Bernard, "L'absence d'organisations industrielles des petites sociétés cinématographiques: l'exemple de la Compagnie des cinématographes Le Lion", *1895* 20 (1996): 5–23.
15. See David Bordwell, Janet Staiger, and Kristin Thompson, *The Classical Hollywood Cinema: Film Styles and Mode of Production to 1960* (London: Routledge and Kegan Paul, 1985); H. Lyman Broenings, "How It All Happened : A Brief Review of the Beginnings of the American Society of Cinematographers", *The American Cinematographer*, 2, no. 20 (1 November 1921): 13; "85th Anniversary Edition", *American Cinematographer* 85 (August 2004); and Fred J. Balshofer and Arthur C. Miller, *One Reel a Week* (Berkeley and Los Angeles: University of California Press, 1967).
16. The union was, in fact, first called *L'Assocation des opérateurs de prise de vues cinématographiques*, but its name was quickly changed to *"Syndicat"*.

PART VI

Exhibition and Showmanship

27

Les séries culturelles de la conférence-avec-projection et de la projection-avec-boniment: continuités et ruptures

André Gaudreault and Philippe Gauthier

Il s'agira de poursuivre ici une réflexion amorcée antérieurement qui a amené à distinguer, dans le contexte culturel ayant présidé à l'avènement du cinématographe, deux séries culturelles apparentées mais reposant sur des bases divergentes: la série culturelle de la *conférence-avec-projection* et celle de la *projection-avec-boniment*.[1] Le principe de la première série est d'*éduquer* l'auditoire par le truchement d'une conférence que l'on illustre par la projection de *vues* (que celles-ci soient *fixes* ou *animées*) alors que le principe de la deuxième, au sein de laquelle la projection de vues animées est prépondérante, a généralement comme finalité d'*amuser* ou de *divertir* l'auditoire. Il est important de distinguer ces deux séries dans la mesure, notamment, où les instances qui seraient responsables de chacune d'elles n'appartiendraient pas au même monde et ne serviraient pas les mêmes causes.

Ce n'est d'ailleurs pas le même principe organisateur qui structure les prestations en provenance de chacune de ces séries. Du côté du *conférencier*, c'est le discours verbal qui constituerait le fil rouge autour duquel la séance s'organiserait, alors que du côté du *bonimenteur*, ce serait plutôt la projection lumineuse elle-même qui jouerait ce rôle structurant. Même si elles ont l'air d'être des jumelles, les deux séries ne seraient en fait que des cousines éloignées. Elles ne parleraient pas à partir du même lieu, n'auraient pas les mêmes principes structurants et n'investiraient pas les mêmes espaces.

Avec ses conférenciers-projectionnistes, ses livrets-conférences, son *Manuel pratique du conférencier-projectionniste*, sa revue corporative (*Le Fascinateur*), son organe spécialisé (*Les Conférences*) et son héraut, en la personne de Guillaume-Michel Coissac, la série culturelle de la *conférence-avec-projection* (de vues, qu'elles soient animées ou non) est déjà, dans la France des années 1900, une véritable *institution* parallèle à ce qu'on peut appeler "l'exploitation des vues animées". En contrepartie, la *projection-avec-boniment* relève, elle, d'une pratique culturelle nettement moins organisée, parce qu'elle n'a jamais connu de véritable institutionnalisation. En fait, la *projection-avec-boniment* est l'une des modalités de la projection lumineuse de vues (qu'elles soient animées ou non), au sein de ce paradigme que l'un d'entre nous (Gaudreault 2008) a suggéré d'appeler la cinématographie-attraction,[2] un paradigme qui aurait dominé le monde des vues animées jusqu'au tournant des années 1910.

233

Autrement dit, la *projection-avec-boniment* n'aurait, en Occident du moins, jamais relevé d'une véritable institution, au contraire de ce qui a pu se passer dans certains pays orientaux, le Japon au premier chef. La *projection-avec-boniment* n'est que l'une des séries de ce plus grand ensemble qu'est le paradigme culturel de l'*exploitation des vues animées*, qui donnera lieu à une institutionnalisation forte dont l'un des fondements essentiels sera, précisément, le *rejet* du bonimenteur, une figure jugée encombrante et inappropriée.

Ce que nous chercherons à faire dans le cadre de la présente réflexion, c'est essayer de rendre compte de l'impact qu'a pu avoir l'arrivée du cinématographe dans ces deux séries culturelles que sont la *conférence-avec-projection* et la *projection-avec-boniment*, qui existaient toutes deux bien avant la fameuse soi-disant PPPP (première projection publique payante du 28 décembre 1895) des frères Lumière, véritable objet de fantasme pour les historiens, qui en ont fait un obscur objet du désir (ou un véritable objet petit "a", pour reprendre le fameux concept de Jacques Lacan).

On peut se demander si l'arrivée du cinématographe a été perçue comme une transformation radicale par les tenants de ces deux séries culturelles. On peut se demander aussi comment les images animées en sont venues à investir la pratique quotidienne des conférenciers (avec projection) et des projectionnistes (avec boniment). On peut, et on doit de plus, se demander comment cet usage bien particulier du cinématographe au sein de la série culturelle de la *conférence-avec-projection* a pu influencer la conception que le public avait du nouveau média? De telles préoccupations sont importantes si l'on veut éviter de tomber dans le piège d'une conception téléologique voulant que le cinématographe ait, à son arrivée, éclipsé tous les autres dispositifs de projection lumineuse et que son invention ait représenté une rupture fondamentale dans l'histoire des médias. On comprendra que pour nous, tel ne serait pas le cas, le *moment de rupture* lié à l'arrivée du cinématographe intervenant bien longtemps après son introduction sur le marché.

Il nous faut insister: la série culturelle de la *conférence-avec-projection* et celle de la *projection-avec-boniment* existaient toutes deux, bel et bien, avant l'invention du Cinématographe Lumière. Et bien avant l'instauration subséquente de la projection de vues cinématographiques. Mieux encore, la distinction entre les deux séries est déjà présente, en filigrane, dans le discours contemporain. Le titre du chapitre 19 du livre de Thomas Cradock Hepworth intitulé *The Book of the Lantern* et publié en 1888 (soit *sept ans* avant la fameuse PPPP) est particulièrement révélateur à cet effet: "Practical hints to those who employ the lantern for *scientific demonstration* or for *entertainments* in the drawing-room or lecture-hall".[3] On utilise donc la lanterne magique, en Angleterre du moins, pour faire soit une démonstration scientifique (*scientific demonstration*), une pratique qui s'inscrit dans ce que nous désignons par l'expression "série culturelle *conférence-avec-projection*", soit à des fins de divertissement (*entertainments*), une pratique qui se situe nettement du côté de ce que nous considérons comme la "série culturelle projection-avec-boniment". Autre exemple allant dans ce sens, deux publicités insérées dans un ouvrage britannique (lui aussi) de 1892, *The Lantern-Slide Manual*, proposé par John A. Hodges.[4] Dans la première publicité, un fabricant loue des plaques de lanterne magique qui seraient "suitable for complete entertainments" (c'est-à-dire, en français, qui conviendraient pour un divertissement complet): "Lantern slides on hire. Well coloured slides, arranged in sets, *suitable for complete entertainments*".[5] On peut présumer qu'il s'agit de plaques qui seront utilisées par des bonisseurs s'inscrivant dans la série culturelle de la *projection-avec-boniment*. Dans la deuxième publicité, située dans la partie inférieure de la page, un autre fabricant annonce des lanternes magiques et des plaques "for educational purposes" (c'est-à-dire des plaques à visée éducative): "Lanterns and slides for educational purposes. Embracing every branch of science, as well as interesting and moral tales. Many of the latter are illustrated from life".[6] On présume ici qu'il s'agit de plaques qui seront utilisées par des conférenciers s'inscrivant plutôt dans la série culturelle de la *conférence-avec-projection*.

Du côté de la France, on peut lire dans le *Catalogue général des épreuves stéréoscopiques sur verre et vues pour la projection*,[7] publié deux années avant l'ouvrage d'Hepworth, que les lanternes aux deux gaz pour projection que la société J. Lévy & Cie a mises sur le marché "sont indispensables" pour les hauts lieux respectifs de la série culturelle de la *conférence-avec-projection* (l'université) et de la série culturelle de la *projection-avec-boniment* (les théâtres): "Ces appareils permettent d'obtenir une image parfaitement nette de cinq mètres carrés. Ils sont indispensables pour *Université* et pour *Théâtres*".[8]

Bien entendu, la simplicité de la division binaire que nous proposons est quelque peu problématique dès lors que, dans le monde réel, telle ou telle prestation empirique oscille entre les deux séries et qu'il devient difficile de faire le partage de ce qui reviendrait à l'une ou à l'autre. Rien n'empêche en effet une conférence scientifique de figurer dans un programme de projections aux côtés d'une conférence plus divertissante ou dans un programme qui ne vise que partiellement le divertissement ou l'amusement de l'auditoire. Il y a donc une certaine porosité entre les deux séries, tant parce qu'il est possible de "spectaculariser" une *conférence-avec-projection* que parce que l'on peut donner à une *projection-avec-boniment* des airs savants ou pédagogiques. Sans compter l'éventualité de voir tel ou tel agent nettement identifié à l'une des séries passer dans l'autre série, avec son savoir-faire. Les conférences de vulgarisation scientifique de Hepworth en sont un bel exemple. Voyez cette conférence sur Dickens, annoncée comme une nouvelle forme de divertissement (a "new form of Entertainment") qui comportera, vu son sujet, certains accents éducationnels:

> Footprints of Charles Dickens. This new lecture combines readings from a most popular author, with limelight illustrations, and represents a totally *new form of entertainment*, which is sure to prove *attractive*. It is illustrated by about 100 pictures. For details of this important lecture see separate circular.[9]

Autre exemple, mais en raison inverse cette fois, cette conférence de sciences naturelles, avec des "illustrations from nature", portant sur les tremblements de terre et les volcans, qui présente assurément certains aspects spectaculaires et attractionnels: "Earthquakes and volcanoes. With *illustrations from nature*, many of them having been taken by the Lecturer at the *scene of disturbance*".[10] La cause est désormais entendue : les conférences de vulgarisation scientifique ont presque toujours un aspect "divertissement" et les projections de divertissement un aspect éducationnel. En somme, les deux séries "*conférence-avec-projection*" et "*projection-avec-boniment*" sont des constructions de l'esprit, des catégories, qui ne se matérialisent pas nécessairement de façon aussi tranchée dans le monde empirique. Ce sont, pour l'historien, des outils d'appréhension et de compréhension du réel historique. Le monde de la pratique lanterniste n'est en effet pas aussi compartimenté que notre dichotomie peut laisser croire.

Nos deux séries représentent plutôt des *extrêmes théoriques*. À l'une des extrémités du pôle tendanciel, du côté de la *conférence-avec-projection*, on aurait ce type de performance pour laquelle les paroles proférées, la conférence, constitueraient l'élément principal. Les images projetées ne représenteraient dans pareil cas qu'une simple plus-value (vraisemblablement attractionnelle), elles ne seraient qu'une simple valeur ajoutée au discours verbal: ce que fait le *conférencier*, c'est une conférence, qu'il illustre *par ailleurs* par des vues, éventuellement animées. Pour les conférenciers-projectionnistes, qui le disent clairement, "[…] a lecturer is not an adjunct to a lantern entertainment, but the principle feature […]".[11] Même discours, une fois les vues animées largement répandues: "les projections ne sont que l'accessoire, la conférence, c'est le principal",[12] ou encore: "le cinéma est 'l'aide de camp' de tout conférencier".[13] Les images projetées, animées ou non, sont, pour ces intervenants, sinon accessoires, du moins un outil supplémentaire à la conférence.

À l'autre extrémité, nous aurions l'autre série, celle de la *projection-avec-boniment*, pour laquelle les images projetées seraient le principe structurant. Ce n'est pas une conférence que le *bonisseur* fait: il accompagne plutôt de sa parole, purement et simplement, la projection de vues, que celles-ci soient animées ou non. *Projection-avec-boniment* et *conférence-avec-projection* développent d'ailleurs des stratégies radicalement opposées, dans le rapport voix/images, notamment en raison de leurs principes de base qui ne sont pas de même nature. D'un côté les images suivent la parole, dans tous les sens du mot, de l'autre, c'est la parole qui suit les images.

Il est probable qu'aucune performance empirique ne puisse être élevée au rang d'exemple pur de la *projection-avec-boniment*. Il est tout aussi probable qu'aucune performance empirique ne puisse être élevée au rang d'exemple pur de la *conférence-avec-projection*. Ce sont là des pôles, ce sont des tendances idéales, aux extrémités d'un axe. Si l'on en croit Eugène Trutat et son *Traité général des projections*, dont le premier tome intitulé *Projections ordinaires* est paru en 1897, "les projections à l'École et au Lycée doivent instruire les élèves en les *amusant*".[14] Ce qui ne serait pas de mise au niveau universitaire, si l'on en croit le même Trutat: "le professeur doit bien éviter d'ennuyer son auditoire, mais il n'a pas à chercher à l'amuser".[15] Autre exemple, tiré d'un ouvrage paru en 1893, peu avant la fameuse PPPP des frères Lumière, et intitulé *The Art of Projection and Complete Magic Lantern Manual*: "[…] a well told anecdote here and there will be found most appreciated by the listeners, as they want to be *amused* as well as *instructed*, plenty of pictures with a compact description is all that is needed".[16] Ce dont on se rend compte, au fond, c'est que tout conférencier est un tant soit peu bonimenteur, comme tout bonimenteur est un tant soit peu conférencier : … Hepworth le dit déjà en 1888, au sujet du conférencier "the best instrument is no good unless the lecturer be an efficient showman and speaker".[17]

La réflexion cruciale qui s'impose à nous à ce moment de notre démonstration est la suivante: *quelles sortes de problèmes se posent aux agents des différentes séries culturelles au sein desquelles le nouveau dispositif permettant la projection de vues animées (que ce soit le Cinématographe Lumière ou non) est susceptible de s'intégrer?* À notre sens, ces agents doivent d'abord et avant tout prendre position sur l'adjonction, ou non, dudit dispositif à leur pratique professionnelle. Ils doivent ensuite se demander de quelle manière se fera l'intégration du petit nouveau. Le considérera-t-on comme un intrus? Comme un corps étranger? Comme un supplément/complément de programme? Comme une attraction supplémentaire?

Au fond, pour chacun des agents des séries culturelles faisant partie du paradigme dit des projections lumineuses, la nouvelle invention peut avoir une importance relativement différente. Cette arrivée peut être majeure et révolutionnaire (mais en tout cas *jamais* cet effet ne se ressent-il du jour au lendemain) pour telle série ou tel agent, et elle pourra être mineure pour telle autre série ou tel autre agent. L'une des hypothèses que nous aimerions avancer est la suivante: *plus la série relève d'une forte institutionnalisation, moins l'arrivée du cinématographe a un effet déterminant.*

L'arrivée du cinématographe se vit par une intériorisation différente chez chacun des agents spécifiques. On peut d'ailleurs penser que Méliès, qui est inscrit dans plusieurs séries culturelles, n'a pas nécessairement le même rapport avec l'arrivée du cinématographe dans chacune d'elles.

Il convient ici, non seulement de réaffirmer un certain changement de perspective,

27 Les séries culturelles de la conférence et du boniment

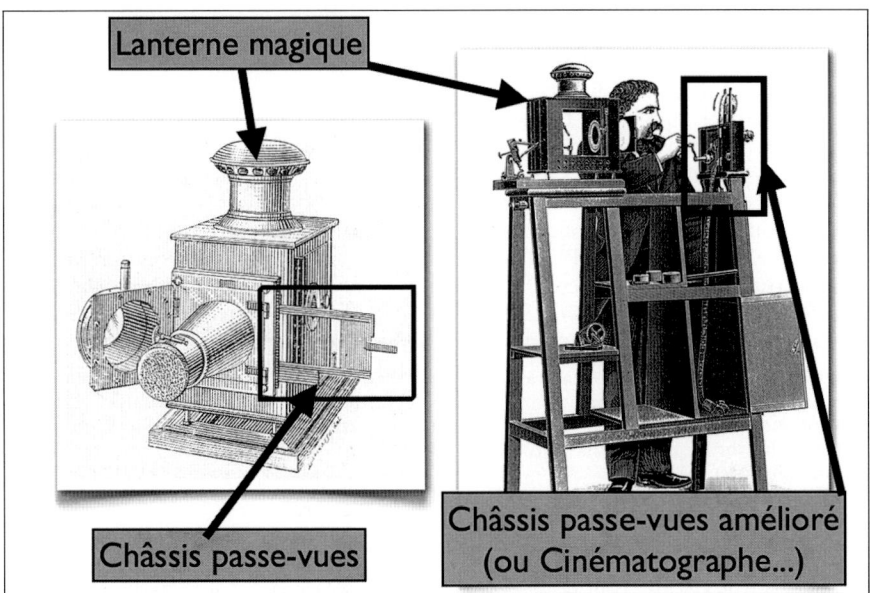

Fig. 1. À gauche, une lanterne magique, pour projeter des vues fixes. À droite, une lanterne de projection de même type, agencée à un Cinématographe Lumière, dans le but de projeter des vues animées.

mais aussi de le radicaliser. *Il apparaît en effet de plus en plus clairement qu'il est essentiel de ne pas voir l'arrivée du cinématographe comme ayant entraîné un quelconque effet de rupture, du moins dans les séries culturelles déjà le moindrement institutionnalisées.* Dans le cas de la série culturelle de la *conférence-avec-projection*, il semble que les agents aient vu le cinématographe comme une simple amélioration apportée à la lanterne magique, ni plus ni moins. Entre la lanterne magique et le cinématographe, il existe en effet une certaine forme de continuité en ce sens que le cinématographe serait, en quelque sorte, un châssis passe-vues amélioré (voir Figure 1).

D'ailleurs, les ouvrages s'adressant aux conférenciers et bonisseurs appartenant aux deux séries culturelles que nous distinguons ici n'ont pas subi de modifications profondes au moment de l'introduction du cinématographe. Au mieux, on tient compte de l'arrivée du nouveau dispositif par une petite section qui lui est consacrée. Prenons par exemple cet ouvrage signé par Roger Child Bayley, intitulé *Modern Magic Lanterns and Their Management*, paru d'abord en 1895,[18] sans aucune mention des vues animées, et qui paraîtra à nouveau en 1900, dans une nouvelle édition augmentée.[19] La seule différence entre les deux versions est l'ajout d'un douzième chapitre intitulé "Animated lantern pictures". Le titre de ce chapitre est particulièrement évocateur, croyons-nous, car il inscrit la nouvelle invention dans la lignée de la lanterne magique et, par conséquent, dans la lignée des séries culturelles qui sont issues de son usage. Que voilà un bel exemple d'appropriation! Voyez plutôt:

> In the beginning of 1896 *a novelty in lantern work* was first shown in London in the form of Mr. Birt Acres' *Kinetic Lantern*, as it was then called, by which street scenes and other moving objects were displayed on the screen in motion with a fidelity which was very remarkable. Almost immediately afterwards a number of other inventors were in the field with instruments for performing the same operation, and *animated lantern pictures* under all sorts of Greek and Latin names were quite the sensation of the moment.[20]

Oui vous avez bien lu: a Kinetic Lantern!!! Les choses ne pourraient être plus claires: une série culturelle, c'est d'abord et avant tout une ... série.

Le problème de l'histoire dite traditionnelle a été de fonder son hypothèse de base sur un moment initial qui aurait fait rupture: soit ce jour du 28 décembre 1895, au cours duquel se serait déroulé quelque chose comme la première projection publique et payante du Cinématographe Lumière. Une conception de l'histoire considérant cet événement comme un point de rupture radical dans le continuum de l'histoire des images mouvantes est une conception en porte-à-faux. Tout se réduirait ainsi à cette date supposée décisive de la PPPP, qui serait non pas UN point de rupture, mais LE point de rupture par excellence. Que nenni! *Il ne faut pas uniquement envisager l'histoire de l'avènement du cinématographe comme une histoire de discontinuités, mais également, et de manière toute aussi importante, comme une histoire de continuités.*

Ce texte a été écrit dans le cadre des travaux du GRAFICS (Groupe de recherche sur l'avènement et la formation des institutions cinématographique et scénique) de l'Université de Montréal, subventionné par le Conseil de recherches en sciences humaines du Canada et le Fonds québécois de recherche sur la société et la culture. Le GRAFICS fait partie du Centre de recherche sur l'intermédialité (CRI).

Notes

1. Voir notamment "Apparition, disparition et escamotage du 'bonimenteur' dans l'historiographie française du cinéma," dans *Le muet a la parole*, sous la direction de Giusy Pisano et de Valérie Pozner (Paris: Association française de recherche sur l'histoire du cinéma, 2005), 167–199.
2. André Gaudreault, *Cinéma et attraction. Pour une nouvelle histoire du cinématographe* (Paris: CNRS, 2008).
3. Thomas Cradock Hepworth, *The Book of the Lantern* (Londres: Wyman and Sons, 1888), 264. Nous soulignons.
4. John A. Hodges, *The Lantern-Slide Manual* (Londres: Hazell, Watson and Viney, 1892).
5. C'est nous qui soulignons.
6. Idem.
7. *Catalogue général des épreuves stéréoscopiques sur verres et vues pour la projection de J. Lévy & Cie* (Paris, 1886).
8. C'est nous qui soulignons.
9. Hepworth, *Book of the Lantern*, xxiv.
10. C'est nous qui soulignons.
11. *The Art of Projection and Complete Magic Lantern Manual* (Londres: E.A. Beckett, 1893), 105.
12. G.-Michel Coissac, *Le Fascinateur* no 17 (1er mai 1904): 134.
13. *Ciné-journal* no 5 (15 septembre 1908): 6.
14. Eugène Trutat, *Traité général des projections*, tome 1, *Projections ordinaires* (Paris: Charles Mendel, 1897), 346. L'italique est dans le texte original. Nous remercions Thierry Lecointe d'avoir porté cette référence à notre attention.
15. Ibid.
16. *The Art of Projection*, 106.
17. Hepworth, *Book of the Lantern*, 264.
18. Roger Child Bayley, *Modern Magic Lanterns: A Guide to the Management of the Optical Lantern for the Use of Entertainers, Lecturers, Photographers, Teachers and Others*, 1ère édition (Londres/New York: L. Upcott Gill /Charles Scribner's Sons, 1895).
19. Roger Child Bayley, *Modern Magic Lanterns: A Guide to the Management of the Optical Lantern for the Use of Entertainers, Lecturers, Photographers, Teachers and Others*, 2e édition (Londres/New York: L. Upcott Gill/Charles Scribner's Sons, 1900).
20. Ibid., 102. C'est nous qui soulignons.

28

Les "conférenciers de cinéma" en France (1896–1930): Historique à travers différents lieux de projection, genres filmiques et réseaux

Thierry Lecointe

Préalable: les sources dans l'historiographie française

En France, la marginalité originelle des accompagnements musicaux durant les séances cinématographiques me permet d'envisager que les projections s'accompagnaient de présentations ou commentaires.[1] D'ailleurs, la musique de film n'est devenue une préoccupation majeure pour les éditeurs et exploitants que vers 1907/1908. Je limiterai mon étude à un état des lieux des pratiques orales afin de mesurer leur étendue et évolution.

Une cinquantaine de sources historiographiques, en dehors des études régionales, évoquent les conférenciers ou bonimenteurs, personnages installés au-delà de l'écran si l'on s'en tient à leur position dans la salle. Ces sources décrivent des dispositifs entre 1896 et 1922. Tout d'abord, une conférence de 1913 mentionne uniquement que pour le "cinématographe forain [il faut] partir avec des films neufs bien choisis et un bon conférencier".[2] En 1917, on nous apprend: "dès son origine et surtout à son origine, le cinéma comportait presque toujours un commentaire verbal qui ne valait que ce que valait le conférencier",[3] et en 1925: "En ce temps-là, pas de salle de cinéma qui n'eût son conférencier. [...] c'était au temps préhistorique du cinéma, c'était vers 1907".[4] Ces affirmations modifient notre regard sur la présentation des films vers 1900 lesquels, selon certaines idées reçues, étaient exclusivement accompagnés de musique. Il faut attendre 1996 puis 2005 pour que des études spécifiques aux approches pragmatiques soient réalisées.[5] Cependant, ces analyses ne peuvent le plus souvent que souligner des interrogations subsistantes puisqu'on y évoque le *"[bonimenteur] refoulé"*, le *"bonisseur introuvable"* et *l'"escamotage du 'bonimenteur'."*

Les conférenciers des cinémas itinérants

J'ai dénombré une bonne soixantaine d'occurrences relatives aux conférenciers dans les tournées itinérantes ou chez les forains. Cet inventaire confirme un procédé s'étendant de 1896 au début des années 1930, époque où l'apparition du sonore en format réduit marqua la fin de cette pratique. Une synthèse regroupée en périodes correspondant aux étapes importantes de l'évolution de cette attraction permet de générer quelques déductions. Les volumes annualisés montrent un pic en 1896/1897

239

proportionnel au nombre d'exploitants engagés dans cette nouvelle voie, suivi d'une chute brutale amorcée dès 1897. On note une remontée progressive du nombre de conférenciers jusqu'à la guerre, correspondant à la création de grands cinémas forains, dont la disparition vers 1910 fut compensée par l'émergence d'exploitants locaux. À partir de 1919, les cinémas itinérants subsistants n'étaient principalement que de modestes exploitations tournant en zones rurales. Dans les années 1920, les bonimenteurs étaient probablement aussi nombreux qu'auparavant mais, comme ils œuvraient dans de petites exploitations circulant dans des villages, la presse de l'époque ne les médiatisa pas. Les occurrences trouvées sont toutes issues de témoignages rétrospectifs, suffisamment nombreux pour conclure à une persistance temporelle des conférenciers au sein des exploitations foraines et itinérantes. Une analyse géographique de ces données montre un déplacement des conférenciers des cinémas itinérants des villes (1896–1909) vers les villages (1910–1930). Elles démontrent que la conférence relevaient d'une corporation "institutionnelle" jusqu'à la guerre, pour n'être plus qu'un simple procédé, adopté par des tourneurs peu fortunés afin de remplacer des systèmes de sonorisation inexistants ou encore de traduire les intertitres aux populations rurales analphabètes ou maîtrisant mal la lecture.

Les conférenciers dans les salles sédentaires

C'est à partir de 1906 que l'implantation des salles sédentaires se normalise dans le paysage urbain. Dans ce type d'exploitation, les occurrences répertoriées montrent une pratique limitée (de nombreuses salles se passaient de conférencier) mais ininterrompue de 1906 à 1926. Elles révèlent deux époques: l'une, s'étendant jusqu'à 1913 où les conférenciers sont associés à des salles; la seconde, de 1914 à 1926, où ils sont associés à des films spécifiques. En ce qui concerne les genres commentés, le documentaire est largement majoritaire (films aéronautiques, de voyages, grandes expéditions). Notons toutefois que les films d'actualités ne semblent pas avoir été commentés. On se contentait peut-être des sous-titres comme seuls commentaires explicatifs, compte tenu de la brièveté de ces films. On trouve également des revues, spectacles marginaux qui mêlaient projections cinématographiques, boniments sarcastiques et chants illustrant les vues. Avec la guerre, des films de propagande patriotique étaient commentés par des journalistes, militaires, sociétaires de théâtres ou écrivains. Les fictions semblent avoir échappé à toute forme de boniment après 1913. En province, l'implantation progressive et plus tardive des salles qu'à Paris explique peut-être la quasi-absence du recours à cette profession, dont le déclin fut amorcée à partir de 1906/1907 et s'amplifia vers 1910. L'avènement de la musique puis des sous-titres est probablement la principale cause du déclin de cette corporation.

Les conférenciers dans les réseaux connexes

1 – Les réseaux de cinéma scolaire

Je m'appuie pour les deux prochaines parties sur l'étude de Martin Barnier présentée dans cet ouvrage, qui restitue la prépondérance des commentaires des professeurs dans le déroulement des séances scolaires ainsi que l'importance de la parole des ecclésiastiques dans les cinémas paroissiaux. Je me contenterai d'ajouter que des séances scolaires furent organisées dès 1896 par la maison Lumière dont on peut penser qu'elles furent accompagnées de commentaires. Par ailleurs, des manuels traitant de l'utilisation du cinématographe dans les conférences pédagogiques furent rédigés dès 1897[6] et jusque dans les années 1920.[7] Ajoutons aussi que la problématique du commentaire dans ces séances perdura puisqu'en 1934, lors du Congrès international du cinéma d'enseignement et d'éducation de Rome, Paul Barrier souleva la question sur la "méthode à employer dans l'enseignement par le film: projections continues ou brefs tableaux séparés par des commentaires du maître".[8] Unanimement, la communauté éducative française, de l'école primaire à l'enseignement supérieur, mit en exergue le rôle prépondérant des commentaires des professeurs lors des projections, rejetant à la fois ceux des conférenciers institutionnels et des premiers films parlants, et préférant avoir recours aux films muets. Le Congrès (section "Méthodologie du film d'enseignement") déclara:

> En ce qui concerne les méthodes à adopter dans l'emploi du film d'enseignement, [...]:
> 1. *L'emploi du cinéma ne doit pas faire obstacle à l'action éducative du maître et à l'effet de sa parole*; c'est lui qui doit [...] commenter les faits.
> 2. En conséquence *le film d'enseignement ne doit pas être un film sonore ou parlé, mais un film muet dont le commentaire appartient au maître.*[9]

Malgré l'avènement du sonore, la conférence au cinéma perdura par le biais du cinéma scolaire, les enseignants devenant les derniers successeurs des bonimenteurs d'antan. Mais cette forme de spectacle – s'agit-il d'ailleurs d'un spectacle? – relève d'une autre problématique.

2 – Les réseaux de cinémas paroissiaux

Barnier analyse le rôle, moraliste ou éducatif, des commentaires effectués par les religieux durant leurs séances cinématographiques. Les occurrences s'étendent de 1898 jusqu'au milieu des années 1920. En raison de l'importance du réseau mis en place par la Maison de la Bonne Presse, les cinémas paroissiaux n'ont cessé de croître, ce qui laisse présager de l'étendue de la pratique du commentaire. D'après la Bonne Presse, en 1924, seuls six départements n'avaient pas accueilli de séance sous leur égide.[10] "Les réseaux confessionnels du 'Bon Cinéma' sont surtout implantés en province, en étroite collaboration avec la 'Bonne presse'. [...] [Le] service de projection dirigé par l'abbé Honoré revendique l'installation de 60 nouveaux cinémas, et le répertoire des films que peut louer aux œuvres le service des projections [représente] 748 000 mètres"[11] annonce *La Croix* un an après. En novembre 1926, le chanoine Simonin fait état de 673 salles[12] et en 1929, ces cinémas étaient implantés dans 61 départements.[13] Le cinéma paroissial, avec des programmes souvent très éclectiques, se positionnait en concurrent des cinémas éducateurs laïques.

3 – Un réseau de conférenciers laïcs

Le 11 janvier 1895, le Ministre de l'Instruction publique prend un décret qui doit inciter les instituteurs déjà présents sur tout le territoire, à officier aux cotés des conférenciers, notamment ceux de la Ligue de l'Enseignement, ou à suppléer à leurs absences dans le cadre des cours d'adultes et des conférences populaires. Le 11 mars, un arrêté instituait une Commission chargée d'examiner les moyens de mettre à la disposition des Sociétés d'instruction populaire les appareils de projections lumineuses et les collections de vues photographiques pouvant servir à l'enseignement au sein du Musée pédagogique. On trouve donc des conférenciers-projectionnistes officiant avec des vues fixes et cinématographiques dans les écoles, mais aussi dans des lieux publics, associés parfois à des entrepreneurs locaux, lors de séances récréatives commentées. Ce réseau de conférenciers extrêmement développé est paradoxalement peu visible médiatiquement parce que souvent constitué de notables ou d'instituteurs anonymes. Les tergiversations de l'institution sur le rôle à conférer au cinéma d'enseignement amenèrent la Ligue de l'Enseignement à ne se doter d'un "Service des appareils et films cinématographiques" qu'en 1914 et le Musée pédagogique d'un service de films qu'en 1920. Dès lors, les films d'enseignement officiels disposèrent d'un large réseau de conférenciers. Ainsi, si le Musée pédagogique ne mentionne que l'expédition de 54 films dans son réseau en 1919–1920, c'est "près de 44 000" qui tournaient dans l'hexagone en 1927–1928[14]. Il est dit en novembre 1927 que "le ministère de l'Instruction publique et ses offices régionaux [...] approvisionnent à peu près [...] 2500 à 3000 postes".[15]

4 – Les réseaux de "cinéma éducateur"

Les cinémas éducateurs sont une émergence du cinéma scolaire. Des séances post et extrascolaires, ouvertes progressivement à tout public, devinrent de vrais spectacles alternatifs aux salles commerciales. Leur implantation, principalement dans des petites bourgades ou communes rurales, n'engendrait pas de concurrence directe avec les réseaux commerciaux. Les programmes étaient constitués de films éducatifs mais aussi de grands documentaires, comiques, drames, etc. Ces structures s'approvisionnaient dans les filmothèques municipales créées dès 1920 (Strasbourg), émergences locales du Musée pédagogique, et dans les "offices régionaux de cinéma éducateur", cinémathèques gérées en association loi 1901, ouvertes à partir de 1924 (Nancy). Les bilans statistiques des offices montrent au fil des ans une proportion croissante d'organisation de séances récréatives par rapport aux séances scolaires. Ils possédaient dans leurs fonds presque autant de films de divertissement que d'enseignement. Il n'est pas rare de trouver des exemples de séances récréatives postscolaires commentées. Parfois les séances avaient lieu dans des cinémas commerciaux: "Dès 1923, l'Alhambra [d'Étampes] propose, en concertation avec les instituteurs, des séances commentées de "cinéma éducateur" [...] avec un programme qui alterne habilement documentaires et fictions de manière à retenir l'attention des enfants".[16] Un exploitant de cinéma éducateur précise en 1929: "Je dois ajouter que pendant le déroulement d'un film éducatif, parfois avant, nous donnons les explications nécessaires pour le rendre plus compréhensif [sic]".[17] Gustave Cauvin, responsable de l'office de Lyon, tenait le rôle de conférencier dans les séances qu'il officiait:

> M. Cauvin [...] vint lui-même diriger et commenter les projections [...], par sa parole facile, primesautière et convaincue, [il] fit apprécier les *bienfaits de l'art muet à l'école au point de vue instructif ou récréatif*.[18]

Mais cette pratique, non systématisée, s'essouffla aussi dans les séances de cinéma éducateur. Cauvin déplora que "de grands films à succès, comme *Les merveilles de la mer, l'inaccessible* ont lassé les enfants [...] surtout parce qu'ils ne sont pas commentés".[19] Il répondit encore à un interlocuteur: "*Pasteur* [...]. S'il n'a pas plu auprès de vos jeunes filles, [...] de 14 à 17 ans, c'est que vous n'avez pas su le faire précéder de commentaires intéressants".[20] Puis il dressa un dernier constat: "*Fer forgé: N'intéresse pas les enfants*. [...] comme tous les films d'enseignement, il faudrait le commenter".[21] Ces recommandations, constat du déclin des commentaires, n'impliquent-elles pas, encore à cette époque, leurs pratiques y compris sur des films récréatifs? Le réseau était considérable puisqu'en 1930 la France comptait entre 10 000 et 12 000 postes scolaires pourvus d'appareils cinématographiques et jusqu'à 18 000 en comptant "les écoles libres, pensionnats, foyers du soldat, les cercles, [...] œuvres postscolaires, [...] les patronages divers, les municipalités, les associations de toutes sortes".[22] La même année, on ne comptait qu'un peu moins de 3 000 salles commerciales.

5 - Les réseaux de propagande ouvrière

Dans les années 1910, des anarchistes allaient utiliser le cinématographe pour servir leurs discours propagandistes. Cauvin (déjà), brillant orateur, fut l'un des co-fondateurs de l'*Avenir cinématographique (fin 1911)*, organisation affiliée à la ligue antialcoolique chargée d'organiser des séances cinématographiques pour illustrer leurs conférences. Elle disparaît fin 1912 et *renaît sous* le nom *Cinéma Social* dont les thèmes principaux allaient vanter les mérites de la classe ouvrière, du syndicalisme, du socialisme et dénoncer les fléaux du peuple. Le 28 octobre 1913, une coopérative prolétarienne de production et de diffusion de films – *Cinéma du Peuple* – remplace *Cinéma Social*. Elle disparaît aussi dès la déclaration de guerre. Le conflit terminé, Cauvin réitère son action contre l'alcoolisme par des tournées itinérantes en France et en Suisse. Un compagnon de Cauvin nous laisse un témoignage à l'époque du *Cinéma Social*: "je tournais la manivelle pour le déroulement des bandes, pendant que Cauvin parlait".[23] De cette période, deux affichettes-programmes mentionnent cette pratique:

> Le Cinéma social n'est pas un Cinéma ordinaire, le Cinéma abrutissant et immoral; le Cinéma Social est éducatif et moralisateur. On n'y voit pas les films policiers ou chauvins, on n'y voit que des œuvres saines et morales, amusantes et vraiment instructives. Les vues sont expliquées au fur et à mesure qu'elles se déroulent sur l'écran, ce qui les rend plus intéressantes et plus compréhensibles.
>
> Les vues seront commentées par les camarades Cauvin et Pengam.[24]

En janvier 1914, "Charles Marck [secrétaire de la Fédération nationale des ports et trésorier de la CGT[25]], commente les images des *Misères de l'aiguille*,[26] tandis que le film se déroule sur l'écran".[27] Quant à Cauvin, on le retrouve à Genève (1921) et Lausanne (1924) où il est dit qu'il commente les films pendant leur déroulement.[28]

6 – *Les réseaux de propagande militaire et patriotique*

Des tournées de propagande patriotique, émaillées de commentaires, furent organisées sur tout le territoire. En 1915, sous le patronage du Touring Club de France au profit de l'œuvre du soldat au front, des vues furent projetées à Carcassonne pendant lesquelles "les commentaires vécus d'un journaliste liégeois, M. Ernest de Thoran, qui fait défiler sous les yeux des spectateurs des films inédits [...], donnent une idée exacte et réellement saisissante de la 'Dévastation de la Belgique et du Nord de la France par les armées allemandes'".[29] En 1917, Paolo Arcari, lieutenant de l'infanterie, "brillant universitaire avant la guerre", présenta et commenta des films de la section cinématographique de l'armée italienne lors d'une tournée en France. Le Service Cinématographique des Armées organisa des tournées; les films de l'une d'elles furent commentés par le soldat Victor Faivre.[30] La "Ligue Maritime Française" diffusa partout en France en 1917 ses propres films. Elle "les fait commenter par des conférenciers [...], des orateurs spécialistes [dont] la parole [...] ajoute à l'intelligence des films".[31] Après la guerre, ces tournées continuèrent. Le *Cinéma à la campagne*, fondée en 1917, "a organisé dans toutes les régions de France plus de 3 000 conférences publiques, dans le courant du mois de novembre 1918"[32] avec des films du S.C.A.; la presse relata que "les projections les plus susceptibles d'intéresser les populations rurales seront présentées et commentées par M. Charles Esquier, de la Comédie-Française, qui se rendra dans toutes les communes".[33] L'Alsace fut le lieu de tournées cinématographiques de propagande de février 1919 jusqu'à fin 1920. Elles prévoyaient à la fois des séances publiques et scolaires constituées de films documentaires et instructifs du Commissariat général de la propagande et des films commerciaux et récréatifs fournis par une compagnie privée. Les séances étaient "en général suivies d'une 'causerie en français et en patois'".[34] On précisait que "les intertitres de tous les films seront bilingues [...], en français et en allemand, ou mieux encore en patois alsacien".[35] Malgré cette recommandation, il est probable que les conférenciers se livraient à quelques traductions de cartons ou explications dans le dialecte local bien que ces activités n'aient pas explicitement été relatées. Les tournées en Alsace "auraient touché environ six cent mille spectateurs par an".[36]

7 – Les réseaux de propagande de l'hygiène

Dès août 1917, des films de propagande de l'hygiène étaient diffusés par le réseau de la mission américaine Rockefeller de lutte contre la tuberculose. En 1922, le Comité National de Défense contre la Tuberculose prit le relais. Puis, en 1926, l'Office National d'Hygiène Sociale se substitua au CNDT. Les équipes, de 1917 à 1934, étaient constituées de un à trois conférenciers par voiture dont une conférencière, parfois, traitant pour les femmes de l'hygiène du foyer et de la puériculture.[37] Les projections étaient presque exclusivement constituées de films sur l'hygiène. Ces réseaux intervenaient sur des lieux très variés: cinémas de quartier à Paris, cinémas provinciaux, salles des fêtes, cafés en zones rurales, ateliers, usines et écoles primaires. Des témoignages montrent que des médecins commentaient encore en 1929/1930 les films sur l'hygiène, comme le docteur Poncet en Saône-et-Loire: "Naturellement, je commente tous les films que je projette, sans quoi il suffirait d'envoyer un mécanicien".[38] En 1930, l'Inspecteur d'académie de l'Isère rapporte que des "docteurs expliquaient et commentaient les films d'hygiène".[39] D'ailleurs, en 1934, le Congrès de Rome (section "Hygiène et prévention sociale") réaffirme la primauté du rôle du conférencier:

> Le Congrès [...] estime que les films [...] qui visent nettement à la propagande et qui sont destinés à des publics d'un niveau intellectuel trop peu élevé pour pouvoir suivre le commentaire synchronisé, les films muets, commentés éventuellement par un conférencier, sont préférables.[40]

La mission Rockefeller aurait touché entre 1917 et 1922, trois millions de personnes.[41] Pour les séances du CNDT et de l'ONHS, "le public est estimé à 103 000 personnes en 1924 et 250 000 en 1929; 14 départements visités en 1924, 61 en 1932".[42]

8 – Le réseau de propagande du Ministère de l'agriculture

Il fut le vecteur de diffusion, en zones rurales, des films de la Cinémathèque agricole fondée en avril 1923, mais pas seulement. Alfred Massé[43] considérait pour que "le programme d'une séance de cinéma rural soit varié, [...] il convient à ce propos de disposer de trois films au moins: un film d'actualités ou un documentaire; un film technique ou de propagande agricole; un film récréatif, comique de préférence",[44] ce fut le cas. L'enquête diligentée par le Ministère de l'agriculture en octobre 1930 est sans équivoque en ce qui concerne l'emploi du commentaire si l'on se rapporte à la question 15: "Le film vous semble-t-il gagner à être commenté verbalement? Dans l'affirmative, à quel moment doit-on intervenir?"[45] Les réponses confirment l'emploi des commentaires.[46] La verbalisation fut jugée nécessaire car la question de la compréhension des sous-titres se posait également. Massé confirma cette problématique et préconisa des "sous-titres courts, clairs et bien détachés. [...] La durée de projection suffisante pour permettre une lecture facile de la part de spectateurs généralement peu habitués à lire rapidement".[47] La seule Cinémathèque agricole centrale comptait 600 emprunteurs en 1926, 3 000 en 1931.[48]

Cet état des lieux nous confirme les multiples usages de la conférence au cinéma à la fois dans les réseaux commerciaux, de cinéma éducateur, propagandistes et religieux. Cet emploi de la conférence nous l'avons rencontré aussi bien lors des projections de films de divertissement que des documentaires. L'inventaire nous montre que, même en France – l'un des berceaux du cinéma – les pratiques du cinéma des premiers temps sont restées d'actualité au-delà de 1915, ce qui pose le problème de la périodisation de cette époque.

Notes

1. En 1896–1897, seulement 2,08 % des 673 implantations mentionnent un accompagnement musical (13 exploitants sur 204). Voir: Thierry Lecointe, "L'année 1896 en France: état des lieux sur les représentations Lumière face aux concurrents, à Paris et en Province", dans *Les cinémas périphériques dans la période des premiers temps: actes du 10ᵉ Congrès international Domitor*, sous la direction de François Amy de la Bretèque, Michel Cadé, Jordi Pons i Busquet et Angel Quintana (Perpignan: Presses universitaires de Perpignan, 2010), 75–99.
2. E. Kress, *Conférences sur la cinématographie* (Paris: Charles Mendel, 1916), 37. Conférence de 1913.
3. "La conférence au cinéma", *Ciné-journal* (1 septembre 1917).
4. V. Guillaume-Danvers, "Du conférencier au film sans sous-titre", *Cinémagazine* (6 février 1925).
5. André Gaudreault et Jean-Pierre Sirois-Trahan, "Le retour du [bonimenteur] refoulé …"; Jean-Philippe Restoueix, "Le bonisseur introuvable … De l'utilisation de la presse spécialisée dans l'écriture de l'histoire du cinéma des premiers temps", *Iris* no 22 (1996): 17–32, 67–79; François Albéra et André Gaudreault, "Apparition, disparition et escamotage du 'bonimenteur' dans l'historiographie française du cinéma", dans *Le muet a la parole*, sous la direction de Giusy Pisano et Valérie Pozner (Paris: AFRHC, 2005), 167–199.
6. Eugène Trutat, *Traité général des projections,* tome 1, *Projections ordinaires* (Paris: Charles Mendel, 1897), 344–369.
7. G.-Michel Coissac, *Manuel pratique du conférencier-projectionniste* (Paris: Maison de la Bonne Presse, 1908); M. Fallex et E. Lasnier, *Enseignement et cinématographe* (Paris: Librairie Delagrave/Pathé Consortium Cinéma, 1923); G.-Michel Coissac, *Le cinématographe et l'enseignement* (Paris: Librairie Larousse/Éditions du "Cinéopse", 1926); Eugène Reboul, *Le cinéma scolaire et éducateur* (Paris: Les Presses universitaires de France, 1926); *Ciné-schola: bulletin de la ligue pour l'enseignement par le cinématographe* (Paris, 1922).
8. Paul Barrier (Inspecteur-Général de l'Instruction publique), "Le cinématographe et l'enseignement", *La participation française au Congrès international du cinéma d'enseignement et d'éducation* (Paris: Comité français de l'Institut international du cinématographe éducatif, 1934), iii.
9. Ibid., 24.
10. *Catalogue des films en location 1925–1926*, (Paris: Maison de la Bonne Presse, 1924), 246.
11. F.F., "XVIe congrès des projections", *La Croix* (10 octobre 1925), dans Christophe Gauthier, "Au risque du spectacle: les projections cinématographiques en milieu scolaire dans les années 1920", dans *Cinéma pédagogique et scientifique: à la découverte des archives*, sous la direction de Béatrice de Pastre-Robert, Monique Dubost et Françoise Massit-Folléa (Lyon: ENS Editions, 2004), 89–90.
12. Dimitri Vezyroglou, "Les catholiques, le cinéma à la conquête des masses: le tournant de la fin des années 1920", dans *Pour une histoire cinématographique de la France*, sous la direction de Christophe Gauthier, Pascal Ory et Dimitri Vezyroglou, *Revue d'histoire moderne et contemporaine* 51, no 4 (octobre-décembre 2004): 121.
13. Second congrès catholique français du cinématographe. Les autorités cléricales ne prirent officiellement conscience de l'importance propagandiste de ce média que très tardivement. Ils ne créèrent qu'en septembre 1927 le Comité catholique du cinématographe installé 278, boulevard Raspail à Paris.
14. Gauthier, "Au risque du spectacle", 79.
15. Gaston Sévrette, "Le cinéma et l'éducation nouvelle", *Le Petit Journal* (24 novembre 1927).
16. Clément Wingler, "Le cinéma, miroir de la société étampoise (1904–1994)", *Bulletin de la Société historique et archéologique de l'Essonne et du Hurepoix* no. 73 (2003): 166.
17. Gustave Cauvin, *Résister – Rapport sur l'activité et le développement de l'Office régional du cinéma éducateur de Lyon en 1929* (Lyon: Office régional du cinéma éducateur, 1930), 163.
18. Séance à Saint-Quentin-Fallavier (~ 1200 hab. en 1930). *Le Droit du peuple* (18 janvier 1930), dans Gustave Cauvin, *Dix ans après – Rapport sur l'activité et le développement de l'Office régional du cinéma éducateur de Lyon en 1930* (Lyon: Office régional du cinéma éducateur, 1931), 94.
19. Cauvin, *Résister*, 247.
20. Ibid., 207–208.

21. Cauvin, *Dix ans après*, 39–40.
22. G.-M. Coissac, "Le cinéma dans l'enseignement et l'éducation en France", *Tout-cinéma* (1930): 17, dans Gauthier, "Au risque du spectacle", 89.
23. Henri Poulaille, *Mon ami Calandri* (Paris: Spartacus, 1970), 32.
24. Cauvin, *Résister*, 16–17.
25. Tangui Perron, "'Le contrepoison est entre vos mains, camarades': C.G.T. et cinéma au début du siècle", *Le Mouvement social* no 172 (juillet-septembre 1995), 33.
26. Réalisé par Raphaël Clamour et Armand Guerra et mettant en vedette Musidora.
27. Laurent Mannoni, "28 octobre 1913: création de la société 'Le Cinéma du Peuple'", dans *L'année 1913 en France*, Thierry Lefebvre et Laurent Mannoni (dir.), *1895* hors série (1993): 105.
28. *La Revue suisse du cinéma* (3 décembre 1921 et 26 avril 1924). Source Pierre-Emmanuel Jaques.
29. *Le Courrier de l'Aude* (2 juillet 1915). Source Isabelle Debien.
30. Laurent Véray, *Les films d'actualité français de la Grande Guerre* (Paris: SIRPA/AFRHC, 1995), 161–162.
31. Georges Dureau, "Les galas de propagande", *Ciné-Journal* (8 septembre 1917).
32. Valérie Vignaux, "Cinéma, éducation de masse et propagande agricole dans l'entre-deux-guerres: les films de Jean Benoît-Lévy pour la Cinémathèque du Ministère de l'agriculture (1924–1939)", *Archives* no 98 (janvier 2006): 2.
33. "Le cinéma à la campagne", *Le Cinéopse* no 3 (novembre 1919): 74, dans Christophe Gauthier, *La passion du cinéma: cinéphiles, ciné-clubs et salles spécialisées à Paris de 1920 à 1929* (Paris: AFRHC/École de Chartes, 1999), 14.
34. Voir Odile Gozillon-Fronsacq, "Le cinéma en Alsace après 1918: son utilisation politique", *1895* no 20 (1996): 50.
35. Lettre du haut commissaire de la république à Strasbourg au sous-secrétaire d'État à la présidence du Conseil, 17 janvier 1919, ibid., 48.
36. Ibid., 50.
37. Voir Thierry Lefebvre, "Les films diffusés par la mission américaine de prévention contre la tuberculose (mission Rockefeller, 1917–1922)", *1895* no 11 (1991): 102; Compte rendu de l'assemblée générale du CNDT, 20 mars 1926, dans Valérie Vignaux, *Jean Benoît-Lévy ou le corps comme utopie: une histoire du cinéma éducateur dans l'entre-deux-guerres en France* (Paris: AFRHC, 2007), 78–79; "Les Équipes mobiles de propagande d'hygiène, du Service de propagande de la Ligue des sociétés de la Croix-Rouge", *Revue internationale du cinéma éducateur* no 2 (février 1930), dans Valérie Vignaux, "Femmes et enfants ou le corps de la nation", *1895* no 37 (2002): 26; dans L. Dreyfus-Barney, "Cinéma et hygiène publique", *Cinéma et éducation* (Rome: Institut international du cinématographe éducatif, [1934]), 145.
38. Cauvin, *Résister*, 244–245.
39. Rapport de l'Inspecteur d'académie de l'Isère, 8 décembre 1930, dans Cauvin, *Dix ans après*, 86–87.
40. *La participation française*, 29.
41. Lefebvre, "Les films diffusés par la mission américaine", 106.
42. Valérie Vignaux, *Jean Benoît-Lévy*, 78.
43. Président de la première Commission de la cinématographie agricole instituée par décret le 30 avril 1923.
44. Alfred Massé, "Le cinéma agricole en France", *La participation française*, LXXVI.
45. Voir Vignaux, "Cinéma, éducation de masse et propagande agricole", 7.
46. Les réponses émanaient des maires, instituteurs et directeurs de services agricoles. Voir Alison J. Murray Levine, "Cinéma, propagande agricole et populations rurales en France (1919–1939)", *Vingtième siècle: revue d'histoire* no 83 (juillet–septembre 2004): 32–36.
47. Massé, "Le cinéma agricole en France", LXXVI.
48. Christine Buzzini, "La propagande par le Ministère de l'agriculture", *1895* no 18 (1995): 132.

29

Les images en mouvement au théâtre de variétés: le cas de l'Apollo de Düsseldorf

Frank Kessler et Sabine Lenk

La relation entre le théâtre de variétés et le cinématographe aux premiers temps du cinéma a été analysée dans le passé par des chercheurs tels que Robert C. Allen[1] ou Charles Musser.[2] Plus récemment, Joseph Garncarz a consacré une étude au volet allemand de la question.[3] Il y reste, pourtant, un bon nombre de questions. Ceci est dû, entre autres, au fait que cette forme de spectacle scénique présente quelques différences selon les pays: le *vaudeville* aux États-Unis, le *variety show* en Angleterre, le music-hall ou le café-concert en France et le *Varieté* (écrit parfois aussi *Variété*) ou *Spezialitätentheater* en Allemagne fonctionnent selon leurs propres lois et ne s'adressent pas aux mêmes publics. Ceci vaut d'ailleurs également pour la terminologie, car le mot "vaudeville", en l'occurrence, renvoie en France et aux États-Unis à des types de spectacles fort différents. Autrement dit, les résultats des études de Musser et Allen, par exemple, sur le vaudeville américain ne sauraient être appliqués au spectacle de *Varieté* allemand.

Pour notre article, qui portera uniquement sur la situation en Allemagne, nous avons examiné de plus près le cas de l'Apollo, grand théâtre de *Varieté* de la ville de Düsseldorf. Partant de cet exemple nous présenterons plus précisément le cinématographe en tant que numéro de variétés. La relation entre le nouveau média et cette institution de spectacles légèrement plus ancienne sera discutée, nous nous pencherons sur la place des images en mouvement au sein de la programmation, et nous proposerons quelques réflexions concernant la *chaser theory* ayant fait couler tant d'encre vers 1980 aux États-Unis.

La relation de parenté entre Varieté et cinématographe

Le *Varieté* en tant que lieu et forme d'amusement commence son essor en Allemagne environ 20 à 25 ans avant l'invention du cinématographe. Il répond aux besoins des ouvriers et petits-bourgeois dans le milieu urbain, fortement transformé par l'industrialisation rapide du pays. Cette forme de spectacle propose ce que son nom annonce: des performances artistiques ou acrobatiques variées, présentées sous forme de numéro et accompagnées par un orchestre, que le public regarde pendant qu'il boit, mange et souvent fume.[4]

Au tournant du siècle, le cinématographe a en fait plus de traits en commun avec le *Varieté* que celui-ci avec le théâtre, même s'il s'agit dans les deux cas de spectacles scéniques. Résumons en quelques mots leur parenté:

- programmes composés de numéros autonomes;

dans ce milieu. Ceci a peut-être facilité l'expérimentation avec de nouvelles formes de spectacle, dont le cinématographe.

L'Apollo se constitue apparemment assez rapidement une clientèle recrutée parmi les couches relativement aisées de la ville de Düsseldorf:

> [...] nous nous réjouissons que l'Apollo devienne de plus en plus un lieu de rendez-vous pour la bonne société de Düsseldorf. L'officier, le peintre, l'aristocratie du sang comme celle de l'argent, le fabricant et le commerçant, bref, toute la ville [en français dans le texte] s'y retrouve. On peut voir ici tous les soirs par douzaines des gens que l'on n'a jamais vus au théâtre municipal, dans la salle de concert, ni dans d'autres établissements d'amusements [...].[17]

Par ailleurs, le *Varieté* semble devoir faire à cette même période des efforts pour sauvegarder sa réputation, car Gellner demande explicitement, dans ses réflexions sur l'avenir de cette institution, que l'on se tienne loin de toutes sortes de "cochonneries".[18] Or, en ce qui concerne le cinématographe, cela indique que le nouveau média semble plutôt contribuer de manière positive à ces efforts, car autrement on ne l'aurait guère intégré de manière aussi systématique dans les programmes.

Lors de la soirée d'ouverture de l'Apollo le 16 décembre 1899, le public peut voir et écouter, entre autres, la chanteuse Frieda Walter, des cyclistes acrobatiques, un ballet volant (annoncé explicitement comme une "nouveauté"), un chanteur humoristique et, comme numéro de clôture, le Megalograph de Willy Hagedorn. Celui-ci projette alors dix vues: un prestidigitateur, des soldats de la marine, le Kaiser à l'inauguration d'un canal à Dortmund, un duel, une lutte mystérieuse, une machine à saucisses, une fête suisse près d'une cascade, un alarme de pompiers, la vue du lieu d'un incendie, et un voyage en train.[19] Il s'agit-là d'un programme assez typique pour l'époque, et caractéristique des premières années de l'Apollo. Le cinématographe présente en effet généralement dans ces années une série de vues diverses, notamment des actualités, des images documentaires, parfois quelque peu dramatiques, et aussi des scènes comiques.

Ce type de programmation continuera par la suite, et les photographies animées contribuent ainsi aux efforts du *Varieté* de s'établir en tant qu'institution "éducative", c'est-à-dire comme *Bildungsmittel*:

> Le *Varieté* moderne est un facteur culturel et aussi un moyen d'éducation pour la foule. Cette éducation, cependant, ne concerne pas ce qu'on apprend à l'école. [...]
>
> Au cours de ces dernières années, le *Varieté* moderne s'est révélé comme la seule école au service de tous les courants modernes des différents genres artistiques. [...] Les danses, ne nous offrent-elles pas un aperçu de la vie et des sentiments de peuples qui, autrement, resteraient étrangers pour nous? Les poses plastiques, ne nous montrent-elles pas les chefs-d'œuvre de nos peintres? Les "photographies animées" ne nous présentent-elles pas les événements importants de manière plus claire et plus en détail que des reportages interminables, et ne nous tiennent-elles ainsi pas au courant de l'histoire du monde dans lequel nous vivons [...]?[20]

La valeur éducative du *Varieté* se situe ainsi au niveau d'une *médiation*. Tout comme le cinématographe, il n'offre pas un accès direct aux objets de l'art ou un savoir, mais sert, pour ainsi dire, d'intermédiaire. Sur la scène du *Varieté* se présente une imitation en trois dimensions (donc à cet égard réaliste) renvoyant directement à l'original; le cinématographe, par contre, propose une reproduction photographique directe de l'original, mais apparaissant seulement en deux dimensions.

Sur le plan des efforts de se faire reconnaître au niveau de la culture "légitime" on pourra donc en effet dire: *Variété*, cinématographe – même combat!

Les photographies animées dans le programme de l'Apollo

Willy Hagedorn et son Megalograph s'inscrivent clairement dans la pratique de l'époque des exploitants itinérants choisissant en effet souvent des dénominations aussi fantaisistes qu'évocatrices pour leurs appareils dans le but de se distinguer de la concurrence. En 1902 (mais peut-être plus tôt déjà) le Kosmograph prend la relève à l'Apollo.[21] Ce nom renvoie à l'une des firmes d'Oskar Messter, la Kosmograph Compagnie, enregistrée en janvier 1901 et se consacrant aux services de projection. L'Apollo a donc dans un premier temps signé, semble-t-il, un contrat avec la maison berlinoise afin que celle-ci y présente des films, vraisemblablement choisis parmi la production Messter. Jusqu'à la Première Guerre mondiale au moins, le Kosmograph devient un numéro régulier dans les programmes de l'Apollo. Or, on peut supposer que la direction de l'Apollo choisit de conserver cette dénomination indépendamment de Messter (qui ne restera pas le fournisseur exclusif des programmes) pour continuer à proposer à la clientèle des images en mouvement sous un intitulé reconnaissable et familier. L'Apollo peut, de cette manière, distinguer ses projections des autres cinématographes qui s'établissent au fur et à mesure dans la ville.

À quelques exceptions près les photographies animées de l'Apollo sont annoncées sous le nom de Kosmograph et occupent la dernière place dans le programme. De temps à autre l'Apollo engage une troupe de spectacle de variétés qui propose une soirée entière, y compris des vues cinématographiques. Ces dernières apparaissent alors sous un nom autre, comme c'est le cas pour l'Eden-Motor-Bioscop du Continental Eden Theater dirigé par Bruno Schenk. Cette troupe se produit à Düsseldorf sur la scène de l'Apollo au cours d'une tournée en mai 1905.[22] Les photographies animées semblent donc constituer un élément quasiment obligatoire dans un programme de *Variété*, car même les troupes itinérantes les proposent de manière assez systématique.

Étant donné que le métrage des bandes continue à augmenter au cours des premières années du 20e siècle, le nombre de films que l'on peut montrer dans le cadre d'une soirée de spectacle de variétés devient de plus en plus limité. Les quelques sources que nous avons à notre disposition indiquent: dix vues dans le programme du 16 décembre 1899, neuf vues le 2 juin 1900, neuf vues le 20 août 1902, cinq ou six titres le 1 février 1905, deux titres le 1 février 1912, et un titre le 14 décembre 1912.[23]

De manière générale, il est difficile d'obtenir des informations précises sur les titres projetés, car le magazine de la maison, l'*Apollo-Theater-Revue*, se contente la plupart du temps de renvoyer au Kosmograph. On précise cependant assez régulièrement qu'il s'agit de "vues nouvelles" ou même "absolument nouvelles", ce qui indique un changement de programme toutes les deux semaines, rythme imposé par l'engagement de nouvelles attractions. De temps à autre on annonce une actualité comme le Delhi Durbar en mars 1912 ou le vol du comte Zeppelin à Berlin en septembre 1912.[24] À ce niveau, le programme de l'Apollo correspond explicitement à la fonction des photographies animées d'offrir une *Optische Berichterstattung* (proche, paraît-il, de la fonction de *Visual Newspaper* dans le vaudeville américain).[25] Les quelques indications de titres que nous avons pu trouver suggèrent par ailleurs que la composition standard de la section Kosmograph du programme consiste au début des années 1910 en une vue documentaire, suivie par un film comique (parfois deux).

Le Kosmograph: un *chaser*?

Vers la fin des années 1970 et au début des années 1980, des chercheurs américains ont mené un débat concernant la position en fin de programme des projections cinématographiques.[26] L'explication canonique, selon Robert C. Allen, veut que cette position soit symptomatique d'une perte d'intérêt pour le nouveau média entre 1897 et 1901: on l'aurait laissé clore le programme car le public aurait eu l'habitude de quitter la salle un peu avant la fin, et en plus il fallait que la salle se vide pour permettre à un deuxième groupe de spectateurs d'entrer. Aucun artiste n'aurait aimé fonctionner comme *chaser*, et on aurait donc laissé cette place à la machine dès qu'elle n'aurait plus eu le même attrait pour les spectateurs qu'à ses débuts. Allen conteste cette interprétation en évoquant notamment le grand succès des actualités, tandis que Charles Musser, tout en affirmant que le terme *"chaser period"* est sans doute réducteur, renvoie à des sources d'époque qui confirment cette perte de valeur spectaculaire des vues animées. Pour lui, la position en fin de programme est en effet un symptôme de crise. Plus récemment Alex Rankin reprend la théorie en mentionnant la présentation d'un diorama itinérant à Exeter au terme de laquelle les spectateurs seraient partis avant la fin, en prenant toutefois soin de préciser que l'établissement ne changeait pas ses films, ce qui montre bien que le débat continue.[27]

Pour l'Allemagne, on peut constater que, d'une part, les images en mouvement clôturent le programme dès la soirée du Wintergarten des frères Skladanowsky. La même situation prévaut à l'Apollo où leur place ne change en principe pas (à quelques exceptions près). On ne peut donc pas dire que ce serait le résultat d'une perte d'attrait. Par ailleurs, et cela est peut-être plus important encore, en Allemagne il n'y a pas, comme cela semble être généralement le cas pour le vaudeville américain, deux séances par soirée, ce qui explique la nécessité de vider la salle rapidement pour faire entrer le deuxième groupe de spectateurs. Il n'y a qu'un seul programme par soirée, et par conséquent la direction a plutôt intérêt à ce que le public reste encore un peu pour continuer à consommer.[28] En plus, les titres, renouvelés régulièrement, sont choisis avec soin car ils doivent satisfaire une clientèle habituée à voir des films. Cette politique est apparemment suivie aussi par les confrères de l'Apollo, comme le démontrent les commentaires louangeurs dans les quotidiens.[29]

La place du Kosmograph en fin de programme ne peut donc pas être prise comme une indication du statut des images en mouvement. Par contre, en lisant les descriptions des programmes publiés dans la revue de l'Apollo il est évident que les artistes qui performent sur scène sont de loin plus importants pour la direction que le Kosmograph. C'est à eux que l'on consacre des articles, non pas aux vues animées qui pourtant sont presque toujours mentionnées, du moins en passant.

Néanmoins, leur emplacement à la fin du programme n'est pas innocent. Il sert très probablement à des fins dramaturgiques comme peut l'indiquer cette remarque dans un article de journal: "Les nouvelles images du Kosmograph provoquent des rires aux éclats, ce qui fait que les spectateurs quittent très animés ce beau théâtre".[30] Les projections ont donc peut-être pour fonction de provoquer une émotion positive à la fin de la soirée, apte à laisser un bon souvenir et ainsi inciter le public à revenir.

Le film – un numéro respecté

Malgré les nombreuses salles de cinéma qui s'établissent dans la ville à partir de l'été 1906, l'Apollo continue à intégrer les films dans son programme. Ils y tiennent une place fixe, ce qui indique qu'on les considère une partie, sinon indispensable, du moins enrichissante de la soirée.

Et ça continue. Dans les années 1920 l'établissement présente non seulement des artistes mais également des nouveaux films de fiction, sans pourtant oublier ses bonnes habitudes: en 1929 les actualités cinématographiques font toujours partie du programme de *Varieté* de l'Apollo – et cela même en plein milieu de la soirée.[31]

Notes

1. Robert C. Allen, *Vaudeville and Film: A Study in Media Interaction* (New York: Arno Press, 1980).
2. Charles Musser, *The Emergence of Cinema: The American Screen to 1907* (Berkeley/Los Angeles: University of California Press, 1994), 297–298.
3. Joseph Garncarz, *Maßlose Unterhaltung: Zur Etablierung des Films in Deutschland 1896–1914* (Francfort-sur-le-Main/Bâle: Stroemfeld/Nexus Verlag, 2010).
4. Pour plus d'informations sur l'histoire du *Varieté* en Allemagne, voir: Ernst Günther, *Geschichte des Varietés* (Berlin: Henschelverlag, 1977), 119–182.
5. Voir Günther, *Geschichte des Varietés*, 126, 128; Sabine Lenk, *Vom Tanzsaal zum Filmtheater: Eine Kinogeschichte Düsseldorfs* (Düsseldorf: Droste Verlag, 2009).
6. Günther souligne la différence entre la scène et le *Varieté* qui consisterait, entre autres, dans la manière d'instruire le public: "Si la tâche du théâtre est d'instruire en distrayant, c'est la tâche du théâtre de variétés de distraire en instruisant". Günther, *Geschichte des Varietés*, 14.
7. Le *Varieté* allemand naît dans les "centres industriels en plein essor […] où se concentraient des bourgeois avides de profits et prêts à prendre des risques". Günther, *Geschichte des Varieté*, 27–28. Idem pour le cinématographe.
8. "Wer vieles bringt, wird manchem etwas bringen, Und jeder geht zufrieden aus dem Haus" (Directeur dans "Vorspiel", *Faust I*, vers 97).
9. Oskar Gellner, "Die Zukunft des Variétés", *Der Artist* no 779 (14 janvier 1900). Notre traduction.
10. Les rapports institutionnels entre les deux n'ont pas encore été suffisamment étudiés. Pour le cinématographe, le *Varieté* était sans doute un lieu de projection fort intéressant, parce qu'il pouvait s'y présenter à un public déjà constitué, tandis que pour le *Varieté* les photographies animées étaient un nouveau type d'attraction que l'on pouvait intégrer assez facilement dans un programme.
11. *Der Artist* no 778 (7 janvier 1900). Notre traduction.
12. Acte de construction du bâtiment conservé aux Archives municipales de Düsseldorf.
13. Les vues des frères Skladanowsky présentent en fait des reproductions d'une série d'actes de variétés et fonctionnent ainsi quasiment comme une mise en abyme du spectacle dont elles font elles-mêmes partie. Voir: Frank Kessler, "La cinématographie comme dispositif (du) spectaculaire", *Cinémas* 14, no 1 (automne 2003): 21–34.
14. "Madame Olinka présente actuellement chez Sagebiel [situé sur le Dom, célèbre kermesse à Hambourg, nda] des 'photographies vivantes gigantesques' sur un écran de 40 m²". *Der Artist* no. 619 (20 décembre 1896), notre traduction. Sur Mme Olinka, voir: *Who's Who in Victorian Cinema*, sous la direction de Luke McKernan et Stephen Herbert (Londres: BFI, 1996), 103. Une annonce dans *Der Artist* no 776 (24 décembre 1899) propose un dispositif de "500 pieds carrés", donc d'environ 150 m². Du point de vue de la technique disponible à l'époque, l'Apollo aurait alors eu la possibilité d'installer un écran correspondant à la taille de sa scène.
15. Voir aussi les projections du "cinématographe géant" des frères Lumière lors de l'Exposition universelle de Paris en 1900 sur un écran de 21 m de large et de 18 m de haut avec comme source electrique un arc de 75 ampères. Jacques Deslandes et Jacques Richard, *Histoire comparée du cinéma*, Tome 2, *Du cinématographe au cinéma 1896–1906* (Tournai: Casterman, 1968), 53.
16. Oskar Gellner, "Die Zukunft des Variétés II", *Der Artist* no 784 (18 février 1900). Gellner cite quelques autres personnes n'étant pas originaires de la profession: "Julius Baron, directeur du Wintergarten à Berlin, n'a jamais été artiste […] le directeur Grell du Hansa-Theater à Hambourg non plus, pas non plus Glück, directeur de l'Apollo à Düsseldorf, tout comme son collègue Bruck, directeur de l'Orpheum à Francfort, etc." (notre traduction). Ceux-ci comptent parmi des grands impresarios de l'histoire du *variété* en Allemagne. Dans tous les établissements nommés par Gellner le cinématographe figurait déjà au programme vers 1900.
17. "Aus Düsseldorf", *Der Artist* no 783 (11 février 1900).
18. Gellner, "Die Zukunft des Variétés II".

19. Voir la reproduction du programme dans Heinrich Riemenschneider, *Theatergeschichte der Stadt Düsseldorf*, tome 1 (Düsseldorf: Kulturamt der Stadt Düsseldorf, 1987), 473.
20. "Zu Beginn der Jubiläumssaison", brochure de l'Apollo-Theater Düsseldorf, Varieté-Saison 1909–1910 (Jubiläums-Saison) (12 septembre 1909): 8.
21. Programme de l'Apollo du 20 août 1902 (collection Thomas Bernhardt). Selon Garncarz, 28, c'est en effet après 1900 que les projectionnistes indépendants sont remplacés par les maisons de production qui concluent des contrats avec les théâtres et proposent une sélection de films.
22. *Apollo-Theater-Revue* (4 mai 1905): 14. En novembre 1905 les photographies animées sont présentées par le Bernardinograph. Selon Thomas Bernhardt il s'agit-là d'une pratique récurrente (communication personnelle, mai 2010).
23. Voir les sources suivantes: Riemenschneider, *Theatergeschichte*, 471: programme d'ouverture; les autres proviennent de la collection de Thomas Bernhardt : Apollo-Programm (2 juin 1900 et 20 août 1902) ; *Apollo-Theater-Revue* (1 février 1905): 10; *Düsseldorfer Theater-Woche* [no 3] ([1912]) et no 111 (14 décembre 1912): 10. Sur la question de la longueur des programmes et du nombre de films projetés voir aussi Garncarz, 25–26.
24. Programmes de l'Apollo du 1 au 15 mars ainsi que du 12 septembre 1912 (collection Thomas Bernhardt). La féerie *Der Sohn des Teufels* (*Le fils du diable*, Pathé, 1906) figure dans le programme du mois d'octobre 1906, *Generalanzeiger für Düsseldorf und Umgebung* (5 octobre 1906), mais vu la longueur du film ceci était probablement une exception.
25. Voir Garncarz, *Maßlose Unterhaltung*, 31, ainsi que Robert C. Allen, "Contra the Chaser Theory", dans *Film Before Griffith*, sous la direction de John Fell (Berkeley/Los Angeles: University of California Press, 1983), 105–115.
26. Voir Allen, *Vaudeville and Film*, 161–180, et "Contra the Chaser Theory". Allen cite les ouvrages de Robert Grau (1911 et 1914), Terry Ramsaye (1926), Gilbert Seldes (1929), Lewis Jacobs (1939), Gerald Mast (1971) et Joseph H. North (1973). Charles Musser, "Another Look at the 'Chaser Theory'", *Studies in Visual Communications* 10, no. 4 (1984): 24–44; Robert C. Allen, "Looking at 'Another Look at the Chaser Theory'", *Studies in Visual Communications* 10, no 4 (1984): 45–50. Voir aussi Richard Abel, *The Red Rooster Scare: Making Cinema American 1900–1910* (Berkeley/Los Angeles: University of California Press, 1999), 4, 192 (notes 24, 25).
27. Alex Rankin, *The History of Cinema Exhibition in Exeter 1895–1918* (thèse de doctorat, University of Exeter, 2001): http://www.exeter.ac.uk/bdc/teaching_article_02_chapterone.shtml#25, consulté le 20 février 2011.
28. Il y a, cependant, dans la presse corporative quelques remarques qui suggèrent que les artistes n'aimaient pas apparaître en tant que dernier numéro d'un programme de variétés, mais que justement, le cinématographe représentait une solution à ce problème. En, plus, les photographies animées pouvaient être considérées comme "une attraction de premier ordre", même quand elles étaient programmées pour clore la soirée. Voir *Der Komet* no 803 (11 août 1900), cité dans Garncarz, 26.
29. En outre, dans une annonce un *Reformkino* ("salle de réforme", type de salle dont les programmes ne présentaient pas des films jugés moralement discutables) berlinois proposait d'échanger ses "films avec des [...] théâtres de variété de haute gamme" (notre traduction), ce qui indique que la programmation des théâtres de variétés avaient très bonne réputation. *Der Kinematograph* no 3 (21 août 1907).
30. *Generalanzeiger für Düsseldorf und Umgebung* (22 janvier 1905).
31. Nous remercions Thomas Bernhardt d'avoir généreusement mis à notre disposition des documents provenant de sa collection privée sur l'histoire de l'Apollo, ainsi que Herbert Birett qui nous a amicalement communiqué des articles provenant de ses archives personnelles.

Royals, Rembrandts and Luxors: Patterns and Clusters in the Nomenclature of Dutch Cinemas

André van der Velden

Scholars of early film exhibition have repeatedly noted that the naming of film theatres had a bearing on how potential audiences perceived and evaluated those venues and the entertainments they offered.[1] Choosing a name was (and of course still is) a marketing tool, the use of which may reveal some of the tested knowledge, expectations, and presuppositions of an entrepreneur with regard to the specific market and socio-cultural context in which he or she intended to operate and make a living. It is this idea that I want to put to work in this paper, in order to see if it may help us unravel some of the secrets of early film exhibition and moviegoing in the Netherlands. For practical reasons, I shall limit myself mainly to the period from the initial establishment of permanent cinemas (1906–1907) until the end of World War One, and exclude itinerant cinemas.

Table 1. Permanent cinemas in the Netherlands, 1906–1919.

Year	Number of permanent cinemas as of 1 January	Additions	Closures	Net increase
1906	1	2	0	+2
1907	3	4	0	+4
1908	7	11	2	+9
1909	16	11	6	+5
1910	21	21	1	+20 (+95%)
1911	41	51	0	+51 (+124%)
1912	92	91	10	+81 (+88%)
1913	173	71	28	+43 (+25%)
1914	216	21	32	–11
1915	205	24	34	–10
1916	195	10	26	–16
1917	179	10	21	–11
1918	168	28	17	+9
1919	177	26	22	+4 = 181

Table 1 offers an overview of the expansion and contraction of the film exhibition business in the Netherlands between 1906 and 1919, measured in numbers of permanent cinemas. The numbers derive from Cinema Context, an internet database storing tens of thousands of data about film exhibition in the Netherlands from 1896 to the present.[2] Since my focus here is on venues that offered programs devoted primarily to films, I have excluded variety theatres, which showed films as a minor part of mixed-bill programs dominated by live stage acts. Furthermore, I have also added a couple of cinemas not yet included in the Cinema Context database. Despite these modifications, the numbers in this table are probably still not fully accurate, although they certainly are reliable enough to show the most important trends.

A few observations then with regard to what these numbers show us, especially if we compare them to what was going on in neighboring countries during the same period. To begin with: the spread of permanent cinemas was a phenomenon that developed rather late in the Netherlands. As of 1 January 1906, there was just one permanent cinema in the whole country. Two years later that number had risen to a mere seven. Six of these seven could be found in one of the four relatively large cities in the western provinces: Amsterdam (two cinemas), Rotterdam (one cinema), The Hague (two), and Utrecht (one). At the time these four cities had a combined population of about 1.2 million people. By comparison: the German city of Hamburg, at the time a city with about a million inhabitants, counted at least forty permanent cinemas by the beginning of 1908, while the Belgian capital of Brussels already had in the neighborhood of fifty cinemas for a population of about 760,000.[3] Comparisons with large cities in other countries would render the same conclusion: while the rest of Western Europe witnessed an expansion-boom of permanent cinemas from about 1905 on, nothing on the same scale happened in the Netherlands.

Indeed, measured in absolute numbers of venues, substantial growth only kicked in from 1910 onwards, with a real peak in 1911 and 1912. The Dutch would never catch up with their European neighbours, though. In fact, 1913 witnessed the first signs that growth was already slowing down, while during World War One the number of permanent cinemas in the country dropped significantly. This had nothing to do with the substitution of small capacity theatres by larger ones. Cinemas which could hold a thousand people or more only started to come into use in the Netherlands from around 1918, and even then their number remained limited. The drop in numbers of cinemas during the war years was due predominantly to the fact that permanent film exhibition ceased altogether in several smaller, provincial towns, sometimes never to resurrect again.

Although the general picture could be nuanced further on the basis of other available indicators and sources, this would not change the overall gist of the message: the Dutch were trailing behind. Which puts one simple question centre stage: why? Up till now, only a few, still rather sketchy and tentative answers have been put forward by Dutch film historians, many of whom have evoked a general sense of the "backwardness" of the Netherlands' moviegoing culture.[4] In fact, it was the ambition to bring a more detailed and evidence-based answer into view that was the main impetus behind the construction of the Cinema Context database, a project initiated and presided over by Karel Dibbets. My current research into patterns of nomenclature of Dutch cinemas departs from previous accounts, and instead works in the predominantly inductive vein of so-called "grounded theory". Roughly speaking, this approach does not aim to test any pre-given theories or hypotheses, but sets out to generate "new" theoretical insights through a research procedure in several stages. The first stage consists of a cyclic process of gathering, labeling (or "coding"), and comparing (sub)sets of empirical data on a given phenomenon, with the aim to stabilise the coded (sub)sets. Stabilisation occurs when new data no longer produces a need to change the codes that organise the dataset as a whole. As soon as this is accomplished, the second stage kicks in, which consists of defining the relationships operating in and between the coded subsets. The result will be a new, empirically "grounded" theory about the phenomenon under scrutiny, which may then – and only then – be compared to the other, pre-existing theories on the same topic. Right now, though, my project is still in the initial phase, trying to find and stabilise the codes and subsets that effectively structured the full range of cinema names in the Netherlands from decade to decade.[5]

Nonetheless, some patterns have emerged already, at least for the period prior to World War One. In choosing a name for their businesses, Dutch film exhibitors showed three basic tendencies. First, and most important: they kept things close to their potential patrons' known environment. Second, and this tendency really kicks in from 1912 onwards: they showed a preference for names that somehow conveyed the message that their establishment and its offerings could pass the test for moral decency and respectability. Finally, as a third tendency – and to some extent this was the negative complement to the first and second – most Dutch cinema operators eschewed names that referred to consumerism, luxury, and exoticism. Below, these three tendencies will be elaborated upon further, according to the existing data on the naming of Dutch cinemas during the years 1910–1913, the period of the expansion boom.

Table 2. Cinemas with names referring to their location: the largest cluster within the grand total of 234 cinemas opening or re-opening in the Netherlands during the years 1910–1913.

Names referring to	Total number	In larger cities or small towns	% of total
Town/village of cinema's location	25	Small towns	10
Existing hotel or meeting hall, where cinema was located	22	Predominantly small towns	9
Street/neighbourhood of cinema's location	20	Larger cities	8
Province of cinema's location	2	Both	0.8
	69 (total)		29% (total)

Table 2 offers a breakdown of theatre names associated with the potential patron's known environment. This tendency found its strongest expression in the use of names referring to the location of the cinema. In small towns and villages, many cinemas simply shared the town's or village's name. Alternatively, cinemas carried the names of already existing facilities, like hotels or meeting halls, on the premises of which they were situated. In almost all cases these host-facilities had a multi-functional character, in the sense that from day to day they would accommodate a whole range of social, festive, and recreational events, of which film exhibition was but one, for instance on Saturday nights and Sunday afternoons. Quite often, the history of these places reached back at least a couple of decades, while their life span as film exhibition sites would remain relatively short. Half of these places did not last as exhibition venues for more than five years, while only four of them lasted longer than twenty-five years in this role.

In larger cities the tendency to name theatres after their place of location was less predominant, but still quite strong. Here, it found expression in the choice of names referring to the cinema's street or surrounding locality. As could be expected, theatres

Fig. 1. The Rembrandt Theatre on Rembrandt Square in Amsterdam. It opened as an operetta theater in 1902 and became a cinema (keeping the same name) in 1919.

that carried this type of name were often neighbourhood cinemas, located at some distance from the city center.

Table 3. Cinemas with names alluding to moral or cultural respectability: the second largest cluster among cinemas opening or re-opening during the years 1910–1913.

Names referring to	Total number	In larger cities or small towns	% of total
Catholic church	13	Predominantly small towns	5
Family life	6	Both	2.5%
Dutch royalty	5	Both	2
Icons of national culture	5	Both	2
Other (miscellaneous)	6	Both	2.5
	35 (total)		15% (total)

The second largest cluster within the data set comprises cinemas with names foregrounding moral or cultural respectability. Again, we can draw subdivisions within this cluster. Most numerous were names indicating the theatre's moral probity, as judged by members of the Catholic clergy. A special kind of brand name came into use to this end. Any theatre with the name "White Cinema" was, so to speak, safe for Roman Catholics. Incidentally, there was no comparable safety marker for Protestants: proper, God-abiding Calvinists were simply supposed to keep well clear of cinemas, or – for that matter – any other form of commercial entertainment, as all of these were judged to be the works of Satan. Other, less stringent Protestants held the view that it was every believer's personal responsibility to decide in these matters.[6]

Less numerous, but still marking the respectability of the place, were cinema names referring to family life, members of the Dutch Royal Family, or icons of national culture like Rembrandt. Although not shown in the table, the tendency to choose names underscoring respectability became much stronger from 1912 onwards. This coincided with an upsurge in anti-cinema discourse in the Dutch press, and mounting pressures – especially from Roman Catholic clergymen and politicians – to regulate cinema by imposing film censorship and admission bans for children.[7]

Table 4. Cinemas with traditional theatre names: the third largest cluster among cinemas opening or re-opening during the years 1910–1913.

Specific names	Total number	In larger cities or small towns	% of total
Apollo	7	Both	3
Scala	6	Both	2.5
Flora	6	Predominantly small towns	2.5
Other (miscellaneous)	15	Both	6.5
	34 (total)		14.5% (total)

In addition to claiming respectability, branding a cinema as Roman Catholic or giving it a name that resonated with notions of family life and nationhood also helped to integrate the place into the known *mental* environment – into the life-world, so to speak – of potential audiences. On first sight, such a function cannot be claimed for the third largest cluster of names in the data set – traditional theatre names, like the Apollo, Scala, Olympia, and Odeon. Most of these were used throughout – at least – the Western world, and therefore had a predominantly international ring to them. Or so we may think. Looking closer into the history of these theatre names in the Netherlands in fact reveals that they could acquire very specific national and even local flavours too, especially within the still less-media saturated, and less globalised life-world of most early-twentieth-century Dutch. For the set of "international" names for Dutch theatres was actually fairly limited. A few, like Apollo, Scala, and Flora, were used over and over again – not only for cinemas, but also for live-stage theatres – while other names in this category found no, or almost no, use at all. Which names caught on seemed to depend on their national and local, not international, pedigree; and, in this respect, it was Amsterdam that set the major trends. Beginning in the mid-nineteenth century, Amsterdam was the first, and for some decades remained the only Dutch city to have developed a more or less substantial infrastructure of permanent music halls and variety theatres, mostly located along the street "de Nes". The majority of these places carried traditional theatre names, a few of which developed a national reputation. The names subsequently caught on and spread into the provinces, especially when permanent movie theatres started to emerge there.[8]

Table 5. Two of the smaller clusters among cinemas opening or re-opening between 1910 and 1913.

Names referring to	Total number	In larger cities or small towns	% of total
Cosmopolitanism/the exotic	21	Both	9
Consumerism/luxury	11	Both	4.5

So, even in their use of "international" theatre names, entrepreneurs in the Dutch entertainment business tended to stick to what was already familiar – and identifiable as "Dutch" – to their audiences. This, of course, was simply another expression of exhibitors' tendency to keep close to their potential patrons' known environment, their physical and mental "home and hearth", so to speak. As if to complement this tendency, it is noticeable how Dutch cinema owners of the early- to mid-1910s showed only a mild interest in cinema names that conjured up exotic and cosmopolitan connotations, like Americain, Parisien, or Chicago. Rarer still were names that resonated with themes of consumerism and luxury. A name like Bijou – very popular in the U.S. during the nickelodeon period[9] – never caught on in the Netherlands. Before Word War Two, it was used only once, for a cinema in Amsterdam in operation between 1906 and 1915; predictably, perhaps, the theatre was founded by an American businessman. From Word War Two to the present, the name was chosen for just two other cinemas, both of which have long gone out of business.[10]

Although this project is still too underdeveloped to come to any definite conclusions, the foregoing findings find interesting resonance in the 1928 memoirs of one of Holland's most successful and best remembered cinema owners of the period: the Rotterdam-based exhibitor Abraham Tuschinski.[11] Writing about the particularities of the Dutch entertainment market, this immigrant showman – Tuschinski was born a Russian Jew – stated that, in order to draw an audience in the Netherlands, exhibitors needed to assure patrons that their theatres offered

> even more homely comfort and coziness than he [the Dutchman] is used to in his own home. ... The foreigner lives so much more in the street. He just enters a theatre or cinema without giving it much thought. While visiting a show, hearing the music, having a drink and meeting with his friends, he is "out" and has fun. The Dutchman is completely different. Most of the time, he lives at home, and *if* he decides to leave the pleasures of his homely hearth for a couple of hours to see some show, he asks himself whether the money he is about to spend will equal the pleasure that he is going to get.[12]

To put it briefly: Tuschinski found the Dutch to be thrifty stay-at-homes.

Present-day social and cultural historians have come to similar conclusions in their studies of everyday life in the Netherlands during the nineteenth and early twentieth centuries. Domesticity and modesty were central values in the process of "bourgeoisification" that took hold among all social strata in Western and Westernised societies. But among the Dutch these values were embraced so strongly that a culture of demonstrative domesticity and thriftiness became a national characteristic, or even – as A.J. Schuurman has argued – a part of the nation's self-identifying ideology.[13]

To explain why this was the case, Schuurman points to the long tradition of representing scenes of domesticity in Dutch culture, especially in paintings. This tradition reaches back into the seventeenth century, when the Dutch Republic – being the first institutional embodiment of the Netherlands as an independent nation-state – experienced its "Golden Age", and – according to Canadian scholar Witold Rybczynski – provided the socio-cultural context in which the bourgeoisie "discovered" the culture of domesticity as a central marker of its own class-identity.[14] As a result, scenes of domesticity featured prominently in the visual and literary discourses through which the Dutch Republic's bourgeoisie (re)presented itself, even if for most Dutch people the actual realities of their domestic lives did not live up to what these discourses suggested.

Two centuries later, the Dutch middle class became the principal pillar of support for the new Kingdom of the Netherlands, founded as an embodiment of the Dutch nation state after the Napoleonic Wars and turned into a bourgeois parliamentary democracy in 1848. In the process of cultural nation-building within this later context, the Dutch middle classes appropriated and intensified the glorious image of the seventeenth-century Republic, including its (alleged) culture of domesticity, that once again came to be seen, propagated, and – at least in part – practiced as something quintessentially Dutch and virtuous. As the nineteenth century progressed, this exceptionally positive view on domesticity was accepted and internalised across the social formation, even by those who did not – or did not *primarily* – identify themselves as bourgeois. Modern-day orthodox Protestants, the Roman Catholic emancipation movement, or social-democratic workers and their organisations: whatever the differences and even strong political animosities between them, they shared some common ground in their adherence to the Dutch culture of domesticity – an adherence which they did not hesitate to translate into practical measures when these groups developed into the three most influential forces in Dutch politics and civil society during the early decades of the twentieth century.[15]

This strong and broadly rooted adherence to a culture of domesticity among the Dutch may have stimulated the tendencies in the naming of Dutch cinemas discussed above. Moreover, it may also have brought about a cultural climate that limited the growing potential of the nation's film exhibition industry in the first place. So, do we have a clue here that could lead us to a satisfactory explanation of the late and rather modest expansion of an infrastructure of permanent cinemas and of moviegoing as a cultural practice in the Netherlands? Well, a clue perhaps, but we are still on thin ice, and a solid explanation would require a much deeper and broader analysis than the mapping of clusters and patterns in the nomenclature of Dutch cinemas presented above. Besides, even this mapping is still unfinished and may be complicated by new findings as we move into the interwar period. It is already clear, for instance, that the Dutch tendency to avoid "exotic" names declined after World War One. Indeed, during the 1920s and 1930s, the name "Luxor" became by far the most popular and widely used name for new cinemas, especially after Howard Carter's discovery of the tomb of King Tutankhamun in 1922.[16] So obviously, "keeping it close to home and hearth" is not the full story when it comes to explaining the oddities of film culture in the Netherlands.

Notes

1. See for instance, Kathryn H. Fuller, *At the Picture Show: Small-Town Audiences and the Creation of Movie Fan Culture* (Washington, DC: Smithsonian Institution Press, 1996), 50–56; Mark Jancovich and Lucy Faire, with Sarah Stubbings, *The Place of the Audience: Cultural Geographies of Film Consumption* (London: BFI, 2003), 69–70.

2. http://www.cinemacontext.nl (accessed 14 July 2011).

3. Michael Töteberg, "Neben dem Operetten-Theater und vis-à-vis Schauspielhaus: Eine Kino-Topographie von Hamburg, 1896–1912", in Corinna Müller and Harro Segeberg (eds), *Kinoöffentlichkeit (1895–1920): Enstehung, Etablierung, Differenzierung* (Marburg: Schüren, 2008), 87–104; Guido Convents, *Van Kinetoscoop tot café-ciné: De eerste jaren van de film in België, 1894–1908* (Leuven: Universitaire Pers Leuven, 2000), 302–320.

4. Recent contributions to the debate include Karel Dibbets, "Het taboe van de Nederlandse filmcultuur: Neutraal in een verzuild land", *Tijdschrift voor Mediageschiedenis* 9.2 (2006): 46–64; Jaap Boter and Clara Pafort-Overduin, "Compartmentalisation and its Influences on Film Distribution and Exhibition in the Netherlands, 1934–1936", in Michael Ross et al. (eds), *Digital Tools in Media Studies: Analysis and Research, an Overview* (Bielefeld: Transcript Verlag, 2009), 66–67; and André van der Velden and Judith Thissen, "Spectacles of Conspicuous Consumption: Picture Palaces, War Profiteers and the Social Dynamics of Moviegoing in the Netherlands", *Film History* 22 (2010): 452–461.

5. There is an extensive methodological literature on grounded theory. To mention just one, fairly

recent introduction, see Kathy Charmaz, *Constructing Grounded Theory: A Practical Guide Through Qualitative Analysis* (Thousand Oaks, Cal.: Sage Publications, 2006).

6. On Protestant attitudes regarding cinema, see Jan Hes, *In de ban van het beeld: Een filmsociologisch-godsdienstsociologische verkenning* (Assen: Van Gorcum and Co., 1972), 116–128, 141–152.

7. In 1913, Rotterdam became the first Dutch city that actually took these kind of measures, followed by quite a few other municipalities in the years thereafter. From 1918 onwards, the Dutch government started to prepare national legislation to curb "the danger of the cinema" ["het bioscoopgevaar"]. However, these efforts remained unsuccessful until 1926, because of deep divisions among members of parliament about the scope of a state law on film censorship – would it have to apply for young audiences only, or for adults as well? – and its practical arrangements. As long as these differences could not be sorted out, film censorship and other regulatory measures remained an exclusively local affair for municipal authorities in the Netherlands. For further details, see J. van der Burg and J.H.J. van den Heuvel, *Film en overheidsbeleid. Van censuur naar zelfregulering* (The Hague: SDU Publishers, 1991), 52–56.

8. On the nineteenth- and early-twentieth-century history of popular theatre in Amsterdam and the rest of the Netherlands, see Jacques Klöters, *100 jaar Amusement in Nederland* (The Hague: Staatsuitgeverij, 1987). More specifically on the history of "de Nes", see Paul Blom, "2 September 1839: Opening van de Salon de Variétés in de Nes in Amsterdam", in R.L. Erenstein, et al. (eds), *Een theatergeschiedenis der Nederlanden: Tien eeuwen drama en theater in Nederland en Vlaanderen* (Amsterdam: Amsterdam UP 1996), 410–417.

9. Fuller 1996, 53.

10. http://www.cinemacontext.nl (accessed 14 July 2011); Fuller 1996, 53.

11. For a detailed analysis of Tuschinski's autobiography, see André van der Velden, "Life Writing, Marketing, and the Construction of Cinema History: On the Ghost-written Autobiography of Dutch Film Entrepreneur Abraham Tuschinski", in Arianne Baggerman, Rudolf Dekker and Michael Mascuch (eds), *Controlling Time and Shaping the Self: Developments in Autobiographical Writing since the Sixteenth Century* (Leiden, Boston: Brill 2011), 331–353.

12. A. Tuschinski, "Vijftien jaar van mijn leven", *Tuschinksi Nieuws* 2.4 (1928): 3–9, 5.

13. Anton J. Schuurman, "Is huiselijkheid typisch Nederlands? Over Huiselijkheid en Moderniser-ing", *Berichten en mededelingen betreffende de geschiedenis der Nederlanden* 107 (1992): 745–759, 758. On the Dutch culture of domesticity, see also Els Kloek, *Vrouw des Huizes: Een cultuurgeschiedenis van de Hollandse huisvrouw* (Amsterdam: Balans, 2009).

14. Witold Rybszynski, *Home. A Short History of an Idea* (Harmondsworth: Penguin, 1987), 77.

15. Schuurman "Is Huiselijkheid Typisch Nederlands?" 791–751, 753–754. Perhaps the most telling symptom of these combined efforts to stimulate the culture of domesticity among their own followers as well as among the Dutch people as a whole, can be found in married women's exclusion from the nation's labor force. Generally considered to be the main providers of a well-developed domestic life for husbands and children, married women were strongly dissuaded and often even legally impeded to do paid work outside the home. As a result, the percentage of married women with a paid job never exceeded ten percent in the Netherlands between 1899 and 1960. For Belgium, Britain, Germany and France these percentages ranged from nineteen to fifty percent. Kloek 2009, 195.

16. During the period 1915–1921, eleven cinemas in the Netherlands were named Luxor. During the period 1922–1949, fifty Dutch cinemas got this name. http://www.cinemacontext.nl (accessed 14 July 2011).

31

Local Showmanship in the Early Feature Era: The Case of Stanley Mastbaum

Joel Frykholm

In the transformative year of 1914, Stanley Mastbaum all but dominated the motion picture scene in Philadelphia. In less than a year's time, he had gone from successful but anonymous real-estate agent to owner of a chain of motion picture theatres, most of which were located on or near Market Street, in the hub of Philadelphia's premier amusement district.[1] His firm, the Stanley Company, co-founded with older brother Jules, controlled several of the city's most prominent and profitable movie houses, making Mastbaum a force to reckon with already by 1914.[2] The following year, a *Motography* reporter stated that he "well deserve[d] his title of Imperator", and by 1916, other commentators did not hesitate to dub Mastbaum "the king of local exhibitors" or to declare that he "[set] the photoplay fashions of the town".[3] Over the next couple of years, the Stanley Company would expand into one of the largest chains of motion picture theatres in the United States.[4] A decade or so later, by 1928, the Stanley Company owned 255 theatres in seventy-five cities across the mid-Atlantic region.[5]

In spite of Mastbaum's track record – which also included a profitable but eventually enjoined booking combine, a brief and unsuccessful venture into film production, and a considerable interest in First National – we know next to nothing about this man, his company, or his historical significance.[6] There are several explanations for this. First of all, Philadelphia was something of a cultural backyard to New York City, a secondhand market for motion pictures that had already had an initial run in the great metropolis; possibly for this reason, Philadelphia has been relegated to film historians' back burner at best. Second, Mastbaum's unexpected and untimely death in 1918 obviously put an abrupt end to his career before it really took off beyond the sphere of local and regional interest.[7] Finally, and most importantly, the Stanley Company was devoured first by Paramount in 1919 and then by Warner Bros. in 1928, exploits that seem to have left Mastbaum and his company a mere footnote in standard histories of the Hollywood studio system.[8]

The objective of this paper is not to usher in a heroic biography of yet another great man from the pre-classical era. Instead I will attempt to demonstrate how Mastbaum's activities around 1914–1915 offer a model case study for enhancing our understanding of what is sometimes referred to by cinema scholars as the "transitional era".[9] Above all, I hope to shed some new light on how the transformation of cinema in the mid-1910s can be framed as a many-pronged negotiation that took place as national networks of publicity and distribution trickled down to the local level.[10] For this

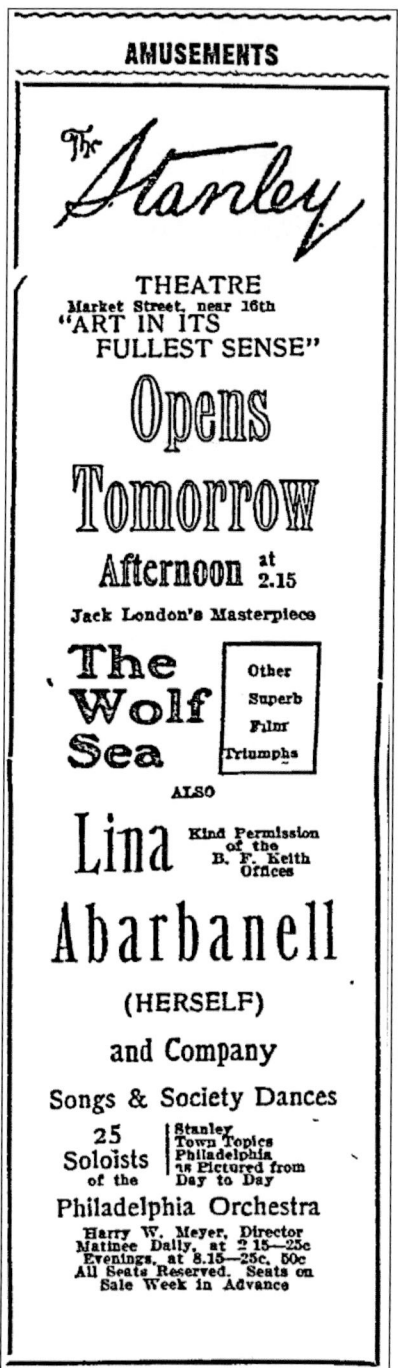

Fig. 1. Advertisement for the Stanley Theatre, Philadelphia Inquirer *(26 April 1914): 23.*

purpose, two trends of national magnitude and scope can be usefully put into play in relation to Mastbaum's local showmanship: (a) the rise to dominance of the multi-reel feature film in the United States; and (b) the intensifying exchange and tightening links between motion pictures and the paper press.[11]

Even though the Stanley Company already owned and controlled twelve Philadelphia theatres, the opening of the Stanley Theatre on Market Street and 16th on 25 April 1914 marked the moment when Mastbaum began to catch the attention of the public eye.[12] The Stanley was Mastbaum's flagship theatre, and the platform from which he launched himself as a showman. From the outset, the Stanley's business model was geared toward an upper- and middle-class patronage. According to advertisements, it was the "Favorite Resort of Discriminating People" and devoted to "Art in Its Fullest Sense".[13] Several related strategies were developed to secure this status and attract a "high-class" clientele. One was to market the theatre space as safe, pleasant, and aesthetically appealing. Seats were comfortable, the ventilation system efficient, the projection booth fireproof, and the lobby and auditorium sumptuous.[14] Another was to invest heavily in first-rate musical accompaniment. As a complement to the twenty-five-piece orchestra, conducted by the Philadelphia Orchestra's Harry W. Meyer, a massive Hastings organ was installed in June 1914.[15] Seemingly, these investments paid off, as the Stanley's musical program was consistently and enthusiastically praised by local newspapers and trade-press commentators alike.[16] Last but not least, the Stanley adhered to the notion that "high-class pictures" would attract "high-class patrons". The crucial commodity in this respect was, of course, the multi-reel feature film. To be sure, such films made up the core and most heavily advertised part of the show, but nonetheless, the Stanley also retained elements of the variety model, in the form of a series of shorter films in different genres, including local views under the brand name "Stanley Town Topics".[17] For all the impact of the fairly new multi-reel feature format, its introduction to Philadelphia audiences was negotiated within a familiar context of local elements, which at times even included live entertainment acts.[18] This balancing between local elements and a centrally distributed commodity should not be seen as unique to Mastbaum's showmanship, but rather as a defining trait of local showmanship overall during this period, or, as Paul Moore suggests, that which distinguished the showman from the pure salesman.[19]

Tracing the balance between local and national circuits seems equally central when analysing the marketing strategies that Mastbaum deployed. As the familiar story goes, a great advantage of the multi-reel feature format was its superior marketability. If the one-reel standard of production and distribution favoured standardisation and a daily change of program, the feature format came with a promise of differentiation and longer exhibition spans. In terms of marketing, this involved a shift from brand names to individual films, but also, on a more hands-on level, a shift from local sidewalk ballyhoo to citywide newspaper advertising. Hovering over all of this was – unsurprisingly – the hope for uplift and boosting cinema's cultural prestige. According to the trade press, the key challenge for ambitious exhibitors was to attract the upper and middle classes, and according to some commentators, this could best be achieved through press advertising.[20] Film producers and distributors, too, not least those working within the fledgling feature field, clearly recognised the value of newspaper ads and took action by supplying exhibitors and newspaper editors with various sorts of publicity. However, there were numerous complaints about the poor quality of this centrally circulated press material. Newspaper editors argued that much of it could not be adapted or adjusted to local conditions, which rendered it unusable.[21] Others complained about the immense dullness of the material, making it suitable only for the wastebasket.[22] In the words of one anonymous Midwest motion-picture page editor: "Those letters, dozens of them, from film manufacturers and distributors, are so neat, so nicely typewritten, and so deadly dull or so foolishly silly!"[23] Still others recognised that the intensified marketing of feature films had led to an inflation of superlatives that drained the advertising of all credibility. A Detroit newspaperman stated in a 1915 issue of *Motion Picture News* that "[t]he extravagant superlatives of the theatrical press agent have long been axiomatic, but I don't believe that P.T. Barnum in his palmiest days could out-praise some film press agents".[24] Anyone familiar with newspaper discourse from the early feature era is bound to have encountered some evidence to back this up; the most frequently recurring phrase in motion picture advertising at this juncture must surely be "The Greatest Photoplay Ever Made".

All of the above helps explain what is, at first glance, the somewhat surprising fact that Mastbaum's newspaper advertising for his flagship theatre was quite modest. While most other downtown movie theatres offering feature films would emulate the elaborate and outsized ads for theatrical stage plays, ads for the Stanley Theatre were small and relatively uninformative.[25] Mastbaum's strategy for achieving maximum promotional impact was instead predicated on the staging of publicity stunts and active involvement in the city's social, cultural, and, at least occasionally, political life. Let us examine a selection of these stunts, strategies, and practices:

First of all, like several other exhibitors around this time, Mastbaum exploited the idea of the "movie ball" – a special event involving a personal visit by some (or sometimes several) popular screen actor(s) or actress(es).[26] The most popular star at this time was Mary Pickford, and in October 1914, Mastbaum managed to get her to visit Philadelphia. After a private dinner hosted by Mastbaum for Pickford and several other "well-known persons", the party was supposed to head over to the Stanley Theatre to enjoy the evening's entertainment, which included Pickford's performance in *Behind the Scenes* (1914).²⁷ Clearly aware of the drawing power of film stars in general and Pickford in particular, Mastbaum leaked all information about the visit to the press, and as a result, even before dinner ended, the party was notified that "the throng about the theatre was of such proportions that it would be impossible to accommodate more than a small portion of the people clamoring for admission".²⁸ In the end, a police escort had to be engaged to secure the party's entrance, and while as many as four thousand fans were admitted, it was claimed that as many, or more, were turned away. This was the first in a series of claims in the press that the Stanley Theatre was habitually forced to turn away as many patrons as were let in, and the event itself was the first in a series of movie star visits hosted by Mastbaum.²⁹

Another approach – a slight variation on the same theme – was to arrange dinner parties that catered not to motion picture stars but to "film men" (these seems to have been all-male affairs), local and otherwise. Such business gatherings presented an opportunity to meet and discuss matters of common interest under pleasant circumstances, and in October 1914 (the same month as Pickford's visit), Mastbaum hosted one such event with the explicit aim of bringing "film men" and "newspapermen" closer together.³⁰ Another similar affair, held two years later, was organised to celebrate and promote the newly formed Stanley Exhibitors' Association, Mastbaum's upscale alternative to the local branch of the Motion Picture Exhibitors' League.³¹ In both cases, the presence of movie business notables such as Adolph Zukor, Jesse Lasky, Sam Goldfish, Lewis Selznick, and Carl Laemmle, helped raise the theatre's promotional profile and the public interest, albeit perhaps not to the level a movie star proper would have. It should also be noted that Mastbaum was always careful to invite representatives of the major Philadelphia newspapers to his events, which guaranteed at least some promotional impact. He would also on occasion reserve a box at the Stanley Theatre for representatives from the fourth estate and arrange special screenings exclusively for the press.³² (On a more anecdotal level, it is intriguing to note that practically all of Mastbaum's functions seem to have taken place at the Bellevue-Stratford Hotel – still standing today on the corner of Walnut and Broad Streets but now under the Hyatt flag. Perhaps the "platform" for Mastbaum's showmanship referred to earlier rested upon two material pillars, i.e. the Stanley Theatre *and* the Bellevue-Stratford.)

If his rather flamboyant social life positioned Mastbaum as a Philadelphia socialite, he seems further to have been careful to promote a public image of himself as a socially responsible member of the community. As Paul Moore has argued, concerns over fire hazards during the nickelodeon era prompted exhibitors to incorporate an element of civic responsibility into their showmanship in order to ensure public safety for film exhibition.³³ By the mid-1910s, fire hazards might not have remained on top of the agenda, but I would suggest that conveying a sense of civic responsibility was still an important facet of showmanship. With regard to this objective, supporting various charities and volunteer/non-profit organisations was one option and, accordingly, Mastbaum regularly made his Stanley Theatre available to functions ranging from Red Cross events to Boy Scouts conventions.³⁴ He also aimed to associate his business model with ideals of civic responsibility. For instance, Mastbaum sought – and received – considerable attention and praise for the generous employee benefits he offered his staff, including free health care, vacation with full pay, substantial Christmas bonuses, and a profit-sharing system that was inaugurated in 1916.³⁵ Mastbaum also framed the continuous expansion of his theatre chain as beneficial for the city's overall economy, or, at least, for its property owners, since the erection of new theatres would boost real-estate value in depreciated neighborhoods.³⁶

All of the activities described here seem indicative of Mastbaum's promotional flair and his ability to create a buzz about his chain of picture theatres, especially the Stanley. Of course, the extent to which this should be ascribed to Mastbaum personally cannot be determined. Nonetheless, there was a desire to assign a name and a face to the dominant force in Philadelphia motion picture life, and Mastbaum was more than willing to lend himself to this enterprise.[37] Put differently, something of a cult of personality emerged in the wake of Mastbaum's meteoric rise "from practical obscurity to foremost rank" due to his daring and foresight when it came to strategies for attracting well-heeled patrons and, not least, his proclivity for staging elaborate publicity stunts.[38] Already in October 1914, on the subject of Pickford's visit, a local reporter declared that Mastbaum had "out-Stanleyd [sic] Stanley".[39] Such flattering remarks seem, in fact, to have cultivated a megalomaniacal strain in Mastbaum; for instance, he would at times unabashedly open his banquets with a performance of "The Stanley March", composed in honor of the host.[40]

Megalomaniac or not, Mastbaum's success as a showman was largely the result of his skillful balancing of old exhibition models and the challenges that the new feature format posed; between locally adjusted promotional campaigns and centrally prepared marketing schemes; and between civic responsibility and corporate strategising. In more concrete terms: The multi-reel feature format *had* an impact on Philadelphia. The dissemination of central marketing schemes *did* affect relations between showmen and the Philadelphia press – but the national trends did not override the local, they were integrated into it. The case of Stanley Mastbaum offers a model for better understanding this process. We should also acknowledge that the process harbours transnational dimensions, not least considering how the early feature era was initially defined by the influx and impact of European multi-reel pictures, before a gradual Americanisation of the feature market – domestically and globally – set in. This paper, however, having dealt primarily with the dynamics of local-national interactions, can only hint at these dimensions. Nonetheless, Mastbaum's clever dexterity in navigating between the local and national can perhaps remind us that cases such as his offer windows of opportunity to readjust the optics of pre-classical cinema scholarship, not via a complete turn from the national or transnational to the local, but to the focal points where they all connect.

Notes

1. "'Movie' Syndicate Adds to Holdings", *Philadelphia Inquirer* (henceforth *PI*) (27 March 1914): 5; and "Quakers to Have News Weekly", *Motion Picture News* (henceforth *MPN*) (11 April 1914): 29–30. Additional data regarding the various Philadelphia movie theatres owned by the Mastbaum brothers has been gathered by cross-correlating findings in local newspapers, the trade press, and Irvin R. Glazer, *Philadelphia Theatres, A–Z: A Comprehensive, Descriptive Record of 813 Theatres Constructed Since 1724* (Westport, Conn.: Greenwood Press, 1986).

2. The Mastbaum brothers started a real estate company in 1901 together with Alfred W. Fleischer and began investing in the motion picture business in 1905 when they opened Philadelphia's presumably first nickelodeon on the corner of Market St. and 8th. Before this, in the summer of 1902, older brother Jules had been the manager of a seasonal movie theatre in Woodside Park (owned by Sigmund Lubin). When Lubin began selling off his movie theatres and exchanges in 1908 to finance new production facilities, the Mastbaums purchased at least five of his Philadelphia theatres. However, it was not until 1914 that the Mastbaums consolidated their chain of picture theatres, and it was only at this point that their activities within the field were widely noticed. The latter signals not only a shift from real estate to motion pictures as the Mastbaum brothers' primary area of business, but also an ongoing renegotiation of the position of motion pictures in the overall culture. On the Mastbaum brothers' earliest endeavors within the field of motion pictures, see Joseph Eckhardt, *King of the Movies: Film Pioneer Sigmund Lubin* (Teaneck, NJ: Farleigh Dickinson Press, 1997), 43 and 80–81. A framework (based on Raymond Williams' concepts of "emergent", "residual", and "dominant") for analysing early film culture in the United States as

a culturally negotiated process is presented in Jan Olsson, *Los Angeles Before Hollywood: Journalism and American Film Culture, 1905–1915* (Stockholm: National Library, 2009), 21–22.

3. "Philadelphia Notes", *Motography* (27 November 1915): 1116; "Philadelphia, PA Lays Claim to an Early Date", *Moving Picture World* (henceforth *MPW*) (15 July 1916): 386–387; and "Week's Philadelphia Happenings", *MPW* (2 December 1916): 1357.

4. According to Terry Ramsaye, the Stanley circuit was the "earliest of the important theatre chains [and] became a demonstration of the power of combination and a pattern to endless development of chain theatre combines to come". Terry Ramsaye, *A Million and One Nights* (New York: Simon and Schuster, 1964 [1926]), 710–11.

5. *The Film Daily Yearbook, 1929* (New York: Film Daily, 1929), 856.

6. The most informative (albeit still very brief) account of the Mastbaum brothers and the Stanley Company of America – as seen within the context of a general history of theatrical motion picture exhibition in the United States – can be found in Douglas Gomery, *Shared Pleasures: A History of Movie Presentation in the United States* (Madison: University of Wisconsin Press, 1992), 38–40. See also Douglas Gomery, "Mastbaum, Jules and Stanley", in Richard Abel (ed.), *Encyclopedia of Early Cinema* (London: Routledge, 2005), 415. On the Stanley Booking Corporation, see "Stanley Company Under Charges: Federal Trade Commission Alleges Philadelphia Organization's Methods Have Been Unfair", *MPW* (15 June 1918): 1584; and "Stanley Corporation Is Enjoined: Federal Trade Commission Issues First Order in Motion Picture Field Against Unfair Methods", *MPW* (28 September 1919): 1869. On Stanley Mastbaum's venture into motion picture production, see "Mastbaum Talks of His New Film Activities", *MPW* (19 August 1916): 1284.

7. "Stanley Mastbaum Dies Suddenly", *MPW* (23 March 1918): 1641.

8. On Paramount's acquisition of the Stanley Company in 1919, see Richard Koszarski, *An Evening's Entertainment: The Age of the Silent Feature Picture, 1915–1928* (New York: Charles Scribner's Sons, 1990), 75. On Warner's 1928 purchase, see Douglas Gomery, *The Hollywood Studio System: A History* (London: BFI Publishing, 2005), 52.

9. The notion of a "transitional period" (beginning sometime between 1906 and 1909 and ending sometime between 1913 and 1917, depending on the exact criteria of periodisation) emanates from Bordwell, Staiger, and Thompson's *The Classical Hollywood Cinema* (1985), but has been more fully explored and developed by Charlie Keil in *Early American Cinema in Transition* (2001), which launched the term into scholarly centrality. A more recent manifestation of a research program/agenda based on the concept is a 2004 volume edited by Keil and Shelley Stamp. The latter volume offers ample critique of the term "transitional era" (on account of it being too vague, too wide, too teleological, etc.), while basically retaining it as a sort of heuristic tool for scholarly exploration of various transformations that American cinema underwent in the 1910s. David Bordwell, Janet Staiger, and Kristin Thompson, *The Classical Hollywood Cinema: Film Style and Mode of Production to 1960* (New York: Columbia University Press, 1985), esp. chap. 14; Charlie Keil, *Early American Cinema in Transition: Story, Style, and Filmmaking, 1907–1913* (Madison: University of Wisconsin Press, 2001); and Charlie Keil and Shelley Stamp (eds), *American Cinema's Transitional Era: Audiences, Institutions, Practices* (Berkeley: University of California Press, 2004).

10. This approach is inspired by the growing interest among film historians in local film history, a field pioneered by scholars such as Gregory Waller, Robert C. Allen, Richard Abel, and others, and also manifested in the publication of various collections of historical case studies of local film culture. For a summary of developments within the field, see Kathryn H. Fuller-Seeley and George Potamianos, "Introduction: Researching and Writing the History of Local Moviegoing", in Kathryn H. Fuller-Seeley (ed.), *Hollywood in the Neighborhood: Historical Case Studies of Local Moviegoing* (Berkeley: University of California Press, 2008), 3–19.

11. The breakthrough of the multi-reel feature film in the United States is explored at length and from a variety of perspectives in my doctoral dissertation, "Framing the Feature Film: Multi-Reel Feature Film and American Film Culture in the 1910s" (Ph. D. diss., Stockholm University, 2009). The dissertation also includes a case study of film culture in Philadelphia around 1914, parts of which have been revisited and revised for this paper. On the links between motion pictures and the press in early American cinema, and for convincing cases for the use-value of local newspapers as a film historical source, see Richard Abel, *Americanizing the Movies and "Movie-Mad" Audiences, 1910–1914* (Berkeley: University of California Press, 2006), 215–227; Richard Abel, "Fan Discourse in the Heartland: The Early 1910s", *Film History* 18, no. 2 (2006): 140–153; and Olsson 2009, especially 57–98.

12. The opening of the Stanley Theatre garnered considerable attention in local newspapers and the trade press, indicating that it was regarded as a major event at the time. See, for example, "Stanley Theatre Opening", *PI* (19 April 1914): 19; "Current Views of the Stage", *Philadelphia Evening Bulletin* (25 April 1914): 5; "Inspections of the Stanley Theatre", *PI* (25 April 1914): 9; "Lina Abarbanell–Stanley", *Philadelphia Record* (28 April 1914): 6; and "Stanley Theatre, Philadelphia, PA", *MPW* (16 May 1914): 948.
13. Advertisements for the Stanley Theatre, *PI* (10 May 1914): 21; and (26 April 1914): 23.
14. See, for example, "Philadelphia Now has a Fifty-Cent House", *MPN* (9 May 1914): 20; and "Stanley Theatre, Philadelphia, PA", *MPW* (16 May 1914): 948.
15. "Inspections of the Stanley Theatre", *PI* (25 April 1914): 9; "New Organ at Stanley", *PI* (9 June 1914): 4; and "Musical Accompaniment at the Stanley", *MPW* (22 May 1915): 1296.
16. See, for example, "The Call Boy's Chat", *PI* (17 May 1914): 18; "Paramount Pictures at Stanley", *PI* (20 October 1914): 10; and "Musical Accompaniment at the Stanley", *MPW* (22 May 1915): 1296.
17. While some advertisements for the Stanley Theatre clearly promoted multi-reel feature pictures as the main attraction, others highlighted the variety of the show. For instance, the advertisement appearing in the 3 May 1914 issue of the *Inquirer* made no mention of any specific multi-reel feature film, but included the phrase "Infinite Variety of Subjects" as a tagline of sorts. Seen as a whole, then, the advertisements are characterised by a dual focus on multi-reel feature pictures as the main filmic attraction on the one hand, and on elements of a variety model of film exhibition (including daily changes of program, continuous shows, live entertainment, and short films) on the other. See, for example, advertisements for the Stanley Theatre, *PI* (26 April 1914): 23; (3 May 1914): 19; (10 May 1914): 21; and (17 May 1914): 19. On the "Stanley Town Topics", see "Stanley", *PI* (26 April 1914): 22; and "Stanley Theatre, Philadelphia, PA", *MPW* (16 May 1914): 948.
18. Advertisement for the Stanley Theatre, *PI* (26 April 1914): 23.
19. Paul S. Moore, *Now Playing: Early Moviegoing and the Regulation of Fun* (New York: SUNY Press, 2008), 79.
20. See, for example, Frederick James Smith, "The Evolution of the Motion Picture: X–The Feature Picture and Exhibiting Methods", *New York Dramatic Mirror* (3 September 1913): 25, 27; "Booming the Feature Film", *MPN* (17 January 1914): 32; and Charles J. Giegerich, "The Function of Feature Productions", *Motography* (21 August 1915): 357.
21. "Mastbaum Banquet Briefs", *MPW* (23 December 1916): 1832.
22. Al. U. Thornberg, "The Press, the Press Representative and the Picture–III", *MPN* (30 October 1915): 49.
23. "The Press, the Press Representative and the Picture–VI", *MPN* (20 November 1915): 45–46.
24. A.L. Weeks, "The Press, the Press Representative and the Picture–V", *MPN* (13 November 1915): 45.
25. Advertisements for the Stanley Theatre were never of imposing size and actually decreased in scale to reach all but minuscule proportions by September 1914. For a revealing illustration, compare the advertisement for *The Virginian* (1914) at the Stanley Theatre with the advertisement for *Cabiria* (1914) at the Chestnut Street Opera House, both ads appearing in the *Inquirer*'s amusements advertising section on 6 September 1914. *PI* (6 September 1914): 11.
26. On the phenomenon of "motion-picture balls", see Eileen Bowser, *The Transformation of Cinema, 1907–1915* (New York: Charles Scribner's Sons, 1990), 117.
27. "The Call Boy's Chat", *PI* (1 November 1914): 14.
28. Ibid.
29. See, for example, "'Carmen' in Films Proves Popular", *PI* (24 October 1915): 3; "The Call Boy's Chat", *PI* (31 October 1915): 12; "Actress to Be Feted", *PI* (14 November 1915): 10; "Dinner to Popular Actress", *PI* (16 November 1915): 5; "Polly and Her Creator at the Stanley", *MPW* (29 September 1917): 2026.
30. "The Call Boy's Chat", *PI* (4 October 1914): 14; "Philadelphia", *MPW* (10 October 1914): 217–218; "Film Magnates at Mastbaum Dinner", *MPN* (17 October 1914): 26, 52.

31. "Stanley Exhibitors' Association Formed", *MPW* (25 November 1916): 1200.
32. "Philadelphia", *MPW* (24 October 1914): 519; "The Call Boy's Chat", *PI* (7 November 1915): 9.
33. Moore 2008, 45–73.
34. "Philadelphia Show Notes", *MPW* (19 June 1915): 1970; "Mastbaum Boosts Red Cross", *MPW* (15 July 1916): 484; "Local Theaters Aid Red Cross", *MPW* (14 July 1917): 274; "More Philadelphia News", *MPW* (16 February 1918): 1000.
35. "Stanley Theater Celebrates Second Anniversary", *MPW* (6 May 1916): 1001. See also "The Call Boy's Chat", *PI* (31 October 1915): 12; and "Philadelphia, PA, Lays Claim to an Early Date", *MPW* (15 July 1916): 386–387.
36. "Philadelphia to Have New Amusement Center", *MPW* (9 September 1916): 1722.
37. As indicated by articles such as "Realized His Ideals", *PI* (25 April 1915): 12; and "Great Film Plays for Long Runs", *MPW* (13 February 1915): 958.
38. "Philadelphia Briefs", *MPW* (15 May 1915): 1116.
39. Irene Page Solomon, "Mary Pickford Captures Philadelphia", *MPN* (21 November 1914): 26.
40. "Stanley Mastbaum Is Host to Film Men", *MPW* (23 December 1916): 1779–1781.

32

A Transformative Moment: Samuel Rothafel and the Rise of Multi-Class Moviegoing in the Midwest, 1911–1913

Ross Melnick

Scholars have often focused attention on the social composition of motion picture theatres in the United States during the nickelodeon era; yet there remains a dearth of in-depth analyses of how theatres subsequently began drawing middle- and upper-class audiences in the early 1910s. "A Transformative Moment" examines the ways in which one enterprising exhibitor in the Midwest helped usher in a new era of social acceptance for motion pictures and motion picture theatres at a time when the industry desperately needed political, religious, moral, and legal approval.

Though the year 1913 is often noted as the moment when audiences began embracing American and European multi-reel films in upscale venues, middle- and upper-class audiences were already patronising deluxe film-only theatres in the Midwest by 1911 due to a new breed of movie theatre that catered to literary, stage, and biblical adaptations. Theatres like the Alhambra in Milwaukee and the Lyric in Minneapolis not only programmed multi-reel films based on well-known novels, plays, and biblical narratives, but also added live performance and classical music to lure in a multi-class patronage. By understanding how these two theatres were programmed by exhibitor Samuel "Roxy" Rothafel – who would soon become a nationally known figure through his management of the Regent, Strand, Rialto, and Rivoli theatres in New York between 1913 and 1919 – and how he reached out to clergy, politicians, business leaders, women, and children during this pivotal, earlier moment in his career, we can better understand how these theatres created fertile venues for feature-length films.[1] It was ultimately the Midwest, not New York, that was at the vanguard of film exhibition in 1911. Of Roxy's Milwaukee theatre, *Moving Picture World* noted in September 1911: "Here we are in New York City, which is claimed to be America's foremost city, yet we do not have an all-picture show put on in the style that is done at the Alhambra. We are living in hope that some day a New York exhibitor will rise to this opportunity, meanwhile we compliment Milwaukee in setting the pace".[2]

Film exhibition would become an enormously profitable and socially acceptable business in the 1920s but, in 1911, movie theatres and theatre managers faced an uphill struggle against social reformers, fire chiefs and safety inspectors, religious, political, and business leaders, and nearly every other element of middle- and upper-class society. Every city argued over the cultural and moral consequences of motion pictures and the venues that exhibited them. Any movie theatre operator in the early 1910s interested in attracting the middle class, and particularly middle-class women, needed to combat these critics. Early film exhibitors needed to be more than just managers or operators – they needed to be showmen and women.

Roxy is typically associated with New York and remembered as American-born. Unlike the Horatio Alger legend he often repeated, though, he emmigrated from Germany to the United States in 1886. His family settled in Stillwater, Minnesota, roughly twenty-five miles from the Lyric in Minneapolis. After moving to Brooklyn in 1896, he joined the Marines in 1902. Discharged in 1905, he worked as a hotel clerk in Massachusetts and then as a traveling book and insurance salesman before opening his first nickelodeon, the Family Theatre, in Forest City, Pennsylvania, in December 1908. His early clientele consisted mostly of coal miners and their families, but Roxy insisted on bringing "refined" films, vaudeville, and music to his theatre. At the Family, he also developed a technique whereby films could be projected with the house lights on and dubbed the process "Daylight Pictures".[3] Roxy noted in a 13 October 1910 advertisement that, "The theatre at all times hereafter will have enough light to see everything and everyone in the entire audience".[4] This was, of course, a particular concern for women and those who worried about the social composition of film audiences. Roxy subsequently left Forest City to install Daylight Pictures in vaudeville and movie theatres across the country.

Alhambra Theatre/Milwaukee

By 1911, Roxy was looking for a greater challenge and a return to theatre management. Herman Fehr lured him to Milwaukee to boost attendance at the Alhambra Theatre, a prominent, 3,000-seat legitimate venue that was normally closed or half-empty during the summer months when the oppressive heat kept audiences away. Roxy was hired to boost the Alhambra's summer prospects by installing film as the primary entertainment, making it the largest motion picture theatre in the United States at the time. He immediately hired a new staff of ushers, replaced the carpets and draperies, and added a nursery to take care of children – an initiative to bring in and curry favour with women. Roxy also marketed film's ability to provide education, culture, and uplift through advertisements aimed at the general public and in letters he sent to a thousand of the city's most prominent residents offering free tickets to see *La Caduta di Troia* (*The Fall of Troy*, 1910).[5]

The positive response to the Alhambra's mix of orchestral music and higher-class films was instantaneous.[6] "People who never went to motion picture theatres are going regularly to the Alhambra", the *Milwaukee Daily News* reported, "where the motion pictures de luxe are proving the summer amusement sensation of the city".[7] Motion picture-only venues had been scantily attended by many members of the upper and middle classes of Milwaukee before, but with the adoption of the medium at one of the city's largest and most prestigious theatres, the Alhambra's shows were "adding hundreds daily to the roll of motion picture patrons".[8] The theatre's immediate success, and the publicity it generated, demonstrated the potential for deluxe moviegoing in Milwaukee and the possibility of building and/or leasing ever larger and more opulent theatres for motion pictures in that city and elsewhere. The Saxe Amusement Company, recognising the value Roxy had created, now leased the Alhambra from the Shubert Theatrical Company in order to operate the venue as a year-round movie house.[9] Herman Fehr and Roxy, in turn, signed a new agreement with Lee Shubert to sublease the Lyric Theater in Minneapolis.[10]

Lyric/Minneapolis

Martin Miller Marks has accurately observed that for much of the next twenty years "every new stage in Rothapfel's career eclipsed the one before".[11] Yet, Minneapolis would prove to be an unexpected challenge. Opened in 1885 as the Hennepin Theater for live performances, the theatre became the Lyceum in 1905, and was remodeled and renamed the Lyric in 1908. Three years later, in September 1911, Roxy reopened the

Lyric for the season, hoping to replicate the Alhambra's success by again implementing an all-film policy.[12]

Minneapolis would not succumb as easily as had Milwaukee. Motion pictures had already offended local reformers, while the city's legislators looked upon movie theatres as dangerous fire hazards – or worse. As Roxy would later recall of his early days in the city, "Everyone was antagonistic to pictures", including the clergy, police, merchants, and the city's educators:

> My first task was to find the reason for this dislike. After days of questioning, after being openly insulted for my interest in pictures, and many discouragements from every side, I found that Minneapolis had been flooded with sensational, objectionable film, and that a wave of protest and indignation had followed. The parasites who seek "easy money" with no thought of the future had descended upon the city, reaped a harvest by catering to the baser natures, and then fled, leaving in their wake a seething cauldron of outraged dignity, shattered ideals, religious uprisings and moral protest. … The theatre was opened with a program of morally enlightening pictures. I was obliged to adopt this policy and stick to it tenaciously.[13]

For its reopening on 18 September 1911, Roxy installed a $2,500 pipe organ, a concert grand piano, and the all-women Fadette Orchestra of Boston. He also presented a variety of soloists along with the newly formed Lyric Quartet.[14] All of this was provided for a ticket price of between ten and twenty cents at the 1,700-seat theatre – roughly the same cost as the city's cheaper nickel and dime houses and dramatically lower than the Lyric's prices when operated as a legitimate theatre.[15] Roxy's new staff included footmen, pages, matrons, and female ushers who courteously assisted all patrons during the four daily ninety-minute shows.[16] The staff, like that at any Roxy theatre, was given a military-style inspection each day. Roxy personally inspected every seam, glove, cap, collar, hem, head, and fingernail, making certain that his employees were ready to receive their patrons.[17] This was not at all typical of 1911-era movie houses, but was an attempt to incorporate the high standards of legitimate theatres into this new entertainment world, an effort for which Roxy's previous military training proved essential.

Roxy refurbished the Lyric Theater as well, elaborately decorating the stage and screen. And with uneven projection in theatres across the city (and throughout the country), the Lyric's "Daylight Pictures" were now intended to encourage repeat attendance, attract women, and boost perceptions. Elsewhere, palms, flowers, and an electric fountain prominently graced the entryway.[18] "The two large audiences that thronged into the Lyric last night gasped a little in astonishment at the changes that have been wrought in the once familiar playhouse", the *Minneapolis Journal* added after the opening night premiere. "The process of rearranging the theatre to make it the home of 'motion pictures de luxe' has resulted in a brilliant success. The arrangement of the stage, the light effects and the refurbishing in evidence everywhere combine in what may be described as an artistic triumph".[19] Several Minneapolis newspapers quickly repeated Roxy's claims that the Lyric was now the "finest picture show in America".[20]

Roxy was discerning in his selection of films, viewing each one in advance before agreeing to its exhibition. This, too, was a departure, signaling that exhibitors should be programmers and not just projectionists and bookers. Four reels were chosen for each performance from a selection of scenics, travelogues, educational pictures, dramatic stories, historical films, and comedies.[21] Not only did Roxy determine the accompanying music, he even exerted a measure of authorial control through editing, in some cases eliminating entire scenes.[22] Celluloid shipped to Roxy, was, in his mind, merely a rough draft; Roxy considered himself every film's final editor. Nor was his control over the live performances at the Lyric any less stringent, insisting upon daily rehearsals for his musicians, dancers, and other performers to ensure consistency in both quality and content.[23]

Building community/*The Passion Play*

Roxy began his community-building efforts at the Lyric by presenting a screening of *The Star Spangled Banner* (1911) to the Boy Scouts in late September. Hailed by the press as "a champion of the Boy Scout movement", Roxy addressed the crowd on the subject of signaling, drawing from his Marine Corps experience.[24] Thus, an appeal to children was part of the Lyric's approach. "Probably never in the amusement history of Minneapolis has an enterprise made such a marked impression as has [sic] the Pictures de Luxe at this theater", the *Minneapolis Tribune* commented. "Mr. Rothapfel's 'The Star Spangled Banner' last week" was "one of the finest things ever produced here on any stage".[25] Roxy also reached out to and joined the city's businessmen's club, hosting the annual "Elks' Night" at the Lyric.[26] He further made sure that his theatre's charitable efforts were well publicised in local newspapers.[27] *Moving Picture World* journalist James McQuade observed that Roxy's efforts were "so keenly appreciated by prominent people in that city, that club members, both ladies and gentlemen, are exerting their influence to support him, and other people of influence go to the expense of printing circular letters and mailing them to acquaintances and business men".[28]

With the promise of filmic material suitable for middle-class audiences in an increasingly socially acceptable venue, many of Minneapolis's once reluctant citizens were transformed into Lyric patrons. "Best of all", the *Tribune* added, "parents feel certain that the entire atmosphere ... will be clean".[29] *Motion Picture News* noted that "clergymen had gone again and again to the theatre, and always there greeted them the same clean, healthy atmosphere, both on the screen and in the physical appearance of the house".[30] As Reverend James W. Cool wrote to Roxy, "A man who will brave the chance of losing money rather than pander to the lower tastes should receive the support of every citizen interested in the welfare of humanity".[31] Roxy further appealed to the city's clergy with an elaborate presentation of *The Passion Play* – one of Roxy's first Christmas pageants – exhibited four times a day between 18 December and Christmas.[32] To highlight its importance, the presentation was framed in a dramatically different manner than the continuous performance model operative in most other contemporary movie theatres. Mimicking the format of opera houses and legitimate theatres, Roxy closed the doors at the beginning of each show and, as Robert Grau noted, was "uncompromising in demanding that the same rules that prevail for grand opera (in seating the audience at the start of the show and forbidding an exodus while the curtain is up) must be observed".[33] The feature film was accompanied by "Holy City" and other melodies performed by twenty boy vocalists as well as the Lyric's in-house musicians and singers.[34]

The 1,700-seat theatre was repeatedly sold out during that week and had to turn away many seeking tickets. Roxy remarked that the exhibition had "done more to gain him a prominent place in picturedom than any other presentation".[35] By cementing the Lyric's relationship to Christmas, Roxy had proven the movie house to be a worthy secular institution capable of honoring the traditional and the sacred. For Roxy the Jew, this event demonstrated once more that the audience for what others pejoratively characterised as "dirty movies" could be expanded greatly if motion pictures could provide meaningful entertainment and uplift in keeping with mainstream Christian life and values. This was a lesson he would long remember and later employ at theatres such as Radio City Music Hall, where his Christmas pageants continue more than seventy-five years after his death.

The success of *The Passion Play* in 1911 served a more narrowly tactical purpose as well – it was Roxy's retaliatory strike against recently voiced concerns about the safety of movie theatres. Only a month earlier, the city's most influential newspaper, the *Tribune*, had attacked all forty-seven motion picture theatres in Minneapolis as unsafe. (Only one, the Elite, had in fact been declared a fire hazard by the city).[36] Extravaganzas like *The Passion Play*, though, enabled Roxy to demonstrate the quality of his musicians, his interest in cultural and spiritual uplift, and his ability to attract the middle- and upper-class audiences he needed to make the Lyric, and motion pictures, a cross-cultural and multi-class form of entertainment. The popular acclaim for *The Passion Play* served to distinguish the Lyric from other movie houses in the city, while also elevating those same theatres by generic association. To close the Lyric now, after *The Passion Play*'s success, would be the equivalent of closing a secular cathedral.

Roxy left little to chance, though, and a few weeks later invited Minneapolis's fire chief and a group of firemen to be his guests at a special screening of images of the New York City Fire Department.[37] The following month, the Fire Marshall, along with the City Building Inspector and the City Electrician, sent a signed report to the *Tribune* arguing that the city's theatres were indeed "safe and sanitary, and as well safeguarded against panic and fire as any class of public buildings in the city".[38] "I would advise any exhibitor to mix freely in local affairs", Roxy would later remark. "It is a wonderful power for good".[39]

The Lyric raises prices and class distinctions

Roxy's next move was to increase the Lyric's ticket prices, further separating the theatre from Minneapolis' smaller houses while also intensifying class distinctions within the auditorium. Although matinees were still ten cents, evening prices were increased to twenty cents for the "ground floor" and twenty-five cents for box seats – a signal to the middle and upper classes that securing premium seats at the city's largest movie theatre was now a privileged activity.[40] These tickets had an exclusivity of both price and location that made them attractive to those who needed to demonstrate their affluence and position in society. Sitting in a box seat at the Lyric quickly became a form of social plumage – something previously unheard of in Minneapolis.

One of Roxy's more esteemed box-seat patrons was a forty-one-year-old Swedish immigrant, Governor Adolph Olson Eberhart, who reportedly made "regular weekly visits". The governor may have found in motion pictures, and in Roxy's presentations thereof, the same cultural uplift and advocacy of Americanisation and assimilation that appealed to the Lyric's growing, multi-ethnic audience.[41] Roxy wrote to Eberhart on 6 January 1912, inviting him to see a newsreel of the latter's trip east, alongside the presentation of William Selig's film, *Cinderella* (1912).[42] The governor accepted the invitation and the Lyric's organist serenaded him with a song written in his honour.[43] Roxy's campaign to convert legislators into moviegoers was part of his efforts against local censorship and other related concerns then being discussed in the state legislature.[44] Eberhart was so taken with the Lyric and motion pictures that he was chosen as a keynote speaker at the first convention of the Motion Picture Exhibitors League of Minnesota.[45]

It had taken just four months for Roxy to make the Lyric and its motion pictures a cultural institution in Minneapolis. The success of *The Passion Play* and films such as *Cinderella*, as well as the scenics, educational films, and travelogues he presented, had brought the theatre and Roxy acclaim among the region's reformers, clergy, politicians, educators, businessmen, and women. The cultivation of the city's female population, though, was perhaps Roxy's most important victory, as it assured the theatre a growing audience of women *and* children. The following letter, from a female patron of the Lyric published in the *Minneapolis Tribune*, demonstrates the rapid change in viewpoint: "For one hour and a half one can be very much benefited and rested", Mrs. J.K. noted:

> The pictures on the screen are delightfully free from coarse suggestions. The songs and music are elevating. One is never afraid something is coming next to disgust you either in seeing or hearing. The Bible scenes and history of the same are surprising, and certainly an education for people who cannot understand the Bible by reading. ... Parents and children will do well to patronize this theater.[46]

In late April 1912, *Moving Picture World* noted that so-called "cultured" women of Minneapolis – members of the Thursday Study Club, the Authors' Study Club, the Pathfinders, the Prospect Park Study Club, the Utopian Club, and the Shakespeare Club – had embraced the Lyric and its multi-reel films.[47] University professors and an increasing number of civic leaders also patronised the theatre.[48] By 1913, a study conducted by the *Minneapolis Tribune* reported that out of ten thousand local families surveyed, 6,653 were now going to the movies.[49]

From the Manger to the Lyric

Roxy continued to count on the goodwill and publicity generated by religious-themed films in 1913, announcing the presentation of Kalem's *From the Manger to the Cross* (1912) as his Easter special. Roxy invited the city's clergy to a private screening to engender their support and promotion of the film on the Lyric's behalf.[50] Rev. Ulysses S. Villars, pastor of the Prospect Park Methodist Episcopal Church, wrote to Roxy after attending the advance screening:

> As you know, we were enthusiastic over the "Passion Play", but to my mind there is no comparison to be made between the two. I have great confidence in your judgment and "good taste", but I confess I was not prepared for such a reverent, sympathetic and appreciative presentation of the life of Our Savior as is shown in these pictures. I wish I could be as sure of the good effect of the sermons we preach as I am of this remarkable production. As I have opportunity I am urging my friends to attend, for all, clergy or laity, must be impressed and inspired by it. ... I feel that you have added greatly to the debt the people of this city owe you.[51]

In September 1913, after being elected to the Minneapolis University Club and to its Civic and Commerce League, Roxy left the Lyric for new opportunities in New York City, where, at the Regent and Strand theatres, he would cement his national reputation.[52] His management of those theatres – and their public embrace by multi-class audiences and the popular and trade press –contributed further to the rebranding of motion pictures and motion picture theatres as culturally, socially, and morally acceptable institutions. All of these New York theatres, however, were operated on the model Roxy had created between 1911 and 1913 in Milwaukee and Minneapolis.

Conclusion

Roxy's efforts to generate public support for what he was creating at the Lyric between 1911 and 1913 would foreshadow the work of film exhibitors, producers, and distributors throughout the 1910s to craft a new identity for the cinema, one that would be fully realised during World War I when movie houses were deemed "an essential business" by the United States government. The movie theatre, no longer seen by elites as a venue solely for the promotion of vice and sin, would become a popular, if still contested, public sphere where audiences engaged both with the content on the screen and with each other. Socialist or capitalist, business owner or laborer, the movie house would become a venue for all.

The Lyric is almost entirely forgotten today – even in Minneapolis – and typically glossed over in contrast to Roxy's later work. But his efforts there and in Milwaukee demonstrate that the gentrification of the movie house was often less architectural than it was social and cultural.

It is high time, then, that Minneapolis's Lyric be given its due rather than passed over as a mere stop along the way to Roxy's New York successes in film and, later, radio, music, and stage productions. It is also essential in understanding the rise of producers specialising in prestige, feature-length films like Famous Players, that we more strongly consider the role of film exhibition and film exhibitors in providing a home for multi-class product in multi-class theatres. The Alhambra and Lyric established new venues for multi-reel films and classical music. These film-only theatres formed a burgeoning network of deluxe motion picture venues that began changing the way film was exhibited and perceived in cities across the United States. New York's Regent and Strand theatres would later expand and more soundly promote their own innovations, but it was Roxy's pivotal work in the Midwest between 1911 and 1913 that created the model for the next two decades of American and even global deluxe film exhibition.

Acknowledgements: Special thanks to Martine Brownley, Keith Anthony, Jeffrey Lesser, Danielle Bobker, and the 2010–2011 Fellows at Emory University's Fox Center for Humanistic Inquiry for their contributions to the revision of this article.

Notes

1. Born Samuel Lionel Rothapfel, Roxy dropped the "p" from his last name in 1920.
2. "A Progressive Exhibitor", *Moving Picture World* (hereafter *MPW*) (2 September 1911): 618.
3. For more information on "Daylight Pictures" in Los Angeles – and Roxy's influence upon the "technology" and trend – see Jan Olsson, *Los Angeles Before Hollywood: Journalism and American Film Culture, 1905 to 1915* (Stockholm: National Library of Sweden, 2009).
4. Advertisement for Family Theatre, *The Forest City News* (13 October 1910): n.p.
5. Reprinted in Larry Widen and Judi Anderson, *Milwaukee Movie Palaces* (Milwaukee: Milwaukee County Historical Society, 1986), 43–44.
6. "At the Theater", *Milwaukee Daily News* (14 June 1911): 6.
7. "At the Theater", *Milwaukee Daily News* (16 June 1911): 6.
8. "Week at the Theaters", *Milwaukee Daily News* (17 June 1911): 7.
9. Jas. S. McQuade, "Chicago Letter", *MPW* (12 August 1911): 366; "Brevities of the Business", *Motography* (August 1911): 100.
10. "Lease Fehr, Lyric", August 1911, Group II, 239, Contracts, Shubert Archive, New York.
11. Martin Miller Marks, *Music and the Silent Film* (New York: Oxford University Press, 1997), 92.
12. "This Week at the Local Theaters", *Minneapolis Tribune* (24 September 1911): 19.
13. "How an Exhibitor Made Good", *Motion Picture News* (10 January 1914): 20.
14. "The Week at Local Theaters", *Minneapolis Sunday Tribune* (hereafter *MST*) (17 September 1911): 18; advertisement for Lyric Theater, *Minneapolis Journal* (hereafter *MJ*) (17 September 1911): 9; "Amusements", *MJ* (17 September 1911): 10; "On Vaudeville Stages", *MJ* (17 October 1911): 12.
15. "Promissory Notes about Local Bills of the Week", *MJ* (24 September 1911): 9.
16. "Pictures de Luxe Open at Lyric Next Week", *Minneapolis Tribune* (10 September 1911): 18.
17. Jas. S. McQuade, "The Belasco of Motion Picture Presentations", *MPW* (9 December 1911): 798.

18. Ibid., 797.
19. "The New Grand Draws A Throng", *MJ* (19 September 1911): 12.
20. "The Week at Local Theaters", *MST* (17 September 1911): 18; advertisement for Lyric Theater, *MJ* (17 September 1911): 9; "Amusements", *MJ* (17 September 1911): 10; "On Vaudeville Stages", *MJ* (17 October 1911): 12.
21. McQuade, "The Belasco of Motion Picture Presentations", 797.
22. "This Week at the Local Theater", *MST* (15 October 1911): 26.
23. Advertisement for Lyric Theater, *MJ* (24 September 1911): 9.
24. "Sheehans in 'Bo, Girl'", *MJ* (28 September 1911): 12.
25. "This Week at the Local Theaters", *MST* (1 October 1911): 21.
26. "Elsie Janis as a Slim Princess", *MJ* (13 October 1911): 20.
27. "'Busy Izzy' Comes Back", *MJ* (31 October 1911): 16.
28. Jas. S. McQuade, "Staging the Passion Play", *MPW* (30 December 1911): 1055.
29. "This Week at the Local Theaters", *MST* (5 November 1911): 28.
30. "How an Exhibitor Made Good", *Motion Picture News* (10 January 1914): 20–21.
31. Letter quoted in W. Stephen Bush, "The Art of Exhibition", *MPW* (12 December 1914): 1512.
32. Untitled, *MJ* (23 November 1911): 16; "A Few Moments With The Truthful Press Agents", *MJ* (10 December 1911): 14. Numerous *Passion Plays* were produced during cinema's early years; it is unknown which version was shown at the Lyric. See Roberta E. Pearson's entry on "biblical films" in Richard Abel (ed.), *The Encyclopedia of Early Cinema* (Routledge: New York, 2005), 98–101.
33. Robert Grau, *The Theatre of Science* (New York: Broadway Publishing Company, 1914), 290, 291.
34. McQuade, "Staging the Passion Play", 1055.
35. "This Week at the Local Theaters", *Minneapolis Tribune* (17 December 1911): 30.
36. Jas. McQuade, "Minneapolis Situation", *MPW* (25 November 1911): 631.
37. "Diva as a Bootblack", *MJ* (28 December 1911): 4.
38. "Minneapolis Houses Officially Approved", *Motography* (February 1912): 60.
39. "How An Exhibitor Made Good", 20, 21.
40. McQuade, "The Belasco of Motion Picture Presentations", 798.
41. Ibid., 797; see also "Adolph O. Eberhart" in Robert Sobel and John Raimo (eds), *Biographical Directory of the Governors of the United States, 1789–1978*, vol. 2 (Westport, Conn.: Meckler Books, 1978), 785–786.
42. S.L. Rothapfel to Gov. A. O. Eberhardt [sic], January 6, 1912, Box 63, A. O. Eberhart Papers, Minnesota Historical Society, St. Paul, Minnesota.
43. "Diva As A Bootblack", *MJ* (28 December 1911): 4; "Governor at Lyric Tonight", *MJ* (12 January 1912): 16.
44. S.L. Rothapfel, "The League and the Exhibitor", *Motion Picture News* (22 August 1914): 23.
45. "Minnesota Organized in Convention", *Motography* (14 September 1912): 193.
46. Letter from Mrs. J. K., *Minneapolis Tribune*, reprinted in Jas. S. McQuade, "Chicago Letter", *MPW* (2 March 1912): 761.
47. "Rothapfel Resigns Management of Lyric", *MPW* (11 May 1912): 612. Roxy left the Lyric in the summer of 1912 to work for the Shuberts, but returned to the Lyric after the Saxe chain took over its operation.
48. Jas. S. McQuade, "Chicago Letter", *MPW* (31 May 1913): 906.
49. "Statistics from Minneapolis", *MPW* (28 February 1913): 771.
50. "Story of Christ in Moving Pictures", *MJ* (27 April 1913): 8:10.
51. Jas. S. McQuade, "Chicago Letter", *MPW* (31 May 1913): 906.
52. "The Stage", *MJ* (17 August 1913): 8:7; "Moving Pictures", *MJ* (14 September 1913): 8:10.

PART VII

Community and the Public Sphere

33

"This Splendid Temple": Watching Movies in the Wanamaker Department Store

Caitlin McGrath

All went well at the beginning of our visit to Dufayel. ... At the entrance to the store a man wearing a braided cap asked us if we wanted to see the "cinema". ... The Grands Magasins Dufayel were in the forefront of progress. ... The free cinema was another of their daring innovations. ... Scarcely had we taken our seats than the room was plunged into darkness. A terrifying machine shot out a fearsome beam of light piercing the obscurity, and a series of incomprehensible pictures appeared on the screen, accompanied by the sound of a piano at one end and at the other a sort of hammering that came from the machine. I yelled in my usual fashion and had to be taken out. ... So my first encounter with the idol was a complete failure. Gabrielle was sorry we had not stayed. The film was about a big river and she thought that in a corner of the screen she had glimpsed a crocodile.
Jean Renoir, *My Life and My Films*[1]

Born in 1894, the child Renoir was at the time presumably somewhere between the ages of five and ten, placing these remembered events likely between 1899 and 1904. As such, Renoir's anecdote offers a vivid record of the role of department stores as exhibition sites during cinema's earliest years. While Lauren Rabinovitz, Anne Friedberg, and others have written on the affinity between early cinema and department stores, there has been little attention paid to the actual practice of screening films within the stores themselves.[2] As a first step toward elaborating this history, I will examine the uses of cinema in the Wanamaker department stores in Philadelphia and New York. The Wanamakers' commitment to the emerging medium is remarkable both for how sustained as well as how varied it was, beginning with the installing of motion picture technology in both their Philadelphia and New York stores in 1907. To provide an overview of the variety of motion-picture situations the stores generated, I will divide them into four categories.

The first of these comprises screenings similar to those Renoir described, consisting of already-existing films, like travelogues, that were shown as part of a lecture series. Then there were actualities that were shot specifically for the store's use, the result of expeditions or teams dispatched to record topical events. Third, and sometimes overlapping with the second category, were films that the store made about itself as promotional material. And lastly, commercially produced fiction films were shown as part of the store's anniversary programs, often celebrating historical figures.

Two letters testify to the uses of film in the stores, and, being written eight years apart, give a sense of developments in the stores' film programming. The first, dated 1 June 1908, appeared as an "unsolicited testimonial" in Charles Urban's 1909 General Catalogue of Classified Subjects, and is a letter to Urban signed "J.K. Dixon, Lecturer and Demonstrator to John Wanamaker".[3] In it Dixon praises Urban's motion picture cameras and projecting Bioscopes, both of which he used "in the New York and Philadelphia auditoriums of the Wanamaker Stores, each of them seating about two thousand people, with great success". He praises the films themselves, stating "We have also purchased from the Kleine Optical Company a great many reels of your educational films, and I may say with a good deal of enthusiasm that I do not know of any motion picture films that can touch yours within a thousand miles". The last line of the letter is also intriguing; there he writes, "I have been using your motion picture camera for the purpose of carrying on my educational work in chronicling historic events here and we have had tremendous success, turning away thousands of people". There are a number of key details here: first, the fact that educational work was going on within a commercial enterprise; second, that Dixon not only screened purchased films, but also himself shot films for the store's use; and lastly that the programs were so successful that they were turning people away from a lecture hall that seated (by his estimation) two thousand people.

In the second letter, dated 14 June 1916, H.H. Kaeuper, Director of Education at the Philadelphia store, writes to George Kleine expressing his dismay at hearing that there were no more Kleine catalogues available and that no reprints would be made. "Your catalog, which I saw in the office of the librarian of the Bureau of Education, Department of the Interior, Washington, interested me more than any other, and I was most eager to have a copy".[4] Kaeuper's title of "Director of Education", as opposed to Dixon's "Lecturer and Demonstrator", implies a more established, purposeful educational division at the store by this time. Indeed his letter goes on to confirm this, "We are particularly desirous of finding films that will effectively supplement classroom work in history, geography, and general school and commercial subjects". These two letters provoke a series of questions. What was the purpose of having an educational institution within a commercial establishment? Did Wanamaker's have dedicated classroom space within the store? Who was taking classes there? A brief look at how John Wanamaker envisioned the social function of both his New York and Philadelphia stores will help frame this early turn to cinema for educational and uplifting purposes.

In *The Golden Book of the Wanamaker Store*, a two-volume set published between 1911 and 1913 lauding the stores' various successes, Wanamaker stated his desire for his stores to function as public museums.[5] A cynical view of the *Golden Book* might characterise it as a tome of self-promotion in the guise of history; however, it does contain valuable insights into Wanamaker's aims for his stores. A typical device is to quote some unknown source speaking about the stores and then expand on the idea. For example "'To give people the things they want is not enough for the Wanamaker stores,' was recently written; 'They must be a leader in taste—an educator.'... They go a step farther ... and present exhibitions and lectures by men of national reputation, in Science, History, Literature, Art and Music. ... Educative exhibits of art and life and history have been part of the Wanamaker purpose from the beginning".[6]

For Wanamaker, every aspect of business was to be held to the highest standard, which for him was heavily influenced by his own Christianity. He saw the stores' educational function as part of his efforts to give back to his community. Understanding this mindset helps explain the early move to use the most modern and effective tools possible to educate both his workers and the general public. For Wanamaker, images were paramount in this mission, perhaps not surprising for a man whose stock in trade was in display; cinema, then, was an obvious choice. On the use of the Philadelphia store's Egyptian Hall specifically (which seated anywhere from fourteen hundred to Dixon's claim of more than two thousand), Wanamaker proclaimed that it would be neither a "door mat to publicity, [n]or the noisy tongue of advertising" and indeed it seems clear that Wanamaker's hopes were for a venue for visual education.[7]

In New York, the Wanamaker Auditorium was an even more impressive hall, boasting seating for fifteen hundred.[8] Designed more like a theatre, it was three stories high with a gallery above the main floor and an arched stage. Beyond these auditoria's uses for public lectures and performances, they were also put into service for the education of store employees, to which end Wanamaker founded the John Wanamaker Commercial Institute at the turn of the century. Begun initially to educate the young boys working in the Philadelphia store, the Commercial Institute quickly expanded to include the girls and night classes for the slightly older boys, and by 1908, became the American University of Trade and Applied Commerce (Figure 1). It is likely that Kaeuper was trying to obtain Kleine's films for the American University classes.

As we know, this use of cinema for the purpose of moral uplift was very much a contemporary concern in 1907, with Jane Addams at Hull House perhaps its best known advocate. Wanamaker was clearly influenced by the reformist mission to prioritise cinema as a means of instruction for the general public as a counter to the medium's alleged invidious influences. Dixon's status as a lecturing educator moving between the New York and Philadelphia stores also echoes the work of traveling exhibitor Lyman Howe, whose career similarly valorised the educational potential of the motion picture. What was unusual about Wanamaker's, however, was the articulation of uplift within a commercial establishment.

As Dixon's letter to Urban indicates, by June 1908 the public lecture series was already well underway. Film screenings seem first to have been established in the Philadelphia store in 1907, with Dixon serving from the start as in-house lecturer and demonstrator. Dixon's appointment was arranged in January 1907, at which time he was working for George Eastman.[9] So eager was Wanamaker to have Dixon start at the store that just ten days after writing to confirm his employment, he wrote Dixon again inquiring if there were any way, without of course offending or upsetting Mr. Eastman, that he might start earlier. Wanamaker's impatience speaks to both his heavy involvement in the store's educational activities as well as his recognition of the importance of a structured visual education component to the larger mission of the store.

The first instance of cinema's use at Wanamaker's seems to have occurred in the annual Christmas celebrations later that year. Advertised for 24 December 1907, "Christmas Entertainments" were to be a mixture of organ playing, singing, readings, and two moving pictures.[10] *The Story of the Teddy Bears* is undoubtedly Edwin S. Porter's film of the same year; *Kris Kringle* is unknown. Although *The "Teddy" Bears* is familiar, it is worthwhile to reconsider it in the context of its Christmas screening inside a department store, where surely the craze for "teddy" bears was well-established and the toys likely for sale.

The appeal of the department store as a screening space doubtless lay in its difference from nickelodeons, not only in size but in tone as well. With auditoria seating nearly two thousand people, both the Philadelphia and New York stores would have offered viewing environments quite different from those of storefront nickelodeons (Figure 2). But beyond just the difference in physical space, the clientele likely would have

Fig. 1.

Classrooms for the John Wanamaker Commercial Institute. From J.H. Appel, The Golden Book of the Wanamaker Stores: Jubilee Year, 1861–1911.

come from a different social class as well. In a letter to one of the New York store's event organisers, Dixon outlines tactics for soliciting the right kind of audience. Dixon states that people who have the time to wait in line for tickets are unlikely to be the audience to whom the store should be catering, so perhaps the organisers should consider sending out invitations to select members of New York society, requesting to know how many tickets they would like, rather than operating on a first-come, first-served basis.[11]

After his first two years with Wanamaker, Dixon's role began to shift as he became more involved in the work for which he is now most famous – his support of Native American rights. Between 1908 and 1913, Dixon was in charge of the photography and filming on three expeditions into Indian territory. The first two expeditions, in 1908 and 1909, resulted in two films made with Native Americans – one actuality, one fiction. *The Last Great Indian Council* (1908) was a record of the meeting of the remaining living chiefs as well as scenes of daily life. *Hiawatha* (1909) was a visualisation of Longfellow's poem using Native Americans as actors, and received heavy play in both

33 "This Splendid Temple"

Fig. 2.

Egyptian Hall, used as a piano salesroom and an auditorium for concerts and educational lectures.
From J. H. Appel, The Golden Book of the Wanamaker Stores: Jubilee Year, 1861–1911.

stores. The third expedition, in 1913, dubbed the Expedition of Citizenship, took Dixon to over 150 reservations with a Declaration of Allegiance, with the aim of obtaining signatures from all the chiefs. With these signatures Dixon hoped to convince the U.S. government that Native Americans were willing to be considered members of the nation and deserved the rights and privileges of American citizenship. After this, Dixon continued to work for Wanamaker's, but more as a traveling educator than attached to either store. He gave regular lectures at the Wanamaker's Native American Exhibit at the 1915 San Francisco Exhibition and documented Native American involvement in the military through the 1920s.

For Wanamaker, film was a means of both recording historical events and engaging with technological modernity. He would boast of having sent a team from his Paris office in 1909 to film the first ever aeronautic meeting, images of which were brought immediately back to the Philadelphia and New York stores, along with one of the planes, for viewing as part of a public lecture. In May 1910, King Edward VII's funeral pageant was shown in the Egyptian Hall "a full week before any other moving pictures of the event reached America".[12] Wanamaker was keen to be at the forefront of all new technologies, boasting the first rooftop wireless and the first in-store radio station. The stores placed themselves at the cutting edge of the use of cinema as a means of reportage, filming things worthy of public attention not only because of their educational and informative appeal, but also because these events, like the variety of flying machines in Paris and the massive crowds attending the royal funeral, were visually striking.

In March 1908, the in-store publication, *The Anniversary Herald*, began to advertise what would become Wanamaker's most screened film, *The Midnight Ride of Paul Revere*.[13] Like *The "Teddy" Bears*, this is likely the Edwin S. Porter film from the previous year, and also like *The "Teddy" Bears*, *Paul Revere* was extensively publicised. Beginning in the New York store and then moving to Philadelphia until at least the end of April, Dixon gave lectures on Paul Revere, usually twice a day. The film was listed as a part of this presentation, and was shown at the end of Dixon's lecture, the text of which was reproduced in the *Anniversary Herald* toward the end of the film's run. On 7 April, a synopsis of the film was printed under the heading "Paul Revere's Ride: As Shown In The Motion Pictures In Egyptian Hall". The text is quite detailed, describing individual shots and quoting periodically from the Longfellow poem ("One if by land, two if by sea", etc.). It seems this synopsis was included in the store's daily paper both as an enticement to shoppers and also as a kind of advertisement for Wanamaker's role as public educator. The end of the synopsis goes to some lengths to illustrate the importance of this film when it was shown in the New York store:

> These pictures were shown, together with Dr. Dixon's lecture, twice each day, for four weeks, in the Auditorium of the New York Store, which was crowded to the doors, and thousands were unable to gain admittance. Educators and statesmen, school teachers and old soldiers, all pronounced it the most beautiful and inspiring motion picture they had ever seen, and gave it a surprising meed of praise. The school board of Brooklyn sent their schools in daily sections with teachers, simply because of the spirit of patriotism inculcated by the lecture and motion picture, and offered a prize to the pupils of their schools for the best essay on Paul Revere's Ride.

Of course motion pictures were also used to advance the stores' commercial aims, in a manner that seems more familiar. The Paris Bureau filmed models posing in gowns: "By the courtesy of a distinguished courier, Wanamaker's were [sic] even able to show in a cinematograph film how a Parisienne chooses and tries on her gowns in a Paris Salon".[14] Wanamaker's was not alone in showing fashion films for its clientele. On 10 May 1913, Gimbel's of New York was written up in the *New York Review* for an upcoming screening: according to the article, titled "Kinemacolor Arranged for Ladies Only: Moving Color Pictures Made of Gimbel's Lingerie Display", the film *La Parisienne Elegante in her Boudoir* was to demonstrate the "correct manner of wearing the latest styles of French lingerie". It is unclear what exactly was so complicated about French knickers that an explanatory film was required, but apparently this was part of the draw. As the article describes, "For this fashion display Paris has sent her loveliest and most novel specimens of under-apparel". The review itself acts as a kind of tease for those who would be barred from entering; namely men. "Women are shown the correct method of donning a corset, while the putting on of a vest, chemise and billows of fairy-like gauzes, laces and filmy stuffs, some of them duplex, some of them single, all of them a mass of mysterious ruffles and fluffles and foam, are shown by nearly a score of beautiful models".[15] These brief excerpts are likely just the tip of the iceberg of a larger history of cinema's use for such commercial purposes.

Further research will surely expand our understanding of film's place in department stores. While it would not be until the classroom films of the 1920s that educational cinema truly gained a foothold, the department store promises to open up a rich area for further exploration into cinema's manifold uses as a tool for the uplift and edification of its audiences. Specifically, the space of Wanamaker's, run by a man driven to serve the public as well as the dollar, contains many lessons about the varied, sustained, and spectacular uses of cinema as an educational tool.

Acknowledgements: I would like to thank Ellen Sieber at the Mathers Museum, Indiana University, for her enthusiastic support for this project. The digitisation of the Wanamaker materials at the Mathers has been invaluable in facilitating further research into Dixon's filmmaking among Native-American tribes.

Notes

1. Jean Renoir, *My Life and My Films* (New York: De Capo Press, 1974), quoted in Colin Harding and Simon Popple (eds), *In the Kingdom of Shadows: A Companion to Early Cinema* (London: Cygnus Arts, 1996), 11.
2. See Anne Friedberg, *Window Shopping: Cinema and the Postmodern* (Berkeley: University of California, 1993); Lauren Rabinovitz, *For the Love of Pleasure: Women, Movies, and Culture in Turn-of-the-Century Chicago* (New Brunswick, NJ: Rutgers University Press, 1998); and Leo Charney and Vanessa R. Schwartz (eds), *Cinema and the Invention of Modern Life* (Berkeley: University of California Press, 1995).
3. Early Rare British Filmmakers Catalogues, reel 7 (London: World Microfilms Publications, Ltd., 1982).
4. Educational Films 1916, 1920–30 folder, Container 18, George Kleine Papers, Manuscript Division, Library of Congress.
5. J.H. Appel, *The Golden Book of the Wanamaker Stores: Jubilee Year, 1861–1911* (Philadelphia: John Wanamaker, 1911), 285. The goals Wanamaker expressed for his stores seemed to focus on the Philadelphia store primarily, but we know that the New York and Paris stores were also seen as key in this larger mission of education.
6. Ibid, 238.
7. Ibid, 265. It is difficult to know exactly how many were seated in the hall during events. *The Golden Book* quotes the number fourteen hundred, but Dixon claims more than once that they seated over two thousand. Because the seating was temporary (folding chairs) it is conceivable that the seating capacity fluctuated. Also, in some of the surviving photographs of the space, there are a fair number of standing viewers lining the rooms that surely were not part of the "official" count.
8. Unlike the Philadelphia store's Egyptian Hall, the Wanamaker Auditorium in New York was a dedicated screening space, with fixed seating, so the seating capacity is more concretely known.
9. "I duly received your letter and confirm the engagement with you at Three Hundred Dollars per month, to take up work in the Photographic Departments of our New York and Philadelphia stores, especially in conjunction with Mr Wilson in Philadelphia". Letter from Wanamaker to Dixon, 5 January 1907, Box 13, Personal Correspondence, Wanamaker Papers, Pennsylvania Historical Society (hereafter WP).
10. Christmas Entertainments pamphlet, 1907, Box 77, Store Promotional Materials, WP.
11. Letter dated 1 April, 1909 from Dixon to M. J. Chapman, MMUS – WD – Folder 40, Wanamaker Collection of Photographs of American Indians, Indiana University.
12. *The Golden Book*, 244.
13. *Anniversary Herald* (7 April 1908): 2, Box 77, Store Publications, WP.
14. *The Golden Book*, 199.
15. "Kinemacolor Arranged for Ladies Only", *The New York Review* (10 May 1913); clipping in Charles Urban Papers, National Media Museum, Bradford; URB 3/1, 18.

34

"Boost Your Town in the Movies": Municipal Film Companies in the United States, 1910–1917

Martin L. Johnson

In May 1910, Watterson R. Rothacker partnered with Carl Laemmle of the Independent Moving Picture Company and R.H. Cochrane of the Cochrane Advertising Company to establish the Industrial Moving Picture Company in Chicago, Illinois.[1] The Industrial Moving Picture Company was the first of many companies founded in the early teens that specialised in advertising films. Many of these films were not advertisements for products, but rather for cities and towns seeking to attract new industries and residents. Identified in *Moving Picture World* and local newspapers as *booster films*, *municipal advertising films*, or *industrial romances*, these films were sponsored by local business organisations interested in promoting the attractions of their town or city. If the companies that produced municipal advertising films are to be believed, these films were subsequently exhibited in hundreds of cities throughout the United States. Based on this claim, Stephen Bottomore has suggested that municipal advertising films – made with the expectation they would primarily be seen by audiences elsewhere – should not be considered "local" films made for local viewing.[2] My research has shown, to the contrary, that most municipal advertising films *were* exhibited in local movie theatres, and I have found little evidence to suggest that these films received distribution elsewhere, counter to the production company's assertions. Indeed, I assert that municipal films were, in fact, a form of local film: hybrid between the "local views" popular in the early cinema period and narrative fiction films that were dominant by the early 1910s. Many producers of municipal films helped expand the definition of the "local" film to include narrative and fictional elements, which allowed this mode of production to adapt to the changes in mainstream film production taking place at the time. To explore the origins of the municipal advertising film, I focus on the work of the Paragon Feature Film Company of Omaha, Nebraska, one of the most prolific producers of municipal films in the 1910s.

In July of 1915, the poet Vachel Lindsay saw a municipal advertising film produced in his hometown of Springfield, Illinois, by Paragon. In *The Art of the Moving Picture*, published later that year, Lindsay called the film, titled *The Mine Owner's Daughter*, a "mediocre photoplay" but a "social-artistic event" nonetheless.[3] What Lindsay saw in *The Mine Owner's Daughter* was a film that connected local society – the son of the governor of Illinois played the lead in the film – with the interests of local businesses. As I review in detail in the remainder of the chapter, Paragon's municipal advertising films were hybrids in several ways. First, although produced and screened locally, the municipal sponsors of these advertising films expected that their films would be seen elsewhere. Second, the films blended an original fictional plot with nonfiction scenes of a town's natural and industrial resources. Third, Paragon's films combined the logic of the local view of early cinema, which privileged the pleasure of seeing oneself on screen, with that of the local film of the transitional era, which also incorporated the pleasures of seeing local people and places.

Before discussing the municipal advertising film and its business, let me review the context in which municipal advertising films were produced and exhibited. Early municipal films were commissioned by business leaders in search of novel ways to advertise their city. Although western expansion and speculative land investors had fueled regional, state, and municipal promotion for decades, by the turn of the twentieth century a new phase in self-promotion was well underway.[4] Illustrated pamphlets – long the standard form of publicity – were replaced by a multitude of advertising materials, from mass-produced booklets to full-page advertisements in general interest magazines and newspapers, including special souvenir illustrated newspapers that could be sent by post to prospective investors but also distant relatives, family who had moved away from home. Advertising agencies began to take on accounts for local governments and business organisations, and produce full-scale campaigns for regional and national events, such as national expositions and trade shows. By the time the city business publication *Town Development* was established in December 1909, scores of people identified themselves as town promotion "experts", many of whom had backgrounds in advertising. This development mirrored the general shift at the time to professional town planning and standardised municipal practices.[5] By convincing growth-obsessed civic and business leaders that a town could be advertised just like any other product, these experts encouraged the flourishing of municipal promotional campaigns. The overall development toward such specialised publicity schemes set the scene for a unique type of local film: the hometown booster story.

The origin of the local film is coterminous with cinema itself. The human subjects of the experimental films produced by the Cinématographe or Biograph were also among the first spectators to "see themselves" in the cinema. When the Lumière Company began touring their Cinématographe in 1896, operators routinely produced "local views" near the places of exhibition, and re-exhibited some of these views in other places, making the "local" a relational, rather than determinative, attribute of a film. Even as film producers made advancements toward narrative films over the next decade, the local view maintained a relatively consistent part of film programs. American Vitagraph included local views and event-oriented local topicals in its programs in 1904 and 1905, and itinerant exhibitors like Lyman H. Howe continued to film passers-by in front of exhibition locations in order to increase ticket sales.[6] The nickelodeon boom, quickly followed by the construction of purpose-built movie theatres, allowed exhibitors to localise the physical location of cinema experience, and audience demand for quick program turnover may have obviated exhibitor interest in outlaying the capital to produce local views.[7] By March 1909, seeing oneself in the movies had become unusual enough that the *Los Angeles Herald* reported the production of a local film on the front page.[8]

In the early teens, some audiences were offered new attractions through local films that drew upon emerging fiction film narrative conventions. Standardisation of film programs, the nascent star system, and the formation of distribution networks allowed cinema to emerge as a truly mass medium. While the nickel show was, as Miriam

Hansen has suggested, a physical space where diverse groups mingled, it also existed as an imaginary space shared by people across geographic and national boundaries. Michael Warner has argued that the salient quality of a public is the "reflexive circulation of discourse".[9] The possibility of imagining mass circulation beyond the locale of local films changed the character of their mode of reception. People continued to delight at seeing themselves and their town for narcissistic reasons, but the knowledge that they might be seen by strangers elsewhere proved to be very appealing. Other genre developments, such as newsreels and educational films, persuaded producers and sponsors of the viability of a wider audience for moving images of their city.

In the early teens, some municipalities, such as Redlands, California, purchased cameras to make local films.[10] Most cities, however, were approached by or contracted with one of a handful of industrial film companies to produce a film of their town. Many of these companies were based in Chicago, including the Industrial Moving Picture Company, the Tisdale Industrial Film Company and the Advance Motion Picture Company. A number of regional producers of municipal booster motion pictures existed, including the Scenic Film Company in Atlanta, Georgia, and the Magnet Film Manufacturing Company in Evansville, Indiana. In addition to advertising in *Moving Picture World*, these companies also pitched their services in municipal trade journals such as *Town Development* and *American City*, and were also the subject of several feature articles in these publications about the "town boosting" movie phenomenon.[11] Chambers of Commerce and Advertising Clubs were particularly susceptible to new and unusual methods of self-promotion, and the comparatively low cost and high potential of a motion picture convinced many organisations to sponsor films. As *Town Development* noted in its very first issue, published December 1909, the principal fear of a booster group was that their town would not be "on the map" of the manufacturers, railroad companies, and investors who would choose their fates.[12] Appearing in the movies was one way to be discovered.

The first municipal advertising films created by these companies were nonfiction views of local industries, scenery and townspeople. In the Fall of 1911, for example, the Carolina Ad League hired the Industrial Moving Picture Company to produce a film of cities and farm lands for exhibition locally, and to visitors of the upcoming National Corn Exposition in Columbia, South Carolina.[13] The league paid one thousand dollars – roughly the equivalent of twenty-thousand dollars today – for the production and duplication of two reels of films, which were meant to give a citizen "a chance to look at actual life in the cities of his own State, views of historic spots, factories, parks, residence streets, business streets".[14] While the league planned for these films to be exhibited theatrically, they also budgeted for the purchase of two projectors so the films could be screened at fairs, expositions, and sites where theatres were not available. The organisation's proposal assumed that audiences would be willing to pay ten cents admission to view scenes of their state, and that the admission money would fund the production of new films and other expenses. As A.W. McKeand, the head of the Carolina Ad League, put it in one article, "One hundred thousand people, looking at Carolina pictures in Carolina at 10 cents each, would give $10,000 in cash. Does it not look easy?"[15] While the municipal film had a local appeal, its draw was not just self-recognition, but also what I have elsewhere called place-recognition.[16] Many booster campaigns targeted local residents, who commercial clubs felt needed to be persuaded to stay put in a period of constant migration. Municipal advertising films thus had a dual task of presenting the attractions of a place to visitors and residents alike. The Carolina campaign demonstrates how the local audience was often the most important one for municipal film sponsors.

> **PARAGON FEATURE FILM COMPANY**
> INCORPORATED
> MAKERS OF
> **COMMERCIAL MOTION PICTURES**
> (WITH A PLOT)
> WOODMEN OF THE WORLD BLDG.
> **OMAHA, NEB.**
> Nov-23-14.

Fig. 1. Paragon's letterhead noted its films were made "with a plot". Courtesy of the Bancroft Library at the University of California at Berkeley.

Other companies soon joined the municipal film field. In February 1911, the Advance Motion Picture Company was founded in Chicago, and within three years was successful enough to increase its capital stock from two thousand dollars to one hundred and fifty thousand dollars.[17] In March of that year, Horatio F. Stoll, a California correspondent for the *Moving Picture World*, noted an advertising scheme in the West where Chambers of Commerce sponsored the production of advertising films for exhibition in the state's theatres.[18] In September 1911, the Industrial Film Syndicate, which was based in New York, produced a motion picture in Des Moines, Iowa, and filmed President William Howard Taft's visit to the city.[19] By October 1911, the production of city booster films was so commonplace that *Moving Picture World* reported that "this idea of picturing cities the motion picture way is becoming quite popular throughout the West, and the Advance Motion Picture Company", one of several industrial firms based in Chicago, had landed many contracts to do so.[20]

Paragon features: local films "with a plot"

Another important development in the municipal advertising film was the use of fictional and narrative conventions. A shift away from the simple presentation of views and actualities and toward narrative plot was soon common in other types of local film, too. The Paragon Feature Film Company was perhaps the largest company specialising in the production of municipal films "with a plot", as their company letterhead put it (Figure 1). Paragon – no relation to the New Jersey studio of the same name – produced dozens of films in towns and cities across the Midwest and South in the mid-1910s. The company's director, Oliver William Lamb, was both the lead salesperson and supervised the production of Paragon's films, hiring cinematographers and even script writers to assist in the making of his films. Unfortunately, very little is known about Lamb; publicity and documentation of him and Paragon vanish after 1917. However, Lamb's films in the previous few years were covered in great detail in local newspapers, in large part because they were produced at the behest of leading business organisations.

Paragon's films were relatively expensive propositions, with booster clubs spending one thousand dollars or more on a film's production. Prominent members of local society were cast in the leading roles, while crowd scenes made up only a small part of the finished product. Full plot summaries of Paragon films were printed in local newspapers, along with accounts of film production and exhibition. Booster organisations attempted to make back their initial investment through local theatrical screenings, and it was not uncommon for a two- or three-reel Paragon film to receive a week's run in its home city.[21] Lamb promised cities that their films would go on the Universal Exchange, and would be seen in 182 cities across the country before its film was

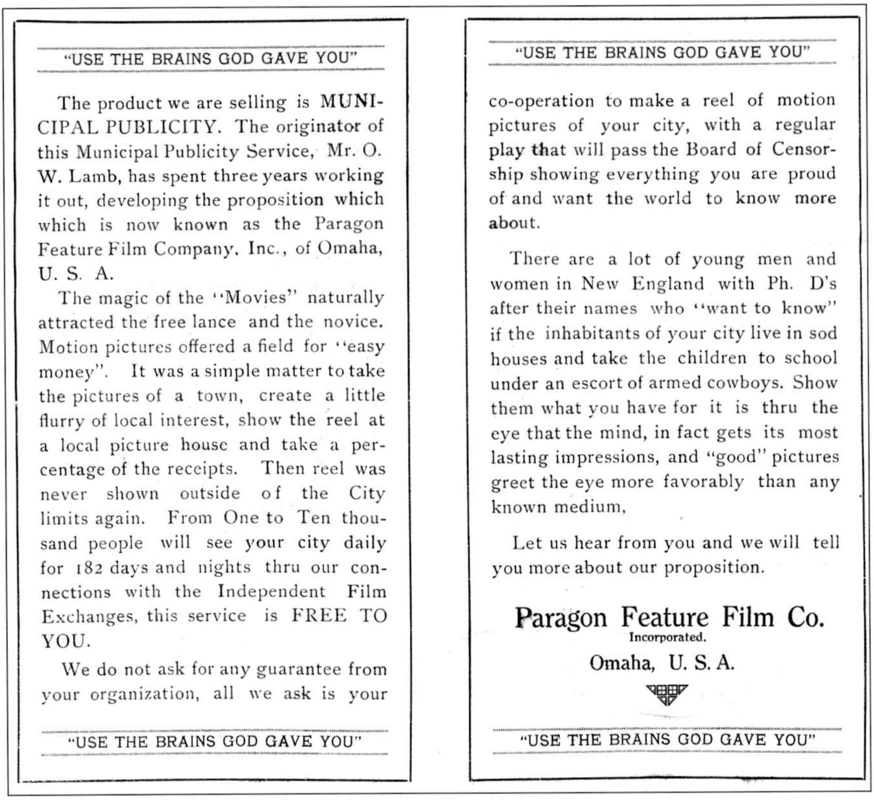

> "USE THE BRAINS GOD GAVE YOU"
>
> The product we are selling is **MUNICIPAL PUBLICITY**. The originator of this Municipal Publicity Service, Mr. O. W. Lamb, has spent three years working it out, developing the proposition which which is now known as the Paragon Feature Film Company, Inc., of Omaha, U. S. A.
>
> The magic of the "Movies" naturally attracted the free lance and the novice. Motion pictures offered a field for "easy money". It was a simple matter to take the pictures of a town, create a little flurry of local interest, show the reel at a local picture house and take a percentage of the receipts. Then reel was never shown outside of the City limits again. From One to Ten thousand people will see your city daily for 182 days and nights thru our connections with the Independent Film Exchanges, this service is FREE TO YOU.
>
> We do not ask for any guarantee from your organization, all we ask is your
>
> "USE THE BRAINS GOD GAVE YOU"

> "USE THE BRAINS GOD GAVE YOU"
>
> co-operation to make a reel of motion pictures of your city, with a regular play that will pass the Board of Censorship showing everything you are proud of and want the world to know more about.
>
> There are a lot of young men and women in New England with Ph. D's after their names who "want to know" if the inhabitants of your city live in sod houses and take the children to school under an escort of armed cowboys. Show them what you have for it is thru the eye that the mind, in fact gets its most lasting impressions, and "good" pictures greet the eye more favorably than any known medium.
>
> Let us hear from you and we will tell you more about our proposition.
>
> **Paragon Feature Film Co.**
> Incorporated.
> Omaha, U. S. A.
>
> "USE THE BRAINS GOD GAVE YOU"

Fig. 2. Paragon promotional brochure. Courtesy of the Bancroft Library at the University of California at Berkeley.

returned to the sponsoring organisation. While other municipal film production companies produced narrative, fictional films in this period, and other home-talent filmmakers produced narrative fiction films in their home city, Paragon was a particularly consistent and prolific producer of narrative fiction local films between 1913 and 1916, and received considerable coverage in the trade press for their efforts. While only three of Paragon's films are known to survive today, the newspaper articles about the company's films suggest that the company incorporated progressively more complex narrative and fictional techniques over its four years, rather than Lamb starting with a finished script when he created the company.

Paragon's earliest films in 1913 were merely tours of a city following five or six local young women, or, as Lamb termed them, "pilgrims" in Kansas City, Kansas, and several other Midwestern cities, as they visited the city's sights. Keeping with the tradition of the local view, the company published a shooting schedule in the newspaper, so one could easily observe, or avoid, the filming of select scenes. By 1914 Paragon had changed its approach to the production of booster films. When the company signed a contract with the Business Men's League in Montgomery, Alabama, Lamb had his "scenario expert" write a plot that featured a reenactment of Jefferson Davis's inauguration as the President of the Confederacy. In this fictional film, titled *Past and Present in the Cradle of Dixie*, a group of businessmen from the North come to Montgomery to witness the reenactment of Davis's inauguration. After touring local sights and industries, one of the visitors, Bertram C. Lawton, falls in love with Southern belle Elinore Harrison, who is described in a plot summary printed in the *Montgomery Advertiser* as the "beauteous link of the chivalrous past and the dreaming present".[22] Unfortunately, the past is not dead, as Elinore's grandfather, a Colonel in the Civil War, refuses to allow his granddaughter to marry a Northerner. The couple agrees to break off their wedding plans, but, soon after, a fire breaks out in the Colonel's home. Lawton races to the Colonel's house, and saves the life of Elinore's grandfather, who then blesses the marriage.

This tidy ending reconciles both Montgomery's past with its present and suggests that the future of the city lies in greater economic and cultural ties between New England and points west and south. In a company brochure Lamb claimed that the purpose of his films was to counteract regional prejudices (Figure 2). For example, he told potential clients that "there are a lot of young men and women in New England with Ph.D.'s after their names who 'want to know' if the inhabitants of your city live in sod houses and take the children to school under an escort of armed cowboys".[23] In actual fact, many of Paragon's films played to local audiences by incorporating stock scenes of municipal advertising into a fictional narrative – shots of factories, local landmarks, and prominent civic and business leaders. Lamb apparently thought such shots of the municipality would prompt local citizens to locate themselves in the emerging conventions of popular cinema as much as in local histories. By contrasting the historical, and often generic, with the contemporary, and often industrial, Lamb distinguished the fiction of rural areas' representation in mainstream cinema from the fact of their material aspirations.

Lamb's skill at blending the tropes of the local film, the municipal advertising film, and narrative fiction films are also apparent in one of two known surviving Paragon films, *The Blissveldt Romance*, which was produced in September 1915 in Grand Rapids, Michigan. Instead of contrasting North with South, this film compares rural and city life. The film opens in Jennison, Michigan, a small town a few miles outside Grand Rapids. John Graham, who lives in Jennison, is offered a job to work at a bank in Grand Rapids. He leaves behind his girlfriend Lizzie Johnson, who works at the Blissveldt dairy farm. When John arrives to the train station in downtown Grand Rapids, he is so overwhelmed by the city that he is struck by a car when he tries to cross the street. The driver of the car, the urbane and wealthy Amelia Brown takes him to her palatial estate and nurses him back to health. Within a few days John asks Amelia's father if he can marry his daughter, but is turned down. Fortunately for John, the mansion soon catches fire, as mansions tend to do in Paragon films, and John saves Amelia from death, thereby convincing her father to allow the marriage to go forward. Many municipal advertising films featured weddings as an integral part of a narrative in which a couple meets and tours local businesses and industries.

However, *The Blissveldt Romance* takes an unexpected turn, one that reveals the difficulty of making a film that both has local appeal and is interesting enough to receive distribution. Back in Jennison, Lizzie reads of John's nuptials in the Grand Rapids newspaper. She gets on a horse, not in a car, and heads to town to find John. In the next scene, she stops the horse and gets out a telescope, which she uses to find John in the crowd. As well as showing her finding John, the matte shots also show the crowd scenes for which local films are best known. People waving to the camera are not simply waving to Lizzie, but directly to the audience in Grand Rapids, too. By integrating these crowd scenes into the narrative of his film, Lamb is able to produce a film that the business sponsors believe will have appeal to national audiences while keeping its local value. Once Lizzie locates the wedding party at an elite rowing club, she makes the brash and unexpected decision to commit suicide by jumping off a pier. This scene is unusually dark for a town promotional film, and Lamb only manages to pull off a happy ending by showing a scene of Amelia and John with their young daughter a few years later. In an effort to match the standards of popular narrative film productions, Lamb produced films aiming to transform town advertisements into a local variation of mass entertainment because the sales pitch, of course, depended on being able to imagine your local film appealing to audiences anywhere.

The production of municipal advertising films enters a stark decline after 1915. Paragon ceased operating in 1917; the Advance Motion Picture Company dissolved in 1919; surviving corporations like the Cincinnati Motion Picture Company switched to the production of other genres such as educational films.[24] Several factors likely contributed to the decline in production of booster films. First, the excesses of the 1915 Panama-Pacific International Exposition in San Francisco might have contributed. Many of the films produced by Paragon and other municipal film companies were exhibited at the Expo, supplementing the more elaborate displays states and cities usually sent to expositions and, in some cases, serving as fundraising opportunities for states that needed to raise private money to erect buildings. One observer counted seventy-seven motion picture projectors at the State and Country Halls, showing films like *Fifty Thousand Feet of Kansas* (1915), produced by Paragon and featuring 50,000 feet of film about a state with a population of just one and a half million.[25] The sheer amount of footage shot in preparation for the exposition may have exhausted business groups' enthusiasm – and budgets – for such productions. Second, the entry of the United States into World War I in 1917 captured much of the energy that went into the booster movement, and made displays of national citizenship, rather than allegiance to local causes, paramount. Finally, the consolidation and centralisation of film distribution and exhibition operations made it difficult for companies like Paragon to fulfill their promises that their films would be screened in other cities. Although local booster films seemed to enjoy a brief window around 1913 when people could at least imagine their film would be screened in theatres elsewhere, as early as March 1914 came an editorial warning in *Moving Picture World* that municipal film producers exaggerated the circulation of their films.[26] The sponsors for municipal booster films quickly lost their aspirations for national audiences. Local film producers once again had to be content to make films that created, as Lamb put it in one of his company's brochures, "a flurry of local interest" and were then "never shown outside of the City limits again".[27]

Municipal booster films existed at the intersection of two distinct developments in the early teens: the professionalization of town promotion and the emergence of the cinema as a mass medium. While town promotion specialists did not leave the same legacy as urban planners, they shared with their contemporaries a commitment to the standardisation of forms. The cinema proved to be, briefly, a fitting medium for town publicity, offering widespread distribution at a lower cost than the exposition, the booster train, or the pamphlet. The producers of municipal advertising films expanded the category of local films by making films that could potentially be seen elsewhere, but they also revealed the limits of local film production, most obviously the difficulty of getting films distributed. While local films of all genres continued to be made after the transitional era ended, after 1915 film producers rarely promised that their films would be screened elsewhere. Instead, the municipal advertising film retained just one function: showing local people themselves and the attributes of the place where they lived. The production and exhibition of municipal advertising films in the early teens helped establish both the possibilities and the limits for the local film in the transitional and classical Hollywood eras.

Notes

1. *Moving Pictures* (Chicago: Rothacker Film Manufacturing Company), an undated brochure archived at the Chicago Historical Society. While Rothacker and the Industrial Moving Picture Company are repeatedly cited as the first industrial film company, the actual date of its founding is unclear. In Arthur Edwin Krows's history of nontheatrical film, "Motion Pictures – Not For Theaters", he notes that the company was founded in the Spring of 1909. See: *The Educational Screen* (June 1939): 194. Anthony Slide dates the start of the company as December 1909 in *The American Film Industry: A Historical Dictionary* (New York: Greenwood Press, 1986), 169–170. I have chosen the May 1910 date because it is referenced in the company's own literature, is noted in *Moving Picture World* (4 March 1916, 1477), and because a notice for the company's incorporation appeared in the *Chicago Daily Tribune* (21 May 1910, 13). While Rothacker, Laemmle or Cochrane were not listed as the three incorporators, the three individuals listed – Laird Bell, Albert G. Miller, and Rudolph Matz – were attorneys, suggesting that they may have handled legal work for Rothacker.
2. See Stephen Bottomore. "From the Factory Gate to the 'Home Talent' Drama: An International Overview of Local Films in the Silent Era", in Vanessa Toulmin, Patrick Russell and Simon Popple (eds), *The Lost World of Mitchell and Kenyon: Edwardian Britain on Film* (London: British Film Institute, 2004), 33–48.
3. Vachel Lindsay, *The Art of the Moving Picture* (New York: The Macmillan Company, 1915 [Reprinted 1916]), 146–147.
4. See David M. Wrobel, *Promised Lands: Promotion, Memory, and the Creation of the American West* (Lawrence: University Press of Kansas, 2002). See also Jon C. Teaford, *Cities of the Heartland: The Rise and Fall of the Industrial Midwest* (Bloomington: Indiana University Press, 1993).
5. This movement to standardisation took place across a number of areas of civic life. See William J. Novak, *The People's Welfare: Law & Regulation in Nineteenth-Century America* (Chapel Hill: University of North Carolina Press, 1996); John W. Reps, *The Making of Urban America: A History of City Planning in the United States* (Princeton, N.J.: Princeton University Press, 1965); Marina Moskowitz, *Standard of Living: The Measure of The Middle Class in Modern America* (Baltimore: The Johns Hopkins University Press, 2004).
6. Charles Musser, *The Emergence of Cinema: The American Screen to 1907* (Berkeley and Los Angeles: University of California Press, 1983), 405 and 444.
7. Charles Musser, *Before the Nickelodeon: Edwin S. Porter and the Edison Manufacturing Company* (Berkeley and Los Angeles: University of California Press, 1991), 378–379.
8. "Moving Pictures Show Local Scenes", *Los Angeles Herald* (March 13, 1909): 1.
9. Michael Warner, *Publics and Counterpublics* (New York: Zone Books, 2004), 90.
10. One town that produced their own films was Redlands, California, where a member of the Chamber of Commerce, John H. Fisher, was also involved in the film industry. Fisher began working with Cecil B. DeMille in 1914, and served as the personal business manager for DeMille until 1926. For more about Fisher, see *Fun With Fritz: Adventures in Early Redlands, Big Bear, and Hollywood with John H. "Fritz" Fisher*, compiled by William G. Moore (Redlands, California: Moore Historical Foundation, 1986). The Redlands Chamber of Commerce's decision to purchase a film camera was reported in the *Moving Picture World* (14 February 1914): 799.
11. For example, see Leo L. Redding. "Town Boosting With The 'Movies'", *Town Development* (November 1912): 129–131.
12. *Town Development* (December 1909): 1.
13. "Meeting for Ad Club Called This Evening", *The State* (18 July 1911): 10.
14. Ibid.
15. Ibid.
16. Martin L. Johnson, "The Places You'll Know: From Self-Recognition to Place Recognition in the Local Film", *The Moving Image* 10, no. 1 (2010): 24–50.
17. *Moving Picture World* (23 May 1914): 1131.
18. Horatio F. Stoll, "Value of the Moving Pictures for Advertising", *Moving Picture World* (11 March 1911): 521.

19. "Film Company Plans to Take Motion Pictures in New Brunswick", *New Brunswick Times* (5 April 1912): 1. The company appears to have gone by at least three different names. In September 1911 the company was identified as the Independent Film Syndicate. See "Picture Films of Des Moines", *The Des Moines News* (19 September 1911): 3. But, in January 1912, the company identified itself as the Commercial Film Syndicate in a letter to the editor of the *New Brunswick Times* asking the town to participate in a series of films titled "Civic America". The letter was reprinted on the front page of the *Times*, and is referred to in the April article about the company. See "Moving Pictures Will Show Busy New Brunswick to the Rest of State and Country", *New Brunswick Times* (26 January 1912): 1. The company incorporated as the Industrial Film Syndicate in the state of New York on 31 May 1912 (New York State Division of Corporations, State Records).
20. *Moving Picture World* (14 October 1911): 133.
21. Oliver Lamb was associated with at least two other film companies before starting Paragon: the Special Event Film Company of New York, and the Special Scenic Film Company, which Lamb incorporated in Denver, Colorado on 28 April 1913. Lamb first identified himself as the head of the Paragon Feature Film Company of Denver in July 1913, when he produced *Seeing Oklahoma City*. Paragon relocated to Omaha, Nebraska, in late 1913. The company's last known film, *The Maid of the Mississippi*, was produced in October 1916.
22. *Montgomery Advertiser* (22 March 1914): 23.
23. Brochure in the business records of the Panama-Pacific International Exposition at the Bancroft Library of the University of California at Berkeley, Carton 58, Folder 21.
24. For example, Clarence Runey of the Cincinnati Motion Picture Company got out of the local film business in 1918, and instead began producing educational pictures. *Moving Picture World* (3 August 1918): 671.
25. Ben Macober, *The Jewel City* (San Francisco and Tacoma: John H. Williams, 1915), 149.
26. *Moving Picture World* (14 March 1914): 1405.
27. Brochure in the business records of the Panama-Pacific International Exposition at the Bancroft Library of the University of California at Berkeley, Carton 58, Folder 21.

Early Cinema and the Public Sphere of the Neighbourhood Meeting Hall: The Longue Durée of Working-Class Sociability

Judith Thissen

In his pioneering study of working-class recreation in industrialised America, Roy Rosenzweig emphasises continuity and the persistence of collective habits in ethnic communities despite the arrival of early movie theatres. "Moviegoing did not destroy all other forms of working-class leisure; it was simply an additional – albeit particularly important – recreational option. Working people continued to go to their saloon, church, or ethnic club".[1] Cinema's embedding within ethnic working-class culture can be explored in detail by looking at the paradigmatic place associated with the immigrant experience in America: the Lower East Side of Manhattan. Grounded in a broader analysis of Jewish communal life, I focus on the transformation of neighbourhood meeting halls into moving picture theatres to understand how the experience of cinemagoing was shaped by older patterns of working-class sociability and ethnic solidarity. This history reveals cinema's roots in the alternative public sphere of a meeting hall culture that developed during the 1880s and 1890s, thus complicating the standard presentation of the nickelodeon era in New York City.

The Lower East Side as excavation site

The Lower East Side presents the prototypical case to examine film culture in an urban working-class context. It was the social, cultural and political hub of the immigrant community of Yiddish-speaking Jews from Eastern Europe, who made up almost twenty-five per cent of the population in New York City.[2] The integration of these newcomers into the mainstream of American society coincided with the development of cinema into a national mass medium. By 1908, the "Great East Side Ghetto" was literally dotted with moving picture theatres.[3] The downtown Jewish neighbourhood had the highest density of nickelodeons in Manhattan and the movie-mindedness of its inhabitants was amply documented by contemporary accounts, ranging from human interest stories in mainstream newspapers to reports by social workers, city officials and the film industry itself.

The typical Manhattan nickelodeon, according to these sources, was a small and smelly storefront picture show overcrowded with poor immigrants – a naïve and uninhibited audience eager to learn the American way from the silver screen. Handed down by the first historians of American cinema and preserved by popular legend, this scene generated the founding myth of Hollywood's democratic nature and proletarian origins. The rags-to-riches stories of Hollywood moguls Marcus Loew, Adolph Zukor and William Fox, whose humble background and poverty-stricken youth on the Lower East Side were widely publicised, further enhanced the notion that the breakthrough of the movies as the nation's favourite commercial pastime took place at the Jewish immigrants' gateway to the promised land. From Lewis Jacobs' *The Rise of the American Film* (1939), through Robert Sklar's *Movie-Made America* (1975) and Garth Jowett's *Film: the Democratic Art* (1976) to *Working-Class Hollywood* (1998) by Steven J. Ross, the nickelodeons on the Lower East Side embodied the power of the movies to change American society from the bottom up.[4]

In the context of this volume, it is somewhat redundant to point out that research in film history since the 1980s has repeatedly challenged this biased interpretation of the pre-Hollywood era, drawing attention to the significant contributions that the middle classes made to the transformation of the cinema into a mass medium.[5] While the bulk of these studies dealt with metropolitan America, they largely ignored the specific responses of urban working-class communities to these middle-class efforts to domesticate the new film medium. Much of the so-called "revisionist" scholarship concentrates on the discourse and practices of the film industry, its allies (especially Progressive reformers) and critics (anti-vice crusaders, religious leaders etc.), but leaves out the immigrant and working class audience itself – those very people who are hailed time and again as the most fervent filmgoers in big cities. More recently, the research agenda among historians of American film has quite radically shifted to the study of cinemagoing in small-towns and rural communities in the United States. While this reorientation was much needed, it seems to go hand in hand with a wilful blindness to the fact that we still know very little about how the cinema fitted into the social and cultural structure of working-class communities in Lower Manhattan or Chicago's South Side, let alone Brooklyn or the Bronx.

To be sure, I don't argue here that we have to put New York City once again at the centre of the historiographic universe. The pitfalls of "Gothamcentrism" have been more than once convincingly explained by Robert C. Allen, pointing out that "Manhattan has long been at the epicenter of the imagined map of American movie audiences and moviegoing".[6] At the same time, by proposing to decentre historical audience studies to the American heartland, he runs the risk of throwing out the proverbial baby with the bathwater. In my view, the relation between centres and peripheries deserves more attention from film historians. For such a comparative perspective, we still need a much deeper insight into the multifaceted history of film exhibition in New York City itself. We might as well begin, then, by questioning the still stereotypical account of cinema's emergence on the mythical Lower East Side.

Around 1910, the downtown Jewish quarter in Manhattan had about thirty-five motion picture outlets – nickelodeons, family vaudeville theatres and proto picture palaces – without counting those on the adjacent Bowery and East Fourteenth Street, traditional zones of commercial entertainment in downtown Manhattan. I focus here on the history of those buildings used for film exhibition but not built as theatres. In particular, I want to document their uses and purposes before being converted into motion picture venues. This strategy of digging into the past of the actual buildings offers an empirical opening to examine how the cinema was integrated into existing cultural practices and social structures of Jewish immigrant life, thereby providing a materialist historical basis for Miriam Hansen's theoretical account of cinema's functioning as an alternative public sphere for working-class immigrants.[7]

The excavation of the material infrastructure cinema grafted itself onto reveals a double genealogy. On the one hand, was a well-known, well-documented, and rather straightforward trajectory from an existing commercial space – a store, loft or office - into a nickelodeon. On the other hand, I found buildings with a much longer and more intricate history as recreational venues – a history that has been largely overlooked by scholars of American cinema. Let me exemplify this by zooming in on the central part of the Jewish quarter, where the nickelodeons were in "such close quarters that it seems as if the spectator could not be quite sure exactly which house he was getting into".[8]

At the intersection of Rivington and Essex Street, four storefront theatres competed with each other: Charles Steiner's Essex Street Theatre (133 Essex Street), the Metropolitan Theatre (134 Essex Street), the WACO Theatre operated by the World Amusement Company (118–120 Rivington Street) and the Golden Rule Theatre (125 Rivington Street). They resembled each other strongly on the surface, in terms of their façade, advertising, and film programs. All four were storefront theatres and offered for a nickel (or a dime on weekends) a continuous show that consisted of moving pictures with "a song and a dance, as an extra", as the *Jewish Daily Forward (Forvertz)* explained.[9] None of them advertised in the Yiddish-language press. The managers only used bill-boards, handouts and posters to reach the public, which according to the ticket seller of the WACO was "entirely local, confined almost within two or three blocks".[10] Yet in one respect there was a significant difference. Before opening as a nickelodeon, the site of the WACO and the Metropolitan had been used as a bank and furniture store respectively, while young Charles Steiner had transformed his father's Essex Street stable into a picture show.[11] However, the Golden Rule Theatre stood out for a very different record. For several decades, it had been operated as a public meeting hall.

Focusing especially on the history of the Golden Rule Hall to fully grasp the dynamics of cinema's integration into immigrant Jewish life, the remainder of the chapter digs deep into the past of the building at 125 Rivington Street. It is this kind of painstaking archival work and detailed evidence, combined with broader information derived from social surveys, demographic data and cultural histories, that can help us to understand "the maddeningly complex historical dynamics" of commercial entertainment as a social and cultural force in the opening decades of the twentieth century.[12] But let's first go back to the 1880s.

The culture of the meeting halls

In the late nineteenth century, multi-purpose public halls and saloons with assembly rooms were a central institution of working-class culture and common in many immigrant neighbourhoods in urban America. They accommodated thousands of grass-roots organisations and offered an extensive infrastructure for mutual aid, social interaction and political mobilisation. In 1898, the *Trow's Business Directory* listed twenty-five halls below East Houston Street and east of the Bowery, the area which constituted the nucleus of the Jewish quarter.[13] The majority of these halls were converted tenement buildings. This was also the case with the Golden Rule Hall. Its ground floor served as multipurpose assembly room that could accommodate up to five hundred people. This main hall (25 x 100 feet/230 m^2) was rented out on a day per-day basis for a wide variety of activities, ranging from mass meetings and political rallies to masquerade balls and wedding parties. There was a saloon and dining room in the basement of the building, which was linked by stairs to the main hall. The apartments on the upper floors of the building were divided into small assembly rooms and makeshift synagogues.[14]

As a neighbourhood institution, the Golden Rule Hall provided a solid basis for immigrant grass-roots organisation. The building's core users came from two groups within the Jewish community: hometown societies (*landsmanshaftn*) and trade unions, each of which represented a different public sphere with its own formative history. What these different spheres shared however was an ethic of mutuality and reciprocity as well as a strong commitment to democracy and equalitarianism, which both saw as core values of American civic culture.

Hometown societies were mutual aid cooperatives set up by migrants coming from the same town or region in Eastern Europe. Members paid a monthly due that entitled them to sick benefits, free medical care of a physician, a burial plot, funeral arrangements, and loans in cases of financial emergencies. As providers of vital material benefits and outlets for sociability, *landsmanshaftn* were at the centre of the Jewish immigrant experience.[15] Although less important in terms of numbers, labour unions also played a key role in public life because their members consciously sought to shape public opinion on social evils associated with the immigrant condition (poverty, appalling working conditions etc.). A significant minority on the East Side was sympathetic to the ideals of socialism, and the saloon keeper who ran the Golden Rule Hall for nearly three decades was one of them. He maintained strong ties with labour leaders, radical intellectuals, and political activists. As a result, hundreds of labour-meetings and political rallies were held at 125 Rivington Street during the 1880s and 1890s. For almost a decade, the building served as the headquarters of the Jewish cloak makers' union, one of the largest unions in the garment industry.[16]

Altogether, the public sphere of meeting halls was predominantly masculine. Most Jewish immigrant women had marginal access to the daily and weekly activities of the fraternal lodges, *landsmanshaftn* and labour unions. Hometown societies typically excluded women from formal participation by restricting membership to men. Female wage-earners, mostly working-girls, were underrepresented among organised labour, except during periods of mass strikes. However, not all activities that took place in the Golden Rule Hall and other public halls were separated from the family or segregated along gender lines. Men and women attended the many balls, concerts and other festivities that lodges and unions organised during the winter season to raise money for their treasury or some charitable purpose. Dances were by far the most popular leisure-time activity. Any Saturday night from September through May, East Siders could choose from among a dozen or more "full dress and civic balls" and "masquerade balls", which were announced in the Yiddish press and by way of posters on local shop windows.[17] These benefit balls gave young and old a chance to enjoy themselves with *landslayt*, colleagues, family and friends but also reinforced the in-group cohesion and the sense of solidarity derived from the material benefits that the organisation granted to their members.[18]

In sum, throughout the late nineteenth century, public meeting halls functioned as centres of working-class sociability where immigrant Jews created a sense of dignity in trade unions, mutual aid societies and religious congregations, thereby taking full advantage of their newly acquired American civil liberties. The culture of the meeting halls gave rise to a collective spirit of independence and grass-roots democracy as well as new forms of organisation and sociability. It led to the formation of a public sphere that remained profoundly Jewish and distinct from the dominant WASP model, but absorbed at the same time many influences from the surrounding American society, especially notions of egalitarianism and voluntary association. At stake is what happened to this alternative public sphere when cheap commercial entertainment began to colonise the East Side meeting halls.

The commercialisation of working-class leisure

In the opening decade of the twentieth century, the entertainment preferences of immigrant Jews rapidly shifted from predominantly non-commercial recreational activities towards cheap commercial amusements. The process is exemplified again by looking at the main hall on the ground floor of 125 Rivington Street, which was successively turned into a commercial dance hall (around 1900), a Yiddish vaudeville theatre (1905), and a moving picture house (1907).

In the context of increased competition and severe restrictions on the liquor trade, following the introduction of the Raines Law in 1896, many East Side hall managers and saloonkeepers turned their ground floors or adjacent rooms into commercial dance halls or dance academies open to all who paid admission.[19] In 1901, a social worker of University Settlement Society counted thirty-one commercial dance halls in the central part of the downtown Jewish quarter.[20] The Golden Rule was one of them. Under its new management, selling commercial leisure became the hall's core business. In 1904, the first two floors of the building were consolidated into one large dancing hall with a balcony that contained tables and chairs for patrons to relax. The upper floors remained in use as small meeting rooms and synagogues, but there was no longer space downstairs for mass meetings, sponsored balls and other large scale not-for-profit activities. Most revealing in respect to the hall's new function and its intended clientele is the information that the building application provides about the sanitary facilities in the new dance hall. Prior to the renovation, the Golden Rule Hall lacked special facilities for female visitors. After the renovation, women were accommodated with ladies' toilets on the first and second floors of the dance hall. These new restrooms reflect the growing participation of women in public life that was fostered by the emergence of new forms of commercial leisure.[21]

In 1905, the manager of the Golden Rule Hall took up the latest trend in Jewish ethnic entertainment by switching to family vaudeville in Yiddish. The dance hall was turned into a makeshift theatre with a small stage and dressing rooms in the basement, and subleased to a vaudeville company led by Abraham Tantzman, a veteran comedian-actor of the Yiddish legitimate stage. On Friday, 1 September 1905, the 250-seat Golden Rule Vaudeville Theatre opened its doors, promising prospective customers "first class variety: sketches and *vodevils* by the greatest dramatists and actors".[22] Shows were given every night, with matinee performances on Saturdays and Sundays (the bill changed on Friday night). Admission prices ranged from 10 to 25 cents. A year later, the Lower East Side and Brooklyn boasted about a dozen Yiddish family vaudeville houses. "Today every important street has its glaring sign which announces 'Jewish Vaudeville House' or 'Music Hall,'" a contemporary observer noted.[23] With the exception of the People's Music Hall on the Bowery, all were converted meeting halls.

The emergence of Yiddish *myuzik hols* signalled the beginning of a profound transformation of the theatrical infrastructure and paved the way for the nickelodeon boom.[24] However, moving pictures did not become a regular feature in this ethnic version of family vaudeville until 1906–07. Initially, pictures were presented by self-acclaimed professors who operated as itinerant film exhibitors and toured the local Yiddish vaudeville circuit with their own projector and a set of films. In September 1905, for instance, one professor Mayer appeared at the Irving Music Hall on Broome Street, and, two weeks later, at the People's Music Hall on the Bowery ("an extra just for this week: Prof. Mayer's moving pictures").[25] The following year, Mayer became a more or less regular feature on the bill of Irving Music Hall, while a competitor by the name of professor Gold frequently presented his moving picture program at the Grand Street Music Hall.[26]

Before we examine how the cinema developed into the most popular leisure-time activity on the East Side, we need to address the question if and how Yiddish music halls incorporated elements of the earlier public sphere of the meeting hall culture. For that we need to get a sense of the ways in which Jewish immigrant audiences engaged with this new form of commercial entertainment. Put differently, did the music halls develop into an arena for political expression and the articulation of alternative cultural and social values? As Miriam Hansen has eloquently argued, the variety format offers structural conditions around which "working-class and ethnic cultures could crystallise, and responses to social pressures, individual displacement, and alienation could be articulated in a communal setting".[27] Vaudeville acts and sing-alongs encouraged a participatory mode of reception and active sociability between audience members. In addition, the use of Yiddish certainly reinforced feelings of belonging to an immigrant community with shared values and a communal history. More importantly, perhaps, Yiddish vaudevillians – very much like today's stand-up comedians – often tapped into the current political affairs for their material, addressing strikes, immigration policies etcetera, as well as the everyday hardships of tenement life and sweatshop work.[28] In combination with the participatory quality of the variety format, these acts permitted the audience to demonstrate their commitment to notions of equalitarian democracy and nurture a different interpretation of "America" than that of the nation's vested social and cultural authorities. This is exactly what explains the anti-vaudeville discourse articulated by conservative forces and progressive reformers alike. Back in 1849, the Astor Place Riots had already shown that the rowdy behaviour typical of working-class theatre audiences might under certain conditions lead to more overt political action. Uricchio and Pearson make the point clearly: "The specter of labourers and immigrants liberated from the regimentation of the workplace and congregating freely to revel in crude, vicious and lascivious entertainments struck fear into the hearts of many Americans, who saw little difference between a mob of strikers and the unruly patrons of cheap amusements".[29] As a result, the repeated efforts on the part of moral uplifters and city officials to strictly regulate working-class leisure and impose a discipline of silence on working-class audiences.[30] The struggle for middle class hegemony took a new turn when the cinema began to conquer the allegedly "underdeveloped" and "easily excitable" minds of the masses, immigrants in particular.

In November 1906, the Golden Rule Theatre was one of the first music halls to switch to moving pictures as its main fare. However, live entertainment was not entirely abandoned. In between the films, when the reels were changed, vaudevillians continued to divert the audience with skits, jokes, songs. The new format was an instant success. The *Views and Films Index* reported in the summer of 1907:

> The Golden Rule Theatre, 125 Rivington Street, New York City, had a record of 4,038 patrons to their theatre on Saturday, 13 July. On Saturday, July 20th, 3,356, and during the past weeks the average has been 14,000 tickets sold. The seating capacity is not quite 300.[31]

Within a year, the weekly take of the 300-seat Golden Rule Theatre had mounted to $1,800, according to *Variety*.[32] Other entrepreneurs quickly copied this success formula. Yiddish music hall managers invested in film projectors and incorporated movies permanently into their programs. Dozens of newcomers also tried their luck in the booming nickelodeon business. Moving picture shows "are spreading like mushrooms after the rain", the *Jewish Daily Forward* reported in May 1908.

Cinema and working-class sociability

In the 1910s, cinema soon became the nation's primary form of popular entertainment.

35 Early Cinema and the Public Sphere of the Neighbourhood Meeting Hall

Lavish picture palaces were built to attract a "better class" of patrons and dissociate the experience of moviegoing from its roots in working-class culture. The aesthetics and content on screen were also gentrified to conform to middle class taste and notions of respectability. In particular, filmmakers increasingly sought to enhance the viewer's absorption in the imaginary flow on the screen in order to impose a discipline of silence on the movie audience and make the viewing experience an individual experience rather than a collective one.[33]

Despite these radical changes in film style and ideological orientation, film exhibitors on the Lower East Side continued to report boom conditions. The most enterprising among them entered into partnerships with more affluent investors to expand their activities by building new medium-sized movie theatres. By the end of the decade, a large locally-owned independent chain operated more than a dozen medium-sized "photoplay houses" on the Lower East Side alone and had a near monopoly over the business of moviegoing in Jewish working-class New York. A pivotal figure in this M & S circuit was Charles Steiner, who had started out in 1908 around the corner from the Golden Rule Hall. In 1914, his old Essex Street nickelodeon gave way to the brand-new Palace Theatre (133–135 Essex), which seated six hundred. A year later, he renovated and enlarged the WACO Theatre on behalf on the M & S circuit. In the early 1920s, the Golden Rule Theatre closed its doors, but this was not a sign of market saturation. The opening of the 600-seat Ruby Theatre in 1925 brought the total seating capacity in the immediate vicinity of the intersection of Essex and Rivington Street to eighteen hundred (an increase of 50 per cent compared to 1910). Well into the 1930s, independent film exhibitors like Steiner drew their patronage from that segment of the public that could not afford to pay much more than a nickel or a dime for an evening's entertainment. In other words, Mike Gold's "Jews without money" made up the bulk of their clientele.[34]

Like in the case of Yiddish vaudeville, the key question is the extent that cinema continued to provide a basis for manifestations of class and ethnic solidarity. There is no simple answer. Clearly, the shift from locally-produced live entertainment to motion pictures – an "imported" industrial entertainment product – meant that the programs in Jewish neighbourhood theatres were to a considerable degree shaped from the outside by corporate capitalist forces that sought to eliminate all class distinctions to create a standardised homogeneous commodity that could be consumed across social, ethnic, and cultural boundaries.[35] However, at the same time, there is ample evidence to suggest that the social experience of the cinema remained a profoundly working-class and Jewish experience because entrepreneurs and audiences alike resisted top-down efforts to control the local entertainment business. On the basis of my empirical research, then, I call into question the prevailing notion that cinema in the United States successfully ensured the integration of socially and ethnically differentiated audiences into a national mass audience. Let me demonstrate this in further detail by returning once again to the Lower East Side to explore how the cinema sustained Jewish working-class sociability.

Movie theatres in the Jewish quarter catered primarily to first and second generation immigrants who lived or worked nearby. By and large, they maintained popular prices and egalitarian seating policies. With the exception of a handful of neighbourhood picture palaces, like Loew's Avenue A and Delancey Street theatres, there were no ranks and all patrons who entered at a particular moment paid the same price. Prices varied according to the moment of admission. During the nickelodeon era, the admission was five cents except on weekend nights and public holidays, when exhibitors charged ten cent to profit from the increased demand. The low admission fee gave women and children unprecedented access to cheap amusement and thus enhanced the neighbourhood character of the audience. Housewives broke up their daily routine to sneak into the storefront around the corner. During day-time when business was slow, managers would let customers stay as long as they liked. Visiting the East Side nickelodeons in 1908, a reporter from the *Forward* remarked:

> You may ask: who has the time to go to see moving pictures during the day? Actually, during the day it is not that busy. In fact, during the day it is another trade, as the owners would say. As most customers are women and children, it resembles very much the women's section in a synagogue. They gossip and eat sunflower seeds.[36]

Mothers often brought their smallest children with them. Typically, daytime photographs of nickelodeons show empty baby strollers in front of the box office. Candy store owners complained in the Yiddish press that their business was suffering from the motion picture craze because children saved their pennies to go to the nickel theatre.[37]

Because patrons often knew each other, the movie theatre was a homey place where one could chat with one's neighbours and friends. There was no effort to ensure a discipline of silence. Neither the managers nor their patrons cared much about gentile codes of respectability. Although the architecture and interior furnishing of the larger neighbourhood movie theatres offered the trappings of bourgeois culture, this was merely a matter of decoration and a suggestion of luxury without the pressures of having to behave like a middle-class American. Snacks, sweets, fruits and drinks were peddled inside and outside all theatres on the East Side. Tiny dairy restaurants such as Ratner's and Yonah Shimmel's knish bakery – "original since 1910" – opened near movie theatres to provide the moviegoing crowd with inexpensive kosher refreshments.

Film exhibitors made sure that their clients got an entertainment program attuned to local taste. Well into the 1920s, live entertainment ranging from Yiddish vaudeville to performances by Cherniavsky's Hasidic-American Jazz Band gave moving picture shows on the East Side a distinctive Jewish flavour. Features with a Jewish theme or star who had a Jewish or alleged Jewish background were guaranteed box-office hits. These films were often independent productions or imported from Europe. In general, working-class Jews preferred comedies, serials, sensational melodrama and stories with an unhappy "Russian ending". Whenever film exhibitors had some say in what they obtained from their exchange, they would favour these genres.

Conclusion

In the early 1900s – before the nickelodeon – market forces increasingly penetrated the leisure culture of working-class communities in New York City and profoundly altered its traditional structure, which had been governed by strong ties between recreation, mutual aid, and labour activism. While the impact of this commercialisation process on social life should not be underestimated, it is also important to acknowledge that pre-existing ideals of reciprocity and solidarity persisted within the realm of commercial entertainment, thus reinforcing the emancipatory potential of cheap amusements like the cinema, especially in respect to women and the poorest among the working-classes. From the days of the nickelodeon well into the early sound era, East Side Jews successfully resisted the hegemonic efforts to standardise film exhibition and reception. Their passion for the cinema was an expression of their commitment to an American mass culture that cut across class, religious and ethnic lines. In this respect, they did not differ from the Jews who ran the major Hollywood studios. At the local level, however, the social experience of the cinema was not only inscribed in mainstream consumer patterns but also defined by the legacy of the early immigrant public sphere of the meeting halls. As a result, in the neighbourhood movie theatres on the Lower East Side the capitalist logic of individual consumption never fully prevailed over the logic of ethnic community building and the strife for a more democratic social order.

Notes

1. Roy Rosenzweig, *Eight hours for What We Will: Workers and Leisure in an Industrial City* (New York: Cambridge University Press, 1983), 216.
2. For example, see Irving Howe, *The World of Our Fathers: The Journey of the East European Jews to American and the Life they Found and Made* (New York: Harcourt Brace Jovanovich, 1976; reprint Schocken 1990); Moses Rischin, *The Promised City: New York's Jews, 1870–1914* (Cambridge, MA: Harvard University Press, 1962); Gerard Sorin, *A Time for Building: The Third Migration, 1880–1920* (Baltimore: John Hopkins University Press, 1992).
3. For a detailed map, see Ben Singer, "Manhattan Nickelodeons: New Data on Audiences and Exhibitors", *Cinema Journal* 34, no. 3 (1995): 10.
4. Lewis Jacobs, *The Rise of the American Film: A Critical History* (New York: Harcourt, Brace and Company, 1939); Garth Jowett, *Film: The Democratic Art* (Boston: Little Brown, 1976); Robert Sklar, *Movie-Made America: A Cultural History of American Movies* (New York: Random House, 1975); Steven J. Ross, *Working Class Hollywood: Silent Film and the Shaping of Class in America* (Princeton: Princeton University Press, 1998).
5. The notion of cinema's proletarian foundation was first challenged in the late 1970s by Russell Merritt and Robert C. Allen: Merritt, "Nickelodeon Theaters, 1905–1914: Building an Audience for the Movies", in Tino Balio (ed.), *The American Film Industry* (Madison: University of Wisconsin Press, 1976), 59–79; Allen, "Motion Picture Exhibition in Manhattan, 1906–1912: Beyond the Nickelodeon", *Cinema Journal* 18, no. 2 (Spring 1979): 2–15.
6. Robert C. Allen, "Decentering Historical Audience Studies: A Modest Proposal", in Kathryn H. Fuller-Seeley (ed.), *Hollywood in the Neighborhood: Historical Case Studies of Local Moviegoing* (Berkeley: University of Los Angeles Press, 2008), 20. Another example of Allen's argument is "Manhattan Myopia; or Oh! Iowa!", *Cinema Journal* 35, no. 3 (Spring 1996): 75–103.
7. Miriam Hansen, *Babel & Babylon: Spectatorship in American Silent Film* (Cambridge, MA: Harvard University Press, 1991), especially chapter 3.
8. Quoted in *Views and Films Index*, 25 December 1909.
9. "Vu zaynen ahingekumen di yidishe myuzik hols?", *Forward*, 24 May 1908.
10. *Views and Films Index*, 25 December 1909. In 1902, the Tenement House Department found that almost ten thousand people (1,800 families) lived in the four blocks forming the intersection of Rivington and Essex streets. The residential density in the immediate vicinity exceeded 900 persons per acre.
11. Office of the City Register, Pre-1917 Conveyances, Section II, liber 154 cp 222 and liber 157 cp 445 (1906); liber 179 cp 43 and liber 180 cp 25 (1908). Office of the City Register, Pre-1917 Conveyances, Section II, liber 137 cp 269 (1905). Bureau of Buildings, City of New York: Annual Ledgers for Alterations and New Construction, Alteration Docket for Manhattan 1908, application no. 83.
12. Allen, "Manhattan Myopia", 99. See also Richard Maltby, "How Can Cinema History Matter More?", *Screening the Past* 22 (2007).
13. For a description, see John M. Oskison, "Public Halls of the East Side", *Yearbook of the University Settlement Society of New York* (1899), 38–40; Kathy Peiss, *Cheap Amusements: Working Women and Leisure in Turn-of-the-Century New York* (Philadelphia: Temple University Press, 1986), 17–21.
14. Bureau of Buildings for the Borough of Manhattan, lot-file B358-L22 at the New York City Municipal Archives and Records Center (hereafter NYC-MARC).
15. Daniel Soyer, *Jewish Immigrant Associations and American Identity in New York, 1880–1939* (Cambridge, MA: Harvard University Press, 1997). A comprehensive survey carried out in New York

16. Abraham Cahan, *Bletter fun mayn leben* (New York: Forward Association, 1926–1931); Bernard Weinstein, *Fertsig yohr in der yidisher arbeyter bavegung* (New York: Farlag veker fun sotsyalistishen farband, 1924).

17. Belle L. Mead, "The Social Pleasures of the East Side Jews", MA thesis (Columbia University, 1904), 16.

18. Soyer, *Jewish Immigrant Associations*, 105.

19. For a detailed analysis, see Judith Thissen, "Liquor and Leisure: The Business of Yiddish Vaudeville", in Joel Berkowitz and Barbara Henry (eds), *Inventing the Modern Yiddish Stage: Essays in Drama, Performance, and Show Business* (Detroit: Wayne State University Press, 2012).

20. Verne M. Bovie, "The Public Dance Halls of the Lower East Side", *Yearbook of the University Settlement Society of New York* (1901): 31–32. See also, Oskison, "Public Halls of the East Side", 39.

21. Bureau of Buildings, lot-file B353-L22, "Application to Alter etc.", no. 1066, 17 June 1904, and amendments (NYC-MARC).

22. Advertisements, Golden Rule Vaudeville House, *Forward*, between 22 August and 15 September 1905.

23. Paul Klapper, "The Yiddish Music Hall", *University Settlement Studies Quarterly*, vol. 2. 4 (1906): 20. See also, David Bernstein, "Di yidishe theaters un di yidishe myuzik-hols", *Tsaytgayst*, 8 September 1905.

24. For a discussion of the relation between Yiddish vaudeville and the business of Yiddish legitimate drama see Judith Thissen, "Reconsidering the Decline of the New York Yiddish Theatre in the Early 1900s", *Theatre Survey* 44, no. 2 (2003): 173–197.

25. Advertisement, Irving Music Hall, *Forward*, 5 September 1905; Advertisement, People's Music Hall, *Forward*, 15 September 1905.

26. Advertisements, Irving Music Hall, *Forward*, 30 January and 10 March 1906; Advertisements, Grand Street Music Hall, *Forward*, between 10 March and 4 April 1906.

27. Hansen, *Babel & Babylon,* 94.

28. Mark Slobin, *Tenement Songs: The Popular Music of the Jewish Immigrants* (Urbana: University of Illinois Press, 1982), chapters 5–6. During prolonged strikes in the garment industry or other Jewish trades, Yiddish music halls and legitimate theatres typically organised well-publicised benefit performances for the support of the strikers and their families.

29. William Uricchio and Roberta Pearson, *Reframing Culture: The Case of the Vitagraph Quality Films* (Princeton: Princeton University Press, 1993), 24.

30. Richard Butsch, *The Making of American Audiences: From Stage to Television, 1750–1990* (New York: Cambridge University Press 2000), chapters 3–11.

31. *Views and Films Index*, 3 August 1907, 4.

32. *Variety*, 14 December 1907, 12.

33. Hansen, *Babel & Babylon*, 94–96.

34. Gold's 1930 novel, *Jews Without Money* (New York: Carroll & Graf, 2004) was a semi-autobiographical, popular account of the hard-knock life of the Lower East Side.

35. Hansen, 84–85.

36. "Vu zaynen …", *Forward*, 24 May 1908.

37. "Vu zaynen …", *Forward*, 24 May 1908.

36

Trans-Inter-National Public Spheres

Wolfgang Fuhrmann

The short, non-fiction film *Jagd auf Silberreiher/Chasse á l'aigrette en afrique* (Pathé Frères, 1911) starts with the shot of a European hunter and his African guides crawling through the African bushland. The hunter points to a tree, where an egret or heron colony rests. He takes aim and shoots. Successful in his hunt, the guides attach the egrets to sticks and carry them over their shoulders. Moving to a boat, two white men are plucking the kill; in a close-up, two hands hold a dead heron, show where to find the most valuable feathers, and suddenly pluck them out to show a little bunch. An intertitle then states that every year thousands of these beautiful birds are killed to adorn fashionable ladies' hats. The last shots are not filmed in Africa. A female hand presents a bunch of heron feathers to the camera; a chic young lady tries on a feathered hat. In medium close-up, the young lady smiles at the camera and moves her head to show the feathers in a flattering way.[1]

The film is typical of non-fiction titles for its time: part colonial travelogue, part hunting adventure, with a twist of European fashion at the end. It is emblematic for the exploitative character of colonial ideology and an example of what Anne McClintock calls the metamorphosis of imperial time into domestic space.[2] The motif of hunting and fashion suggests that it addressed a European male and female audience. In *Going to the Movies*, Maltby, Stokes and Allen remark that audiences' "primary relationship with 'the cinema' has not been with individual movies-as-artefacts or as text, but with the social experience of cinemagoing".[3] Since a film's audience is not entirely determined by what appears onscreen, close textual analyses should be complemented with knowledge of films' circulation amongst stratified audiences in contexts outside commercial venues. The hunting film summarised above is a good starting point to demonstrate the importance of exhibition contexts in establishing audience stratification, and for my particular purposes of tracing film practices within voluntary associations such as social and fraternal clubs. Such associations kept minutes and records of their programmed events, and often their intentions in public education and entertainment, and their archives provide a wealth of neglected documentation of the non-theatrical use of moving pictures in a wider public sphere.

In her pioneering work on the public sphere of early cinema, Miriam Hansen argued for a diversity of publics and subject positions for any film or genre.[4] This chapter, too, takes up the task of tracing alternative public spheres, in particular for audiences of non-fiction films. I argue against conceiving film reception through aesthetic structures alone, and seek an understanding of how alternative exhibition venues could produce different meanings for a single film. At the Amsterdam workshop "Nonfiction from the Teens", Ben Brewster remarked that early nonfiction film seems to exist apart from the aesthetic regimes of stylistic pressures and influences, making it difficult to tell them apart over a ten-year period.[5] Shifting from the textual analysis of film to a more concerted look at the film experience demonstrates that the meaning of non-fiction films might rest in its exhibition context – its ability to address distinct public spheres – rather than in its stylistic finesse.

Voluntary associations with national, at times transnational, connections routinely incorporated moving pictures into their activities and work; their significant prestige in local social networks provides a record of alternative public spheres in their own right.[6] Sometimes they are the only existing source to learn anything about a particular film's audience. Studying the relation between film and associations deepens our understanding of exhibition and yet unknown distribution networks. I begin in Germany and first present an overview of the national character of associations at the turn of the twentieth century and the emergence of a role for moving pictures within it. Then I turn to a wider transnational context with the specific case of films used to advocate against game-hunting for feathers. Pursuing the potential of specifically transnational public spheres, I ultimately include a look beyond the silent era – although still using silent films – by considering the use of films by German immigrant associations in early 1930s rural hinterlands in Brazil.

Voluntary associations

Sociologically, an association is a group of individuals voluntarily agreeing to act as a collective or organisation to accomplish a specific purpose. Most often relying on events and social gatherings, as opposed to merely lobbying or campaigning, an association typically requires a meeting place such as a clubhouse or an assembly room for regular meetings, usually in the evening outside of working hours. To attract new members, and inform or entertain its membership, associations used media of all kinds from speeches and magic lanterns to leaflets, photography, and film. Associations can be considered public spheres in their own right and their internal structure can be studied with regard to class or gender composition and the resulting problems in establishing and maintaining a common interest. Mary Ryan has argued that gender was the most restrictive category to public access, and most often relegated to the private realm.[7] Nancy Fraser's well-known critique of equitable, communitarian presumptions in ideas of the public sphere explained "that despite the rhetoric of publicity and accessibility, the official public sphere ... was importantly constituted by ... a number of significant exclusions".[8] Such revisionist accounts of Jürgen Habermas' concept of the public sphere were transformed into a theory of "counterpublics" by Michael Warner.[9] Geoff Eley acknowledges the existence of competing publics "not just later in the nineteenth century when Habermas sees a fragmentation of the classical liberal model of *Öffentlichkeit*, but at every stage in the history of the public sphere".[10] The point emphasises the heterogeneity of the public sphere as an arena of continuous conflict and contest. According to Eley, it makes more sense to understand the public sphere "as the structured setting where cultural and ideological contest and negotiation among a variety of publics takes place [...]".[11] The exclusionary character as well as the diversity of the public sphere allows the study of voluntary associations:

> It [the public sphere] was linked to the growth of urban culture – metropolitan and provincial – as the novel arena of a locally organized public life (meeting houses, concert halls, theatres, opera houses, lecture halls, museums), to a new infrastructure of social communication (the press, publishing companies, and other literary media; the rise of a reading public via reading and language societies; subscription publishing and lending libraries, improved transportation; and adapted centres of sociability like

coffee houses, taverns, and clubs), and to a new universe of voluntary associations.[12]

German historian Thomas Nipperdey has pointed out that around 1840 the enthusiasm for joining an association turned into a popular pastime of sorts, and a widespread passion for joining associations resulted in a nationwide network across Germany.[13] Towns with a population of ten thousand citizens could easily host more than a hundred associations. Associations were "one of the most remarkable cultural phenomena of the Wilhelmine epoch".[14] Most associations pursued rather apolitical goals such as entertainment and self-formation. The articulation of a common public interest (*Gemeinwohl*), however, also made voluntary associations the "most political medium in Imperial Germany".[15]

A "common public interest" was part of the self-conception of the German Colonial Society (*Deutsche Kolonialgesellschaft*), which aimed at creating a colonial consciousness in the German public. Founded in 1887, the German Colonial Society was the biggest colonial pressure group, with hundreds of local branches in Imperial Germany. The Society was open to all citizens, but a high annual membership fee excluded those with low incomes. Starting with illustrated lectures to inform the public about the situation and progress in the colonial territories, the society began to integrate cinematographic screenings into its propaganda in 1905 when lectures with lantern slides were losing their appeal.[16] Film screenings immediately became popular among the society's members and other associations such as patriotic, educational, or commercial associations with whom the Colonial Society collaborated.[17] The target audience for the Colonial Society was members of the upper-middle class with a clear interest in overseas business.

Colonial propaganda policy changed in early 1907 when the Society decided to institutionalise film screenings and hired a professional exhibition company, the *Deutsche Bioscope*. Within the positive political climate for colonial issues in German politics in this year, screenings at the Society's branches became very similar to regular screenings of a local or travelling cinema.[18] Already in the first year of colonial film screenings, 1905–06, members started to complain about programs composed exclusively of pictures of the colonies, and asked for a more varied film program including animation shorts and European actualities. A more popular program went hand in hand with the Society's redefinition of their policy towards the German public. The Colonial Society's major task for the future was the intensification of popular (*volkstümliche*) lectures that also addressed a working class audience.[19] In addition to showing the significant link between the colonies' natural resources and the worker's own job in the processing of these resources, colonial lectures also had to show that the colonies presented an alternative for the ordinary worker to start a new life as an independent craftsman, farmer, or settler.[20]

Ironically, these colonial film programs became substitutes for regular film programs in sparsely populated farming regions – where a local commercial cinema culture was not yet established – rather than in already serviced industrial regions where most of the working class lived. The majority of reported colonial film screenings in 1907 and 1908 were in smaller communities, where even an ideologically charged film program could become the talk of the town. Voluntary associations thus became a serious competitor of the itinerant film business, and cut into the profitability of travelling film exhibitors in rural areas. In his research on early film exhibition in Germany, Joseph Garncarz has shown that small towns and sparsely populated regions were especially attractive for traveling exhibitors since they did not encounter any competition; permanent cinemas instead first emerged in bigger cities, while fairground exhibitors concentrated on relatively densely populated regions.²¹ Associations' change to a more popular program did not go unnoticed by itinerant exhibitors, who complained early in 1908 about the unfair competition.²² Beyond their use of film in nationalist activities within Germany, associations also used moving pictures outside commercial contexts to advocate for a transnational perspective on some topics.

From national operation to international cooperation

The circulation of films like *Jagd auf Silberreiher*, discussed above, provides an interesting way to expand upon the national-level use of film by the German Colonial Society. Films about game hunting, such as this one, certainly belonged to the colonial film repertoire of that time, but they could be used for entirely different ideological purposes. Rather than merely show the colonies as territories of infinite resources, such images could becomes examples of wasteful cruelty when used by a group such as the Association for the Protection of Birds (*Bund für Vogelschutz* [BfV]), founded in 1899.

One of the first major campaigns of the BfV was fighting against hunting silver-egrets and birds of paradise for their precious feathers – exactly the scenario shown in *Jagd auf Silberreiher*. In 1912 the German public was asked to sign petitions, or "lists for the renunciation of buying feathers" (*Federnverzichtslisten*) from birds of paradise, egrets, or humming birds. This was a joint campaign with the Feminist Association for Women's Right to Vote (*Bayrischer Verein für das Frauenstimmrecht*), which considered the use of feathers in fashion to be unworthy of the modern woman as it put her on the same evolutionary step as wild and childish primitive cultures.²³ In their 1910–11 annual report, the BfV reported that the protection of the wildlife "concerned the German public as it had never done before".²⁴ The society's tireless efforts had wide-reaching consequences. In November 1913 the Colonial Society set up a special commission for the protection of egrets and birds of paradise.²⁵ In 1914 the State Secretary of the Colonial Office, himself a member of the BfV, placed a ban on importing feathers. Moreover, the BfV's campaign against killing of birds of paradise and silver egrets was coordinated transnationally with the British Royal Society for the Protection of Birds and the Audubon Society in the United States, who achieved a New York State Audubon Plumage Law in 1910 prohibiting the sale or possession of feathers from protected bird species.²⁶

To support its public campaign, the BfV used film screenings to depict the cruelty of hunting animals for sport and leisure. In February 1913 the association's public mouthpiece *Ornithologische Monatsschrift* (Ornithological Monthly Bulletin) remarked:

> Also the events and meetings that are organized by us are used to draw the attention to the disgrace and through cinematographic screenings to give an insight into the conditions. These screenings we were allowed to show on the occasion of our general meeting to Her Majesty the Queen of Württemberg, who, as it is known, has gained particular merits for the fight against the egret fashion, and at the general meeting of the German Society for the Protection of Birds to His Majesty King Friedrich August of Saxony.²⁷

Obviously, hunting films had a quite different purpose for the wildlife protection movement than for the passionate colonial adventurer. Watching the film in the context of transnational advocacy, as indicated above, a film such as *Jagd auf Silberreiher* had now two alternative distribution networks beyond the commercial mainstream, and thus at least two distinct audiences.

The film may have started as a conventional film about shooting birds in Africa, but its conclusion may have been a visual indictment of the senseless slaughter of helpless birds. The meaning of the film's ending becomes ambiguous. Does the film care about wildlife protection or does it support the use of feathers in fashion? Should women feel guilty when watching the film? Do egret feathers' beauty justify hunting their hunt, or is the film's ending a cynical comment on ladies' perverse pleasure in fashion? Did Pathé Frères know about the world-wide campaign to ban the import of feathers, and did this influence their distribution of the film? Was the initial idea of the film to document the hunt and the feathers' beauty, or did the film care about wildlife protection or both? The colonial commitment was perhaps tempered by the international effort to band hunting endangered species for feathers when the film was distributed in an off-cinema network to a different audience.

In order to push the limits of this argument, I turn next to an example of associations using film in a later period and very different national context: film screenings of the German-Brazilian Film Service in the 1930s. In this case it becomes evident that silent film programs could address viewers of any national origin, no matter what language they spoke, and further could address viewers that had no access to other forms of entertainment.

Associations from a transnational perspective

The urban Brazilian film audience was familiar with German films, documentary and fiction, but most German immigrants in Brazil lived in rural areas, and the distribution of cultural films (*Kulturfilme*) did not begin in remote regions until the 1930s. The Association of German Teachers in São Paulo (*Deutscher Lehrerverein São Paulo*) purchased a film projector in 1930 to promote the screening of educational films in schools on the outskirts of the city. Two years later, in São Leopoldo in the state of Rio Grande de Sul, a certain Dr Kosche founded the German Brazilian Cultural Film Service (*Deutsch-Brasilianischer Kulturfilmdienst*), soon administered by the National Association of German-Brazilian Teachers (*Landesverband Deutsch-Brasilianischer Lehrer* [LDL]).[28] The LDL Film Service received support from the overseas branch of the German Reich Railway (*Deutsche Reichsbahn*) in Brazil as well as from companies such as Zeiss, Agfa and Siemens.[29]

The LDL Film Service was created to reach the entire German speaking population in Brazil, especially in remote areas, and to provide "[...] pictures in lifelike form from German the countrysides, historic places and sites of German labor" and "to bring the great national festivities to life".[30] As a "living link" with the tribal home (*Stammesheimat*) the films were aimed to maintain German folklore and strengthen the German schooling system in Brazil.[31] In turn, films produced by the Film Service were sent to Germany to profile "Germanhood in Brazil".[32] Very soon after Hitler's rise to power, the German Ministry of Propaganda also began collaborating with foreign organisations such as in Brazil by providing financial support and supplying films and other materials.[33] However, the LDL Film Service was the prominent association for such activities among German-Brazilians, and its headquarters in São Paulo was soon connected to many other regional, district and city branches, finally reaching to Bahia in the remote Northeast. Film programs could be rented free of charge minus expenses, although only silent films in 16mm and some 24mm prints were available through the service.[34] The problem of nonexistent or unstable electricity at some venues made some of these film screenings in the interior of Brazil masterpieces of improvisation. Some of these programs were the first screenings ever given in small villages in the interior of Brazil.[35]

Although the nationalist rhetoric of the LDL Film Service's mandate suggests their intended audience was exclusively those of German origin, a closer study of their reports shows the film service was only viable with the support of the Portuguese-speaking population. Only ten to fifteen out of 200 viewers were German at a screening in Congonhas do Campo in Minas Gerais in 1938.[36] Another show in Cosmópolis had to be relocated to a local cinema because of its success with the Portuguese-speaking audience. The final report on this particular exhibition noted:

> Though the stories in the films were easy to comprehend [...] especially the Brazilians lamented that the texts were edited in German and not in Portuguese. Without any doubt we would be more successful if we considered this request in future.[37]

In contrast, another screening in São Caetano in March 1935 seemed to include Brazilian viewers from the planning stage. Along with films more clearly fulfilling the German national mandate – *Von Ammergau zum Staffelsee* [From Ammergau to the Lake Staffel], *Die Ostsee* [The Baltic See], and *Sport im Schnee* [Winter Sports] – more popular fare was included, such as the animated shorts films *Os 3 Cavalheiros* [The Three Gentlemen] and *Koko e o Cacique* [Coco and the King].[38] Although there is no record of which language the accompanying lecturer spoke, this remarkable combination of German and Brazilian titles, of cultural and animation films, seems to anticipate and prevent the dilemma in Cosmópolis, where the Portuguese-speaking part of the audience was disappointed. The Film Service's policy of using only silent films thus seems to have been good strategy to satisfy the largest audience irrespective of ethnic origin or language spoken.

Studying the structure of the film programs shows that the Film Service's screenings were not standardised, but varied according to the specific local needs and inquiring institutions. It would be too easy to understand their film shows exclusively as extra-territorial extensions of national-socialist propaganda. For the Brazilian viewer the film shows could also be an interesting part of local cultural life. German-Brazilian viewers could react in very different ways: Films could strengthen the bond of an *imagined community* – but not necessarily that of Germans in Brazil, let alone instilling German fascism overseas. These film programs could also strengthen the bond of an imagined Brazilian community that was composed of both Brazilians and German-Brazilians.

Corinna Müller and Haro Segeberg have remarked that public spheres cannot be conceived without media and should be considered pluralistically as media-constituted, segmented public spheres (*Medien-Teilöffentlichkeiten*).[39] Voluntary associations' use of film to maintain or attract membership has been neglected as a key aspect of the history of non-theatrical film. Associations are generally accepted as public spheres in their own rights, working both inclusively and exclusively to give and deny membership and identity – and taking part in audiences for film screenings. The national propaganda of the Colonial Society, the international campaign of the wildlife protection movement, or the transnational work of the German-Brazilian Film Service all offer important venues for exploring cinema's alternative public sphere. Of course, not every association used film, and not every association maintained international cooperation, but the example of the Cultural Film Service in Brazil shows that cinema only existed in some marginal locations because of the networks of associations. Associations contributed to the social experience of cinemagoing, and their archives and records help to expand the history of cinemagoing.

Notes

1. The film was internationally distributed and existed in different language versions. The German version *Jagd auf Silberreiher* is archived at the Bundesarchiv-Filmarchiv in Berlin, the English version *Shooting Egrets in Africa* is archived at the National Film and Television Archive in London. A Dutch version exists in the Eye Film Institute Netherlands.

2. Anne McClintock, "Soft-Soaping Empire: Commodity racism and imperial advertising", in Nicholas Mirzoeff (ed.), *The Visual Culture Reader* (London, New York: Routledge, 2002), 506–518.
3. Richard Maltby, Melvyn Stokes and Robert C. Allen (eds), *Going to the movies: Hollywood and the social experience of cinema* (Exeter: University of Exeter Press, 2007), 2.
4. Miriam Hansen, "Early Cinema: Whose Public Sphere?" in Thomas Elsaesser and Adam Barker (eds) *Early Cinema: Space, Frame, Narrative* (London: British Film Institute, 1990), 228–246.
5. Daan Hertogs and Nico de Klerk (eds), *The 1994 Amsterdam Workshop: Nonfiction from the Teens*: (London: British Film Institute, 1994): 32.
6. Wolfgang Fuhrmann, "Locating Early Film Audiences: voluntary associations and colonial film", *Historical Journal of Film, Radio and Television* 22 (2002): 291–304.
7. Mary P. Ryan, "Gender and Public Access: Women's Politics in Nineteenth-Century America", in Craig Calhoun (ed.), *Habermas and the Public Sphere* (Cambridge: Massachusetts Institute for Technology, 1992), 259–288.
8. Nancy Fraser, "Gender and Public Access: A Contribution to the Critique of Actually Existing Democracy", in Calhoun (ed.), *Habermas and the Public Sphere*, 109–142.
9. Michael Warner, *Publics and Counterpublics* (New York: Zone, 2002); Jürgen Habermas, *The Structural Transformation of the Public Sphere: An Inquiry into a Category of Bourgeois Society* (Cambridge: Massachusetts Institute for Technology, 1991).
10. Geoff Eley, "Nations, Publics and Political Cultures: Placing Habermas in the Nineteenth Century", in Calhoun (ed.), *Habermas and the Public Sphere*, 306
11. Ibid.
12. Ibid., 291.
13. Thomas Nipperdey, "Verein als soziale Struktur in Deutschland im späten 18. und frühen 19. Jahrhundert. Eine Fallstudie zur Modernisierung", in Thomas Nipperdey (ed.), *Gesellschaft, Kultur, Theorie: Gesammelte Aufsätze zur neueren Geschichte* (Göttingen: Vandenhoeck & Ruprecht, 1976), 175–205.
14. Roger Chickering, *We Men who Feel Most German: A Cultural Study of the Pan German League, 1886–1914* (Boston: George Allen & Unwin 1983), 183.
15. Chickering, *We Men who Feel Most German*, 184.
16. Wolfgang Fuhrmann, "Bilder aus den deutschen Kolonien: Lichtbilder und kinematographische Aufnahmen", *KINtop, Jahrbuch zur Erforschung des frühen Films* 8 (1999): 101–116.
17. For a more detailed discussion of the distribution within the colonial lobby see Fuhrmann, "Local entertainment and national patriotism: The distribution of colonial films in Germany", in Frank Kessler and Nana Verhoff (eds), *Networks of Entertainment: Early Film Distribution 1895–1915* (London: John Libbey, 2007), 246–254.
18. In December 1906 the German Reichstag was dissolved due to a controversy about the budget for the German South West African colony. The election in January 1907 was won by a conservative coalition, who supported colonial efforts.
19. *Berichte über die Sitzungunges des Ausschusses der Deutschen Kolonialgesellschaft* (Berlin: Deutsche Koloniagesellschaft, 1893–1914), 1 February 1907, 4–5.
20. Sybille Benninghoff-Lühl, *Deutsche Kolonialromane 1884–1914 in ihrem Entstehungs- und Wirkungszusammenhang* (Bremen: Selbstverlag des Ubersee-Museums, 1983), 40.
21. Joseph Garncarz, *Maßlose Unterhaltung. Zur Etablierung des Films in Deutschland 1896–1914* (Frankfurt: Stroemfeld Verlag, 2010).
22. "Die Kinematographen-Theater und der Deutsche Flottenverein", *Der Kinematograph*, 60 (19 February 1908): 1.
23. Bundesarchiv Berlin, R 1001/7771, 34–38.
24. *Ornithologische Monatsschrift* 37, no. 2 (1912): 9.
25. Richard Victor Pierard, "The German Colonial Society, 1882–1914", PhD Dissertation (Iowa State University, 1964).
26. Audobon Society's online Timeline of Accomplishments, www.audubon.org/timeline-accomplishments

27. *Ornithologische Monatsschrift* 38, no. 2 (1913): 131.
28. *Allgemeine Lehrerzeitung für Rio Grande de Sul* 5 (May 1934): section 13.
29. Olga Rodrigues and Moraes von Simson, "Imagem e momória", in *O Fotográfico*, Etienne Samain (ed.) (São Paulo: Editora Hucitec, 2005), 21–34.
30. Bericht Deutsche Schule São Paulo (1934), 74.
31. Bericht Deutsche Schule São Paulo (1936), 88.
32. Bericht Deutsche Schule São Paulo (1934), 75.
33. Jürgen Müller, *Nationalsozialismus in Lateinamerika. Die Auslandsorganisation der NSDAP in Argentinien, Brasilien, Chile und Mexiko, 1931–1945* (Stuttgart: Hans-Dieter Heinz, 1997), 65.
34. Bericht Deutsche Schule São Paulo (1934), 75.
35. Bericht Deutsche Schule São Paulo (1934), 76.
36. Archivo Instituto Martius-Staden (AIMST), Correspondência Landesverband Deutsch-Brasilianischer Lehrer 1937–1938, correspondence from 22 April 1938.
37. AIMST, GIV f Nr. 25/ Schubert Chor, Bericht des Deutschen Lehrervereins-São Paulo über die Filmvorführungen, correspondence from 22 May 1931; AIMST, Correspondência Landesverband Deutsch-Brasilianischer Lehrer 1937–1938, correspondence from 22 April 1938.
38. AIMST, GIV f Nr 25/ Schubert-Chor, correspondence from 13 March 1935.
39. Corinna Müller and Harro Segeberg (eds), *Kinoöffentlichkeit (1895–1920) = Cinema's public sphere (1895–1920): Entstehung, Etablierung, Differenzierung: Emergence, settlement, differentiation* (Marburg: Schüren Verlag, 2008), 13.

37

Turning the Social Problem into Performance: Slumming and Screen Culture in Victorian Lantern Shows

Ludwig Maria Vogl-Bienek

The "Social Problem" or "Social Question" has been raised since the 1830s. According to the French social historian Robert Castel "It was raised then through an awareness of the *living conditions* of populations who were both the agents and the *victims* of the *industrial revolution*".[1] The magic lantern was increasingly used within this controversial social discourse and its related social practices. The utilisation of illustrated lectures and melodramatic screen-entertainment featuring impoverished protagonists was a considerable part of Victorian Screen Culture.

The often-employed concept of "pre-cinema" is not appropriate to describe research in this field. Instead the concept of "screen practice" – as so well articulated by Charles Musser[2] – and similar approaches to the history of projection are more helpful in understanding these phenomena that existed in the interstices between social- and media-history, the shows and lectures that used projection as a way of participating in the public debate on the social question. The historic term "art of projection" to indicate nineteenth and early twentieth century screen practice seems much more felicitous to me than just "magic lantern". Analogical terms used in French and German are "l'art de projection" and "Projektionskunst". I use the latter when writing in German because it was so common in the technical literature of the time. It included all aspects of design and projection techniques related to the use of classic hand-painted lanternslides, photographic lanternslides, all kinds of projection effects and early film projection. So the term 'art of projection' signifies the creative potential of screen practice, not only the handling of a technical apparatus: it is the complex potential to produce images that move by dissolves and superimpositions and effects made of light on a screen or any other projection surface. Historically it was realised by "lanternists" who operated (or figuratively speaking "played") a projection apparatus or magic lantern in a live performance. The lanternist was a creative operator, part of a team of performers: lecturers, reciters, narrators, singers or musicians. Live performance was significant for the historic art of projection or those presentations commonly termed as magic lantern shows. And while the screen was part of these performances it was not necessarily always the centre. Music or voice accompanied the event on screen in some cases, but in others the events on screen could also accompany performers. Figure 1 shows the basic arrangement: On the stage in front of an audience we see a performer and an

Fig. 1. Engraving from a distribution catalogue for stereopticons and lanternslides by McAllister / New York 1891. [Courtesy David Francis Collection.] (T.H. McAllister, Catalogue and Price List of Stereopticons, Dissolving-View Apparatus, Magic Lanterns, and Artistically-Coloured Photographic Views on Glass (New York: McAllister 1891), back.

image on screen. In the background we have the lanternist operating a bi-unial magic lantern ("sciopticon" in the USA) to create dissolving views.[3]

The presentation of a magic lantern show needs a venue which can be darkened. It has to be equipped with a screen and a projection apparatus, either temporarily or permanently. The size of the historic venues ranged from small village halls up to big public halls, theatres or churches which had room for more than one thousand spectators. The lantern slides, readings and music were sometimes specifically written and designed for big, and often repeated, productions. But in most cases the performances treating the controversial social problem were chosen from pre-existing resources: lantern slides reproduced in large editions to illustrate lectures, texts abridged from well-known stories, ballads written for public recitation or popular songs.[4] These resources were organised by central religious or philanthropic institutions, such as the Church Army, to provide slides, texts, sheet music and lanterns for local presenters. But commercial distributors too had many slide sets in stock that broached social issues. These included slide sets with both fictional and non-fictional images and even several sets presenting completely staged photographs under the guise of documentaries. An impressive example from the early 1900s is "The Shadows of a Great City or the Slums of New York". Its advertisement in a catalogue of the Chicago Projecting Company highlights: "This Entertainment Set [... is] interesting to all classes but at the same time it has a strong moral influence and is adapted to the requirements of Ministers, Temperance Lecturers and General Missionary Work as well as to the Exhibitor who is interested only from a financial standpoint".[5] A handbill for this entertainment reads like a brief description of the Social Problem from a social reformer's point of view: "The Vices, The Temptations, The Hardships, and the Sufferings of the Poor and Criminal Classes in the Great Cities. Also the wonderful opportunities for good work and what is being done to relieve This Terrible Condition".[6]

The catalogues of distributors and producers of lantern slides as well as the performance practice of social organisations and individual showmen show that in the second half of the nineteenth century the art of projection became an appropriate way to raise the Social Question. During the first decades of the twentieth century it was still widely used both by non-profit organisations as well as by commercial showmen for presentations of social topics. The attractions of the art of projection came from the large format of the bright images on screen, the possibilities of visual storytelling through motion effects such as the dissolve and fast-changing image series, the visual representation of any lecture topic and fascinating projection effects. So the Social Problem was not only illustrated by words or pictures that represented the living conditions of the poor. It was also constituted as a public problem by turning it into performance. The spectators' experiences at these performances were made up not only of re-presentations but also of performative aspects belonging to the here and now of each presentation: the changing colours, the play of light and dark, music, the sound and rhythm of voices or the corporal appearance and personality of the performers. The spectator engaged in a close relationship with the presenters as he seemed to witness the living conditions of the poor. The art of projection was not the only way to turn the Social Problem into performance. There were melodramas and many lecturers or reciters presented social topics without using images. But the art of projection occupied its particular place. We might call it "the screen-aided performance." It enabled producers to arrange an impressive and specific kind of visibility for any desired subject and combine it with an exciting visual presentation. This kind of screen visibility was dependent on the perspectives and choices of the producers.

We know about the existence of these performances primarily through lantern slides. As glass artefacts they tell us nothing of their appearance on screen. Presumably this is one of the reasons why they have been so widely neglected: On a light box in front of us they appear as irrelevant miniature images. Despite the fact that the image on screen completely depends on this artefact, it is definitely not identical to it. Thus we have to interpret the relationship between glass slides and their appearance when projected on screen as a difference: the slide does not act as an image but as image information transformed by projection into a mutable screen-image made only of light. The glass slide itself is invisible as an interchangeable part of the projection apparatus. Using text, music and advice on the presentation, we can reconstruct a description of how the slide set appeared on the screen. But to get a real impression we have to actually show it.

As magic lanterns and performers are not always available, we decided to produce digital versions of several slide sets on social issues, not to replace proper lantern shows but to improve their accessibility for historians, students and the general public.[7] Incorporating the instructions that are included in the slide sets, the digital images reconstruct the relationship of text and image projection on screen.

Our example, *The Magic Wand – A School Board Officers Story*, is based on a ballad by the Victorian author George Robert Sims, illustrated with lantern slides by York & Son (London).[8] The slide set is composed of nine photographic 'Life Model Slides' (see Figures 2–10). Often used to illustrate stories, ballads and songs on the living conditions of the poor, 'life models' posed in stage sets with painted backdrops. Sims' ballad recounts a tour through the slums of London. He was invited by a school board officer who wanted to show the "prose of poverty" to the well-known "poet of poverty".[9] In the ballad, the school board officer acts as a tourist guide: through the eyes of his companion the audience witnesses the horrible dens of a London slum where the officer searches each day for children who stay away from school. They enter the filthy hovel of a drunkard who cares nothing for his four young children. This prepares the

BEYOND THE SCREEN: Institutions, networks and publics of early cinema

Fig. 2.
The Magic Wand.

Slide 1: Horrible dens, sir, aren't they?

[Figs. 2-10: Courtesy Mervyn Heard Collection.]

Fig. 3.
Slide 2: Just give a glance about.

37 Turning the Social Problem into Performance

Fig. 4.
Slide 3: She was one of a group of fairies.

Fig. 5.
Slide 4: And the wand was the wand up there.

*Fig. 6.
Her father was spending his weekly earnings.*

*Fig. 7.
At the wave of her wand he vanished.*

37 Turning the Social Problem into Performance

Fig. 8.
She knelt by the wretched pallet.

Fig. 9.
Then raising her wand, she waved it.

Fig. 10.
She's still at the school, is Sally.

scene for the affecting story of eight-year-old Sally and the death of her mother: like many slum children Sally was allowed to take part in a pantomime at the Drury Lane Theatre. She acted the role of a fairy queen whose magic wand could shield the good from harm. It was possessed of a magic charm "Which bade the gloom give way / to the 'Golden Home of Blisses / In the Land of the Shining Day'".[10] Swept away by the fabulous world on stage, she believed in the magic charm of the wand and was convinced it would help her severely ill mother. But her mother died the very moment Sally waved the wand over her wretched pallet. Sally nevertheless continued to believe: in school she said "that the poor sick mother / By her wand was charmed away / From earth to the Home of Blisses / In the Land of Eternal Day".[11]

Each of the images used in *The Magic Wand* show the spaces in which the little protagonist lives. From the time-based 'montage' of the whole cycle on screen emerges a complex social space of horrible dens, the hovel, pub, theatre and school – the investigation field of the foreign visitors. The characters portray several well-to-do people who observe the poor from different perspectives: the school board officer, a man from the playhouse who believed the girl wanted to steal the wand to sell it, a teacher in the classroom and the visitor representing the spectator. The destitute family is divided by a "handicapology",[12] a term used by Robert Castel to describe criteria used to divide different types of the poor in the controversy surrounding the Social Question. The child and the mother belong to the group of respectable paupers as they are not able to care for themselves. The father, a drunkard, belongs to the group of non-respectable paupers because as an able-bodied man he could care for his family and himself.

Apart from the stereotypes of sentimental representation of the poor, *The Magic Wand* also broaches its social issues through the relationships between Sally, the poor protagonist of the melodramatic tragedy, the characters who portray the slum-visitors, and the audience. In his memoirs about his ballads Sims wrote, "They were never put forward by me as poetry, but were intended for reciters who wanted something dramatic".[13] The live-performances of these ballads were made even more dramatic by the combination of recitation and slide-projection. The audience witnessed the living conditions of the poor through their representation in words and onscreen. But the emotional impact occurred in the here and now of performances. In this context, social questions were not only something represented. Rather, they also became an immediate 'question' or 'problem' for all attendees (audience and presenters) by dint of their presentation in a public performance underpinned by sentimental feelings. But while *The Magic Wand* might look like many other pathetic tales of social exclusion combined with lantern slides, the author adds another twist by presenting different observations of "reality". Sims' works were praised in the press for their realism. The audiences of his plays and ballads were used to observing the problems of social reality through this kind of critical and sentimental representation. But in *The Magic Wand*, the protagonist is denied the usual tragic role model in a tragedy. While the audience witnesses her cruel fate, Sally prefers another theatre category, she remains in the pantomime and with the 'magic wand' she transforms her home in the slums into a happier world. Although the spectator is aware of the child's misconception, he also knows that in his "reality" he wouldn't dare disillusion her, or she would be bound to break down. The two wouldn't be able to share a "reality". The performance of this ballad separates the slummers from the people living in slums. In exaggerated form it provides the experience of the invincible gap in actual slumming.

In fact, *The Magic Wand* presents a typical slumming situation on screen, directly connecting Sims' publications to this social phenomenon. In 1883 under the title "How the Poor Live", he compiled his series of *Pictorial World* reports from "a dark continent that is within easy walking distance of the General Post Office".[14] These were based on the experience of his first visits to the London slums and in his memoirs he wrote that "these illustrated articles made something of a sensation. [...]. The way in which men and women were herded together in the vilest and most insanitary conditions in the capital of the British Empire touched the public conscience, and for a time 'slumming' became fashionable".[15] There were many different reasons to go slumming. Some were justified as a reason for philanthropy; for others it was a kind of pleasure-seeking, but all were driven by curiosity. As the American social historian Seth Koven writes:

> For the better part of the century preceding World War II, Britons went slumming to see for themselves how the poor lived. They insisted that firsthand experience among the metropolitan poor was essential for all who claimed to speak authoritatively about social problems.[16]

For those who hesitated to go, the art of projection provided virtual slumming tours on screen in a safe environment. In the 1880s, the screen was already well-established in cultural life and the public sphere. It was regarded as being appropriate to make visible how the poor lived and to turn the Social Problem into public performance.[17] So the screen was widely used by charitable and philanthropic organisations to show their visions of poverty.[18] But the non-commercial and commercial use of the lantern in the controversial social discourse surrounding the Social Question also further established the screen as a social locale. The rapid success of cinematography was in no small part due the fact that audiences were already used to seeing projected images and their transformations. With both films and lantern slides, the screen was used in the early twentieth century as a means for social debate, education and entertainment with social drama.[19]

Notes

1. Robert Castel, *Les métamorphoses de la question sociale. Une chronique du salariat* (Paris: Fayard 1995). Quoted from the English edition: *From Manual Workers to Wage Laborers: Transformation of the Social Question* (New Brunswick, NJ: Transaction Publishers, 2003), xx.
2. Cf. Charles Musser, *The Emergence of Cinema. The American Screen to 1907* (Berkeley, New York: University of California Press, 1990), 16–54.
3. Engraving from T.H. McAllister, *Catalogue and Price List of Stereopticons, Dissolving-View Apparatus, Magic Lanterns, and Artistically-Colored Photographic Views on Glass* (New York: McAllister, 1891), back cover.
4. For an example, of such production and distribution, see Frank Gray's article on the lantern department of the Church Army, an institution comparable to other charitable and philanthropic organisations, pp. 27–35 in this volume.
5. *Chicago Projecting Co's, Entertainers, Supplies* (Chicago: Chicago Projecting Co's, n.d. [c 1900]), 105.
6. Ibid., 104.
7. They are part of a double-DVD which combines magic lantern slide sets and early films on different aspects of poverty: *Screening the Poor 1888–1914* (Edition Filmmuseum DVD 64, 2011).
8. "The Magic Wand", item 1.
9. Cf. George R. Sims, *My Life. Sixty Years' Recollections of Bohemian London* (London: Eveleigh Nash Company, 1917), 136.
10. George R. Sims, *Ballads and Poems. The Dagonet Ballads. The Ballads of Babylon. The Lifeboat and other Poems* (London: John P. Fuller, n.d. [1883]), 14.
11. Ibid., 16.
12. Castel, *From Manual Workers to Wage Laborers*, 3.
13. Sims, *My Life*, 182.
14. George R. Sims, *How the Poor Live* (London: Chatto & Windus, 1883), 3.
15. Sims, *My Life*, 136.
16. Seth Koven, *Slumming: Sexual and Social Politics in Victorian London* (Princeton, NJ: Princeton University Press, 2006), 1.
17. Cf. William T. Stead, *Magic Lantern Mission. Reprinted from the Review of Reviews* (London: Review of Reviews, 1890), 1–18.
18. Cf. the article by Frank Gray, pp. 27–35 in this volume.
19. Cf. the article by Martin Loiperdinger and Holger Ziegler, pp. 51–63 in this volume.

Editors and contributors

Kaveh Askari is an Assistant Professor of Film Studies in the English Department at Western Washington University. He has published articles on the magic lantern, on film and art education, and on emergent cinema in Tehran. He is currently revising a manuscript on picture craft in American silent cinema.

Martin Barnier est professeur en études cinématographiques à l'Université Lumière Lyon 2. Il a publié plusieurs ouvrages sur l'histoire du son au cinéma, dont: *Bruits, cris, musiques de film. Les projections avant 1914*, Rennes, Presses Universitaires de Rennes, 2010.

Amy E. Borden is the ACM/Mellon Teaching Fellow in Film Studies at St. Olaf College. She is currently researching how American periodicals theorized fin-de-siècle motion picture practices for middle-class readers. She has published on early film and Ousmane Sembène's portrayal of contemporary West-African women.

Stephen Bottomore spent two decades directing documentaries worldwide, while pursuing a parallel career as a film historian. He is the author of two books and many articles on silent and pre-cinema, and was awarded a PhD by Utrecht University in 2007 for his thesis on early cinema and warfare. He is an independent scholar and lives in Thailand and the UK.

Nadia Bozak holds a PhD in Comparative Literature from the University of Toronto. Her book, *The Cinematic Footprint: Lights, Camera, Natural Resources*, was recently published by Rutgers University Press. She is also a published novelist.

Marta Braun teaches in the School of Image Arts at Ryerson University. Among her publications are *Picturing Time: The Work of Etienne-Jules Marey* (1992) and *Eadweard Muybridge* (2010). She was made a chevalier of the Ordre des Palmes Académiques in 1996 and a fellow of the Royal Society of Canada in 2010.

Gerda Cammaer is Assistant Professor in the School of Image Arts of Ryerson University. Her main interests include film history, film technology, documentary film, orphan films and any other ephemeral cinema.

Oksana Chefranova is completing her dissertation in the Department of Cinema Studies at NYU on Evgenii Bauer's cinema and amusement culture in Russia. Her other interests include landscape and architecture in film; theories of the image; experimental cinema; Alexander Sokurov and contemplative cinema; and remediation in contemporary film and digital arts.

Ian Christie is a Fellow of the British Academy and Professor of Film and Media History at Birkbeck College. He has written and edited books on Powell and Pressburger, Russian cinema, Scorsese, and Gilliam, and worked on many film-related exhibitions. Current work includes research on the early motion picture industry in Britain and the place of film in the digital era; his latest book is *The Art of Film: John Box and Production Design*. Website: **www.ianchristie.org**

Liz Clarke is a doctoral candidate at Wilfrid Laurier University, where she also teaches film history. Her doctoral research examines shifting representations of gender in early American war films and related media.

Denis Condon teaches Film at the School of English, Media and Theatre Studies, National University of Ireland Maynooth. His research focuses on early Irish cinema, and he has published a book on the subject, *Early Irish Cinema, 1895-1921* (2008).

Scott Curtis is Associate Professor of Radio/Television/Film at Northwestern University, where he teaches film history and theory. He is the author of numerous articles on early cinema, especially educational and scientific film. He is currently the President of Domitor.

Marina Dahlquist is an Associate Professor in the Department of Cinema Studies, Stockholm

University. She is the recipient of a research grant from the Swedish Research Council for a project on cinema and uplift in the U.S. from 1910-1930. She is also finishing a book manuscript for an anthology entitled *Exporting Pauline: Pearl White and the Serial Film Craze*. Primary research interests are: historical reception, educational films, and issues of globalization.

Joel Frykholm is Postdoctoral Research Associate at the Department of Cinema Studies, Stockholm University. His primary research interest is pre-classical American cinema, including issues of industrial and cultural change, historical reception and local film history.

Wolfgang Fuhrmann, PhD, is Senior Lecturer at the Institute of Cinema Studies, University of Zurich. Research interests include early non-fiction cinema and transnational film history.

André Gaudreault est professeur titulaire au Département d'histoire de l'art et d'études cinématographiques de l'Université de Montréal, où il dirige le GRAFICS. Il a signé *Du littéraire au filmique. Système du récit*, édition revue et augmentée, 1999; *Le récit cinématographique*, 1991 – avec F. Jost); *Cinéma et attraction. Pour une nouvelle histoire du cinématographe*, 2008; *American Cinema, 1890-1909* – direction, 2009. Il est aussi directeur de la revue savante *Cinémas*.

Philippe Gauthier est doctorant en cotutelle à l'Université de Lausanne et à l'Université de Montréal. Sa thèse porte sur l'historiographie du cinéma. Il est l'auteur du livre *Le montage alterné avant Griffith'* (2008) et prépare avec André Gaudreault un ouvrage sur le montage dans le cinéma des premiers temps. Ses articles et ses comptes rendus ont été publiés dans 1895 *Cinéma & Cie*, *Cinémas* et *Film History*, parmi des autres.

Oliver Gaycken is an Assistant Professor in the Department of English at the University of Maryland, College Park. He is currently completing a book entitled *Devices of Curiosity: Early Cinema and Popular Science*, under contract with Oxford University Press.

Frank Gray is the Director of Screen Archive South East at the University of Brighton. He is a specialist in Victorian and Edwardian Cinema and involved in the development of public events for festivals and museums that engage with this history.

Jennifer Horne is Assistant Professor of Film + Digital Media at the University of California – Santa Cruz. She has published articles on film exhibition in *The Historical Journal of Film, Radio, and Television*, *The Moving Image*, and in *Useful Cinema* (Duke University Press, 2011). She is currently preparing a book about civic spectatorship and film use in the U.S. in the interwar years.

Gunnar Iversen is Professor of Film Studies in the Department of Art and Media Studies at the Norwegian University of Science and Technology in Trondheim. He has published books and essays on early cinema, film history and documentary.

Martin L. Johnson is a Lecturer in American Studies at the University of North Carolina at Chapel Hill. He recently earned his PhD in Cinema Studies at New York University, where he wrote his dissertation on the production and theatrical exhibition of local films in the United States from 1909 to 1934.

Amanda R. Keeler is a Visiting Assistant Professor of Film and Media Studies at Bucknell University. Her research interests include film, radio, and television history, technology studies and contemporary television programming.

Charlie Keil is Director of the Cinema Studies Institute and is a Professor in the History Department at the University of Toronto. His books include *Early American Cinema in Transition*; *American Cinema's Transitional Era* (co-edited with Shelley Stamp); *American Cinema of the 1910s* (co-edited with Ben Singer); and *Funny Pictures* (co-edited with Daniel Goldmark). He is currently editing an anthology on D.W. Griffith and completing research on a history of the origins of Hollywood.

Frank Kessler est professeur en Histoire du cinéma et de la télévision à l'Université d'Utrecht et directeur de l'Institut de Recherche Histoire et Culture (OGC). Avec Sabine Lenk et Martin Loiperdinger il a fondé et dirigé *KINtop*. De 2003 à 2007 il était le président de l'association internationale DOMITOR. Il est l'auteur de nombreux articles sur l'histoire du cinéma et notamment du cinéma des premiers temps. Avec Nanna Verhoeff il a co-dirigé *Networks of Entertainment:Early Film Distribution 1895–1915* (2007).

Rob King is an Assistant Professor in the Cinema Studies Institute and Department of History at the University of Toronto. He is the author of *The Fun Factory: The Keystone Film Company and the Emergence of Mass Culture* (University of California Press, 2009) and is currently working on a history of early sound short-subject comedy.

Editors and contributors

Sabine Lenk est chercheur affilié au groupe de recherche Médias de l'Université d'Utrecht et responsable des collections à la Cinémathèque de la Ville de Luxembourg. De 2007 à 2010 elle était la responsable du département film au Nederlands Instituut voor Beeld en Geluid (Hilversum). Elle est l'auteur de nombreuses publications sur le cinéma des premiers temps, la restauration et l'archivage des films. En 2009 elle a publié *Vom Tanzsaal zum Filmtheater. Eine Kinogeschichte Düsseldorfs*.

Germain Lacasse est professeur agrégé au Département d'histoire de l'art et d'études cinématographiques de l'Université de Montréal. Spécialiste du cinéma des premiers temps et du cinéma québécois, il dirige un projet de recherche consacré aux rapports entre le cinéma et l'oralité. Ses principales publications sont *Histoires de scopes* (1989) *Le bonimenteur de vues animées* (2001) et *Pratiques orales du cinéma. Textes choisis* (2011).

Thierry Lecointe est chercheur indépendant. On lui doit quelques articles dans des ouvrages collectifs et dans la revue *1895*. Il a publié *Le Cinématographe Lumière dans les arènes*, Montpellier, UBTF, 2007.

Murray Leeder received a Ph.D. in Cultural Mediations from Carleton University in 2011, with a dissertation entitled "Early Cinema and the Supernatural." He is an instructor at both Carleton and Algonquin College, and his articles have appeared in the *Journal of Popular Culture, Canadian Journal of Film Studies, Journal of Popular Film and Television, Irish Journal of Gothic and Horror Studies* and *Popular Music in Society*.

Martin Loiperdinger is Professor of Media Studies at the University of Trier. He co-edited *KINtop*, the German yearbook of early cinema, and currently, *KINtop – Studies in Early Cinema*. He also edited *Early Cinema Today: The Art of Programming and Live Performance* (2011) and co-curated the DVDs *Crazy Cinématographe 1896-1916*, and *Screening the Poor 1888-1914*.

Caitlin McGrath completed her dissertation, "Captivating Motion: Late-Silent-Era Sequences of Modern Urban Perception", in 2010 from the University of Chicago. She is currently working on a history of film screenings in department stores centered on the Wanamaker screenings, and a history of amateur films from the 1939 New York World's Fair.

Ross Melnick is an Assistant Professor of English and Cinema Studies at Oakland University with research interests in silent film, film exhibition, media industries, and film and globalization His forthcoming book is *American Showman: Samuel 'Roxy' Rothafel and the Birth of the Entertainment Industry* (Columbia University Press, 2012).

Priska Morrissey is Associate Professor in Film Studies at Université Rennes 2. She is the author of *Historiens et Cinéastes: rencontre de deux écritures* (L'Harmattan, 2004). Her current research deals with the history of film industry professionals and the history of film technique, especially in the field of cinematography.

Paul S. Moore is Associate Professor of Communication and Culture at Ryerson University. In addition to *Now Playing: Early Moviegoing and the Regulation of Fun* (2008), his histories of cinema exhibition in Canada have appeared in the *Canadian Journal of Film Studies*, *Cinémas* (with Louis Pelletier), and as chapters in *Covering Niagara* and *Explorations in New Cinema History*. With Sandra Gabriele, he also studies the intermedial history of the illustrated weekend newspaper in North America.

Charles O'Brien is an Associate Professor at Carleton University. He is the author of *Cinema's Conversion to Sound* (2005) and various articles and book chapters on early cinema and other topics in film history.

Marsha Orgeron is Associate Professor and Director of Film Studies at North Carolina State University. She is the co-editor, with Dan Streible and Devin Orgeron, of *Learning with the Lights Off: Educational Film in the United States* (Oxford University Press, 2012) and the author of *Hollywood Ambitions: Celebrity in the Movie Age*. She also co-edits *The Moving Image* (University of Minnesota Press), the journal of the Association for Moving Image Archivists.

Louis Pelletier is a PhD candidate at Concordia University, where he is currently working on a dissertation on film exhibition in Montreal. He is research coordinator of the Canadian Educational, Sponsored, and Industrial Film Project as well as of the early cinema research group GRAFICS. He has published on silent cinema and film exhibition in *The Moving Image*, *Film History*, *Cinémas*, and *Living Pictures*.

Paul C. Spehr is the retired former Assistant Chief of the Motion Picture, Broadcasting and Recorded Sound Division, Library of Congress, Washington, D.C. He is an archival consultant and film historian who has written several articles for publication by Domitor. He has also written several books, most recently *The Man Who Made Movies: W. K. L. Dickson*.

Frédéric Tabet est docteur en Arts (Université Paris Est Marne la vallée) où il a soutenu son doctorat "Circulations techniques entre l'art magique et le cinématographe avant 1906" en 2011. Il est galement diplômé de l'Ecole Nationale Supérieure Louis Lumière. Il est à la fois enseignant universitaire depuis 2006, réalisateur et chef-opérateur, ainsi que d'artiste magicien. Il s'intéresse particulièrement à la relation entre les pratiques audiovisuelles et les arts de la scène.

Judith Thissen teaches Film History in the Department of Media and Culture at Utrecht University. Her research on early cinema focuses on the social dynamics of moviegoing in the United States and the Netherlands.

André van der Velden teaches Media History in the Department of Media and Culture Studies, Utrecht University. His current research focuses on the history of moviegoing and related leisure practices in the Netherlands during the early decades of the twentieth century.

Ludwig M. Vogl-Bienek (PhD) is the Post-Doctoral Researcher of the Screen 1900 Research Group at the University of Trier, and a founding member of the magic lantern ensemble *Illuminago*, which performs lantern shows internationally. He has published on the art of projection and on screen culture and the poor in the 19th century.

Holger Ziegler received his Magister Artium in Theater, Film and Media Studies at Goethe University, Frankfurt. He currently works as an educational coordinator at the Medienwerkstatt "MEWI" Frankfurt and operates an independent arthouse cinema.

Index of Films

A Bake for Schools in the People's House (1918)	134
Abbey of La Cambre, The (1909)	132
A Flower Sale for the Orphans (1918)	134
After the Ball (1897)	183n31
An Arrest (1896)	221n5
An Open-Air Cure for Infants in Bosvoorde (1918)	134
A Novice at X-Rays (1898)	180
Apparitions de Lourdes (1904)	46
Apple Blossom Time in Normandy (1921)	17
Arrival and Stay of the Danish King and Queen in Brussels, The	132
Artist's Dream, The (1899)	179
A Trip through Spain and Portugal (1897)	79
At the Music Hall (1907)	83
Baltic Sea, The see Ostsee, Die	
Behind the Scenes (1914)	266
Belgique martyre, La (1919)	137, 139n22
Ben Hur (1907)	83
Beside the Zuider Zee (1921)	17
Blissveldt Romance, The (1915)	293
Boil Your Water (1911)	113
Bombardment of the Taku Forts by the Allied Fleets (1900)	76
Bonsoir fleur (1910)	48
Boxers, The (1896)	41
Breeches Buoy, The (1899)	221n15
Brussels during the Occupation (1918)	134
Brussels Restaurants (1919)	134, 135, 137
Cabiria (1914)	269n25
Cape to Cairo (1906)	2
Castle of Gaasbeek, The (1909)	132
Chasse á l'aigrette en afrique (1911) see Shooting Egrets in Africa (1911)	
Château hanté (1897)	187
Check-point for Infants and Canteen for Mothers (1918)	134
Chemineau, Le (1910)	48
Chickens Coming out of the Shell (1899)	221n15
Children of the Sahara (1920)	15,16
Children who Labor (1912)	109
Cinderella (1912)	275
City Beautiful, The (1914)	112
Cleopatra (1913)	96, 98
Coco and the King see Koko e o Cacique	
Come Clean (1918)	14
Country Couple, The (1899)	171
Course aux potirons (1910)	48
Course des agents (1910)	48
Dangers of the Street (1912)	109
Day Camp for Weakened Girls in Zellik (1918)	134
Dear Boys	21
Death of Svengali (1896)	41
Decasia: The State of Decay (2002)	200-205, 206n16
Defense of Sebastopol, The (1911)	64
Dentist's Chair, The (1896)	41
Distribution of Flour, The (1918)	134
Distribution of Unemployment Benefits (1918)	134
Eggs Hatching (1899)	221n15
Enfance de Bernadette (1906)	47
Escamotage d'une dame au théâtre Robert Houdin see Vanishing Lady, The (1896)	
Every Woman's Problem (1921)	14
Fahrenheit 9/11 (2004)	92
Fall of Kiev, The (1919)	15
Fall of the Romanov Dynasty, The (1927)	66
Fall of Troy, The (1910)	272
Farces de frise poulet (1910)	48
Father Knickerbocker's Children (1920)	11,12
Fer forgé	242
Fifty Thousand Feet of Kansas (1915)	294
Firebugs, The (1913)	99
First Night After the Wedding (1907) see Første nat efter brylluppet, Den (1907)	
Fluffy's New Corset (1908)	220
Første nat efter brylluppet, Den (1907)	126
French Refugees in Brussels (1918)	134

329

Fresh Supplies for the City: Distribution of Butter and Mussels in the Central Halles (1918)	134
From Ammergau to the Lake Staffel see Von Ammergauzum Staffelsee	
From the Manger to the Cross (1912)	276
Funeral of City Mayor Demot, The (1909)	132
Girls Boxing Match (1908)	220
Gossiping Yapville (1911)	110
Grotesque Tumbling (1895)	41
Hiawatha (1909)	284
Historic Fourth of July in Paris, The (1918)	13
House on Fire, The (1896)	41
I Confess (1953)	94
In Picturesque Romania (1921)	17
Interior, N.Y. Subway, 14th St. to 42nd St. (1905)	222n21
Interior of a Whiskey Saloon (1896)	41
Jagd auf Silberreiher (1911) see Shooting Egrets in Africa (1911)	
Jérusalem	46
Jumping Net Practice (1898)	221n15
Justice in the Far West (1896)	41
Just Kids (1913)	98, 99
Koko e o Cacique	312
Kris Kringle	283
Land without Mirth, The (1920)	17
Last Great Indian Council, The (1908)	284
Life History of a Fly, The	112
Little Cripple, The (1911)	112
Long Haul vs. Short Haul	112
Lourdes en 1858, la genèse des apparitions (1906)	47
Lyrical Nitrate (1990)	200-206
Magnetism	151n18
Magnetism and Electromagnets	151n18
Maid of the Mississippi, The (1916)	296n21
Man Who Learned, The (1910)	109
Maudite soit la guerre (Maudite pour la patrie)	138n5
Merveilles de la mer, Les	242
Mésaventures de Pierrot, Les	187
Midnight Ride of Paul Revere, The (1908)	285
Mine Owner's Daughter, The	288
Misères de l'aiguille	243
Mothers, Despair Not! (1911) see Mütter, verzaget nicht! (1911)	
Mütter, verzaget nicht! (1911)	51-60
Nanook of the North (1922)	198
National Committee Warehouses in the Vergote Bassin: the Arrival of the Ships and the Unloading of Fats and Lard, The (1918)	134
New Faces for Old (1918)	14
Of No Use to Germany (1918)	14
Opening of the Monument to Alexander III in Moscow on May 30, 1912, The (1912)	68
Original Movie, The	175n21
Ostsee, Die	312
Os 3 Cavalheiros	312
Pardon, The (1915)	108
Parisienne Elegante in her Boudoir, La (1913)	286
Passe-partout (1910)	48
Passion de N.S. Jésus-Christ, La (1898)	47
Passion Play, The (1911)	274-276
Passions (1898)	47
Past and Present in the Cradle of Dixie (1914)	292
Pasteur	242
Picturesque Russia, The (1913)	69
Pierrot et la flûte enchantée	187
Prague, City of a Hundred Towers (1921)	17
Prestidigitateur au café, Le (2004)	187
Price of Human Lives, The (1913)	112
Primary Colors (1998)	92
Production and Handling of Milk, The	112
Prolific Magic Egg, The (1903)	183n24
Red Cross Travel Series, The (1920-1921)	15
Repas fantastique, Le (1900)	187
Rescued by Rover (1905)	21
Rough Sea at Dover (1896)	79
Satan (1913)	96
Scene from Comic Opera (1896)	41
Scene in Legation Street, Shanghai (1900)	76
Sea Cave near Lisbon (1897)	79
Seeing Oklahoma City (1913)	296n21
Semaine animée, La (1912)	132
Shanghai Street Scene, no. 2 (1898)	76
Shooting Egrets in Africa (1911)	307, 310, 312n1
Shooting the Life Line (1899)	221n15
Silent Plea for a Widowed Mother's Allowance, The (1914)	108
Somebody's Birth Certificate	110
Sortie des usines, La	138n6
Soul Kiss (1908)	220
Sport im Schnee	312
Star Spangled Banner, The (1911)	274
Story of a Consumptive, The	112
Street Beautiful, The (1912)	109
Street Scene in Peking (1900)	76
Summer Babies (1911)	110
"Teddy" Bears, The (1907)	283, 285
Ten Commandments, The (1923)	173
Tentation de Saint Antoine, La (1898)	187
Tenth Symphony, The (1918)	228
10th U.S. Infantry Disembarking From Cars (1898)	74
10th U.S. Infantry, 2nd Battalion, Leaving Cars (1898)	74
Tercentenary of the Rule of the House of Romanov 1613-1913, The (1913)	64, 69
Three Gentlemen, The see Os 3 Cavalheiros	

Tony Sarg's Almanac	175n21
Too Many in Bed (1908)	220
Train at Havre, The (1918)	14
Treating Spinal Curvature with Exercise (1901)	218
Twister, The (1926)	17
Two Hours After Hatching (1899)	221n15
Uncle Josh at a Spooky Hotel (1900)	170
Uncle Josh at the Moving Picture Show (1902)	168-174
Uncle Josh's Nightmare (1900)	170
Van Bibber's Experiment (1911)	153-160
Vanishing Lady, The (1896)	176, 179, 186
Venice (1920)	11
Vie et passion de Jeanne d'Arc (1904)	46
Village Smithy, The (1896)	41
Virginian, The (1914)	269n25
Visit of Evpatorija, The (1916)	69
Von Ammergauzum Staffelsee	312
X-Ray Fiend, The (1897)	183n30
Wages of Sin (1912)	99
Winning Her Way (1921)	14
Winter Sports see *Sport im Schnee*	
Wonders of Magnetism, The (1913)	147, 151n18
Your Boy (1918)	14
Zaro, the Tumbling Clown (1896)	41

Index of Names

Aas, Nils Klevjer	127, 129	Booth, Charles	27
Abel, Richard	223, 268n10	Booth, Walter R.	176
Ackerman, Raymond	217	Booth, William	27
Acres, Birt	22, 79, 237	Boring, Edwin G.	153-158, 159n2, 160n13
Addams, Jane	283	Bottomore, Stephen	28, 29, 71, 78, 288
Alberti	188	Bourgeois, Albéric	87
Alexey, Tsarevich	64	Bousquet, Henri	196, 198
Alger, Horatio	272	Bowser, Eileen	107, 109
Alger, Russell A.	221n11	Boyer	47
Allen, Robert C.	77n11, 107, 247, 252, 268n10, 298, 305n5, 305n6, 307	Brewster, Ben	307
		Broca, Raymond	228n6
Anderson, Benedict	5	Brown, Richard	78, 79, 83 n7
Anschütz, Ottomar	249	Brownlow, Kevin	107, 108, 112
Arcari, Paolo	243	Bruchési, Archbishop	96, 98
Armitage, Francis	222n20	Burch, Noël	202
Asselin, Georges	226	Burel, Léonce-Henry	227, 228
Auerbach, Jonathan	169	Cadogan, Earl and Countess	39
Ayres, Leonard P.	119	Carlile, Reverend Wilson	27-33
Balázs, Béla	167n17	Caroly, Jean	185
Barnard, Timothy	224	Carou, Alain	224
Barnier, Martin	240, 241	Carstens, Martin	126
Barnum, P.T.	265	Carter, Howard	261
Barrier, Paul	240	Cartwright, Lisa	168
Barthes, Roland	204	Cash, Edward	22, 23, 25n19, 25n20, 26n22
Baudry, Jean-Louis	92	Casler, Herman	214, 221n4
Bayley, Roger Child	237	Castel, Robert	315, 322
Bazin, André	157	Cauvin, Gustave	242, 243
Bell, Laird	295n1	Cazeneuve, Marius	188
Bellingham, Lady	39	Cherchi Usai, Paolo	197, 200
Bellon, Léopold	45	Cherniavsky, Jan	304
Benjamin, Walter	6	Chevalier	46
Benoit-Lévy, Edmond	44	Claye, Jules	146
Benson, Allen	120	Cochrane, R.H.	288, 295 n1
Bernhardt, Thomas	254n21-22, 254n31	Cohl, Émile	176
Biggs, Dr Herman M.	109	Coissac, Georges-Michel	43-46, 49n5, 233
Billet, Henry	45	Collier, John	117, 120-125
Billroth, Theodor	164	Conness, Robert	154, 159
Bitzer, Gottfried Wilhelm "Billy"	216, 217, 221n5, 221n8, 221n12, 222 n19	Cool, Reverend James W.	274
		Creel, George	12
Blackstone, Gary	180	Czitrom, Daniel	95

Index of Names

Daguerre, Louis-Jacques-Mandé	169
D'Alcy, Jehanne	180, 183n31
D'Alton, Emelie	180
Darnell, Nani	180
Davis, Jefferson	292
Davis, Richard Harding	154
Decherney, Peter	2
de Chomón, Segundo	176
de Frenes, Joseph	19
de Kempeneer, Hippolyte	131-139, 139n2
de Kemperneer, Maurice	138n12
de Kolta, Buatier	186, 187
Delpeut, Peter	200-202, 204
Demers, Jacques	88
DeMille, Cecil B.	173, 295n1
Depue, Oscar	19, 24n2
Desmets, Jean	201, 204
de Thoran, Ernest	243
Deutsch, Gustav	202
de Vere, Charles	185
Dewey, John	119
de Windt, Harry	24n2
Dibbets, Karel	256
Dickens, Charles	235
Dickson, William Kennedy Laurie	23, 214, 215, 218, 221n4, 224
Dijkstra, Bram	179
Dinwiddie, W.W.	146, 147, 151n17
Dixon, J.K.	282-285, 287n7
Dow, Arthur Wesley	210-212, 213n10
Doyen, Eugène-Louis	45, 49n10, 49n12, 162-165, 166n9
Dranem	248
Drankov, Aleksandr	64, 65, 67, 69
Eastman, George	283
Eberhart, Governor Adolph Olson	275
Eberwein, Robert T.	108
Edison, Thomas	3, 41, 74, 78, 79, 82, 83, 84n12, 109, 110, 112, 117, 122-125, 124n8, 143, 144, 147, 150n2, 151n16, 151n18-19, 152n25, 153, 155, 158, 214, 220, 221n3
Edward VII, King	285
Eley, Geoff	308
Elsaesser, Thomas	85, 89, 91
Engelen, Leen	139n21
Enticknap, Leo	204
Epstein, Jean	165, 167n17
Esquier, Charles	243
Ezra, Elizabeth	176
Faivre, Victor	243
Faugeras, Jean Auguste	189
Fehr, Herman	272
Fernollosa, Ernest	210
Fescourt, Henry	47
Fischer, Bud	87
Fischer, Lucy	180, 183n27
Fishbein, Morris	108
Fisher, John H.	295n1
Flaherty, Robert	198
Fleischer, Alfred W.	267n2
Forfeitt, William	21, 22
Fossati, Giovanna	197
Foster, Reverend J. Priestley	38, 39
Fox, Imro	188
Fox, William	298
Foy, Emma	177
Frampton, Hollis	201
Fraser, Nancy	308
Frazer, James	180
Fregoli II	187
Fregoli, Leopoldo	187
Friedberg, Anne	281
Friedrich August of Saxony, King	310
Friedrich, Emperor	57
Frimousse	186
Gale, H.G.	147
Gance, Abel	228
Ganot, Adolphe	143, 146, 147, 151n11, 151n19
Gardner, Helen	98
Garncarz, Joseph	247, 309
Garrigue-Lagrange	45
Gaudreault, André	4, 79, 184, 189
Gauley, Armand	45
Gauthier, Christophe	224
Gauthier, Conrad	87
Gehr, Ernie	201
Gellner, Oskar	249, 250
Gibbons, Walter	78, 79
Gibory, Alphonse	227
Gilbreth, Frank	162, 163, 165, 166
Gilbreth, Lillian	162, 163, 165
Giotto, di Bondone	210, 213n8
Goddard, Henry H.	119
Goedike, Albert	87
Gold, Mike	306n34
Goldfish, Sam	266
Goldin, Horace	181
Goldwater, Dr Samuel S.	111
Gonzales, Manuel	25n17
Goodyear, William Henry	208, 209
Gordon, Michael	204
Gorky, Maxim	177
Gosser, H. Mark	36
Gouin, Louis	96, 98
Grattan Bellew, Sir Henry	39
Grau, Robert	274
Grenfell, Reverend George	21, 22

333

Grieveson, Lee	121	Koopman, Elias B.	214, 221n4
Griffin, Peter	96	Koven, Seth	323
Griffith, David Wark	3, 219, 220	Kracauer, Siegfried	157
Griffiths, Alison	203	Kräusslich, Paul	128
Guillaumet, Edouard	229n6	Krows, Arthur Edwin	17, 295n1
Gunning, Tom	15, 72, 75, 76, 170	Kutner, Robert	163, 164
Habermas, Jürgen	5, 308	Lacan, Jacques	234
Habib, André	204	Laemmle, Carl	266, 288, 295n1
Haddon, Alfred	19	Lagrée, Michel	48
Hagedorn, Willy	250, 251	Lamb, Oliver William	291-294, 296n21
Hammerstein, Oscar	220n1	Lameris, Bregtje	196
Hansen, Miriam	5, 289, 298, 302, 307	Lamster, J.C.	24n1
Hanson, J.H.	149	Lane, Winthrop	118
Harbeck, William	19	Lanier, Henry	120
Hay, James	25n12	Lankester, Dr Arthur	26n22
Hearst, William Randolph	216, 217	Lashley, Karl	153
Hepworth, Thomas Cradock	234-236	Lasky, Jesse	266
Herodotus	66	Lathrop, Garry Parsons	171, 172
Herrmann, Adelaide	180	Laurier, Wilfrid	87, 89, 90
Hertz, Carl	180	Lauste, Emile	23, 26n25
Hine, Lewis Wickes	12	LaVoy, Merl	12
Hitchcock, Alfred	94	Lee, Consul General Fitzhugh	217
Hitler, Adolf	311	Lefebvre, Leo	19
Hodges, John A.	234	Le Forestier, Laurent	224
Holmes, Burton	24n2	Lemieux, Louis-Joseph	96, 98, 100, 101
Honoré, abbé	241	Leopold II, King	132
Houdini, Bess	180	Loew, Marcus	298
Houdin-Robert, Jean Eugène	185, 188	Lindsay, Vachel	288
Howe, Frederick C.	122	Little Tich	248
Howe, Lyman	283, 289	Lockwood, E.B.	120
Howe, Williard	113	Loeb, Sophie Irene	108
Huguenet, Félix	229n6	Longfellow, Henry Wadsworth	284, 285
Hurley, Kelly	179	Lowrey, Dan	40
Inglis, William	118, 120	Lubin, Siegmund	71, 82, 267n2
Jacobs, Ken	201	Lumière, Auguste and Louis	3, 41, 78, 138n6, 182n7, 186-188, 234, 236
Jacobs, Lewis	298		
Jagelskiy, Aleksandr	64, 66, 67, 69, 70n4, 70n17	Machin, Alfred	131, 138n4, 138n5, 139n22
Jago, William	79, 80, 81, 82	MacIntyre, James	177
James, Charles	41	Mackenzie King, William Lyon	88
Jarvies, James Jackson	211	Maddin, Guy	202
Johnson, Marietta L.	119	Magidov, Vladimir M.	69n1, 70n7
Jowett, Garth	298	Maltby, Richard	307
Joye, Joseph	198	Malkames, Don	221n12
Kaeuper, H.H.	282, 283	Malkames, Karl	221n12
Kaplan, Amy	72, 76	Manley, Charles	171
Keil, Charlie	268n9	Mann, Frank H.	112
Keith, Benjamin	214	Mantle, Reverend J. Gregory	20, 21, 22, 24, 25n8, 25n9
Kessler, Frank	85, 92		
Khanzhonkov, Aleksandr	64, 67	Marchand, Charles	87
King, Rob	167n17	Marck, Charles	243
Kipling, Rudyard	173	Mariani, Georges	225, 226, 228
Kleine, George	117, 146, 283	Marks, Martin Miller	272
Koerber, Martin	198	Marvin, Arthur	219, 220
Kohl, Max	147	Marvin, Harry N.	214, 216, 221n4, 221n18

Index of Names

Massé, Alfred	244	Ouimet, Léo-Ernest	86, 87, 89, 90, 95, 102n3
Mastbaum, Jules	263, 267n2	Pankhurst, Christabel	181
Mastbaum, Stanley	263-267, 267n1, 267n2, 268n6	Parker, R.G.	147
		Pathé, Charles	131
Matsuzewski, Bolesaw	49n10, 65, 66, 67, 68	Patience, Ernest	87
Matz, Rudolph	295n1	Paul, Robert	35, 41n2, 78, 79, 83
Mayo, Countess of	40	Paulus	248
Mayol, Félix	248	Pearson, Roberta	302
McClintock, Anne	307	Pengam	243
McGrath, Roberta	176	Pepper, John Henry	176
McKeand, A.W.	290	Pernick, Martin	108
McKenzie, John	19, 24n2	Peterson, Jennifer	15, 17, 203
McQuade, James	274	Philippe Marion	4
Meighen, Arthur	88	Picard, Eugène	88
Méliès, Georges	179-182, 183n24, 183n28, 184-187, 195, 196, 198, 236, 248	Pickford, Mary	265-267
		Pierson, Michelle	202, 206n16
		Plait, Phil	181
Merritt, Russell	305n5	Plateau, Dr Joseph	138n2
Méry, Jean	195	Polaire	248
Messter, Oskar	251	Polan, Dana	2
Metz, Christian	92	Polet, Jacques	137
Meusy, Jean-Jacques	224, 226, 228n3	Poli, Joe	215
Meyer, Harry W.	264	Poli, S.Z.	215
Meyer, Jean-Paul	197	Ponting, Herbert	24n2
Meynier, Agosta	185	Porten, Henny	51
Michelens, René	134	Porter, Edwin S.	168, 171, 172, 224, 283, 285
Miller, Albert G.	295n1	Pulitzer, Joseph	216
Millikan, R.A.	147, 151n19	Rabinovitz, Lauren	281
Mitchel, Mayor John Purroy	111	Ramabai, Pandita	21
Moingo, Abbé	151n11	Ramsaye, Terry	268n4
Moody, Dwight Lyman	28	Rankin, Alex	252
Moore, Michael	92	Raynaly	185
Moore, Paul S.	95, 265	Read, Paul	197
Morrison, Bill	200-202, 204	Reeder, R.R.	119
Morris, William	208	Reichenbach, Baron von	182n14
Muir, John	38, 39	Remington, Frederic	216
Müller, Corinna	312	Renoir, Jean	281
Münsterberg, Hugo	153, 159n3	Revere, Paul	285, 286
Musant	46	Robinson, James	80, 81
Musser, Charles	24n2, 77n11, 107, 224, 247, 252, 315	Röntgen, Wilhelm	168, 169, 171, 172, 174n4, 176, 177
Muybridge, Eadweard	175n21	Roosevelt, Theodore	217, 219, 221n8, 221n11
Naficy, Hamid	12	Rosenberg, August	41
Needham, Mary Master	118	Rosenthal, Joe	19
Neve, Dr Arthur	22	Rosenzweig, Roy	297
Nicholas II, Tsar	63-70, 70n5, 70n14	Ross, Denman	210
Nichols, Mike	92	Ross, Steven J.	298
Nielsen, Asta	51, 59n2	Rothacker, Watterson R.	288, 295n1
Niépce, Joseph Nicéphore	169	Rothafel, Samuel "Roxy"	271-277, 277n1, 277n3, 278n47
Nipperdey, Thomas	309		
Noble, C. Rider	19	Rowan, Edgar	30, 31
Nora, Pierre	204	Rowntree, Seebohm	27
Norton, Charles Elliot	210	Runey, Clarence	296n24
Olsson, Jan	95	Ruskin, John	208-210, 213n7
Olinka	249	Russell, Catherine	203

Ryan, Mary	308	Testa, Bart	201, 202
Rybczynski, Witold	260	Thaw, Henry K.	100, 101
Sandow, Eugene	220n1	Thuillier, Elizabeth	198
Sage, Russell	109	Thurstone, Louis Leon	155, 160n13
Sankey, Ira	28	Thurston, Henry W.	119
Sargent, Epes Wintrop	112	Titchener, E.B.	154, 155
Schenk, Bruno	251	Trewey, Félicien	187
Schleswig-Holstein, Princess Christian of	39	Trutat, Eugène	236
Schoedsack, Ernest	12	Tsivian, Yuri	183n23
Schreiber, Adele	58	Turconi, Davide	198
Schuurman, A.J.	260	Turner, Robert	80
Scott, Robert Falcon	24n2	Tuschinsky, Abraham	260, 262n11
Segeberg, Haro	312	Tutelier, Charles	137, 139n23
Selbit, P.T.	181	Tutu, Archbishop Desmond	34n22
Selig, William	275	Urban, Charles	20, 21, 78, 79, 117, 282, 283
Selznick, Lewis	266		
Shepard, David	198	Urrichio, William	15, 90, 302
Shub, Esfir	66	Vandette, Roméo	88
Sigsbee, Captain Charles D.	217, 221n8	Veeder, Gerry K.	12, 17, 18n3
Simon, Josep	146	Velle, Gaston	184, 186-188
Simonin, Chanoine	241	Velle, Joseph	186
Sims, George Robert	317, 323	Victoria, Empress	57
Singer, Ben	107, 123	Victoria, Queen	29
Singley, B.L.	149	Villars, Reverend Ulysses S.	276
Sinn, G. Maxwell	96, 100	Villiers, Frederic	19
Siren, Osvald	210, 213n8	Von Goethe, Johann Wolfgang	248
Skladanowsky, Emil	249, 252	Von Kellar, Albert	179
Skladanowsky, Max	249, 252	Wales, Prince of	79
Sklar, Robert	107, 298	Wales, Princess of	39, 79
Skytte, P.	127, 128	Wallace, Lew	83
Slide, Anthony	295n1	Waller, Gregory	268n10
Smith, George Albert	25n8, 176, 183n30	Wallin, Dr J.E. Wallace	130n17
Sojcher, Frédérick	139n23	Wallis, Henry	80
Spehr, Paul C.	224	Walsh, Michael James	96, 100
Sprague Smith, Charles	122	Walter, Frieda	250
Spurgeon, Charles	28	Wannamaker, John	282, 283, 287n5
Staiger, Janet	224	Warner, Michael	5, 290, 308
Stamp, Shelley	268n9	Wasson, Haidee	2, 203
Stankiewicz, Mary Ann	208	Watson, John B.	153
Staples, Ernest J.	26n25	Weber, Max	207-212, 213n10, 213n15
Starr, Frederick	25n17	Wells, H.G.	27
St. Clair Drake, Dr C.	110	Weule, Karl	24n1
Stead, William Thomas	20, 25n6, 25n18, 32, 33	Whipple, Guy Montrose	153, 154, 155, 159n2, 160n12
Steiner, Charles	299, 303		
Stock, Eugene	26n22	Whissel, Kristen	73, 77n11
Stokes, Melvyn	307	White, Clarence H.	210, 211, 213n13, 15
Stoll, Horatio F.	291	Williamson, James	25n8
Stopford, Lady Charlotte	39	Williams, Raymond	3, 267n2
Svensen, Sven	126-129	Wood, Gaby	180
Taft, William Howard	291	Wurttemberg, Queen of	310
Tantzman, Abraham	301	York, Duchess of	39
Taschereau, Louis-Alexandre	88, 96	Yumibe, Joshua	198
Taylor, Frederick	162	Zukor, Adolph	266, 298
Taylor, Graham	122		
Tennyson, Lord Alfred	179		